Marketing and Managing Tourism Destinations

Marketing and Managing Tourism Destinations is a comprehensive and integrated textbook which uniquely considers both destination marketing and management in one volume. It focuses on how destination marketing is planned, implemented and evaluated as well as the management and operations of destination marketing and management organizations, how they conduct business, and the major opportunities, challenges and issues they face to compete for the global leisure and business travel markets. This textbook provides students with:

- A solid introduction to destination marketing strategy and planning, to organization and support planning and then to operations, implementation and evaluation, as well as major issues, challenges and expected new directions for destination marketing, management and Destination Management Organizations (DMOs).
- A unique systematic model to manage and market destinations.
- Core concepts are supported with well integrated international case studies to show the practical realities of marketing and managing destinations as well as the need to take a flexible and adaptive approach to managing different destinations around the world.
- Encouragement to reflect on the main themes addressed and spur critical thinking; discussion questions and links to further reading are included in each chapter.

This accessible yet rigorous text provides students with an in-depth overview of all the factors and issues which are important to consider to make a destination successful.

Alastair M. Morrison is the President and CEO of Belle Tourism International Consulting (BTI) in the People's Republic of China and a Distinguished Professor Emeritus specializing in the area of tourism and hospitality marketing and management in the School of Hospitality and Tourism Management, Purdue University, USA.

'This excellent text provides a comprehensive introduction to and explanation of the core concepts relevant to the marketing and management of a tourist destination. The theoretical concepts are well supported by extensive international case studies and references. This will be of interest to both students and practitioners and this book should become the leading text in the field.'

Kit Jenkins University of Strathclyde, UK

'As the number of travelers continues to grow, communities are challenged to manage their destinations. Alastair Morrison has produced a resource that combines practical, real world examples with the best current research. *Marketing and Managing Tourism Destinations* provides great insight into how the best destinations and tourism researchers are approaching the challenges of destination management. This resource will appeal to practitioners looking for solutions and provide a solid foundation for students preparing to make an impact in the field.'

Jonathon Day Purdue University, USA

Marketing and Managing Tourism Destinations

Alastair M. Morrison

LONDON AND NEW YORK

First published 2013
by Routledge
2 Park Square, Milton Park, Abingdon, Oxon OX14 4RN

Simultaneously published in the USA and Canada
by Routledge
711 Third Avenue, New York, NY 10017

Routledge is an imprint of the Taylor & Francis Group, an informa business

British Library Cataloguing in Publication Data
A catalogue record for this book is available from the British Library

Library of Congress Cataloging in Publication Data
Morrison, Alastair M.
Marketing and managing tourism destinations / Alastair M. Morrison.
p. cm.
Includes bibliographical references and index.
1. Tourism–Marketing. 2. Tourism–Management. I. Title.
G155.A1M665 2012
910.68'8–dc23
2012024772

ISBN: 978-0-415-67249-8 (hbk)
ISBN: 978-0-415-67250-4 (pbk)
ISBN: 978-0-203-08197-6 (ebk)

Typeset in Frutiger
by Saxon Graphics Ltd, Derby

Printed and bound in Great Britain by
TJ International Ltd, Padstow, Cornwall

To Sheng Hua (Jing), Alick and Andy

Contents

Contents

Contents

Contents

Contents

Contents

Figures

Tables

Preface

Before launching into the chapters, there is need to look at why this book is required in the marketplace. Above all, the growing recognition of destination marketing and management as distinct professional fields of tourism underpins this book's production; as does the increasing acceptance of these closely-connected topics as viable areas for educational and training programmes, and academic research and scholarship.

Research and educational interest in the book's topics

The writing of a contemporary textbook on destination marketing and management is long overdue, and especially one that treats the two concepts together as an integrated whole. One of the reasons is because university academic programmes and researchers are giving more attention to destination marketing and management. Traditionally, many universities have had courses in hospitality management and fewer have been teaching travel trade or travel agency management. More recently tourism management courses have been added, with classes in destination management or marketing being one element introduced within approximately the past 10–15 years.

The following data from Google Scholar show that these two topics started to enter the tourism literature in the 1980s; received more attention in the 1990s; and then became 'mainstream' topics from 2000 to 2009. About 95–96 per cent of the references to the two topics have occurred from 2000 onwards. Judging by the data for 2010–2012, the period from 2010 to 2019 will have significantly more entries than for 2000–2009.

Table 0.1 References to destination management and destination marketing in Google Scholar, 1980–2012

Time period	Destination marketing	Destination management
1980–1989	23	7
1990–1999	357	217
2000–2009	4,310	3,470
2010–2012*	3,240	2,520
Total	7,930	6,214

Note: *to 21 November 2012.

Source: Google Scholar, author analysis (excluding citations).

The literature on destination marketing and management will be further extended with the introduction of new academic journals specifically addressing these topics. For example, Elsevier's *Journal of Destination Marketing and Management* launched in 2012 at about the same time as the publication of this book. It can be expected that journals along similar themes will emerge in the future; for example, we may see one dedicated solely to destination marketing and destination leadership.

It also should be recognized that there has been an explosion in the publication of many journal articles and books in related fields including place, city, and nation branding and marketing. The journals include *Place Branding and Public Diplomacy* (2004, Palgrave) and *Journal of Place Management and Development* (2008, Emerald). In 2002, Kotler, Haider and Rein published the book, *Marketing Places* (Free Press), and that became the frontrunner for a spate of new books about place and nation marketing and branding. In his book, *City Branding: Theory and Cases* (Palgrave Macmillan, 2011), Keith Dinnie had the following to say about the importance of city branding:

> City branding is a topic of significant interest to both academics and policy makers. As cities compete globally to attract tourism, investment and talent, as well as to achieve many other objectives, the concepts of brand strategy are increasingly adopted from the commercial world and applied in pursuit of urban development, regeneration and quality of life. Much of the published research into city branding originates in the disciplines of marketing and urban studies, two fields that have tended to follow parallel rather than interdisciplinary paths.

The above quote is noteworthy since it places destinations within the scope of city branding, while also suggesting that interdisciplinary approaches need to be applied in this field.

Tourism sector interest in the book's topics

There is a growing interest worldwide in the topics of destination marketing and management as more places are vying for a share of global tourism. This is demonstrated through a number of different phenomena, and one of these is the expansion of professional organizations with a focus on destination marketing and management.

There are now several industry groups dedicated to this professional field including Destination Marketing Association International (DMAI), located in Washington, DC; European Cities Marketing (ECM), headquartered in Dijon, France; Pacific Asia Travel Association (PATA), with its head office in Bangkok, Thailand; and several others including AACVB (Asian Association of Convention and Visitor Bureaus), based in Macau SAR; and WACVB (Western Association of Convention and Visitors Bureaus) located in California. Moreover, influential organizations including the UN World Tourism Organization (UNWTO) (Madrid, Spain) have set up special initiatives related to destination management or marketing, and are providing related technical publications, conferences and training. The newly-created World Tourism Cities Federation (WTCF) in Beijing is also likely to attach a high priority to urban destination marketing and management.

DMAI has approximately 600 member DMOs from more than twenty countries. On its website, it states that it is the 'world's largest association of destination marketing organizations' (DMAI, 2012).

European Cities Marketing (ECM), like DMAI, WACVB and AACVB, is an organization principally dedicated to furthering the professional interests and standing of DMOs. DMAI was founded in 1914 as the International Association of Convention Bureaus; whereas ECM's history is shorter, tracing back a little more than twenty-five years. ECM has approximately 100 member cities from thirty-two countries in Europe.

WACVB is an association of DMOs in the western states and provinces of the USA and Canada, and it has around 130 members. The major goal of WACVB is to 'promote and expand the influence of the convention and visitor industry through education' (WACVB, 2012). WACVB's educational offerings include a series of video training modules (Media Relations and Community Relations; Leadership and Management; Marketing and Advertising; Sales (Convention, Meetings, Sports and Leisure); Services (Convention and Leisure); and Social Media).

AACVB was established in 1983 to foster regional cooperation among convention and visitor bureaus (CVBs) in Asia. The founding members were from Indonesia, Hong Kong, Malaysia, Philippines, Singapore, South Korea and Thailand. China and Macau joined later. The mission of AACVB is 'to raise the platform, level of sophistication and capabilities of the MICE industry in Asia, to increase Asia's competitiveness and to drive business to its member destinations' (2011).

The UNWTO has a 'Programme for Destination Management' (2012) and has been active in holding conferences and producing publications on destination management. The main objectives of these efforts are to:

1 Enhance sustainable development of tourism, maximizing economic, social and cultural benefits for the local communities
2 Develop effective management and marketing tools to reinforce destination competitiveness
3 Facilitate new product development in line with market trends, needs and interests
4 Undertake appropriate research to measure the economic impact of tourism as well as to identify the strategic priorities of the destination.

PATA was established in 1951 and is 'the leading voice and authority on travel and tourism in the Asia Pacific region' (PATA, 2012). PATA has a diverse membership drawn from many parts of the tourism sectors and not only DMOs. Included in the membership are approximately 80 government, state and city DMOs. PATA organizes several important events and educational programmes each year, and its Strategic Intelligence Centre (SIC) provides much useful research data on tourism in the Asia-Pacific region.

Pioneering works and programmes in destination marketing and management

The pioneering book on these topics was published in 1988 by Richard Gartrell, *Destination Marketing for Convention and Visitor Bureaus* (Kendall/Hunt Publishing), and it was released under the auspices of the International Association of Convention and Visitor Bureaus (IACVB) (now Destination Marketing Association International). Eric Laws published a book with the title of *Tourist Destination Management: Issues, Analysis and Policies* (Routledge) in 1995.

The introduction of the Certified Destination Management Executive (CDME) programme in 1992 by the then IACVB was a watershed for the field of destination management. It recognized that destination management was not just a topic; it was more importantly a profession. The programme was developed by Don Anderson at the University of Calgary in Canada, and by the author while at Purdue University in the USA. Core and elective classes were offered and the participants were senior DMO executives and managers. The three core classes are on Strategic Issues in Destination Management; Destination Marketing Planning; and Destination Leadership. CDME focuses on upgrading the knowledge and skills of individual DMO professionals.

Later in 2004, DMAI established a Performance Measurement Team to begin the process of identifying DMO performance measurement benchmarks. A *Handbook* of measures was released in 2005. Also in 2005, DMAI released a book about destination branding, called *Destination BrandScience*, co-authored by Duane Knapp and Gary Sherwin. During 2010–2011, DMAI appointed a Performance Reporting Task Force, and the Task Force's efforts resulted in an updated edition of DMAI's *Standard DMO Performance Reporting: A Handbook for DMOs.* Additionally, in 2012 DMAI produced a revised edition of the *DMO Uniform System of Accounts (Standard Financial Reporting Practices for DMOs).*

The Destination Marketing Accreditation Program (DMAP) was another major breakthrough on the professional side of destination marketing. DMAI has the following to say about the importance of DMAP:

> Our industry has made significant progress in elevating the relevancy of DMOs worldwide, with performance reporting reshaping the way DMOs report to stakeholders, and branding improving their positioning.
>
> These two initiatives are the founding fabric of the Destination Marketing Accreditation Program (DMAP), an independent international body defining quality and performance issues in destination marketing and recognizing DMOs that meet or exceed industry standards.
>
> (http://www.destinationmarketing.org)

Unlike the CDME programme, DMAP focuses on DMOs as organizations rather than on individual DMO professionals. As of July 2012, 148 DMOs had been evaluated and awarded the DMAP designation and these were in the USA, Canada, Belgium, Poland and South Korea. DMAP was especially important in identifying sixteen 'domains' for measuring the performance of a DMO (governance; finance; human resources; technology; marketing; visitor services; group services; sales; communications; membership; management and facilities; brand management; destination development; research/marketing intelligence; innovation; and stakeholder relationships).

During the first decade of the new millennium, there was a surge in new books, academic articles and practice-oriented manuscripts on destination marketing and management. One of the most influential of the new books was *Destination Branding* (2002) by Nigel Morgan, Annette Pritchard and Roger Pride. This new publication seemed to spur many academic researchers into doing research, writing articles and arranging conferences around the topic of destination branding. It should be recognized that many tourism scholars beginning in the early 1970s were producing valuable research contributions on destination image and its measurement. This research undoubtedly provided a valuable platform for what was to come later about destination branding and positioning.

Another benchmark was UNWTO's *A Practical Guide to Destination Management* published in 2007. Prepared for UNWTO by TEAM Tourism Consulting of the UK, this was the first practical guide on all aspects of destination management. UNWTO and the European Travel Commission (ETC) later co-sponsored two additional practical guides: *Handbook on Tourism Destination Branding* (2009, prepared by Tom Buncle) and *Handbook on Tourism Product Development* (2011, prepared by Tourism Development International).

Several related books from academic authors have been added in recent years. These have included two books by Stephen Pike: *Destination Marketing Organisations: Bridging Theory and Practice* (Elsevier Science, 2005) and *Destination Marketing: An Integrated Communication Approach* (Butterworth-Heinemann, 2008). Two other books were published in 2011: *Destination Marketing and Management: Theories and Applications* by Youcheng Wang and Abraham Pizam (CABI) and *Managing and Marketing Tourist Destinations: Strategies to Gain a Competitive Edge* by Metin Kozak and Seyhmus Baloglu (Taylor & Francis). All four of these books are welcome additions to the scholarship on destination marketing and management, and offer a variety of different perspectives on the topics.

Some pioneering courses in destination management have appeared in universities in the 2000s. These include the Tourism Destination Management Certificate Program at George Washington University in the US, and the Master in Tourism Destination Management at NHTV Breda University of Applied Sciences in the Netherlands. Individual classes on either destination marketing or destination management have been introduced at universities around the world, particularly in Australia and the UK.

Generally, universities have been rather slow and hesitant to introduce individual classes and full courses on destination marketing and management. The likely reasons for this may be a view that these topics are 'too specialized' and therefore they do not warrant separate attention; and that student interest in these precise topics is modest. There is certainly some validity to these viewpoints at the current time, but this may change in the next decade as destination marketing and management attract more scholars and scholarship. Due to student demand, this trend has already started with many academic programmes introducing courses in event management, which arguably is just one 'sliver' of destination management. As graduates from these event management programmes increase in number and start competing in a relatively small arena, there will perhaps be a realization that universities would be better off aggregating all of the components of destination management into one holistic and integrated course of study. Also, it seems likely in future that there will be some disaggregation of the so-called 'tourism management' programmes that have awkwardly tried to span everything that falls outside of the purview of hospitality management.

Acknowledgements

My association and experiences with destination marketing and management span three decades and I have been very fortunate to have been involved with these two topics at various levels across several continents as a marketer, consultant, teacher and trainer. In my numerous journeys around the world, I have learned from and been inspired by many great professionals.

I have always taught my students to be generous in sharing the credit with others and not to take credit from others when you do not deserve it. To be true to my own teaching and advising, the assistance of many other people is hereby acknowledged.

The idea for writing this book started many years ago when I was providing consulting advice for the Canadian Government Office of Tourism and the Ontario Ministry of Industry and Tourism. These bodies have undergone many name changes since then, but at that time we would have not called them destination management organizations or DMOs. This was my 'apprenticeship' period in destination management when I learned most about destination planning, research, product development, professional development and training. Much was accomplished in that time period and I had the privilege to work with some highly professional clients and mentors including George Kibedi, Wayne Fergusson and Bob Brock. It was also during this time period that I had the pleasure to cooperate on tourism planning projects with Anna Pollock, who has gone on to become one of the great visionaries in destination management.

After setting up the Economic Planning Group of Canada with Gordon Phillips, David Hall and Don Anderson, I had the pleasure of participating in many more DMO projects, particularly in Ontario and the Maritime and Western Provinces.

After moving to Purdue University from Canada, several new avenues in destination management and marketing opened up to me. The first one was with the UN World Tourism Organization in Madrid, and this opportunity took me to many different parts of the world. There were several individuals who helped me on the way to this great opportunity and they included Carson (Kit) Jenkins of Strathclyde University in Glasgow and Don Hawkins of George Washington University. Dr Harsha Varma at UNWTO was a valuable colleague through these years, when I gained more practical experience in South and Southeast Asia, the Caribbean, Middle East and Africa.

The second opportunity came with my continuing close working partnership with Don Anderson, who had moved to work with the University of Calgary after his successful experiences with the Calgary Convention and Tourist Bureau (now Tourism Calgary) and World Expo 1986 in Vancouver. Don is truly one of the world's greatest visionaries with respect to destination management and particularly about the advancement of the professional field. Together we worked with many great people in developing, implementing and fine-tuning the Certified Destination Management Executive (CDME) programme with the support of DMAI. These included Professors J.R. Brent Ritchie, Geoff Crouch and Lorn Sheehan at the outset. During the teaching of many core and elective courses, I got to know many wonderful and talented DMO executives who added to my knowledge of the profession. These included Rick Hughes, Joe McGrath, Elaine McLaughlin, Jim Wood, Teresa McKee Anderson, Valerie Pena, Jo Wade, Amy Vaughan, Doug Harman, Bill Talbert, Matt Carter, Maura Gast and many other truly talented DMO professionals.

The third opportunity that came my way was to go to Australia and work with Philip Pearce at James Cook University. During that time, we were fortunate to provide market research and segmentation analysis support to the Queensland Tourist and Travel Corporation (now Tourism Queensland) and many other DMOs within the state. I need to thank Jonathon Day, then with QTTC and now with Purdue University, for his help in arranging this experience for me in Queensland.

A fourth opportunity that came my way was the teaching in Italy and AILUN in Sardinia and thereafter at IULM in Milan. In working with Manuela DeCarlo, Francesca d'Angella and Ruggero Sainaghi at IULM, I was able to learn much about destination marketing and management in Italy and other parts of Europe.

While at Purdue I was also able to work with Joe O'Leary and many talented graduate students of his and my own. This was an exciting time and we conducted many research studies on tourism consumer behaviour, market segmentation analysis, special-interest travel and various other topics.

My latest adventure has taken me to the People's Republic of China where I have conducted many marketing and consulting projects for DMOs through Belle Tourism International Consulting (BTI) at the provincial and city levels. Although at an early infancy level in China, there are many highly skilled and creative professionals in destination marketing and management and it has been my honour to work with some of them, including Guo Minwen, Chen Meihong, Wu Bihu and Ivan Xu. I am also grateful for several opportunities that have been provided for me by PATA and especially to participate in the PATA Macau Task Force that produced the report *Macau Tourism Positioning: Towards a World Centre of Tourism and Leisure*. It was a pleasure to work with the director of the Macau Government Office of Tourism, Joao Costa Antunes, and his talented management team, and my Task Force colleagues, Andrew Drysdale, Jon Hutchison, Sue Warren, Stewart Moore and Lindsay Turner.

It has also been a distinct privilege for me to work in Indonesia on destination marketing and in training related to the introduction of a new nationwide system of DMOs. Spanning 4 years, it has been my pleasure to work with Wiendu Nuryanti, David Sanders, Frans Teguh, Syamsul Lussa and several others to advance destination marketing and management in Indonesia.

PART I

Introduction to destination management and marketing concepts and roles

Chapter 1

The concepts of destination management and marketing

Learning objectives

1 Explain the characteristics of a tourism destination.
2 Define destination management and destination marketing.
3 Identify and explain the roles of destination management.
4 Differentiate between destination management and destination marketing.
5 Categorize the stakeholders in destination management into groups.
6 Explain the 10 As of successful destinations.
7 Provide a definition of destination governance and explain recent trends therein.
8 Describe the types of destination management organizations at different geographic levels.

Introduction

If you are new to the concepts of managing and marketing destinations, it can be confusing to read what has been written to date about them. These are two relatively new concepts in tourism and many experts have been struggling to define and differentiate them over the past 20 years. Sometimes the concepts are used interchangeably, but although closely linked together, they are different. This book will demystify everything for you so you will truly understand destination management and destination marketing.

Destination management has become a profession in recent decades requiring people with specific skills and experiences. Destination managers are a relatively new breed but their status in society is steadily increasing as destination management gains more recognition. Although relatively small in comparison to hospitality management, this is an up-and-coming career field for tourism management graduates.

Defining a tourism destination

Basically a tourism destination is a geographic area that attracts visitors, but more needs to be added to this definition so you fully understand what this book is addressing. Here are the key characteristics of a tourism destination:

- *A geographic area which has an administrative boundary or boundaries*: This ranges from the largest country in the world (Russia) to the smallest like Monaco and the Vatican City. States, provinces, territories, regions, counties and cities within individual countries can also be destinations.
- *A place where the tourist can find overnight accommodations*: These are typically hotels, but there may be many other forms of accommodation. Some of the visitors may be day-trippers, so not all of them necessarily stay overnight.
- *A destination mix is available for visitors*: There are other facilities for tourists apart from overnight accommodations, including restaurants. Most important in drawing tourists are the attractions and events. Transportation, infrastructure and hospitality resources are the other elements of the destination mix.
- *A tourism marketing effort exists*: Steps have been taken to market and promote the place to tourists.
- *A coordinating organization structure has been created*: A destination management organization (DMO) leads and coordinates the tourism efforts of the place.
- *An image exists of the place in tourists' minds*: People have perceptions about what the place has to offer for tourism. These images may be accurate or inaccurate.
- *Government agencies have introduced laws and regulations*: Special laws and regulations control different aspects of tourism.
- *There is a mixture of tourism stakeholders*: Private-sector enterprises, government agencies, non-profit organizations, individuals and other entities have an interest in tourism.

Now that you have a basic idea about destinations, the concepts of destination management and marketing will make greater sense to you. Later in this chapter, you will get to know that there is a great variety of destinations in the world and an enormous range of DMOs are involved.

Destination management and marketing overview

Destination management

Destination management and destination marketing are two highly interrelated concepts in tourism. In fact, destination marketing is one of the functions within the broader concept of destination management. Therefore, it is important for you to first understand destination management before moving onto the details of destination marketing.

Destination management involves coordinated and integrated management of the destination mix (attractions and events, facilities, transportation, infrastructure and hospitality resources). Effective destination management requires a strategic or long-term approach based upon a platform of destination visioning and tourism planning. Destination management is accomplished through specialized organizations, known as destination management organizations (DMOs). DMOs coordinate the efforts of many stakeholders to achieve the destination's vision and goals for tourism.

Destination management organizations (DMOs) came into being because of the need to mount a coordinated effort for planning, developing and marketing tourism destinations. The UN World Tourism Organization (UNWTO) in its publication, *A Practical Guide to Tourism Destination Management* (2007), identified four different roles of DMOs (Figure 1.1):

- *Leading and coordinating*: Leading and coordinating the efforts of all the stakeholders in tourism within the destination, the DMO is the focal organization for ensuring the appropriate use of all the elements of a destination (attractions, amenities, accessibility, human resources, image and price).
- *Marketing*: Destination promotion; campaigns to drive business; unbiased information services; operation/facilitation of bookings; and customer relationship management (CRM). The DMOs marketing efforts are mainly designed to get people to visit the destination.
- *Creating a suitable environment*: Planning and infrastructure; human resources development; product development; technology and systems development; and related industries and procurement. Policies, legislation and regulations are needed as a foundation for guiding and controlling tourism. This includes the DMO's policies and programmes to promote sustainable tourism development within the destination.
- *Delivering on the ground*: Managing the quality of tourist experiences; training and education; business advice. This means that the DMO must ensure that whatever has been promised in its marketing is actually 'delivered' to tourists; in other words, they get the experiences that they were promised. As Figure 1.1 indicates, the main goal is to exceed the expectations of tourists when they first arrive in the destination.

Figure 1.1 shows these four DMO roles along with the elements of a destination, according to the UNWTO. Located in a central position in the diagram, leading and coordinating is shown as being the key role of a DMO.

The following statement from the UNWTO publication clearly indicates that there is much more to destination management than just destination marketing. The very first DMOs to be created decades ago were basically promotional, sales and public relations agencies; today destination management is much broader, more professional and

Figure 1.1 UNWTO definition of destination management roles
Source: UN World Tourism Organization, 2007.

Destination management roles (UNWTO)

DMOs today should not only lead on marketing, but must also be strategic leaders in destination development. This role requires them to drive and coordinate destination management activities within the framework of a coherent strategy. Promotion must attract people to visit in the first place; creating a suitable environment and quality delivery on the ground will ensure that visitors' expectations are met at the destination and that they then both recommend the destination to others and return themselves, on a future occasion.

(UNWTO, A Practical Guide to Tourism Destination Management 2007,
p. ix)

sophisticated. The statement mentions the need for having the 'framework of a coherent strategy' and this means there needs to be an overall plan or strategy for tourism in the destination.

Destination Consultancy Group (DCG), a US-based tourism consulting company, provides another and slightly expanded view of the roles of the DMO in destination management. Six different DMO roles are identified (Figure 1.2):

● *Leadership and coordination*: Setting the agenda for tourism and coordinating all stakeholders' efforts toward achieving that agenda.
● *Planning and research*: Conducting the essential planning and research needed to attain the destination vision and tourism goals.

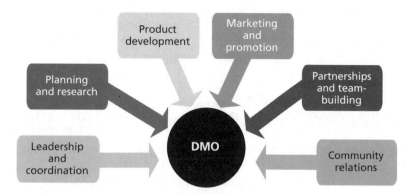

Figure 1.2 DCG definition of destination management roles
Source: Destination Consultancy Group, 2012.

- *Product development*: Planning and ensuring the appropriate development of physical products and services for the destination.
- *Marketing and promotion*: Creating the destination positioning and branding, selecting the most appropriate markets and promoting the destination.
- *Partnership and team-building*: Fostering cooperation among government agencies and within the private sector and building partnership teams to reach specific goals.
- *Community relations*: Involving local community leaders and residents in tourism and monitoring resident attitudes towards tourism.

There are two similar roles in the UNWTO and DCG explanations and these are leadership and coordination, and marketing. DCG expands upon the UNWTO's two other roles of 'creating a suitable environment' and 'delivering on the ground'.

Putting all these pieces together, the following is this book's definition of destination management:

Definition of destination management

Destination management is a professional approach to guiding all of the efforts in a place that has decided to pursue tourism as an economic activity. Destination management involves coordinated and integrated management of the destination mix (attractions and events, facilities, transportation, infrastructure and hospitality resources). Destination management organizations (DMOs) are teams of tourism professionals that lead and coordinate all tourism stakeholders. DMOs' roles include leadership and coordination, planning and research, product development, marketing and promotion, partnership and team-building, and community relations. Effective destination management involves long-term tourism planning and continual monitoring and evaluation of the outcomes from tourism efforts.

VisitEngland offers a second and somewhat different description of destination management that is more focused on sustainability and the needs of tourists and residents. Both of these definitions stress the importance of coordination and collaboration (partnerships) in destination management.

VisitEngland definition of destination management

Destinations are disparate and multifaceted places that are host to numerous stakeholders with their own specific needs. Experience shows that without continued collaboration and coordination, places do not evolve with a common purpose. To create a successful and sustainable visitor economy, all the components that make a successful destination need to be managed and integrated over the long-term, focusing on the needs of both residents and visitors. These components include:

- The things that attract people to the destination; the natural environment, heritage and culture, iconic buildings, retail, sport and leisure facilities, food, gardens, events and scenery. These make a place special, distinctive and capable of engendering civic pride.
- The infrastructure that helps to reinforce and shape the sense of place and make it an easy place to visit; the quality of design, the signs, transport, parking and orientation, interpretation, public spaces and amenities.
- The services that cater for the needs of visitors, and of residents, generating economic and social activity and increasing spending, including the hotels and bars, pubs, restaurants and galleries, the everyday events and the day-to-day services that make a place clean, safe and welcoming.

The elements of destination management are diverse and are often the individual responsibility of a range of public and private sector entities. Destination management is a process that ensures that the visitor experience is of the highest quality and continues to develop and adapt to meet the needs and expectations of visitors. This will achieve a sustainable return from visitor expenditure for the local economy.

You might have come across the term 'destination management company' or 'DMC' and wondered if this is the same as a destination management organization (DMO). Actually they are different types of entities, but the similarity in their names often causes great confusion. DMCs are companies that are specialists in planning and implementing meetings, incentive travel and events in particular destinations. DMOs do not usually provide these services and a DMO's roles are much broader, as you have already learned.

There must be some distinctive advantages of implementing the destination management concept. The UNWTO identifies the following five benefits of following a professional destination management approach (UNWTO website, 2012):

- Establishing a competitive edge
- Ensuring tourism sustainability
- Spreading the benefits of tourism
- Improving tourism yield
- Building a strong and vibrant brand identity.

Destination Marketing Association International (DMAI) adds the following benefits of DMOs for visitors and meeting planners (DMAI website, 2012):

- DMOs offer unbiased information about a destination's services and facilities.
- DMOs save visitors time and energy, as they are a one-stop shop for local tourism interests.
- DMOs can provide the full range of information about a destination.
- Most services provided by DMOs cost nothing.

To sum up here, how can you differentiate between destination management and destination marketing? Destination management is the broader and more inclusive concept. It includes destination marketing and other activities to manage tourism in a destination.

Destination marketing

So, what is destination marketing? Morrison (2010) describes marketing as a 'continuous, sequential process through which management plans, researches, implements, controls and evaluates activities designed to meet customers' needs and wants and their own organizations' objectives'. This definition stresses that marketing is a 365-days-a-year activity and that marketing should be done in a systematic fashion. Morrison also adds that the effectiveness of marketing in tourism can be greatly affected by others outside of the DMO. This holistic, multi-organization view of marketing seems well suited to DMOs who must muster the best efforts of many partner organizations and individuals to have the greatest success. Morrison's broader definition of tourism marketing is adapted and used as the foundation for the following definition of DMO marketing:

Definition of destination marketing

Marketing is a continuous, sequential process through which a destination management organization (DMO) plans, researches, implements, controls and evaluates programmes aimed at satisfying traveller's needs and wants as well as the destination's and DMO's visions, goals and objectives. To be most effective, the DMO's marketing programs depend upon the efforts of many other organizations and individuals within and outside the destination.

(Adapted from Morrison, 2010)

Before the concept of destination management gained widespread acceptance, there were several books and articles published on destination marketing. For example, in 1988 Richard B. Gartrell published a book called, Destination Marketing for Convention and Visitor Bureaus.

Destination management roles

Earlier you learned about two definitions of destination management roles from the UNWTO and DCG. These definitions were quite similar, but also slightly different. Now this chapter will give you a deeper understanding of destination management roles.

Leadership and coordination

The DMO should assume the role of the leader of the tourism sector in its geographic location and coordinate the efforts of all the tourism stakeholders. For example, VisitBritain says that it is Britain's national tourism agency 'responsible for marketing Britain worldwide and developing Britain's visitor economy' (VisitBritain website, 2012). VisitBritain's mission is the following:

VisitBritain mission

'Building the value of tourism to Britain, working in partnership with the industry and nations and regions to generate additional visitor spend'.

This mission statement highlights some of the main parts of a DMO's leadership and coordination role. 'To generate additional visitor spend' indicates that VisitBritain sees itself as a driver of the economic benefits of tourism. 'Working in partnership' reflects VisitBritain's coordination role as an instigator of cooperative efforts and partnerships.

The Virginia Tourism Corporation in the USA also emphasizes its tourism economic leadership role in increasing visitor spending, tax revenues and employment:

Virginia Tourism Corporation goal

The overriding goal of all of VTC's activities is to 'serve the broader interests of the economy of Virginia by supporting, maintaining and expanding the Commonwealth's domestic and international inbound tourism and motion picture production industries in order to increase visitor expenditures, tax revenues and employment'.

DMOs are the advocates, cheerleaders and champions of tourism in their areas. This is needed because tourism is often misunderstood and underestimated as an economic sector and form of business activity. There is also strong competition for local funding and the DMO needs to ensure that tourism gets its 'fair share' of the available resources. DMOs build up community pride and sense of place, often by focusing on local assets and features that local residents under-appreciate or do not recognize at all.

The DMO is usually the leader in tourism marketing and an innovator that other stakeholders follow. It is a main source of tourism marketing ideas and programmes. The DMO tracks overall tourism trends and specific trends in tourist markets, and shares these with other stakeholders.

The DMO takes on another leadership role in helping visitors when they need information and assistance. Additionally, the DMO should promote a sustainable tourism development agenda for the destination.

Planning and research

Taking the major initiative in planning and research is another key role of a DMO. It is accurate to say that there are several destinations that do not have tourism plans, but there are many other DMOs that are very involved in tourism planning. The DMO should periodically coordinate tourism planning exercises and plans should be produced for three time frames: long-term (10 or more years), medium-term (5 years); and short-term (1 year).

DMOs should involve all tourism stakeholders in the planning process, including local residents. Indeed, some experts say that the planning process is just as important as the final planning document. Why? If people are invited to participate in preparing the tourism plan they are more likely to feel that their opinions have been valued and heard. So they may develop a sense of 'shared ownership' in the plan. Additionally, bringing people together who do not normally meet results in more sharing of information and can produce more cooperation within tourism in the destination.

Plans that are not shared widely within the destination are unlikely to be very successful. The DMO should publish final tourism plan documents and ensure that all stakeholders have easy access to them. Nowadays most tourism plans are made available on DMO websites for downloading.

Tourism planning began in the 1960s and there are many countries that have achieved excellence among their DMOs in preparing tourism plans and strategies. These include Ireland, the UK, Canada, Australia and China. For example, Tourism Winnipeg in Canada prepared a very comprehensive *Master Tourism Plan for Winnipeg 2011–2016* and it covers all the DMO roles. The Plan includes a section on research and data management, and correctly points out that research is the foundation for strategic planning. The document has other sections on leadership and foresight, destination product development, marketing and promotions, and community relations (Figure 1.3).

Figure 1.3 Royal Canadian Mint, Winnipeg, Manitoba, Canada
Source: Shutterstock, Inc. (Mike Rogal).

Tourism Winnipeg has a coherent strategy

The role of destination marketing organizations, such as Tourism Winnipeg, is becoming far broader as they move towards providing marketing as well as strategic leadership in destination development. These increased responsibilities require destination marketing organizations to drive and coordinate destination management activities within the framework of a coherent strategy. Initiatives include attracting visitors, creating suitable environments and ensuring quality delivery so that visitor expectations are met resulting in repeat and referral visitation increases.

(Tourism Winnipeg, 2011, p. 7)

Research is a strategic investment for a DMO and usually pays rich dividends. Every DMO should have a research programme and it is a good practice to prepare a plan ahead of time that indicates what research will be completed and what information will be gathered. The Canadian Tourism Commission has an international reputation of being outstanding at conducting tourism research.

Canadian Tourism Commission: a leading innovator in tourism research

The CTC's Research program (www.canada.travel/research) has gained a global reputation as a leading innovator in tourism research. The research conducted has been the fundamental catalyst to our success and the success of Canada's visitor economy. Research contributes to giving Canada's tourism a competitive edge. Timely, credible, and relevant business intelligence has always been at the forefront to support effective strategic business decisions.

(*Inspiring the World to Explore Canada*, Canadian Tourism Commission, 2011, p. 15)

Typically most DMOs track tourist volumes and expenditures to measure year-to-year performance and trends. More detailed tourism economic impact studies are completed by selected DMOs. Some DMOs conduct detailed visitor profile studies on a continuous basis through surveys within the destination. The Las Vegas Convention and Visitors Authority surveys around 300 tourists each month in producing its annual Visitor Profile Study.

Market data is gathered by DMOs and made available to tourism stakeholders. Tourism New Zealand, Tourism Australia, Tourism Ireland and VisitBritain are four national DMOs that do an outstanding job of sharing information on major geographic source markets.

Product development

The DMO's product development role relates to all aspects of the destination product. Figure 1.4 provides a comprehensive definition of the destination product that consists of the physical products in the destination mix, plus people, packages and programmes.

Physical products

These include attractions, facilities (hotels, restaurants, etc.), transportation and infrastructure. DMOs seldom are developers and investors in physical tourism products, but they provide insight and guidance to other stakeholders for such projects. Often DMOs have programmes for identifying potential new attractions and major facilities such as resorts. A good example here is provided in the *Bundaberg-Fraser Coast Tourism Opportunity Plan 2009–2019* prepared in Queensland, Australia by Tourism Queensland and regional tourism authorities. The three goals of this plan were to: (1) identify new tourism products that meets future visitor expectations and demand; (2) identify infrastructure requirements to support the ongoing sustainable development of tourism in the region; and (3) provide a focal document for the development of tourism in the region (Tourism Queensland, 2009).

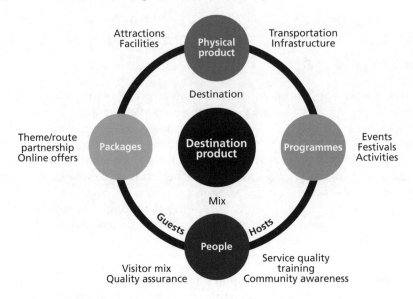

Figure 1.4 The destination product
Source: Adapted from Mill and Morrison, 2012

DMOs may provide funds for conducting planning and feasibility studies on the most promising projects. Attracting investment in tourism is an activity of several DMOs and more recently this has extended into film development.

Accessibility and the safety and security of tourists are major concerns of DMOs. Usually transportation, health and security are the responsibilities of specific agencies of government and the DMO's role is an advisory one.

People

Human resources are very important to all destinations and are very much an essential part of the destination product. The interaction of hosts and guests is critical to successful destination experiences, and both sides of this interaction need to be considered by the DMO.

The visitor mix is the combination of tourist groups and individuals spending time in a destination. The DMO cannot directly and completely control the visitor mix but it can indirectly influence this through its marketing and promotions. The key here is to ensure some general degree of compatibility and absence of conflict among the destination's tourist markets.

Monitoring service quality and maintaining quality assurance programmes are two programmes that several DMOs operate. Examples of DMO quality assurance programmes are Qualmark (New Zealand), T-Qual (Australia), Quality Tourism Services (Hong Kong), Q mark (Spain) and the Quality Programme (Switzerland).

DMOs frequently arrange training programmes for people involved in tourism, both within and outside of the destination. Within destinations, some DMOs offer hospitality and service quality training programmes. Outside of destinations, several DMOs provide training for travel agencies and tour companies. Tourism Australia's Aussie Specialist Program is a good example of training aimed at making travel companies more knowledgeable and skilled in selling the destination.

Community awareness of tourism is very important for destinations and many DMOs recognize this and take action to build greater awareness. For example, Tourism Fraser Coast in Australia has produced a television commercial as part of its community awareness campaign. Other DMOs have special programmes each year where they try to raise awareness of the size, scale, economic and other benefits of tourism. These include many countries in the Caribbean. English Tourism Week is held in March to celebrate the positive benefits from the tourism sector. The National Travel and Tourism Week in May each year is organized by the US Travel Association and celebrated by many DMOs in the USA (Figure 1.5).

Packages

Most packaging in tourism is done by tour operators and travel agencies, and hotels and resorts, but sometimes DMOs get involved as well. Some DMOs offer financial or non-financial incentives to encourage others to build new packages. Several DMOs put together packages through partnerships with their stakeholders and offer them for online sale via their websites.

Another activity of DMOs is the creation of themed routes or itineraries where related attractions and features are linked together. This may be done just by one DMO or by several DMOs working in partnership. For example, VisitScotland has assembled many themed itineraries and publicizes them on its website. These include the Malt Whisky Trail on Speyside and Scotland's Castle Trail.

Programmes

A very worthwhile endeavor for DMOs is to assist with increased programming that enhances tourist experiences within the destination. Programming includes events, festivals and individualized arranged activities for tourists. Events range from mega-events such as the Olympics, World Expo and the World Cup to smaller-scale business events. Festivals are of many varieties but they often celebrate historical and cultural aspects of local communities. Local non-profit groups typically organize festivals and several DMOs assist them by providing grants or marketing assistance.

Individualized activities are another type of programming in which the DMO designs experiences for tourists. Historic walking tours are a great example, as are more nature-based walks and hikes. The Hong Kong Tourism Board, for example, produces the *Inside Guide to Hikes and Walks in Hong Kong* that is a most valuable information resource for tourists who enjoy the outdoors.

Figure 1.5 National Travel and Tourism Week 2012 logo
Source: US Travel Association, 2012

Marketing and promotion

This is a predominant role for many DMOs and receives a great deal of emphasis. In this book, special attention is given to destination marketing because of its great influence on effective destination management. Since several chapters are devoted to marketing, just a brief overview of this role is given now.

The main components of a DMO's marketing and promotion role are the following:

- *Marketing planning*: Following a systematic, step-by-step approach in developing marketing strategies and plans.
- *Market research*: Conducting the essential research, and gathering and interpreting information to make effective marketing decisions.
- *Market segmentation*: Dividing up tourist markets into groups that share common characteristics.
- *Marketing strategy*: Positioning the destination in the competitive marketplace; assessing and adjusting destination image; and designing a destination branding approach.
- *Marketing plan*: Preparing short-term action plans to guide marketing activities.
- *Promotion and communications*: Using online and offline tools and techniques to communicate with all selected audiences.
- *Marketing control and evaluation*: Monitoring marketing implementation and measuring the effectiveness of marketing and promotion activities.

Sometimes you will see a DMO being identified as a destination marketing organization, and this underscores the importance of destination marketing. One of the leading associations in destination management in North America is Destination Marketing Association International (DMAI). This is a result of the historic orientation of DMAI which was to emphasize convention sales and servicing. However, many of the DMOs that belong to DMAI have experienced an expansion of roles beyond marketing and promotion, and they acknowledge that they are part of the broader concept of destination management.

Partnership and team-building

Effective destination management is not only in the hands of the DMO, but also requires effort by other stakeholders within the destination and partners in other places. Collaboration with other organizations and individuals is a must, especially in an era where the financial challenges are great and the competition is intense.

DMOs can achieve much more for their destinations when they work in cooperation with others. A partnership can be defined as a synergistic relationship between a DMO and other organizations or individuals, within or outside of the destination. Morrison (2010) identified five types of potential partners for DMOs: (1) customers (tourists); (2) organizations in the same business (other DMOs); (3) organizations in related businesses (hotels, attractions, airlines, travel agencies, tour operators, etc.); (4) organizations in non-related businesses (automobiles, consumer goods, banks and credit cards, food manufacturers, etc.); and (5) digital alliances (online business relationships including hyperlinking of websites, shared websites and social media sites, etc.).

DMOs can derive many benefits from forming partnerships and these relationships can span all of the DMO roles and not just marketing. Five significant partnerships benefits are shown in Figure 1.6.

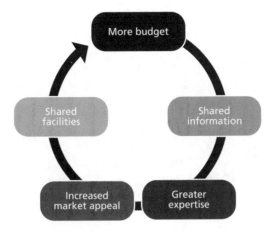

Figure 1.6 Benefits of partnerships

Göteborg & Co. in Sweden provides a great example of a DMO that has been very successful in building partnerships (Figure 1.7).

Figure 1.7 Statue of Poseidon in Gothenburg, Sweden
Photo: Dick Gillberg/Goteborg.com.

17

Collaboration is the key to success in Gothenburg

The main task of Göteborg & Co., in collaboration with private industry and the public sector, is to aid in the development of Gothenburg as a destination. Our ownership structure, which brings together private and public stakeholders, provides a unique foundation for collaboration. One excellent example is the company's Trade & Industry Group. Twenty-five of Gothenburg's largest companies work together in the group to develop Gothenburg as a destination, which also enhances their own competitiveness in the long term.

(Göteborg & Co., 2012)

Community relations

DMOs should frequently communicate and interact with their local communities. Some would say this is a type of internal marketing and public relations for the DMO, but it is much more than that. It is extremely important that local residents are supportive of tourism and are fully aware of its contributions as an economic sector.

Some DMOs believe this is so important that they develop an annual Community Relations Plan that contains all the activities to be used to communicate and interact with the local community. For example, the San Antonio Convention and Visitors Bureau in the USA has a Community Relations and Strategic Initiatives Division. In its annual Business Development Plan, the Bureau has a section on community relations and strategic initiatives. For 2011, the priority objectives were (San Antonio Convention and Visitors Bureau, 2010):

1 Communicate the results of CVB direct sales efforts and marketing activities to stakeholders and the public at large; promote co-op partnerships – as developed by other CVB divisions – with local and regional industry; encourage participation in CVB efforts across all divisions.
2 Represent the interests of the CVB, tourism and hospitality industry in community strategic plans to encourage authenticity and uniqueness of the city.
3 Reinforce brand image and strategy to local audiences to educate and engage them as brand champions across a broad cross-section of visitor touch points.

There are several groups within each community and they include (Tourism Insights, 2008):

- *Elected representatives*: Often referred to as the 'politicians'.
- *Community groups*: Neighbourhood groups, ethnic groups, etc.
- *Interest groups*: Historical societies, conservation groups, etc.
- *Individuals*: Local residents that are not represented by any groups.
- *Business community*: Tourism and non-tourism businesses.

DMOs may also do periodic surveys to gauge resident attitudes to tourism development. Tourism can have negative as well as positive effects on the lives of local residents. Traffic congestion, overcrowding at sites, increased littering and property price inflation can be among the less positive local impacts. Community support is important for tourism development, so polling of resident attitudes is a must and not an option.

Winning community support for tourism is dependent on: (1) the attitudes of local residents to tourism; (2) the contribution of tourism to the economic, social and cultural goals of the community; and (3) the minimization of the negative impacts of tourism on the community. A community-supported tourism management strategy brings with it political support and a warm welcome for tourists in the destination. Additionally, local people will also feel they are involved in tourism and want to act as the 'eyes and ears' of the DMO, in reporting problems and successful tourist experiences when they occur (Tourism Insights, 2008).

The 10 As of successful destinations

How can it be determined if a tourism destination is successful or not? And if the destination is judged to be successful, can the DMO take the sole credit for this great achievement? These are hugely difficult questions to answer but nevertheless they should be tackled.

One answer to the first question is that the successful destinations are the ones with the most tourists. So you will often see the 'world's top destinations' identified as the ones with the most tourist arrivals according to UNWTO. These would include countries such as France, the USA, China, Spain, Italy and the UK. However, many will argue that this is a choice of 'quantity' over 'quality' and that smaller destinations are not necessarily inferior because they have fewer visitors. Additionally, these are countries and there are many more destinations and DMOs below the country level.

Some travel magazines and guidebooks publish 'top destination' lists each year. For example, *Frommer's Top 10 Destinations 2012* included the Bay of Fundy (Canada), Beirut (Lebanon), Chongqing (China), Curacao, Fukuoka (Japan), Ghana, Girona (Spain), Greenwich (England), Kansas City (USA) and Yucatan Peninsula (Mexico). These were picked by Frommer's editors, authors and experts, and with some input from readers. Lonely Planet's *Top 10 Countries for 2012* were Uganda, Myanmar, Ukraine, Jordan, Denmark, Bhutan, Cuba, New Caledonia, Taiwan and Switzerland. This was based on the voting of a Lonely Planet expert panel based on topicality, excitement and value. TripAdvisor.com's *Travelers' Choice 2011 Top 25 Destinations in the World* included Cape Town (South Africa), Sydney (Australia), Machu Picchu (Peru), Paris (France), Rio de Janeiro (Brazil), New York City (USA), Rome (Italy), London (UK), Barcelona (Spain) and Hong Kong (China); these were the top 10 in the ratings followed by fifteen others. There are many other of these 'top destination' lists but just from this small collection, it is interesting to note that no destination appeared twice on these three. But more importantly no specific and detailed criteria were given for the selections.

The World Centre of Excellence for Destinations (CED), located in Montreal, Canada, has developed the *System of Measures for Excellence in Destinations* (SMED). Established in 2007, CED has evaluated several destinations around the world with SMED. A panel of SMED experts visits and assesses each destination that applies, and the destination pays a fee for this service. The destinations that have been evaluated successfully include Abitibi-Témiscamingue (Canada), Andorra, Cantons de L'Est (Canada), Chengdu (China), Crete (Greece), Douro Valley (Portugal), Jeddah (Saudi Arabia), Madeira (Portugal), Mexico City, Montreal (Canada), Riviera Maya (Mexico), Samos (Greece) and Tela (Honduras). This system was a breakthrough for destination management and was created with the support of UNWTO. However, the criteria for approval of destinations under SMED have not been made public.

Based upon years of related experience, the author suggests 'The 10 As' as a useful set of attributes for judging the success of tourism destinations. Each of these ten attributes begin with the letter 'A' (Figure 1.8).

The following is a short explanation of each of the 10 A's attributes:

- *Awareness*: This attribute is related to tourists' level of knowledge about the destination and is influenced by the amount and nature of the information they receive.
  DMO question: Is there a high level of awareness of the destination among potential tourists?
- *Attractiveness*: The number and geographic scope of appeal of the destination's attractions comprise this attribute.
  DMO question: Does the destination offer a diversity of attractions that are appealing to tourists?
- *Availability*: This attribute is determined by the ease with which bookings and reservations can be made for the destination, and the number of booking and reservation channels available.
  DMO question: Can bookings and reservations for the destination be made through a variety of distribution channels?
- *Access*: The convenience of getting to and from the destination, as well as moving around within the destination, constitutes this attribute.
  DMO questions: Is there convenient access to and from the destination by all modes of transportation? Is there convenient transportation within the destination?
- *Appearance*: This attribute measures the impressions that the destination makes on tourists, both when they first arrive and then throughout their stays in the destination.
  DMO question: Does the destination make a good first impression? Does the destination make a positive and lasting impression?
- *Activities*: The extent of the array of activities available to tourists within the destination is the determinant of this attribute.
  DMO question: Does the destination offer a wide range of activities in which tourists want to engage?

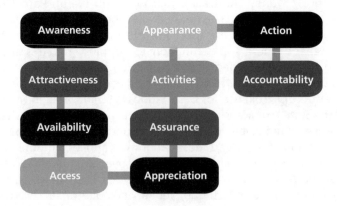

Figure 1.8 The 10 As of successful tourism destinations

- *Assurance*: This attribute relates to the safety and security of the destination for tourists.
  DMO question: Is the destination clean, safe and secure?
- *Appreciation*: The feeling of the levels of welcome and hospitality contribute to this attribute.
  DMO question: Do tourists feel welcome and receive good service in the destination?
- *Action*: The availability of a long-term tourism plan and a marketing plan for tourism are some of the required actions.
  DMO question: Is the tourism development and marketing in the destination well planned?
- *Accountability*: This attribute is about the evaluation of performance by the DMO.
  DMO question: Is the DMO measuring the effectiveness of its performance?

These ten attributes can be useful for all destinations, but they need to be expressed in greater detail than that shown above. Additionally, there are other criteria that could be added to this list of ten. For example, the economic contributions of tourism to the destination might also be included, as well as the degree to which the destination is following a sustainable tourism agenda.

Uniqueness of destination management and marketing

Having constructed these definitions and discussed the roles of destination management and marketing, it is important to pinpoint the key differences between DMO management and marketing and for other tourism and hospitality organizations. The following differences make destination management and marketing unique:

The lack of control over the quality and quantity of services and products

With very few exceptions, DMOs do not own or operate the facilities, services, attractions, events and other amenities that they represent and market. However, this does not mean that the DMO is totally absolved from worrying about these. The quality and quantity of destination services and products greatly influences the satisfaction of visitors and the effectiveness of the DMO's programmes.

The lack of a pricing function

DMOs rarely get involved in pricing the services and facilities they represent, this function being performed by other tourism and hospitality organizations within the destination. Once again, although DMOs seldom do pricing themselves, they are often very concerned with the price levels in their destinations. For example, the prices of hotels and meeting/trade show facility rentals are a major concern in competitive bidding for major conventions, conferences, shows or events.

The need to serve the requirements of many organizations

DMOs have many constituencies or stakeholders that they serve ranging from government departments to industry members (Buhalis, 2000). They must balance the requirements of other organizations that may have differing priorities and objectives, and who may even be competitors. DMOs must be objective and fair in their treatment of all stakeholders.

The need to build consensus among stakeholders

The DMO is the local leader in destination management and marketing. However, it cannot fulfil this leadership role without building consensus among stakeholders for its vision, goals, strategies, objectives, plans and programmes. This consensus building means selling the DMO's ideas to others in the community through formal and informal communications.

The need to be sensitive to the interests of local residents

DMOs not only represent tourism and hospitality organizations but also are accountable to the residents of their communities. They must be vigilant not to promote forms of tourism or developments that will undermine the environmental, social or cultural resources and values of the community.

The need to demonstrate broad economic benefits

Most DMOs are public or quasi-public organizations. While private-sector businesses are accountable through profitability only to their owners or shareholders, DMOs are not profit-driven agencies. Their accountability must be demonstrated through the effective use of funds and the DMO's impact in generating additional visitor spending and employment in tourism and hospitality.

The difficulty in measuring performance

DMOs have no direct sales figures at their disposal because they do not sell products and services directly to visitors. This means that they have greater difficulty in measuring marketing effectiveness (McWilliams and Crompton, 1997).

As a result of these differences, it is clear that a DMO has two distinct audiences with which it must communicate, external and internal. The external audience consists of the potential visitors to the destination and travel trade intermediaries. The internal audience encompasses all the local stakeholders including the board of directors, members, industry operators, government officials and local residents. To be successful requires that a DMO communicate effectively with both the external and internal audiences; its job is not just limited to external marketing.

Stakeholders in destination management

This book uses the term stakeholder many times and you will probably want to know what it means. Before giving the definition, you need to know that the broader view of destination management is being taken and so it is not just about the DMO's stakeholders. Stakeholders are groups and individuals that have a direct or indirect interest in the management of a destination for tourism.

Figure 1.9 shows the five main groups of stakeholders in destination management (tourists, tourism sector organizations, community, environment and government). Tourists and tourism sector organizations have a direct interest in destination management; they are directly affected by the tourism situation in the destination. The other three groups are more indirectly affected by tourism in the destination, although some of these groups and individuals are more involved with tourism than others.

The DMO needs to be especially cognizant of all these groups of stakeholders since they all contribute in some way to the success of tourism within the destination. It is not enough to communicate and interact only with tourists and tourism sector organizations. Continuous communications is also required with government agencies, community groups and residents, and environmental groups. Consultation, involvement and participation are also needed, and especially when strategic decisions are being made about tourism. VisitEngland (2008) defines these three terms as follows:

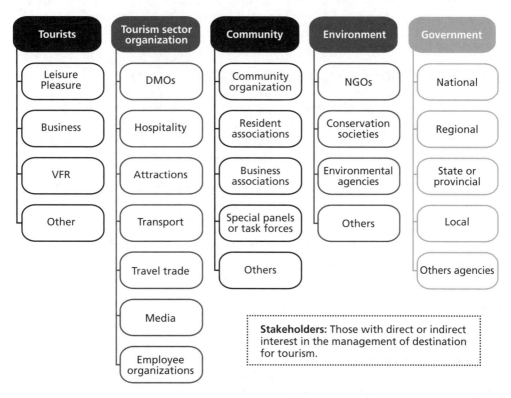

Figure 1.9 Stakeholders in destination management

- *Consultation*: Asking for opinions and viewpoint on options, alternative strategies or programmes of action.
- *Involvement*: Working together with others to formulate options and strategies.
- *Participation*: Facilitating stakeholders to formulate options and strategies.

The stakeholders in the DMO itself are most likely to be certain government agencies and tourism sector organizations. These parties have the most direct interest in the operations of the DMO since the strategies and programmes directly affect them.

Destination governance

Destination governance is an issue that has received more attention in destination management during the past ten years. Beritelli *et al*. (2007) defined destination governance as 'setting and developing rules and mechanisms for a policy, as well as business strategies, by involving all the institutions and individuals'. Destination governance relates to how a DMO is administered and who does the administering. It also concerns the policies, systems and processes used to ensure that all stakeholders are involved.

Traditionally DMOs in most countries were 'governed' by the public sector, meaning that they were run by government agencies with little private-sector input and involvement. According to a survey completed by UNWTO, this situation has changed:

UNWTO findings on destination governance

It seems that destination governance has shifted rapidly from a traditional public-oriented model to a more corporate one. There is a clear indication that public/private partnerships (PPPs) play a leading role for destination management in the majority of the organizations participating in this survey

(Survey on Destination Governance, UNWTO, 2010)

In the following section of this chapter, different types of DMOs and their governance are discussed.

Destination management organizations

Scattered throughout the world and spanning many different organizational sizes and types, DMOs have existed for at least 100 years. Destination management is done by a wide variety of DMOs ranging from national to city-level organizations. The DMO types include entities at four geographic levels:

- Country
- State, province and territory

- Region
- County and city.

Countries have different government administrative structures. For example, under the national government in Italy there are regions and then within the regions there are provinces. In other places, it is the opposite with the regions being under states and provinces, such as in Ontario, Canada and Queensland, Australia.

Should the government administer the DMO or should the private sector or perhaps a collaboration of government and the private sector? Another difficult question to answer, but it is safe to say that in most countries it is the government that runs the DMOs. The strengths of government or the public sector in operating DMOs are considered to be (adapted from a presentation by Esencan Terzibasoglu (2011), UNWTO, September 2011):

- Governments have a mandate to do long-term, strategic planning and they are good at it.
- Destination awareness is high among governments due to their extensive responsibilities and grass-roots knowledge and activities.
- Public administrators are skilled in managing complex organizations and may be better able to get financial support from government.
- Governments often provide grants and other support for small- and medium-sized enterprises (SMEs).
- Public agencies may have greater powers in operating quality assurance programmes.

However, it is often argued that government agencies are very bureaucratic and slow to accomplish tasks. Other common criticisms are that they tend to be politically influenced and that key staff members are frequently changed. Governments are also considered to not be skilled at marketing.

The strengths of the private sector include:

- The private sector is good at implementing short-term tactics.
- Decision-making in the private sector is fast.
- The private sector is very skilled and experienced in marketing and sales approaches.
- The private sector is aware of market opportunities.
- A business management approach is followed.
- The private sector has well-developed programmes for customer relationship management (CRM).

The strongest argument against the private sector is that it is not particularly good at the long-term planning that is required for a tourism destination. Also it can be said that the private sector is profit-motivated and may not be as concerned about community residents or the environment. The private sector may not be as able to get financial support from government agencies.

Having made these initial comments about DMO governance, the following materials describe the types of DMOs that exist around the world at the four geographic levels. As you will see, there is no single template for the organizational structure of a DMO. In fact, there is great variation in DMO types across the globe.

National destination management organizations

National DMOs are typically the most powerful within a country and set the overall agenda for tourism. National DMOs are set up in many different ways and their relative power tends to be a function of how they are positioned relative to the national government.

National tourism administrations and ministries of tourism (NTAs and MOTs)

In some countries, the national DMO is called the National Tourism Administration (NTA) and performs all the DMO roles that were discussed earlier. This is the situation in the People's Republic of China with the China National Tourism Administration (CNTA). Other countries do not explicitly use the term NTA but have created a separate ministry of tourism and in these cases the ministry performs all the DMO roles. This is usually an indication that tourism is considered to be a highly important economic sector for the country. The Bahamas, Croatia, Ghana, Kenya, Oman, India, Israel, Jamaica, Malaysia, and Trinidad and Tobago are just ten of the countries that have a ministry of tourism. Most of these, but not all, are developing countries. Among the countries with dedicated tourism ministries, a good example is the Ministry of Tourism, Government of India, and a description follows:

India Ministry of Tourism

The Ministry of Tourism is the nodal agency for the formulation of national policies and programmes and for the coordination of activities of various Central Government Agencies, State Governments/UTs and the private sector for the development and promotion of tourism in the country. This Ministry is headed by the Union Minister for Tourism and supported by the Minister of State for Tourism.

Shared ministry portfolios including tourism

Some countries afford tourism a somewhat lower priority and profile, and place it along with other government entities in a shared ministerial portfolio. For example, tourism is often combined with economic development, as in the case of the Ministry of Economy, Development, and Tourism in Chile. Another popular combination is tourism and culture, with examples being the Ministry of Culture and Tourism in Turkey and the Ministry of Tourism, Arts and Culture in the Maldives.

In some cases, the word 'tourism' does not appear in the official name of the ministry. An example of this is in New Zealand where tourism is just one of the sectors and industries within the Ministry of Economic Development. In the UK, tourism is under the Department of Culture, Media and Sport (DCMS).

Dual national destination management organization systems

Most countries have just one national DMO, but some have split the roles between two different organizations. Earlier in this chapter, the concept of coordinating all the roles of destination management was emphasized, so why create two separate organizations? The answer revolves around the destination marketing role and governments wanting to give DMOs more flexibility in conducting destination marketing. This option also allows a country to harness the strengths of both government and the private sector within the organization given the responsibility for destination marketing.

In certain countries, all roles except for destination marketing are given to the NTA. Product development, and planning and research are particularly important roles for those types of NTAs that can be found in Australia and Hong Kong SAR, and other destinations. The following is a description of the three main roles played by Australia's NTA, the Department of Resources, Energy and Tourism (RET).

Australia, Department of Resources, Energy and Tourism (RET)

- The Department of Resources, Energy and Tourism (RET) works on a range of tourism policy, projects, programmes and research to strengthen Australia's tourism industry and to grow Australia's tourism market share in a volatile and competitive global environment. A *National Long-Term Tourism Strategy* has been prepared and an update, *Tourism 2020*, was published in December 2011.
- There are a range of programmes administered by the Department of Resources, Energy and Tourism and more broadly across the Australian Government to assist small businesses, including tourism businesses. These programmes include T-QUAL Grants and Accreditation, and the China Approved Destination Status (ADS) Scheme.
- The provision of robust research and analysis for the tourism industry and governments is critical. Research provides the evidence base to support policy, investment, planning and marketing actions to address the structural impediments confronting the industry and enable the industry to position itself to respond to changing market and economic conditions. RET administers Tourism Research Australia (TRA).

Tourism Australia (TA) is the other DMO at the national level in Australia. TA is a statutory body and is responsible for the international and domestic marketing of Australia as a destination for leisure and business travel.

Another example of this dual-DMO system is with the Hong Kong Tourism Commission and the Hong Kong Tourism Board. Of course, Hong Kong is not a country, but a Special Administrative Region (SAR) of the People's Republic of China.

The Hong Kong Tourism Board is the second organization in the SAR. HKTB is a Government-subvented (funded) body that was founded in April 2001 under the HKTB Ordinance. HKTB does the destination marketing for Hong Kong, as well as performing other duties.

Hong Kong Tourism Commission

The Tourism Commission was established in May 1999 and is under the Commerce and Economic Development Bureau. It is headed by the Commissioner for Tourism who is tasked to map out Government's tourism development policy and strategy; to provide a focal point for liaison with the tourism industry; and to enhance coordination in developing tourism.

These are examples of statutory bodies or 'quangos' (quasi non-governmental organizations). Traditionally, they were called commissions, boards or authorities, including the Hong Kong Tourism Board and the Canadian Tourism Commission. More recently the country names have been superseded with either 'Tourism' or 'Visit' including Tourism Australia, Tourism New Zealand and VisitBritain.

One of the main advantages of these bodies is that they tend to offer a blend of public-sector and private-sector strengths. These organizations are governed by independent boards of directors drawn from government, private-sector tourism businesses and non-profits. They have greater management flexibility in dealing with the commercial aspects of tourism marketing and promotion. Additionally, they have closer relationships with the private sector and other non-governmental organizations.

Roles and activities of national DMOs

Despite the variety of organizational structures of national DMOs, they do tend to perform similar types of roles and activities. Some of the major roles and activities of the national DMOs are as follows:

Tourism legislation and regulations: Introduce and enforce legislation and regulations related directly to tourism. This may include the articulation of minimum standards for operating certain types of tourism businesses (accommodations; restaurants; tour guiding; travel agencies; tour operators; adventure travel, etc.).

Tourism policy-making: Prepare overall tourism policies for their countries.

Tourism planning and strategies: Coordinate the processes for developing country-level plans and strategies.

Tourism development: Encourage selected types of tourism developments through financial or technical assistance.

Tourism research: Conduct tourism research at the national level.

Destination marketing: Implement international and domestic marketing strategies and plans.

Education and training programmes: Develop and facilitate education and training programmes that increase professionalism in the country's tourism sector.

Quality improvement and assurance: Introduce strategies and programmes to improve tourism quality that in some cases involve operating quality assurance schemes.

Sustainable tourism: Promote sustainable tourism practices in the country and operate specific programmes to encourage sustainable tourism.

State, provincial and territorial destination management organizations

Several of the larger countries in the world have governmental systems of states, provinces or territories below the national level. In these situations, DMOs are in operation at the state, provincial or territorial levels. Similar to the national level, different types of organizational structures are also found here.

- *Government-run DMOs*: Some of these DMOs are departments or divisions of their state, provincial or territorial governments. For example, in the State of New York in the USA, the Division of Marketing, Advertising and Tourism is within the state government's Empire State Development Agency. The Department of Tourism, Government of Kerala in India is another case. All of the DMOs in the provinces of China are government operated.
- *Statutory bodies and other non-profit organizations*: There has been a trend in recent times to create statutory bodies and other forms of non-profit organizations, particularly to handle the destination marketing for states, provinces or territories. Tourism Northern Territory in Australia is an example of a statutory body. Visit California in the USA is a non-profit organization classified as a (501)(C)(6) corporation.

The roles of these DMOs are similar to the national DMOs but they place more emphasis on domestic tourism in destination marketing and on destination marketing in general. For example, the mandate of Travel Alberta, the provincial DMO for Alberta, Canada is as follows:

Mandate of Travel Alberta

In accordance with the Travel Alberta Act (section 3), the mandate of Travel Alberta is to: market the tourism assets, attractions and opportunities present in Alberta in domestic, national and international markets; promote Alberta as a destination for tourists; assist Alberta's tourism industry operators to market their products; and exercise or perform any other powers, duties and functions authorized by regulation.

Some of these DMOs have a more extensive scope of operations than others and Tourism Queensland (TQ) in Australia is a good example. TQ's primary goals are to:

- Increase leisure visitor expenditure
- Maximize market share
- Increase dispersal to benefit all Queensland regions
- Maximize sustainable tourism growth for the social and environmental benefit of all Queenslanders

(Tourism Queensland (2011), *Annual Report 2010–2011*)

The TQ organization chart (Figure 1.10) shows that it has four main groups: marketing, international, destinations, and performance and planning. This organizational structure shows that TQ is involved in destination marketing, planning and research, and product development. TQ is also very much involved in partnerships and team-building and community relations; so in fact it covers all the DMO roles discussed earlier.

Regional destination management organizations

The definition of what a 'region' constitutes varies from country to country and so therefore does the meaning of a regional DMO. For example, smaller-sized countries including New Zealand and Italy have regional government agencies below the national level. Larger countries such as Canada and Australia have states, provincial or territorial government agencies below the national level and then have regions under the states, provinces or territories.

Several countries, states and provinces have systems of regional DMOs, and these include:

- New Zealand: There are thirty regional tourism organizations in New Zealand.
- Ontario, Canada: The Province of Ontario has thirteen regional tourism organizations.
- Northern Ireland and Irish Republic: There are seven regional tourism authorities in the Irish Republic and seven regional tourism organizations in Northern Ireland.
- Western Australia, Australia: There are five regional tourism organizations in the state of Western Australia.

Destination Queenstown (DQ) in New Zealand is an example of a regional DMO and the following is a description of its roles and activities:

Destination Queenstown

The role of our team is to provide the right assistance to the right people, be it frontline staff, corporate contacts, travel agents, media or DQ Members. Liaison with key markets, leveraging advertising investment, maintaining relationships, developing new contacts and providing updates on events, developments, new products and relevant news in our region is all part of the day's work.

- We have a mandate to generically promote the Queenstown District as an international visitor destination through a variety of distribution channels and we act as the neutral coordinator of initiatives and campaigns that benefit our members.
- We have a core role in several areas including information provision, trade liaison and media promotion.
- We coordinate the collective marketing of Queenstown – identifying, prioritising and promoting the various visitor groups that we believe Queenstown can attract.
- We are responsible for the branding and positioning of Queenstown.

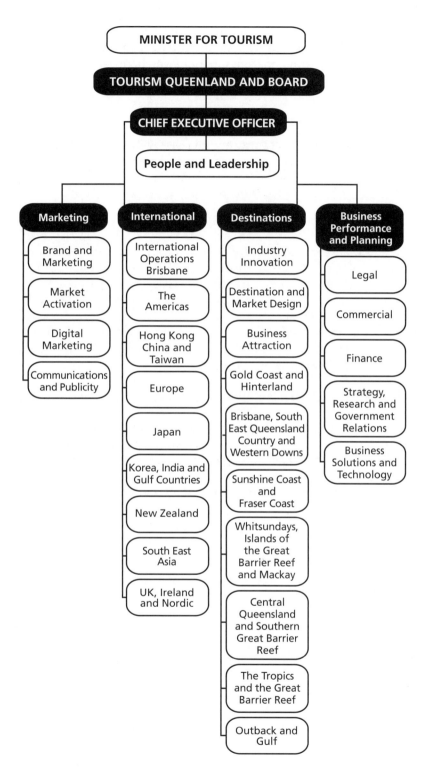

Figure 1.10 Organizational chart for Tourism Queensland
Source: Tourism Queensland, 2012.

Regional DMOs tend to be mainly involved in destination marketing, but in some cases they also assume other roles including planning and research and product development. In most cases, they receive funding from superior levels of government. Regional DMOs are either government-run or are structured as statutory bodies or non-profits.

County and city destination management organizations

At the most local level there are county and city DMOs. These exist in most countries in the largest metropolitan areas. Glasgow in Scotland is a good example:

Glasgow City Marketing Bureau

Glasgow City Marketing Bureau (GCMB) is the official destination marketing organisation (DMO) for the city of Glasgow. As a public–private organization established by Glasgow City Council in 2005, Glasgow City Marketing Bureau's role is to communicate Glasgow's reputation as a world-class city in which to live, work, study, invest and visit.

Glasgow City Marketing Bureau is engaged in a wide-range of activity aimed at delivering economic and social benefits for Glasgow through leisure and business tourism. This activity comprises:

- Development and implementation of the Glasgow: Scotland with style city brand
- Strategic destination marketing communications campaigns across key target markets
- Bidding for, attracting and managing high-profile major events, conventions and exhibitions
- Responsibility for conference and event accommodation bookings.

In some countries and especially in the USA, there are even more extensive systems of county and city DMOs. As was the case at the three other geographic levels, the county or city DMO may be run by the local government or alternatively it may be a non-profit organization.

The introduction of room or bed taxes in the USA at county and city levels led to a rapid expansion of the number of DMOs. Guests at hotels and other forms of accommodation pay these taxes and then part or all of the taxes collected are distributed by local governments to DMOs. In the USA, these organizations are called convention and visitors bureaus or CVBs for short. They mainly focus on destination marketing but are gradually placing greater emphasis on other destination management roles. The Greater Pittsburgh Convention and Visitors Bureau in Pennsylvania is a good example of a city-level CVB in the USA.

Greater Pittsburgh Convention and Visitors Bureau (VisitPittsburgh)

VisitPittsburgh is the official tourism promotion agency for Allegheny County and the lead tourist promotion agency for the Pittsburgh and Its Countryside group. Established in 1935, VisitPittsburgh is dedicated to generating convention, trade show and leisure travel business for the Pittsburgh region. VisitPittsburgh is a non-profit organization serving its business membership.

Careers in destination management and destination marketing

It can be very confusing and frustrating if you enter 'careers in destination management' in a search engine like Google. The results you will get are mainly for destination management companies (DMCs) and not for destination management organizations (DMOs). You will get more success when entering 'careers in destination marketing' but as you already know that does not cover all of destination management.

There is such a great variety of DMOs around the world that it is difficult to talk very accurately about careers. In many countries, the DMOs are governmental agencies so the positions available are as civil servants. In other countries, the DMOs are statutory bodies and non-profit organizations and staff are hired on a contract basis.

VisitEngland is the national tourism board for England and was created in April 2009. This DMO's role is 'to grow the value of tourism by working in partnership with the industry to deliver inspirational marketing campaigns and to provide advocacy for the industry and our visitors' (*An Introduction to VisitEngland*, 2010). According to this description, VisitEngland's main role is destination marketing and so its career opportunities are mainly in marketing and promotion, as shown below:

VisitEngland career opportunities

VisitEngland has teams specializing in many areas including marketing, brands, web development and design, finance and information technology, office services, press and PR, market intelligence, digital and new media, quality standards, online shops, human resources, research and evaluation.

Based on the roles of DMOs, the following skills and competencies shown in Table 1.1 seem the most suited for this career field.

Table 1.1 Skills and competencies most suited for the DMO career field

DMO roles	Skills and competencies
Leadership and coordination	Management
Planning and research	Tourism planning Urban and regional planning Statistics and market research
Product development	Financial analysis Architecture and landscape architecture Urban and regional planning
Marketing and promotion	Marketing Brand management Sales Advertising Public relations and journalism Digital marketing/IT
Partnerships and team-building	Management Negotiation
Community relations	Management Public relations
DMO administration	Human resources management Financial administration Fundraising

Summary

Destination management and destination marketing are two interrelated concepts that have developed in tourism over the past 20 years. Destination management is the broader concept that encompasses destination marketing and other roles. The other roles of destination management are leadership and coordination, planning and research, product development, partnerships and team-building, and community relations.

There are many types of DMOs in the world at the national, state, provincial, territorial, regional, county and city levels. No standardized structural template exists for a DMO and they vary quite widely from country to country. Recently, there has been a trend for DMO governance to move from public-sector only to public–private partnerships (PPPs).

DMOs have a large variety of stakeholders with whom they must network. The fact that they need to serve the requirements of many organizations is one of the unique features of destination management and marketing. The success of a DMO is at least in part measured by how well it communicates and interacts with its stakeholders.

Successful destinations have to satisfy a variety of criteria and this book recommends the '10 As' model as a basic platform. However, there are other systems and criteria that potentially can be used for this purpose.

The field of destination management is receiving greater recognition and becoming more professional. It is a promising career field for tourism management students, although small in comparison to the hospitality management field.

Review questions

1 What are the key characteristics of tourism destinations?
2 How would you define destination management?
3 What is destination marketing?
4 What are the major differences between destination management and destination marketing?
5 Who are the five groups of stakeholders in destination management?
6 What are the features that make destination management and marketing unique?
7 What are the 10 As of successful destinations?
8 What is destination governance?
9 What are the typical roles of national destination management organizations?
10 What are the relative benefits and weakness of government-run DMOs?

References

Beritelli, P., Bieger, T., and Laesser, C. 2007. Destination governance: Using corporate governance theories as a foundation for effective destination management. *Journal of Travel Research*, 46(1), 96–107.

Buhalis, D. 2000. Marketing the competitive destination of the future. *Tourism Management*, 21(1), 97–116.

Canadian Tourism Commission. 2011. Inspiring the World to Explore Canada.

DCG. 2012. Certified Destination Management Executive (CDME) Programme.

Department of Resources, Energy and Tourism. 2012. http://www.ret.gov.au/tourism/Pages/Tourism.aspx

Destination Queenstown. 2012. http://www.queenstownnz.co.nz/information/aboutDQ/

DMAI (Destination Marketing Association International). 2012. http://www.destinationmarketing.org/

Ford, R.C., and Peeper, W.C. 2008. Managing Destination Marketing Organizations. Orlando, FL: ForPer Publications.

Frommer's. 2011. Top Destinations 2012. http://www.frommers.com/micro/2011/top-destinations-2012/bay-of-fundy-nova-scotia.html

Gartrell, R.B. 1988. Destination Marketing for Convention and Visitor Bureaus. Dubuque, IA: Kendall Hunt Publishing.

Glasgow City Marketing Bureau. 2012. http://www.seeglasgow.com/about-us/

Göteborg & Co. 2012. http://corporate.goteborg.com/about/we-create-opportunities/?lang=en

Greater Pittsburgh Convention and Visitors Bureau. 2012. http://www.visitpittsburgh.com/about-us/

Hong Kong Tourism Board. 2011. The Inside Guide to Hikes and Walks in Hong Kong.

Hong Kong Tourism Commission. 2006. http://www.tourism.gov.hk/english/about/abt_est.html

Las Vegas Convention and Visitors Authority. 2011. Las Vegas Visitor Profile Study 2010.

Lonely Planet. 2011. Lonely Planet's Best in Travel: Top 10 Countries for 2012. http://www.lonelyplanet.com/europe/travel-tips-and-articles/76856

McWilliams, E.G., and Crompton, J.L. 1997. An expanded framework for measuring the effectiveness of destination advertising. *Tourism Management*, 18(3), 127–137.

Mill, R.C., and Morrison, A.M. 2012. The Tourism System. Dubuque, IA: Kendall Hunt Publishing.

Ministry of Tourism, Government of India. 2012. http://www.tourism.gov.in/AboutUS/RoleAndFunction.aspx

Morrison, A.M. 2010. Hospitality and Travel Marketing. Clifton Park, New York: Cengage.

San Antonio Convention and Visitors Bureau. 2010. 2011 Business Development Plan: Community Relations and Strategic Initiatives.

Terzibasoglu, E. 2011. Destination Development and Marketing: A Conceptual Model. National Conference on Destination Management Organizations, Labuan Bajo, Indonesia, 22 September, 2011.

Tourism Insights. 2008. Surveying Local Community Attitudes to Tourism. http://www.insights.org.uk/destinationmanagementguideitem.aspx?title=3D%3A+Surveying+Local+Community+Attitudes+to+Tourism

Tourism Northern Territory. 2012. http://www.tourismnt.com.au/about-us/about-tourism-nt.aspx

Tourism Partnership Niagara. 2012. http://visitniagaracanada.com/

Tourism Queensland. 2009. Bundaberg-Fraser Coast Tourism Opportunity Plan 2009–2019.

——2011. http://www.tq.com.au/about-tq/corporate-information/annual-report/2010-11.cfm

——2012. Organisational Chart. http://www.tq.com.au/about-tq/organisational-structure/organisational-chart/organisational-chart_home.cfm

Tourism Winnipeg. 2011. A Master Tourism Plan for Tourism in Winnipeg 2011–2016.

Travel Alberta. 2012. http://industry.travelalberta.com/About%20Us.aspx

TripAdvisor.com. 2011. Top 25 Destinations in the World. http://www.tripadvisor.com/TravelersChoice-Destinations

UNWTO. 2007. A Practical Guide to Tourism Destination Management.

——2010. Survey of Destination Governance.

——2012. http://www.unwto.org

US Travel Association. 2012. http://www.ustravel.org/marketing/national-travel-and-tourism-week

Virginia Tourism Corporation. 2012. http://www.vatc.org/

VisitBritain. 2012. http://www.visitbritain.org/aboutus/whatwedo.aspx

VisitEngland. 2008. England. A Strategic Action Plan 2010–2020.

——2010. An Introduction to VisitEngland. London. http://www.visitengland.org/Images/7506%20IE_Map_AW_FINAL_LR_tcm30-17923.pdf

——2011. Destination Management Action Plan.

——2012. http://www.visitengland.org/about/careers/index.aspx

VisitScotland. 2012. http://www.visitscotland.com/guide/inspirational/itineraries/

World Centre of Excellence for Destinations (CED). 2012. http://www.ced.travel/

Chapter 2

Destination planning

Learning objectives

1 Describe the history and influences on tourism planning for destinations.
2 Explain the benefits that come from doing long-term tourism planning.
3 Detail the desired outcomes from completing a tourism plan for a destination.
4 Identify the contents of a tourism plan for a destination.
5 Elaborate on the different geographic levels for destination tourism planning.
6 Explain the tourism planning process for destination management.
7 Differentiate between strategic planning and visioning.
8 Provide a step-by-step explanation of destination visioning.
9 Pinpoint the advantages of using tourism planning toolkits.

Introduction

Every destination needs to have a long-term direction for its tourism sector, a shared path for all stakeholders to follow for the next five, ten or more years. Long-term or strategic planning are the names most often given to the process used to create this multi-year path to the future. The process used in tourism planning is hugely important and particularly the people and organizations that are involved and how it is conducted.

Tourism planning is not a new subject or endeavour and it dates back at least 45 years in the English-speaking world. So the value and necessity of long-term planning for destinations has been accepted for many decades. However, planning for tourism has recently gained more attention as DMOs expand their roles beyond just marketing and promotion and there is greater priority being given to sustainable tourism development.

Unfortunately, there is no standard template for conducting destination planning and practices vary from country to country. However, this chapter describes some common planning processes and techniques. It also identifies some practical tourism planning toolkits that DMOs can apply.

Planning and research is one of the roles of destination management and it is here that a DMO should start to demonstrate its leadership and coordinative abilities. If no long-term tourism plan exists, the DMO should take the initiative to get a planning process started.

Characteristics of tourism planning

Before describing how a long-term plan for a destination is prepared, there is a need to cover some of the basic characteristics of tourism planning.

History and influences on tourism planning

Tourism planning as a professional field will soon be a 50-year-old. It got started in places like Ireland and France where there was a strong belief in community long-term planning and especially in a regional context that included rural areas. These earliest tourism plans were done by government agencies and prepared by professionals with a background in regional and urban planning rather than tourism. There was an emphasis on the physical planning of destinations in the earliest tourism planning works (Figure 2.1).

The next influence on tourism planning was from tourism academics and professional experts. These people were mainly geographers and economists who had developed a special interest in tourism. These included Professor Clare A. Gunn, who published the book, *Tourism Planning*, in 1979 and this was a 'watershed' text for the topic. Edward Inskeep, who was a tourism planning expert with the UN World Tourism Organization (UNWTO) made a significant contribution with his books on national and regional tourism planning. Another important contribution was by Professor Bihu Wu in his book, *Regional Tourism Planning Principles*, published in 2001 and covering the tourism planning experiences in China.

Management and marketing professionals also greatly influenced tourism planning, drawing especially from the fields of corporate strategic management and strategic planning. From the classic texts on strategic management came the concepts of SWOT

Figure 2.1 Influences on tourism planning

(strengths, weaknesses, opportunities, threats) analysis, and terms such as mission, vision, core values, goals, strategies and critical success factors. The focus was on defining a step-by-step process and in emphasizing that strategic planning was a cycle to be repeated many times. Here also there was a priority on researching, analysing and projecting external environments with the procedure of environmental scanning.

More people with business management backgrounds and MBA-style educations began working for DMOs, as they gradually moved away from just public-sector governance. Marketing, public relations and sales professionals also added their distinct imprints on tourism planning, especially in putting more emphasis on market and competitive analysis rather than just analysing the physical resources of the destination.

The fourth influence on tourism planning was from community planners and non-profit organizations. Here the main focus was on the planning process and on how to get all parts of communities involved in discussing and defining future directions. Inclusiveness and 'getting buy-in' from all stakeholders were key features of these planning processes. The visioning process was derived from this source as an interactive planning tool allowing many people to contribute to strategic planning. In developing countries, non-governmental organizations (NGOs) often play a key role in tourism planning processes.

This influence has also brought a more active role in tourism planning for local residents as individuals or as groups. The sustainable tourism 'movement' since around the early 1980s has also supported the critical need to have resident and community inputs.

Consumers have had a significant influence on tourism planning in recent years. For example, their demands for greater transparency by governments and others have led to tourism plans being publicly available documents, rather than being in the hands of only select people. Consumer use of the Internet and affection for using social media channels has meant there is more open discussion of tourism planning processes and planning documents. Additionally, the need to input tourists' opinions, perceptions and expectations through gathering primary research has become more recognized as an important input to tourism plans.

So tourism planning has evolved over the past 40–50 years. It is much more comprehensive and integrated than when first introduced around the 1960s. Tourism planning is more inclusive than before with all stakeholders getting the opportunity to have their say on how tourism should look in the future.

Benefits of strategic planning for tourism

There is no doubt that every destination needs long-term tourism planning, yet not all destinations have long-term plans for tourism. Essential as they might be, the DMO may be required to justify spending time and money on a long-term tourism planning process. Therefore, the DMO must be able to clearly articulate the benefits of long-term planning for tourism.

Figure 2.2 identifies some of the key benefits of long-term planning for tourism.

● *Clear future directions*: Destination long-term tourism planning produces clear overall directions for all stakeholders on how tourism will be developed and progressed in future years.
● *Greater attention and emphasis for tourism*: Initiating and conducting long-term planning tends to draw greater attention and focus to tourism within the destination.
● *Vision and goals for tourism*: Targets are set for the destination to achieve within specific timeframes.
● *Identification of opportunities*: Specific strategies and development opportunities are identified that will enhance and improve tourism in the destination.
● *Shared plan ownership*: If the planning process is done openly with the involvement and contributions of all stakeholders, there will be a feeling of shared ownership in the plan.
● *Implementation and evaluation guidelines*: The planning process produces steps for implementation and measures for assessing the effectiveness of the plan.

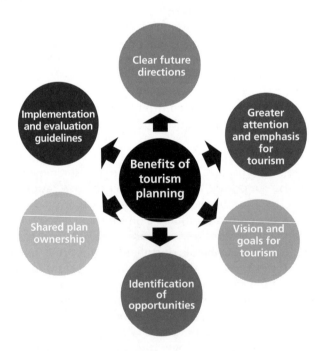

Figure 2.2 Benefits of preparing long-term plans for tourism

Inskeep (1994) identified a more extensive set of advantages of undertaking national and regional tourism planning and these are shown below:

- Establishing the overall tourism development objectives and policies. What is tourism aiming to accomplish and how can these aims be achieved?
- Developing tourism so that its natural and cultural resources are indefinitely maintained and conserved for future, as well as present, use.
- Integrating tourism into the overall development policies and patterns of the country or region, and establishing close linkages between tourism and other economic sectors.
- Providing a rational basis for decision-making by both the public and private sectors on tourism development.
- Making possible the coordinated development of all the many elements of the tourism sector. This includes inter-relating the tourist attractions, activities, facilities and services and the various and increasingly fragmented tourist markets.
- Optimizing and balancing the economic, environmental and social benefits of tourism, with equitable distribution of these benefits to the society, while minimizing possible problems of tourism.
- Providing a physical structure which guides the location, types and extent of tourism development of attractions, facilities, services and infrastructure.
- Establishing the guidelines and standards for preparing detailed plans of specific tourism development areas that are consistent with, and reinforce one another, and for the appropriate design of tourist facilities.
- Laying the foundation for effective implementation of the tourism development policy and plan and continuous management of the tourism sector, by providing the necessary organizational and other institutional framework.
- Providing the framework for effective coordination of the public and private sector efforts and investment in developing tourism.
- Offering a baseline for the continuous monitoring of the progress of tourism development and keeping it on track.

Despite the many obvious benefits of long-term planning of tourism, there still remain many destinations that have not initiated tourism planning. Why? Probably the most important reason for this inaction is that the destination has not attached a high priority to tourism as an economic sector. Additionally in some places there is a belief that the private sector can handle its own planning and there is no need for others to get involved. A third argument against doing long-term planning is that it takes too much time and costs too much money. A fourth reason may simply be in the perceived complexity of tourism planning with so many government agencies, private-sector and non-profit organizations, and individuals involved.

Time frames for tourism planning

A strategic planning process is an approach used to develop a long-term plan for a tourism destination. So what is the 'long term'? In destination management practice, there is no clear agreement on how long a period a tourism plan should cover. Looking at the tourism plans and strategies that have been published over the past 5 years, the range for long-term is from 3 to 15–20 years. For example in 2007, Turkey released the *Tourism Strategy of Turkey 2008–2023* (Figure 2.3). The *New South Wales Tourism Masterplan (Towards 2020)* spanned an even longer period from 2002 to 2020.

Figure 2.3 The tourism strategy for Turkey had an emphasis on culture and heritage. Ancient city of Perge in Turkey
Source: Shutterstock, Inc. (Muratart).

Some tourism plans that have been produced have shorter timeframes than the ones for Turkey and New South Wales. Five-year tourism plans and strategies have included the *Maldives Third Tourism Master Plan 2007–2011*, a *Master Tourism Plan for Winnipeg 2011–2016* and *Roadmap 2009–2013* for Monaco. Ten-year tourism plans and strategies have been the *Wyoming Tourism Industry Master Plan*, *Tourism Master Plan for Barbados 2011–2020*, England's *Strategic Framework for Tourism 2010–2020*, *Glasgow Tourism Strategy to 2016* and *Finland's Tourism Strategy to 2020*.

If tourism plans are prepared for less than 5 years, they are called 'action plans' and usually are for the next 2–3 years. Action plans are either included within the longer-term plans or they are initiated due to previously unforeseen challenges and difficulties within the destination.

Naming of tourism plans

What name should be given to the destination's plan? That's a good question, but it seems there is no consistency in naming practices around the world. The words master plan (or master plan), plan, strategy, framework, blueprint and roadmap all get used rather interchangeably. This is no doubt confusing to anybody unfamiliar with tourism planning and there is a definite need for more standardized terminology across the world.

In order to provide some guidelines in naming, the following three groupings of tourism plans can be used:

- Tourism plan or tourism master plan: a long-term plan for 10 or more years
- Tourism strategy: a medium-term plan for 5–9 years
- Tourism action plan: a short-term plan for 2–4 years.

There is a difference between planning for the destination and planning for the DMO. In this chapter, the topic is planning for the destination and planning for the DMO is discussed in later chapters. This chapter is about the DMO jointly planning for the future of the destination along with all the other tourism stakeholders.

DMOs must also prepare other plans that are more closely related to their operations. For example, DMOs often produce annual corporate plans or business plans that are operating guides for the upcoming year. There may also be a community relations plan prepared by the DMO and, of course, a marketing plan will be required (Chapter 3). In addition, the DMO may prepare its organization strategic plan.

Before moving on, it is important to clear up some confusion in the use of the words strategic, strategy, strategies and strategic planning, as they have multiple meanings in tourism planning and practitioners tend to use them in different ways. Here is how they are used in this book:

- *Strategic*: This means long-term and thus planning for 5 or more years into the future.
- *Strategy*: Tourism strategy is used interchangeably with the term tourism plan.
- *Strategies*: Selected overall programmes of actions or initiatives contained in a tourism plan or strategy to achieve its stated goals.
- *Strategic planning*: A process emerging from the management literature that involves scanning the macro-environment (internal and external) and then defining mission, vision, core values, goals and strategies.

Outcomes of tourism planning

The DMO and its stakeholders must define the key goals for completing a tourism plan and state the desired outcomes of planning. Mill and Morrison (2012) suggest that tourism planning should have at least five outcomes (Figure 2.4):

- *Identifying alternative approaches*: Pinpointing different options or scenarios for important aspects of tourism in the destination.
- *Creating the desirable*: Following steps that increase the benefits of tourism.
- *Avoiding the undesirable*: Anticipating potential negative impacts of tourism and taking steps to avoid them.
- *Maintaining uniqueness*: Identifying the destination's unique assets and USPs (unique selling propositions) and identifying steps to maintain and enhance them.
- *Adapting to the unexpected*: Designing contingency and crisis management plans to cope with unexpected situations.

Content areas of a tourism plan

It is important that a plan is built from a platform consisting of a clear set of long-term goals for tourism in the destination. An overall destination vision for the future needs to be articulated. The UNWTO states that a tourism master plan should identify the actions, stakeholder roles and responsibilities, timelines, indicative budgets, monitoring guidelines and success criteria for ten aspects of tourism in a destination (transport, accommodation, tourist activities, product development, tourism zoning, marketing and promotion, institutional framework, statistics and research, legislation and regulation and quality standards of tourism services).

The following table combines the 10 As model from Chapter 1 with the UNWTO recommendations for tourism master plans to produce a more detailed set of recommended topics for tourism plan contents (Table 2.1).

Identifying alternative approaches	Adapting to the unexpected	Maintaining uniqueness
• Marketing • Development • Organization of tourism • Community awareness of tourism • Support services and activities • Transportation and infrastructure	• General economic conditions • Energy supply and demand situation • Values and lifestyles • Performance of local industries • Government legislation and regulations • Technological advances	• Local cultural and social fabric and traditions • Local architecture and heritage • Historical monuments and landmarks • Local festivals, events and activities • Natural features and resources • Parks and outdoor sports areas

Creating desirable	Avoiding the undesirable
• Sustainable tourism development • High level of community awareness of the benefits of tourism • Clear and positive image of area as a tourism destination • Effective organization of tourism • High level of cooperation among tourism organizations and businesses • Effective marketing, directional sign and travel information programmes	• Friction and unnecessary competition • Hostile and unfriendly attitudes of local residents towards visitors • Damage or undesirable permanent alteration of natural features and historical resources • Loss of cultural identities • Loss of market share • Stoppage of unique local events and festivals • Overcrowding, congestion and traffic problems • Pollution • High seasonality

Figure 2.4 Desirable outcomes of tourism planning
Source: Adapted from Mill and Morrison, 2012.

Table 2.1 Recommended content areas for a tourism plan

10 As	Plan content topics	Detailed content topics
Awareness	• Marketing and promotion	• Destination branding • Marketing strategy
Attractiveness	• Product development	• New and improved attractions
Availability	• Marketing and promotion	• Distribution channels • Information communication technologies (ICTs)
Access	• Transportation • Infrastructure • Tourism zoning	• Airports and airline services • Road, rail and water access • Touring corridors and pathway systems
Appearance	• Tourism zoning • Product development	• Entry point beautification • Arrival zone planning • Overall public space maintenance
Activities	• Product development • Programming	• Festivals and events • Individual activities

continued

Table 2.1 Continued

10 As	Plan content topics	Detailed content topics
Assurance	• Quality standards of tourism services • Safety and security • Infrastructure • Legislation and regulation	• Quality assurance programme • Public health and food safety programmes • Public security programmes • Regulations on operating practices
Appreciation	• Human resources • Community attitudes	• Hospitality skills training • Foreign language training • Community tourism awareness
Action	• Statistics and research	• Long-term tourism plan • Marketing plan • Research programme • Implementation
Accountability	• Institutional framework • Statistics and research	• Organizational structure • Performance evaluation • Tourism market volume statistics and economic impacts
Additional As		
Accommodations	• Accommodations	• Hotels and resorts • Specialist accommodations
Actors	• Stakeholder roles and responsibilities	• Programme implementation responsibilities
Agenda for sustainability	• Policies • Tourism zoning	• Sustainable tourism policy • Sustainable tourism programmes
Allocation	• Budgets	• Budget requirements • Funding sources
Attainment	• Timelines/timeframes	• Timetable for implementation and achievement of goals

The Ministry of Jobs, Tourism and Innovation in British Columbia, Canada provides another good and more succinct listing of the contents that should be in a destination's long-term plan for tourism:

● Vision, mission, objectives (goals) and strategies
● Organizational structure
● Budget and sources of funding
● Target markets
● Brand positioning
● Priority product and destination development categories and strategies
● Priority promotional strategies
● Research and evaluation
● Tactics and implementation plan.

These are recommendations about what should be included in long-term tourism plans, but what in actual practice appears in completed plans? To make sure that you really know what is 'happening on the ground', a few examples from recently completed tourism plans for destinations are now reviewed.

The first case study is for a national-level tourism plan and the table of contents is shown in Figure 2.5. It is from the Maldives Third Tourism Master Plan (TTMP). This was a ninety-two page document containing four main sections (Introduction; Review of tourism in the Maldives; Situational analysis; and Strategies and actions). This plan included a very detailed analysis of the existing situation comprising thirty-six pages. Six main strategies were identified in the plan and for each of the strategies specific actions, completion dates and performance measures were identified.

Introduction
Review of tourism in the Maldives
- Overview of the Maldives tourism industry
- The First Tourism Master Plan 1983
- The Second Tourism Master Plan 1996–2005

Situational analysis
- Economic and financial analysis
- Tourist arrivals, markets and product analysis
- Human resource situation analysis
- Environmental analysis
- Community-based tourism analysis
- The legal framework
- Infrastructure and support services analysis

Strategies and actions
1. Facilitate sustainable growth and increase investment in the industry, while enhancing public share of benefits from tourism
2. Increase employment opportunities and open up opportunities for gainful public and community participation in the tourism industry
3. Develop and maintain supporting infrastructure required for growth of the tourism industry
4. Ensure environmental sustainability in development and operation of all tourism products, and strive for global excellence in environmentally responsible tourism
5. Continue to brand the Maldives as a unique destination with innovative products and retain the Maldives positioning as a top ranking destination in traditional and emerging source markets
6. Continue to strengthen the legal and regulatory framework and the institutional capacity of the Ministry of Tourism and Civil Aviation

Figure 2.5 Structure of the Maldives Third Tourism Master Plan 2007–2011
Source: Ministry of Tourism and Civil Aviation, 2007.

A second case study was at the state level and was for Wyoming in the USA. Figure 2.6 provides the table of contents for the *Wyoming Tourism Industry Master Plan 2010–2020*. This fifty-eight-page document had twenty-four pages allocated to the recommendations. It included the results of a SWOT analysis (weaknesses were renamed as 'challenges') and other research data and information collected. Unlike the Maldives plan, the introductory materials and background analysis were brief at just ten pages.

Overview

- Background and goals
- Master plan process
- Vision and direction
- National trends overview
- Significance of the tourism industry to Wyoming's economy
- Key plan drivers
- Integration
- Themes/organization

Recommendations

- Product development
- Partnerships
- Communications/ education
- Marketing
- Outdoor recreation/ wildlife
- Culture/heritage
- Visitor services
- Sustainability

Appendices

- Primary data for e-surveys, meetings and interviews
- Regional map
- Key words
- Strengths summary
- Challenges summary
- Opportunities summary
- Threats summary
- Key plan elements by region
- Primary data collected
- Secondary research/ resources
- Per capita comparisons 50 states

Figure 2.6 Table of contents for Wyoming Tourism Industry Master Plan 2010–2020

Source: Hank Todd Solutions Group, 2010.

Figure 2.7 shows the table of contents for the third case study of the Master Tourism Plan for Winnipeg 2011–2016, a city-level destination. This was a fifty-two-page document with thirty-nine main sections. The vision, mission, goals and objectives were included and most of the destination management roles were as well (leadership and foresight; research; product development; marketing and promotion; and community relations). Several sections were devoted to specific markets (niche market segments; meetings and conventions; sports and special events) and there were multiple sections on different marketing and promotion functions.

- Destination management
- Positioning statement
- Mission statement
- Goals and objectives
- Leadership and foresight
- Destination product development
- Research and data management
- Sector analysis
- Visitor profiles
- Customer segmentation
- Market development
- Signature experiences

- Meetings and conventions
- Sports and special events
- Travel trade
- Visitor and concierge servicing
- Integrated marketing communications
- Public relations
- Travel media
- Advertising and promotions
- Digital marketing
- Collateral development and management

- Workforce development
- Hospitality training and industry enrichment
- Financial resources
- Funding and investment
- Financial incentives
- Organizational development
- Destination marketing accreditation
- Programme designation
- Corporate responsibility
- Professional development
- Conclusion

Figure 2.7 Table of contents for Master Tourism Plan for Winnipeg, 2011–2016

Source: Tourism Winnipeg, 2011.

The inclusion of sections on workforce development, and hospitality training and industry enrichment was an excellent feature of this plan. It should also be noted that there were three sections related to budget and funding (financial resources; funding and investment; and financial incentives). Several sections were included related to Tourism Winnipeg, the city DMO, itself (organizational development; Destination Marketing Accreditation Program designation; corporate responsibility; and professional development).

These three cases exhibit very different structures and content areas for documents that were all called tourism master plans. They are from three geographic levels (country, state and city) and from three individual countries, and so some variation can be expected due to these differences. However, there are common contents and themes within these tourism plan documents, including tourism product development, marketing, human resources, research, and community relations and participation. While this is just a small sample of three from among hundreds of plans, the lack of standardization in plan contents and structure is quite typical.

Each of these three plans has strengths. The Maldives Third Tourism Plan had a very in-depth analysis of the existing tourism situation. It also emphasized sustainability and the involvement of local people in the tourism sector. The Wyoming Tourism Industry Master Plan contained good content recommendations and presented detailed information on how the plan was completed and its main data and analysis components. The Master Tourism Plan for Winnipeg did a great job of covering the roles of destination management. By combining the strengths of these three case studies with the outline of proposed contents in Table 2.1, the DMO has a solid foundation for structuring a comprehensive tourism plan.

Geographic levels of tourism planning

Tourism planning for destinations is conducted at multiple levels within a country. The highest level is at the national level with the planning process being coordinated by the country's national DMO. At the sub-national level, there can be plans for states, provinces, territories and regions (if applicable). The local level is the third tier for tourism planning and there can be several types of plans here depending on how local authorities are structured. In many countries, there will be counties, cities and towns and tourism plans may be prepared for each of these. As mentioned in Chapter 1, some states and provinces have regional tourism set-ups under the sub-national level; and some countries go to the regional level right after the national level.

Under the local level, plans may be put together for specific areas such as rural communities or resorts, or districts within a city (Figure 2.8). As you will realize in Figure 2.8, for design convenience, the local levels were not repeated for provinces, territories or regions.

In looking at the tourism planning practices around the world, it can be said without any doubt that some countries have more tourism plans than others. For example, many plans are found for countries such as Australia, Canada, Ireland and the UK; while countries such as the USA seem to have very few comprehensive tourism plans for destinations.

These then are some of the most important characteristics of tourism planning. Next, and as mentioned earlier, the process used for destination strategic planning is very important and so the following materials are devoted to this subject.

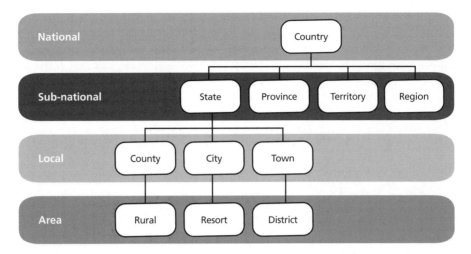

Figure 2.8 Levels of tourism planning

Tourism planning process for destination management

Managing a destination means that long-term tourism planning is required, but what is the best process to employ to develop a long-term plan? Unfortunately there is no 'instructions manual' for organizing a long-term tourism planning process and the steps followed tend to vary from plan to plan. However, the following elements are present in most tourism planning processes:

- Policy
- Principals
- Participants
- Process
- Plans and communicating about plans.

Policy

It is a very good idea for all destinations to have an official tourism policy. These are the basic guidelines for tourism and may be expressed as policy goals or aims. For example, the UK government in 2011 set the following policy goals for tourism:

UK government policy goals for tourism

- Fund the most ambitious marketing campaign ever to attract visitors to the UK in the years following 2012.
- Increase the proportion of UK residents who holiday in the UK to match those who holiday abroad each year.
- Improve the sector's productivity to become one of the top five most efficient and competitive visitor economies in the world.

Another good example of a policy for a tourism destination is from Cape Town, South Africa. This is called the City of Cape Town Responsible Tourism Policy and states that 'the City of Cape Town commits to adopting Responsible Tourism as an approach to destination management to bring about positive economic, social, cultural and environmental impacts'.

Cape Town Responsible Tourism policy

- Makes positive contributions to the conservation of natural and cultural heritage embracing diversity.
- Minimizes negative economic, environmental and social impacts.
- Provides more enjoyable experiences for tourists through more meaningful connections with local people, and a greater understanding of local, cultural, social and environmental issues.
- Is culturally sensitive, encourages respect between tourists and hosts, and builds local pride and confidence.
- Generates greater economic benefits for local people and enhances the well being of host communities.
- Provides accurate information about accessibility of facilities and infrastructure for people with disabilities (visual, communication, mobility) to customers.
- Involves local people in decisions that affect their lives and life chances.
- Improves working conditions and access to the industry.

Principals

The principals are the people that coordinate the long-term planning process for tourism in the destination. The DMO will certainly want to play this role but may decide to form a steering or coordinating committee. For example, a Joint Government and Industry Steering Committee was established and coordinated the process for preparing the Queensland Tourism Strategy. The Third Maldives Tourism Master Plan also had a Project Steering Committee.

Independent consultants are often hired to conduct the analysis required for a long-term tourism plan and to facilitate the planning process. There are consulting companies that specialize in this type of planning work. The independence and considerable past experience of these consultants are the main reasons why they are engaged, and this particularly happens when tourism planning is conducted in developing countries and in very large and complex destinations.

There have been some situations where long-term planning was done mainly by DMO leaders and staff members, but that is not the approach recommended in this book. While these people may be highly capable, the active involvement of all stakeholders produces better tourism plans in which there is a sense of shared ownership.

Participants

The principals will meet and decide which organizations and individuals should be invited to participate in the long-term planning process. The invitees should represent all five groups of tourism stakeholders that were identified in Chapter 1 (government; tourism sector organizations; community; environment; and tourists). The input from tourists should be gathered either through surveys, focus groups or independent in-depth interviews.

There are many different ways in which organizations and people can participate in tourism plan preparation. The following example from Wyoming, USA had three different participation techniques; face-to-face individual interviews, online survey and regional meetings.

Participants in the Wyoming Tourism Industry Master Plan

- Initially over fifty individuals throughout the state were interviewed in March/April to get a solid foundation on what their expectations were, what they saw as key elements to be addressed, what they saw as strengths, weaknesses, threats and opportunities and their vision for Wyoming tourism in 2020.
- Following this, an e-survey was designed and deployed in April/May 2010 to all the databases of the organizing agencies; 366 individuals responded to this survey. Participant's geographic location ranged from the Northwest with 32 per cent of the respondents to 12 per cent from the Southwest. Their composition went from 25 per cent from the accommodations industry, 19 per cent from destination marketing organization/local units of government to 13 per cent from state and federal agencies. The majority of participants were owner/operators, general managers, CEOs or directors (58 per cent).
- Seven regional meetings were conducted in May in Cody, Riverton, Jackson, Rock Springs, Laramie, Douglas and Gillette. Over 200 people took part in the 5-hour sessions.

Process

The process is the heart of long-term tourism planning and requires great forethought about how best to accomplish the various tasks involved. Once again there is no standardized template for a long-term tourism planning process. In actual practice, many different approaches have been used in recent years. In the following materials, five types of long-term tourism planning processes and techniques are described:

- Step-by-step planning designed specifically for tourism
- Meet-analyse-report-approve process used in tourism
- Strategic management and planning techniques
- Balanced Scorecard approach
- Scenario planning.

The destination visioning process is also explained later in the chapter.

Step-by-step planning designed specifically for tourism

One of the approaches available is to use a phased or step-by-step planning process designed specifically for tourism, with each step building upon the previous ones. Many of these process models have been developed based upon actual practices in tourism planning. For example, Mill and Morrison (2012) recommend this approach and there are seven steps in their tourism planning process (Figure 2.9).

The following is a short description of each of the seven steps in this process:

1 *Background analysis*: This is an analysis of the existing destination mix, tourist markets and government policies and programmes related to tourism. When these three items have been fully analysed, the strengths, weaknesses, problems and issues of the destination are identified.
2 *Detailed research and analysis*: The second step builds upon the first and more detailed research and analysis is conducted on key aspects of tourism. These include resources, activities, markets and competitors. This step produces many important findings and conclusions, e.g. maps showing the disposition of tourism resources, competitive strengths and weaknesses, research results on potential markets, etc.
3 *Synthesis and visioning*: In this step, position papers are prepared based upon the analysis and conclusions from the previous two steps. Some of the position paper topics are product development, marketing, organization for destination management, and community awareness of tourism, and support services for tourism. Basically, the position papers outline the current status on these aspects of tourism within the destination.

Then vision statements are prepared for each of these topics or aspects of tourism. These outline the desired future situations for each aspect of tourism. Along with each vision statement, a set of critical conditions are specified that must be met in order to attain the vision.

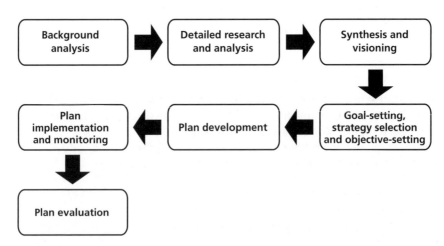

Figure 2.9 Mill and Morrison (2012) tourism planning process model

4 *Goal-setting, strategy selection and objective setting*: Taking the position and vision statements as the basic foundation, the fourth step begins with the statement of long-term tourism goals for the destination. These goals are set for 5 or more years. Once the goals have been stated, the focus then turns to identifying alternative strategies to meet them. For example, for a goal on product development, it is a common practice to divide up the destination into 'tourism zones' with different functions. Finally, the strategies are selected that best fit with tourism policies and the visions for the destination.

Next, shorter-term objectives are set for tourism in the destination. These are for up to three years into the future and are more measurable than the goals.

5 *Plan development*: The planning document is then prepared using the goals, selected strategies and objectives as its basic framework. The plan details how each of the goals and objectives are going to be achieved. The programmes, activities, stakeholder roles and funding procedures are specified. The written plan is prepared in several draft versions until it receives final approval.

6 *Plan implementation and monitoring*: The plan is put into action and progress is carefully monitored against the achievement of goals and objectives.

7 *Plan evaluation*: When the term for the tourism plan ends, an assessment is made of the extent to which its visions, goals and objectives were attained.

This step-by-step model has the advantage that it was developed based upon actual successful experiences in tourism planning. It is logical and thorough in gathering and analysing research and information directly related to tourism in the region. However, this model does not take full advantage of the contributions from strategic management and strategic planning that are discussed below. For example, an external environment scan is not included. Additionally, it does not allow for any required government approvals, but assumes a 'straight-line' process for producing the plan.

Meet–analyse–report–approve process used in tourism

The second type of planning process is illustrated in Figure 2.10 and it was the one used to prepare the Maldives Third Tourism Master Plan (TTMP). This process is a 'meet–analyse–report–approve' sequence that is typical of the procedures for plans run by government agencies and involving consultants or technical assistance teams.

These processes tend to require somewhat longer since various levels of government approvals are required before proceeding further. However, without these approvals the plans are unlikely to be implemented successfully. This is especially important in a smaller country with a fragile environment like the Maldives (Figure 2.11).

Strategic management and planning techniques

The third type of long-term planning process is one that follows more of the strategic management approach. As mentioned earlier, tourism planning has been greatly influenced by the concepts of strategic management and strategic planning in recent decades. In particular, these concepts have introduced the techniques of environmental scanning, SWOT (strengths, weaknesses, opportunities and threats) analysis, and situation analysis to long-term tourism planning processes. Other ideas introduced from strategic management to tourism planning have been vision, mission and core values.

Destination planning

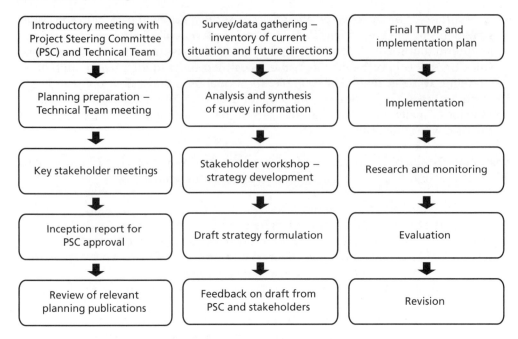

Introductory meeting with Project Steering Committee (PSC) and Technical Team	Survey/data gathering – inventory of current situation and future directions	Final TTMP and implementation plan
Planning preparation – Technical Team meeting	Analysis and synthesis of survey information	Implementation
Key stakeholder meetings	Stakeholder workshop – strategy development	Research and monitoring
Inception report for PSC approval	Draft strategy formulation	Evaluation
Review of relevant planning publications	Feedback on draft from PSC and stakeholders	Revision

Figure 2.10 Process for tourism master planning in the Maldives

Source: Maldives Third Tourism Master Plan, 2007–2011; Ministry of Tourism and Civil Aviation, 2007.

Figure 2.11 A beautiful sunset at a tropical resort in the Maldives

Source: Shutterstock Inc. (K. Kulikov).

Environmental scanning means the monitoring of internal and external environments, to detect changes and trends that will affect tourism in the destination in the long term. The main emphasis in environmental scanning tends to be placed on external environments, usually called the macro-environment, and a variety of analysis techniques are used for this purpose including:

PEST	Political, economic, sociological and technological.
PESTEL	Political, economic, social, technological, environmental and legislative.
EPISTEL	Environmental, political, informatic, social, technological, economic and legal.
STEER	Socio-cultural, technological, economic, ecological and regulatory.

A good application of environmental scanning for tourism is provided in the *Destination Management Plan for Townsville North Queensland* in Australia (Townsville Enterprise Limited, 2008). According to this document, it is important for tourism destinations to pay attention to global trends in long-term tourism planning for the following reasons:

Global trends and influences

Tourism is an open and dynamic system subject to various global, national and regional influences and trends. While many of these factors exist outside the destination's direct sphere of influence, they can still impact on travel and tourism business at the destination level.

Figure 2.12 shows the external trends that can affect a tourism destination and that should be analysed in an environmental scan.

A short description of each of the external trend areas in Figure 2.12 is provided below:

● *Social and cultural*: These trends, for example, include the increasing concern for safety and security; threat of pandemic diseases; greater desire for authentic cultural experiences; aging of the population; increasing urbanization in developing countries, etc.

Figure 2.12 Environmental scanning of trends for a tourism destination

- *Political and legal*: Some of the trends here are the increasing security levels when travelling; greater controls on food safety; threats of terrorism; controls on tour operators; increasing popularity of multi-country trading zones, etc.
- *Economic*: Trends might be the fluctuations in the economic conditions of key origin countries; variations in fuel prices; changes in currency exchange rates; greater concern with value offers, etc.
- *Natural environment*: The natural environment trends could be the increasing environmental awareness in society; global warming and climate change; threats of natural disasters; movement toward sustainable tourism development, etc.
- *Technological*: Technological trends could include the increasing use of mobile phones for travel information and bookings; growing influence of social media on tourism; innovations in transportation modes, etc.
- *Competitive*: Intensifying competition among destinations; increasing regional focus to tourism and travel; and emerging destinations getting greater market shares may be some of these trends.
- *Tourism market*: There are many trends here including increasing special-interest travel; more short-break travel; higher expectations for service quality; greater concern with environmental sustainability and impacts through travel; new technology-enabled information and booking channels, etc.
- *Tourism sector*: Tourism industry trends could encompass the growth of low-cost air carriers (LCCs); financial problems of some major airlines; consolidation in some sub-sectors of tourism; globalization of brands, etc.

The next step is usually to prepare a SWOT analysis based upon the findings and conclusions from the environmental scan about external environments. The strengths and weaknesses part of the SWOT analysis focuses on 'internal' aspects of the destination including the operations of its DMO. An assessment of the 10 As may be a useful starting point for the internal analysis. Environmental scanning and SWOT analysis are covered in greater detail in Chapter 3.

A large assortment of concepts and terms has come with the introduction of strategic management and strategic planning approaches to tourism planning. Unfortunately, many of these terms are used rather loosely and this has caused much confusion.

- *Mission statement*: A statement about an organization's purpose or its reason for being. This concept is generally not applied to a destination.
- *Vision statement*: A statement that describes a future for a destination that is achievable and attractive, and is supported by a majority of tourism stakeholders. This concept can also be applied to the DMO itself.
- *Core values*: These are enduring beliefs and principles held by tourism stakeholders about their destination. Again, this concept may also be applied to the DMO.
- *Goals*: Broad, general results to be achieved by the destination over a number of years, and usually within 3–5 years.
- *Strategies*: Overall actions or initiatives to be followed to achieve goals.
- *Critical success factors*: Required activities or conditions that must be met to achieve the destination's goals and vision.

Undoubtedly, strategic management and strategic planning principles have had a major impact on tourism planning, and have now blended with the frameworks earlier recommended by physical planners and tourism scholars. They are particularly helpful to DMOs since they have introduced more rigour into performance measurement, as well as placing greater emphasis on research to support assumptions and strategy development.

Balanced Scorecard approach

There are other general frameworks for strategic and long-term planning than the three described above. The destination visioning approach is one of them and it is discussed later in this chapter. Others include using the Balanced Scorecard approach and scenario planning. The Balanced Scorecard was originated around 1996 by Drs Robert Kaplan and David Norton of the Harvard Business School. The Balanced Scorecard Institute provides the following definition of this tool:

The Balanced Scorecard

The Balanced Scorecard is a strategic planning and management system that is used extensively in business and industry, government and non-profit organizations worldwide to align business activities to the vision and strategy of the organization, improve internal and external communications, and monitor organization performance against strategic goals.

The original Balanced Scorecard (BSC) has four components that are monitored: (1) financial; (2) internal business process; (3) learning and growth; and (4) customers. Objectives, measures, targets and initiatives are developed for each of these components. The BSC was designed for corporations and other types of organizations, and was not originally intended for tourism destinations. However, there have been some recommendations about adapting the BSC to fit with destinations, including using the following six perspectives (Vila *et al.*, 2010):

- Infrastructure and resources
- Activities and processes (tourism planning; marketing strategies, etc).
- Relationships (residents; tourists and visitors; and organizations)
- Economic results
- Social results
- Environmental results.

The BSC approach was used in the mid-2000s to assist Ireland West Tourism, a regional DMO, with its strategy and performance measurement. This pioneering work was done by Dr Douglas Frechtling of George Washington University, USA and the Dublin Institute of Tourism with financial assistance from UNWTO. This project provided many practical suggestions on how a DMO can apply the Balanced Scorecard approach in tourism planning for the destination and also in how to measure the DMO's own performance.

Although the BSC has undoubted potential for application in destination planning, it remains a technique that needs to be more thoroughly tested and practised. As mentioned in Chapter 1, there is no universal consensus on what constitutes a successful tourism destination, so this represents a barrier to the implementation of the BSC for tourism destinations.

Scenario planning

Scenario planning is another potential long-term planning technique for destinations. The following definition of scenario planning is supplied by Professor Ian Yeoman, a well- known tourism futurist:

Scenario planning definition

Scenario planning is the capability of organizations to understand their business environment, to think through what this means to them and then to act upon this new knowledge. Scenarios are a range of pictures and stories of the future that are constructed using drivers and trends that shape the future. Scenarios provide alternative views of the future. They identify some significant events, main actors and their motivations, and they convey how the world functions. On a practical level, it is just about crystal ball gazing and estimating the future.

Scenario planning involves tourism stakeholders in thinking about what the future might be for their destinations and producing different scenarios (descriptions in stories and pictures). As with the Balanced Scorecard, the scenario planning technique has not yet been often applied in destination planning, but certainly has great potential for application in the years ahead.

It is fair to say that the processes for the long-term planning of tourism destinations are still evolving, despite almost 50 years of practice. Planning is simpler for individual companies and organizations; but tourism destinations are much more complex. This is perhaps the main reason why tourism planning has not yet fully matured. However, DMOs need to carefully study tourism plans that have been produced in other destinations, to learn as much as they can from what has been successful elsewhere and what has not worked. There is no need for 'reinventing the wheel' as there are several good models of tourism planning that can be followed. Moreover, the tourism planning toolkits discussed later in this chapter provide many useful tips and suggestions for a DMO's efforts at tourism planning.

Plans and communicating about plans

A long-term tourism plan is a written document that describes what will be done by the destination to achieve the vision, goals and objectives. Planning documents vary greatly in style and length, and they may be produced in different versions aimed at distinct audiences. Typically a shorter document, often called an executive summary, is prepared for general distribution and a longer, detailed report is designed for a more selective audience.

Communicating the essential contents of long-term tourism plans has become more important and DMOs must pay careful attention to this task. Tourism planning processes can be long and it may even take up to one year to prepare a plan. With so much time and effort going into the planning process and all the associated research, analysis, meetings and discussions, it can be easy to forget that the plan is a 'beginning' and not 'the end'. The principals may be exhausted at the end of the planning process, but the life of the plan is just about to start then.

So, how can a tourism plan be communicated in an appealing way and in a fashion that those outside of the tourism sector can also comprehend? Some plans have become the subjects of videos to expand their awareness and communication effectiveness. For example, the Nova Scotia Tourism Partnership Council in Canada prepared a 10-minute video on the 2005 Nova Scotia Tourism Plan. This video put across the main plan features in a simple and visually appealing way. There was also a short video in early 2011 that went along with the release of Tourism Winnipeg's *Master Tourism Plan for Winnipeg*.

There has also been much more effort put into designing more attractive looking plans with eye-catching images and photography. Figure 2.13 provides some samples from plans that have high quality graphic designs. The main idea here is that tourism plans themselves need to be 'marketed' within the destination.

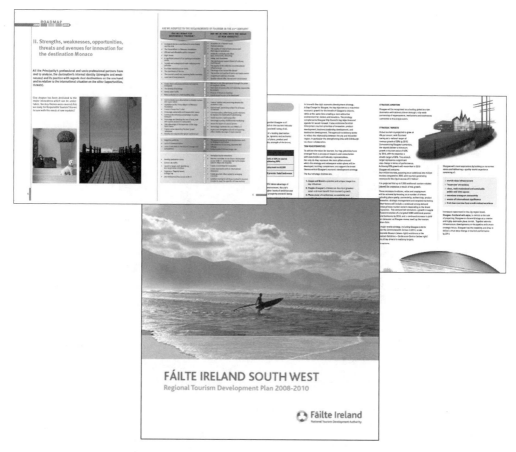

Figure 2.13 Well-designed tourism plans
Source: Glasgow City Marketing Bureau, 2007; Monaco Tourism Office and Fáilte Ireland, 2007.

Destination visioning

Destination visioning is a long-term planning process that has gained greater popularity among DMOs from about the early 1990s. It involves a different type of process than that previously described for long-term tourism planning. Long-term planning is more prescriptive and follows a fixed, step-by-step process; visioning is more creative and dynamic, and the process is more fluid. In some ways, long-term and strategic planning start with the present and build to the future. Visioning starts with the future and then works back to the present.

One definition of visioning is as follows (adapted from University of Wisconsin Extension, 2005):

Vision definition

A vision is a clear and succinct description of what the destination should look like after it successfully implements its strategies and achieves its full potential. It is an expression by the people about what they want the destination to be – a preferred future, a word or picture of the destination the stakeholders choose to create.

The image of the horizon shown in Figure 2.14 is an excellent visual metaphor for a vision. The horizon can be seen but we have not yet reached it. It is attainable if we follow the road ahead, just like the destination can achieve its vision if it follows the plan.

Figure 2.14 The vision as an attainable horizon for the destination
Source: Shutterstock Inc. (Sergej Khakimullin).

Visioning originated as a process for getting resident input into the future directions for their communities, and was later adapted for tourism destinations. Visioning processes are normally run by skilled facilitators and there are several rounds of workshops. Task forces are also formed to deal with specific issues or topics. The following is a step-by-step process for destination visioning (adapted from *Planning for the Future. A Handbook on Community Visioning*, 3rd edition (Center for Rural Pennsylvania, 2006)):

- *Appoint a steering committee*: A steering committee is appointed by the DMO and represents all stakeholders in the destination. The Steering Committee begins planning for the first visioning workshop. A facilitator is selected to run the visioning workshops.
- *Hold first visioning workshop*: The Steering Committee and facilitator provide an overview of the visioning process and ask participants to identify the major issues affecting tourism within the destination.
- *Tally results and establish task forces*: The Steering Committee and facilitator tally the results from the first visioning workshop. Major tourism issues are identified and task forces are created to deal with each issue. Plans for the second visioning workshop are made.
- *Hold second visioning workshop*: The facilitator and Steering Committee review activities and progress to date. The Task Forces make short presentations on their specific issues and this is followed by a general discussion of these issues. The larger group is asked to define values and guiding principles for the future of tourism in the destination.
- *Hold third visioning workshop*: Participants are asked to discuss what they want the destination to be like in the future. With the facilitator's help, the group drafts the vision statement for tourism in the destination.
- *Hold fourth visioning workshop and celebration*: This is a public unveiling of the destination vision statement and celebration among tourism stakeholders.
- *Market and make the vision a reality*: The Steering Committee and Task Forces present the vision statement to community groups, local government and other organizations for their approval.
- *Create an action plan*: Working with various other organizations and government agencies, the Steering Committee develops an action plan for implementing the recommendations and the elements of the vision statement.

The destination visioning process is not as comprehensive as that described earlier for long-term tourism planning. However, it is more focused on issues and desired futures for the destination. It is more creative and less analytical than strategic planning.

The following is an example of a destination vision statement for Elkhart County in Northern Indiana, USA. This statement was produced after a destination visioning process was completed.

Destination vision statement for Elkhart County, Indiana, USA

Elkhart County, IN will be a globally recognized center for creativity. This reputation will be built by residents who have the courage to take risks and help each other succeed in an environment of tolerance and respect that provides opportunities for all. Outstanding businesses and talented professionals will locate in our county because of excellent schools and rich cultural life enhanced by visitor amenities, safe attractive neighborhoods and vibrant downtowns. Area business development, land use and government initiatives will consider how their actions would have implications on continued sustainable tourism development.

Although long-term strategic planning and visioning are most often viewed as alternative planning approaches, there is no reason why they cannot be used together or sequentially.

Tourism planning toolkits

To assist local communities with their tourism planning, several DMOs and other organizations have developed tourism planning toolkits. These are very helpful for guiding DMOs in implementing tourism planning. There are several of these toolkits available around the world and they include the following:

- *Tourism Planning Toolkit for Local Government*, New Zealand
- *Good Practice Guide on Planning for Tourism*, UK
- The South African *Tourism Planning Toolkit for Local Government*
- *Tourism Planning Manual for Local Government*, New South Wales, Australia
- *Developing a Tourism Plan*, British Columbia, Canada.

The *Tourism Planning Toolkit for Local Government* in New Zealand provides a good case study of these helpful resources for DMOs. It is divided into four main sections each including a set of practical 'toolboxes'. The sections are situation analysis, strategic planning, implementation and monitoring performance (Figure 2.15).

The South African *Tourism Planning Toolkit* is more extensive, containing another main section on capacity building:

- Situation analysis toolkit
- Strategic planning toolkit
- Capacity building toolkit
- Implementation toolkit
- Monitoring performance toolkit.

The major advantage of these toolkits is that they have been built based on successful tourism planning processes and techniques in other places. Additionally they are

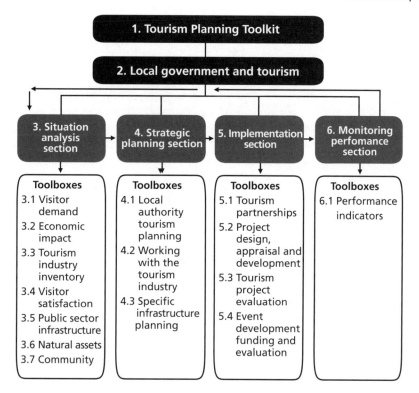

Figure 2.15 New Zealand *Tourism Planning Toolkit for Local Government*
Source: New Zealand Ministry of Economic Development, 2006.

comprehensive in their coverage and provide useful, step-by-step instructions for DMOs to apply to their own situations. Adaptations to forms and procedures can easily be made to fit particular local conditions in the destination.

Specialized forms of destination planning

This chapter has focused mainly on the broader type of tourism planning for a destination, providing comprehensive coverage of all the major issues and touching upon every role of destination management. However, it must be acknowledged that there are more specialized forms of tourism planning at the destination level. Sometimes these become components of overall plans, but at other times they are free-standing plans addressing a specific topic or reflecting a specific type of planning. These include:

Sustainable or responsible tourism development plans: These are plans that focus on sustainable tourism development principles as applied to specific geographic areas. The emphasis is on the long-term sustainability of natural, social, heritage and cultural resources. For example, they may look at the application of the principles of Agenda 21 to the destination. These types of plans are especially important in environmentally- and culturally sensitive destinations, including destinations along coastlines:

Need for sustainable tourism planning in coastal destinations

In order to minimise tourism-induced problems and secure both the sustainability of the tourism industry and coastal resources used by other sectors, increased attention must be given to proper planning and the better integration of tourism in coastal development. Negative impacts and conflicts are due mainly to ignorance of coastal environments and inadequate planning.

(United Nations Environment Programme, 2009)

Some of these plans advocate the 'triple-bottom-line' approach to tourism development in which there is a balance between economic, social and environmental benefits and impacts. For example, this approach was advocated in the Queensland Tourism Strategy in Australia in 2006.

Spatial master plans for tourism development: These are physically-oriented tourism plans for destinations with a particular focus on the proposed functions of specific geographic areas within the destination. Broadly this can be called 'tourism zoning' and the work is done by landscape architects, architects, urban planners, physical geographers and others with physical planning skills and experience.

Some zones may have high potential for tourism development, while others may be designated as travel corridors or protected areas. These planning processes usually involve the development and design of several concept options from which a preferred alternative is selected.

Workforce development plans or strategies: These plans focus on tourism human resources with a view to ensuring that there will be sufficient supply and quality in the future to meet the destination's needs. The contents of these plans cover tourism workforce needs and availability, attitudes towards careers in tourism, recruitment and motivation strategies, training and education requirements, and other relevant topics.

Since people are such a crucial element to all tourism destinations, it is hard to imagine a destination planning process that would not give some emphasis to human resources development. As mentioned earlier, the origins of tourism planning were in the physical planning of regions and rural areas; nowadays tourism planning has expanded to be much more comprehensive in the issues it covers and the techniques that are applied to produce plans.

These specialized plans may reflect issues that are of great importance to tourism in particular destinations. For example, sustainable tourism plans are especially required in highly environmentally-sensitive areas and in places where local cultures and traditions are fragile and may easily be altered or damaged by tourism. Workforce strategies are needed in destinations that have shortages of human resources for tourism and where tourism growth is very rapid.

In the chapters that follow, more detailed planning for most of the destination management roles is presented. These cover marketing, research, product development, partnership and team-building, and community relations. Once again, it is important to say that the DMO is demonstrating its leadership and coordination role in bringing tourism stakeholders together to prepare these plans.

Summary

Long-term planning for tourism within a destination is crucial and DMOs must take a leadership and coordinative role to ensure that these planning processes are as successful as possible. One of the major requirements of successful planning is that all tourism stakeholders are involved, as this gives the plan a sense of shared ownership.

Tourism planning has existed for approximately 50 years and it has been subject to a variety of influences from planning authorities and professionals, tourism scholars, management and marketing professionals, communities and non-profit organizations, and consumers. Done in the correct way, there are many benefits to be derived from tourism planning for destinations.

Destination long-term tourism planning processes are best achieved in a step-by-step way with each successive step building on the previous ones. Destination visioning is a more recent addition to tourism planning and, although less comprehensive in scope, it can be more creative and allow for greater community resident input.

This chapter has suggested that tourism planning for destinations is still maturing and there remain many destinations around the world that are without long-term tourism plans. It is difficult to contemplate professional destination management without long-term planning; as the old saying goes, 'Failing to plan is planning to fail.'

The specific steps that a DMO should complete in destination planning are as follows:

- Build support for the value and benefits of long-term planning of tourism in the destination.
- Lead and coordinate the process of preparing a long-term plan for tourism.
- Work together with all tourism stakeholders to prepare the long-term plan.
- Ensure that the planning is based on established tourism policies and is consistent with higher levels of tourism planning in the country.
- Choose a planning process that will result in the greatest sense of shared ownership of the plan.
- Encourage local residents to participate in plan preparation.
- Insist that the planning process is research-based and analyses all the relevant external and internal environment factors.
- Ensure the plan identifies a vision, goals, strategies and objectives for tourism in the destination.
- Communicate the results and recommendations of the plan in a compelling fashion for all audiences.
- Implement the plan along with the assistance of other tourism stakeholders.
- Monitor the implementation of the plan and make corrective changes if required.
- Evaluate the plan on the achievement of the vision and goals.
- Initiate the next cycle of tourism planning.

Review questions

1 What have been the major influences on tourism planning over recent decades?
2 What are the major benefits that a destination will realize from initiating a tourism planning process?
3 The DMO should target which outcomes to be desired as the result of conducting tourism planning and from implementing the plan?
4 Which topics should be covered in a tourism plan for a destination?
5 At which different geographic levels is tourism planning done? What are the advantages to integrating across these various geographic levels?
6 What process should be applied in tourism planning for destinations? How important is the selected process to the overall success of the planning?
7 Strategic planning and visioning are different processes. How would you describe the key differences between these two planning methods?
8 What are the advantages of using tourism planning toolkits to guide destination planning processes?
9 What are the steps in conducting a destination visioning process?

References

Alaska Office of Tourism. 2001. Tourism Planning and Assessment.

Alleyne, N.N. 2011. A Tourism Master Plan for Barbados 2011–2020. 12th Annual CTO Sustainable Tourism Conference.

Balanced Scorecard Institute. 2011. http://www.balancedscorecard.org/BSCResources/AbouttheBalancedScorecard/tabid/55/Default.aspx

Center for Rural Pennsylvania. 2006. Planning for the Future. A Handbook on Community Visioning, 3rd edn. Harrisburg, PA: CRP.

CHL Consulting Ltd. 2011. Government of Anguilla. Sustainable Tourism Master Plan 2010–2020.

City of Cape Town. 2009. City of Cape Town Responsible Tourism Policy.

Department for Communities and Local Government. 2006. Good Practice Guide on Planning for Tourism.

Department of Culture, Media and Sport. 2011. Government Tourism Policy.

Department of Environmental Affairs and Tourism. 2009. The South African Tourism Planning Toolkit for Local Government.

Elkhart County Convention and Visitors Bureau. 2011. ECCVB, Inc. 2011 Business Plan.

Fáilte Ireland. 2007. Fáilte Ireland South West Regional Tourism Development Plan 2008–2010. Cork, Ireland.

Frechtling, D.C. 2006. A Balanced Scorecard system for managing strategy and measuring performance of destination management organizations. Working paper. Dublin. http://home.gwu.edu/~frechtli/material/BSCWorkingPaper4-06.pdf

Getz, D. 1986. Models in tourism planning. Towards integration of theory and practice. *Tourism Management*, 7(1), 21–32.

Glasgow City Marketing Bureau. 2007. Glasgow's Tourism Strategy to 2016.

Gunn, C.A. 1979. Tourism Planning. New York: Crane Russak & Company.

Hall, C.M. 2008. Tourism Planning: Policies, Processes and Relationships. Upper Saddle River, NJ: Prentice Hall.

Hank Todd Solutions Group. 2010. Wyoming Tourism Industry Master Plan 2010–2020.

Inskeep, E. 1994. National and Regional Tourism Planning. Methodologies and Case Studies. Madrid: World Tourism Organization.

——1981. Tourism Planning: An Integrated and Sustainable Development Approach. New York: Wiley.

Kaplan, R.S., and Norton, D.P. 1996. The Balanced Scorecard: Translating Strategy into Action. Boston MA: Harvard Business School Press.

Kastarlak, B.I., and Barber, B. 2011. Fundamentals of Planning and Developing Tourism. Upper Saddle River, NJ: Prentice Hall.

Maldives Third Tourism Master Plan 2007–2011. Malé, The Maldives.

Mill, R.C., and Morrison, A.M. 2012. The Tourism System. Dubuque, IA: Kendall Hunt Publishing.

Ministry of Culture and Tourism. 2007. Tourism Strategy of Turkey 2008–2023.

Ministry of Jobs, Tourism and Innovation, British Columbia. 2012. Developing a Tourism Plan. http://www.jti.gov.bc.ca/industryresources/DevelopingTourism_Plan.htm

Ministry of Tourism and Civil Aviation. 2007. Maldives Third Tourism Master Plan 2007–2011.

Monaco Tourism Office. n.d. The Tourist and Convention Authority of the Principality of Monaco. Roadmap 2009–2013. Monaco.

New Zealand Ministry of Economic Development. 2006. Tourism Planning Toolkit for Local Government. Wellington, New Zealand.

Nova Scotia Tourism Partnership Council. 2005. The 2005 Nova Scotia Tourism Plan (video).

Pearce, J., and Robinson, R. 2012. Strategic Management. Planning for Domestic and International Competition, 13th edn. New York: McGraw-Hill/Irwin.

Ritchie, J.R.B. 1993. Crafting a destination vision: Putting the process of resident responsive tourism into practice. *Tourism Management*, 14(5), 379–389.

Tourism New South Wales. 2002. Towards 2020. New South Wales Tourism Masterplan.

Tourism Queensland. 2006. Queensland Tourism Strategy.

Tourism Recreation Research and Education Centre, Lincoln University, New Zealand. 2006. Tourism Planning Toolkit for Local Government. http://www.med.govt.nz/sectors-industries/tourism/pdf-docs-library/Tourism%20policy/tourismplanningtoolkit.pdf

Tourism Winnipeg. 2011. A Master Tourism Plan for Winnipeg 2011–2016. Positioning Winnipeg for Tourism Growth. 2012 update.

Tourist and Convention Authority of the Principality of Monaco. Roadmap 2009–2013.

Townsville Enterprise Limited. 2008. Destination Management Plan for Tourism in Townsville North Queensland 2008–2011.

UN Department of Economic and Social Affairs, Division of Sustainable Development. 2009. Agenda 21, http://www.un.org/esa/dsd/agenda21/

United Nations Environment Programme. 2009. Sustainable Coastal Tourism. An integrated planning and management approach.

United Nations Social and Economic Commission for Asia and the Pacific. 1999. Guidelines on Integrated Planning for Sustainable Tourism Development.

University of Kansas. 2012. The Community Tool Box. http://ctb.ku.edu/en/default.aspx

University of Wisconsin Extension. 2005. An Overview of Vision and the Visioning Process. Madison IA: University of Wisconsin.

UNWTO. 2012. Tourism Development Master Plans and Strategic Development Plans. http://cooperation.unwto.org/en/technical-product/tourism-development-master-plans-and-strategic-development-plans

Var, T., and Gunn, C. 2002. Tourism Planning: Basics, Concepts, Cases. New York: Routledge.

Vila, M., Costa, G., and Rovira, X. 2010. The creation and use of scorecards in tourism planning: A Spanish example. *Tourism Management*, 31(2), 232–239.

VisitEngland. 2011. England. A Strategic Framework for Tourism 2010–2020 (revised edn. 2011).

Visit Finland. 2010. Finland's Tourism Strategy to 2020.

Wu, B. 2001. Regional Tourism Planning Principles. Beijing: China Tourism and Travel Press.

Yeoman, I., and McMahon-Beattie, U. 2005. Developing a scenario planning process using a blank piece of paper. *Tourism and Hospitality Research*, 5(3), 273–285.

Yeoman, I. 2008. Tomorrow's Tourist. Scenarios and Trends. London: Routledge.

Chapter 3

Destination marketing planning

Learning objectives

1 Explain the key destination marketing professional principles.

2 Describe the different levels of goals and objectives in the destination marketing planning process.

3 Differentiate between a vision and a mission.

4 Identify the meaning of the components of the PRICE model.

5 Provide a detailed explanation of the steps in the destination marketing system (DMS).

6 Describe the contents of a destination marketing plan.

7 Give an explanation of each of the 8 Ps of destination marketing.

8 Explain how KRAs and KPIs are used to measure the marketing performance of DMOs.

Introduction

As was explained in Chapter 1, destination marketing is one of the most important DMO roles. So the planning of destination marketing takes on a high priority for a DMO and destination marketing planning must be done professionally and thoroughly. Marketing and promotions are expensive, so making the right choices of which markets to target and how to communicate them most effectively are of paramount importance. Competition among destinations is intense, so there is a constant need to 'stand out in the crowd'.

Destination marketing and promotion are dynamic and they require a high level of creativity and innovation. Although the field changes rapidly, it must be based on a scientific approach using solid research and systematic procedures known to produce the most effective results. This chapter explains the destination marketing planning process as a systematic approach for accomplishing the DMO's marketing and promotion role.

There are many career professionals engaged in destination marketing around the world. It can be said that without doubt they have a passion about their work because of its creativity and every-changing nature. More recently the Internet has 'spiced up' destination marketing and brought a new breed of professionals with information technology skills into the field.

Destination marketing principles

It is better to start with the basics on marketing before getting into the details of destination marketing planning. Contemporary destination marketing is founded on four key professional principles that apply to all DMOs.

Marketing concept and customer orientation

The first principle of modern destination marketing is that success is based mainly on the continuing satisfaction of the customer's needs and wants (Figure 3.1). For a DMO, this principle raises an important question – Who are the DMO's customers? The first and most instinctive answer would be the people who travel to the destination for business or pleasure reasons. However, a DMO has many other stakeholders including tourism industry members, government officials and local residents. You will remember that these various stakeholders were earlier identified in Chapter 1. In some ways, these stakeholders are also customers of the DMO.

Destination life cycle

The product life cycle is another widely accepted principle of marketing. The notion here is that every product in time goes through the four stages of introduction, growth, maturity and decline. The overall product life cycle model has been converted into the destination life cycle concept. Butler (1980) described a tourism area life cycle (TALC) with seven stages consisting of exploration, involvement, development, consolidation, stagnation, decline and rejuvenation (Figure 3.2).

Figure 3.1 The traditional cycle of marketing

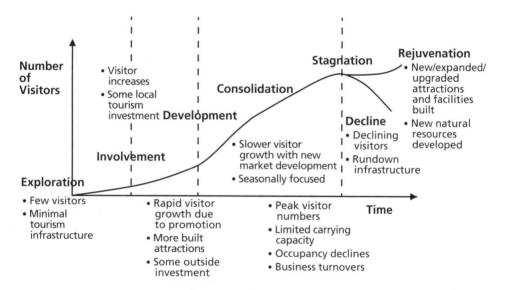

Figure 3.2 The tourism area life cycle (TALC)
Source: Butler, R. W., 1980. 'The concept of the tourist area life cycle of evolution: implications for management of resources', *Canadian Geographer* 24(1): 5–12. This material is reproduced with permission of John Wiley & Sons, Inc.

Market segmentation

Greater marketing success follows from pursuing specific groups of tourists (target markets) rather than trying to appeal to the mass market. Moreover, it is considered wasteful for a DMO to go after everyone in the market. The DMO needs to decide how it will divide pleasure and business tourists into groups (market segmentation analysis) and make a selection of target markets from among these available groups.

Marketing mix

All destination marketers have an arsenal of tools to use in appealing to customers. These tools have come to be known as the 'Ps of marketing' which McCarthy (1960) first designated as the '4 Ps of marketing' including product, price, place and promotion. Several authors have argued that the traditional 4 Ps do not fit as well to tourism as they do for physical products. Morrison (2010) adds four other Ps (packaging, programming, partnership and people) to address the unique aspects of marketing tourism and hospitality services.

Destination marketing planning

Destination marketing planning must not be haphazard, but requires a systematic, step-by-step approach. The destination marketing planning process is one template that can be used. This is a tried-and-tested process that the author pioneered and used extensively over the past 20 years with DMOs in several countries.

Destination marketing planning process

Every DMO needs to plan its destination marketing, and it is very important to think of this planning as consisting of long-term (strategic) and short-term (tactical) time dimensions. For destination marketing, the strategic dimension is defined as 3–5 years into the future, while the tactical dimension is 1–2 years ahead (Figure 3.3). A core part of the destination marketing planning process is the creation of a time-ordered hierarchy of marketing goals and objectives. This hierarchy consists of the following:

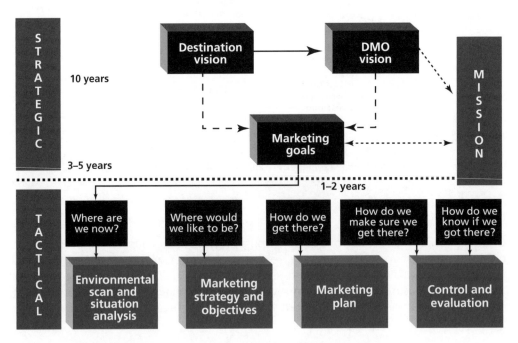

Figure 3.3 The destination marketing planning process model

- Destination vision
- DMO vision
- Destination marketing goals
- Destination marketing objectives.

There are specific techniques and processes that help DMOs define their goals and marketing activities and programmes including the environmental scan, situation analysis, marketing strategy selection, positioning and the marketing plan. Finally, the destination marketing planning process must reflect and be consistent with the roles of the DMO, as expressed in its mission statement.

Destination vision

Every DMO's destination marketing efforts should be driven by a set of explicitly articulated marketing goals. These goals should be established to achieve the destination vision, which is identified through a planning process known as visioning where the outcome is the definition of a 'super long-term goal' for the destination.

A more formal description of the destination vision statement is that it represents a concise, desired 'word picture' of the destination at some point in the future. It is a verbal image of the destination that local people aspire for it to become. The vision provides a clear focus on what the destination will strive to be. This sets the overall direction for the tourism marketing and development of the destination in the upcoming years. The destination vision should be articulated in a vision statement. Ritchie (1993) suggests that the destination visioning process should be completed in three stages: (1) envisioning an image of the desired future destination state, which (2) when effectively communicated to those responsible, (3) serves to empower these people so they can enact the vision.

An example of a destination vision statement is the following from Morocco's Department of Tourism (Figure 3.4):

Destination vision statement for Morocco

To raise Morocco to be one of the world's top 20 tourist destinations and a model of sustainability in the Mediterranean destinations.
(Department of Tourism, Morocco, 2010)

A second and somewhat different vision is the following from the *New Zealand Tourism Strategy 2015*:

Destination vision for New Zealand

In 2015, tourism is valued as the leading contributor to a sustainable New Zealand economy.
(Tourism Strategy Group, Ministry of Economic Development, 2008)

Figure 3.4 Morocco's vision is to become one of the world's top twenty destinations. Kasbah and the Atlas Mountains in Morocco
Source: Shutterstock Inc. (Rechitan Sorin).

DMO vision

The destination vision statement creates a pathway for future marketing action. However, the prime responsibility and accountability for achieving the destination vision is given to the officially recognized DMO. The next step is for the DMO to define its own vision for the future that will set it on the right course to achieving the destination vision in cooperation with its internal and external stakeholders.

The DMO vision statement should be more concrete than the destination vision statement, because the DMO will be accountable for achieving this vision. It is helpful to think of the destination and DMO visions as being the 'super long-term goals' from which all the other marketing goals and objectives flow.

Some DMO vision statements are quite short and simple, such as the following one for the Richmond Metropolitan Convention and Visitors Bureau in Virginia, USA:

Richmond (USA) DMO vision

To be a world-class organization known for our superior service and innovative marketing.
(Richmond Metropolitan Convention and Visitors Bureau, 2012)

The Korea Tourism Organization (KTO) has a very short but easily understandable DMO vision as being the '*control tower of the Korean tourism industry*' (Korea Tourism Organization website, 2012).

Destination marketing goals

The destination marketing goals are like stepping stones on the DMO's path to realizing the destination and DMO visions. They are longer-term (3–5 years) measurable results that the DMO wants to achieve for its destination marketing. It is best if the destination marketing goals are target-market and time-specific, and state an intended result in a quantified format, but not all marketing goals exactly fit these criteria.

Travel Montana set the following three destination marketing goals for state tourism in 2011–2012 (Tourism Marketing Plan, July 2011–June 2012, Montana Department of Commerce, Office of Tourism, 2011):

Travel Montana marketing goals

- Increase awareness of the brand among the target audience
- Move Montana into the target audience's consideration set
- Support Montana tourism entities in increasing their revenues.

Tourism Victoria in British Columbia, Canada has three main marketing goals:

Tourism Victoria (Canada) marketing goals

- Increase tourism revenues by attracting visitors from both our short-haul and long-haul markets.
- Continue to maintain and build relationships with key tour operators, meeting planners and travel media through sales efforts in our key markets in North America, Europe and Asia.
- Match our key offerings and visitation drivers with the appropriate receptive geomarket (geographic market) in order to best deliver tailored messaging for that particular consumer.

Another good example of destination marketing goals is for South Africa Tourism, the national DMO. In fact, South Africa Tourism calls these its 'strategic objectives' but they can also be called marketing goals.

South Africa Tourism's strategic objectives

- Increase in tourist volume
- Increase in tourist spend
- Increase length of stay
- Improve geographic spend
- Improve seasonality patterns
- Promote transformation.

The DMO is not alone in achieving the destination marketing goals, but must rely on the efforts of its private- and public-sector partners within and outside the destination.

Destination marketing objectives

Destination marketing objectives are short-term (usually within 1 year) measurable results that the DMO wants to achieve. These objectives must be based on the marketing goals and be interim steps toward achieving these goals. As with the goals, marketing objectives should, if possible, be target market- and time-specific, and indicate a quantified result. It should be realized here that many DMOs have marketing objectives, but have not derived these through a visioning process and goal-setting. Marketing objectives are often set as part of the annual process of developing a marketing plan. While marketing objectives are essential foundations for a marketing plan, they are more effective when derived from a long-term visioning process and goal setting.

The following destination marketing objectives are from the Virginia Tourism Corporation in 2011:

Virginia Tourism Corporation marketing objectives for 2011

1 Evolve the 'Virginia Is for Lovers' campaign
2 Leverage media buys at least 3:1
3 Increase the number of unique visitors to Virginia.org to 6.5 million
4 Complete twenty new photo shoots to enhance and update image library
5 Generate $9 million in earned media
6 Generate 50,000 incremental leads through promotions and sweepstakes
7 Increase domestic sales leads by 5 per cent
8 Increase international visitation from Canada and target overseas markets by 4 per cent
9 Benchmark outdoor marketing plan
10 Increase film contacts by 5 per cent.

As you can see, these marketing objectives for VTC are almost all very quantified and measurable. Some of them directly specify target markets, including the eighth objective about visitors from Canada and overseas. Other objectives are directly related to specific marketing and promotional programmes and efforts.

DMO mission

The DMO mission, articulated in its mission statement, describes its reason for being. It is a broad statement about the organization's business and scope, services and products, markets served and overall philosophy (Kotler, 2000). The mission statement is not a goal or objective, but rather it is a clear description of what the DMO does and who it serves. DMO mission statements are sometimes confused with vision statements and goals, but these are three quite different concepts. In fact, the DMO's mission statement should be derived from the destination and DMO vision statements and be consistent with the destination marketing goals.

Figure 3.5 Jumeirah Palm Island, Dubai
Source: Shutterstock Inc. (Haider).

The following is an example of a DMO mission statement from Dubai (2012):

Dubai Department of Tourism and Commerce marketing mission

To strengthen the Dubai economy through:

- The development of sustainable tourism.
- The provision of a unique visitor experience combining quality service and value for money in a safe environment for all our employees, contractors and visitors.
- The innovative promotion of Dubai's commerce and tourism opportunities.
- The further development of partnership with our industry stakeholders.

It was decided to use the terms vision, goals and objectives in this book. However, many different terms are actually used by DMOs. For example, the terms initiatives, strategic initiatives, strategies or priorities are sometimes applied in place of marketing goals. The word objective is often replaced with action or tactic. Essentially the meanings are the same, but the choice of terminology is the difference.

The destination marketing system (DMS) and the PRICE model

A more detailed description is now provided of how a DMO develops its marketing activities and programmes. The destination marketing goals trigger the rest of the planning process, since the goals are the connection between the strategic and tactical time dimensions. The PRICE model suggested by Morrison (2010) provides a logical sequence for the remaining elements of the destination marketing planning process. The PRICE model is derived from the destination marketing system (DMS) (Figure 3.6), which involves answering five questions in a sequence of steps:

- Where are we now?
- Where would we like to be?
- How do we get there?
- How do we make sure that we get there?
- How do we know if we got there?

The PRICE model (Figure 3.7) identifies the key destination marketing functions as:

- Planning (P)
- Research (R)
- Implementation (I)
- Control (C)
- Evaluation (E).

The planning and research tasks are accomplished by answering the first two DMS questions (Where are we now? Where would we like to be?); by doing research-based planning and then analysing the resulting information to develop a destination marketing strategy and objectives. DMOs must make choices among alternative types of marketing activities and programmes. A conscious effort in planning is needed to make the right choices. For planning to be as effective as possible, research must be done and then analysed before making the choice of a future marketing strategy and the supporting activities and programmes.

The destination marketing objectives are developed based on the selected marketing strategy and are the main guides for specifying the marketing activities and programmes. The accomplishment of the selected destination marketing strategy and objectives is articulated and described in a written format in a marketing plan, which is implemented by the DMO (How do we get there?).

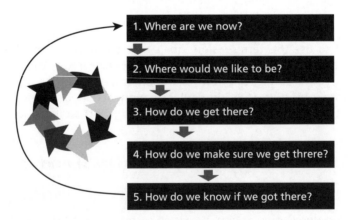

Figure 3.6 The destination marketing system (DMS)

Figure 3.7 The PRICE model for destination marketing

Then the implementation of the marketing plan is evaluated in two stages: (1) formative evaluation, through monitoring and controlling progress toward the marketing objectives (How do we make sure we get there?); and (2) summative evaluation, through performance measurement at the end of the marketing plan period (How do we know if we got there?). A more contemporary name for evaluation commonly used by DMOs is demonstrating accountability for the money and other resources expended in implementing a marketing plan.

Each DMS step and marketing function in the destination marketing planning process involves using specific marketing techniques and concepts to achieve the marketing objectives. The steps, functions, techniques and concepts are identified in Figure 3.8.

Destination marketing system steps and marketing functions	Marketing techniques and concepts

Where are we now
(Planning and research)
PR
	• Environmental scan
	• Situation analysis:
	  o Destination analysis
	  o Competitive analysis
	  o Visitor market analysis
	  o Marketing position (destination image) analysis
	  o Marketing plan analysis
	  o Resident analysis
	• USP identification

Where would we like to be?
(Planning and research)
PR
	• Marketing strategy:
	  o Target markets
	  o Positioning–image–branding approach
	• Marketing objectives

How do we get there? (Implementation) **I**	• Marketing mix (8 Ps) • Marketing plan
How do we make sure we get there? (Control) **C**	• Marketing control (formative evaluation)
How do we know if we got there? (Evaluation) **E**	• Marketing evaluation (summative evaluation)

Figure 3.8 Destination management system steps and functions

Every DMO is faced with a huge array of marketing choices. Some of the most crucial of these decisions include which tourists to try to attract (target markets), which services and products should be developed and promoted (destination mix) and what image of the destination should be communicated (destination positioning, image and branding). Rather than making quick and arbitrary decisions, a careful and thoughtful approach of research-based planning must be followed to make the best choices. This approach is now described in the five destination marketing system (DMS) steps.

1 Where are we now? (planning and research)

Figure 3.9 shows the inputs and outputs of the first step in the DMS (Where are we now?). When beginning a new cycle of marketing planning, the DMO starts with its mandate to attain the destination vision, DMO vision and marketing goals, along with the lessons it has learned from implementing the DMO's previous marketing plans from the evaluation step (DMS Step 5).

The DMO identifies and assesses strengths, weaknesses, trends, challenges, opportunities and threats as these relate to its marketing goals. This involves using an environmental scan and situation analysis. Often when combined, these are referred to as a SWOT (strengths, weaknesses, opportunities and threats) analysis (Figure 3.10).

Inputs	DMS step 1	Outputs
• Destination vision and DMO vision • Marketing goals • Performance, conclusions and recommendations from previous marketing plan (DMS step 5)	**Where are we now?** **PLANNING AND RESEARCH**	• Environmental scan (challenges, opportunities and threats in the marketing environment) • Situation analysis (destination analysis, visitor market profile, competitive analysis, marketing position and plan analysis, resident analysis) • Stengths and weaknesses of the destination and DMO • Unique selling propositions (USPs)

Figure 3.9 Destination marketing system, step 1: Where are we now?

Figure 3.10 SWOT analysis
Source: Shutterstock Inc. (Marekuliasz).

The Town of Drumheller in Alberta, Canada conducted a SWOT analysis in 2010 in preparing a Tourism Master Plan. The SWOT analysis results are shown in Figure 3.11.

The Drumheller SWOT analysis covers more tourism issues than just marketing, but it is still important and beneficial in destination marketing planning to take this 'bigger picture' view.

Strengths	Weaknesses
• Strong provincial market • Close to major centres/populations • Family vacation market • Royal Tyrrell Museum • Atlas Coal Mine • Passion Play • Historical significance • Historic downtown • Large creative class • Unique physical settings • Badlands topography • Red Deer River • Moderate climate • Good highway access • Adequate road network • Free public parking • Paved trail system • Sport and recreation facilities • Recognition of tourism in the Community Sustainability Master Plan	• No destination marketing organization • Insufficient development and marketing dollars • Brand fragmentation—lack of unity of voice • Lack of downtown revitalization • Lack of architectural control policies • Land Use Bylaw/tourism as a discretionary use • Downtown physically separated from attractions and accommodations • Lack of higher-end products • Limited range of accommodations • Limited range of retail • Little variety in food and beverage services • Lack of winter and shoulder season products • Lack of signature festivals and events with few exceptions • Inconsistencies in signage • Lack of tourism data • Automobile dependent • Too few inbound tour operators • Slow uptake of new and innovative Internet marketing techniques • Industry's role in affecting overall strategic change • Closed for the season mentality • Ongoing reluctance to shift to a customer orientated philosophy
Opportunities	**Threats**
• Tourism regarded as long-term economic driver • Development of community brand • Rejuvention of downtown core • Canadian Badlands Ltd • Boomtown Trail • Development of luxury product • Development of family-oriented activities • Themed tours • River use • Badlands Community Facility • Rail line • Active transportation • Extended stay of VFR and business travellers • Enhanced partnerships with provincial and federal marketing agencies • Travel trade could expand reach • Industry-led product standards • Use of Internet	• Other jurisdictions well funded and well organized • Slow economic recovery • Macroeconomic factors—exchange rate, rising fuel costs, US economy • Continuing decline of US visitors to Canada • Changing market demographics • Climate change • Shortened booking cycles, time poverty and propensity for shorter vacations • Industry apathy/inward focus • Industry fracture/self-interest • Community resistance to change • Community reluctance to embrace its heritage • Provincial jurisdiction of highways

Figure 3.11 SWOT analysis of Tourism in Town of Drumheller
Source: Town of Drumheller, 2011; Malone Given Parsons Ltd. *et al.*, 2010.

Environmental scan

An environmental scan pinpoints trends and the potential challenges, opportunities and threats in the marketing environment. The environmental factors to be analysed include legislation and regulation, political and economic conditions, social and cultural patterns, environmental changes, political situation and technological advances. For each of these factors, the following questions are asked:

● What have been the major trends in the past 3–5 years?
● What are the expected future trends in the next 3–5 years?
● Will these trends affect our destination and DMO in the next 3–5 years?
● How will they affect our destination and DMO?
● How will they affect competitive destinations and DMOs?
● How should our DMO change its marketing approaches to adapt to these trends?

For example, the Ministry of Tourism, Republic of Kenya conducted an external environment scan through PESTEL analysis (political, economic, social, technological, environmental and legal) in preparing a strategic plan for 2008–2012.

Situation analysis

Next, the DMO identifies the strengths and weaknesses of the destination and the DMO's internal strengths and weaknesses. An effective DMO is constantly taking inventory of its destination's and the DMO's strengths and weaknesses. The DMO's traditional ways of marketing are forever being challenged to see if there is not a better way of doing things.

The six key techniques in completing a DMO situation analysis are:

● Destination or product/product development analysis
● Competitive analysis
● Visitor market analysis
● Marketing position/destination image analysis
● Marketing plan analysis
● Resident analysis.

DESTINATION ANALYSIS

A destination analysis (also sometimes called a product or product development analysis) is a careful assessment of the strengths and weaknesses of the destination, ideally based on input from a variety of sources within and outside the destination. More recently, this process has become known as a destination audit and may be completed by an independent consulting or research company on the DMO's behalf. Destination Consultancy Group (DCG) is a US consulting firm that conducts destination audits on behalf of convention and visitors' bureaus (CVBs). This company analyses the destination (product development assessment), marketing programmes (marketing assessment) and the DMO and its local partners (organization assessment). A variety of sources are polled through different types of research enquiries, which include a visitor survey, secret or mystery shopping within the destination, and personal interviews with community and tourism leaders. Recommendations are provided on needed improvements by the tourism industry and by the community/local area within the destination, for future marketing, and for the DMO and overall tourism industry organization.

The DMO should develop a set of criteria for analysing the destination. The 10 As model described in Chapter 1 is one set of suggested criteria for assessing the many different dimensions of a destination. Another set of criteria for assessing destinations is found in the *Travel and Tourism Competitiveness Reports* produced by the World Economic Forum. The *Travel and Tourism Competitiveness Report 2011* used the following fourteen criteria for ranking country destinations:

- Policy rules and regulations
- Environmental sustainability
- Safety and security
- Health and hygiene
- Prioritization of travel and tourism
- Air transport infrastructure
- Ground transport infrastructure
- Tourism infrastructure
- ICT infrastructure (information communication technology)
- Price competitiveness in the travel and tourism industry
- Human resources
- Affinity for travel and tourism
- Natural resources
- Cultural resources.

COMPETITIVE ANALYSIS

A competitive analysis is another important element in destination marketing planning and research, but surprisingly is not something that DMOs tend to do well. Often this is a result of inadequate or inaccurate definitions of the destination's competitive set or sets. Most destinations' competitors vary by target market and it is best to divide the competitive analysis in that way. For example, a destination may have a different set of competitors for business conventions and meetings than it has for individual pleasure travellers.

The DMO's marketing and sales team should have a good feel for the closest competitors, but the best source is visitors themselves. Asking the destination's visitors in surveys to pinpoint other destinations that they considered for their trips is one way to tackle this. Another option is to use a focus group approach in which past and/or potential visitors reach a consensus on the destination's closest competitors. Secondary sources of research information may also be helpful in shedding light on the most popular destinations for specific visitor market segments.

VISITOR MARKET ANALYSIS

Every DMO should have a detailed visitor market profile at its disposal. Some DMOs do this research on a monthly or quarterly basis every year, while others conduct visitor profile studies only once every 2 or 3 years. Unfortunately, there are many DMOs that have never developed a detailed profile of their visitors through a research study. The categories of information that should be provided by a visitor profile analysis include:

Destination marketing planning

- Demographic and socio-economic characteristics
- Travel trip characteristics (e.g. trip purposes, length of stay, party size and com-
position, accommodation and transportation usage, etc.)
- Previous visit patterns (number and timing of previous trips)
- Revisit intentions (probability of a return visit)
- Attraction usage and awareness
- Activity participation in destination
- Travel information sources used for trip to destination
- Media usage (TV; newspapers; magazines; Internet/social media; mobile, etc.)
- Trip satisfaction levels
- Likes and dislikes
- Suggested improvements to the destination.

An outstanding example of conducting a visitor profile study within a city destination
is the research done by the Las Vegas Convention and Visitors Authority (LVCVA). The
Las Vegas Visitor Profile Study has the following six aims:

- To provide a profile of Las Vegas' visitors in terms of socio-demographic and
behavioral characteristics.
- To monitor trends in visitor behaviour and visitor characteristics.
- To supply detailed information on the vacation and gaming habits of different
visitor groups, particularly gaming and non-gaming expenditures.
- To allow the identification of market segments and potential target markets.
- To provide a basis for calculating the economic impact of different visitor groups.
- To determine visitor satisfaction levels.

Approximately 3,600 visitors are personally interviewed per year, about 300 per month.
The 2010 questionnaire included sixty-six questions. The research findings are divided
into the following categories:

- Reasons for visiting
- Travel planning
- Trip characteristics and expenditures
- Gaming behaviour and budgets
- Entertainment
- Attitudinal information
- Visitor demographics.

MARKETING POSITION (DESTINATION IMAGE) ANALYSIS

Every destination needs to understand its image or position in the minds of past and
potential visitors. Unfortunately, although DMO practitioners acknowledge its
importance, image research for specific destinations is done infrequently and seldom
with great rigour.

The Icelandic Tourist Board conducted destination image research in Denmark,
Germany and the UK in early 2009. There was great concern at the time about the
economic health of Iceland and a survey was conducted on its reputation as a travel
destination. The research found that Iceland's image as a destination had not been
damaged by its economic difficulties. Some 55 per cent of the UK residents surveyed

thought that Iceland was a place with outstanding nature. They also thought Icelanders were charming and kind. Germans felt Icelandic people were hospitable and comfortable to be around. They also believed Iceland had beautiful houses and a good standard of living.

MARKETING PLAN ANALYSIS

The marketing plan analysis involves an objective assessment of the DMO's past marketing plans. This is done mainly by evaluating and measuring the effectiveness and results for the previous marketing plan. The summative evaluation of the last period's performance against marketing objectives must answer three key questions.

- How effective was the last marketing plan?
- Which activities and programmes worked?
- Which activities and programmes did not work?

The evaluation of previous marketing activities and programmes should yield the answers to these questions.

RESIDENT ANALYSIS

Some destinations go one step further and conduct research on local resident attitudes or sentiments about tourism in their communities. This is especially important when tourism represents a very large part of the local economy and affects residents' everyday lives.

Hawaii provides a very good example of this kind of situation where tourism is a very dominant economic force. The Hawaii Tourism Authority (HTA) conducts a regular *Resident Sentiment Survey* to monitor local residents' attitudes to tourism on the islands and how people's sentiments are changing. In 2009, HTA conducted a random sample survey of 1,650 residents. The main finding was that residents have an overall favourable attitude towards the visitor industry with 78 per cent viewing the industry favourably and only 22 per cent viewing it unfavourably.

USP IDENTIFICATION

The major outcome of all these analyses is a clearer understanding of how the destination is different from its competitors, and how this will be reflected in the marketing strategy. According to Porter (1996), competitive strategy is about being different and the DMO must identify these differences early in its marketing planning. Sometimes these differences are referred to as USPs (unique selling points or propositions), sustainable competitive advantages (SCAs) or differential-distinct competitive advantages. Adapting Barney's (1991) work, a sustainable competitive advantage for a destination and its DMO would mean having the assets and/or skills that meet the following conditions:

- They are valuable to visitors.
- They are rare among the destination's current and potential competitors.
- They must be imperfectly imitable (cannot be easily copied).
- There are no strategically equivalent substitutes for the assets or skills.

The Canadian Tourism Commission has identified the following five unique selling propositions (USPs) for Canada as a tourism destination:

- Vibrant cities on the edge of nature
- Personal journeys by land, water and air
- Active adventures among awe-inspiring natural wonders
- Award-winning Canadian local cuisine
- Connecting with Canadians.

Output summary for DMS Step 1

When Step 1 of the destination marketing system is finished by the DMO, it will have a completed environmental scan and situation analysis. The strengths and weaknesses of the destination and DMO will be known. Additionally, the destination's unique selling propositions (USPs) will have been identified (Figure 3.12).

When beginning DMS Step 2, the DMO has several inputs to use for deciding upon its marketing strategy and objectives:

- The trends, opportunities, challenges and threats presented in the external environment. How to take advantage or adapt to these in future marketing strategies and plans?
- The major issues resulting from the destination and competitive analyses. How to change in the future to deal with these issues?
- The characteristics and feedback from visitor research. How to respond to visitor feedback and changes in tourists?
- The assessment of marketing position and previous marketing plan. How to improve positioning, branding and marketing plan?
- The attitudes of residents towards tourism. What needs to be done to address residents' concerns with the operations of the tourism sector?
- The statement of USPs. How to apply and communicate USPs more effectively in future?

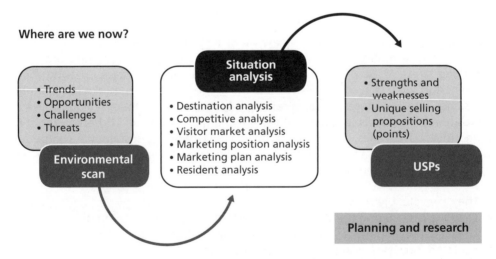

Figure 3.12 Output summary for DMS step 1: Where are we now?

2 Where would we like to be? (planning and research)

The DMO's marketing strategy and objectives are developed in the second DMS step (Figure 3.13). These should be based upon the strengths, weaknesses, trends, challenges, opportunities and threats identified in the first DMS step. The DMO considers several different options with respect to target markets and destination positioning, image and branding approaches before choosing what it considers the ideal strategy for the upcoming marketing period.

Figure 3.14 shows the marketing strategy stages in the left column; the steps that DMO marketers must complete are listed in the middle column; and the right column indicates the outcomes or choices that result from the completion of the steps.

Inputs	DMS step 2	Outputs
• Environmental scan (trends, challenges, opportunities and threats) • Situation analysis (strengths and weaknesses) • USPs	**Where would we like to be?** **PLANNING AND RESEARCH**	• Market segmentation analysis • Target markets • Positioning–image–branding approach • Marketing objectives

Figure 3.13 Destination marketing system: step 2: Where would we like to be?

Marketing strategy stages	Steps	Outcomes and choices
Where would we like to be?	**PR = Planning and Research**	
Visitor market segmentation analysis	• Divide the market into segments	• Market segments available
Target market selection	• Develop criteria for selecting target market • Select target markets	• Single target market, concentrated, full-coverage or undifferentiated?
Positioning–image–branding (PIB) approach development	• Select positioning, image and branding: o Overall positioning and image o Positioning and image for each selected target market • Destination branding	• Specific product features, benefits/problem solution/needs, specific usage occasions, against another product or product class dissociation?
Marketing objective-setting	• Write marketing objectives for each selected target market	• Marketing objectives that are target-market specific, results-oriented, quantitive and time-specific

Figure 3.14 Stages and steps in destination marketing strategy

Marketing strategy

The DMO's marketing strategy is a combination of the selected target markets and the positioning–image–branding approach.

VISITOR MARKET SEGMENTATION ANALYSIS

As indicated earlier, market segmentation is one of the key professional principles of marketing, and an extremely important step in selecting a marketing strategy. Each of the DMO's major markets should first be subjected to a visitor market segmentation analysis. Morrison (2010) describes this process as one of dividing the visitor market into groups that share common characteristics.

The most widely accepted practice in destination marketing is to begin by dividing markets by geographic origin and by broad trip purpose into business and pleasure/personal travellers. The following seven sets of segmentation criteria may be used to divide up overall markets:

- *Trip purpose*: Defining the market segment by the visitor's main purpose of trip, with four main divisions into business, meetings, conventions, etc.; pleasure, vacation or leisure; visiting friends or relatives (VFR); and personal.
- *Geography*: Describing markets by place of residence.
- *Socio-demographics*: Profiling tourists according to census-style characteristics such as age, education, occupation, income, household composition, etc.
- *Psychographics*: Dividing up visitors by their psychological orientations, lifestyles or AIOs (activities–interests–opinions).
- *Behaviour*: Differentiating among groups of visitors based upon past purchasing and travel behaviours or future travel purchase intentions.
- *Product-related*: Using some aspect of the product to define the market segment, such as ski slopes and alpine skiers, golf courses and golfers, reefs and scuba divers, spa-goers, etc.
- *Channel of distribution (business to business, or B2B)*: Applying different criteria, specific travel trade intermediaries are divided into sub-groups. For example, this might include defining travel agent markets by geographic area or commission volume level. Tour operators might also be defined geographically or by speciality or destinations served.

TARGET MARKET SELECTION

Having divided up its markets, the DMO must now select from among the market segments. To do this effectively, the DMO must have a set of criteria to evaluate the relative merits of each market segment. The potential criteria and some possible ways of measuring or evaluating them are as follows:

- *Segment size, growth and sales potential*: Segment size can be measured in number of visitors, total expenditures within the destination or daily expenditure per visitor, which is often referred to as the segment's yield. The rate of growth in a visitor market segment can be calculated in percentage terms in recent years and may then be compared to the rate of that segment's growth in competitive destinations.
- *Competition and segment structural attractiveness*: Here measures of the competitiveness for each segment and the relative power of buyers (visitors),

travel trade intermediaries and sellers (DMOs, transportation providers, attractions, hotels and other suppliers) are evaluated.

- *Destination vision and DMO's vision and marketing goals*: The appropriateness of market segment should be gauged against the destination vision and DMO vision and marketing goals.
- *Serviceability*: The degree of match between the segment's needs/benefits sought and the destination mix is determined. Additionally, the DMO must determine if the destination has the managerial, financial and other resources and skills required to effectively tap into and service the market. For example, this would be the case if medical tourism was being considered by a DMO.
- *Costs*: The additional investment required to break into the target market or to significantly increase market share.

POSITIONING–IMAGE–BRANDING (PIB) APPROACH DEVELOPMENT

The DMO must decide in its marketing strategy how to position the destination in the minds of potential visitors and among its competitors. The DMO must also decide how to brand the destination given the selected positioning and images that reflect this positioning. The PIB approach is the combination of positioning, image and branding.

Figure 3.15 illustrates how the DMO tries to match the destination's chosen positioning (desired image) with visitor's images (perceived image). Of course, the ultimate strategy is to bring the two images (desired and perceived) closer together.

Positioning and image communication: The DMO must select a positioning approach to communicate an image of the destination to people, within its selected target markets. Al Ries and Jack Trout (2001) introduced the positioning concept to the world in 1981 in their classic book, *Positioning: The Battle for Your Mind*. The following definition provides a clear picture of what positioning involves:

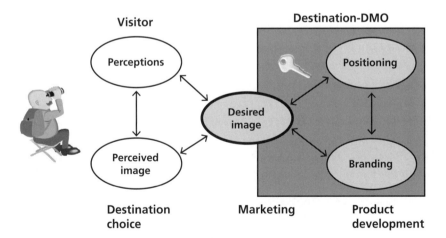

Figure 3.15 The PIB model: positioning–image–branding

Positioning definition

Positioning starts with the destination. But positioning is not what is done to the destination. Positioning is what the DMO attempts to do to the mind of the prospective visitor. That is the DMO positions the destination in the mind of the prospective visitor.

(Adapted from Ries and Trout, 2001)

Positioning by the DMO should be done in a series of steps and Morrison (2010) suggests using the following 5 Ds of positioning:

- *Documenting*: This step involves doing research with past and potential visitors to determine which benefits they are seeking in visiting the destination.
- *Deciding*: The second step is accomplished in two stages: (1) determining what images past visitors and non-visitors have of the destination (perceived image); and (2) deciding what image the DMO wants visitors to have of the destination (desired image).
- *Differentiating*: Positioning communicates the differences between the destination and competitors. Positioning is performed in two stages: (1) determining which destinations are in the competitive set (from the competitive analysis); and (2) pinpointing the factors and USPs, especially as these relate to the desired visitor benefits, that can be used to make the destination appear different from competitors.
- *Designing*: Fourth, the DMO must decide how it is going to communicate the select positioning or image to potential visitors within its target markets. The DMO must also make sure the destination mix supports the selected approach to positioning.
- *Delivering*: Last, the DMO must implement and monitor the chosen approach to positioning. In Chapter 1, this was referred to as 'delivering on the ground'.

The DMO should develop a destination positioning statement that expresses the differences and uniqueness of the place. The following is an example of a positioning statement from Tourism Australia:

Positioning statement for Australian tourism

The people of Australia are friendly and straight talking and open. Their sense of mateship and their no worries attitude make all visitors feel welcome. They make it easy to enjoy adventures beyond imagination. Whether it's in Australia's wide-open landscapes, pristine oceans or vibrant cities a holiday in Australia is an opportunity to experience a vast yet accessible adventure playground. You don't just visit Australia, you live it.

The friendly and open people are the key to Australia's positioning statement, since they give visitors such a special feeling of welcome.

The concepts of destination positioning, image and branding are closely linked, with branding being used to support the selected positioning approach in communicating the desired destination image (Figure 3.16). Ritchie *et al.* (1998) provide the following definition of a destination brand:

Destination brand

A name, symbol, logo, word mark or other graphic that both identifies and differentiates the destination; furthermore, it conveys the promise of a memorable travel experience that is uniquely associated with the destination; it also serves to consolidate and reinforce the recollection of pleasurable memories of the destination experience.

(Ritchie *et al.*, 1998)

Shaoxing, an ancient city in Zhejiang Province, China provides an excellent example of destination positioning and branding. For a few years now, Shaoxing's DMO has been using the phrase 'Shaoxing, Vintage China' (Figure 3.17).

Another good example of positioning and branding is Cumbria Tourism's strategy to become 'Adventure Capital UK' (Figure 3.18).

MARKETING OBJECTIVES

Specific short-term objectives are set for each target market. These objectives serve as guidelines for the activities and programmes included in the DMO's marketing plan. An example of the marketing objectives of the Virginia Tourism Corporation in the USA was provided earlier in this chapter.

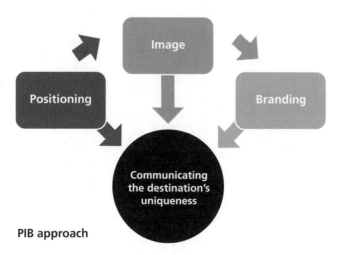

Figure 3.16 The interrelationship of positioning, image and branding

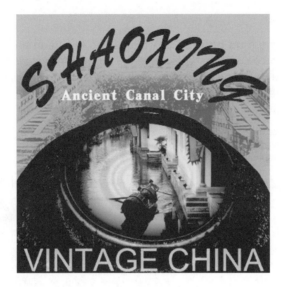

Figure 3.17 Excellent positioning and branding by the Shaoxing Tourism Commission in China
Source: Belle Tourism International Consulting.

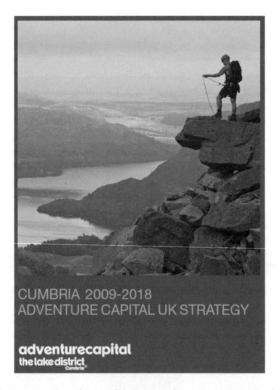

Figure 3.18 Cumbria tourism branding as Adventure Capital UK
Source: Cumbria Tourism, 2009.

Output summary for DMS Step 2

On completion of DMS Step 2, the DMO will have (Figure 3.19):

- A set of identified target markets. What are the priority groups of tourists to be targeted?
- Positioning/image and destination branding approaches. How to communicate the destination's uniqueness?
- The marketing objectives for the next marketing plan. What do we need to accomplish in the period ahead?

3 How do we get there? (implementation)

The third element of the DMS is the selection of a marketing mix, and the development and implementation of a marketing plan (Figure 3.20).

This is one of the most detailed and time-consuming stages in destination marketing and its planning (Figure 3.21). DMOs usually divide up the preparation of their marketing plans by the divisions or units within their organizational structures. For example, one group might handle business tourism, conventions and exhibitions, while another group will focus on pleasure or leisure travellers.

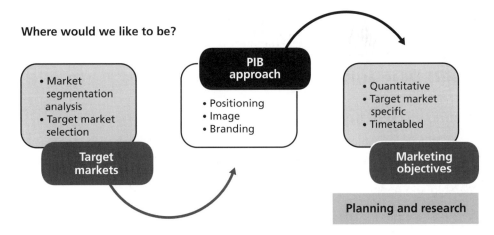

Figure 3.19 Output summary for DMS step 2: Where would we like to be?

Inputs	DMS step 3	Outputs
• Selected target markets • Positioning-image-branding approach • Marketing objectives	**How do we get there?** **IMPLEMENTATION**	• Marketing mix selection (8 Ps) • Marketing plan • Marketing budget • Marketing plan timetable or schedule • Assignment of implementation responsibilities • Control and evaluation procedures and measurements • Marketing implementation

Figure 3.20 Destination marketing system, step 3: How do we get there?

Marketing plan stages	Steps	Outcomes
How do we get there?	**I = implementation**	
Marketing mix selection	• Decide on how the 8 Ps are to be used to achieve the marketing objectives for each selected target market	• Use of product, partnership, people, packaging, programming, place, promotion and pricing
Marketing plan development	• Write a plan including executive summary, marketing plan rationale and implementation plan	• Written marketing plan
Marketing budget development	• Prepare the marketing budget according to the marketing objectives and the activities and programmes to achieve them	• Marketing budget
Marketing plan timetable or schedule	• Prepare a month-by-month timetable showing when each activity and programme will be implemented	• Month-by-month timetable
Assignment of implementation responsibilities	• Allocate responsibilities to different marketing departments and between DMO and its partners	• Responsibility assignments
Control and evaluation procedures and measurements	• Specify how the implementation of the marketing plan will be tracked and evaluated	• Control and evaluation procedures and measures
Marketing plan implementation	• Implement the marketing plan according to the specifications in the written documents	• Implementation of specific activities and programmes

Figure 3.21 Stages and steps in destination marketing plan

Marketing mix selection

The marketing mix is one of the key professional principles of marketing. The DMO has eight principal weapons within its marketing mix for achieving the marketing objectives for each target market (product, price, place, promotion, packaging, programming, partnership and people). Each of the 8 Ps are described below.

PRODUCT

A DMO really does not have a specific product or service to sell to potential visitors. However, there can be no doubt that the DMO represents the destination as a whole, and the destination is what it markets. Mill and Morrison (2012) describe all of the components of what a destination offers to visitors as the destination mix. The five elements of the destination mix are:

- Attractions and events
- Facilities (hotels, restaurants, etc.)
- Transportation
- Infrastructure
- Hospitality resources (people, service, hospitality, etc.).

The attractions and events play the key role in the destination mix, representing the unique assets that draw people to the destination.

The Slovenian Tourist Board provides a very interesting and detailed example of how a DMO defined its destination mix and product. Four different levels of the product were defined:

- Level 1: Overall level (image and promotion of Slovenia)
- Level 2: Tourist regions of Slovenia
- Level 3: Tourist products for activity and experiences of Slovenia
- Level 4: Composite tourist products and complete tourism programmes of Slovenia.

Within Level 1, the Slovenian Tourist Board (2007) identified the country's '7 + 2' products; seven existing and two others in partial development:

- Active holidays and breaks
- Towns and culture
- Natural environment, eco-tourism and tourism in villages
- Gastronomy
- Health and wellbeing
- Business tourism
- Entertainment tourism
- High-end offer (in development)
- Youth offer (in development).

The destination mix is sometimes called the destination product or tourism product of the destination. As discussed in Chapter 1, the destination product is multi-dimensional. It includes physical products (attractions, facilities, transportation, infrastructure), but also has a human dimension (people). The people dimension includes both the hosts (hospitality resources) and the guests (tourists). The destination also offers many packages and arranges events and festivals (programming).

A DMO must be concerned about the quality of experiences that visitors are having within the destination, since this impacts satisfaction levels, word-of-mouth recommendations and repeat visit intentions. Many DMOs have become involved in developing service and hospitality training programmes, with a particular emphasis on front-line employees.

A destination audit can be very useful in evaluating the physical and qualitative aspects of the destination mix. One specific qualitative measurement technique that is increasingly being used is mystery shopping. This is a form of participant observation, where the researchers act as customers or potential customers to monitor the quality of processes and procedures used in the delivery of a service (Wilson, 1998).

Price

With respect to price, the DMO can act more as a 'price influencer' than a 'price setter'. Above all the DMO must recognize that price is a multi-faceted concept. In the private sector, it is a major determinant of profitability. Prices also tend to attract certain markets and repel others. A destination where the prices are high may earn a reputation of being exclusive or luxury-oriented, while a destination with low prices can be viewed as a place for mass tourism. Additionally, price levels influence value-for-money perceptions.

Destination marketing planning

PLACE

In destination marketing, place represents distribution and the online and traditional travel trade channels the DMO uses to draw visitors to the destination. The DMO can market directly to potential visitors (direct distribution) or indirectly through travel trade intermediaries (indirect distribution). The 1990s brought electronic or digital distribution to tourism through the use of the Internet.

PROMOTION

Promotion has been a traditional activity of DMOs, with most organizations placing the greatest emphasis on advertising and sales (personal selling). Other elements of the promotional mix include public relations, sales promotion and merchandising. Now DMOs are heavily involved with digital marketing techniques, and especially with promotion through the World Wide Web, e-mail, mobile phones and social media.

All promotions are types of communications and it is essential that a DMO integrates promotions so that they are consistent. This process is known as integrated marketing communications or IMC (Figure 3.22).

PACKAGING

Packaging in tourism is very different from product packaging and is a key tool for the DMO in customizing the destination mix for specific target markets. Additionally, packaging is important in helping the destination to smooth out seasonal (peak and valley) patterns of visitor volumes. Packaging is the combination of related and complementary hospitality and tourism services and facilities into a single-price offering (Morrison, 2010).

PROGRAMMING

There are many opportunities for destinations to arrange special activities or programmes that are attractive to visitors. A festival is one of the best examples of programming in tourism.

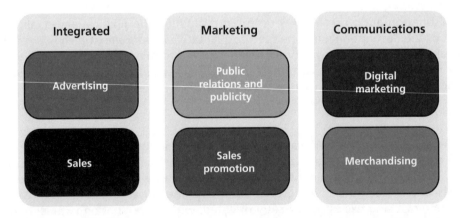

Figure 3.22 Components of integrated marketing communications (IMC)

Packaging and programming when combined together can be very powerful in convincing people to visit a destination or a tourism business (Figure 3.23). A good example of this is the Mohonk Mountain House resort in the state of New York, USA. The resort has created several specialized packages that include theme programmes for people with particular interests (Figure 3.24).

PARTNERSHIP

DMOs have been involved in building marketing partnerships for many years, but the last two decades has seen an increasing emphasis on tapping into the power of combining forces with other players.

A great example of a DMO partnership is walkmyalps.com involving the countries of Austria, Germany and Switzerland. Another good example of a destination partnership is the Welcome to Asia programme created by eight major cities (Tokyo, Kuala Lumpur, Taipei, Seoul, Delhi, Jakarta, Hanoi and Bangkok). The objective of this partnership is to attract more tourists from North America, Europe, Asia, Oceania and elsewhere.

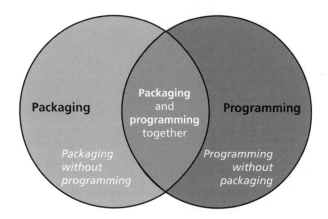

Figure 3.23 The relationship of packaging and programming

Figure 3.24 Mohonk Mountain House website
Source: Mohonk Mountain House, 2012.

PEOPLE

There is no question that tourism is a people-intensive business and that personal service encounters within a destination have a great impact on the visitor's experience and satisfaction.

Marketing plan development

A marketing plan is a written document that describes the activities and programmes that the DMO will use to accomplish its marketing objectives. This document should include an executive summary, marketing plan rationale and implementation plan.

EXECUTIVE SUMMARY

This is a summary in a few pages of the key highlights and major initiatives outlined in the marketing plan. It is called an executive summary partly because it can be read quickly and conveniently by DMO leaders and other busy stakeholders.

MARKETING PLAN RATIONALE

This is where the DMO explains the reasons and assumptions behind its choices of activities and programmes. It also explains the selected marketing strategy and lists the marketing objectives. Basically, the marketing plan rationale covers the first two DMS steps (Where are we now? Where would we like to be?); it summarizes the results of the planning and research done to prepare the marketing plan. The contents of the marketing plan rationale are:

- Environmental scan and situation analysis highlights
- USPs
- Marketing strategy
- Marketing objectives.

IMPLEMENTATION PLAN

The implementation plan is the most detailed and longest part of the marketing plan. It describes in detail how each of the 8 Ps of destination marketing (marketing mix) will be used for each target market to achieve that market's objectives for the upcoming period. The contents of the implementation plan are as follows:

- Marketing objectives
- Activities and programmes (marketing mix or 8 Ps)
- Marketing budget
- Timetable or schedule
- Assignment of responsibilities
- Control and evaluation procedures and measures.

The marketing plans are written for internal purposes to guide marketing; but they are also used to inform stakeholders and partners. The example below from Myrtle Beach, South Carolina, USA is excellent for communicating to external audiences (Figure 3.25).

Figure 3.25 2011 Myrtle Beach Area Destination Marketing Plan
Source: Myrtle Beach Area CVB, 2011.

Marketing budget development

Once the DMO has determined the activities and programmes (tasks) that it will use for each target market, it should develop the marketing budget to go along with the marketing plan.

The best approach to doing this is with the objective-and-task budgeting method. Figure 3.26 shows how this method builds the marketing budget from the bottom up, starting with the objectives; the activities and programmes to achieve each objective; and the estimated costs of implementing each activity and programme.

The marketing budget should be detailed out by expense category and by month.

Marketing plan timetable or schedule

A month-by-month timetable should be developed showing when each activity and programme will be implemented. Usually it is necessary to divide the timetable by target market or according to the marketing department that is responsible for each target market. For example, the marketing plan timetable may be sub-divided into month-by-month schedules for the following target markets and audiences:

- Business meetings, conventions and exhibitions; and incentive travel
- Leisure tourism/pleasure travel

Destination marketing planning

- Digital marketing/social media
- Travel agents and tour operators
- Travel exhibitions/fairs
- Festivals and events
- Media or press
- Other target markets/audiences.

Assignment of implementation responsibilities

It is very important to indicate who has the responsibility for implementing each activity and programme. There should be an assignment of responsibilities to each marketing department, as well as an indication of what the DMO will do and what it expects its partners and other stakeholders to accomplish. The assignment of responsibilities depends on how the DMO marketing department or division is structured. However, internationally it is common to find the following units:

- Convention/meeting sales and service
- Leisure tourism/pleasure travel (independent travellers)
- Group travel
- Sports marketing
- Public relations and communications
- Tourism development
- Administration and accounting.

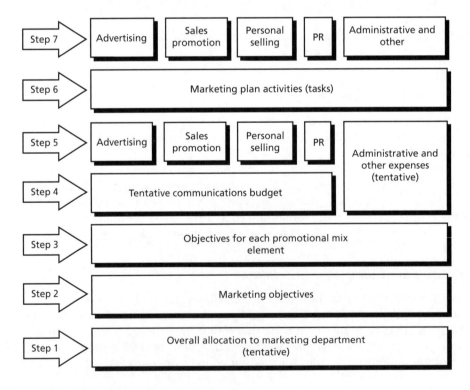

Figure 3.26 Objective-and-task budgeting
Source: Morrison, 2010.

100

Control and evaluation procedures and measurements

The marketing plan must include specific control and evaluation procedures and measurements for the remaining two DMS steps. Particularly important here is the identification of evaluation measures or metrics, milestones and performance standards.

- *Evaluation measures or metrics*: The activities and programmes that will be measured and the units of measurement (how the activities and programmes will be measured).
- *Milestones*: The dates at which measures will be taken or calculated (e.g. monthly, bi-monthly, every quarter, every six months, etc.).
- *Performance standards*: The range of acceptable performance (e.g. the quantified target for an objective + or – a certain percentage).

Marketing plan implementation

The DMO now uses the marketing plan as a guide for implementing its selected marketing activities and programmes. The marketing budget, timetable and assignment of implementation responsibilities are key tools for guiding the marketing plan implementation.

Output summary for DMS Step 3

The major outputs from Step 3 are the marketing mix selection and the written marketing plan (Figure 3.27).

Some of the outstanding international DMOs also produce a 'companion guide' to their marketing plans to assist the tourism sector and other stakeholders with their marketing activities and programmes. A very good example is the Belize Tourism Board's *Tourism Marketing Kit* (Figure 3.28).

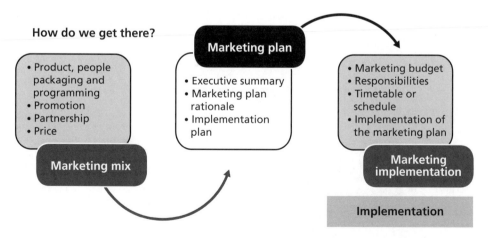

Figure 3.27 Output summary for DMS step 3: How do we get there?

Figure 3.28 Tourism marketing kit of Belize Tourism Board
Source: Image courtesy of the Belize Tourism Board, 2010.

4 How do we make sure we get there? (control: formative evaluation)

The last two DMS steps are both types of marketing evaluation:

● Control or formative evaluation: measuring progress while the marketing plan is being implemented.
● Evaluation or summative evaluation: measuring after the marketing plan is completed.

Unfortunately these are two highly important steps that DMOs often neglect or they just do partially. Control and evaluation among DMOs is quite incomplete and mostly focused on measuring activities rather than productivity and performance. Also, it is common to see DMOs keeping track of numbers of visitors and expenditures, but nothing else. While it is essential for a DMO to measure these factors, the DMO cannot itself take full credit for these results.

The DMO monitors its progress in implementing the marketing plan during the formative evaluation step (control) of the DMS (Figure 3.29).

There are four different measures or 'metrics' that can be used in DMO evaluation, as the diagram on the next page illustrates (Figure 3.30):

● *Activities*: The destination marketing activities and programmes identified in the marketing plan. The completion of these activities and programmes is one type of measure. For example, the DMO held a festival or forum; attended a travel exhibition or fair; launched a new website; completed a familiarization tour, etc.
● *Activity Measures*: These are quantitative measures of activities, when there is more than one instance or occasion. For example, the DMO exhibited at eight different travel exhibitions or fairs.
● *Productivity Measures*: These are measures of the efficiency and effectiveness of the DMO in using its financial, human and other resources. For example, how many people came to the DMO's booth during a travel exhibition or fair?
● *Performance Measures*: These are the actual outcomes or results from implementing the activities and programmes contained in the marketing plan.

Inputs	DMS step 4	Outputs
● Marketing objectives ● Marketing plan (8 Ps) and the specified activities and programmes ● Marketing plan timetable ● Marketing plan implementation responsibilities ● Marketing budget	**How do we make sure we get there?** **CONTROL**	● Progress reports (formative evaluations) ● Marketing plan modifications

Figure 3.29 Destination marketing system, step 4: How do we make sure we get there?

Destination marketing planning

C = How do we make sure we get there?
E = How do we know if we got there?

Figure 3.30 DMO performance reporting measures

Sometimes these are also called Key Performance Indicators (KPIs) by DMOs.

Another very outstanding example of KRAs is provided by Tourism Queensland in Australia (Figure 3.31).

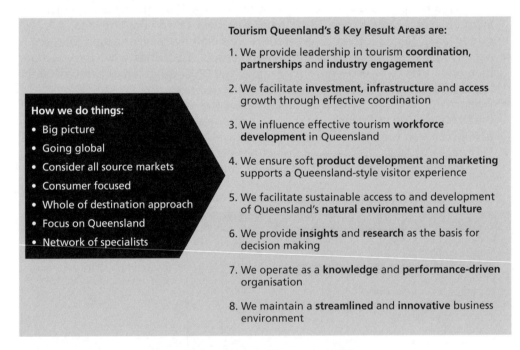

How we do things:
- Big picture
- Going global
- Consider all source markets
- Consumer focused
- Whole of destination approach
- Focus on Queensland
- Network of specialists

Tourism Queensland's 8 Key Result Areas are:

1. We provide leadership in tourism **coordination, partnerships** and **industry engagement**

2. We facilitate **investment, infrastructure** and **access** growth through effective coordination

3. We influence effective tourism **workforce development** in Queensland

4. We ensure soft **product development** and **marketing** supports a Queensland-style visitor experience

5. We facilitate sustainable access to and development of Queensland's **natural environment** and **culture**

6. We provide **insights** and **research** as the basis for decision making

7. We operate as a **knowledge** and **performance-driven** organisation

8. We maintain a **streamlined** and **innovative** business environment

Figure 3.31 Key result areas for Tourism Queensland
Source: Tourism Queensland, 2009.

Output summary for DMS Step 4

Step 4 takes place as the marketing plan is being completed and involves tracking the progress of plan implementation, especially the degree to which the marketing objectives are being achieved (Figure 3.32).

If the progress on a specific activity or programme is very poor, the DMO may consider discontinuing it or making a corrective adjustment in the activity or programme.

5 How do we know if we got there? (evaluation: summative evaluation)

When the marketing plan is completed, a thorough evaluation should be conducted (Figure 3.33).

DMOs are increasingly being asked to demonstrate their marketing effectiveness and performance, thereby showing their accountability for the funds that are invested in marketing activities and programmes. The following are the reasons for performance measurement of a DMO (Industry Canada, 2010):

- To create recognized benchmarks to utilize for assessing internal performance.
- To provide a means to accurately compare performance to other DMOs.
- To capture valuable information about which marketing tactics are most effective, what types of prospects are most likely to buy, which customers are most profitable, and how the market in general develops over time.
- To aid in the decision-making process for resource management and allocation.
- To aid in decision-making during sales and marketing campaign development.
- To identify 'need areas' for staff training and development.
- To provide a platform by which you can clearly articulate your contribution to your stakeholders and the local community.

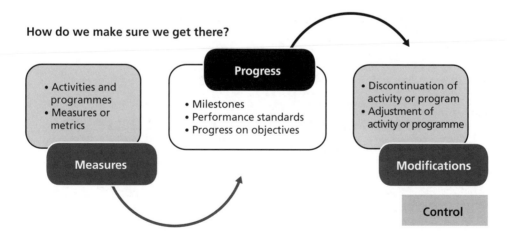

Figure 3.32 Output summary for DMS step 4: How do we make sure we get there?

Inputs	DMS step 5	Outputs
• Marketing objectives • Progress reports (formative evaluations) • Marketing plan modifications	**How do we know if we got there?** **EVALUATION**	• Marketing effectiveness or performance measures • Changes required in next marketing plan

Figure 3.33 Destination marketing system, step 5: How do we know if we got there?

Faulkner (1997) defined evaluation as 'a systematic process for objectively assessing an organization's (or programme's) performance'. He suggested the following three criteria for evaluating a DMO's performance:

- *Appropriateness*: The extent to which the DMO's objectives and priorities match the needs of its stakeholders.
- *Effectiveness*: The extent to which the DMO achieves its marketing goals and objectives.
- *Efficiency*: The extent to which the DMO's marketing programme outcomes are achieved at a reasonable cost and within a reasonable time frame.

An excellent example of how a DMO measures and reports its performance is Meet Minneapolis Impact (http://impact.minneapolis.org/). This website is maintained by Meet Minneapolis (Minneapolis Convention and Visitors Bureau) in the USA (Figures 3.34 and 3.35). It contains a summary in dashboard format and a page of detailed results and progress reporting.

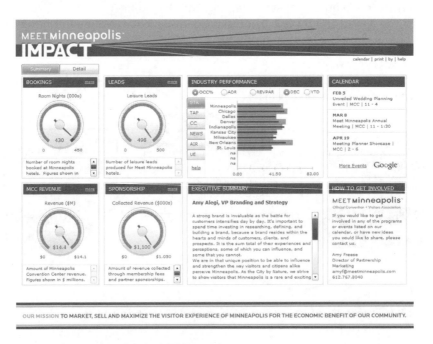

Figure 3.34 Summary impact dashboard
Source: Meet Minneapolis, Convention and Visitors Association and Inverra, Inc., 2012.

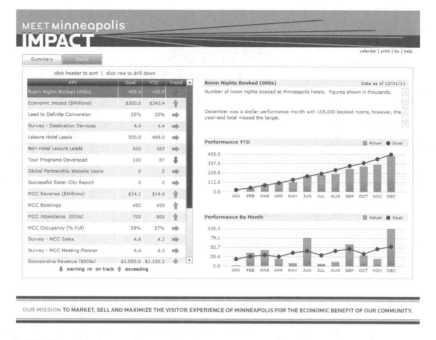

Figure 3.35 Detailed results and progress reporting

Source: Meet Minneapolis, Convention and Visitors Association and Inverra, Inc., 2012.

The Summary Impact Dashboard contains eight elements:

- Bookings
- Leads
- Minneapolis Convention Center (MCC) revenues
- Sponsorships
- Industry performance
- Executive Summary
- Calendar
- How to get involved.

The detailed results and progress reporting show the measures of the DMO's KPIs (key performance indicators). Then the objectives for the year for each KPI are shown and after that the progress year-to-date (YTD). Performance is monitored on each KPI in three possible categories with appropriate arrow symbols (exceeding; on track; warning). The results for each KPI can be seen by clicking on the appropriate row ('drilling down').

This is an excellent tool and it combines both destination marketing control and evaluation. Progress monitoring is included on the KPIs (control). At the end of the year, the results become final and form part of the evaluation.

Output summary for DMS Step 5

When the marketing plan is completed, the DMO evaluates the results and produces measures of activities, productivity and performance (Figure 3.36).

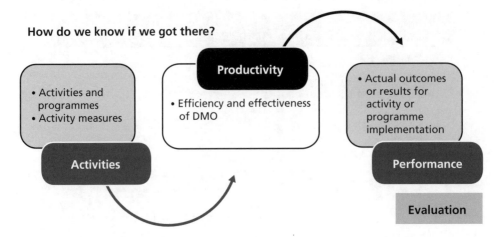

Figure 3.36 Output summary for DMS step 5: How do we know if we got there?

Summary

Marketing and promotion are one of the most important roles of a DMO, requiring careful, step-by-step planning. The destination marketing planning process is an approach that has proved to be effective in practice. This involves developing a hierarchy of goals and objectives, including a destination vision, DMO vision, marketing goals and marketing objectives. A DMO mission also needs to be written.

The specific steps that DMOs must complete in destination marketing planning are as follows:

- Develop a destination vision and DMO vision
- Prepare a set of 3–5 year destination marketing goals
- Write a DMO mission statement
- Prepare an environmental scan
- Develop a situation analysis
- Conduct market and marketing research to support decisions
- Identify the destination's USPs
- Conduct market segmentation analysis
- Select target markets
- Write a destination positioning statement
- Create a destination branding approach
- Prepare a set of marketing objectives
- Write a marketing plan
- Monitor the implementation of the marketing plan and report on progress (control)
- Evaluate the effectiveness of the marketing plan and measure the DMO's performance.

> ### Review questions
>
> 1 What are the key destination marketing professional principles?
> 2 Which five questions comprise the destination marketing system?
> 3 What are the management functions represented by each of the letters in the PRICE model?
> 4 Which time frames are specified within the destination marketing planning process?
> 5 What is the difference between a DMO vision and a DMO mission?
> 6 Which three parts are included in a destination marketing plan?
> 7 What are the 8 Ps of destination marketing and which steps does each of them involve?
> 8 How are KRAs and KPIs used in destination marketing control and evaluation?

References

Barney, J. 1991. Firm resources and sustained competitive advantage. *Journal of Management*, 17(1), 99–120.

Belize Tourism Board. 2010. http://belizedev.com/belizetourism/component/option,com_remository/Itemid,56/func,download/id,345/chk,05bb9e026bc83e10ecd4ad3f08483002/

Butler, R.W. 1980. The concept of the tourist area life-cycle of evolution: implications for management of resources. *Canadian Geographer*, 24(1), 5–12.

Canadian Tourism Commission. 2012. http://en-corporate.canada.travel/resources-industry/canada%E2%80%99s-tourism-brand

Cumbria Tourism. 2009. Cumbria 2009–2018 Adventure Capital UK Strategy.

Department of Tourism, Morocco. 2010. Vision 2020 for Tourism in Morocco.

Dubai Department of Tourism and Commerce Marketing. 2012. http://www.dubaitourism.ae/about/background

Faulkner, W. 1997. A model for the evaluation of national tourism destination marketing programs. *Journal of Travel Research*, 35(3), 23–32.

Hawaii Tourism Authority. 2010. Resident Sentiment Survey.

Ice News. 2009. Iceland as a Tourist Destination: Image is Still Strong. http://www.icenews.is/index.php/2009/05/27/iceland-as-a-tourist-destination-image-still-strong/

Industry Canada. 2010. A Guide to Using Market Research and Marketing Measurement for Successful Tourism Destination Marketing. http://fednor.gc.ca/eic/site/fednor-fednor.nsf/eng/fn03316.html

Korea Tourism Organization. 2012. http://kto.visitkorea.or.kr/

Kotler, P. 2000. Marketing Management. Millennium Edition. Upper Saddle River, NJ: Prentice Hall.

Las Vegas Convention and Visitors Authority. 2011. Las Vegas Visitor Profile Study 2010.

McCarthy, E.J. 1960. Basic Marketing: A Managerial Approach. Homewood, IL: Irwin.

Meet Minneapolis, Convention and Visitors Association and Inverra, Inc. 2012. Meet Minneapolis Impact.

Mill, R.C., and Morrison, A.M. 2012. The Tourism System. Dubuque, IA: Kendall Hunt Publishing.

Ministry of Tourism, Republic of Kenya. 2009. Strategic Plan 2008–2012.

Mohonk Mountain House. 2012. http://www.mohonk.com/Event-Program-Calendar

Montana Department of Commerce, Office of Tourism. 2011. Tourism Marketing Plan July 2011–June 2012.

Morrison, A.M. 2010. Hospitality and Travel Marketing. Clifton Park, NY: Cengage Delmar.

Myrtle Beach Area CVB. 2011. 2011 Myrtle Beach Area Destination Marketing Plan.

Porter, M.E. 1996. What is strategy? *Harvard Business Review*, November–December, 61–78.

Richmond Metropolitan Convention and Visitors Bureau. 2012. http://www. visitrichmondva.com/Foot/About-RMCVB/Mission-Vision-and-Values

Ries, A., and Trout, J. 2001. Positioning: The Battle for Your Mind: The 20th Anniversary Edition. New York: McGraw-Hill, 2–3.

Ritchie, J.R.B. 1993. Crafting a destination vision: Putting the process of resident responsive tourism into practice. *Tourism Management*, 14(5), 379–389.

Ritchie, J.R.B. and Ritchie, J.B. 1998. The branding of tourism destinations: Past achievements and future challenges. *Proceedings of the 1998 Annual Congress of the International Association of Scientific Experts in Tourism, Destination Marketing: Scopes and Limitations*, edited by Peter Keller. Marrakech, Morocco: International Association of Scientific Experts in Tourism, 89–116.

Slovenian Tourist Board. 2007. Marketing Plan for Slovenian Tourism 2007–2011.

Tourism Australia. 2012. Australia's Tourism Brand. http://www.tourism.australia.com/ en-au/marketing/brand-australia.aspx

Tourism Ireland. 2011. Competing to Win. Tourism Ireland Marketing Plan 2012.

Tourism Malaysia. 2009. Destination Governance. 5th Meeting of the UNWTO Destination Council, 11 March.

Tourism Queensland. 2009. Tourism Queensland Corporate Plan 2008–2011.

——2011. http://www.tq.com.au

Tourism South Africa. 2010. The Marketing Tourism Growth Strategy for South Africa 2011–2013.

Tourism Strategy Group, Ministry of Economic Development. 2008. New Zealand Tourism Strategy.

Tourism Victoria. 2010. Tourism Victoria 2011. Strategic Sales and Marketing Plan.

Town of Drumheller. 2011. Tourism Master Plan.

Turismo de Portugal. 2012. http://www.visitportugal.com/pturismo/Downloads/ default.aspx

Virginia Tourism Corporation. 2010. Virginia Tourism Corporation Marketing Plan FY11.

WalkMyAlps.com. 2012. http://walkmyalps.com

Wilson, A.M. 1998. The role of mystery shopping in the measurement of service performance. *Managing Service Quality*, 8(6), 414–420.

World Economic Forum. 2011. The Travel & Tourism Competitiveness Report 2011.

Chapter 4

Destination management research

Learning objectives

1. Explain the contributions that research makes to destination management.

2. Describe the process for developing a destination management research agenda.

3. Discuss the fundamental principles of the research needed to support destination management.

4. Detail the steps and research techniques for analysing existing tourist markets.

5. Explain how a destination conducts a potential market analysis.

6. Describe the techniques for doing destination image research.

7. Identify the research process to assess the opinions and attitudes of community residents about tourism.

8. Pinpoint the types of research projects that can be done on the four parts of the destination product.

9. Name some of the major research approaches for measuring economic impact.

10. Delineate procedures for completing competitive research.

11. State the reasons why performance measurement and reporting are needed in destination management.

12. Provide suggestions on how a research plan for a destination should be prepared.

Introduction

In Chapter 1, planning and research were identified as one of the roles of destination management. The previous two chapters have discussed the planning part of this role in detail; Chapter 2 was about overall destination planning for tourism and Chapter 3 covered destination marketing planning. To be successful, both of these types of planning need to be research-based and so research is the next topic to explore.

Tourism research has exploded in the past four decades and much of this research has been on topics that directly affect destinations and destination management. For example, there have been many studies on consumer motivations and behaviours related to tourism, as well as on people's decision-making strategies. The research on destination image has been very extensive since the early 1970s. Research on the supply side of tourism destinations is equally impressive in terms of volume and diversity. For example, recently there has been much research related to destination competitiveness and to the sustainable tourism development of destinations.

Not everyone likes to do research and others get bored listening to people talking about research results. So for some, it is a 'necessary evil' but there are others who have a real passion about research. No matter where you stand on research, it is part of the basic foundation of professional destination management today. So the best place to start is to consider how research contributes to contemporary destination management.

Contributions of research to destination management

Research makes an enormous contribution to destination management and it is a fundamental component of the professional destination management concept. Without research, the DMO and other stakeholders cannot make important decisions accurately and with any degree of confidence. Table 4.1 shows the potential research contributions and methods for each of the destination management roles (the 'and research' part has been deleted from 'planning' since research actually contributes to all roles and not just to planning).

What about the reasons for doing destination management research and the benefits that flow to the DMO and other tourism stakeholders? Research can be expensive to conduct, so it often needs further justification. Morrison (2010) suggests that the 5 Cs (customers; competitors; confidence; credibility; and change) are the main reasons for doing tourism research. For destination management, there is a need to add a sixth C for 'community':

- *Customers*: Helps destinations develop a detailed knowledge of visitors, as well as their destination images and satisfaction levels.
- *Competitors*: Assists with identifying and assessing the relative strengths of competitive destinations.
- *Confidence*: Reduces the perceived risk for the destination in its decision-making.
- *Credibility*: Increases the credibility of the DMO as well as the claims the DMO and tourism stakeholders make in marketing and promotional programmes.
- *Change*: Keeps the DMO and all tourism stakeholders up-to-date with the constant changes in tourism and travel.
- *Community*: Increases the understanding of community residents' perceptions and attitudes about tourism and its impact on their lives.

Table 4.1 Contributions of research to destination management roles

Destination management roles	Research contributions and methods
Leadership and coordination	• Estimating economic impact of tourism • Documenting non-economic benefits of tourism • Identifying tourism sector and stakeholder needs/issues • Measuring performance
Planning	• Completing environmental scan • Conducting SWOT analysis
Product development	• Analysing successful product development cases in other destinations • Assessing tourist satisfaction • Destination analysis (product analysis) • Doing project market analyses/feasibility studies
Marketing and promotion	• Analysing marketing efficiency and effectiveness • Determining destination image • Identifying potential visitors • Preparing competitive analysis • Profiling existing visitors
Partnership and team-building	• Measuring partnering benefits • Studying successful partnering case studies
Community relations	• Collecting resident opinions and attitudes towards tourism • Gathering community input/suggestions

The Northwest Regional Development Agency (NWDA) in England (2006) highlighted other specific reasons for doing destination management research:

Reasons for doing regional destination research

Throughout the industry (both public and private sector), we are facing increasing demands and expectations to provide robust evidence for monitoring performance and to support planning, policy and funding decisions. The development of a high quality evidence base is essential to enable us to:

● Demonstrate to Central Government the importance of tourism within the wider economy, thereby helping to secure funding for the region.
● Monitor trends in demand (e.g. by month/year/area/sector) in order to guide regional and sub-regional investment/intervention decisions.
● Measure the impact of public sector investment/intervention and of shocks/ major incidents.
● Improve the performance of the region's tourism businesses through the provision of high quality industry intelligence that can support their business development decisions.

The NWDA statement provides additional reasons for conducting destination management research. The first is to demonstrate the size and importance of the tourism sector in the destination. To assess the impacts and effectiveness of funds invested in tourism by government agencies is a second reason. Third, the research that the DMO gathers helps organizations in the tourism sector to be more successful in their operations and marketing.

Developing a destination management research agenda

In every destination, there are many tourism research sponsors (those who pay for the research) and providers (those who do the research), but the focus in this chapter is on the research done by or on behalf of the DMO. What should a DMO put on its agenda for tourism research? This is a tough question to answer as it depends on the characteristics of the destination and what the strategies are within its long-term plan for tourism. However, most destination management research agendas can be divided into the following three main categories:

- *Ongoing research*: Research projects completed and other information collected each year by the DMO.
- *Periodic research*: Research projects and information gathering that are done repeatedly by the DMO, but not each year.
- *As-needed research*: Irregular and unexpected research projects and information gathering that are required for specific opportunities, problems or issues that arise in the destination.

The DMO's priority research projects are included among ongoing research. This research is on matters that are expected to change every year, such as the number and mix of tourists to the destination. The DMO's marketing and promotion role has a constant need for research inputs, so much of that research is ongoing.

Important research topics where change is expected to be more gradual, such as destination image, are in the periodic research category. Other aspects that require continual research but not every year are the destination product and the human resources available.

'One-off' or 'one-time' research projects are completed when the need arises. For example, this might be a study on the need for a new convention and exhibition centre or an analysis of an emerging market with promising market potential. It is sometimes impossible to predict what research is required and when it will be needed.

Figure 4.1 shows a recommended agenda for destination management research. It consists of two sections (marketing-related and other). The marketing-related research is input to the operation of the destination marketing system (DMS) discussed in Chapter 3 and provides the data and information required for the destination marketing planning process. The second section contains research and information needed to support the other five roles of destination management. It is strongly recommended that all DMOs develop an annual plan as well as a multi-year strategy for destination management research.

The research items neatly fall into the two sections of Figure 4.1. However, in actual practice the research done in one section may also be helpful and may be drawn upon in the other section. For example, many of the marketing-related research projects are

Categories	Marketing-related research	Other research
On-going reseach	• Marketing control and evaluation research • Marketing plan analysis • Situation analysis • Social media channel tracking and analysis • Visitor market analysis • Visitor satisfaction analysis • Website traffic analysis	• Economic impact analysis • KPI measurement and tracking (key performance indicators)
Periodic research	• Competitive analysis • Conversion studies on enquiries • Destination image analysis • Destination positioning and branding analysis • Marketing audit • Market segmentation studies	• Community resident analysis • Destination analysis (product analysis) • Environmental scan and other research for destination planning • Festival/event analysis • Labour market analysis
As-needed research	• Potential market analysis	• Project market analyses and feasibility studies

Figure 4.1 Recommended agenda for destination management research

used as a foundation for parts of the destination planning. Additionally, some of the KPI (key performance indicator) measurements will be taken from the marketing evaluation research.

Later in the chapter, some of the important research and information items contained in Figure 4.1 will be described in more detail. However, before moving on to these materials, it is important to review two key fundamental principles and procedures for destination management research; the destination management research process, and primary and secondary research.

Fundamentals of destination management research

Nowadays we are all swamped by seas of information and DMOs are especially swimming in a huge ocean of facts and numbers. So, to what should the DMO give the most attention and how should the data and information be digested? The first step for the DMO is to make sure that the research that it does is accurate and reliable, and this means that it must follow the correct research process.

Destination management research process

There is a 'classic' research process for gathering, analysing and interpreting data, and it definitely needs to be applied in destination management research projects. This process is described step-by-step below:

Formulate the research problem and identify research objectives

The first step is to clearly define the research problem and this means what is the overall goal of the research. In other words, what are the critical items that the DMO wants to get from doing the research? The example shown below from Austin, Texas,

USA (Austin Convention and Visitors Bureau, 2011) describes two research projects the city's DMO commissioned and the projects' research problems. The research problem in the first project was to detail the benefits of tourism to the city of Austin. The second project was to produce a better understanding of the typical Austin visitor.

Research studies by Austin, TX CVB

Two newly completed research studies commissioned by the Austin Convention and Visitors Bureau (Austin CVB) detail the benefits of tourism to the city and present a new profile of the typical Austin visitor. The studies were ordered to better understand who is visiting, what drew them to the city, what the economic benefits of tourism are and how the Bureau can improve its marketing efforts to diversify and expand the number of visitors that travel to Austin annually. As the City of Austin's contracted tourism marketing organization, the Austin CVB is charged with researching and reporting visitor trends, and identifying opportunities to improve the visitor experience.

A second example is from two studies of the outbound markets from the UK and UAE (United Arab Emirates) to India. These research projects were designed to gauge the perception of tourists – past as well as prospective – in the UK and UAE about tourism in India.

Once the overall research problem or goal has been articulated, this should be used to identify more detailed research objectives and related questions. For example, a research project on the tourism labour market on Vancouver Island, Canada (Roslyn Kunin & Associates, Inc., 2009), had the following specific objectives:

Research questions for tourism labour market study for Vancouver Island, Canada

1 To estimate labour demand in the Vancouver Island tourism region to 2015.
2 To estimate labour supply and potential demand–supply gaps in the tourism region.
3 To ensure industry training requirements are aligned to provincial and regional needs.
4 To engage regional tourism stakeholders in the process, to provide direction to the labour market analysis process and to provide regional input into the provincial human resources strategy.
5 To use this process as a means of assessing the need for region-specific human resources strategies and where appropriate identifying organization(s) willing to develop and implement these strategies.

A second example is from Hawaii in the USA and the Hawaii Tourism Authority's (2010) Visitor Satisfaction and Activity Report for 2009. This research project had three specific objectives:

Hawaii Visitor Satisfaction and Activity Report research questions

- To present measurements of survey respondents' satisfaction with Hawaii as a visitor destination, specifically from the six major market areas (US West, US East, Japan, Canada, Europe and Oceania).
- To provide more insight into the destination selection and trip planning process taken by these visitors.
- To analyse demographic information on visitors who responded to the study.

Select research design and data collection method

The second step in the research process is to select the research design and the data collection method to meet the research objectives. There are several alternative research designs including surveys, observations and experiments. There are also qualitative and quantitative branches of research, more about which will be said later.

Next is the choice of a specific data collection method to fit with the selected research design. For example, for a survey research design, there are several data collection methods available including mail, telephone, online and face-to-face (personal interviews/intercepts). The data collection method picked will depend on a number of factors that are important to the DMO including the research budget available and the time available to do the research project. Later, you will hear about several data collection methods used by DMOs in actual research projects.

Collect and analyse secondary information

It is a good idea now to gather previously-published research data and information related to the research topic. It can save time and money to look at secondary information since someone may have previously completed similar research to that which the DMO is planning. For example, a DMO might be planning to investigate the market potential of niche and special-interest markets. Just as academic scholars do 'literature reviews', a DMO with an interest in this topic would be well advised to learn from others' research. The following niche market study by Cape Town, South Africa (2008) would be one of the many secondary research pieces that the DMO or its research suppliers could review in detail.

Cape Town Tourism niche market study

This study was commissioned by the City of Cape Town with the aim of reviewing the identified tourism niche sectors in the City's Tourism Development Framework.

The study required desktop research for the identification of trends, demands, gaps, definitions and descriptions of the niche sectors including culture and heritage, backpacking and youth, nature-based and adventure, wine and cuisine, and business tourism.

As mentioned earlier there are now several mountain ranges of tourism research data and information that have accumulated over the past 40–50 years. Some of this research is good; some not so good, but it is always worthwhile checking on what has been done before on the topic of interest to the DMO.

Decide on sample design

If the secondary or previously-published data and information is judged to be insufficient or if it does not directly apply to the destination, the DMO will probably decide to move forward with primary research. Then the next item to be dealt with will be the composition and size of the sample, and how the sample will be constructed.

This is a rather complex subject and any description of sample design can quickly get into statistical theory. This is not a book about statistics, but it needs to be said that the DMO must be assured that the sample size is large enough to produce accurate and reliable research data results. Often sample sizes used in research for DMOs are insufficient, so the results they get are questionable.

Collect data

Using the chosen data collection method, the researchers now collect the primary data and information. The DMO should ensure that there are adequate quality control steps built into the data collection process.

Analyse and interpret data

Data analysis is a very important part of the research process and there are many alternative ways of analysing data. These include using statistical analysis programmes like SPSS and SAS for data entry and analysis. If the research data is qualitative (non-numerical) then other analysis techniques must be used.

The research results need to be set against the research problem (main goal) and specific research objectives that were established earlier. Every question should be addressed with the parallel data results. Said in a simpler way, the research questions must be answered.

Interpreting the results of a research project is much harder than analysing the data, but there are a few basic questions that need to be answered. What do the research results mean for the destination? Which practical steps should be taken by the DMO and tourism stakeholders to follow up on the research?

Prepare research report

The results, conclusions and recommendations of the research should then be concisely written up in a research report. It is often a good idea to produce two report versions;

one that is a summary version and the other that contains all the results, technical details and data tables.

Communicate research findings and recommendations

The final step in the destination management research process is to communicate results and findings to DMO management, tourism stakeholders and other affected parties. This is perhaps the most critical step since it is the DMO and the tourism stakeholders that must absorb and implement programmes, based upon the research findings. 'Keep it simple' is the best advice in making these communications on research findings successful. The two examples in Figure 4.2 from New Zealand and the USA are outstanding in the simplicity in which they put across research results using great graphics.

The concepts of secondary and primary research were discussed during this description of the destination management research process and these are two fundamental concepts that require some more elaboration.

Secondary and primary research

When does second come first? The answer is in research because secondary research data and information must be carefully analysed before primary research is started. The following are the definitions of these two terms in the context of destination management:

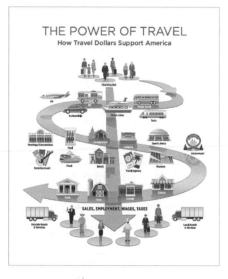

Figure 4.2 Good examples of visually communicating research results

Source: New Zealand Ministry of Tourism, 2010; US Travel Association, 2012.

- *Secondary research*: Data or information previously gathered and published by organizations or persons that are not associated with the DMO. This is called secondary because someone else did the research and the DMO is a subsequent user.
- *Primary research*: Research done by DMO staff or by research suppliers commissioned by the DMO to collect data or information that addresses questions specific to the destination. This can be described as 'first-time' data or information collected for the DMO for its own specific purposes, hence the term 'primary'.

DMOs are well advised to use a mixture of secondary and primary research. DMO staff members can be trained on where to find secondary research and how to use it. Doing primary research requires a higher level of training and education, and it is often better to use a research supplier either at a private research company or at an academic institution.

There is so much secondary research information now available for destination management research that it is difficult to identify and describe every source. Some of the secondary research comes from within the DMO or the destination (internal secondary) and the rest is produced outside of the destination (external secondary). Figure 4.3 shows the main sources of a DMO's internal and external secondary research.

Earlier there was a discussion on research design and this relates to primary research. Figure 4.4 identifies the main primary research designs in two parts; quantitative primary research mainly producing numerical data, and qualitative primary research mainly generating non-numeric data.

Having explained the fundamentals of destination management research, it is appropriate to now discuss a variety of analysis topics that are of special importance for DMOs and destinations.

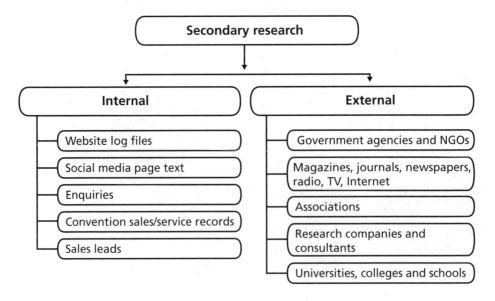

Figure 4.3 Types of internal and external secondary research

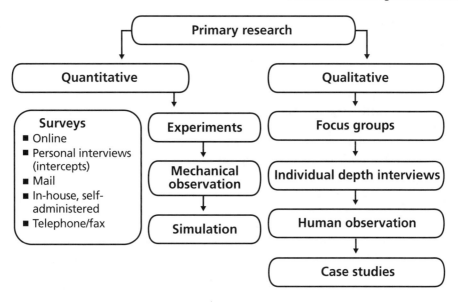

Figure 4.4 Primary research designs

Analysis of existing markets

It is of fundamental importance that a destination fully comprehends its portfolio of existing visitors. Primary research is definitely needed to build this understanding of existing markets and specifically a technique that is usually called a visitor profile study. The following are the main steps in conducting a visitor profile study.

Establish study objectives

Conducting a visitor profile study within a destination meets several important objectives including to:

- Get a demographic and geographic profile of visitors
- Find out how much visitors spend in a destination
- Determine which attractions and events visitors use
- Find out about visitors' activity participation in a destination
- Collect information on travel party characteristics (e.g. party sizes and composition, lengths of stay, trip purposes, accommodation usage, etc.)
- Determine satisfaction levels with trips to a destination
- Determine perceptions/images of a destination
- Determine previous trip history to a destination and future intentions to return to a destination
- Find out about uses of sources of travel information and travel planning processes
- Collect information on visitors' media usage patterns.

Define visitor

A clear definition of visitor is needed for this type of research study. Sometimes a 'visitor' is defined as a non-resident of the destination who stays in the destination for at least one night. Other definitions allow for visitors to include people who are non-residents but do not stay overnight in the destination. This can be especially important to places that receive a high proportion of day-trippers or so-called 'excursionists'. The main concern here is to exclude local residents and others who are commuting every day to work in the destination. In some instances, a visitor must travel a minimum of a certain distance or be from specific geographic areas to qualify for surveying.

Determine data collection method

Visitor profile studies generally apply the survey design method, but there are now many data collection methods available for such surveys. For example, an international visitor profile study was conducted in Shanghai, China in 2009 and 2010 using the personal interview technique. The Las Vegas Visitor Profile Study 2010 was also accomplished by using face-to-face surveys. Personal interviews are usually the most expensive and most difficult way to survey existing markets, but this data collection method has distinct advantages, including:

- There is absolute certainty that respondents (those people surveyed) actually visited the destination.
- People can recollect their destination experiences very well.
- There is usually a high rate of response and completion of surveys (the refusal rate is relatively low).

However, the personal interview method has disadvantages in addition to its higher costs. People may feel that they are being inconvenienced in being stopped and asked to complete a survey, and this is especially the case for business travellers who are often on very tight schedules. Additionally, some people may have just arrived in the destination and not yet had the 'full experience'. Their estimates of expenditures may be more guesses than accurate facts.

'Exit surveys' are very popular as visitor profile studies, although they are hard to implement at most destinations. Many island destinations are ideal for exit surveys since they have very few exit points where visitors tend to congregate before leaving.

Visitor profile studies can be completed with other data collection methods apart from personal interviews. If contact information can be gathered for visitors while they are in the destination or when they book, they can be contacted after they return home by phone, mail or e-mail. The major challenge with post-visit surveys is the possibility of visitors forgetting the exact details of their trips to the destination. For example, Tourisme Montréal in Canada recruited 13,000 visitors who stayed in the city for two or more nights in 2010 for pleasure/leisure travel purposes. They were asked to respond to a web-based survey after their visits and 2,895 people responded (around 22 per cent).

The Hawaii Tourism Authority conducts its 'Visitor Satisfaction and Activity Report' via mail. For the 2009 study, HTA mailed out 59,517 questionnaires and 17,763 were returned (around 27.7 per cent). These questionnaires were mailed to the US, Japan, Canada, Europe and Oceania. The response rate for Japan was the highest at 37.8 per cent.

A third example of data collection for a visitor profile study is from Ireland and Fáilte Ireland's Visitor Attitudes Survey 2010. Potential respondents were given a self-completion questionnaire at major airports and ferry terminals. Some 11,142 return postage-paid forms were handed to visitors exiting Ireland, and 4,816 were mailed back (around 42 per cent).

A fourth example is of a mixed method of data collection and it was used for the Scotland Visitor Survey 2011 and 2012. Figure 4.5 shows the methodology used for this survey, which was a combination of short personal interviews followed up with an online e-mail survey. The total sample size for the personal interviews was 4,520 and thereafter 1,882 of these face-to-face respondents completed the online surveys (around 42 per cent).

As can be seen, with response rates usually above 50 per cent and sometimes much higher, personal interviews normally produce the highest response rates and lower the risk of a non-response bias. To counter-balance this, questionnaires can be gathered more efficiently (at a lower cost) via online or mail surveys.

Develop the survey questionnaire

The survey questionnaire should contain all the questions needed to satisfy the research objectives for the visitor profile study. However, it is important that survey questionnaires are not very lengthy, as respondents get irritated when filling them out

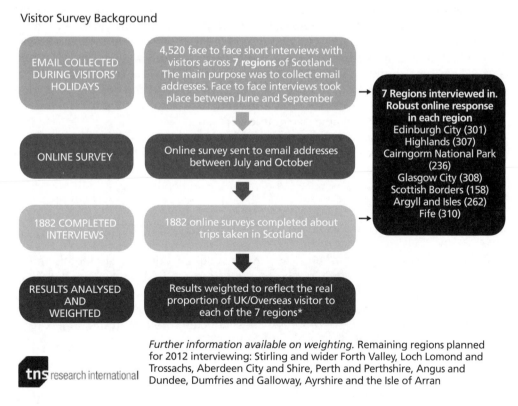

Figure 4.5 Data collection methods for the Scotland Visitor Survey
Source: VisitScotland, 2012.

if it takes too much time. As a general rule, a questionnaire should not have more than thirty questions or take more than 15 minutes to complete.

Completing questionnaires has become easier thanks to computer and information communication technology (ICT), especially with the use of the Internet, mobile phone and tablet devices. The traditional pen-and-paper approaches were much slower in recording responses.

Determine the sample design and size

Here a decision has to be made about which particular visitors are to be surveyed and how many completed survey questionnaires are required. If several distinct groups of visitors are to be surveyed, the total sample size for the research project will be larger. For example, in the Hawaii visitor study mentioned above, the sample sizes and confidence intervals were as follows:

Japan	4,369 surveys; confidence interval +/– 1.48 per cent
US East	3,260 surveys; confidence interval +/– 1.71 per cent
Canada	3,256 surveys; confidence interval +/– 1.71 per cent
US West	3,250 surveys; confidence interval +/– 1.72 per cent
Europe	2,283 surveys; confidence interval +/– 2.03 per cent
Oceania	1,182 surveys; confidence interval +/– 2.84 per cent

From the above, it will be noticed that the confidence interval gets lower as the number of surveys completed increases. But what do the confidence intervals mean? Here is an example for the Japanese, who responded that 31.7 per cent were in Hawaii for the first time, and 68.3 per cent were repeat visitors. Based on the sample size and at a 95 per cent confidence level, it can be estimated that the true percentage of Japanese first-timers was from 30.22 per cent to 33.18 per cent, and the repeaters were from 66.82 per cent to 69.78 per cent. The margin of error (2.96 per cent for the Japanese) increases as the sample size gets lower.

If the personal interview method is used, decisions will also have to be made on where and when visitors are to be intercepted. For example, the Las Vegas Convention and Visitors Authority uses the following procedures for visitor intercepts:

Las Vegas visitor profile interviewing procedure

Visitors were intercepted in the vicinity of Las Vegas casinos, hotels, motels and RV parks. To assure a random selection of visitors, different locations were utilized on each interviewing day, and interviewing was conducted at different times of the day. Upon completion of the interview, visitors were given souvenirs as incentives. Verification procedures were conducted throughout the project to assure accurate and valid interviewing.

Good places for intercepting visitors are at airports, ferry and bus terminals, lodging facilities, attractions, festivals/events/arts and cultural performances, shopping areas and visitor centres.

Determine study schedule

Another question to be addressed is how many times in a year the survey is to be conducted. Of course, this will probably be dictated by the budget available for the research project, but for greater accuracy it is better to consider whether the profile of visitors varies significantly by season or even by month of the year.

In most cases, visitor profile studies are conducted only once a year, but there are some situations where surveys are completed more frequently. For example, the Las Vegas Visitor Profile Study has surveys conducted in each month of the year.

It may also be necessary to consider the day of week and the time of day when visitor surveys are conducted. If the destination tends to get most visitors on weekends, for example, then more surveys should be completed on Saturdays and Sundays.

Analyse, interpret, report and communicate the data and results

As discussed above, these steps are crucial for the success of all research projects. The example in Figure 4.6 shows that a DMO can communicate visitor profile study results in a very creative and compelling way.

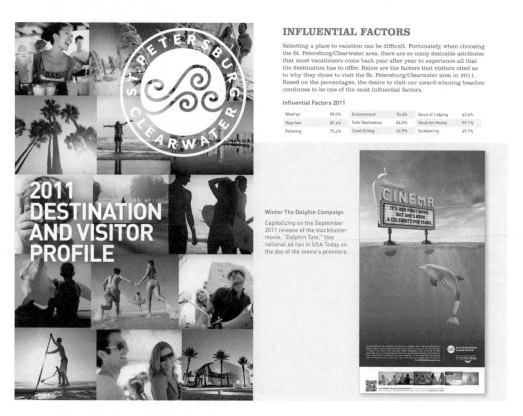

Figure 4.6 Destination profile of St. Petersburg/Clearwater using visitor profile study research data
Source: St. Petersburg/Clearwater CVB, 2012.

Analysis of potential markets

A DMO may have an interest in a specific geographic market or market segment, and decide to conduct a research project on that group of potential tourists. These potential market analyses can either be done through secondary research only, or a primary research project can be completed. The potential markets may be completely new markets for the destination or they may already be markets that are visiting the destination.

One example of potential market research using a qualitative primary research design was part of a domestic tourism market study by the New Zealand Ministry of Tourism. This research project used thirty individual depth interviews and two focus groups. The overall goal of the research was to improve the tourism sector's understanding of the domestic tourism market.

Domestic tourism qualitative research in New Zealand

A mixed method qualitative approach was adopted, with forty two participants in total involved in the research. Thirty individual face to face interviews each up to 2 hours in duration were conducted with people across the life cycle stages to explore in-depth New Zealanders' backgrounds and travel experiences and aspirations. These interviews took place in Auckland, Wellington, Christchurch, Palmerston North and Nelson.

Two group discussions, up to four hours in duration each with six participants aged between eighteen and thirty five without children were facilitated in Auckland and Nelson. Issues around travel choices were explored in depth amongst this important audience, which accounts for a diminishing share of nights away from home in New Zealand.

The Canadian Tourism Commission (CTC) has a series of research reports on potential markets called the 'Global Tourism Watch' (GTW). In 2011, CTC released reports on the potential markets in Australia and the United States. The target sample size for the United States was 3,000 and for Australia it was 1,500. Another quota was to have 35 per cent of the United States' respondents who recently visited Canada; and 20 per cent of the Australians. These two surveys were completed in March–April 2011 and they had four specific objectives:

Research objectives of CTC's 'Global Tourism Watch'

- To monitor awareness, travel intentions and other key market indicators for Canada and the regions.
- To assess perceptions of Canada and track brand performance over time.
- To identify the general experiences sought by travellers, assess Canada's competitive positioning on key products and identify growth opportunities.
- To identify motivators and barriers for travel to Canada, as well as media sources and images that lift Canada's appeal.

As you can see, these survey objectives were mainly related to CTC's marketing and promotion role, but the third and fourth objectives also provided information for product development. The second and third objectives concerned Canada's destination image and branding.

A third example of an analysis of potential markets was a survey completed in the United Arab Emirates (UAE) on behalf of the Ministry of Tourism in India (2011a). The personal interview technique was used and 2,007 people were surveyed in the UAE. The research supplier approached 3,284 people, so the response rate was 61 per cent. The sample included 760 people who had visited India in the past 3 years.

Another example mentioned earlier in the chapter was Cape Town's research on specific niche market segments. The five segments were researched using secondary research data and information, and this was supplemented with local interviews with twenty-two knowledgeable people; so this was mainly what is called a 'desk research' project.

These four examples from DMOs in New Zealand, Canada, India and South Africa demonstrate that there is a wide variety of data collection methods available for analysing potential markets. They range from simpler secondary research analysis (Cape Town, South Africa) to extensive personal interviewing in source countries (UAE for India).

Analysis of destination image

The analysis of destination image has been a hot topic for tourism scholars since the early 1970s; however, destination image studies by DMOs have been much less frequently attempted. So, much of what has been written about destination image is within tourism academic journals and conference proceedings. There is no doubt that bridging this research gap between theory and practice is desirable for destination management.

According to Stepchenkova and Morrison (2008) and based on the previous research by Echtner and Ritchie (1993), destination image has two main components (attributes and holistic) and three dimensions (functional, tangible and psychological):

Echtner and Ritchie destination image components and dimensions

- Destination image should be envisioned as consisting of two main components; those that are attribute-based and those that are holistic.
- Each of these components of destination image contains functional, or more tangible, and psychological, or more abstract, characteristics.
- Images of destinations can also range from those based on 'common' functional and psychological traits to those based on more distinctive or even unique features, events, feelings or auras.

Doing research on a destination's image attributes is normally accomplished through a survey data collection method in which respondents are asked to rank the destination on a list of predetermined attributes. The Connecticut, USA study that you will hear about later is an example of attribute ranking for determining destination image.

The holistic image concept is much more difficult to measure since this is a sort of overall assessment of a destination. Since these are personal opinions and vary from person to person, they cannot be measured by attribute lists. These are suited to open-ended questions to which each respondent provides their own unique answers. For example, in a destination image study on Brazil that was conducted in the USA, the following three open-ended questions were asked (Rezende-Parker et al., 2003):

- What images or characteristics come to your mind when you think of Brazil?
- What is the mood or atmosphere in Brazil?
- Which distinctive or unique attractions can be found in Brazil?

Qualitative research data collection methods can be used to explore holistic images including focus groups, where about 8–12 people from the target audience are invited to attend a discussion about the destination. An experienced facilitator coordinates the focus group discussions and invites the participants to give their thoughts and opinions on a short list of open-ended questions. Then the facilitator will get the group to reach a consensus on the most important issues within the discussion.

Measuring these two main components of destination image is not all there is to destination image research. It is also important to examine the information that causes people to form images about destinations. Actually this image formation process is quite complex, as you are about to learn.

Destination images are formed in different ways and influenced by a variety of sources of information on places, including previous visits. Gartner (1993) suggested that there are eight destination image formation agents (Figure 4.7). These range from organic images that are formed by actually visiting a destination to 'overt induced 1', where a person notices tourism advertising by the destination. The three organic agents are considered to be the most powerful in forming destination image, and two of these are what usually gets called 'word of mouth'.

The covert and overt induced image formation agents should constantly be tracked by the DMO. These may not be as powerful as actual visit experiences and word of mouth, but they can be influential especially if the information is from a trusted and unbiased source. For example, the opinions of people on travel review sites like TripAdvisor.com are now often used in selecting destinations.

One case study on destination image research 'on the ground' was a research project on Connecticut and Metro New York residents' images of Connecticut as a leisure travel destination. Called a 'brand image study', the research (Connecticut Commission on Culture and Tourism, 2007) asked respondents to rate several attributes of Connecticut as a destination. The total sample size was 1,200. As can be seen from the results in Table 4.2, Connecticut residents had the most favourable destination images of their own state, and visitors from Metro NY had more positive images than non-visitors. Respondents were asked to rate each attribute on a scale of 1 (does not describe Connecticut at all) to 10 (completely describes Connecticut). The percentages are the proportions of respondents assigning 10/9/8 scores to attributes.

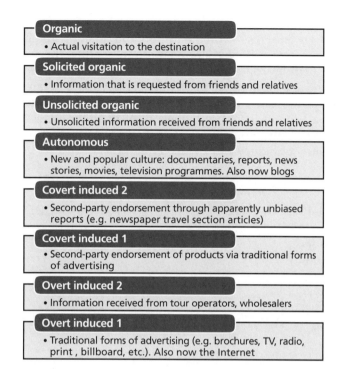

Figure 4.7 Gartner's definition of destination image formation agents
Source: Gartner, 1993.

Table 4.2 Brand image study for Connecticut, USA

Top 10 attribute items describing Connecticut as a leisure travel destination	Total	Connecticut residents	Metro NY visitors	Metro NY non-visitors
Sample sizes	1,200	500	350	350
Attribute statements				
It is close by	80%	88%	81%	69%
It is an easy to get to destination	80%	84%	83%	71%
It is a beautiful scenic place	73%	79%	71%	65%
It is a great day-trip destination	71%	81%	73%	55%
It is a great 1 to 3 night getaway destination	69%	73%	71%	60%
It has historical sites and properties that you can visit	64%	73%	61%	54%
It offers a sense of history as part of the landscape	61%	69%	60%	52%
It is a place to relax and unwind	61%	64%	66%	51%
It offers many opportunities for outdoor adventure	60%	71%	55%	48%
It is a good place for couples to visit	58%	63%	58%	50%

Some DMOs do not conduct full-blown destination image studies, but incorporate image-style questions in visitor profile and potential market studies. Of course, this saves money and the data may be collected more frequently. For example, the Visitor Attitudes Survey 2010 by Fáilte Ireland included questions that were about image attributes of Ireland as a destination. Respondents were asked to rate the attributes on a five-point importance scale with 5 being 'very important' and 4 for 'important'. The following eleven attributes were the highest ranked, either rated as 5s or 4s by the holidaymaker respondents. Friendly people got the highest score at 92 per cent and good all round value for money was 74 per cent.

Highest ranked attributes of Ireland as a destination

- Friendly people
- Beautiful scenery
- Safety and security
- Plenty to do and see
- Unspoilt environment
- Range of natural attractions
- Interesting history and culture
- Anticipation of a new destination to discover
- Attractive cities and towns
- An easy and relaxed pace of life
- Good all round value for money.

Another practical way to assess destination image is to analyse what people are saying about the destination. This has become more popular because of the huge amount of comments being written in popular social media channels and blogs. For example, Choi et al. (2007) conducted a research study on the destination image of Macau by analysing online content. A qualitative research design known as content analysis was applied to the online text about Macau as a destination. They found that Macau's destination image varied across five online information sources (Macau Government Tourist Office; blogs; magazines; guides; and travel trade). This type of destination image analysis is much less expensive to do when compared to visitor surveys, but it has limitations for practical application. The main drawbacks are that the content mainly represents induced image formation agents (Figure 4.7), and that the accuracy and credibility of the information is not as high as data from actual visitors.

Analysis of community resident attitudes

Community relations are an important destination management role and need to be supported by research on resident attitudes and opinions about tourism. Community resident support is fundamental to the sustainability of the tourism sector within a destination. Surprisingly there is not much of this type of research done by DMOs, although there is a growing recognition that DMOs need to constantly pay attention to how local people perceive the tourism sector. This is another field of tourism research where scholars are doing much research, but the practical application in destination management is limited.

Tourism within destinations affects residents directly and indirectly. The impacts can be positive but they can also negatively impact the lives of community residents. In the past, there was a tendency for DMOs to focus most of their attention externally on markets, but this is definitely not enough, as residents are an important 'internal market' for the DMO and the destination. Many tourism scholars are insistent on the need to consult community residents. For example, Harrill (2004) strongly recommends that getting inputs from residents must be part of the tourism planning in a destination:

Importance of community resident input to tourism

Tourism, defined for the purpose of this review as all travel except commuting, permeates communities unlike other industries. Its composition of transportation, lodging and entertainment exercises considerable influence on a community's employment, land use, environment and social structure. Because of this pervasive influence, obtaining the input of residents should be integral to any tourism planning process.

A study conducted in the province of Huelva in Spain by three academic researchers produced some really interesting findings about local residents' attitudes to tourism (Vargas-Sánchez et al., 2010). They found that the most powerful predictor of residents' attitudes to tourism was if they believed that the positive impacts outweighed the negative ones. Other findings of this research about resident attitudes were:

Community resident attitudes to tourism in Huelva, Spain

- The more positive the residents' perceptions about the respectful behaviour of tourists, the greater is their overall perception that the positive impacts outweigh the negative impacts of tourism.
- Residents who receive personal benefits from tourism perceive tourism more favourably.
- The level of tourism development as perceived by residents has a negative influence on residents' attitudes.

The South West Tourism Alliance in England in 2006 prepared a Community Attitudes Survey (2007). The objectives of this research project were to:

Research objectives of community attitudes to tourism in South West England

- Explore residents' perceptions of attractions for visitors and residents appreciation and usage of them.
- Establish the impact of visitor levels on local communities for a number of key areas.
- Explore residents' attitudes towards visitors.
- Establish the effect of tourism on the local area for a number of key areas.
- Explore residents influence on tourism in their local area and their opportunities to express their views.

A sample of 2,400 local residents was drawn and they were surveyed via telephone. Some 800 of these respondents were picked randomly and the other 1,600 were drawn from four 'honey pot' areas where the residents were under higher levels of pressure from tourism throughout the year (resorts; historic cities; coastal area towns/villages; and countryside area towns/villages). The findings were that there was a general appreciation within the community that tourism was good for the region, with 96 per cent stating that tourism was good for their area.

Analysis for product development

The destination product was described in Chapter 1 as consisting of physical products, people, packaging and programming. Product development is one of the roles of destination management and research is helpful for guiding decisions related to all parts of the destination product. Table 4.3 shows the specific research projects that can be done related to physical products, people, packaging and programming. The research projects are split according to whether they focus on the existing destination product or are for expanded and new destination products.

Visitor satisfaction analysis research is of great importance for destinations, since happy people tell others about their experiences and are also more likely to return. You learned earlier about the visitor satisfaction survey completed by the Hawaii Tourism Authority. Tourism Queensland (TQ) conducts a Customer Satisfaction Survey that concerns the service on its destination website. TQ sent an e-mail survey to people who made enquiries at its website and received 1,161 completed responses.

Almost all the visitor profile studies discussed earlier contain one or more questions about visitor satisfaction. So while they may not be investing in full-scale visitor satisfaction studies, these DMOs are still constantly tracking the satisfaction levels of their visitors.

The assessment of destination quality levels is a branch of product development research that some DMOs undertake and consider it to be of great importance. Mystery shopping, service quality audits and destination audits are a few of the techniques applied here. The following is a very good example from Wales in the UK (Figure 4.8).

Table 4.3 Types of research projects for product development

Destination product	Existing	Expanded and new
Physical products	• Business performance surveys • Mystery shopping • Site inspections	• Product development exemplar case studies • Feasibility studies • Market analyses
People	• Labour market analysis • Community resident analysis • Service quality audits • Visitor satisfaction analysis	• Labour needs analysis • Potential visitor analysis
Packaging	• Surveys of package users	• Packaging exemplar case studies • Travel trade surveys
Programming	• Festival/event participant analysis	• Festival/event exemplar case studies

Figure 4.8 Visit Wales Mystery Shopper programme brochure
Source: Visit Wales, 2012.

The Welsh Tourism Mystery Shopper Service

Our mystery shopper service gives fresh perspective on your business to help you monitor current performance and plan improvements. The mystery shopper is an independent review service open to hotels, guest accommodation and restaurants with rooms currently participating in the Visit Wales grading scheme.

The mystery shopper costs between £110 and £360 per visit. Costs depend on the number of visits per year plus the cost of dinner, bed and breakfast at the standard rate. One of our trained assessors will stay overnight incognito at your hotel to test and observe the level of service and facilities on offer.

Festival and event research is very widespread and even has two academic journals (*Event Management*; *International Journal of Event and Festival Management*). Again this is a very popular field of research for tourism scholars, but gets much less attention from DMOs. However, some destinations conduct research to profile visitors to their biggest festivals and events, and to estimate impacts. For example, the impacts of twelve festivals in Edinburgh, Scotland were measured in 2010. The research (Scottish Enterprise, 2011) identified the following eight impacts of the festivals:

Impacts of Edinburgh festivals in 2010

- Cultural impact: provide enriching, unique, world class cultural experiences and develop audiences for culture.
- Cultural impact: develop the creative, cultural and events industries in Edinburgh and Scotland.
- Learning impact: provide learning benefits for large sections of audiences.
- Place-making and media impact: enhance the identity and image of Edinburgh and Scotland.
- Social impact: increase cultural diversity and community cohesion.
- Social impact: contribute to well-being and quality of life.
- Economic impact: provide routes to employment and skills.
- Economic impact: support the wider economy in Edinburgh and Scotland.

Chapter 5 is devoted to the product development roles and some of the most popular research methods and techniques are discussed in greater detail there.

Analysis of economic impact

The measurement of the economic impact of tourism has been an important research topic for destinations for at least the past 40 years and many different approaches have been used. Many 'tourism multiplier' studies were conducted in the earliest period and demonstrated that the spending and employment in the tourism sector have a ripple effect in other economic sectors of the destination. The 'Power of Travel' image in Figure 4.2 visually demonstrates this basic idea.

Several countries have now introduced Tourism Satellite Accounts (TSAs) including Australia, Ireland, New Zealand, the UK and the USA.

Tourism satellite account in the UK

The UK Tourism Satellite Account (TSA) is a technique that seeks to calculate the value of tourism in a way that allows it to be compared with other economic activities, and with tourism elsewhere. The TSA attempts to reconcile demand data from tourism surveys with information on the supply of goods and services generated by tourism related industries. It follows guidelines from the United Nations World Tourism Organisation (UNWTO).

(HM Government, 2011)

DMOs below the national level are not so able to do tourism satellite accounting, although it does occur in a few cases. For example, the tourism satellite account for Wales estimated £4.2 billion in total tourism expenditure for 2007, and two-thirds of the spending was by Welsh residents. The £4.2 billion was equal to 2.8 per cent of all final products and services purchased in Wales in 2007. Sixteen tourism-related 'industries' were identified in the Welsh TSA and together they produced £8.1 billion in output. The gross value added to the Welsh economy by these sixteen was £3.875 billion.

There are many ways to do economic impact analysis research for destinations and this discussion has been short. However, the topic of economic impacts is discussed in greater detail in the later chapter on DMO governance and accountability. It suffices to say here that these economic impact research data are vital for proving the relative value of tourism as an economic sector of the destination.

Analysis of competitors

It is a very good idea for a destination to be constantly tracking its main competitors and what these destinations are doing. The DMO may do this informally but periodically there is a need to do a full-blown competitive analysis study. Which competitors should be analysed and what are the most important dimensions of these competitive destinations that should be assessed? You will remember this topic was already discussed in Chapter 3 as part of a DMO situation analysis. The point was made there that destination competitive sets vary according to the markets and products to be covered in the analysis. For example, the competitors for conventions and exhibitions will be different than for pleasure or leisure travellers.

In the earlier chapters, there was a discussion of the 10 As model of destination success, as well as the criteria used by the World Economic Forum for the Travel and Tourism Competitiveness Report 2011. These two sources provide a good initial list of dimensions for comparing competitive destinations.

Destination competitive analysis is another research area that has attracted great attention from tourism scholars but has not permeated the professional destination management field as deeply. Crouch (2007) divides this scholarly research into several categories: (1) diagnosing the competitive positions of specific destinations; (2) focusing on specific aspects of competitiveness such as marketing and price competitiveness; and (3) developing general models and theories of destination competitiveness.

For the third category, several models of destination competitiveness have been proposed by tourism scholars but they have yet to be widely applied in practice. The Ritchie and Crouch (2003) model of destination competitiveness is one of the most widely accepted (Figure 4.9) and it is very comprehensive. Destination competitiveness in this model is composed of five components:

- Supporting factors and resources
- Core resources and attractors
- Destination management
- Destination policy, planning and development
- Qualifying and amplifying determinants.

Models are models, and often their great complexity means that tourism practitioners find them difficult to apply in the real world. So now you will learn about a few applications of competitive analysis by destinations.

A very interesting application of competitive analysis for a destination was done for the Northwest Territories in Canada on Aurora (Borealis) viewing tourism (Western Management Consultants, 2007, 2008). This research study was conducted in two phases with reports in 2007 and 2008. The research was conducted as there had been a sharp decline in the visitors coming to Yellowknife to view the Aurora; this is a good example of 'as-needed' research. A comparison was made with other Aurora viewing destinations in Canada (Alberta, Manitoba and Yukon) and foreign competitors (Australia, Finland, Greenland, Iceland, New Zealand and Russia).

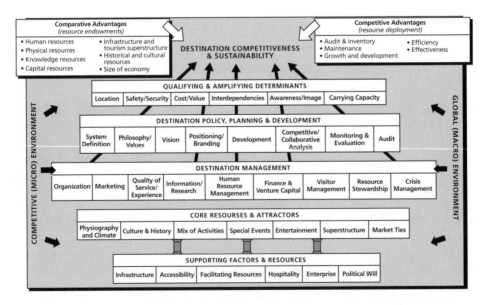

Figure 4.9 Crouch and Ritchie model of destination competitiveness
Source: Crouch, 2007.

In 2010, a Tourism Competitive Analysis Study was conducted for Williamsburg, Virginia in the USA. Williamsburg was compared with another eight US tourism destinations (Asheville, Charleston, Gettysburg, Hershey, Orlando, St Augustine, Savannah and Virginia Beach). This study was particularly used to 'benchmark' the successful marketing strategies and promotional programmes used by the eight competitors.

The Province of Ontario launched a tourism competitiveness research project in 2008 for the following reasons:

Ontario Tourism Competitiveness Study

In 2008, the Province launched the Ontario Tourism Competitiveness Study ... to set a future path for revitalizing and growing tourism in Ontario. A key area of interest for the Competitiveness Study was to investigate successful marketing approaches in other contexts in order to scope the magnitude of potential that exists and to single out the practices that Ontario, in its battle for market share, could potentially replicate.

The 'best of class' tourism destinations that were analysed included Alberta, Australia, British Columbia, Ireland, Las Vegas, New Zealand and Newfoundland and Labrador. The study also analysed seven non-destination companies: Canadian Tire, Fairmont Hotels and Resorts, Kraft, Tim Horton's, Unilever–Dove, Telus and WestJet.

(Queen's Printer for Ontario, 2009)

Evaluation research

Performance measurement and performance reporting are important tasks that a DMO needs to accomplish with great professionalism. Measuring and reporting the DMO's performance requires many research inputs. DMOs around the world are increasingly being closely scrutinized and being asked to demonstrate their accountability for the funds with which they have been entrusted.

Destination Marketing Association International (DMAI) has produced a set of standard performance measures for DMOs. Activity, performance and productivity measures are specified for five performance reporting areas and the ROI on the DMO is also estimated:

- DMO convention sales performance reporting
- DMO travel trade sales performance reporting
- DMO marketing and communications performance reporting
- DMO membership performance reporting
- DMO visitor information centre performance reporting
- DMO return on investment (ROI).

DMAI standard DMO performance reporting

With the adoption of standard DMO performance reporting techniques, the DMO community has recognized benchmarks to utilize in order to assess its internal performance over time as well as provide meaningful comparisons to other DMOs. Most importantly, with ever-growing accountability and scrutiny from its stakeholders, the utilization of industry standards re-enforces confidence in DMO operating and reporting practices.

(Destination Marketing Association International, 2011)

What are the main reasons for doing evaluation research and why should the DMO make an investment in this branch of research? There are internal and external reasons for conducting evaluation research, including the following:

● Allows performance comparisons with other destinations, including competitors.
● Demonstrates to tourism stakeholders, including government agencies, that the DMO has achieved its goals and objectives.
● Details the impacts of the DMO's efforts and their significance to the tourism sector.
● Focuses DMO staff on achieving results.
● Highlights needs for improvements in operations, marketing and other aspects of the DMO's work.
● Pinpoints plans, strategies, programmes and actions that were successful and those that were not successful.

There are certainly other analysis topics and types of research projects that can be done by DMOs. However, eight of the most prominent analysis topics have been described in the foregoing materials. Next there is a need to discuss some of the organizational details to get research done smoothly.

Preparing a destination management research plan

Earlier in this chapter, there was a discussion about setting a destination management research agenda, consisting of ongoing, periodic and as-needed research. All DMOs should develop an annual plan and a multi-year strategy for destination management research.

The annual destination management research plan should include the following elements:

● Description and justification for ongoing research to be completed
● Description and justification for any periodic or as-needed research contemplated
● Requests for proposals (RFPs) for any research to be outsourced to research suppliers
● Research timetable
● Research budget
● Research communication programmes.

DMO research departments and staff

Not all DMOs have full-time research staff but there are many that do and some have their own research departments. It is quite normal for national-level DMOs to have research officers and they are also found in most state, provincial and territorial DMOs. Some well-funded city DMOs, including Las Vegas, have their own research departments.

Research Department at Las Vegas Convention and Visitors Authority

The Research department aims to gain a better understanding of the Las Vegas visitor and overall city demographics in order to guide and support the LVCVA's overall marketing strategy. The department's wide range of research projects and programs tracks the dynamics of Las Vegas and Southern Nevada, as well as the nationwide competitive gaming and tourism industries. Among the research programs administered by the department are the monthly executive summaries of tourism and convention indicators, annual visitor profile studies that track visitor demographics and behaviors, periodic marketing bulletins and a variety of programs to monitor local, national and global travel trends.

Research departments at DMOs are typically small, with most ranging from one to five full-time staff. Although the number of positions is limited, careers in doing research at DMOs are interesting, rich and rewarding. People with a good background in tourism management and with statistical analysis skills are especially well suited for these positions.

Table 4.4 RESPECT U criteria for selecting a DMO research supplier

R	Reputation	• How satisfied were previous research sponsors?
E	Experience	• Has the supplier done this type of research before?
S	Staff	• Which staff members will work on the DMO's research project and what are their experiences?
P	Post-study service	• Will the supplier be available after the research is done to answer questions?
E	Explanation of method	• How comprehensively does the supplier explain the research design and data collection method?
C	Cost	• Is a detailed breakdown of the supplier's fees and expenses provided?
T	Timetable	• Is the time frame for the research fully explained and justified?
U	Understanding	• What has the supplier done to better understand the DMO and its research needs? • What provisions has the supplier made for on-going liaison with the DMO?

Outsourcing to research suppliers is very popular among DMOs and several research companies have developed specialities in conducting tourism research. The DMO needs to develop requests for proposals (RFPs) and supplier selection criteria for its outsourced research projects. Table 4.4 presents a model developed by the author for research supplier selection.

Summary

Research is an integral component of professional destination management and contributes to all destination management roles. A DMO should establish a research agenda including ongoing, periodic and as-needed research, and prepare an annual research plan and a multi-year strategy for destination management research.

Customers, competitors, confidence, credibility, change and community are the six main reasons for doing destination management research. Other reasons for destination management research include demonstrating the size and importance of the tourism sector in the destination; assessing the impacts and effectiveness of funds invested in tourism by government agencies; and helping organizations in the tourism sector to be more successful in their operations and marketing.

When doing destination management research, it is important to follow the classic research process consisting of the following steps:

- Formulate the research problem and identify research objectives
- Select research design and data collection method
- Collect and analyse secondary information
- Decide on sample design
- Collect data
- Analyse and interpret data
- Prepare research report
- Communicate research findings and recommendations.

Secondary and primary research data and information are used together in many research projects. Before starting any original or primary research for its own purposes, the DMO should carefully scan what others have previously published.

The DMO should make a selection from among a portfolio of analysis topics based upon its own and the destination's research needs; existing markets, potential markets, destination image, community resident attitudes, product development, economic impact and competitors.

The specific steps for a DMO to accomplish its research role are to:

- Prepare a research agenda and plan for destination management research for the next year and 3–5 years ahead.
- Ensure that research makes a contribution to all the destination management roles.
- Describe which analysis topics, research designs and data collection methods will be selected from the available portfolios.
- Clearly articulate the expected benefits of the research contemplated in the agenda and plans.
- Prepare a research budget estimate and include in the research plan.

- Communicate research results to all tourism stakeholders and to other parts of the local community as required.

<hr>

Review questions

1 What are the contributions of research for each of the roles of destination management?

2 Ongoing research, periodic research and as-needed research are the three parts of a destination management research agenda. What are the essential differences among these three research agenda categories?

3 Which steps should be followed in the research process for destination management?

4 Secondary and primary research data and information are both important in destination management research. How would you differentiate these two concepts?

5 Research results can often be boring. What are some techniques that can be used to more interestingly and effectively communicate a DMO's research findings?

6 How should a study of existing visitors (visitor profile study) be conducted?

7 What different methods can be used to analyse potential markets for a destination?

8 People's images of destinations have a significant influence on where they travel. Which destination image measurement techniques can be applied?

9 How important is it to determine community resident attitudes to tourism and how can this research be accomplished?

10 What types of product development research can be completed in a destination and how can this research help to improve the destination product?

11 How can destinations measure the economic impact of tourism?

12 How important is competitive analysis for a destination and how should a destination select the competitors to evaluate?

13 Why is it important for a DMO to do performance measurement and reporting?

14 What should be the contents of a destination management research plan?

References

Austin Convention and Visitors Bureau. 2011. http://www.austintexas.org/media/press_releases/press_release?id=324

Canadian Tourism Commission. 2011. Global Tourism Watch. Australia Summary Report–2011.

Choi, S., Lehto, X.Y., and Morrison, A.M. 2007. Destination image representation on the web: Content analysis of Macau travel related websites. *Tourism Management*, 28(1), 118–129.

City of Cape Town. 2008. Niche Market Study.

Connecticut Commission on Culture and Tourism. 2007. 2006 Brand Image Study.

Crouch, G.I. 2007. Modelling Destination Competitiveness: A Survey and Analysis of the Impact of Competitiveness Attributes. Brisbane, Australia: CRC for Sustainable Tourism.

Destination Marketing Association International. 2011. Standard DMO Performance Reporting. Washington, DC: DMAI.

Dillman, D.A., Smyth, J.D., and Christian, L.M. 2008. Internet, Mail, and Mixed-Mode Surveys: The Tailored Design Method, 3rd edn. New York: Wiley.

Dwyer, D., and Kim, C. 2003. Destination competitiveness: Determinants and indicators. Current Issues in Tourism, 6(5), 369–414.

Echtner, C.M., and Ritchie, J.R.B. 1993. The measurement of destination image: An empirical assessment. Journal of Travel Research, 31 (Spring), 3–13.

Fáilte Ireland. 2011. Visitor Attitudes Survey 2010. Executive Summary.

Gartner, W.C. 1993. Image formation process. In M. Uysal and D. Fesenmaier (eds), Communication and Channel Systems in Tourism Marketing. New York: Haworth Press, 191–215.

Hair, J.F., Black, W.C., Babin, B.J., and Anderson, R.E. 2009. Multivariate Data Analysis, 7th edn. Upper Saddle River, NJ: Prentice-Hall.

Harrill, R. 2004. Residents' attitudes toward tourism development: A literature review with implications for tourism. Journal of Planning Literature, 18(3), 251–266.

Hawaii Tourism Authority. 2010. 2009 Visitor Satisfaction and Activity Report.

HM Government. 2011. Tourism Satellite Account. http://data.gov.uk/dataset/tourism_satellite_account

Las Vegas Convention and Visitors Authority. 2011. Las Vegas Visitor Profile Study 2010.

——2012. http://www.lvcva.com/about/about-marketing.jsp

Ministry of Tourism, Government of India. 2011a. Study on Tourism in the Overseas Market of UAE.

——2011b. Study on Tourism in the Overseas Market of United Kingdom (UK).

Ministry of Tourism, New Zealand. 2010. Domestic Tourism Market Qualitative Research.

Morrison, A.M. 2010. Hospitality and Travel Marketing, 4th edn. Clifton Park, NY: Cengage Delmar.

New Zealand Ministry of Tourism. 2010. New Zealand Domestic Tourism Infographics.

Northwest Regional Development Agency. 2006. Tourism Research Strategy 2006–2009.

Queen's Printer for Ontario. 2009. Ontario Mix of Tourism Marketing and Promotion Research. Study Final Report.

Rezende-Parker, A.M., Morrison, A.M., and Ismail, J.A. 2003. Dazed and confused? An exploratory study of the destination image of Brazil. Journal of Vacation Marketing, 9(3), 243–259.

Ritchie, J.R.B., and Crouch, G.I. 2003. The Competitive Destination: A Sustainable Tourism Perspective. Wallingford: CABI.

Roslyn Kunin & Associates, Inc. 2009. Vancouver Island Tourism Labour Market Study Final Report.

Scottish Enterprise. 2011. Edinburgh Festivals Impact Study. Executive Summary for Media.

St. Petersburg/Clearwater Area Convention and Visitors Bureau. 2010. Destination Profile '09 St. Petersburg/Clearwater.

South West Tourism Alliance. 2007. Community Attitudes Survey 2006.

Stepchenkova, S., and Morrison, A.M. 2008. Russia's destination image among American pleasure travelers: Revisiting Echtner and Ritchie. Tourism Management, 29(3), 548–560.

Tourisme Montréal Research Department. 2011. Annual Survey of Leisure Visitors to Montréal. Executive Summary.

Tourism Queensland. 2009. Customer Satisfaction Survey 2009.

US Travel Association. 2012. The Power of Travel.

Vargas-Sánchez, A., Porras-Bueno, N., and Plaza-Mejía, M.D. 2010. Explaining residents' attitudes to tourism. Is a universal model possible? *Annals of Tourism Research*, 38(2), 460–480.

VisitScotland. 2012. Scotland Visitor Survey 2011 and 2012. Summary of 2011 Results.

Visit Wales. 2012. Visit Wales Mystery Shopper Programme.

Welsh Economy Research Unit. 2010. The Tourism Satellite Account for Wales 2007.

Western Management Consultants. 2007. Northwest Territories Tourism Competitive Analysis: Aurora Viewing Tourism. Phase One: Supply Side Assessment.

——2008. Northwest Territories Aurora Viewing Tourism. Competitive Analysis: Aurora Viewing Tourism. Phase Two: Analysis of Competition for the NWT.

William and Mary School of Business. 2010. Williamsburg, Tourism Competitive Analysis Study.

World Economic Forum. 2011. Travel & Tourism Competitiveness Report 2011. Geneva, Switzerland.

Destination management research

Shanghai International Visitor Survey
case study

Figure 4A The spectacular waterfront scenes of Pudong are a
hallmark image of Shanghai
Source: Shutterstock Inc. (Chungking).

This case study accompanies the materials included in Chapter 4 on
destination management research. In particular, it demonstrates an
analysis of existing markets.

Introduction

The Shanghai International Visitor Survey was conducted for the Shanghai
Municipal Tourism Administration (SMTA) in late 2009 and early 2010 by
Belle Tourism International Consulting (BTI). The goals of the project
were to profile the characteristics of international visitors; determine
visitor opinions on Shanghai as a tourism destination; and suggest the
most appropriate marketing strategies for the top ten international
leisure markets and for international business/MICE markets.

The International Visitor Survey was completed in seven main steps:

- Design of research methodology
- Preparation of survey questionnaires
- Survey administration
- Analysis of survey results
- Reporting of results
- Preparation of market profiles
- Preparation of recommendations.

Design of research methodology

To achieve the best response rates and most accurate results, it was decided to complete the survey through one-to-one personal interviews with intercepted international visitors while they were in Shanghai.

SMTA required that both leisure/pleasure and business/MICE visitors be covered in the market research.

It was another requirement that international visitors from the top ten origin countries for Shanghai be covered (excluding compatriots in Hong Kong, Macau and Taiwan). The top ten origin countries were:

- Australia
- France
- Germany
- Japan
- Malaysia
- Russia
- Singapore
- South Korea
- UK
- USA.

Because of greater difficulties in intercepting sufficient numbers of business/MICE visitors from individual countries, it was decided to group them by region, as follows:

- Americas
- East Asia
- Eastern Europe
- Oceania
- South and Southeast Asia
- Western Europe

Design of survey questionnaires

Two slightly different questionnaires were developed for the leisure and business/MICE visitors. SMTA provided guidance on the types of topics to be covered in the questionnaires and the market research team drafted the questions for SMTA's approval. The questionnaires encompassed the following topics:

- Demographic characteristics
- Trip purposes
- Most popular activities and attractions in Shanghai
- Most important travel information sources
- Length of stay and expenditures
- Travel party type and composition
- Previous visits and future intentions
- Concerns when planning trips to Shanghai
- Impressions and satisfaction levels with Shanghai trips
- Awareness of marketing efforts (e.g. official website use).

Survey administration

Interviewers were trained to be familiar with the contents of questionnaires and the way to approach respondents. Interviews were conducted at popular tourist attractions such as the Shanghai Museum, Yu Garden, People's Square and Nanjing Road; and at major hotels including the Westin Hotel and Jinjiang Tower Hotel.

Interviews were conducted from September 2009 to February 2010; and the response rates by country and region were carefully tracked on a week-to-week basis. Careful quality control measures were implemented to ensure accuracy.

Analysis of survey results

Data from the completed interviews with Shanghai's international visitors were entered into the SPSS statistical analysis program and analysed to produce the most salient results for the business/MICE and leisure markets.

Reporting of results: leisure

Australia

- Total respondents: 444.
- Australians were interested in tasting authentic Shanghai food and they tended to visit Nanjing Road, Shanghai Museum and the Bund.
- The most used travel information sources were websites, guidebooks and friends or relatives. A quarter of the Australians stayed in Shanghai more than 5 days (25.6 per cent of the total).

Figure 4B The Bund is a popular attraction in Shanghai for international tourists
Source: Shutterstock Inc. (Chungking).

France

- Total respondents: 350.
- French people got travel information through the Internet, guidebooks, friends and relatives. Their most favoured activity was visiting historic buildings and sites.
- They usually stayed in Shanghai for 3–5 days (61.1 per cent) and they tended to travel independently on their own (25.5 per cent).

Germany

- Total respondents: 425.
- Germans preferred to visit the Shanghai Museum, Nanjing Road and Yu Garden. They liked to taste the authentic Shanghai food during their stays.

- The most preferred travel party arrangement was travelling independently with friends (25.4 per cent). A majority of Germans were visiting Shanghai for the first time. They disliked the language barriers with locals (18.2 per cent).

Japan

- Total respondents: 350.
- Japanese leisure visitors were interested in visiting historic buildings or sites and tasting Shanghai food. They visited Yu Garden the most.
- They relied on the Internet, guidebooks and travel agencies when collecting travel-related information. Japanese people liked Shanghai food and night-time; however, they disliked the traffic and pollution.

Figure 4C The local food in Shanghai, like these steamed buns (*xiao long bao*), is popular with many foreign visitors
Source: Shutterstock Inc. (Yu Lan)

Malaysia

- Total respondents: 102.
- Malaysians liked to see modern city landmarks and to visit historic buildings or sites. The most popular destination was Nanjing Road.
- Malaysian leisure visitors often travelled independently with their friends (32.4 per cent). Most had not seen any of Shanghai's destination marketing materials, but 42.6 per cent noticed some.

Singapore

- Total respondents: 181.
- Singaporeans tended to form a small group when travelling to Shanghai (30 per cent). They also tended to collect information through the Internet.
- The major concerns of Singaporeans were weather and food. During their trips to Shanghai, Singaporeans liked the food, buildings and shopping. They disliked Shanghai traffic.

Russia

- Total respondents: 165.
- Russians liked to taste authentic Shanghai food (mean: 4.11/5) and to see modern city landmarks (4.1/5).
- The most used travel information sources were websites, guidebooks and friends and relatives. The majority of the Russian leisure visitors (60.2 per cent) spent USD 501 or more in Shanghai.

South Korea

- Total respondents: 355.
- Koreans were highly interested in tasting Shanghai food, enjoying nightlife activities and seeing modern city landmarks.
- South Koreans were concerned with Shanghai transportation and the language barrier. Approximately 18.9 per cent of South Korean respondents intended to come back to Shanghai for the 2010 Expo.

United Kingdom

- Total respondents: 400.
- UK citizens liked to visit the Shanghai Museum (91.9 per cent), Bund (88.4 per cent), People's Square (87.2 per cent) and Nanjing Road (85.2 per cent).
- Around 25.4 per cent of UK respondents travelled to Shanghai independently with friends (25.4 per cent). The things that UK people particularly mentioned that they liked were people, food, buildings and architecture.

USA

- Total respondents: 452.
- The most popular tourism activity was visiting historic buildings and sites; seeing modern landmarks was next.

- After this visit, 14.8 per cent of USA residents said that they intended to return to Shanghai for the 2010 Expo. Overall, people from USA were highly satisfied with their trips to Shanghai (90.4 per cent).

Other countries

- Total respondents: 737.
- The most popular tourism activity was visiting historic buildings and sites, and second was seeing modern city landmarks.
- After this visit, 16.3 per cent of other country visitors said they intended to return to Shanghai for the 2010 Expo. Overall, people from other countries were highly satisfied with their trips to Shanghai (89.7 per cent).

Reporting of results: business/MICE

The Americas

- Total respondents: 440.
- A majority of the Americas' visitors came to Shanghai to attend trade shows, fairs or exhibitions (40.2 per cent). They tended to visit historic buildings or sites during their stays.
- For the Americas' business travellers, the Bund was the most popular attraction in Shanghai. They showed great interest in the 2010 Expo (35.3 per cent).

East Asia

- Total respondents: 350.
- East Asian business travellers enjoyed Shanghai cuisine and they were open to experiencing Shanghai nightlife.
- Nanjing Road, the Bund, People's Square and Oriental Pearl TV Tower were the major attractions for them. East Asian business travellers visited Shanghai frequently (only 27.7 per cent of respondents were first-time visitors).

Eastern Europe

- Total respondents: 186.
- A majority of Eastern European business travellers came to Shanghai for trade show, fair, exhibition, meeting and conference purposes.
- During their stays, they liked Shanghai people, food, buildings and the city itself.
- Overall, they were highly satisfied (88.7 per cent).

Oceania

- Total respondents: 275.
- Oceania business travellers visited Shanghai for meetings or conferences. During their stays, they enjoyed seeing modern city landmarks.
- They most liked to visit the Bund, Nanjing Road and People's Square. However, they did not express a high interest in visiting temples. They liked the people, food, city, buildings and modernity of Shanghai.

South and Southeast Asia

- Total respondents: 163.
- A majority of respondents had completed college or higher education and 43.1 per cent had completed postgraduate-level studies.
- South and Southeast Asians were most interested in seeing modern city landmarks and tasting Shanghai food. They collected travel information from the Internet and friends and relatives.

Western Europe

- Total respondents: 512.
- Western European business travellers were most often in the age range 35–49. They tended to appreciate modern city landmarks during their stays.
- Among all the attractions, the Bund, Nanjing Road and People's Square were the top three attractions. They most often collected travel information through websites, and friends and relatives.

Preparation of market profiles for leisure markets

A comprehensive market profile report was prepared for the top ten leisure origin markets. An eleventh report was also prepared for the leisure visitors interviewed from all other countries.

The market profile reports included the following information:

- The survey results for each country
- Recent major outbound travel trends
- Travel trade profiles
- Major travel trade fairs/exhibitions
- Media profiles.

Market profile reports were also done for each of the six business/MICE regions.

Preparation of recommendations

Business/MICE markets

As the final step in the International Visitor Survey, the research team prepared very detailed marketing recommendations. Twenty key recommendations for marketing to the MICE and business travel markets were specified in a report titled *The 20/20 Vision for MICE and Business Travel*. For example, four of these recommendations were:

● Increase awareness of websites and their URLs.
● Prepare more foreign language versions of websites.
● Put up an online RFP.
● Expand networking in professional associations.

Leisure markets

Individual marketing recommendations were prepared for each of the top ten origin countries and also for the other countries as a group. These were called the *Top 10 for 2010* and overall 110 separate recommendations were provided. For example, the titles of the ten recommendation programmes and initiatives for the Australian leisure travel market were the following:

● OZ meets the Middle Kingdom
● See China's architectural marvel
● Experience Shanghai cuisine in style
● China's city of endless surprises
● Do we have the cruise for you?
● Tell your mates about your Shanghai experiences
● Stop-over in Shanghai on your way
● Meet your friends and family in Shanghai
● Discover your creative side and take a souvenir home
● Light up your life in Shanghai.

Case summary

The Shanghai International Visitor Survey is an outstanding example of a well-executed market research study by a DMO. For this survey, a total of 5,978 valid questionnaires were completed (3,973 with international leisure travellers; and 2,005 with business/MICE travellers).

Apart from the large number of international visitors interviewed, the survey produced a wealth of in-depth information about international visitors to Shanghai, and many practical marketing recommendations. In terms of information insights, the following findings were among the most important for SMTA:

- The most popular activities for international visitors to Shanghai
- The most popular attractions for visitors to Shanghai
- Average lengths of stay and expenditures
- The most used information sources in planning trips to Shanghai
- Major concerns when planning trips to Shanghai
- Satisfaction levels with trips to Shanghai
- Major likes and dislikes about Shanghai
- Overall impressions of Shanghai as a tourism destination
- Return trip intention levels
- Awareness and use of Shanghai's official tourism websites.

For a DMO, the most important outcome of market research is that it can apply the results in a positive and practical way. This has certainly been the case in Shanghai, as SMTA is using this survey's results to guide its marketing and promotional activities for certain of the countries that were covered. For example, a new official version of the website is being prepared in French and the other recommendations for French inbound travellers are to be implemented.

Destination management research case study questions and exercise

1 The Shanghai IVS involved personal interviews (or intercepts) with international visitors to the city. What do you feel are the major advantages of completing surveys with international visitors in this way? What are the potential disadvantages of following this survey approach?
2 How frequently should a city DMO like SMTA do surveys of international visitors like the one described in this case study? What are your reasons for suggesting this schedule for these surveys?
3 If you were given the task of designing a survey of international or domestic visitors to your local area, what would your research design involve? Be sure to mention how the survey would be conducted and who would conduct the survey.

Chapter 5

Destination product development

Introduction

Now that you have learned about planning and research, it is time to hear about how they are applied to make a better destination. Product development definitely benefits from the careful long-term planning and solid research that were discussed in the last three chapters.

Chapter 1 introduced the concept of the destination product as consisting of physical products, people, packages and programmes. Historically destination product development was a role that many DMOs gave a low priority as they focused most attention on marketing and promotion. However, with intensifying competition among destinations and the realization that customer satisfaction and the presentation of product offers are also very important parts of the destination marketing role, DMOs started to take a more active role in product development.

DMOs can engage in product development at different levels of involvement ranging from being a bystander to becoming a partner in development. The level of involvement is affected by the destination's stage in the Tourism Area Life Cycle (TALC) and the unique local circumstances and characteristics.

There are approximately 200 country destinations in the world with many sub-regions, so it is difficult to describe a common template for destination product development. However, there are some guiding principles for product development and these are described in this chapter.

Definition and components of the destination product

What is the destination product and what are its specific components? These are topics that have sparked great debate among tourism scholars since at least the 1970s. The conversations among academics have been really interesting, but unfortunately DMOs have found little practical value in their propositions and research findings. This gap between theory and practice needs to be bridged in the future.

In developing this book's approach to defining the destination product and its components, the contributions of several prominent tourism scholars were considered. Middleton (1989) argued that from the standpoint of a potential customer considering any form of tourist visit, the product may be defined as a bundle or package of tangible and intangible components, based on activity at a destination. The package is perceived by the tourist as an experience, available at a price.

This is a useful definition since it says that the destination product has both tangible and intangible components, and this is certainly true. Also it highlights the importance of 'activities' and 'experiences' to tourists.

Smith (1994) suggested that the 'generic tourism product' consisted of five elements: (1) the physical plant; (2) service; (3) hospitality; (4) freedom of choice; and (5) involvement. Freedom of choice and involvement are factors related to tourists; that there is some choice of product available to them in the destination, and that the tourists are themselves involved in the experiences they have purchased. Smith also described a tourism production process of primary inputs (resources), intermediate inputs (facilities), intermediate outputs (services) and final outputs (experiences). This was another useful definition and confirmed Middleton's identification of tangible (physical plant) and intangible (service and hospitality) components. There was again an emphasis on tourists' involvement in experiences.

Ritchie and Crouch (2003) in their model of destination competitiveness (Figure 4.9) provided another view on the destination product, consisting of the two levels of 'core resources and attractions' (physiography and climate; culture and history; mix of activities; special events; entertainment; superstructure; and market ties) and supporting factors and resources (infrastructure; accessibility; facilitating resources; hospitality; enterprise; and political will). This was a much more detailed description of the destination product and extended the definition to include stakeholder support and entrepreneurial capacity.

Murphy *et al.* (2000), using data on visitors to Victoria in British Columbia, Canada found that two aspects of the destination product, namely 'environment' and 'infrastructure', influenced tourists' perceptions of the quality and value of Victoria as a destination. Environment was composed of the attributes of pleasant climate, attractive scenery, clean city, heritage ambiance and friendly people; infrastructure included good food, interesting attractions and good hotels. You will note that this is not the definition of infrastructure as used in this book.

So, there are at least two important perspectives on what constitutes the destination product; (1) how the customer views and perceives the product within the destination; and (2) the product itself with its tangible and intangible components. The DMO can indirectly influence the customers' product perceptions through marketing and promotion, and steps taken to improve product and service quality. The DMO does not have direct control over the product itself, but must rely on tourism stakeholders to make product changes.

Reflecting the second of these perspectives, Mill and Morrison (2012) referred to the destination product as the destination mix or a blending of interdependent elements. All elements need to be present to produce satisfying experiences for tourists. The five elements are attractions and events, facilities, infrastructure, transportation and hospitality resources.

Morrison (2010) suggested three extensions to 'product' in McCarthy's traditional marketing mix (4 Ps) to better fit with the tourism sector and what the sector offers for customers. These three 'product extensions' were people, packaging and programming (Figure 5.1). Blending Mill and Morrison's (2012) and Morrison's (2010) concepts produces the destination product model shown earlier in Figure 1.4. This admittedly does not cover all of the elements, especially those on the consumer's side or the support from local stakeholders, but it is a practical and understandable solution to defining the destination product.

Definition of the destination product

The destination product is an interdependent mixture of tangible and intangible components comprising physical products, people, packages and programmes. The interaction of the hosts and guests within the destination is an important dimension of the destination product.

Despite its simplicity, this definition provides a practical foundation for a DMO to determine what to include in its product development role. The four destination

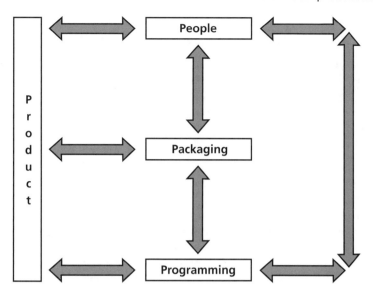

Figure 5.1 Product extensions in tourism development

product components are items over which, in partnership with tourism stakeholders and others, the DMO can exert some direct control.

Before discussing the product development role in detail, it is important for you to know a little more about the destination product life cycle.

Destination product life cycle

The Tourism Area Life Cycle (TALC) (Figure 3.2) was mentioned in Chapter 3 as one of the principles of destination marketing. Also known as the destination life cycle, this concept is of great relevance for a DMO's product development role. TALC is very similar to the product life cycle (PLC) concept that encompasses the stages of introduction, growth, maturity and decline. The PLC was introduced by Joel Dean around 1950 and is well accepted among management experts and scholars as a foundational principle, especially those specializing in marketing.

Although the TALC model has had its critics among scholars, it has stood the test of time over the 30-plus years since the first article was published about it in 1980. The originator of the TALC model, Professor Richard Butler (2011), defines TALC and explains its basic purpose as follows:

Definition of Tourism Area Life Cycle (TALC)

The Tourism Area Life Cycle is a process describing how a destination starts off slowly with visitor numbers limited by the facilities and access. As the destination attracts more visitors, amenities are improved and visitor numbers grow rapidly towards and sometimes beyond the carrying capacity of the destination.

Purpose of Tourism Area Life Cycle (TALC) model

The purpose of the model was to draw attention to the dynamic nature of destinations and propose a generalised process of development and potential decline which could be avoided by appropriate interventions (of planning, management and development), or as suggested in the title of the article, the management of resources.

The title of Butler's 1980 article in *Canadian Geographer* was 'The concept of the tourist area life-cycle of evolution: Implications for management of resources'.

You should especially note in Butler's statement of the TALC model's purpose the idea that management and development (as well as planning) interventions will help in avoiding a decline in the life cycle of an area. Stated in a simpler way, the destination needs to anticipate a decline and deal with this through destination planning, management and development. So, here is one of the parts of the DMO's product development role: determining where the destination is located along the TALC model.

Before leaving this topic and moving on, it is best to mention one serious criticism of the TALC model. This is that the TALC model of a destination is too general and in reality many destinations have 'sub-products' at different stages of their life cycles. For example, Malaysia has had tropical beach resorts for many years, but the recent introduction of medical tourism facilities and services is a new part of the country's destination product. China has offered culture- and history-based travel for three decades, but the introduction of wine tourism is a fresh initiative. Butler (2011) acknowledges this point and agrees that destinations may be experiencing several cycles at different stages of development, and that the TALC is an aggregate model made up of several life-cycles. Therefore, the DMO needs to pay heed to this extension of the TALC model and not blindly follow the single-cycle assumption.

DMO involvement in product development

How should the DMO get involved in product development and what are the sub-roles that it should perform? This varies across the many destinations and DMOs in the world, but there is a continuum of involvement (Figure 5.2) ranging from being a bystander to becoming a partner in product development.

- *Bystander*: The DMO watches on as other tourism stakeholders do the product development. The argument for non-involvement is usually that if private-sector companies in the tourism sector can take care of product development, there is no need for the DMO to get involved.

Figure 5.2 Continuum of DMO involvement in product development

- *Facilitator*: The DMO provides a basic level of information and advice for tourism stakeholders who wish to engage in product development.
- *Instigator*: The DMO takes an active role in identifying opportunities for product development and finds strategies to realize these opportunities. The example below from New South Wales, Australia is one in which the DMO is instigating regional tourism product development.
- *Partner*: The DMO is not only an instigator, but makes a financial, staff or other resource investment in product development, usually along with other tourism stakeholders.

NSW Regional Tourism Product Development Funding Program

To create and/or enhance tourism products in regional NSW to work towards achieving the NSW Government target of doubling tourism overnight expenditure by 2020.

Desired product development outcomes may include:

- Strengthen product quality and customer service standards.
- Ensure product providers understand and then meet or exceed consumer expectations.
- Adapt products to leverage off current technology and trends in consumer behaviour.
- Identify and resolve infrastructure and consumer accessibility to product issues.
- Establish a sustainable competitive advantage for destinations/regions/NSW.
- Maximise visitation, revenue and/or yields.

The bystander position is really one of non-engagement in destination product development and presumably the DMO has a 100 per cent focus on marketing and promotion, or has another reason for not assuming this role. The other three 'active' roles of facilitator, instigator and partner need some further discussion and clarification. Figure 5.3 provides more details on the specific tasks DMOs perform as facilitators, instigators and partners. For a newly-emerging place that needs a higher level of product development, it could be expected that the DMO's role would be the most 'proactive' (taking action and being results-oriented) and the DMO may be willing to be a partner in product developments. Where the destination is more mature (but not in a decline stage of the TALC) or where there are concerns about the environmental, social and cultural impacts of tourism, the DMO might be the least 'proactive' and is more likely to be a 'facilitator'.

The information below from the State of Georgia in the USA (Georgia Department of Economic Development, 2011) is a good example of a DMO working as a facilitator and an instigator.

Figure 5.3 Facilitator, instigator and partner roles in product development

Georgia USA Tourism Product Development team

The Office of Product Development assists communities and tourism partners in giving new life to existing resources and in fostering new tourism products within communities. This is done by delivering technical assistance and financial resources in hopes of creating new opportunities/markets for Georgia tourism products through strategic partnerships, packaging and marketing. The Tourism Product Development (TPD) team works to increase Georgia's tourism product development portfolio, and creating opportunities to introduce new audiences to Georgia's amazing variety of sites and attractions.

You should also realize that not all destinations are the same and therefore the DMO's role in product development varies according to the special circumstances of the country. In certain circumstances, a DMO is compelled to get involved in destination product development and cannot be a bystander, especially in a newly-emerging destination and where environmental protection is crucial. The *Handbook on Tourism Product Development* (2011), prepared on behalf of UNWTO and the European Travel Commission, identified the following different varieties of destination; the examples are supplied by this author:

- *Mature destinations*: Many of the sea coast beach resorts of Spain, Portugal and Italy are in this category. These may be approaching the decline stage in the TALC, so a greater emphasis needs to be given to diversification and new product development.
- *Newly emerging destinations*: The People's Republic of China is one of the best examples here as its tourism development is rapid at the moment. Indonesia, South Africa and Sri Lanka are others that might fit. Again, DMOs need to be very proactive in product development in these situations.
- *Centrally planned economies*: China is a great example here again and its government-run DMOs are highly proactive in destination product development, especially for new physical products.

- *Destinations with fragile environments and endangered species*: Here included would be destinations such as Antarctica, the Galapagos Islands and Komodo in Indonesia. It might be expected here that DMOs would not be instigators of new product development, but rather be involved in more of a resource conservation role.
- *Countries with perception problems in international markets*: Destinations such as Iraq, Afghanistan and Iran fit in this category. DMOs may be more concerned with marketing to counterbalance negative perceptions rather than focusing on new product development.
- *Destinations with a dominant product*: Las Vegas with its many casinos fits into this group. Parts of East Africa also belong, with their reliance on safaris and wildlife viewing. Product diversification may be a strategy here, requiring the DMO to take an active role in product development.
- *Destinations with a major tourism development opportunity*: Countries with large populations and rapidly growing economies such as the BRIC (Brazil, Russia, India and China) grouping are in this category. These situations justify DMOs being proactive in tourism product development.
- *Destinations specializing in sports, adventure or activity tourism*: New Zealand is a good case example here. In addition to adding new and fresh experiences, the DMO must assure that measures are in place to ensure the safety of people participating in high-adrenalin and physically demanding activities.
- *Historic cities*: Athens, Budapest, Cairo, Istanbul, Prague, Rome, Venice and Vienna are just a few of these great historic cities. Many of them are under huge pressure from tourism, and the capacity of their historic and heritage resources is finite and limited. Here, the DMOs must come up with visitor management strategies to protect and conserve their precious resources.

Jamaica is an appropriate case study of a destination that has a dominant product, beach resorts and where there is a need to diversify the destination product. The Jamaican government has established a tourism product development company and that agency is seeking niche-market product development opportunities. The following materials describe seven niche products that Jamaica is trying to encourage to provide a more diversified destination product.

Tourism product diversification in Jamaica

The Tourism Product Development Co. Ltd (TPDCo) is collaborating with the Ministry of Industry and Tourism and the private sector to generate and maintain projects that showcase this variety. However there are still vast untapped opportunities in:

- Nature and eco-tourism
- Sports tourism
- Cuisine (food)
- Cultural heritage
- Entertainment (music)
- Conference/convention tourism
- Health and wellness tourism with emphasis on spas, walking trails, retirement, and healthy cuisine.

In a study conducted for the UNWTO, a survey of fifty-two national DMOs worldwide showed that less than half of them (47 per cent) had a dedicated product development function. The highest percentages with such a function were in the Americas (67 per cent) and in new and emerging destinations (60 per cent).

Another way of looking at the DMO role in product development is to consider the two aspects of 'hard' and 'soft' development (Figure 5.4). Hard product development in tourism means building physical products such as attractions, hotels, roads, transport terminals, travel information centres, tourism schools or colleges, festival or event performance areas, etc. Generally, these initiatives fit into the physical products component of the destination product, but there are situations when physical structures are needed to support people and programming projects.

Soft product development in tourism encompasses things that do not leave a long-term imprint on the physical landscape of the destination, including preparing workforce development strategies, conducting education and training programmes, designing packages, creating themed itineraries or driving tours, operating quality assurance programmes, providing interpretation services, setting up product clubs, etc. Generally, these activities fall within the people, packaging and programming components of the destination product.

Destination quality

The notion of the 'hard' and 'soft' sides of the product inevitably leads to a discussion of destination quality. The argument is often made that it is not the physical structures or their size that truly matters to customers; what is more important is their quality and the quality of the service provided by staff as well as the hospitality and welcome given by local community residents. There will probably never be a winner in this argument over 'quality' versus 'quantity'. More important for the destination and the DMO is to determine the dimensions of quality and to have programmes to manage these dimensions. Koch (2004) suggested that quality in tourism had three main dimensions: hardware (physical products), software (services and information) and the environment (Figure 5.5). This model of quality in tourism was based on earlier work by Professor Felizitas Romeiss-Stracke (1995).

This viewpoint of the quality of tourism in a destination again adds the condition of the environment into the destination product. There are three parts within the environment dimension: landscape (and landscaping too), resource consumption (sustainable use) and freedom from or lack of pollution. The software dimension consists of service and hospitality, as previously mentioned in this chapter. However, information is a third part of software and as you can imagine, this includes information provided within the destination and information distribution elsewhere, including in the online world. The hardware dimension represents the physical products in the destination and has three parts: facilities (what they provide), functions (what they do for customers) and aesthetics (how they look).

Managing quality is an important sub-role of destination product development, as this undoubtedly affects the tourist experience. The European Communities publication (2003), *A Manual for Evaluating the Quality Performance of Tourist Destinations and Services*, lists ten reasons and benefits for a DMO and its stakeholders from managing destination quality:

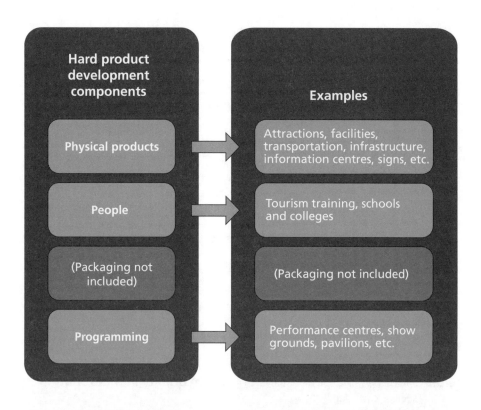

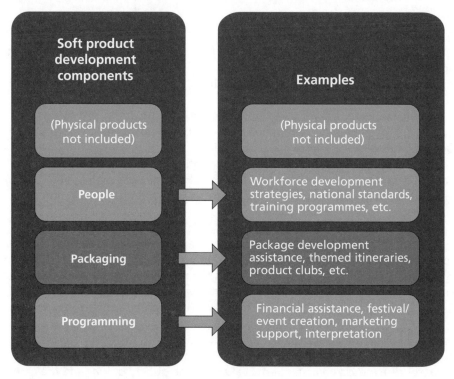

Figure 5.4 Hard and soft tourism product developments

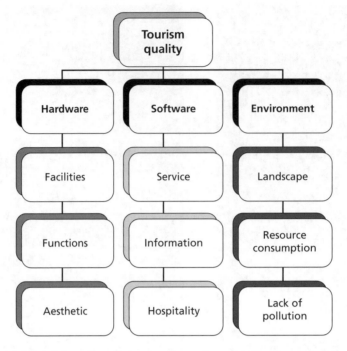

Figure 5.5 Model of the dimensions of tourism quality in a destination
Source: Koch, 2004.

- Quality gives the edge over competitors.
- Quality performance makes destinations and services easier to market, both to operators and tourists.
- A quality product results in customer loyalty.
- Better quality means more profit.
- Quality management leads to a stable tourism industry and protects jobs.
- Quality improvements in a destination provide a better quality of life for local residents.
- Quality management improves access to finance.
- Effective monitoring of progress avoids repeating costly mistakes.
- Careful data collection provides the tool for making the right management decisions.
- Monitoring progress in quality improvement provides the understanding that encourages proactive management.

How then can the DMO implement a quality management programme? One of the recommended ways of doing this is by adopting an Integrated Quality Management (IQM) approach. IQM for destinations reflects the multi-dimensional nature of tourism quality. IQM combines four key elements in its approach (European Communities, 2003, *A Manual for Evaluating the Quality Performance of Tourist Destinations and Services*):

- *Tourist satisfaction*: Regularly monitoring tourists' satisfaction levels with the products and services in the destination.
- *Local tourism industry satisfaction*: Evaluating the quality of jobs and the careers of employees in the tourism sector, and the well-being of local tourism enterprises.

- *Local people's quality of life*: Finding out what local residents think of the effects of tourism.
- *Environmental quality*: Measuring the positive or negative impacts of tourism on the environment, including natural, cultural and human-made assets.

So, what should the DMO's specific roles be with respect to destination quality? The following represents a range of activities in which the DMO can engage to manage destination quality levels:

- Control quality through mandatory licensing or registration programmes.
- Regularly inspect tourism operations to check quality levels.
- Introduce quality assurance programmes that guarantee approved businesses meet certain standards.
- Initiate award programmes for excellence in tourism quality.
- Provide advice or financial incentives for businesses to upgrade quality levels.
- Offer training programmes to improve tourism workforce skills and knowledge.
- Continuously measure tourist and tourism stakeholder satisfaction levels.
- Establish parameters for environmental quality and resident life quality, and periodically measure these parameters.

An outstanding example of an awards programme is TidyTowns, which was introduced in Ireland in 1958 by its DMO.

Ireland's TidyTowns programme

Right from the start, the primary focus of TidyTowns was to encourage communities to improve their local environment and make their area a better place to live, work and visit. The competition aspect was an important element in developing friendly rivalry that would help boost standards across the board. However, the emphasis was always on participating rather than winning as the very act of taking part brought benefits to the community. And with a focus on long-term results rather than quick returns, TidyTowns was soon seen as a unique and far-sighted initiative.

(Fáilte Ireland, 2011)

General product development strategy models

There are many general models for product development in management textbooks, but they do not fit well with tourism destinations. They are mainly for manufactured products and information technologies. However, there is at least one general product development strategy model that can be applied to destinations and which already has been used in tourism. Ansoff's Growth Strategy is a simple model and it identifies four destination product development opportunities in a two by two matrix (Figure 5.6). There are four specific strategies in this matrix:

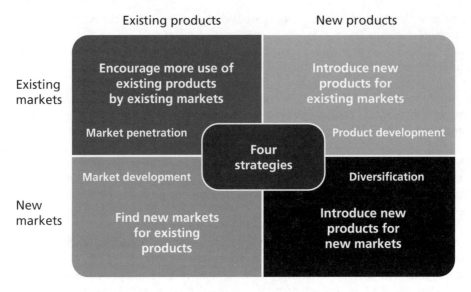

Figure 5.6 The growth strategy matrix from Ansoff
Source: Ansoff, 1987. Adapted by author.

Market penetration

This means that the destination adjusts the product to attract a higher volume from existing markets; hence, existing markets, existing product. For example, the UK government has decided to take steps to convince more of its residents to take holidays in the UK rather than abroad. Only 20 per cent of residents holiday at home, compared to 28 per cent on average for Europe. The UK government is considering changing public holidays to give residents more opportunity to holiday at home. Another way of implementing this strategy is to try to get existing markets to return to the destination more often, and this is accomplished through destination marketing and promotional programmes.

Market penetration is the least risky of the four strategies, since no long-term changes are being made to physical products. This is basically a change in destination marketing approaches.

Market development

The existing destination product is used but the strategy is to attract new markets to use the product. For example, the tropical southern island of Hainan Province in China decided some years back on a strategy to attract holidaymakers from Russia to its beach resorts. The strategy has worked very well.

Again, this not a particularly risky strategy since it is just adding new target markets to the destination's marketing strategy. However, there is greater marketing investment required than with the first strategy.

Product development

The destination adds new products for existing markets. The construction of the new Kai Tak cruise terminal in Hong Kong is a good case study here. Hong Kong was already attracting cruise ships, but the reconstruction of the runway of the old Hong Kong airport will allow two mega-cruise ships to berth at Kai Tak.

This is a more risky strategy than the first two, since new product development is required. However, the market demand for the new product already exists.

Diversification

The destination introduces new products and uses these to pursue new markets. The addition of casinos on Sentosa Island in Singapore is an example. The casino resorts were a new product for Singapore and gaming customers were a new market.

Diversification is the most risky of the four strategies. New product development is needed and the markets at which they are aimed are not proven. Additionally, there has to be more marketing investment since new markets are being targeted.

Principles of destination product development

The DMO, in consultation with tourism stakeholders and community residents, must identify a set of basic principles for destination product development. This is another important sub-role in product development for the DMO. The following is a list of principles of destination product development that was adapted from the UNWTO/ETC *Handbook on Tourism Product Development* (2011):

- *Appropriate scale*: Development is large enough to have a significant positive impact on the tourism sector, but not so big that it causes problems for other stakeholders, the environment or the destination's economy.
- *Authenticity*: Development is a true and authentic reflection of the destination and its history, culture and peoples.
- *Community support*: Community residents are not opposed to the development and support its proceeding.
- *Competitive differentiation*: Development is substantially different from what is found in competitive destinations.
- *Creativity and innovation*: Development is a 'one-of-a-kind' in its category or at least demonstrates new features that are innovative in the tourism sector.
- *Destination vision*: Development is consistent with the destination vision and preferably actively contributes to its realization.
- *Integration*: Development integrates well with the existing destination product.
- *Market need and feasibility*: The market need and financial feasibility of the development have been proven.
- *Positioning*: Development fits with the destination positioning approach.
- *Sustainability*: Development does not harm the environment or the social and cultural fabric of the destination.
- *Tourism stakeholder support*: Stakeholders, particularly those within the tourism sector, support the development.
- *USPs*: Development reflects or takes advantage of the identified unique selling propositions of the destination.

Now that the basic principles of destination product development have been reviewed and you know about the importance of destination quality, this chapter turns to how the DMO performs its role for each of the components of the destination product. This discussion starts by looking at physical products within the destination since these often receive the highest priority.

Development of physical products

Physical or tangible products are what first come to mind when people talk about tourism development or destination product development, but as you already know there is more to the destination product than just physical structures. What are the various types of physical products and how should they be assessed?

Types of destination physical product developments

This discussion was opened up briefly in Chapter 1. The destination's physical products include attractions, facilities, infrastructure, transportation and certain other supportive facilities and amenities.

- *Attractions*: These are critical to the tourism sector since they draw visitors to the destination. Swarbrooke (2002) identifies four categories of attractions:
    1 Features within the natural environment.
    2 Human-made buildings, structures and sites that were designed for a purpose other than attracting visitors, such as religious worship, but which now attract substantial numbers of visitors who use them as leisure amenities.
    3 Human-made buildings, structures and sites that are designed to attract visitors and are purpose-built to accommodate their needs, such as theme parks.
    4 Special events.
- *Facilities*: Generally (but not always) facilities play a supportive role to attractions and events. The three major categories of facilities are accommodations, food and beverage facilities, and retail outlets of different types. These are mostly 'built' facilities and operated by the private sector.

There are certain other facilities that support the destination product including visitor information centres and venues for conventions, exhibitions and meetings. Some events and festivals require physical structures and spaces. Interpretive and directional signs and displays are also highly important in tourism destinations.

- *Infrastructure*: This is a term that has a huge range of definitions, but there is one 'classic' meaning in tourism and that is that infrastructure includes roads, utilities, water supply, sewerage and other basic physical systems to support the destination and its community. These are essential for the tourism sector but often require a substantial initial investment.
- *Transportation*: Access to a destination is crucial and so the development of transportation services is important in product development. As with infrastructure, the investment in transportation facilities is substantial and tends to be mainly done by governments. Typically, the DMO plays an advisory role on transportation planning and strategies.

Figure 5.7 Main parts of a new tourism development project analysis

Analysis of physical product developments

All physical product opportunities need to be thoroughly researched and analysed, and the DMO can play a role in ensuring that this is accomplished. Figure 5.7 shows the main parts of a new project analysis.

- *Site evaluation*: This step looks at the physical characteristics of the site and its accessibility.
- *Resource impact analysis*: The environmental, social and cultural impacts of the project are analysed.
- *Market analysis*: The market potential of the project is assessed in this step.
- *Financial feasibility analysis*: The profitability and return on investment in the project are estimated.
- *Business and marketing plan preparation*: A marketing plan for the project is prepared and also a broader business plan.

Human resources (people) development

The following quote from the *Victorian Tourism Workforce Development Plan 2010–2016* in Australia (Government of Victoria, 2010) sums up some of the major human resources development challenges in today's world. It also provides the justification for destinations and their DMOs to get involved in tourism human resources development.

Extract from the Victorian Tourism Workforce Development Plan

Tourism is largely a people business and as such, the visitor experience is reliant on the quality and attitude of the person behind the counter, in the restaurant or making the beds.

However, the tourism industry is currently not an industry of choice for many employees. For some, the industry has a reputation for hard work, unfavourable conditions, poor work-life balance and relatively low pay scales when compared to many other industry sectors. It is often stated that tourism is an entry point to the workforce, rather than a career.

People are an exceptionally important component of the destination product due to the personal service provided and the overall feeling of hospitality and welcome. Having sufficient numbers of staff with the right skills, knowledge and attitudes is essential for the proper functioning of the destination product. Many destinations and DMOs recognize this and play an active role in human resources development.

Tourism workforce development strategies

A number of destinations have developed specific strategies or plans for tourism human resources, and these tend to be called workforce development strategies or plans. These include several states and provinces in Australia, Canada and the USA, as well as destinations in New Zealand, South Africa and the UK. The recommendations of the Workforce Development Strategy for Alberta's Tourism and Hospitality Industry provide a good example of the types of strategies and actions these documents recommend for tourism human resources development. The Alberta strategy had four themes for implementation (adapted for application to this book):

Four implementation themes in Alberta Tourism's workforce strategy

- *Inform*: Increasing access to information so that employers, employees and workforce entrants can make better decisions about work and careers in tourism.
- *Attract*: Drawing workers from outside of Alberta and Canada to work in tourism and hospitality in the province.
- *Develop*: Through education and training, building up the quality and quantity of the tourism workforce. In addition, create higher-performing work environments by improving workplaces and work arrangements, increasing capital investment and technology adoption, and improving business processes.
- *Retain*: Enhancing the attractiveness of working in tourism and hospitality so that workers continue to stay in the tourism sector.

Tourism workforce standards, and education and training programmes

Another initiative that can be taken is to establish systems of standards for jobs within the tourism sector. These systems identify the skills and knowledge required for specific job positions. Often these are competency-based models and a complete training curriculum is developed. For example, in 2007 Mekong Tourism created 'ASEAN's Common Competency-Based Tourism Curriculum'. Six tourism work areas are covered in the curriculum: food production, food and beverage services, tour operation, travel agencies, front office and housekeeping.

The Canadian Tourism Human Resource Council (CTHRC, 2008) has created the 'emerit' training programme that covers several occupations in tourism. Canada's Federal Tourism Strategy emphasized the need for national tourism workforce standards and having training and certification programmes to support the standards.

Tourism workforce national standards in Canada

The Minister of State will also highlight the importance of meeting national standards for knowledge, skills and attitude within the tourism industry, using the CTHRC's emerit certification program. Emerit includes more than two dozen occupations, and we will encourage federal organizations to implement emerit for these jobs, when feasible. We will also recognize individuals and organizations – including tourism operators, educators and human resources groups – that have adopted certification programs or trained a skilled workforce effectively.

The Certified Destination Management Executive (CDME) programme is operated by the Destination Marketing Association (DMAI) in Washington, DC. This is a very important programme since the focus is on destination management. This training programme is for senior executives and managers in DMOs. The main focus of CDME is on vision, leadership, productivity and the implementation of business strategies. To earn the CDME designation, DMO professionals must take certain core and elective courses, complete papers on the core courses and pass a final comprehensive exam.

Mentoring programmes

Some DMOs have created mentoring programmes where they team up seasoned entrepreneurs, managers or supervisors with colleagues who want to learn more about specific tasks. The example below from Alaska in the USA is a mentoring programme on tourism business operations.

Alaska's Tourism Mentorship Assistance Program (TMAP)

The Tourism Mentorship Assistance Program (TMAP) represents an 18-month long program that partners current successful business owners in Alaska's visitor industry with potential business owners committed to furthering the development of the visitor industry in Alaska's rural areas. As a progression from the Division of Economic Development's D.A.R.T. program of targeted technical assistance in the form of trainings and workshops, the Tourism Business Mentorship program brings participants the opportunity to apply their business skills into the establishment and operation of a new business.

Travel trade staff education programmes

These programmes were mentioned in Chapter 3 and are aimed at training people in travel agencies and tour operating companies in source markets. The Aussie Specialist Program operated by Tourism Australia (2012) is an outstanding case study.

The Aussie Specialist Programme

Aussie Specialists are a dedicated group of retail travel agents actively selling and promoting Australia around the world. The programme is designed to provide travel agents and distributors with the knowledge and skills to sell Australia more effectively and has won awards for 'best training programme' in the United Kingdom, Asia and United States of America.

In January 2010, Tourism Australia launched a new version of the programme, which is now available in 14 languages. Globally, there are over 20,000 registered agents across more than 110 countries including the key markets of the United Kingdom, Europe, North America and Asia.

Development of packages

Packaging in tourism is unique and there is no other economic sector that has anything quite like it. There are professional companies like tour operators and travel agencies that specialize in packaging; resorts, hotels, airlines, cruise line companies, attractions and other tourism stakeholders also develop packages. Before discussing the DMO's roles here, there are some basics to be covered first about the roles and benefits of packaging in tourism.

Roles of packaging

New tourism packages do not usually require that a new physical product has to be developed. However, packages attract tourists to destinations, so they are a very powerful part of the destination product.

Tourism packages combine several travel and hospitality offers together at a single price. Packages play a very important role in tourism since the capacity of different components of the destination product is fixed. Packaging plays the following specific roles:

- *Uniting tourism stakeholders' product and service offers*: Packaging is a great demonstration of partnerships and collaboration in tourism. It brings together different businesses and other organizations into an integrated offer.
- *Smoothing out business cycles*: Packages are used to build business at times when demand is in a down cycle. Doing this tends to improve the profitability of tourism businesses, as well as reducing seasonality in destinations.
- *Diversifying market segments*: Packages can be developed and customized for specific market segments, allowing the destination and tourism stakeholders to diversify marketing strategies.
- *Consolidating the destination product*: Packaging brings together components of the destination product in a very convenient format for buyers.
- *Providing value*: Packages offer distinct value to buyers, so they extend the value perceptions of the destination.

Benefits of packages

Packages are very popular among tourists mainly because of their convenience and value. They are also popular among operators in the tourism sector. The major benefits of packaging for customers and the tourism sector are shown in Figure 5.8.

DMO roles in packaging

DMOs can perform three distinct roles related to new package development: (1) provide training for tourism operators on how to develop effective packages; (2) encourage tourism stakeholders to develop new packages with marketing or financial assistance; and (3) create new packages themselves and either offer the packages for sale directly to the public or find tourism stakeholders to do the distribution and sales. As an example of the first role, the South Australian Tourism Commission prepared a guide for tourism operators for designing effective packages. The Ontario Tourism Marketing Partnership in Canada also developed a handbook on packaging for tourism suppliers.

Customer benefits	Tourism sector benefits
❏ Ability to budget for trips	❏ Added appeal to specific markets
❏ Added value	❏ Attraction of new target markets
❏ Assurance of consistent quality	❏ Easier business forecasting
❏ Convenience	❏ Increased business in off-peak seasons
❏ Satisfaction of special interests	❏ Increased customer satisfaction
	❏ Increased efficiency
	❏ Partnering opportunities

Figure 5.8 Major benefits of packaging

For the second role, several destinations encourage package development through financial incentive schemes and the Singapore Tourism Board is just one example. A second example is from the Province of Nova Scotia in Canada. Under its Tourism Industry Development Program, grants are offered that allow tourism operators to attend seminars, workshops or conferences where they learn about package development.

Another avenue of DMO assistance is to help support the marketing of tourism stakeholders' packages and an example here is the Idaho Vacation Package Program in the USA. If packages meet certain criteria, the state DMO will provide direct links to the packages on the official destination website of Idaho.

The Bihar State Development Corporation in India provides a case study for the third DMO packaging role. This DMO has itself created 'ready-made packages' that are based on itinerary 'circuits' related to Buddhism, and the Sikh and Jain religions. DMOs usually play this most proactive packaging role when there is no private-sector interest in creating and offering packages.

Two other roles that the DMO can play that are related to packaging and programming are designing thematic itineraries or routes and providing assistance in the establishment of product clubs. These concepts are both represented in the 'Wine Routes' of Spain, which is a series of themed itineraries that also represents a number of product clubs in different parts of the country. Product clubs are discussed in more detail in Chapter 6 as they are a form of partnership as well as a packaging of experiences.

The creation of themed driving tours is another form of packaging and programming done by certain DMOs. The Elkhart County Convention and Visitors Bureau in Indiana, USA has created the 'Heritage Trail Driving Tour' and supports this with a map and an audio CD that can be downloaded from its website.

Event, festival and activity programme development

Programming is a very important component of the destination product; it is sometimes done within packaging but often separately. There are different varieties of programming ranging from huge mega-events to teaching one individual visitor how to scuba dive. The following are the roles and benefits of programming.

Roles of programming

Programming plays multiple roles for a tourism destination:

- *Enhancing experiences of tourists*: Programming creates new activities and experiences in which tourists can engage.
- *Increasing economic impact of tourism*: New or expanded events and festivals can create significant incremental economic benefits for destinations.
- *Increasing tourist spending and length of stay*: Programming encourages people to stay longer and, if they stay longer, they spend more money in the destination.
- *Informing and educating tourists*: Programming, and especially interpretation, provides tourists with a deeper understanding of the destination and its resources.
- *Involving tourists in experiences*: Nowadays more people like to participate and be actively involved in their destination experiences, and programming does exactly that.
- *Satisfying special-interests*: Programmes can be developed to satisfy all sorts of special-interests, from architecture to zoology.

Benefits of programming

The benefits from programming are profound if well planned and executed. The major benefits of programming for tourists and the destination are illustrated in Figure 5.9.

DMO roles in programming

As with packaging, there are several different roles that a DMO can perform to support programming development. For example, the DMO can encourage the development of new events or festivals, or the expansion of existing ones through providing financial assistance. Often this financial assistance is to help cover marketing expenses or programming enhancements, and is not for physical product development. For example, Fáilte Ireland offers two programmes of financial assistance: regional festivals and participative events, and national festivals and participative events. Regional festivals and events receive smaller grants, in the range of €5,000 to €20,000.

Fáilte Ireland event programmes: eligible expenses for grant assistance

- Marketing activity – up to 100 per cent of the cost of selected marketing activities with a regional, national and international reach (may include advertising, PR, e-marketing, etc.). Local marketing is not eligible. Marketing support may also include the cost of branding of the location during the event.
- Up to 100 per cent of the cost of selected programming activity – where the programme element has not received other grant aid and is considered to deliver significant benefits to tourism.
- Up to 100 per cent of development activity – audience research, feasibility studies, training, branding consultancy – must be of long-term benefit and/or considerably raise the profile of the event.
- Cross border events – only that portion of the project that takes place in the Republic of Ireland can be funded. In this regard applicants will need to clearly demonstrate the benefit to tourism in the Republic of Ireland at application for funding stage.

Tourist benefits	Destination benefits
❑ Active participation in experiences	❑ Attraction of special-interest markets
❑ Added excitement	❑ Destination image enhancement
❑ Greater aesthetic/personal fulfilment	❑ Increased economic impact
❑ Increased learning and understanding	❑ Increased length of stay and per capita spend
❑ Increased trip satisfaction	❑ Increased tourist satisfaction
❑ More entertainment	❑ New marketing initiatives
❑ Richer experiences of destination	❑ Reduction of seasonality
❑ Satisfaction of special interests	❑ Stakeholder partnering opportunities

Figure 5.9 Major benefits of programming

A second potential role is where the DMO creates a new festival or event, and usually this is done with the assistance of tourism stakeholders. The Hong Kong Tourism Board (HKTB) introduced the Hong Kong Wine and Dine Festival in 2009. HKTB now organizes ten so-called 'mega events' throughout the year, including for the first time bundling together four traditional festivals in April–May 2010 into the Hong Kong Cultural Celebrations series.

A third potential DMO programming role is to encourage tourism stakeholders to develop activities and experiences for tourists. The Signature Experiences Collection® (SEC) introduced by the Canadian Tourism Commission (CTC) in 2011 is an excellent demonstration of this particular role. When launched the SEC included 48 experiences offered by tourism businesses and CTC's research showed that these experiences were attractive to high-spending international travellers to Canada. By January 2012, there were 115 experiences in the SEC. As you will realize, arranging these experiences for tourists is a form of programming. There is a huge variety of programmed experiences in the SEC, ranging from viewing grizzly bears in British Columbia to cruising among icebergs off of Newfoundland and Labrador. The CTC actively markets the SEC through social media, web marketing and travel trade relationships.

A fourth role related to programming is usually only performed by the DMOs in very large cities, along with their national and state/provincial DMOs. This role is in bidding for major events that have a potentially huge impact on destinations. These events include the mega-hallmark events such as the summer and winter Olympic Games, the World Expo and the soccer World Cup. Although the DMOs are only one part of the bid teams, they have an influential role in selling their destinations and ensuring that holding these events has a long-lasting positive impact on tourism within their destinations.

A fifth programming role of DMOs relates to the provision of interpretation. This is such an important topic that a separate heading has been assigned to it below.

Interpretation

Interpretation is fundamentally important in tourism, although it does not attract the same attention as glitzy new resorts, theme parks and other major physical product developments within destinations. Freeman Tilden, a US scholar, provided one of the very first definitions of interpretation:

Definition of interpretation by Freeman Tilden

Interpretation is the work of revealing, to such visitors as desire the service, something of the beauty and wonder, the inspiration and spiritual meaning that lies behind what the visitor can with his senses perceive.

So, interpretation is helping people understand more deeply what they are seeing and experiencing in the destination. Interpretation can be done in many different ways, including through physical products such as displays, signs and audio-visual materials, or it can be done by people such as tour guides through oral interpretation. Before discussing how the DMO can be involved with interpretive services, the primary roles and benefits of interpretation are discussed.

Roles and benefits of interpretation

Interpretation really got its start at places like national parks and heritage-cultural sites, but is now much more pervasive in tourism. Some of the key roles and main benefits of interpretation are the following:

- *Communicating issues and concerns*: Interpretation can be used to make visitors aware of major issues and concerns on the sustainability of the resources they are viewing and experiencing.
- *Deepening understanding*: Interpretation deepens tourists' understanding and appreciation for specific aspects of a destination, including its history, culture and natural environment.
- *Encouraging appropriate visitor behaviours*: Especially at sensitive natural and heritage-cultural sites, interpretation is used to put across an appropriate code of behaviour while enjoying the experience.
- *Enhancing visitor satisfaction and experiences*: Interpretation involves visitors with their experiences and done well increases their satisfaction levels and the quality of their experiences.
- *Entertaining*: Interpretation can be designed to be engaging and entertaining, and may include some element of audience participation.
- *Informing tourists*: Interpretation informs and educates tourists about the destination.
- *Managing visitors*: Interpretation can be used as a visitor management technique by controlling the flows of people at an attraction or site.
- *Presenting content*: Interpretation is a set of presentation techniques for delivering content to tourists about specific resources within a destination.

DMO roles in the provision of interpretation

Since DMOs traditionally have not been involved in the operation of sites and attractions, they have not historically played an active role in the provision of interpretation. It is also true that other governmental agencies have had a stronger focus on interpretation, including those responsible for parks, museums and other heritage and cultural sites and facilities. However, with the increasing interest in product development, DMOs are now paying greater attention to interpretation.

Some real-life examples from tourism help explain how DMOs are increasingly engaging with interpretation. One role is for the DMO to produce materials or 'how-to guides' that assist others in providing interpretive services. Tourism Queensland, for example, produced the *Outback Interpretation Guide* to assist tour guides, tour companies and other tourism operators in providing better interpretation of the rich resources in this vast area of the state. Also in Australia, Tourism Tasmania produced the *Tasmania Thematic Interpretation Planning Manual* to help with interpretation planning for tourism in the island state. Another example is the *Heritage Tourism Guidebook: A How-To Guide for Georgia*, produced in the USA to help communities interpret their heritage resources.

Tasmania Thematic Interpretation Planning Manual

Interpretation is fundamental to the visitor experience in Tasmania and is seen as integral to the tourism brand. Tasmanian industry members are encouraged to look at how they can benefit from using interpretation techniques to enhance their delivery of the visitor experience.

The Thematic Interpretation Planning Manual aims to assist the Tasmanian tourism industry better plan the way visitor experiences are developed.

A second role is for the DMO to engage in or encourage the training of professional tour guides who provide oral interpretation. Indeed, in some countries the national DMOs have licensing programmes for tour guides so that they can control the quality of guiding and human oral interpretation. You might think this only happens in developing countries like Belize or Indonesia, but that is not true as places like Washington, DC, New York City and Singapore have tour guide licensing programmes.

Many DMOs operate ambassador or volunteer programmes in which they recruit local people to guide or in other ways help visitors in their community. Bermuda is a good example here with its Tourism Ambassador programme, but there are many other similar programmes worldwide.

A fourth role is for DMOs to provide financial assistance for the production of materials that assist with interpretation. For example, several DMOs have 'matching grant' programmes where they share production costs fifty–fifty for such items as videos that can be used as part of interpretive presentations. The Colorado Tourism Office in the USA is an example here with its Marketing Matching Grant Program.

So these therefore are four specific roles that the DMO can play in providing interpretation and in encouraging others to do so more professionally. There is no doubt that DMOs will become even more involved with interpretation in the future as more of them realize the value of enriching the experiences of tourists.

Information provision and information centres

The DMO should also consider tourism information as being part of the destination product, particularly if it operates one or more travel or visitor information centres (TICs or VICs). According to *A Practical Guide to Tourism Destination Management* published by UNWTO (2007), 'the visitor information centre is the showcase for the destination and must set the standard in terms of quality, integrity and customer care which other industry operators can follow'. So VICs then are a sort of destination product showcase that merchandises all of the components of tourism.

Roles of visitor information centres

VICs perform multiple roles for the destination and tourism stakeholders, and these include the following:

- *Encouraging higher per capita spending*: Many VICs try to 'up-sell' their destinations, encouraging tourists to spend more money on their trips.
- *Handling requests for pre-visit information*: Often people contact VICs for information prior to leaving for the destination. The VIC responds to information requests received by phone, e-mail, mail or fax.
- *Interpreting local history, culture and nature*: VICs include displays or show videos that interpret the most important tourism-related resources of the destination.
- *Making bookings*: Many VICs make bookings for accommodations, attractions, entertainment shows, local tours, transportation, etc. Typically the VIC earns a commission on these bookings.
- *Merchandising hub for tourism stakeholders*: VICs are the one place where tourism stakeholders can publicize their products and services.
- *Providing information during visits*: This is the traditional role of VICs and tourists expect them to provide accurate, detailed and up-to-date information on all aspects of the destination.
- *Recommending itineraries*: VIC staff can recommend customized itineraries based on people's particular interests and time constraints.
- *Selling travel-related literature and local souvenirs*: Many VICs include retail operations where tourists can buy maps, guidebooks, DVDs, clothing and local souvenirs.

The Visit York Information Centre in England is a good case study of a VIC. This state-of-the-art VIC was opened in May 2010 and welcomed 400,000 people in its first year of operations. Located in a nineteenth-century historic building, the Centre offers the full range of services as identified above. VIC staff members, who have multilingual capabilities, provide services including ticket sales for attractions, tours and concerts, accommodation and some transportation bookings, and personal itinerary planning. There is a shop in the VIC where gifts, souvenirs and local produce can be bought. Eleven 64-inch digital screens show videos of what to see and do in York and other parts of Yorkshire. Another good example is the Tasmanian Travel and Information Centre in Hobart, Australia (Figure 5.10). This VIC is located in a historic building and contains many displays of information by geographic location and according to activity.

There are now many different varieties of VICs, ranging from the full-service VIC playing all the roles described above, to kiosks with no VIC staff present.

DMO websites, plus related social media channel pages, are now the major providers of information about destinations. Are these a part of the destination product? Some would argue that they are not and that these online information channels are part of destination marketing and promotion. However, there other ways of looking at this. Websites and social media pages are a reflection of the destination and in some ways they function like 'virtual VICs' albeit without the human touch. It can also be argued that these online channels are becoming more like 'virtual destinations' where Internet users can experience the places online. In later chapters about the markets for destinations, there are in-depth materials about destination websites and social media channels. It suffices to say here that there is a good case for including these online tools within the concept of the destination product.

With the rapidly expanding use of the mobile phone, and especially smartphones, several DMOs have developed applications ('apps') that can be downloaded and used on these devices as well as tablets. Tourism Australia, the Singapore Tourism Board,

Figure 5.10 The Travel Information Centre in Hobart, Australia is in a historic building
Source: Photo by Alastair M. Morrison.

the Hong Kong Tourism Board and Spain Tourism have produced especially outstanding apps and these are offered free of charge.

Accessible tourism

Another aspect of the destination product that requires the DMO's attention is in the provision of accessible tourism. According to VisitEngland (2012), a definition of accessible tourism is as follows:

Definition of accessible tourism from VisitEngland

Accessible tourism is tourism that can be enjoyed by everyone, including those with access needs. Many people have access needs including disabled people such as those with hearing and visual impairments, wheelchair users, older and less mobile people and people with pushchairs.

There are different roles that DMOs should play in improving the accessibility within their destinations. VisitEngland provides a good case study in the information and services it provides:

- *Educating and training service staff*: Giving staff the skills and knowledge to allow them to provide better customer service to people with access needs and their family members and friends.
- *Informing tourism operators about the business case*: Proving to operators that it makes good business sense to make their facilities and services more accessible, since the market being served is very substantial.
- *Providing facilities and amenities*: Requesting that tourism operators provide specific facilities and amenities for people with access needs. These can be as simple as providing non-feather pillows or bowls for assistance dogs.
- *Providing information about specific access needs*: Passing along information to tourism operators about services for people with hearing loss and those with assistance dogs, for example.
- *Providing information for people with access needs*: Encouraging tourism operators to provide more information about accessibility.

Tourism signage

Signs of different varieties are very much a part of the destination product. This is sometimes overlooked by DMOs and not given the attention that it deserves. However, signs are of particular importance to destinations and tourism operations that rely most heavily on motorists and drive markets. They are also important within urban and rural areas to direct people to attractions and sites, and other tourism facilities.

There are basically two major categories within tourism signage; (1) tourism directional signs; and (2) tourism interpretive signs. The roles of interpretive signs have already been discussed, but directional signs have not yet been covered. To start with, it can be said that the use of directional signs in most jurisdictions is usually strictly controlled by government agencies and especially those regulating transportation. The DMOs role is typically to work in collaboration with transportation agencies to ensure that there is adequate tourism directional signage and to lobby for this signage programme to be distinctive and attractive (if possible). For example, the brown-and-white tourism signs in the UK are very distinctive.

Do directional signs (or the lack of them) affect tourist experiences and satisfaction levels in destinations? There really is no accurate, worldwide statistic that says so, but from the results of many visitor profile studies in a range of destinations, tourists often complain about getting lost or not finding what they wanted to see due to inadequate directional signage. So what can the DMO do to resolve these sorts of issues?

While this is a difficult question to answer because of the need for inter-agency coordination, the DMO can at least make the tourism sector aware of the signage policy within the destination. Good examples here are in the information provided by the Kentucky Department of Travel in the USA and Tourism Western Australia (Tourism WA, 2012).

Of course, there is another side to the topic of signs and especially those along roads. This is the aesthetic impacts of signs and their influence on tourists' perceptions of the place and its environment. For example, the DMO surely wants to avoid an ugly and unsightly proliferation of signs at its entry points (remember about first impressions in the 10 As?).

Tourist road signage guidelines in Western Australia

Tourist road signage needs to be carefully designed and implemented to ensure directional signage is effective and that road safety is maintained to the highest degree. Effective signage must also be of assistance to the visitor.

The tourist signage guidelines were developed by Tourism WA in conjunction with Main Roads WA to address the issues of safety, aesthetics and compliance with national industry and road authority standards.

Directional road signs should contain the name of recognised tourist attractions, services and facilities.

The environment and sustainability

The importance of the environment to the destination product has already been mentioned. Sustainable tourism development has emerged as the broad concept for ensuring that tourism grows in a fashion that does not permanently damage the environment, society and the culture of the destination.

The DMO should be a catalyst and champion for sustainability within its destination. There are many sustainable tourism criteria and models now available for destinations to follow. These include the Global Sustainable Tourism Criteria (GSTC) and many guidelines on encouraging low-carbon tourism practices. One of the specific initiatives that the DMO can take is to design a sustainable tourism development charter or code of ethics for the destination. This charter or code spells out the guiding principles for sustainability in tourism within the destination.

The DMO should also encourage tourism operators to follow green practices and accomplish this in various ways, including offering related education and training. Other techniques include informing operators of best practices in sustainability programme applications and establishing special award programmes for those operators in the destination that demonstrate leadership in sustainable development practices.

An outstanding case study in building tourism sustainability into product development is provided by the Queensland Tourism Strategy in which Tourism Queensland had a key involvement. The basic approach envisaged for the sustainable development of tourism in Queensland was the 'triple-bottom-line' (Figure 5.11) through which a balancing of economic, social and environmental goals would be achieved.

More will be said in later chapters about sustainable tourism development. However, it is worthwhile noting here that this is not only an issue related to product development, but it also impinges on the DMO's relationship with community residents and has implications for destination marketing as well. Community residents want to be assured that tourism is sustainable and also that it will not adversely affect cherished natural, heritage and cultural resources. Moreover, there is an increasing number of tourists who are environmentally conscious, and a portion of these people will have a preference for destinations that adopt sustainable or responsible tourism practices. Finally, sustainable tourism development is an area for collaboration among tourism stakeholders and so it is discussed again in the next chapter on partnerships and team-building.

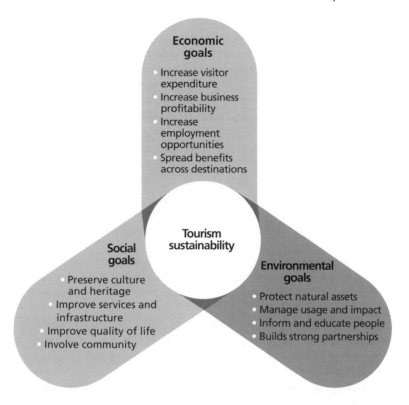

Figure 5.11 The triple-bottom-line approach to tourism sustainability
Source: Tourism Queensland, 2006.

Summary

DMOs are generally becoming more involved in destination product development as the competition for tourists intensifies. There is also greater recognition that destination marketing and product development are closely intertwined, and that those involved in destination marketing should have an interest and involvement in product development.

Many definitions of the tourism product have been offered by scholars. For this book's purposes, the destination product is defined as an interdependent mixture of tangible and intangible components comprising physical products, people, packages and programmes. In assessing a destination's product, it is important to determine its position along the Tourism Area Life Cycle (TALC).

DMOs vary in their levels of involvement in product development from non-engagement (bystanders) to being partners in development. They can also be facilitators or instigators of product development. Involvement depends to some extent on the TALC stage and the particular circumstances of the destination. No matter the situation, the DMO and tourism stakeholders should prepare a set of principles for destination product development.

Ansoff's Growth Strategy Matrix (Figure 5.6) provides a useful model for destination product development. The four specific strategies (market penetration, market development, product development and diversification) can be contemplated by most destinations in future planning for tourism.

Destination quality is important for destinations and all of the dimensions of quality (hardware, software and environment) need to be managed. Significant benefits accrue to those destinations that make a concerted effort to manage quality. An integrated quality management (IQM) approach is recommended for destinations.

There are different types of physical product developments that can take place in a destination. New project analysis should be done professionally and include a site evaluation, resource impact assessment, market analysis, financial feasibility analysis and the preparation of business and marketing plans.

All destinations are facing serious challenges with respect to human resource availability and quality. DMOs can make significant contributions to meeting these challenges by working with tourism stakeholders to prepare workforce development strategies, develop national standards for tourism occupations, and design education and training programmes.

Packaging and programming each play several key roles for destinations and offer significant benefits for customers and for the destination. DMOs should play an active role in encouraging innovative packaging and programming among the tourism stakeholders in their destinations.

Visitor information can also be considered as part of the destination product and visitor information centres (VICs) play a key role here. Online information and mobile phone 'apps' should be viewed as additional elements of the information products supplied by destinations.

There are some aspects of the destination product that often do not get adequate attention from DMOs. These include interpretation, accessible tourism and tourism signage. As these items are integral to the tourist experience, they require a higher priority and a proactive involvement from DMOs.

DMOs should play the key role in encouraging the implementation of sustainable tourism practices within their destinations. Product development should be guided by the principles of sustainable tourism so that the destination product will remain intact for future generations to enjoy.

The specific steps for a DMO to accomplish for its product development role are to:

- Determine the destination's position on the Tourism Area Life Cycle (TALC) and identify individual sub-product cycles within that.
- Decide on the dimensions of tourism quality within the destination and introduce a tourism quality management programme.
- In consultation with tourism stakeholders and community residents, identify a set of basic principles for destination product development.
- Prepare a tourism product development strategy as a component of the overall destination plan.
- Identify opportunities and needs for new physical product developments within the destination.
- Work collaboratively with other tourism stakeholders to develop a tourism workforce development strategy and support this with the appropriate standards and education and training programmes.
- Encourage the development of a wider assortment of packaging and programming offers within the destination that appeal to identified market trends and needs.

- Create specific programmes to increase the quality of interpretation in the destination.
- Develop a comprehensive visitor information provision strategy incorporating visitor information centre facilities and online information sources.
- Advise and assist tourism operators and other tourism stakeholders to achieve a higher level of accessible tourism.
- Work collaboratively with transportation and other regulatory agencies to ensure an adequate programme of tourism directional signage.
- Introduce a sustainable tourism development approach and practices to the destination.

Review questions

1 What is the definition of the destination product as it relates to the destination management role of product development?
2 The destination product has several components. What are these components?
3 What are the stages of the Tourism Area Life Cycle (TALC) model and how do these stages impact the product development role of a DMO?
4 The levels of involvement of DMOs in product development vary significantly. Can you explain the continuum of involvement indicating the roles that a DMO can play?
5 What are the dimensions of destination quality?
6 What are the reasons and benefits for managing destination quality?
7 Which principles should be articulated to guide product development within a destination?
8 What are the steps that should be followed in completing an analysis of a new physical product development?
9 What are the roles and benefits of packaging in tourism? How should a DMO get involved with packaging?
10 What are the roles and benefits of programming in tourism? What roles can the DMO play in encouraging more programming in its destination?
11 What are the roles of interpretation in tourism and what can the DMO do to improve the quantity and quality of interpretation?
12 Visitor information centres can perform a number of key roles for a destination. What are the types of roles that VICs can play?
13 What are the steps that can be taken by a DMO to encourage a higher level of accessible tourism within the destination?
14 How important are tourism directional signs to visitors and how can the DMO ensure that there is a good directional signage system in place?
15 How can a DMO encourage the adoption of a sustainable tourism development approach?

References

Alberta Employment, Immigration and Industry. 2007. A Workforce Development Strategy for Alberta's Tourism and Hospitality Industry.

Ansoff, H.I. 1987. Corporate Strategy. New York: McGraw-Hill.

Baum, T. 1998. Taking the exit route: Extending the tourism area life cycle model. *Current Issues in Tourism*, 1(2), 167–175.

Bihar State Development Corporation. 2012. Packaged Tours. http://bstdc.bih.nic.in/Tours.asp

Briggs, S. 2008. Product Development for Tourism. http://www.insights.org.uk/articleitem.aspx?title=Product%20Development%20for%20Tourism#summary

Butler, R.W. 1980. The concept of the tourist area life cycle of evolution: implications for management of resources. *Canadian Geographer*, 24(1), 5–12.

——2011. Tourism Area Life Cycle. Contemporary Tourism Reviews. Oxford: Goodfellow Publishers Limited.

Canadian Tourism Commission. 2003. Passages to Innovation. A Dynamic Interactive Planning Tool for Tourism Product Developers in Canada.

——2012. Signature Experiences Collection®. http://en-corporate.canada.travel/resources-industry/signature_experiences_collection

Canadian Tourism Human Resource Council. 2008. Training Programs and Resources. http://emerit.ca/en/emerit_training/available_training_programs

Colorado Tourism Office. 2012. Marketing Matching Grant Program – FY2012. http://www.colorado.com/ai/MarketingGrantCriteriaFY2012.pdf

Daniel, H. 2006. Portfolio analysis of a destination's tourism 'product line'. *Proceedings of the 2006 Northeastern Recreation Research Symposium*, 89–97.

Department of Culture, Media and Sport. 2011. Government Tourism Policy.

Department of the Environment, Community and Local Government. 2012. TidyTowns. http://www.tidytowns.ie/index.php

Destination Marketing Association International. 2012. CDME Certified Destination Management Executive. http://www.destinationmarketing.org/page.asp?pid=39

Destination New South Wales. 2011. Regional Tourism Product Development Program.

Elkhart County Convention and Visitors Bureau. 2012. Heritage Trail Driving Tour. http://www.amishcountry.org/things-to-do/heritage-trail

European Communities. 2000. Towards Quality Urban Tourism. Integrated Quality Management (IQM) of Urban Tourist Destinations. Brussels: European Commission, Enterprise DG Tourism Unit.

——2003. A Manual for Evaluating the Quality Performance of Tourist Destinations and Services. Brussels: Enterprise DG Publication.

Fáilte Ireland. 2011. Product Development in a Destination Context.

Georgia Department of Economic Development. 2011. Product Development. http://www.georgia.org/GeorgiaIndustries/Tourism/ProductDevelopment/Pages/default.aspx

Getz, D. 1992. Tourism planning and destination life cycle. *Annals of Tourism Research*, 19(4), 752–770.

Getz, D., Anderson, D., and Sheehan, L. 1998. Roles, issues, and strategies for convention and visitors' bureaux in destination planning and product development: A survey of Canadian bureaux. *Tourism Management*, 19(4), 331–340.

Global Sustainable Tourism Criteria. 2011. GSTC Criteria. http://new.gstcouncil.org/resource-center/gstc-criteria

Government of Canada. 2011. Canada's Federal Tourism Strategy. Welcoming the World.

Government of Jamaica. 2005. Tourism Product Development Co. Ltd. Product Diversification. http://www.tpdco.org/dynaweb.dti?dynasection=tourismenhancement&dynapage=proddiver

Government of Nova Scotia. 2012. Tourism Industry Development Program. http://www.gov.ns.ca/econ/tourism/funding-programs/development-investment/industry-development.asp

Government of Victoria. 2010. Victorian Tourism Workforce Development Plan 2010–2016.

Haq, F., Wong, H.Y., and Jackson, J. 2008. Applying Ansoff's Growth Strategy Matrix to Consumer Segments and Typologies in Spiritual Tourism. 8th International Business Research Conference, Dubai, UAE.

Hong Kong Tourism Commission. 2011. Develop Hong Kong as a Leading Regional Cruise Tourism Hub. http://www.tourism.gov.hk/english/ctkt/ctkt.html

Idaho Department of Commerce. 2012. Idaho Vacation Package Program. http://commerce.idaho.gov/tourism-grants-and-resources/vacation-package-program/

Information Services Department, Hong Kong SAR Government. 2011. Hong Kong: The Facts: Tourism.

Jennings, J. 2008. Collaborating our Way through Workforce Challenges. http://www.insights.org.uk/articleitem.aspx?title=Collaborating%20our%20Way%20Through%20Workforce%20Challenges

Kentucky Department of Travel. 2012. Tourism Signage. http://www.kentuckytourism.com/industry/tourism_signage.aspx

Koch, K. 2004. Quality Offensive in Swiss Tourism. European Seminar-Workshop on Tourism Quality Systems. Vilnius, Latvia: UNWTO.

Komppula, R. 2001. New-product Development in Tourism Companies: Case Studies on Nature-based Activity Operators. 10th Nordic Tourism Research Symposium, 18–20 October, Vasa, Finland.

MacNulty, P. 2011. Fundamentals and Principles of Tourism Product Development. 5th UNWTO/PATA Forum on Tourism Trends and Outlook, Guilin, China, 26–28 October.

Mekong Tourism. 2012. Tourism Curriculum. http://www.mekongtourism.org/site-t3/resources/hrd-training/tourism-curriculum/

Middleton, V.T.C. 1989. Tourist product. In Witt, S.F., and Moutinho, L. (eds). Tourism Marketing and Management Handbook. Hemel Hempstead: Prentice-Hall.

Mill, R.C., and Morrison, A.M. 2012. The Tourism System, 7th edn. Dubuque, IA: Kendall Hunt Publishing.

Morrison, A.M. 2010. Hospitality and Travel Marketing, 4th edn. Clifton Park, NY: Cengage Delmar.

Murphy, P., Pritchard, M.P., and Smith, B. 2000. The destination product and its impact on traveller perceptions. *Tourism Management*, 21(1), 43–52.

Northwest Territories Industry, Tourism and Investment. 2009. Tourism Development Handbook for the Northwest Territories.

Ontario Tourism Marketing Partnership. 2000. Packaging Handbook for Tourism Suppliers.

Rink, D.R., and Swan, J.E. 1979. Product life cycle research: A literature review. *Journal of Business Research*, 7(3), 219–242.

Ritchie, J.R.B., and Crouch, G.I. 2003. The Competitive Destination: A Sustainable Tourism Perspective. Wallingford: CABI.

Romeiss-Stracke, F. 1995. Service-Qualität im Tourismus. Munich: ADAC.

Rudolph, D. 2008. The Role of CVBs in Visitor Product Development. http://www.dmopro.com/, Sun Prairie: WI. Zeitgeist Consulting.

School of Travel Industry Management, University of Hawaii. Tourism Workforce Development Strategic Plan 2007–2015.

Smith, S.L.J. 1994. The tourism product. *Annals of Tourism Research*, 21(3), 582–595.

Song, H. 2011. New Product Development – An E-tourism Perspective. The 5th UNWTO/PATA Forum on Tourism Trends and Outlook. Guilin, China, 26–28 October.

South Australian Tourism Commission. 2007. Creating a Tourism Package. A Step-by-Step Guide to Create an Effective Tourism Package.

Sustainable Tourism Cooperative Research Centre. 2008. Accessible Tourism: Challenges and Opportunities. Brisbane, Australia: STCRC.

Swarbrooke, J. 2002. The Development and Management of Visitor Attractions, 2nd edn. Oxford: Butterworth-Heinemann.

Tabata, R.S. 2003. Thematic Itineraries: An Approach to Tourism Product Development. Sea Grant Extension Service, University of Hawaii at Manoa.

Tilden, F. 1977. Interpreting our Heritage. Chapel Hill: University of North Carolina Press.

Tourism Australia. 2012. Aussie Specialist Program. http://www.tourism.australia.com/en-au/marketing/5651_aussie-specialist-program.aspx

Tourism Queensland. 2004. Outback Interpretation Manual.

——2006. Queensland Tourism Strategy. www.tq.com.au/resource-centre/plans-&-strategies/queensland-tourism-strategy/queensland-tourism-strategy_home.cfm

Tourism Tasmania. 2005. Tasmania Thematic Interpretation Planning Manual.

Tourism Western Australia. 2006. What is a Tourist Attraction? nhttp://www.tourism.wa.gov.au/Publications%20Library/Growing%20Your%20Business/What%20is%20a%20Tourist%20Attraction%20v3%20211005%20(final).pdf

——2012. Tourist Signage. http://www.tourism.wa.gov.au/Growing_Your_Business/Pages/Tourist_Signage.aspx

UNWTO. 2007. A Practical Guide to Tourism Destination Management. Madrid: UNWTO.

UNWTO and European Travel Commission. 2011. Handbook on Tourism Product Development. Madrid: UNWTO.

US AID. 2010. Guide to Designing Tourism Workforce Development Programs.

Visit York. 2011. Flagship Visitor Centre Sets New Record. http://www.visityork.org/media/news/releases/NR-may2611vic1yearanniversary.aspx

VisitEngland. 2012. Accessible Tourism. http://www.visitengland.org/busdev/bussupport/access/index.aspx

Wine Routes of Spain. 2012. http://www.wineroutesofspain.com/

World Tourism Organization. 2001. Tourism Signs and Symbols: A Status Report and Guidebook. Madrid: WTO.

Chapter 6

Destination partnerships and team-building

Learning objectives

1 Define the terms destination partnership and team-building.

2 Discuss how partnerships contribute to the accomplishment of the other roles of destination management.

3 Describe the relationship between destination governance and destination partnerships.

4 Explain the benefits of destination partnerships.

5 Discuss the potential partners for DMOs.

6 Elaborate on how a DMO identifies potential partners.

7 Explain the concept of public–private partnerships (PPPs) and their advantages.

8 Pinpoint and explain the barriers and challenges in forming destination partnerships.

9 Identify the types of partnerships into which DMOs can enter.

10 Describe the ingredients of a successful destination partnership.

11 Explain how a DMO performs as a destination team-builder.

Introduction

Partnerships and collaboration earned 'buzzword' status in tourism in the past 10–20 years. Why so? One reason is because tourism is such a fertile field for partnerships and collaborations of all types. This is mainly because it is unusual for one company, government agency or other type of organization to control all of the stages in the tourism value chain (Figure 6.1), while customers often expect destination offers to be integrated. Additionally, tourism stakeholders are increasingly recognizing the positive synergies that result from working together rather than separately. As destinations enter new markets, they also need to build fresh relationships there, as DMOs are lacking in local marketing and promotional experiences and contacts.

There is a wide assortment of benefits that result from destination partnerships, so it is worthwhile for DMOs to invest in collaboration. However, partnering is not for everyone and there are barriers and challenges to building new partnerships. So finding the 'right' partners is a critical step for a DMO. This chapter explains the steps to identifying partners and building partnerships that produce synergies for everybody.

A DMO's partners are those organizations and individuals who have the same or similar goals. Most DMOs have limited resources, especially funding and partnering is a good way to extend the impact of these resources by teaming up with others.

It is important that a DMO is proactive in forming destination partnerships and does not just wait to join partnerships assembled by other organizations. In this chapter, you will learn how a DMO sets up a destination partnership planning team and the steps that this team follows to form cooperative agreements with partners.

Team-building is another aspect of this destination management role and includes proactive efforts by DMOs to build, support and maintain teams of people and organizations to implement specific strategies, programmes or actions. Just like in any sports team, the DMO may act as the captain or the coach, and needs to get the best out of all the 'team players'.

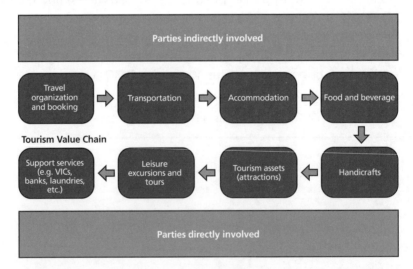

Figure 6.1 The tourism value chain. Indirect parties do not provide services directly to tourists; and these generally include DMOs except for their operation of visitor information centres
Source: Adapted from UNWTO and European Travel Commission, 2011.

Definitions of destination partnerships and team-building

Before moving ahead, it is important that you have the definitions of the two key concepts in this chapter: destination partnership and destination team-building.

Destination partnership

The partnership concept has already been introduced in Chapters 1 and 3. In this chapter, all of the potential DMO relationships with other parties are identified and explained. Just to be sure, here again is the definition of a destination partnership.

Definition of destination partnership

A partnership is a synergistic relationship between a DMO and other organizations or individuals within or outside of the destination.

There are several other terms and concepts associated with partnership and as Figure 6.2 illustrates these include collaboration, cooperation and teamwork. Alliance or strategic alliance are also often used but not shown on Figure 6.2. So what are 'synergy' and a 'synergistic relationship'? There is an enormous range of definitions of synergy around, but the concept is best characterized as 'the whole is greater than the sum of the parts'. A more formal description of synergy is that when two or more entities work together, they achieve more than they could individually and separately. Another view is that when collaborating, organizations or individuals can do things that they could not do on their own.

A synergistic relationship for a DMO, therefore, is a deliberate cooperative arrangement that produces benefits for the DMO and its partners that would not be achieved without working together. This results from the pooling of effort and resources, either financial or non-financial, or both. As some say, these are situations where '1+1' equals more than two!

As was mentioned in Chapter 1, DMOs cannot effectively perform all the roles of destination management without the assistance of tourism stakeholders and partners outside of the destination. Partnering with others is essential for DMOs in today's business climate where budgets are shrinking but competition is growing. Moreover, DMOs get more done and accomplished when they collaborate with others.

You might come across the terms 'strategic partnerships' and 'strategic alliances' when you read about tourism and some specific parts of the tourism sector, including airlines. Here the meaning of 'strategic' is long-term and the partners agree (often in writing) to work together for 3 or more years. These demonstrate the highest levels of commitment among destination partnerships.

Figure 6.2 Synergy, the outcome of cooperation, collaboration, partnership and teamwork
Source: Shutterstock, Inc. (iQoncept).

Destination team-building

Some partnerships are the result of team-building by the DMO and this is a demonstration of the leadership and coordination role in destination management. There are so many diverse tourism stakeholders in a destination that the DMO often has to be proactive in bringing groups of specific people together to deal with particular issues or opportunities. Here then is the definition of destination team-building:

Definition of destination team-building

Team-building represents proactive efforts by DMOs to build, support and maintain teams of people and organizations to implement specific strategies, programmes or actions.

As you will realize, the concepts of destination partnerships and team-building are linked; in fact, it is a bit hard to say where one stops and the other begins. Through team-building, a DMO creates new partnerships; but the DMO can also join partnership teams organized by others.

Destination management role contributions of partnerships

Before getting into the specific benefits of destination partnerships, you need to know about the broad scope of partnering in destination management. When partnering was first discussed in tourism, this was mainly in the context of marketing and promotion (Palmer and Bejou, 1995). Today, it is recognized that partnerships and collaboration can make a valuable contribution to all destination management roles. Here are some examples to prove this point:

- *Destination planning*: The process for preparing plans and strategies must be collaborative as you already learned in Chapter 2. Many real-life examples could be provided here, but one will suffice. In preparing the Town of Drumheller Tourism Master Plan in Alberta, Canada, a public workshop was held with local residents, town staff and council members; meetings were also held with other tourism stakeholders.
- *Research*: Destination research is sometimes co-sponsored by DMOs and others that have an interest in the results. The Great Britain Tourism Survey (GBTS) is an outstanding partnership case for destination research. GBTS is jointly sponsored by three national tourist boards in the UK: VisitEngland, VisitScotland and Visit Wales.
- *Product development*: Chapter 5 cited several examples of partnerships related to product development and indeed there are many potential avenues of cooperation here. In early 2012, ASEAN (Association of Southeast Asian Nations) member countries agreed to take collaborative steps to build up cruise tourism in the region. They will co-organize workshops with the industry to share best practices and strengthen collaboration in port infrastructure development, development of regional itineraries and joint marketing.
- *Marketing and promotion*: Partnership has been already identified as one of the 8 Ps of destination marketing (Chapter 3) and cooperative marketing has been very strong in tourism for many years. A good example here is the 4-year collaboration agreement signed in 2011 by Tourism Queensland in Australia and Singapore Airlines. Together they will jointly fund a number of campaigns and promotions to bring more visitors to Queensland through Singapore Airlines' service into Brisbane.
- *Partnering and team-building*: Well, that is the name of this chapter; so this role definitely does involve partnering and team-building, and you get many examples on the pages to follow. But how about an innovative example here to keep your interest? In 2009, the Michigan Travel Commission in the USA introduced the Governor's Awards for Innovative Tourism Collaboration within the state. One of the main goals of the awards programme was 'to promote innovative collaboration as an effective, efficient and creative operating principle for the industry'.
- *Community relations*: DMOs are very active in developing partnerships and teams within their own communities and mention was made in Chapter 5 of 'tourism ambassador' programmes. A nice case study here is the Colorado Tourism Ambassador Program run by the Colorado Tourism Office (CTO) in the USA. CTO recruits people from the tourism sector to become Ambassadors and to make presentations to Colorado residents about the economic and other benefits of tourism to the state (Figure 6.3). The $157 note is an effective tool to use in these

Figure 6.3 The $157 note from the Colorado Tourism Office
Source: Colorado Tourism Office, 2008.

presentations and puts across the fact that tourism Colorado contributes $157 in taxes for every Colorado resident.

- *Leadership and coordination*: As a matter of fact, partnering and team-building are coordination tools that DMOs can use to bring different parties together. An example of a national DMO showing leadership through partnering is in the agreement signed in 2011 between Tourism Spain and Amadeus, a leading technology provider in tourism. Under this agreement, Spain will share its experience in sustainable tourism development with developing countries.

The main point of this discussion, along with the examples, was to communicate that destination partnerships are pervasive and can be used as strategies to fulfil all the roles of destination management.

Partnerships and destination governance

Destination governance is the topic of Chapter 8, but you should know now that there is a relationship between destination partnerships and destination governance. In fact, achieving effective destination governance is another major reason for partnerships. According to Laws *et al.* (2011), destination governance requires the following:

Requirements of destination governance

Achieving cooperation, collaboration and integration among the government organizations involved in the various aspects of tourism, and between government and private sector enterprises, as well as between tourism policies and community interests are major concerns for policy makers, managers, community members and academics.

Still on the topic of destination governance, it should also be noted that some DMOs or their departments were established with a specific mandate to collaborate with others in the tourism sector. So partnering is definitely not optional for these entities.

For example, the Industry Development Department of the Abu Dhabi Tourism Authority (2012) is mandated to collaborate with industry stakeholders:

Abu Dhabi Industry Development Department

The Department's mandate is to collaborate with its stakeholders to raise the level of professionalism within Abu Dhabi's tourism industry. The Industry Development Department is responsible for promoting compliance of the tourism regulatory framework by sharing best practices within the industry, assessing training needs and organizing training programs to address these needs.

There are also certain instances where government agencies agree to have their various DMOs collaborate, and Australia provides one example (Australian Government, 2005). The document, 'Achievement by Partnerships: Tourism Collaboration Intergovernmental Arrangement' spells out how all of the tourism ministries at the national, state and territorial levels will collaborate and coordinate their tourism activities and build stronger partnerships. This arrangement was based on specific principles for collaboration and cooperation, shown below.

Principles and processes for collaboration and cooperation

The Australian governmental tourism agencies agreed on the following principles:

a) Consult with each other on matters of shared interest and benefit.
b) Minimise duplication.
c) Align and mutually reinforce tourism promotional messages where appropriate.
d) Explore opportunities for collaborative funding.
e) Strengthen existing collaborative arrangements.
f) Avoid cost shifting.
g) Recognise and respect the roles of tourism agencies in all jurisdictions, including their relationships with key stakeholders.

(Cost-shifting usually means that when one party under-pays for services; other parties have to put in more than their shares.)

This example from Australia exposes you to another perspective on the need for partnering. Again this is more of a destination governance perspective, and avoiding the duplication of effort and redundancy of programmes and actions are key reasons for forming closer partnerships. Better communications among partners is another justification under this perspective.

So there is a need for partnerships based on the characteristics of tourism and some agencies are compelled to engage in them. In addition, some government agencies agree to coordinate their tourism activities for better governance reasons. However, as you will now see, there are also many other benefits that accrue from partnerships to DMOs and destinations.

Benefits of destination partnerships

Destinations and their DMOs can enjoy profound benefits from being involved in destination partnerships. In fact, in some of the more advanced tourism destinations, including Canada, there is recognition (Industry Canada, 2008) that tourism has entered a 'new era of collaboration' and that partnering is no longer 'optional' for DMOs.

A new era of collaboration

It is evident that the current way of doing business is no longer feasible to meet the challenges facing the tourism sector or to seize emerging opportunities. A new era of collaboration, involving all tourism stakeholders, is necessary to enable Canada to increase its market share and raise its domestic and international profile.

Figure 1.6 identified five significant partnership benefits as more budget, shared information, greater expertise, increased market appeal and shared facilities. Actually this is just a short list and there are many other benefits of destination partnerships as you will see.

- *Accessing customer databases*: The usage or sharing of a partner's proprietary customer databases can be a powerful advantage of cooperation. For example, the Hong Kong Tourism Board teamed up with Visa credit card in the summer of 2011 to boost inbound tourism and spending on Visa cards. Visa could use its huge database of card-holders to publicize this promotion.
- *Accessing new markets*: A partnership may provide new geographic markets or other new target markets for the DMO. An interesting new example here involves what are called 'blog trips' and the Jordan Tourism Board participated in these by inviting eight select travel bloggers to the country. The bloggers wrote about their experiences in Jordan after returning home. This is a good way for Jordan to connect with potential tourists worldwide.
- *Better serving customer needs*: When DMOs and other tourism stakeholders pool facilities, services and other resources, this often better serves tourists' needs. European Cities Marketing, for example, provides great convenience to tourists in its partner cities through the distribution of European CityCards. This requires the cooperation and collaboration of many tourism stakeholders in the participating cities.

- *Enhancing image*: Associating with other destinations and their DMOs can enhance customers' perceptions and the positioning of destinations. The BestCities Global Alliance (http://www.bestcities.net) is an outstanding application of partnering that gives all the participants an enhanced image within a particular market segment, business events. The ten city DMOs belonging to the alliance are Cape Town, Copenhagen, Dubai, Edinburgh, Melbourne, San Juan, Singapore, Vancouver, Berlin and Houston.
- *Expanding social responsibility*: Mentioned above was the collaboration between Amadeus and Tourism Spain to help developing countries with implementing sustainable tourism. A second example is the partnership between the Cyprus Tourism Organization and the Travel Foundation of the UK in creating the Cyprus Sustainable Tourism Initiative (CSTI). The Travel Foundation entered into this 5-year agreement in 2010 with the Cyprus Tourism Organization and the Cyprus Sustainable Tourism Initiative.
- *Increasing budgets*: Often when the DMO agrees to cooperate with others, the total budget amount for all the partners is increased through the pooling of funds. In addition to the amount being greater for all, the partners may be able to do things that they could not do on their own. The 'European Quartet' is a great case study of mutual benefit through long-term cooperation in tourism. The four countries, for example, have booths at major travel shows and exhibitions, which they may not have been able to afford by themselves. This has meant that all the DMOs are able to reach out to long-haul markets, such as China, since the pooled budget is large enough to allow them to do so.

The European Quartet joint marketing

European Quartet is the promotional name for joint marketing of the national tourist head offices of four Central European sovereign states – the Czech Republic, Hungary, Poland and Slovakia, under which they present themselves in the field of tourism. The association of these countries, known as the Visegrad Four (V4), has actively been developing cooperation over the long term in fields of common interest and is intensively reinforcing its internal cooperation. The Visegrad initiative is an expression of the effort to develop the region of Central Europe within the wider framework of Europe-wide integration. This is based on the joint historical roots or one civilisation which all four countries belong to, on a shared cultural tradition and similar historical development. At the same time however, each of the member countries has its own unique points and specifics, be these in the field of architecture, art, religion, folklore and traditions or nature. Thanks to this, visitors to the V4 region are surprised every step of the way and are most certainly not bored. The Visegrad area offers several unique UNESCO monuments, world famous spas, authentically preserved historical towns and places of natural beauty.

(European Quartet, 2012)

- *Increasing market appeal*: When the DMO works with others with similar interests in certain markets, the result is usually an increased appeal to these people. The DMO in Tenerife in the Canary Islands, along with a Swedish travel agency and with help from Tourism Spain, promoted its wine tourism in Sweden to older travellers. This resulted in an increase in Swedes travelling to the wine country in Spain.
- *Increasing pool of expertise*: A partnership may be formed because the DMO and the other partners have expertise that the other partners need to pursue the tasks that their cooperation involves. In Australia in early 2012, Sydney Airport and Destination New South Wales announced a new partnership agreement to bring more visitors to the state. The two will work together to attract new airlines and routes to Sydney from key tourism markets such as China and India, and to enhance passengers' arrival and departure experiences at the airport. In this partnership, Destination NSW has expertise in destination marketing and international promotion of tourism; Sydney Airport has the expertise in airport management and in marketing to airline companies. The two entities working together means that their complementary expertise is pooled for greater effectiveness.
- *Sharing facilities*: If the DMO teams up with other organizations, this may help each partner to afford certain physical facilities. For example, DMOs that share office space in foreign countries find this more affordable than leasing and operating their own stand-alone offices. A great case study is the New York office of the Scandinavian Tourist Boards that represents Denmark, Finland, Iceland, Norway and Sweden in North America. Scandinavian Tourism Inc., an umbrella organization for the five countries, has a call centre handling all consumer requests and fulfilments. It is unlikely that these individual countries could justify the cost of having an office in the USA on their own.
- *Sharing information*: Most destination partnerships result in a great deal of sharing of information among the participants. The Great Britain Tourism Survey discussed earlier was a direct example of information sharing through jointly-sponsored research.

Ten distinct destination partnerships benefits have now been identified and described, and there may be more. However, these benefits are substantial enough to prove the great power in destination partnerships. The next step is to discuss the potential partners for a DMO.

Destination partners

Chapter 1 identified five types of destination partners, but that was really just the 'tip of the iceberg' when it comes to the assortment of potential partners that a DMO needs to consider. You will know this from the examples already used in this chapter. The following is an extended list and description of potential destination partners.

E-collaborators: When the Internet started being used by DMOs around 1995, this new tool brought with it many novel ways of partnering online. For example, http://www.alpseurope.com/ is a portal shared by the national DMOs of Austria, Germany and Switzerland. Portals are online 'gateways' to the individual websites of the partners.

You heard earlier about the BestCities Global Alliance, which also includes an impressive shared website. Other online partnership applications include reciprocal hyperlinking of partners' websites (each partner provides a 'hot link' to the other partners' websites) and shared social media sites.

Education and training institutions: There has been significant expansion around the world in tourism and hospitality education, as well as in training and professional development programmes in destination management. DMOs sometimes find it advantageous to work with academic institutions and suppliers of training to implement human resources development and research projects. Lee and Wicks (2010) explain an interesting case of DMO–university collaboration in the joint production of podcasts for the destinations of the participants. This was surely a win–win project for the DMOs and the university in the partnership.

Existing and potential tourists: DMOs can develop programmes to build closer relationships with existing tourists. A good case study here is the *Valued Visitor* programme of the Brown County Convention and Visitors Bureau in Indiana, USA (Figure 6.4). For a sign-up fee of $12, people join the programme and receive a 'Valued Visitors' card and a free 'Memories' shopping bag. With the membership,

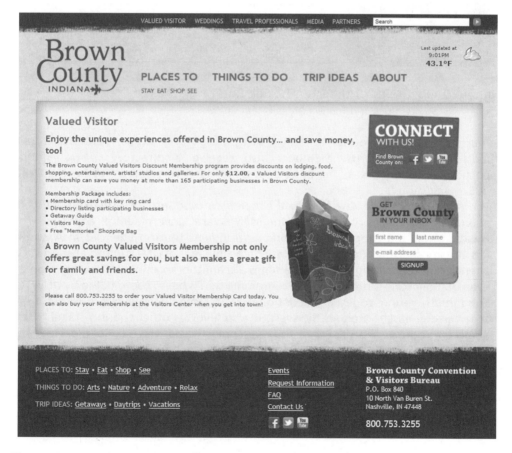

Figure 6.4 Brown County Indiana Valued Visitor Program
Source: Brown County Convention and Visitors Bureau (Indiana), 2012.

The Silk Road will be an internationally renowned, seamless travel experience	• The Silk Road will be an established brand, supported by extensive cooperative marketing campaigns • High quality infrastructure will facilitate smooth travel across international borders
The tourism sector will be prosperous across all Silk Road destinations, stimulating ongoing investment	• Governments will value and support tourism • The Silk Road will offer high quality tourism infrastructure • Tourism will generate significant direct and indirect employment
Silk Road stakeholders will work closely together for mutual benefits	• Strong cooperation among Silk Road countries • Profitable partnerships between public and private sectors • Increased visitor length of stay and yield across all regions
Tourism will drive improved cultural and environmental management	• Advanced cultural management systems in place • Environmental sustainability will underpin every aspect of tourism development
Silk Road tourism will act as a vehicle for fostering peace and cultural understanding	• Promotion of cultural pluralism and intercultural dialogue • Intercultural cooperation as key instrument to strengthen social cohesion, solidarity and peace

Figure 6.5 Objectives of the UNWTO Silk Road Programme

Source: UN World Tourism Organization, 2013.

tourists receive discounts at 165 participating local shops, restaurants and lodging establishments. Members also receive a directory listing of the participating businesses. The programme has been very successful for the DMO in Brown County.

Government agencies: DMOs often see the benefits in working closely with government agencies, whether or not they themselves are governmental agencies. The collaboration and cooperation among government tourism agencies in Australia has already been mentioned. In Chapter 5, the linkages of DMOs with transportation agencies on tourism signage programmes are another example. An example on an even grander scale is the Silk Road Programme that is being coordinated by UNWTO. This initiative brings together the national DMOs from twenty-eight countries, from Japan in the east to Italy in the west. It also involves other tourism stakeholders along the route of the Silk Road. The main objectives of this Silk Road partnership are shown in Figure 6.5 and these highlight the sorts of benefits that can be gained from working together across political boundaries.

Local community residents: DMOs often recruit local residents to be ambassadors or volunteers to assist visitors to their communities, and this is a form of partnership with local people. Visit Wales' Community Tourism Ambassadors is an outstanding case in DMO partnering with local residents:

Visit Wales. What are Community Tourism Ambassadors?

Community Tourism Ambassadors are citizens committed to their local communities who have received free, accredited training to become a welcoming host and a reliable source of information about their locality. They may be professionally involved in the tourist industry, volunteers in a variety of community groups or simply individuals enthusiastic about doing something to promote their locality.

(Destination Management Wales, 2010)

One of the strengths of this programme in Wales is the training and certification element. This ensures that all volunteers have been exposed to Visit Wales' programme objectives and have studied similar information about travel and destinations in Wales.

Another creative approach here is the Chicago Office of Tourism and Culture (COTC) and its invitation to expert photographers in the city to help tourists in taking their own shots. COTC had noted that an increasing proportion of tourists were taking pictures and decided to be very proactive in helping people in getting better quality photographs. In addition, COTC launched the '175 Ways to Love Chicago' programme in January 2012 in the lead-up to the city's 175th birthday in March 2012. Each weekday for 35 days, a famous Chicagoan listed five of their favourite things to see and do in Chicago and these were posted to the city's official tourism website.

Media companies: DMOs often work with different types of media companies to accomplish various destination management roles and particularly related to marketing and promotion. For example, the Spa Week Media Group (*Spa Week Daily*) and Czech Tourism North America collaborated to publicize wellness spas and health tourism in the Czech Republic. This partnership commenced with a familiarization trip to the leading wellness spas in the Czech Republic for editors of *Spa Week Daily* and EuroSpaClub, and bloggers and writers.

Non-profit organizations: DMOs can find good partners among non-profit organizations when they need to address specific issues and challenges. The partnership of the Cyprus Tourism Organization and The Travel Foundation was an example given earlier. Another case is the link-up between the Singapore Tourism Board and the Consumer Association of Singapore (CASE) to better handle complaints made by tourists. CASE will mediate on behalf of tourists when their complaints and cases thereon enter into legal proceedings.

Non-tourism companies: Earlier the partnership of the Hong Kong Tourism Board and the Visa credit card was mentioned. Automobile companies, banks, credit cards, sporting equipment and goods manufacturers, food processing and technology suppliers are just a small sample of these potential partners. Another example here was the partnership between the Nevada Commission on Tourism (NCOT) and Google, Inc. in which NCOT was able to very accurately measure the results of its winter advertising campaign through the link-up with Google.

Other DMOs: This is possibly the most popular type of partnership since DMOs tend to understand each others' goals and priorities very well and they are in frequent contact with one another. Many countries and some states and provinces have associations of DMOs and their members work together on joint initiatives. You have already heard about the cooperation of the five Scandinavian countries in the USA. Another example is the cooperation between the DMO in the Malaysian state of Kedah with the DMO in Satun Province in Thailand. The Kedah–Satun Joint Cooperation Committee is designed to create tourism programmes to bring more tourists to Langkawi Island and the Kedah mainland through the Satun–Langkawi gateway.

Tourism sector associations: DMOs often work in partnership with tourism sector associations as they share similar goals. For example, several CVBs in the USA worked with Destination Marketing Association International (DMAI) in its Performance Reporting Initiative that produced many performance measurements for DMOs.

Tourism sector employees: DMOs can partner with people working in the tourism sector and not just with their bosses. The Hospitality and Tourism Ambassadors programme in Northern Ireland provides a good application example. The following is a short description of this partnership:

Northern Ireland Hospitality and Tourism Ambassadors

About the Ambassadors

Our Ambassadors are passionate, enthusiastic and highly motivated individuals working in hospitality, leisure, travel and tourism and they want to spread the word about the exciting, varied and real opportunities offered by the industry to you!

Benefits to you

Both students and teachers need direct links with industry to help them understand more about the real world of work. Ambassadors will share their stories, demonstrating to you just why they love their jobs and why the industry provides an excellent career choice in the twenty-first century.

Tourism stakeholders: Most DMOs work very closely with the tourism sectors in their destinations and create partnerships of various types. Membership programmes are operated by many DMOs, especially in the USA, and these are a type of partnership. Other DMOs appoint advisory boards partly or wholly from the tourism sector, and this is another example of partnering. For example, a Council for Tourism Development consisting of approximately fifty public- and private-sector representatives was created in Macau in 2011 to give advice on tourism development, planning and organization.

Transportation companies: Two examples were given earlier of DMOs working cooperatively with airlines and airport operators. These were Sydney Airport with Destination NSW and Singapore Airlines with Tourism Queensland; both partnerships involved travel to Australia. Another very clear example is the Austin Convention and Visitors Bureau in Texas, USA providing a direct link to its airline partner, United Airlines, on the home page of the CVB website.

Travel trade: Many mutually beneficial partnerships occur between DMOs and companies in the travel trade including traditional travel agencies, online travel agencies (OTAs), tour operators and wholesalers, destination management companies (DMCs), incentive travel planners and others. For example, in 2011 Destination New South Wales and the Jetset Travelworld Group (JTG) signed a 2-year partnership agreement for marketing the state in Australia and abroad.

These then are fourteen potential partners for DMOs and there could be more. The main point is that a DMO has many potential partners that it can call upon for collaboration and cooperation. Figure 6.6 provides a composite picture of destination partnership benefits and destination partners. You will see that there are twenty-five blocks in this matrix of benefits and partners, and only one of these is the DMO itself. So, once again, it should be clear that there is great potential for a DMO in destination partnering.

Identifying destination partners

How does a DMO find the right partners? This is a matching process and the key is to find other organizations or individuals with the same or similar goals or objectives to the DMO's. Another key is that the partners share an interest in a specific tourist market, or they want to tackle a particular issue, challenge or problem in tourism that

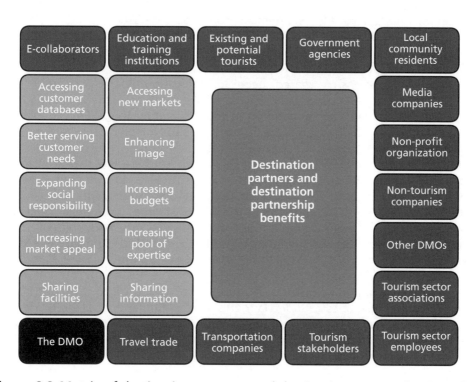

Figure 6.6 Matrix of destination partners and destination partnership benefits

the DMO also wants to address. This could be to advocate a sustainable tourism development agenda for the destination; to make local people more aware about tourism; to improve destination quality; or many other situations best worked on together as a team.

There has to be willingness on both sides to work together and so all partners must have a 'win–win' mentality. A good example here is the cooperation between NYC & Company, the DMO for New York City and the Seoul Metropolitan Government in South Korea. The two cities signed a memorandum of understanding (MOU) in which they promoted each other through websites and advertisements in public places.

Mutual trust is another prerequisite and all partners must trust each other. Partners must also be comfortable with the idea of interdependence, and have the ability to accept change. It is much better if partners have a future orientation rather than an orientation to the past.

Apart from these general conditions required for collaboration, there are other ways of identifying potential partners. Finding a 'common ground' is the key step here. These are through recognizing shared resources including geographic features, history and heritage, cultures and transportation linkages. The following are some examples based upon the sharing of specific characteristics:

- *Cultures and traditions*: The European Quartet of the Czech Republic, Hungary, Poland and Slovakia is an example of four countries that have shared cultural traditions, including a rich history of music. Another good case study is the Greater Shangri-La region of China that includes the strong Tibetan ethnic cultures in Qinghai, Sichuan and Yunnan Provinces, and Tibet itself. 'El Mundo Maya' (The Mayan World) in Mexico and Central America is another application here, bringing together Belize, El Salvador, Guatemala, Honduras and Mexico.
- *Geographic features*: These include mountain ranges; seas, rivers and lakes; coastlines; climate; and other physical geography characteristics. A good example is the Baltic Sea Tourism Commission (BTC) that has its headquarters in Sweden.
- *Geographic locations*: A shared geographic location is one of the primary motivations for destination partnerships, especially where there are adjoining political boundaries. The cooperation in tourism among the ASEAN countries in Southeast Asia is just one example of marketing and developing a shared geographic region.
- *History and heritage*: Partners may be found where there is a shared history of heritage through the presence of human-made structures, historic trails or routes, or events from the past. The trail to Santiago de Compostela (Camino de Santiago de Compostela, Figure 6.7) that follows the Way of St James through parts of France and Spain is an excellent example. There are numerous other examples of historic tourism trails including the Silk Road, the Cabot Trail in Cape Breton, Nova Scotia, Canada, the Lewis and Clark Trail in the USA and many more.

Places sharing human-made historic structures often find ways to form destination partnerships and examples include Hadrian's Wall in England, and the Great Wall and the Grand Canal in China. Destinations that were all touched by famous people in history provide another reason for collaboration. Argentina, Bolivia and Cuba have joined together to form a tourism trail based upon the revolutionary, Che Guevara.

Figure 6.7 The distinctive direction symbol on the Camino de Santiago de Compostela in Burgos, Spain
Source: Shutterstock, Inc. (Roberaten).

- *Industrial characteristics*: A shared industrial heritage is another reason for places to link up together. The whisky trail in Scotland is a fine case study. The European Route of Industrial Heritage is another example on a larger scale and covers more than thirty countries.
- *Transportation routes*: This is another popular reason for destinations grouping together and there are many examples worldwide. Route 66 in the USA is one of the most famous of these. The extensive canal systems of Europe also link many destinations.

You will hear later about themed routes, circuits and itineraries as a type of destination partnership, and many DMOs have been very active in creating these destination product offers for tourists.

Figure 6.8 provides a visual illustration of how a DMO can identify potential partners by looking at similarities in: (1) resources; (2) location; (3) markets; and (4) challenges and problems. You should also realize that there are occasions when a DMO wants to find partners based on dissimilarities, when it needs partners that have resources or expertise that it does not have. In these situations, the end result is a rounding out of the partnership team.

Public–private partnerships in destination management

Public–private partnerships or PPPs are becoming a popular way to structure DMOs and also to accomplish specific projects within destinations. Chapter 1 opened up this topic by explaining the strengths and weaknesses of government (public sector) and company (private sector) operations. Both have their respective advantages and both have distinctive disadvantages.

Statutory bodies like Tourism Australia and Tourism Queensland are good examples of this formula of blending together the strengths of the two sectors. These

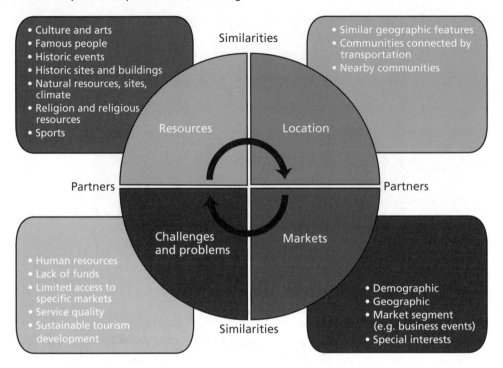

- Culture and arts
- Famous people
- Historic events
- Historic sites and buildings
- Natural resources, sites, climate
- Religion and religious resources
- Sports

Similarities

- Similar geographic features
- Communities connected by transportation
- Nearby communities

Resources

Location

Partners

Partners

Challenges and problems

Markets

- Human resources
- Lack of funds
- Limited access to specific markets
- Service quality
- Sustainable tourism development

Similarities

- Demographic
- Geographic
- Market segment (e.g. business events)
- Special interests

Figure 6.8 Destination partner identification wheel

organizations are established through special 'statutes' or decrees of national, state, provincial or territorial governments. They are normally administered by boards of directors selected from government and the private sector. So it can be said that they are at 'arm's length' from the government, but are also not fully in the private sector.

This is a topic discussed in detail in Chapter 8 under destination governance, so you will not get a detailed description here. The main point to be made is that many DMOs today are themselves a partnership of government and private-sector organizations.

Barriers and challenges for destination partnerships

There are some limitations to the concept of destination partnerships and you need to be aware of them. The main barriers and challenges regarding the development and operation of destination partnerships are identified below:

- *High turnover rate of principals*: People tend to move from position to position quite quickly in the tourism sector. Thus, the original 'principals' who formed the partnership may leave and be replaced by others who do not have the same enthusiasm for the collaboration. So the DMO must think about the 'sustainability' of each new partnership and ensure that the partnership will continue even after staff departures.
- *Huge diversity of the tourism sector*: The tourism sector is very diverse, involving many different government agencies, private-sector companies, non-profits and others. In addition, geography and cultures, even within the same country, tend to

separate people and their ideas about how to proceed with tourism initiatives. It is extremely difficult to coordinate such a complex variety of entities and therefore to form effective partnerships.

- *Imperfect information communications*: There are many success stories and best practices in destination partnering and this chapter has revealed several of them. However, due to difficulties in communications, the sharing of these case studies is seldom very widespread in tourism.
- *Independence and self-interest*: The tourism sector is composed of many small and medium-sized enterprises and their owners tend to have a strong sense of independence. They may be unwilling to cooperate or share information. Apart from this, there are people who only act out of self-interest and they tend not to make very good team players in a partnership.
- *Lack of adequate funds*: This can be a huge barrier to destination partnerships. There may be willingness to partner, but not enough money to create and operate the partnership's initiatives.
- *Long-term payoffs*: Sometimes partnerships take years rather than months to produce tangible benefits. Partners looking for short-term benefits may not have the patience to remain in the collaboration for several years.
- *Measurement difficulties*: As with many programmes in tourism, it is often difficult to measure the results of destination partnerships.
- *Sub-sector differences*: Tourism is composed of many sub-sectors and often there is some friction among them, e.g. between airlines and travel agencies. This may result in a lack of mutual trust and an unwillingness to cooperate.
- *Uneven partner benefits*: Not all partners receive equal benefits from a destination partnership and this may not be acceptable for some of the partners. The Collaborations and Partnerships Issue Work Team for the preparation of the Michigan Tourism Strategic Plan in the USA had this to say about the distribution of partnering benefits:

Mutual benefit does not mean equal benefit

There is also a mind-set challenge operating within this sphere [tourism]. While the value of collaborating can be in its ability to generate 'win–win' results, industry members need to recognize and accept the fact that 'mutual benefit' does not necessarily mean 'equal benefit'. It must also be recognized that the benefits from collaboration may be direct or indirect, and may be immediate or realized over a longer period of time.

So what looks easy, may not in reality be that straightforward. There are many barriers and challenges on the way to establishing a great destination partnership. In reality, destination partnerships often succeed because of the 'passion' of a few of the principals to make them work and to sustain the enthusiasm that is always there at the very beginning.

Destination partnership types

There is an enormous variety of types of destination partnerships. Some are short-term and are not repeated; others are long-term (strategic) and the cooperation spans several years. Partnerships can be 'one-shot' propositions covering just one activity or initiative; or they can be multi-faceted and involve several different activities.

- *Cooperative promotions ('co-ops')*: These are definitely the most common types of partnerships found in tourism and involve collaboration in destination marketing and promotion. Most often co-ops are done as part of advertising campaigns but they occur across all types of promotions. The DMO for the Northern Territory in Australia says that cooperating with them allows tourism sector operators to reach further with their advertising budgets.

Cooperative marketing in Australia's Northern Territory

Cooperative marketing allows operators and trade partners to cost-effectively promote their product and extend their advertising reach nationally and internationally through financial support from Tourism NT. Cooperative funds are also used to encourage trade and industry partners to support and align with Tourism NT's campaign initiatives.

(Tourism Northern Territory, 2009)

- *Customer care*: You heard earlier about the partnership of the Singapore Tourism Board and the consumer association in Singapore teaming up to help tourists, mainly with their complaints about shops where they made purchases. There are many other good examples where DMOs arrange customer care training for operators in the tourism sector and other tourism stakeholders. For example, Tourism South East in England organized a one-day 'Welcome Host Gold' training course to improve the service levels of staff in the tourism sector.
- *DMO organizational structures*: Often DMOs are established that are partnerships in themselves. For example, the Melbourne Tourism Partnership in Australia is a coalition of Destination Melbourne (the regional tourism organization), the City of Melbourne, Melbourne Convention and Visitors Bureau, Tourism Victoria and Victorian Major Events Company. Destination Melbourne acts as the coordinator of the Melbourne Tourism Partnership.
- *Event and festival sponsorships*: DMOs often seek sponsorships for business and sporting events, as well as other types of events and festivals. There are so many potential case studies here; it is really hard to pick one. However, the Qingdao International Beer Festival in Shandong Province, China is an interesting one to discuss briefly. It was started by the Tsingtao Brewery Co. Ltd and they are still its main sponsors. However, it has grown to be so big and popular that there are many other partners now involved, including the local DMO.
- *Product clubs*: Product clubs may be formed with or without the intervention of a DMO, but in several cases DMOs have been involved in creating these partnerships

of tourism stakeholders. Gomis *et al.* (2010) provided the following definition of a product club in an article about the 'Wine Routes' of Spain.

Tourism product club definition

A tourism product club is a group of companies that have agreed to work together to develop new tourism products or increase the value of existing products and collectively review the existing problems that hinder profitable development of tourism. Tourism product clubs share an interest in a sector of the tourism industry and aim to increase the variety and quality of products available (packages, events, activities, experiences) and/or develop new products for a specific market segment. The group is committed to conducting a program of development of tourism products for a period of at least three to five years.

- *Professional development, education and training*: Many DMOs get involved in partnerships that provide professional development and training programmes, or that lend support to other forms of tourism education. In fact, they are a major thrust of DMOs and their associations. These partnerships occur in almost every destination as DMOs recognize that training and education are continuously needed in the tourism sector due to the fairly high rate of labour turnover. Just one small example here is of the Malta Tourism Authority teaming up with Malta Communications Authority in 2011 to offer a training course on e-marketing in tourism.
- *Sponsored research*: DMOs pool funds with others to do specific research projects. For example, several state tourism offices and CVBs buy custom reports from the Survey of International Air Travelers conducted each year by the US Department of Commerce's Office of Travel and Tourism Industries.
- *Strategic marketing consortia*: These are long-term agreements between DMOs and other partners to conduct marketing and promotions over several years. You have already heard about the cooperation of the Scandinavian tourist boards in North America. The Atlantic Canada Tourism Marketing Partnership, the Mekong Tourism Coordinating Office and ASEAN Tourism Marketing are three other examples mentioned in this chapter.
- *Sustainable tourism*: There is a growing interest worldwide in sustainable tourism development. DMOs and their partners are getting more involved in joint programmes related to sustainable tourism. For example, in early 2011, the tourism bureau in Jiuzhaigou in Sichuan Province, China co-organized a low-carbon tourism forum with the International Tourism Studies Association (ITSA), an association of tourism scholars.
- *Themed routes, circuits or itineraries*: You have already heard about UNWTO's Silk Road and the Wine Routes of Spain, and these are great examples of touring routes linked by a common theme. Another outstanding example is actually much more than just a themed itinerary, and it has become a destination management organization. This is the area surrounding Hadrian's Wall in Northern England (Figure 6.9).

Figure 6.9 Hadrian's Wall Heritage Ltd, a great DMO example
Source: Hadrian's Wall Heritage Ltd, 2011.

- *Tourism advocacy*: This means helping to communicate the benefits of tourism and its contributions to the economy and society. There was a great example given in Chapter 1 (Figure 1.5) of the US Travel Association working together with other DMOs in the country during National Travel and Tourism Week.
- *Websites and social media*: This is where a DMO partners with others to develop a website or sites on popular social media channels. For example, the Korea Tourism Organization and the China National Tourist Office developed a joint website, http://www.visitchinaandkorea.com/, aimed mainly at the tourist market in the USA.

Ingredients of successful destination partnerships

What steps can a DMO take to make sure a destination partnership is successful? It is very difficult to generalize in answering this question since partnerships are so diverse. However, there are some basic ingredients needed and several authors have discussed them. For example, in her famous article, 'Collaborative advantage: The art of alliance', Rosabeth M. Kanter of the Harvard Business School (1994) identified the 'Eight Is of partnership development' that she argued were the basic ingredients of successful partnerships:

- *Individual excellence*: The partners are strong and have something to contribute to the collaboration.

- *Importance*: The partnership fits with the goals and strategies of the partners.
- *Interdependence*: The partners need each other and they have complementary resources, skills and experiences.
- *Investment*: The partners invest in each other.
- *Information*: The partners share information and communications are open.
- *Integration*: The partners create linkages and shared ways of doing things.
- *Institutionalization*: The partnership is given a formal status, e.g. with a contract or MOU.
- *Integrity*: Mutual trust is increased because partners behave in an honourable way toward each other.

A successful destination partnership, like a good marriage, is one that lasts. A few good examples will help to make this point sink in more deeply. For almost 20 years, the Atlantic Canada Tourism Partnership has been jointly marketing the provinces of New Brunswick, Newfoundland and Labrador, Nova Scotia and Prince Edward Island. It is a great example of a public–private partnership since governmental DMOs and provincial tourism associations cost-share the partnership. The Government of Canada contributes 50 per cent through the Atlantic Canada Opportunities Agency (ACOA), and the four provincial governments also put funds into the pool.

The Atlantic Canada Tourism Partnership

ACTP is a powerful example of the benefits of government working with the tourism industry in pursuit of shared goals. Since 1994, ACTP has successfully promoted and marketed the Atlantic Provinces. Funding for the 2009–2012 initiative, valued at $19.95 million, is cost-shared by the partners, with 50 per cent contributed by ACOA, 33 per cent contributed by the four Atlantic provinces and 17 per cent contributed by the four tourism industry associations in Atlantic Canada.

(Atlantic Canadian Tourism Partnership, 2012)

Another long-enduring tourism partnership has been among the six countries bordering on the Mekong River in Southeast Asia (Cambodia, China, Laos, Myanmar, Thailand and Vietnam). The Mekong Tourism Coordinating Office (MTCO) is located in Bangkok, Thailand and has two main goals: (1) to coordinate sustainable pro-poor tourism development projects in the Mekong in line with the United Nations Millennium Development Goals (tourism development); and (2) to promote the Mekong region as a single travel and tourism destination (tourism marketing).

A third example of a long-lasting destination partnership is Dallas Fort Worth and Beyond in the USA, also known as the Dallas Fort Worth Area Tourism Council (DFWATC) (2009). This organization was created in 1978 to market the entire Dallas/Fort Worth area as a single destination. One of the ingredients of the success of this partnership is its precise market focus.

The Dallas Fort Worth Area Tourism Council

Formed to jointly market the entire Dallas/Fort Worth area as a single destination, the Dallas/Fort Worth Area Tourism Council, a not-for-profit organization, has banded together all segments of the tourism industry. DFWATC represents over 40 cities and multiple counties in North Texas with more than 150 organizational members participating from area Convention and Visitors Bureaus, Chambers of Commerce, hotels, attractions, transportation, entertainment, tour operators, airlines, shopping centres, airports and restaurants. The Council focuses on the promotion of the DFW area as a leisure destination to a growing regional inbound market with heavy concentration on attracting visitors within a 500 mile radius.

Having looked at these three case studies from Canada, Southeast Asia and the USA, it can be seen that they share common ingredients. First, they have unanimous or at least widespread support from all the adjoining jurisdictions covered. Second, all partners share a desire to market and develop the entire destination as a whole. Third, the participants share a common interest, either in similar markets or in a similar style of tourism development.

It is also instructive to consider why destination partnerships fail; this alerts partnership planners on what to avoid or how to anticipate potential major problems. These include a lack of time and investment in the destination partnership; changes in priorities; insufficient communications; unrealistic timetables or time frames; unrealistic expectations of partnership benefits; and a lack of detailed partnership planning.

Destination partnership steps

A destination and its DMO should take a proactive approach to partnership-building rather than always waiting for others to invite them to join their collaborations. Planning of partnerships is needed just as much as it is for overall destination planning (Chapter 2), destination marketing and promotion (Chapter 3), destination research (Chapter 4) and destination product development (Chapter 5).

The following steps reflect this proactive stance on destination partnerships.

1 *Form a destination partnership planning team*: A team dedicated to partnership-building is put together consisting of DMO staff and tourism stakeholders. The composition of the team depends on the types of partnerships to be pursued.

2 *Review partnership needs and desired benefits*: The team identifies partnership needs across all the roles of destination management and attaches priorities to these roles and their respective needs. The benefits desired from specific partnership needs are articulated as well.

3 *Set partnership goals*: The team establishes goals, in quantitative terms if possible, for the priority partnership proposals.

4 *Identify potential partners*: The team searches for potential partners using a set of partner selection criteria that it has established.

5 *Prepare a draft written partnership proposal*: The team writes up a partnership proposal that is shared with potential partners.

6 *Appoint a partnership leader*: For each individual partnership, the team appoints a partnership leader.

7 *Commence discussions with most appropriate partners*: The team selects the most appropriate partners and begins discussions with them using the partnership proposal as an outline for the talks.

8 *Modify proposal as necessary and move toward consensus*: Several rounds of discussions may be required and the partnership proposal may need a few drafts. It is also possible that agreement may not be reached and the discussions are ended. However, assuming the talks remain positive, the team should work towards reaching a consensus with its potential partners.

9 *Prepare a contract or memorandum of understanding (MOU)*: A formal agreement is prepared specifying the duties and responsibilities of all parties involved in the destination partnership. The agreement includes rules about opting out of the partnership agreement and conditions that will lead to its dissolution.

10 *Appoint partnership leadership team*: After the signing of the agreement, all partners signing appoint a leader and a deputy leader from their respective teams.

11 *Evaluate the results of the partnership*: Periodically the results from the partnership against the goals and desired benefits are measured.

Destination team-building

Building partnerships with partners outside of the destination is a form of team-building and much has now been said about that in this chapter. However, team-building is also used by DMOs to build 'internal partnerships' within the destination and this is a demonstration of the leadership and coordination role. Figure 6.10 shows an old business saying about the essence and desired results of team-building exercises.

Team-building is a topic that is also discussed in Chapters 7 and 8 since it is related to community and stakeholder relationships, and destination governance. DMOs with a strong orientation toward community and stakeholder relationships are usually the most effective at team-building.

Teams can either be *ad hoc* (temporary and single-purpose) or more permanent. As an example of the first type of team, the Greater Des Moines Convention and Visitors Bureau in Iowa, USA set up a 'CVB Street Team' from January to April 2012. The five-person team was recruited to pass out flyers to people at festivals and events; attend some of the biggest festivals and events in Greater Des Moines to answer questions about what to do, where to eat, sleep and play, and how to get around; build the CVB brand; and update databases.

Another interesting example of team-building by a DMO, also from the USA, is the Seattle Convention and Visitors Bureau (SCVB) and its 'give back to the community' projects.

Figure 6.10 The essence and results of team-building
Source: Shutterstock, Inc. (bbbar).

Seattle CVB and Voluntourism teams

Seattle's Convention and Visitors Bureau (SCVB) recently teamed up with local non-profit organization Seattle Works to remove invasive species before planting 135 plants and trees in the West Duwamish Greenbelt, which has the largest remaining contiguous forest in the West Seattle neighborhood.

SCVB's 'Voluntourism' program was initially created for visiting clients and is part of a rising demand from convention and tour groups looking for ways to give back to the communities they visit. The program partner, Seattle Works, organizes these work projects for visiting groups.

(http://www.visitseattle.org/News-Room/Press-Releases/Convention-Trade-News/News/SCVB-Establishes-New-Community-Roots, 2 November 2011)

DMOs assemble different teams to handle specific tasks, as you can see from the two examples discussed above. Here are other specific team-building examples:

- *Advisory teams*: These are groups of tourism stakeholders who provide ongoing advice to DMOs and they may meet regularly.
- *Crisis management teams*: Teams that are formed either to plan for crisis situations that may occur in the destination or that are appointed to deal with specific crises that have actually occurred.
- *Festival and event teams*: Groups formed to plan or help out at festivals or events, including at business events.

- *Planning teams*: Again, usually these are teams of local stakeholders formed when the DMO and destination are preparing plans.
- *Research teams*: Groups that share an interest in tourism research, information and market trends for the destination. These people may be from hotels and attractions, as well as from the DMO, and they freely share information among themselves. Sometimes they are joined by academic researchers and people from market research firms.
- *Sales teams*: Teams of sales directors and managers from hotels, attractions, transport companies and other organizations. Sometimes these teams are used for 'sales blitzes' that are attempts to find new customers and tourists for the destinations.
- *Tourism advocacy teams*: Groups of people who assist the DMO in communicating about the positive economic and other benefits of tourism within the destination.
- *Tourism ambassador and welcoming teams*: This has been mentioned several times already. These are teams of local tourism stakeholders and residents that welcome guests and provide travel information and advice.

Summary

Destination partnerships are very popular in tourism and fit well with an economic sector that is so diverse. A destination partnership is a synergistic relationship between a DMO and other organizations or individuals within or outside of the destination.

The real power of destination partnerships is that they can be applied to all destination management roles and they are not exclusively for marketing and promotion. DMOs are discovering that when they recruit the help of others, more tends to get accomplished.

A wide assortment of benefits result from destination partnerships, including increasing budgets, sharing information, increasing pool of expertise, increasing market appeal, sharing facilities, better serving customer needs, accessing customer databases, accessing new markets, enhancing image and expanding social responsibility. DMOs have many potential partners in government, the private sector and among non-profit organizations and individuals with an interest in tourism.

Public–private partnerships in destination management have become more widespread as more destinations realize the synergies of combining government with private enterprise. There is a definite trend of more DMOs changing from being exclusively run by governments to being jointly administered by both the public and private sectors.

Although the potential benefits from destination partnerships are substantial, there are many barriers and challenges to setting up such cooperation and collaborations. Lack of adequate financial resources, communication problems, uneven benefit distribution and unwillingness to cooperate are just a few of the roadblocks to destination partnerships.

There are many types of destination partnerships across the world today. They last all the way from a single day to several years or decades. Cooperative promotions, customer care programmes, DMO organizational structures, event and festival sponsorships, product clubs, professional development/education/training, sponsored research, strategic marketing consortia, sustainable tourism initiatives, themed routes, tourism advocacy, and shared websites and social media are the main types of destination partnerships.

Successful destination partnerships tend to have certain common ingredients. They have widespread support from all partners who share the same or similar goals or interests. The partners want to focus on specific markets and see the wisdom of joining forces to appeal to these markets. They are willing to make an investment in each other and share information freely.

DMOs should be proactive in destination partnership building and there is a set of steps they should follow, including appointing partnership planning teams. It is best to put partnership agreements in writing and have all parties sign them.

Team-building is an important sub-role of destination management and DMOs are frequently called upon to assemble different teams within their communities. Teams are either short-term or long-term, and they are assembled to address specific issues or tasks that the DMO has in completing its destination management roles.

Partnerships and team-building are not exactly the same concepts, although they are very intertwined.

The specific steps for a DMO to accomplish its partnership and team-building role are to:

- Provide accurate information to tourism stakeholders about destination partnerships and build enthusiasm for partnering.
- Appoint a destination partnership planning team from DMO staff and tourism stakeholders.
- Pinpoint highest-priority partnering needs and the likely benefits that will result from addressing these needs through partnerships.
- Identify partnership opportunities by type and potential partners.
- Prepare destination partnership proposals for sharing with potential partners.
- Engage in discussions with potential partners and negotiate cooperative agreements.
- Prepare written agreements, either as contracts or MOUs.
- Participate in partnerships.
- Evaluate the results and benefits resulting from each destination partnership in which the DMO participates.
- Build teams within the destination to achieve specific tasks.
- Communicate and celebrate the positive results of destination partnerships and team activities.

Review questions

1 What are the definitions for destination partnership and destination team-building?
2 How should the terms 'synergy' and 'synergistic relationship' be interpreted in the context of destination management?
3 How does partnering help a DMO to accomplish all of its roles of destination management?
4 What is the relationship between destination governance and destination partnerships?
5 What are the benefits of destination partnerships?

6 Who are a DMO's potential partners?

7 How should a DMO identify potential partners?

8 Shared resources are often the bases for destination partnerships. What are some good examples of destinations forming partnerships when they share the same or similar resources?

9 Public–private partnerships (PPPs) are becoming more popular in destination management and marketing. What are the reasons behind this trend?

10 What are the major barriers and challenges to the formation of destination partnerships?

11 What are the types of destination partnerships available to DMOs?

12 What are the main ingredients of successful destination partnerships?

13 It is important for a destination and DMO to be proactive in planning for its destination partnership and team-building role. What steps should a DMO follow in destination partnership planning?

14 Which types of teams are frequently assembled by DMOs and what are their purposes?

15 What are the differences between partnerships and team-building, and how are they inter-related?

References

Absolute China Tours. 2011. The 21st Qingdao International Beer Festival. http://blog. absolutechinatours.com/index.php/2011-08-18/the-21st-qingdao-international-beer-festival/

Abu Dhabi Tourism Authority. 2012. Industry Development Department. http://www. abudhabitourism.ae/en/portal/tourism.professional.development.aspx

Amadeus North America. 2011. Spanish Government and Amadeus Collaborate to Implement Tourism Projects in Developing Countries. http://www.amadeus.com/us/x194133.html

Andaman Times. 2011. Thai–Malay collaboration. http://www.andamantimes.com/travel/thai-malay-collaboration/

APEC Secretariat. 2002. Public/Private Partnerships for Sustainable Tourism. Singapore: APEC.

Atlantic Canadian Tourism Partnership. 2012. Growing Tourism Together. http://www. actp-ptca.ca/

Austin Convention and Visitors Bureau. 2011. http://www.austintexas.org/

Australian Government. 2005. Achievement by Partnerships. Tourism Collaboration Intergovernmental Arrangement.

Baltic Sea Tourism Commission. 2007. What is BTC? http://www.balticsea.com/showpage.asp?pageid=1

Beritelli, P. 2011. Cooperation among prominent actors in a tourist destination. *Annals of Tourism Research*, 38(2), 607–629.

BestCities Global Alliance. 2012. http://www.bestcities.net/

Brown County Convention and Visitors Bureau (Indiana). 2012. Valued Visitor Program. http://www.browncounty.com/valued-visitor

Canary Island News. 2011. Tenerife Focuses on Wine Tourism in Collaboration with Swedish Travel Agency. http://news.canary-travels.com/2011/01/tenerife-focus-on-wine-tourism-in.html

Chua, T. 2011. Singapore Airlines Strengthens Collaboration with Tourism Queensland. http://sbr.com.sg/aviation/news/singapore-airlines-strengthens-collaboration-tourism-queensland

CIM Magazine. 2012. Sydney Airport and Destination NSW Partner to Boost Tourism. http://meetingsreview.com/news/view/76342

City of Chicago. 2012. ExploreChicago.org Offers Visitors & Residents '175 Ways to Love Chicago'. http://www.cityofchicago.org/content/city/en/depts/dca/provdrs/tourism/news/2012/jan/explorechicago_orgoffersvisitorsresidents175waysto lovechicago.html

Collaborations and Partnerships Issue Work Team. 2006. Michigan Strategic Tourism Plan: Collaboration and Partnership IWT Report to the Council.

Colorado Tourism Office. 2008. http://www.colorado.com

——2012. Tourism Ambassador Program. http://www.colorado.com/tourism-ambassador-program

CRC for Sustainable Tourism Pty Ltd. 2009. The Costs and Implications of Inter-Firm Collaboration in Remote Area Tourism.

Czech Tourism. 2010. European Quartet. http://www.european-quartet.com/Home.aspx

Dallas Fort Worth Area Tourism Council. 2009. http://www.dfwandbeyond.com/press_rooms/press-room/articles/welcome

Des Moines Convention and Visitors Bureau. 2012. CVB Street Team Opportunities. http://www.seedesmoines.com/learn_more/join_the_street_team.php

Destination Management Wales. 2010a. Create a Destination Partnership. http://www.dmwales.com/?q=content/create-destination-partnership

——2010b. Tourism Ambassadors. http://www.dmwales.com/?q=content/tourism-ambassadors

Destination Marketing Association International. 2012. New Performance Measures Established; Updated Handbook Available. http://www.destinationmarketing.org/page.asp?pid=155

Destination Melbourne. 2011. Melbourne Tourism Partnership. http://www.destination melbourne.com.au/industry/key-tourism-organisations/melbourne-tourism-partnership/

Destination NSW. 2011. Destination NSW and Jetset Travelworld Group (JTG) Partnership. http://archive.tourism.nsw.gov.au/JTG-Partnership_p5088.aspx

European Cities Marketing. 2012. European CityCards. http://www.europeancitycards.com/default.asp

European Quartet. 2012. http://www.european-quartet.com/Home.aspx

European Route of Industrial Heritage. 2012. http://www.erih.net/index.php

EuroSpaClub International. 2011. EuroSpaClub, Czech Tourism and Spa Week Daily Announce Collaboration. http://www.eurospaclub.com/eurospaclub-international-czechtourism-n-a-and-spa-week-media-group-are-partnering-to-cover-wellness-spas-of-czech-republic

Gomis, F.J.D.C., Lluch, D.L., Civera, J.M.S., Torres, A.M.A., Molla-Bauza, M.B., Poveda, A.M., de Los Rios, F.C., and Pedregal, A.M.N. 2010. Wine tourism product clubs as a way to increase wine added value: The case of Spain. *International Journal of Wine Research*, 2(2), 27–34.

Google, Inc. 2011. The Nevada Commission on Tourism uses Campaign Insights on the Google Display Network to measure performance beyond the click. https://docs.

google.com/a/google.com/viewer?url=http%3A%2F%2Fwww.google.com%2Fad
words%2Fdisplaynetwork%2Fpdfs%2FGDN_Case_Study_NCOT.pdf

Gordon, S. 2010. Che Guevara Tourist Trail to Follow his Life through Argentina, Cuba and Bolivia. http://www.dailymail.co.uk/travel/article-1282166/Che-Guevara-tourist-trail-Argentina-Cuba-Bolivia-follows-leaders-life.html

Hadrian's Wall Heritage Ltd. 2011. Reviewing the Past and Building the Future – Annual Review 2010–2011. http://www.hadrians-wall.org/

Hansen, M.T., and Nohria, N. 2004. How to build collaborative advantage. *MIT Sloan Management Review*, 46(1), 22–30.

Heng, J. 2012. ASEAN to Strengthen collaboration in cruise tourism. BIZ Daily. http://bizdaily.com.sg/newsite/asean-to-strengthen-collaboration-in-cruise-tourism/

Huxham, C. 1996. Creating Collaborative Advantage. Thousand Oaks, CA: Sage Publications.

Industry Canada. 2008. A New Era of Collaboration. http://www.ic.gc.ca/eic/site/dsib-tour.nsf/eng/qq00133.html

International Tourism Studies Association. 2011. The 2nd Jiuzhai Valley 'Smart Attractions' International Forum: Low Carbon Tourism and Mobility Management http://www.itsa.cn/article/conference/201101271885.shtml

Ioannides, D., Nielsen, P.A., and Billing, P. 2006. Transboundary collaboration in tourism: The case of the Bothnian Arc. *Tourism Geographies*, 8(2), 122–142.

Jamal, T.B., and Getz, D. 1995. Collaboration theory and community tourism planning. *Annals of Tourism Research*, 22(1), 186–204.

Kanter, R.M. 1994. Collaborative advantage: The art of alliances. *Harvard Business Review*, 72(4), 96–108.

Lane, B. 2004. Tourism Collaboration and Partnership: Politics, Practice and Sustainability. Clevedon: Channel View Publications.

Laws, E., Richins, H., Agrusa, J., and Scott, N. 2011. Tourist Destination Governance: Practice, Theory and Issues. Wallingford: CABI Publishing.

Lee, B.C., and Wicks, B. 2010. Podcasts for tourism marketing: University and DMO collaboration. *Journal of Hospitality, Leisure, Sport and Tourism Education*, 9(2), 102–114.

Malone, Givens, Parsons Ltd. 2011. Town of Drumheller Tourism Master Plan.

Malta Tourism Authority. 2010. Tourism Training and HR Development. http://www.mta.com.mt/training

Mekong Tourism Coordinating Office. 2012. http://mekongtourism.org/website/

Michigan Tourism Coalition. 2012. 2012 Governor's Awards for Innovative Tourism Collaboration Announced. http://www.mitourismcoalition.org/

Mynewsdesk. 2011. Singapore Tourism Board: Collaboration between CASE and STB Sends a Stronger Signal to Recalcitrant Retailers to Curb Unfair Trade Practices. http://www.mynewsdesk.com/sg/view/pressrelease/singapore-tourism-board-collaboration-between-case-stb-sends-a-stronger-signal-to-recalcitrant-retailers-to-curb-unfair-trade-practices-597801

Palmer, A., and Bejou, D. 1995. Tourism destination marketing alliances. *Annals of Tourism Research*, 22(3), 616–629.

Parker, S. 1999. Collaboration on tourism on tourism policy making: Environmental and commercial sustainability on Bonaire. *Journal of Sustainable Tourism*, 7(3/4), 240–259.

Partner Concepts LLC. 2011. Visit China and Korea. http://www.visitchinaandkorea.com/

People 1st. 2012. NI Hospitality and Tourism Ambassador Programme. http://www.people1st.co.uk/nations-and-skills-strategies/northern-ireland

Plummer, R., Kulczycki, C., and Stacey, C. 2006. How are we working together? A framework to assess collaborative arrangements in nature-based tourism. *Current Issues in Tourism*, 9(6), 499–515.

Rails-to-Trails Conservancy. 2007. http://www.railstotrails.org/index.html

Scandinavian Tourist Boards. 2012. Official Website of the Scandinavian Tourist Boards of North America. http://www.goscandinavia.com/usa/en-us/menu/scandinavia/go-scandinavia.htm

Selin, S., and Chavez, D. 1995. Developing an evolutionary tourism partnership model. *Annals of Tourism Research*, 22(4), 844–856.

Seoul Metropolitan Government. 2011.

Special Administrative Region of Macau. 2011. Administrative Regulation 40/2011: Council for Tourism Development.

The Travel Foundation. 2012. Cyprus. http://www.thetravelfoundation.org.uk/projects/destinations/cyprus/

Tourism Northern Territory. 2009. Cooperative Marketing. http://www.tourismnt.com.au/industry-resources/marketing-tool-kit/cooperative-marketing.aspx

Tourism South East. 2011. Welcome Host Gold. http://www.tourismsoutheast.com/training/welcome-host-gold

UNWTO. 2013. UNWTO Silk Road Programme. http://silkroad.unwto.org/en/content/objectives

UNWTO and European Travel Commission. 2011. Handbook on Tourism Product Development. Madrid, Spain, 5.

Vernon, J., Essex, S., Pinder, D., and Curry, K. 2005. Collaborative policymaking: Local sustainable projects. *Annals of Tourism Research*, 32(2), 325–345.

VisitEngland. 2012. Domestic Overnight Tourism (Great Britain Tourism Survey – GBTS). http://www.visitengland.org/insight-statistics/major-tourism-surveys/overnightvisitors/index.aspx

Whitaker, R. 2011. Jordan Tourism Launches Innovative Marketing Collaboration with Bloggers. http://travelllll.com/2011/12/12/jordan-tourism-launches-innovative-marketing-collaboration-with-bloggers/

Wong, E.P.Y., Mistilis, N., and Dwyer, L. 2011. A model of ASEAN cooperation in tourism. *Annals of Tourism Research*, 38(3), 882–899.

Xinhuanet.com. 2011. HK Tourism Board Team Up with Visa to Drive Summer Spending. http://news.xinhuanet.com/english2010/china/2011-06/03/c_13910142.htm

Zapata, M.J., and Hall, C.M. 2012. Public–private collaboration in the tourism sector: Balancing legitimacy and effectiveness in Spanish tourism partnerships. *Journal of Policy Research in Tourism, Leisure and Events*, 4(1), 61–83.

Chapter 7

Destination community and tourism stakeholder relations

Learning objectives

1 Explain the importance of community relations to destination management.

2 Describe the steps that a DMO follows to build and maintain positive relationships with local community residents.

3 Discuss the activities and initiatives included in a community relations plan.

4 Define the term stakeholder.

5 Identify and describe the tourism sector stakeholders in a destination.

6 Elaborate upon the activities that a DMO should use to maintain positive relationships with tourism sector stakeholders.

7 Discuss the reasons for having DMO membership programmes and the benefits that accrue to members and the DMO.

8 Explain how DMOs maintain good relations with boards of directors.

Introduction

Traditionally DMOs focused much of their attention on marketing and promotion, and these efforts were directed at people living outside of their own destinations. There was a tendency to neglect the people in the destination and especially local community residents. DMO leaders also believed that they would be judged mainly on the results of external marketing and promotions, so most emphasis was put there.

Things have changed now and if DMOs ignore local residents, they do so at their own peril. Community resident support of tourism is essential and this chapter explains why this is so. As the leaders and coordinators for the tourism sector, DMOs must also reach out and garner the broad support of their communities. One of the ways to accomplish this in a professional fashion is to prepare a community relations plan, and this chapter explains the types of activities that are included in such a plan for local community residents and tourism sector stakeholders.

Destinations contain a wide variety of stakeholders and these are groups and individuals that can affect or be affected by the outcomes of destination management. The tourism sector stakeholders are those directly involved with tourism. The DMO's relationships with tourism sector stakeholders in the community are vital to its effectiveness. The DMO must mould a strong destination tourism team from these stakeholders and have their complete support.

One of the overall themes that is dominant in this chapter is the need for ongoing communications with the local community and for actively involving local community residents and tourism sector stakeholders. Above all the DMO must recognize that it has external markets (tourists) and internal markets (residents and tourism sector stakeholders) to serve, and needs the support of both of them to be successful.

Community resident relations

The word 'community' is a very broad term and includes everyone who lives and works in the destination. However, for the purposes of this chapter, two specific groups are identified and discussed. Community residents are the people who permanently live in the destination; they may work in the tourism sector, but usually a majority of the residents are not involved in tourism. Also included are their elected representatives, community and interest groups, and non-tourism businesses. The second group is tourism sector stakeholders which, as defined in this chapter, includes public and private organizations and individuals that are directly involved with the tourism sector.

This chapter is all about 'relationship management' within the destination, and it begins with looking at the management of community resident relations. After that, tourism sector stakeholder relationship management is reviewed.

Importance of community relations

Dealing with community relations is one of the roles of destination management. As you heard in Chapter 1, DMOs need to have ongoing communications and interactions with their local communities. Local community residents must support tourism and fully comprehend tourism's economic contributions. This point was well highlighted in a study of twenty-five Canadian destinations by Bornhorst et al. (2010):

Importance of community relationship management

A compelling finding in this study for practitioners is the number of responses highlighting the importance of relationship management within the destination by the DMO. If DMO executives cannot effectively manage relationships within the destination, specific resource inputs (such as funding) from both the private and public sector may become impaired, thus threatening the very existence of the organization.

From their research results, Bornhorst *et al.* (2010) separately identified the success determinants of the DMO and the destination. They defined three sets of variables: (1) input variables (resources to the DMO; products to the destination); (2) process variables (marketing; community support; suppliers/other organization relations; and operations: management/services); and (3) performance variables (return on investment for DMO; visitor numbers; and visitor experience for the destination). Figure 7.1 shows the process variables and clearly highlights the influence of community relations on the success of both the DMO and the destination. So, in other words, the DMO needs community resident support, and tourism in the destination also requires the backing of community residents. You will also notice from Figure 7.1 that marketing is another determinant of both DMO and destination success.

For the DMO, there are two other success determinants: relationships with suppliers and other organizations, and operations (management/services). The first of these is

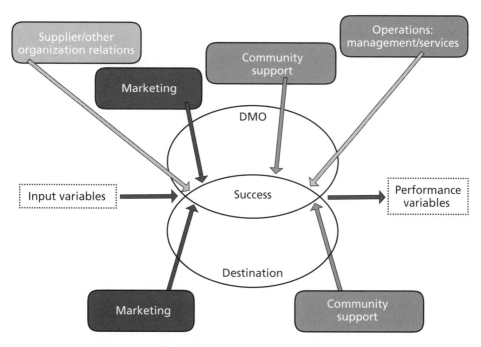

Figure 7.1 Determinants of DMO and destination success
Source: Adapted from Bornhorst, Ritchie and Sheehan, 2010.

what this chapter refers to as tourism sector stakeholder relations. The second is the operational activities of the DMO, which in the Canadian study were mainly marketing and management, and to a lesser extent service and product development.

You will remember from the discussion of the destination product and the destination mix in Chapters 1 and 5 that the feeling of welcome from local residents was viewed as being important to the success of tourism. If local residents do not support tourism or if their relationship with the DMO is not good, they may be unfriendly towards tourists. Again, it is recommended that DMOs be proactive in fulfilling this destination management role by planning ahead rather than waiting for opportunities to interact with the local community.

Having community support is the major desired outcome from the community relations role of destination management, but there is a longer list of reasons and potential benefits that result from building and maintaining closer relationships with community residents. This longer list includes the following:

- Residents are potential customers of the tourism sector.
- Residents interact and share local facilities and services with tourists.
- Residents can give tourists an unforgettable experience of welcome (and unfortunately the other way as well).
- Residents take their friends and relatives to local attractions, restaurants, shops and other tourism venues.
- Residents vote, so political leaders are concerned about their opinions.
- Residents write about their communities on paper and in blogs and micro-blogs. It is much better for tourism if they do so in a positive way.
- The local community is a labour pool for the tourism sector; if residents positively perceive tourism, they may be more willing to work in the sector.
- Tourists often ask local people for directions and advice on what to do and see, and where to eat in the community.

All of this discussion underscores the great importance of community relations to the DMO and the tourism sector in general. The next section, therefore, discusses how community relations should be planned.

Community relations planning

As mentioned in Chapter 1, several DMOs prepare annual community relations plans and an example was provided from the San Antonio Convention and Visitors Bureau in the USA. This is a very good idea and demonstrates a professional commitment by DMOs to engage with their communities. What specific activities should be included in a community relations plan? The following are eight priority activities that the planning should cover:

Analysing community residents' attitudes and perceptions

The DMO periodically needs to do research on community residents' perceptions of tourism within the destination. This was already previewed in Chapters 3 and 4 with research study examples from Hawaii, Huelva Province in Spain and Southwest England.

It is very important to determine how residents feel about tourism, and academic scholars have contributed many studies from different viewpoints since around the mid-1980s. Most of these studies have been about resident perceptions of the impacts of tourism. Liu *et al.*

(1987) considered resident perceptions of the environmental impacts of tourism, analysing case studies in Hawaii, North Wales and Istanbul, Turkey. They found that residents in all three cases were concerned about the negative environmental impacts of tourism. Besculides *et al.* (2002) examined resident perceptions of the cultural benefits of tourism in an area of southwestern Colorado. The researchers concluded that residents regarded tourism as a means of helping them learn about, share and preserve their culture. Andereck and Nyaupane (2011) explored the perceptions of Arizona residents about the impact of tourism on quality of life (QOL). It was concluded that the amount of contact residents have with tourists substantially influenced the perception of tourism's role in the economy.

Other research studies have determined residents' support for tourism. Perdue *et al.* (1990) surveyed the residents of sixteen rural communities in Colorado and found that residents were more likely to agree with the positive statements about tourism impacts than the negative ones. There were concerns, however, about increased tourism development contributing to traffic congestion and pushing up property taxes. Pérez and Nadal (2005) surveyed residents of the Balearic Islands of Spain and found that overall they acknowledged the positive economic benefits of tourism. They also recognized the cultural and social benefits of tourism, but to a much lesser degree. Residents perceived that tourism had negative impacts, including over-saturation of community services, traffic congestion and causing prices to inflate. Nunkoo and Ramkissoon (2011) conducted a resident survey in a resort community in Mauritius and found that the more residents perceived tourism as having positive impacts, the more they were likely to support tourism. If residents had negative perceptions, they were less likely to support the tourism sector.

This is just a small sample of the research on residents' attitudes and perceptions about tourism, and you will note that these were studies by tourism scholars rather than by DMOs. However, there seems to be some consensus forming from these research studies. Residents generally acknowledge that there are positives and negatives to tourism and if their overall assessment of tourism is positive, they will be supportive. Educating local residents about tourism and making them more aware of both the positive and negative impacts appears to be the best way forward for destinations and DMOs in the future.

Communicating with the local community

The DMO must find ways and open more channels to maintain an ongoing dialogue with the local community. Some DMOs do this by having their executives write columns about the tourism sector on a regular basis in local newspapers. For example, the chairman of Tourism Whitsundays in Australia writes a column every two weeks for the *Whitsunday Times*. Of course, you might think that is the old-fashioned way to communicate with many people and that it is now better and easier to write blogs or use popular micro-blogging sites like Twitter to get the message out. As a matter of fact, Tourism Whitsundays also uses Twitter and has its own Facebook page as well.

The most important part of this communications is simply telling local people about what the DMO has done and is doing. It cannot be assumed that every local resident knows about the DMO and fully comprehends what a DMO does. So raising the 'visibility' of the DMO needs to be a goal of local community communications. This point is very well reflected in the Industry and Community Relations section of the 'Destination Business Plan 2011–2012' of the Greenville Convention and Visitors Bureau in North Carolina, USA. You will especially note that the CVB plans to increase the local awareness of its activities and promotional role:

Industry and community relations, Greenville CVB

To advance our position in the growing regional tourism marketplace, we must continue to build strong relationships between the CVB and its Greenville and Upcountry hospitality partners. We must also engage local citizens, organizations and businesses to learn about, activate and support the vision of Greenville as a meeting and convention and leisure destination.

The desired outcomes of industry and community relations are to:

- Increase the understanding, among key stakeholders and community residents, of tourism's importance to Greenville for economic impact, contribution to the tax base and potential future economic growth.
- Increase the awareness of the CVB's activities and its role in promoting Greenville as a world-class destination for both meetings and conventions, and leisure travel.

Educating the community

It cannot be assumed that residents know what the tourism sector encompasses or how tourism benefits the community. Only those who work in the tourism sector and who have studied tourism management truly understand about tourism. It is not wrong to say that most uninformed people tend to underestimate the positive impacts of tourism. As a result, it is not only important to regularly communicate with local residents, but an ongoing effort to educate them about tourism is also needed.

There are many good examples around the world of DMOs developing materials and implementing programmes to educate their communities about tourism. In 2011, the Canadian Tourism Commission (CTC) released a new video, *Power of Tourism*, which was very effective in communicating the positive impacts of tourism on the Canadian economy.

Another good case study is from Barbados in the Caribbean and its 'Tourism Education, Awareness & Me' (TEAM) programme operated by the Ministry of Tourism. This is a multi-faceted programme including local television awareness promotions, a speak-off competition, school tourism awareness competitions, an environmental poster and essay competition, and other elements.

Tourism Education, Awareness & Me, Barbados

The aim of the TEAM programme is to sensitize and educate Barbadians to the important role tourism plays in the country as a whole and to demonstrate how Barbadians can become involved in the industry. The programme is divided into two components: (1) *awareness*: seeks to sensitize and educate Barbadians to the important role which tourism plays in Barbados' development; and (2) *training*: seeks to improve visitor/host relations through greater knowledge of and understanding about the hotel sector.

The Barbados programme includes elements that are directed at schools and children. Educating these young community residents is a very good idea as they are the community's future generations of adults. They will also absorb and remember what they learned about tourism in their schools.

Involving the community

DMOs find great benefit in involving the local resident community with tourism and especially by giving them 'samples' of what is on offer free of charge, or at a much reduced price for a short time. One example here is the Residents Festival in York, England. During a weekend, the residents of York are given free admission to local attractions and special discount rates at restaurants.

Residents Festival, York, England

York Residents Festival (28th and 29th Jan 2012) gives residents the opportunity to celebrate one of Europe's best loved cities – not only a popular destination for visitors, but also a great place to live. York Residents Festival is organised by Visit York, as a thank you to the residents of York for the warm welcome they give to York's seven million annual visitors and the support they show for the city's tourism industry.

During the festival residents will be able to gain free entry to a record number of the city's world class attractions and exhibitions as well as enjoying special rates at some of York's superb restaurants.

(Visit York, 2012)

Another set of great examples here are the 'Be a Tourist in Your Home Town' programmes that take place in selected cities in Canada and the USA. For example, in Lansing, Michigan, USA, for a $1 fee to purchase a 'passport', local residents get admission to over fifty attractions. The Louisville Convention and Visitors Bureau in Kentucky, USA, organizes a 'Hometown Tourist Celebration' during National Travel and Tourism Week in May each year (Figure 7.2). Discounts are offered at attractions, restaurants and hotels for all residents of Kentucky and Indiana during the week-long celebration.

These examples from York, Lansing and Louisville are community-wide programmes that are designed to get local people to try out local tourism attractions, restaurants and other destination facilities and services. In so doing and after having a first-hand experience, residents have a better and more accurate understanding of tourism in their hometowns. They are more likely to recommend places to friends, relatives and others if they have been there themselves. When they encounter visitors who ask them for advice, they are also in a much better position to say where to go and what to do.

A fourth outstanding case study is from VisitBritain and their VFR (visiting friends and relatives) campaign in 2012. The 'Share Your GREAT Britain' programme enlisted the help of residents of England, Wales and Scotland to invite their relatives and friends to come and visit. This is another form of 'resident recruitment' and works

Figure 7.2 The Hometown Tourist Celebration, Louisville, Kentucky, USA
Source: Courtesy of the Louisville Conventions and Visitors Bureau, 2012.

especially well at times when there are major events and celebrations; in this case, the 2012 Summer Olympic Games in London. The basic appeal of programmes like this is to have local residents make a special effort to invite VFRs during these unique and exciting time periods.

Share Your Great Britain (VisitBritain)

In January 2012 we launched the invitation from the British public element of our four-year, £100 million GREAT Britain marketing programme. The campaign aims to encourage UK businesses and the UK public to invite their friends, family and past customers based overseas to visit them in Britain during 2012.

We have developed a toolkit to help businesses leverage the campaign. The toolkit is a free resource and includes templates for print advertisements, e-newsletters, posters (Figure 7.3) and digital postcards, as well as images and a Facebook app through which you can invite people to visit your region of the United Kingdom.

(Visit Britain, 2012c)

Figure 7.3 Posters from the 'Share Your GREAT Britain' campaign from VisitBritain

Source: VisitBritain, 2012b.

'Homecoming Scotland' in 2009 was a similar type of programme that attracted an additional 95,000 visitors to Scotland that year. A second 'Homecoming Scotland' will be held in 2014 when Scotland plays host to the Commonwealth Games and the Ryder Cup (golf).

Listening to the community

The DMO should have open channels of communication to the community at all times, and not just when a formal research study of resident perceptions is being conducted. There are also certain key times at which listening becomes particularly important and strategic. When the destination is engaged in the preparation of a long-term plan for tourism this is one of these special occasions when the voices of community residents need to be heard, as was discussed in Chapter 2.

When major tourism development projects are being considered is another vital time to get community resident input. Residents may have concerns about the environmental, social and cultural impacts of projects, and these opinions should be gathered and included in the project assessment.

Lobbying for tourism

Interacting with the elected representatives of political parties and government officials is crucial for DMOs and for tourism in any destination. At least some part of this effort is called 'lobbying'; this means trying to influence or persuade public officials

229

to support, think or even vote in a certain way. Generally, for tourism these are attempts to convince politicians to be more supportive of the sector.

This can be accomplished in different ways, as can been seen from some examples. The Florida Association of Destination Marketing Organizations (FADMO) in the USA arranges a 'Florida Tourism Day' where DMO executives meet with state legislators in the state capital of Tallahassee and discuss the challenges that they are facing in tourism.

In some cases, DMOs will engage the services of professional lobbyists to assist them in gaining more influence on government legislators. These are specialized public relations professionals who have built strong relationships with politicians and the political parties in their communities. This is especially important when the DMO funding is coming mainly from government or when there are proposed changes to legislation that will significantly affect DMO operations or tourism in the destination.

Recruiting community support

Various types of partnering with community residents and community groups were discussed in Chapters 5 and 6, including local ambassador programmes in Bermuda and Wales. Another example is the City of Melbourne in Australia that has a 'Tourism Volunteer Program' and recruits 'City Ambassadors' and volunteers for two visitor information centres (VICs). The requirements for volunteering are the following:

- Passionate about Melbourne
- Customer service focused
- Computer literate
- Available for one four-hour shift (either morning or afternoon) each week for a minimum of 1 year
- Team players who love engaging with people
- Flexible and willing to assist with additional shifts when needed
- Keen to demonstrate a commitment to the City of Melbourne's values
- Ability to speak a language or languages other than English is also desirable
- Extensive training programme and ongoing support and development is provided.

These volunteer programmes are aimed at individual residents, but there are other efforts that address local communities as a whole. These efforts are often implemented to focus community attention on service quality or the hospitality levels in the destination. The goal is to raise overall community awareness and support for an initiative.

For example, the 'Faces of Aspen/Snowmass Guest Service Initiative' is a community-wide programme to raise service quality and the feeling of welcome in these resort areas in Colorado:

Faces of Aspen/Snowmass Guest Service Initiative, Colorado, USA

In 2006 the Aspen Chamber Resort Association and the Town of Snowmass Village developed a community wide Guest Service Initiative, the FACES of ASPEN/SNOWMASS. The name of the program reflects not only our local population and our visitors, but also of our year round recreation and cultural activities. Since the program's inception, one thing has become loud and clear: we all relish our roles as hosts in this unique and stunning Colorado playground.

Along with the unbelievable scenery and terrain, there's a genuine, conspicuous vibe in our community to collectively make visitors feel at home. It's a natural advantage for us as resorts, and a key reason why Aspen and Snowmass are such highly adored destinations.

(Aspen Chamber of Commerce, 2012)

Representing tourism in the destination

DMOs must be champions and the cheerleaders for tourism in their destinations. This is a demonstration of the leadership and coordination role of destination management. The DMO must be the official representative of tourism in the community and assume all the duties that this involves.

As mentioned above, the first part of this role is to continuously educate the local community about the positive impacts of tourism. A second part is being a team leader for the tourism stakeholders within the destination and keeping their enthusiasm for tourism always at a high level. The third part is to be a defender or protector of tourism, when the sector is the subject of unfair or ill-informed criticism.

Gretzel *et al.* (2006) organized a forum of DMO executives in the USA to discuss the future challenges facing DMOs. One of the conclusions from this forum was that DMOs must establish themselves as 'local experts, the "go-to" people, or the information clearing house' for tourism in their communities. DMOs also should be perceived as valuable partners when major development projects were being contemplated locally. These are attributes of a leader and key representative of an economic sector in a community, and a DMO must have these attributes.

Figure 7.4 summarizes the eight priority activities that go into community relations planning for destination management, and it is called the 'community resident engagement wheel'. As you learned at the outset of this chapter, community resident relations is a new endeavour for many DMOs, but it is now crucial that they get fully involved and view this role as being just as important as destination marketing and promotion.

With the intensity of competition for tourist markets, DMOs are under increasing pressure to show excellent performance in completing their destination marketing and promotion role. So in reality, it is difficult for DMOs to devote time and energy to local community relations, as there is constant pressure and stress to deal with external marketing. This has implications for DMO staffing as steps must be taken to ensure that community relations activities are not neglected. Some DMOs deal with this by appointing specific staff members to coordinate and monitor the implementation of the community relations plan. Some DMOs go even further and have a separate division or department to look after community relations, like the San Antonio Convention and Visitors Bureau in Texas.

Figure 7.4 The community resident engagement wheel for destination management

San Antonio CVB Community Relations and Strategic Initiatives Division

The Community Relations and Strategic Initiatives Division coordinates with partners, public agencies and business interests in an effort to be engaged and central to the issues and developments that have an impact to the visitor experience and hospitality industry. The division also oversees the San Antonio Convention and Visitors Bureau's (CVB) local media and partner communications, positioning its key staff as the central force in one of the city's most important economic generators.

Division staff will serve as resources to key city projects that further the interest and goals of the hospitality and tourism industry. The division will also act as an advocate for the hospitality and tourism industry, representing the industry and coordinating with appropriate stakeholders to ensure representation. The Community Relations Division will coordinate with the CVB's Marketing, Sales and Communications staff to communicate CVB results, activities and opportunities in an effort to facilitate participation and inclusion.

(San Antonio Convention and Visitors Bureau, 2010)

Tourism sector stakeholder relations

Chapter 1 identified five groups of stakeholders in tourism management: tourists, tourism sector organizations, community, environment and government. This chapter has already discussed the community and government groups, and tourists will be covered in later chapters. The chapter now focuses on tourism sector stakeholder organizations, and it begins with a discussion of stakeholder theory and then an identification of the different types of stakeholders that can be found within destinations.

Stakeholders and stakeholder theory

Since this chapter is talking about stakeholders, you might want to know what exactly stakeholder means and what the basic theory is behind the concept of stakeholders. This concept of stakeholders has its origins in organizational theory and corporate management. It is attributed to R. Edward Freeman and his book, *Strategic Management: A Stakeholder Approach* (1984). Freeman's definition of a stakeholder was 'any group or individual that can affect, or is affected by the achievement of a corporation's purpose'. In the case of this book, 'corporation' needs to be replaced by 'DMO'. Freeman's basic argument was that there were many more groups and individuals that had a 'stake' in corporations than just its employees and shareholders. This is certainly very true of tourism and destination management, as there are many groups and individuals involved, and many groups and individuals are affected by tourism within a destination.

For stakeholder theory as applied to corporations, Donaldson and Preston (1995) identified eight stakeholder groups: investors, customers, suppliers, employees, communities, trade associations, governments and political groups. All of these groups exist in a destination, although the DMO itself does not have the same types of investors as does a corporation. However, those providing the DMO with its funding can be considered the equivalent of investors.

There have been many academic papers written about stakeholder theory and some practitioner books as well. Sheehan and Ritchie (2005) point out, based on a review of these articles, that 'all are not equal' among an organization's stakeholders. This means that some stakeholders are more important than others; and therefore DMOs need to prioritize stakeholders within the destination. In a study of 91 CVB executives in North America, Sheehan and Ritchie (2005) found that hotels and hotel associations were considered to be the most important stakeholder group. After them, city/local governments were the next most important, and after that regional/county governments and attractions/attraction associations.

There have been various types of management strategy suggested for different groups of stakeholders. Savage *et al.* (1991) suggested a classification of stakeholders based upon their potential to cooperate and potential to threaten the organization:

- *Collaborative*: stakeholders with high potential to cooperate and with high potential to threaten.
- *Involvement*: stakeholders with high potential to cooperate and low potential to threaten.
- *Defensive*: stakeholders with high potential to threaten and low potential to cooperate.
- *Monitoring*: stakeholders with low potential to threaten and low potential to cooperate.

Sheehan and Ritchie (2005) suggested that DMOs would prefer to follow collaborative and involvement strategies with stakeholders. This means that DMOs tend to want to focus on organizations and individuals that have a high potential for cooperation; and not to engage with those where there is a low potential to cooperate.

Tourism sector stakeholder types

Figure 1.9 in Chapter 1 showed seven tourism sector organizations (DMOs, hospitality, attractions, transport, travel trade, media and employee organizations). For the purposes of this chapter, the focus is on tourism sector stakeholders within the local community and there will be an expansion of some of the categories listed in Figure 1.9.

Figure 7.5 shows the main tourism sector stakeholder types, not including governmental agencies, utility companies, banks/financial institutions, non-tourism business associations, educational institutions and non-profit organizations.

A brief description of each of these eight local tourism sector stakeholder groups is provided below:

- *Attractions*: Natural and human-made attractions. These can be private-sector operations, or run by government agencies or non-profit organizations.
- *Events and festivals*: The organizers of significant events and festivals held regularly in the local community. Once more, these may be private-sector operations, or run by government agencies or non-profit organizations.
- *Convention and meeting venues*: Convention and exhibition centres.
- *Hotels and other accommodations*: Hotels, resorts and specialist accommodations.
- *Restaurants and other food services*: Restaurants, banquet halls, catering companies, etc.
- *Transport*: Motor coach, taxi, ferry, train and other transport companies.
- *Travel trade*: DMCs, travel agencies, tour operators, guides, meeting planners, etc.
- *Media*: Newspapers, magazines, TV and radio stations, online media, etc.

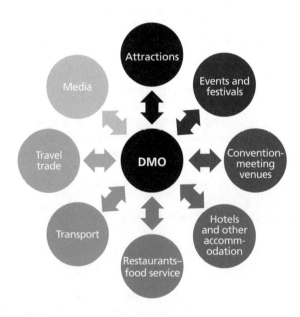

Figure 7.5 Local tourism sector stakeholders

There may be local trade associations formed representing some or all of these sub-sectors of tourism. For example, there could be associations for hotels, restaurant and food services, or attractions. These are also included under the definition of local tourism sector stakeholders.

Some DMOs, and especially those that operate at a geographic level below a state, province or territory, have membership programmes that are optional for tourism sector stakeholders. This is especially the case at city, county and regional levels (that are not governmentally-administered regions). So this in many cases introduces two distinct categories of local tourism sector stakeholders for the DMO: members and non-members.

Another layer of complexity is introduced in stakeholder relationships if the DMO has a board of directors or an advisory board or committee of some type. These two concepts are not the same, as a board of directors governs the DMO, but an advisory board/committee is there to provide advice and does not have direct power over the DMO and its executives. DMOs with boards of directors are becoming more common around the world but they are particularly found in certain countries and the USA is one of these. According to Ford *et al.* (2011), more than 93 per cent of CVBs in the USA have a governance structure that includes a board of directors.

For DMOs with boards of directors those stakeholders on the board are especially important. Additionally, it is reasonable to expect that members will be given a higher priority than non-members. You will hear much more about this later.

The sources of financial support for DMOs vary from country to country and sometimes by province and state as well. If the DMO is government-run and gets all its funding from government then all local tourism sector stakeholders should have equal priority. There are other situations in which DMOs are mainly funded through user-pay taxes, most commonly through taxes on rooms and entertainment. This may or may not influence these DMOs to give greater attention to the sources of the tax revenues (e.g. hotels, casinos, restaurants, etc.).

Relationships with tourism sector stakeholders

DMOs are transitioning from being just destination marketing organizations to becoming destination management organizations. Part of this new 'management' responsibility is the relationship management for tourism sector stakeholders, and DMOs need to hone their skills in building and maintaining these contacts. Once again, it is much better for the DMO to approach this in a professional way and prepare a plan for how it will handle these relationships in the period ahead. So, another part of the community relations plan should be devoted to tourism sector stakeholders and a range of specific activities should be included. In several instances, these activities are similar to those for community residents.

Analysing stakeholders' opinions: The DMO should periodically gauge the sentiments of stakeholders about the current status of the tourism sector, and major issues and challenges that they face in the future. One outstanding example of this activity is the 'Tourism Barometer' survey conducted by Fáilte Ireland (2012) (Figure 7.6). Through an online survey, Fáilte Ireland gathered information from tourism stakeholders about their operating performance in the past year and their opinions on future prospects for the year ahead. In November and December 2011, 709 responses to the survey were received.

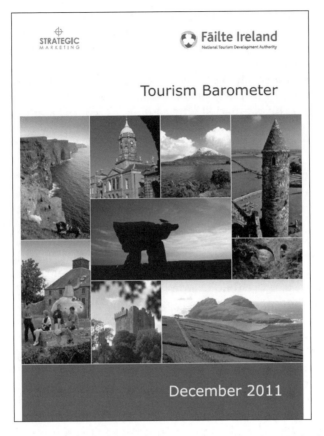

Figure 7.6 Fáilte Ireland's Tourism Barometer survey of stakeholders
Source: Fáilte Ireland, 2012.

A second example is from Tourism Northern Territory in Australia (2011). Tourism NT surveys operators online four times per year:

Tourism Northern Territory online poll of tourism operators

Tourism NT (Northern Territory) conducts an online poll every three months to provide a timely gauge for the health of the tourism industry. Information sought from tourism operators in the Northern Territory includes visitation levels for the quarter just completed compared with the same period in the previous year and an outlook for the next twelve months.

Operator views are also collected on the issues they feel are currently affecting the tourism industry and can provide an important insight into the current market environment. The poll results also assist with validation, collaboration and insight for the national surveys conducted by Tourism Research Australia.

The information gathered from research on stakeholders is valuable for the DMO in gauging stakeholders' feelings and sentiments about the current conditions and future prospects for the tourism sector. This is also useful in tracking recent trends occurring in local tourism. It can be an 'early warning system' for the DMO about emerging problems and issues in tourism. Moreover, it demonstrates to tourism sector stakeholders that the DMO highly values their opinions and input.

Celebrating successes with stakeholders: It is important that the DMO and tourism sector stakeholders together celebrate the successes and success stories of tourism within their destinations. This builds a sense of pride and excitement, and reinforces the feelings of belonging to a vital sector of the economy.

One of the most popular types of activities that DMOs implement to achieve this purpose is tourism awards programmes. Almost every destination in the world has these types of awards programmes, so it is difficult to pick out specific examples. The Tourism Authority of Thailand (TAT) has run such a programme every 2 years since 1996; it is used to reward best practices in the Thai tourism sector and to encourage tourism operators to strive for higher levels of professional standards. In 2012, the selection criteria stressed environmentally-friendly tourism products and creative marketing campaigns, particularly via social media. The awards are given in six categories: (1) tourism attractions; (2) tourism development and promotion organizations; (3) tourist accommodation; (4) health tourism; (5) domestic tour packages; and (6) international tour packages. TAT also uses the awards programme for promotional purposes and feels that it increases the credibility of Thai tourism among domestic and international visitors.

Communicating with stakeholders: The DMO must constantly keep in touch with tourism sector stakeholders and therefore needs to find the right channels to do so. Websites now are one of the most popular ways to communicate with stakeholders, but the social media and printed materials like newsletters are also used. Some DMOs create members-only sections of their websites; while others have separate, dedicated websites for tourism sector stakeholders.

Many DMOs have decided to save trees and go paperless with e-newsletters and this also helps increase the reach of the DMO 'news'. And by also asking website visitors to sign up to receive e-newsletters, DMOs are able to build larger databases.

Another more formal way to ensure ongoing communications is by setting up advisory boards, councils or committees that give frequent input to DMOs and destinations. For example, a Tourism Advisory Council (TAC) was established in Prince Edward Island, Canada in 2004. The TAC has fourteen tourism sector stakeholders and five ex-officio senior provincial and federal government members and staff. TAC's role is to advise the Minister of Tourism on marketing, product development and research initiatives, with the goal of increasing tourism revenues for PEI.

A second example is from Byron Shire Council in New South Wales, Australia where a Tourism Advisory Committee has been set up. This is an advisory committee of the Council and does not have executive power or authority to implement actions. The Committee has several purposes, but one of these is to advise on 'the sustainable development, marketing and management of tourism, including events and other cultural initiatives, representing the interests of both the tourism industry and resident communities across the Shire, with regard for the social, environmental and economic benefit of the Byron Shire community'. (Byron Shire Council Tourism Advisory Committee, 2012)

A third case study is the Tourism Advisory Council of the Arizona Office of Tourism in the USA. The Council has fifteen members who are appointed by the Governor for terms of five years. It has representatives from recreational and tourist attractions, lodging, restaurant or food and transportation industries, as well as other tourism businesses and the general public. The Council assists and advises the Director of the Arizona Office of Tourism in preparing the budget and establishing policies and programmes which promote and develop tourism for Arizona.

Informing: Providing relevant information and data to tourism sector stakeholders encourages more professional and better informed decision-making. Once again, DMO websites are one of the best tools since much information can be placed there and accessed at the convenience of tourism sector stakeholders. The following example from Ontario is a good demonstration of sharing information with stakeholders in Bruce, Grey and Simcoe Counties (Figure 7.7).

Involving: Chapter 6 discussed the team-building activities of DMOs, and one of the main goals of these efforts is to involve tourism sector stakeholders and create a greater sense of teamwork. The following eight types of teams were identified: advisory, crisis management, festival and event, planning, research, sales, tourism advocacy and tourism ambassador and welcoming teams.

Another way to get tourism sector stakeholders involved with DMOs is to invite them to be members or partners. The Newport Beach, California example that follows is an example of a partner programme and tourism stakeholders can join the programme free of charge:

Figure 7.7 Stakeholder website of RTO7 in Ontario, Canada
Source: Regional Tourism Organization 7, 2012.

Visit Newport Beach Partnership Program

Visit Newport Beach Inc. is the driving force behind marketing Newport Beach as a destination for leisure travelers, as well as meetings and conferences. This quintessential Southern California vacation retreat has grown to include Corona del Mar, Balboa Island, Newport Coast, San Joaquin Hills and Balboa Peninsula. We take great pride in our partnerships with the community, as we cannot sell the destination alone! Our partners range from hotel and resort properties, restaurants, and attractions to real estate agencies and event planners – while all can benefit from the rewards of the 6.9 million visitors that come to Newport Beach on average each year.

(Visit Newport Beach, Inc., 2010)

Leading and coordinating: Leadership and coordination is one of the roles of destination management. One of the sub-roles is for the DMO to be a coordinator of groups and individuals within the destination, including tourism sector stakeholders. Then what is a coordinator and what does coordination involve? For the purposes of this book, the following definition of coordination is used:

Destination coordination

The coordinator convinces groups and individuals to work together harmoniously and in an organized way for achieving specific goals or objectives. Mainly this involves the DMO working as the coordinator of tourism sector stakeholders.

Earlier in this chapter, the example was given of the Florida Association of Destination Marketing Associations organizing a 'Tourism Day' where DMO executives together went for discussions with state law makers. This is a good example of coordination. Another example of coordination by DMOs is when they work with tourism stakeholders in arranging familiarization tours for the travel trade and media within the destination.

Many DMOs have convention or business events services departments that coordinate the logistics for events with tourism stakeholders and others. In addition, as mentioned in Chapter 6, DMOs coordinate cooperative marketing efforts of different types. Some DMOs coordinate festivals and events in their communities.

What about leading and leadership, then? This is a topic that is discussed in more detail in Chapter 8 but, of course, it can be said now that there are many facets of leadership. Undoubtedly, DMOs and their executives need to be accepted as leaders by tourism sector stakeholders and must therefore earn the respect of many people. Apart from requiring personal charisma, DMOs need to be visionary and strategic in their thinking and planning in order to be viewed as leaders. The leadership role will also be reinforced if DMOs are successful in gathering all the resources they need to operate successfully and if they can prove that these resources have been used effectively.

Listening: Just as with community residents, DMOs must always keep the channels of communication open for listening to stakeholders' suggestions, issues and concerns. Some DMOs and their executives make a point of regularly visiting tourism stakeholders at their offices or places of business to hear stakeholders' ideas and also share the latest news about the DMOs' activities and successes. This is an excellent way of demonstrating that the DMO is actively listening to stakeholders.

Representing: The DMO is the most important representative for all the tourism sector stakeholders in a destination. The stakeholders may also belong to trade associations, but the DMO is the only body that represents tourism as a whole. For example, the DMO can periodically present the tourism sector's most pressing issues to leaders in government to ensure that these government officials are aware of the issues and will consider taking steps to deal with them. The US Travel Association did this in February 2012 when it presented the following nine issues and recommendations to President Obama and his government:

- Improving the visa process
- Expanding the Visa Waiver Program
- Supporting international travel promotion
- Improving the entry experience at international airports
- Increasing youth and student travel to the US
- Improving the air travel screening and security process
- Accelerating travel-related infrastructure projects
- Boosting visitation at national parks
- Improving capabilities to assist economic recovery following disasters.

Figure 7.8 summarizes the eight most important activities in the relationship management with tourism sector stakeholders.

As mentioned earlier in this chapter, there are two groups among tourism stakeholders that often take on special importance for DMOs and these are members and boards of directors.

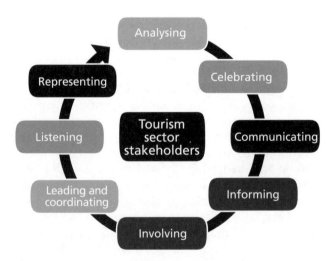

Figure 7.8 Tourism sector stakeholder engagement

Relations with members

Many DMOs operate membership programmes so the relationships with members require special attention. Membership fees are normally charged, so the members represent a source of income. However, membership programmes seldom, if ever, represent a major source of funding for DMOs. More important for the DMO is the 'bonding' that is formed with members and the members' support for the organization and its programmes and activities. The general appeal in getting tourism stakeholders to join is to work together with the DMO to grow the tourism sector in the destination. The following is a good example of this from the Cincinnati USA Convention and Visitors Bureau in Ohio, USA:

'Cincinnati USA CVB Membership Pays Off'

The Cincinnati USA Convention and Visitors Bureau is comprised of nearly 500 businesses that realize the economic importance of meetings and conventions in Greater Cincinnati. These businesses, the CVB's members and partners, support the CVB's mission to positively impact Cincinnati USA's economy through convention and trade show expenditures and to provide quality service to our clients.

An investment in the CVB is an important contribution to the economic growth of the region. By investing in our future, you are investing in your own future. No matter what the size of your organization, we have a membership that is just right for you.

(Cincinnati USA Convention and Visitors Bureau, 2012)

However, DMOs must offer members other more meaningful and significant benefits to entice them to join. Generally, these benefits are business-oriented and fall under the heading of marketing and promotion. The sharing of 'sales leads' for potential business events is a typical benefit offered by city-based DMOs. The following is a more comprehensive set of typical member benefits:

- *Access to research findings*: Chapter 4 discussed the various types of research that DMOs conduct. Sometimes DMOs limit the access to the findings to members, or offer reduced prices for purchasing reports or data by members while non-members have to pay significantly more.
- *Education and professional development*: Chapter 5 explained the types of educational and professional development programmes being organized by DMOs and gave several examples. Normally, DMO members are allowed to participate in these programmes free of charge or at reduced rates.
- *Familiarization tour participation*: DMOs frequently organize trips for travel trade and media people to sample the destination. It is very advantageous for a tourism operation to get exposure on these tours. Members are normally given preference for inclusion in familiarization tour itineraries.
- *Leads and referrals*: Members receive leads and referrals from DMOs for meeting planners and travel trade professionals who have shown an interest in the destination.

- *Media exposure assistance*: DMOs often help their members to get publicity in the media.
- *Networking*: Meeting and getting to know other members and DMO staff is a significant benefit since many tourism stakeholders need to work together to get business or solve problems of mutual interest.
- *Publication listings and descriptions*: DMOs produce several publications each year and members are listed in these free of charge. These typically include visitor guides, meeting planner guides, calendars of events, etc.
- *Receipt of DMO materials*: Members receive supplies of DMO publications, as well as getting the DMO's own newsletter.
- *VIC information distribution*: Members can have their printed materials displayed and distributed at visitor information centres operated by DMOs.
- *Website listings and description*: DMOs often list and describe the members on their official tourism websites and this gives members outstanding online exposure.

A number of events are organized by DMOs to which members are invited. These range from monthly business meetings to more elaborate tourism awards ceremonies and banquets. The ten benefits offered by the New Orleans Convention and Visitors Bureau in Louisiana, USA provide a good actual example:

- *Networking*: NOCVB has over 1,000 members and members have access to upcoming meetings and conventions 18 months into the future.
- *Convention markets*: Connects members to convention and leisure markets through different types of marketing and advertising opportunities.
- *Website listings*: A complimentary hyperlink from the official website that has 200,000 unique visitors per month (www.neworleanscvb.com).
- *Strong marketing partner*: NOCVB is the only organization that markets New Orleans at regional, national and international trade shows.
- *Brochure distribution*: Free distribution of brochures at the Welcome Center.
- *Membership team*: Access to seminars and a regularly updated convention calendar.
- *Return on investment*: Reaching potential visitors for one year at only the weekly cost of a newspaper advertisement.
- *Free publication listings*: Free listings in *Visitors Guide*, *Meeting Planners Guide* and *Travel Planners Guide*.
- *Leads*: NOCVB sends out sales leads from convention and leisure markets to members.
- *Members-only tools*: NOCVB operates an Extranet to which only members have access. There members have access to meeting planners in town, posting coupons to reach specific audiences, industry research, confidential convention schedules, etc.

As you can see from these descriptions of benefits, they are mainly related to marketing and promotion, and specifically in assisting tourism sector stakeholders with their sales efforts and in gaining more exposure and awareness. Networking with other DMO members is another major benefit offered by most DMOs.

DMOs may have different membership categories and member benefits may vary according to category. This is usually done in a classification by tourism sector stakeholder type, but there are other approaches that accord to the scope of the benefits that a member desires. An interesting example here is from Central Coast Tourism Inc. in New South Wales, Australia. This DMO has six membership categories and charges according to the target market that a member wants to address (Figure 7.9). The six membership

Figure 7.9 Central Coast Tourism and membership categories and benefits
Source: Central Coast Tourism Inc., NSW, Australia, 2012.

categories are: social, local, regional, national, international and corporate. In 2012 the fees ranged from AUD 60 for a social membership to AUD 12,000 for a corporate membership.

The support of members is crucial to all DMOs that have membership programmes and so continuously delivering meaningful member benefits is the key. As with all membership organizations, it is often very hard work to retain members year after year, and DMOs must continue to deliver high value and maintain frequent member communications if they want to stay relevant.

Relations with boards of directors

It can be said that without doubt the stakeholders on boards of directors take on great significance for DMOs and their executives, since boards often have direct power over the DMOs and their executives. Boards of directors are explained in greater detail in Chapter 8 since they directly affect destination governance. However, in this chapter you will learn about some of the basic characteristics of boards and their relationships with DMOs.

Board composition

The way that DMO boards of directors are created varies greatly across the world, so it is difficult to generalize about their composition. The main differences lie in the legal status of the DMO. Boards range from ones in which all the members are selected according to a strict procedure set by government (over which the DMO has little control) to situations where the DMO can select a majority of board members subject to certain conditions.

For example, if the DMO is a part of a private business association such as a chamber of commerce, it has much freedom to select board members. The example of this shown below is from Billings, Montana, USA.

Billings, Montana qualifications for board members

The Billings Chamber of Commerce/Convention and Visitors Bureau adds members to its board of directors annually. The board consists of no more than 19 voting board members and no less than 15 along with four non-voting ex-officio members. Terms for voting members are one, 3-year term with eligibility to serve two terms if reelected.

Board members will be chosen from individuals within the organization who have exhibited a desire to serve, coupled with a past history of supporting the organization through committee activity or other means. They should be highly motivated individuals and community leaders committed to the furtherance of Chamber/CVB objectives. Criteria generally are a balance of gender, industry types and geographic and socio-graphic categories.

(Billings Chamber of Commerce/Convention and Visitors Bureau, 2012)

The board of VisitBritain is at the other end of the spectrum with all its members being appointed by specific government agencies in the UK. The board includes the chairman of VisitBritain; five members appointed by the Secretary of State for Culture, Media and Sport; one member appointed by the Welsh Assembly; two ex-officio (non-voting) members who are the chairmen of VisitEngland and VisitScotland; and an observer from the Northern Ireland Tourist Board.

Another example of an externally-appointed board is for Tourism Australia. There is a Tourism Australia Board Charter that spells out all of the rules and policies for the board. In this case, the federal minister responsible for tourism appoints eight of the members of this nine-person board and the ninth member is the managing director of Tourism Australia.

VisitBritain and Tourism Australia are statutory bodies that were established by special pieces of legislation in the UK and Australia respectively. In these situations, the DMO itself has little, if any, control over board composition.

Board member recruitment and selection

From what has just been said, you can see that some DMOs can choose board members, while others have to accept boards that others, typically governments, select. So for the first group of DMOs, board member recruitment and selection is a very important issue.

According to Ford et al. (2011), many DMOs in North America and especially in the USA are non-profit organizations and they should recruit board members who can help the DMO access important resources and provide specific types of expertise. As mentioned earlier, the DMO must also determine which stakeholder groups are the most important (or salient) and ensure that these stakeholder groups are represented on the board of directors. For example, where DMOs are being funded through user taxes that are collected and distributed by local governments, it is important to have local government representation on boards. As Sheehan and Ritchie (2005) found, it is very helpful to have representatives from hotels and hotel associations and attractions and attraction associations, as DMOs work very closely with these tourism sector stakeholders.

Board orientation

Preparing board members for their tasks through proper orientation needs to be given a high priority. Again, it cannot be assumed that all people understand what DMOs do and what their priorities are. Board member orientations should cover topics including the destination and DMO vision, DMO mission, DMO business and marketing plan, expectations of board members, and board code of conduct.

Board member motivation

Unlike corporate boards, the boards of directors of many DMOs are unpaid and essentially are volunteering their time and services. This is an important consideration in the DMO-board relationship as the DMO must find non-financial means to motivate and reward volunteer board members. This is one of the biggest challenges for DMOs and especially those that are non-profit organizations that are not statutory bodies. Nowadays people have so many demands on their time and it is difficult to motivate them when there is no monetary compensation. The responsibility for board member motivation falls mainly to DMO executives, and success depends on the strength and quality of the relationships that executives build and maintain with board members.

Board member conduct

Board members make decisions that involve the use of the DMO's resources. Therefore, it is common for DMOs to have codes of conduct and stated policies regarding conflicts of interest that the board must follow. Tourism Australia (2012) provides an example of such a code of conduct that sets out how board members must behave.

Tourism Australia Board Members' Code Of Conduct

a) A board member must act honestly, in good faith and in the best interests of the Board and Tourism Australia as a whole.
b) A board member has a duty to use due care and diligence in fulfilling the functions of office and exercising the powers attached to that office.
c) A board member must use the powers of office for a proper purpose, in the best interests of Tourism Australia as a whole.
d) A board member must not allow personal interests, or the interests of any associated person, to conflict with the interests of Tourism Australia. A board member must advise the Board when there is a conflict of interest with a matter being discussed by the Board and the Board is to decide whether the board member is to contribute to the discussion or whether he or she should be excused from the meeting for the duration of the discussion.

e) A board member has an obligation to be independent in judgement and actions and to take all reasonable steps to be satisfied as to the soundness of all decisions taken by the Board.

f) Confidential information received by a board member in the course of the exercise of his or her duties remains the property of the entity from which it was obtained and it is improper to disclose it, or allow it to be disclosed, unless that disclosure has been authorised by that entity, or the person from whom the information is provided, or is required by law.

g) A board member should not engage in conduct likely to bring discredit upon Tourism Australia.

h) A board member has an obligation, at all times, to comply with the spirit, as well as the letter, of the law and with the principles of this Code of Conduct.

i) A board member must act in accordance with the provisions relating to directors of the Corporations Act 2001.

Board size and members' terms of office

Boards of directors vary in size from under ten to thirty or more. As you saw above, VisitBritain has a board of nine people (seven voting and two non-voting) and Tourism Australia also has a nine-person board; but the Billings, Montana DMO had up to nineteen board members. In reality, it is hard to recommend an ideal size for a board and indeed there are two contradictory considerations. The board of directors needs to be small enough to make decision-making more convenient and easier to coordinate. However, the board has to be large enough to represent all the tourism stakeholders within the destination. As a general rule, boards with twenty or more people are difficult to manage and coordinate; while boards of less than ten people are unlikely to represent all of the tourism stakeholders within the destination. In actual practice, most boards of directors have between ten and nineteen members.

The terms of office of board members are another important consideration for DMOs. Generally, appointments to DMO boards are for two or three years, and may be renewable for one additional term. Most DMOs with boards have a member rotation pattern such that there is an overlap in lengths of term so that there is more continuity. In other words, they try to avoid situations where board members are all new at the same time.

Board performance assessment

Boards need to assess their overall performance each year to ensure that they are achieving their purposes. In addition, the performance of every individual board member should be assessed and feedback provided to them.

In their excellent article about non-profit CVB boards, Ford *et al.* (2011) suggested five basic propositions:

- *Proposition 1*: A non-profit board that has directors representing critical or key stakeholder groups will be more successful than one that is less representative.
- *Proposition 2*: Non-profits that take the time and effort to ensure proper board composition, size and term of office will be more effective than those that are less successful.

- *Proposition 3*: More successful non-profits executives are more likely to provide a formal orientation programme for board members than those who are less successful.
- *Proposition 4*: Providing the rewards that motivate each board member will increase the likelihood that the board member will be more engaged in the activities and mission of the organization.
- *Proposition 5*: Boards and board members whose performances are evaluated annually will be more effective in helping a CVB to understand its future selection needs more than performance that is evaluated less often.

As you can see, DMOs need to give special attention to the needs of their members and boards of directors. It is especially critical that DMOs have the support of these two groups of stakeholders from within their communities.

Summary

Community relations are becoming a more important role of destination management, as DMOs increasingly recognize that they must have the support of local community residents and tourism sector stakeholders. This is putting much more pressure on DMOs not only to perform at a high level in external markets, but also to be outstanding at building and maintaining relationships at home.

It is highly recommended that a DMO prepares an annual community relations plan that details how it proposes to interact with local community residents and tourism sector stakeholders. The portion of the community relations plan dedicated to local community residents should cover at least eight potential activities: analysing, communicating, educating, involving, listening, lobbying (government), recruiting and representing.

Destination stakeholders can be defined as any group or individual that can affect, or is affected by the achievement of the DMO's goals and objectives and by the results of the tourism sector in general. So these stakeholders include community residents and the tourism sector itself. The tourism sector stakeholders include attractions, events and festivals, convention and meeting venues, hotels and other accommodations, restaurants and other food services, transport, travel trade and media.

The portion of the community relations plan dedicated to tourism sector stakeholders should encompass eight activities; analysing, celebrating, communicating, informing, involving, leading and coordinating, listening and representing.

Many DMOs operate membership programmes and they must ensure that members receive meaningful benefits for joining and continuously renewing their membership. Most of the member benefits provided by DMOs relate to the marketing and promotion of members' businesses.

Boards of directors play an extremely important role for many DMOs around the world. The relationships between board members and the DMO can directly affect the DMO's effectiveness and credibility within the destination. The key issues and considerations relative to DMOs include board composition; board member recruitment, selection, orientation and motivation; codes of conduct and conflict of interest guidelines; board size and member terms of office; and board performance assessment.

The specific steps a DMO must take in order to accomplish its community relations role are to:

- Prepare an annual community relations plan.
- Champion tourism and build excitement and enthusiasm for the sector within the destination, especially among tourism sector stakeholders.
- Communicate regularly and openly with community residents and tourism sector stakeholders.
- Convince tourism stakeholders to work together harmoniously and in an organized way to achieve the destination's goals and objectives.
- Educate local community residents to better understand tourism and its positive and negative effects.
- If applicable, provide meaningful benefits to DMO members and maintain frequent communications with members.
- Invite the active participation and involvement of community residents and tourism sector stakeholders in the programmes and activities of the DMO.
- Lobby with people in government to ensure that tourism receives an adequate share of resources.
- Provide information and data to tourism sector stakeholders to allow them to operate more professionally and profitably.
- If applicable, recruit, select, orient, motivate and assess board members.
- Represent tourism within the destination in all matters that are likely to have a significant impact on the sector.

Review questions

1 Why are community relations efforts important to destination management?
2 How do community residents influence the success of tourism in a destination?
3 What types of actions and initiatives should be included in a community relations plan for local residents?
4 How is the term 'stakeholder' defined?
5 What are the different strategies available for managing relationships with stakeholders?
6 Who are the tourism sector stakeholders within the destination?
7 What types of actions and initiatives should be included in a community relations plan for tourism sector stakeholders?
8 How can a DMO determine which stakeholders are the most important?
9 What are the benefits to DMOs and their members from operating membership programmes?
10 For DMOs with membership programmes, what types of benefits are provided to members?
11 What are the most important issues and considerations for the relationship between boards of directors and DMOs?
12 Why does a DMO need to establish a code of conduct for board members?

References

Andereck, K.L., Valentine, K.M., Knopf, R.C., and Vogt, C.A. 2005. Residents' perceptions of community tourism impacts. *Annals of Tourism Research*, 32(4), 1056–1076.

Andereck, K.L., and Nyaupane, G.P. 2011. Exploring the nature of tourism and quality of life perceptions among residents. *Journal of Travel Research*, 50(3), 248–260.

Ap, J. 1992. Residents' perceptions of tourism impacts. *Annals of Tourism Research*, 19(4), 665–690.

Arizona Office of Tourism. 2012. Tourism Advisory Council. http://azot.gov/aot-executive-office/tourism-advisory-council

Aspen Chamber of Commerce. 2012. Guest Services Program – Faces of Aspen. http://www.aspenchamber.org/aspen-community/guest-service-initiative/

Besculides, A., Lee, M.E., and McCormick, P.J. 2002. Residents' perceptions of the cultural benefits of tourism. *Annals of Tourism Research*, 29(2), 303–319.

Billings Chamber of Commerce/Convention and Visitors Bureau. 2012. TBID Stakeholders. http://www.visitbillings.com/+bid.php

Bornhorst, T., Ritchie, J.R.B., and Sheehan, L. 2010. Determinants of tourism success for DMOs and destinations: An empirical examination of stakeholders' perspectives. *Tourism Management*, 31(5), 572–589.

Byron Shire Council Tourism Advisory Committee. 2012. http://www.byron.nsw.gov.au/committees/tourism-advisory-committee

Caribbean Tourism Organization. 2008. Competing with the Best. Good Practices in Tourism Awareness Programmes.

Central Coast Tourism Inc. 2012. Membership. http://www.visitcentralcoast.com.au/membership

Cincinnati USA Convention and Visitors Bureau. 2012. Cincinnati USA CVB Membership Pays Off. http://www.cincyusa.com/members/

City of Melbourne. 2012. Tourism Volunteer Program. http://www.melbourne.vic.gov.au/CommunityServices/CommunityFacilities/Pages/VolunteeringTourismMelb.aspx

Dallas Convention and Visitors Bureau. 2012. Dallas CVB Objectives. http://www.visitdallas.com/visitors/about_dallas/dallas_cvb/objectives

Donaldson, T., and Preston, L.E. 1995. The stakeholder theory of the modern corporation: Concepts, evidence and implications. *Academy of Management Review*, 20(1), 65–91.

Dyer, P., Gursoy, D., Sharma, B., and Carter, J. 2007. Structural modeling of resident perspectives of tourism and associated development on the Sunshine Coast, Australia. *Tourism Management*, 28(2), 409–422.

Fáilte Ireland. 2012. Tourism Barometer. http://www.failteireland.ie/Tourism-Barometer

Florida Association of Destination Marketing Associations. 2011. 2012 Florida Tourism Day. http://www.fadmo.org/event/id/177495/2012-Florida-Tourism-Day.htm

Ford, R.C., Gresock, A.R., and Peeper, W.C. 2011. Board composition and CVB effectiveness: Engaging stakeholders that can matter. *Tourism Review*, 66(4), 4–17.

Freeman, R.E. 1984. Strategic Management: A Stakeholder Approach. Boston: Pitman.

Government of Barbados. 2011. Tourism Education, Awareness, & Me (T.E.A.M). http://www.tourism.gov.bb/tourism-education-awareness-me-t.e.a.m.html

Greater Lansing Convention and Visitors Bureau. 2011. Be a Tourist in Your Own Town. http://www.lansing.org/events/batyot/

Greenville Convention and Visitors Bureau. Destination Business Plan, July 2011–June 2012.

Gretzel, U., Fesenmaier, D.F., Formica, S., and O'Leary, J.T. 2006. Searching for the future: Challenges faced by destination marketing organizations. *Journal of Travel Research*, 45(2), 116–126.

Industry Canada. 2011. Power of Tourism. http://www.ic.gc.ca/eic/site/ich-epi.nsf/eng/02176.html

Jawahar, I.M., and McLaughlin, G.L. 2001. Toward a descriptive stakeholder theory: An organizational life cycle approach. *Academy of Management Review*, 26(3), 397–414.

Johnson, J.D., Snepenger, D.J., and Akis, S. 1994. Residents' perceptions of tourism development. *Annals of Tourism Research*, 21(3), 629–642.

Jurowski, C., Uysal, M., and Williams, D.R. 1997. A theoretical analysis of host community resident reactions to tourism. *Journal of Travel Research*, 36(2), 3–11.

Liu, J.C., Sheldon, P.J., and Var, T. 1987. Resident perception of the environmental impacts of tourism. *Annals of Tourism Research*, 14(1), 17–37.

Louisville Convention and Visitors Bureau. 2012. Hometown Tourist Celebration. http://www.gotolouisville.com/hometown-tourist-celebration/index.aspx

Martins, C., and Martins, C. 2011. Selling Tourism to the Local Community. http://www.insights.org.uk/articleitem.aspx?title=Selling+Tourism+to+the+Local+Community

Mitchell, R.K., and Agle, B.R. 1997. Toward a theory of stakeholder identification and salience: Defining the principle of who and what really counts. *Academy of Management Review*, 22(4), 853–886.

New Orleans Convention and Visitors Bureau. 2012. Top 10 Reasons to Join the CVB. http://www.neworleanscvb.com/membership/benefits/top-ten-reasons/

Nunkoo, R., and Ramkissoon, H. 2011. Residents' satisfaction with community attributes and support for tourism. *Journal of Hospitality and Tourism Research*, 35(2), 171–190.

Perdue, R.R., Long, P.T., and Allen, L. 1990. Resident support for tourism development. *Annals of Tourism Research*, 17(4), 586–599.

Pérez, E.A., and Nadal, J.R. 2005. Host community perceptions: A cluster analysis. *Annals of Tourism Research*, 32(4), 925–941.

Regional Tourism Organization 7 (RTO7). 2012. RTO7 Stakeholder Site. http://rto7data.ca/Default.aspx

San Antonio Convention and Visitors Bureau. 2010. 2011 Business Development Plan. Community Relations and Strategic Initiatives.

Savage, G., Nix, T., Whitehead, C., and Blair, J. 1991. Strategies for assessing and managing organizational stakeholders. *Academy of Management Executives*, 5(2), 51–75.

Scottish Government. 2010. Second Homecoming in 2014. http://www.scotland.gov.uk/News/Releases/2010/05/25113855

Sheehan, L., and Ritchie, J.R.B. 2005. Destination stakeholders: Exploring identity and salience. *Annals of Tourism Research*, 32(3), 711–734.

Sheehan, L., Ritchie, J.R.B., and Hudson, S. 2007. The destination promotion triad: Understanding asymmetric stakeholder interdependencies among the city, hotels, and DMO. *Journal of Travel Research*, 46(1), 64–74.

Simpson, M.C. 2008. Community benefit tourism initiatives: A conceptual oxymoron? *Tourism Management*, 29(1), 1–18.

Tourism Advisory Council of Prince Edward Island. About TAC. http://www.peitac.com/

Tourism Australia. 2011. Tourism Australia Board Charter.

——2012. Our Board. http://www.tourism.australia.com/en-au/aboutus/our-board.aspx

Tourism Authority of Thailand. The 8th Thailand Tourism Awards 2010. http://tourismawards.tourismthailand.org/home.php

Tourism Northern Territory. 2011. Tourism Industry Sentiment Poll. http://www.tourismnt.com.au/Portals/3/docs/research/Online Poll_SeptQtr11 (2).pdf

Tourism Whitsundays. 2012. Whitsundays Tourism Industry. http://www.tourismwhitsundays.com.au/business-centre/whitsundays-tourism-industry/

US Travel Association. 2012. US Travel Industry Submits Input for National Travel and Tourism Strategy. http://www.ustravel.org/news/press-releases/us-travel-industry-submits-input-national-travel-and-tourism-strategy

Visit Newport Beach, Inc. 2010. Industry Partners. http://visitnewportbeach.com/industry-partners/

Visit York. 2012. Residents Festival 2012. VFR and Marketing Toolkit. http://www.visityork.org/seeanddo/residentsfestival.aspx

VisitBritain. 2012a. Our Board. http://www.visitbritain.org/aboutus/ourboard/index.aspx

——2012b. Posters. http://www.visitbritain.org/opportunitiesadvice/getinvolved/posters.aspx

——2012c. VFR and Marketing Toolkit. http://www.visitbritain.org/opportunitiesadvice/getinvolved/vfrtoolkit.aspx

Williams, J., and Lawson, R. 2001. Community issues and resident opinions of tourism. *Annals of Tourism Research*, 28(2), 269–290.

Chapter 8

Destination governance and leadership

Learning objectives

1 Define the term destination governance and identify the dimensions of governance.

2 Describe accountability and the actions required of a DMO to demonstrate it is accountable.

3 Explain the concept of transparency and how this applies to a DMO.

4 Identify the ways in which DMOs can measure the effectiveness of their operations.

5 Explain how DMO organizational structures are related to destination governance.

6 Define by-laws and how they affect destination governance.

7 Review how the chairs of boards of directors can be influential in DMO governance.

8 Discuss the different funding mechanisms and sources available for DMOs.

9 Identify and review the types of risk to which DMOs and destinations are exposed and how they should handle risk management.

10 Identify and explain the major leadership roles of DMOs.

11 Elaborate on how DMOs and their executives can demonstrate different leadership styles within their destinations.

Introduction

Leadership and coordination is one of the roles of destination management. Chapter 7 introduced and defined the topic of coordination in the context of community and stakeholder relations. This chapter reviews destination management leadership and the closely associated concept of governance.

Like partnerships, destination governance has become a 'hot topic' recently and especially among tourism academics. Two prominent academic journals (*Journal of Sustainable Tourism* and *Tourism Review*) had special issues on tourism governance in 2011and 2010 respectively. An edited book, *Tourism Destination Governance: Practice, Theory and Issues,* was published in 2011 (Laws *et al.*, 2011). However, reading some of this recent literature can be a little confusing, as people tend to use the word 'governance' in different ways.

In this chapter, a practical approach to destination governance is described that covers the key dimensions. Particular attention is given to the two related dimensions of accountability and transparency. Demonstrating effectiveness by setting and measuring results is another dimension of destination governance and guidelines on doing this are provided.

Structure and power are also dimensions of destination governance and so this chapter discusses DMO organizational structures, funding levels and funding mechanisms. Details are provided about the operation of boards of directors and the functions of by-laws are discussed.

The major leadership roles of DMOs are identified. Destination leadership styles are reviewed and particularly the servant leadership concept that seems to fit well with destination management.

Definition of destination governance

What is destination governance and how does the concept relate to the role of a DMO? If you look it up in a dictionary, it will be described as the act of governing. You might then ask, is that not what governments do? Yes, of course, governments do govern, but now the concept is much broader and includes corporate governance and non-profit organization governance. Chapter 1 already supplied one definition of governance by Beritelli *et al.* (2007) as being 'setting and developing rules and mechanisms for a policy, as well as business strategies, by involving all the institutions and individuals'. Another definition of governance from UNESCAP (United Nations Economic and Social Commission for Asia and the Pacific) (2012) is shown below and it emphasizes how decisions are made and implemented.

UNESCAP identified eight characteristics of good governance and these are shown in Figure 8.1. It should be noted that these are broad characteristics of good governance and were not intended to specifically reflect the governance of DMOs. Accountability and transparency are discussed in detail later, but the other six characteristics require a short description of how they can be applied to DMOs:

- *Responsive*: The DMO and its processes respond to stakeholders within a reasonable time.

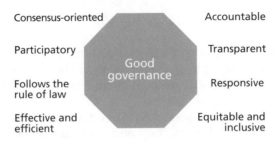

Figure 8.1 Characteristics of good governance
Source: UNESCAP, 2012.

UNESCAP definition of governance

The concept of 'governance' is not new. It is as old as human civilization. Simply put 'governance' means: the process of decision-making and the process by which decisions are implemented (or not implemented). Governance can be used in several contexts such as corporate governance, international governance, national governance and local governance.

- *Equitable and inclusive*: All groups of stakeholders have an input to the DMO's policies, plans, strategies, programmes and activities. The DMO does not deliberately exclude any stakeholder group from its operations and communications.
- *Effective and efficient*: The DMO sets and meets its goals and objectives. It is not wasteful in its use of resources. The DMO has internal controls to manage and monitor how resources are used.
- *Follows the rule of law*: The DMO follows all the applicable laws and has no discriminatory practices.
- *Participatory*: Every stakeholder group and type of individual has an equal opportunity to participate in the activities of the DMO.
- *Consensus-oriented*: The DMO works to coordinate all of the tourism stakeholders in the destination and builds consensus on the most important tourism issues and opportunities.

Based on these materials, the following definition of destination governance is used in this book. The main focus of the definition is on who administers the DMO and how it is administered, and on the accountability and transparency that is demonstrated by the DMO in its operations.

Definition of destination governance

Destination governance is how a DMO is administered and who does the administering. Governance involves the policies, systems and processes to ensure that all stakeholders are involved and that the DMO is accountable for its results and resource usage and has a high level of transparency.

Dimensions of governance

A review of the literature on governance by Ruhanen *et al.* (2010) revealed six most frequently identified dimensions of this concept, and these are shown in Figure 8.2.

Accountability and transparency were the most frequently identified dimensions, followed in order by involvement, structure, effectiveness and power. Involvement is similar to the concept of an organization being participatory in the UNESCAP model of good governance; while effectiveness is found in both Figures 8.1 and 8.2. The structure and power dimensions were not included in the UNESCAP model.

The following description of corporate governance at Tourism Australia (2011) also highlights accountability, performance effectiveness and efficiency, and open communications. However, another dimension of destination governance is identified that does not appear in Figures 8.1 and 8.2. This is the management of risk, and this is certainly an important issue for an organization involved with tourism. This includes the reduction of risk through crisis management planning, as well as protection from potential litigation against the DMO and from fraud and the misappropriation of funds.

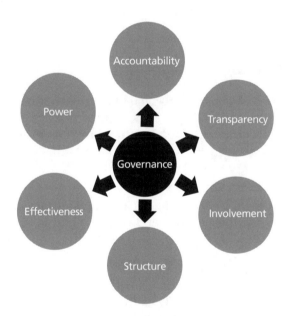

Figure 8.2 Most frequently encountered dimensions of governance
Source: Adapted from Ruhanen *et al.*, 2010.

Corporate governance at Tourism Australia

Tourism Australia is committed to implementing best practice in matters of corporate governance, and to ensuring accountability, integrity, transparency and efficiency are reflected in its day-to-day operations. Tourism Australia places a strong emphasis on the importance of these values by ensuring:

- There is a focus on project planning and performance monitoring of key projects and contracts in line with best practice
- There is open communication with the Australian Government, Minister for Tourism and regulatory bodies
- There are sound risk management policies and procedures in place.

DMO accountability

Accountability is one of the core dimensions of destination governance and DMOs are increasingly being held accountable for their activities and use of resources. It is not a new concept in destination management, having been discussed since at least 1990 by academic scholars including Perdue and Pitegoff (1990). However, the scope of the accountability concept has expanded from just destination marketing and promotion to now include all aspects of destination management and all DMO activities. It is best to start with a definition of accountability as it applies to a DMO.

Definition of DMO accountability

The obligation of a destination management organization (DMO) to justify and account for its programmes and activities; and to accept responsibility for results. The DMO must disclose these results in a transparent manner and take responsibility for the use of all resources with which it has been entrusted.

This definition places the obligation on DMOs to account for what they do and take the full responsibility for their actions and results. You can see that the following actions are required of the DMO to prove accountability:

Justifying programmes and activities: The DMO must explain why it is proposing to implement specific programmes and activities for an upcoming cycle of business operations. This means that the DMO has to reveal its assumptions and facts based upon research that has been completed. Typically this is accomplished by preparing plans for each of the destination management roles and then making presentations of these in different ways, sometimes through public meetings.

Measuring results from programme and activity implementation: The DMO must first specify the results it intends to achieve from particular programmes and activities. Here is where the DMO uses KRAs (key result areas) and KPIs (key performance indicators), which were discussed earlier in Chapter 3. The DMO must then measure the results from the implementation of the programmes and activities.

Disclosing results: The DMO cannot keep the results secret but must disclose them in the way that it is required by its legal constitution. If the DMO is governmental, it may be subject to 'open public records' and thus any resident can request to see all of its records. Many developed countries have enacted freedom of information (FOI) laws that apply to national, state, provincial and territorial government agencies and give the public access to documents, data and other information from governments.

Disclosure is related to the concept of transparency that is discussed in this chapter as another dimension of destination governance. By disclosing details of its decision-making and other information, a DMO is also demonstrating its transparency.

Accepting responsibility for results: The DMO must take full responsibility for the actual results of particular programmes and activities. If the results that the DMO expected were not achieved, the DMO must explain why it did not perform up to the standard that it set for itself.

Assuming responsibility for resource use: The DMO must account for its use of all resources and especially for the budget that was consumed. The accounting for the use of funding is done through the preparation of audited financial statements. Many DMOs produce annual reports that provide an overall summary of results, as well as looking ahead to future operating cycles.

Maintaining and measuring accountability are other topics that are of great significance for destination management. Some DMOs maintain accountability by developing internal control systems including setting up internal audit departments or having an audit committee. For example, the Hong Kong Tourism Board (HKTB) has an Audit Committee that checks the adequacy of internal controls and effectiveness and efficiency of HKTB operations.

Audit Committee of Hong Kong Tourism Board

This committee provides advice to the Board on adequacy of internal controls and the effectiveness and efficiency of HKTB operations, and is authorised to investigate any activities within its terms of reference. It reviews and endorses the annual audit plan to ensure adequate audit coverage of critical operations, reviews major findings, recommendations and the implementation of actions arising from internal audit and other relevant authorities. It also reviews the annual audited financial statements before submission to the Board. The committee meets three times a year, and extraordinary meetings can be convened if necessary. It comprises a chairman and four Members from the Board, with the Chief Internal Auditor acting as Committee Secretary.

(Hong Kong Tourism Board, 2010)

Measuring accountability may be done periodically by having an independent audit carried out on the DMO. Normally these independent audits are done by consultants with vast experience in the operations of DMOs. These types of audits are often quite critical of DMOs and traumatic for senior executives. One audit conducted in 2006 in the USA found that over $1.5 million had been misappropriated from the DMO. Another US audit found that the DMO was not sufficiently involving stakeholders and especially the local government.

DMO transparency

Another dimension of destination governance is that there must be transparency to the DMO and its operations. In everyday use, transparent means an object that you can see through. However, in a business context transparency means openness in operations and communications. In other words, tourism stakeholders in the destination should be able to see what the DMO is doing and understand its decision-making. Being transparent is the opposite of keeping business matters hidden and secret. The following is an example of how VisitBritain demonstrates its transparency.

Transparency at VisitBritain

The Government's vision for democratic accountability through the publication of data held by Central and Local Government Departments will enable the public to hold politicians and public bodies to account. VisitBritain, as a Non-Departmental Public Body funded by the Department for Culture, Media and Sport provides transparency data on financial spend and senior staff as well as links to other sources of information.

- Board minutes and committees
- Organograms and salary bands (organograms are organizational diagrams or charts)
- Publication of spend over £25,000
- Corporate policies

(Visit Britain, 2012)

As you can see, the accountability and transparency dimensions of destination governance are closely linked. For a DMO to be accountable, it must practise transparency. The DMO must show how it has used money and other resources, and must reveal its results. What specifically must a DMO do to be a transparent organization? The following are some of the key steps required for DMO transparency:

- *Holding public meetings*: One of the ways to demonstrate openness is to hold public meetings at which the DMO reveals its past results and planned programmes and activities. A good example of this is the annual press conference organized each year by the Macau Government Tourist Office (MGTO). Several hundred people attend this event to hear about MGTO's future priorities and plans.
- *Making financial results available*: Budgets and financial statements are made available. Many DMOs do this by publishing an annual report that contains the financial data; others make budgets and financial statements available on their websites.
- *Providing records from meetings*: Agendas and minutes are kept for all formal meetings and are available for perusal. Some DMOs open their board meetings to the general public and this enhances transparency.
- *Publishing all policies, plans and strategies*: This means that such documents must be located in a place for all to view. Many DMOs accomplish this by making documents available for download on their websites.

- *Revealing DMO salary information*: Salary levels are often a contentious issue with DMOs, especially those at senior management levels. To be transparent, DMOs should make salary information available.

A good example of such transparency is the Las Vegas Convention and Visitors Authority (LVCVA) in the USA. On its business website, LVCVA provides a wide range of information and data that demonstrates its transparency. Board of directors' meeting agendas and minutes are available for reading and downloading. The mission and purpose of LVCVA are provided and so is a detailed description of the organization, its 14-person board, and operating departments. LVCVA explains its purchasing policies and information on the status of bids it has authorized. Very detailed financial information is provided on the website, including a financial status report, comprehensive annual financial reports, popular annual financial reports, annual budgets and quarterly budgets and statistical reports. The salary bands for all staff are published in these financial materials.

Transparency on the travel expenses of DMO staff members is a consideration as well, since these expenses often cause controversy. Some DMOs 'open the books' on these travel expenses and Tourism New Zealand is one of them. It makes all of the travel expenses of its chief executive available for viewing on its corporate website. The Canadian Tourism Commission makes public the total value of the travel and hospitality expenses of all its senior officers.

Accountability and transparency are two complementary dimensions of governance, and rather like two sides of the same coin. There can be no doubt that DMOs will be the subject of more intense scrutiny in the future, so learning more about being accountable and transparent is a must for them.

DMO organizational structures, boards and by-laws

This book's definition of destination governance states that it is how a DMO is administered and who does the administering. More specifically, it is about how decisions are made by the DMO and who makes them. Therefore, the way that the DMO is organized and the 'checks and balances' that are built into DMO policies, systems and procedures have a major impact on destination governance.

Power and influence

Figure 8.2 identified structure and power as two other dimensions of governance. How a DMO is structured and how it makes important decisions are the most important issues here. Power is a concept that comes more from political science and political governance, but it is also an important issue for corporate governance. For example, if a DMO is a separate tourism ministry and has a high level of funding, it has more power and influence than if tourism is just one of several units within a ministry and its budget is low.

If tourism is the major economic sector within a destination, it is likely that its DMO will have more power and influence. For example, in places like the Bahamas and the Maldives where tourism predominates, you would expect their DMOs to have strength and influence. However, these types of situations are unique and rather rare on a worldwide basis. Most economies are quite diversified and normally tourism represents only a small proportion of GDP.

It also needs to be remembered from Chapter 1 that DMOs do not have direct control over the products in the destination that they are representing, so they need to collaborate with tourism sector stakeholders and 'borrow power' from this association with tourism operators and other supporting organizations.

Organizational structures

How DMOs are organized is fundamental to their governance. There is a huge variety of organizational structures for DMOs around the world and there is certainly not one template for how to organize these specialized entities. DMOs range from government-operated tourism ministries or departments to ones that are purely private-sector funded and sometimes through business associations. There are considerable variations in structures from country to country, and based upon the unique legislation in individual jurisdictions.

According to the UNWTO and the European Travel Commission, national tourism organizations (NTOs) in the developing countries tend to be 100 per cent funded by government and be part of government. In developed countries, NTOs tend to be public–private partnerships (PPPs) with a combination of public- and private-sector governance.

The Macau Government Tourist Office (MGTO) is an example of a government-operated DMO, and its organization chart is shown in Figure 8.3. MGTO is a unit under the Secretariat for Social Affairs and Culture of the Macau Special Administration Region Government. It has a director, two deputy directors, seven departments and twelve divisions. The departments and divisions are organized by functions and roles. For example, there is a Destination Marketing Department (marketing and promotion) and a Tourism Product and Events Department (product development). The Communication and External Relations Department handles relations within the Macau community and externally. Since this is a purely governmental unit, it does not have a board of directors, but is under the direct administration of the Secretariat.

Tourism Queensland (TQ) is a state-level DMO in Australia and provides another type of structural model. TQ is a statutory body created with the Tourism Queensland Act 1979 and that Act describes TQ's powers and functions. TQ is governed by a ten-member board and the board members are appointed by the governor in council and are responsible to the minister of tourism in the Queensland government. One of the ten board members is the director-general of the Department of Employment, Economic Development and Innovation, who is ex-officio (non-voting). There are two standing committees of the Board: the Remuneration Committee and the Audit Committee. The Chief Executive Office (CEO) of TQ reports to the Board. The organization chart for TQ is shown in Figure 8.4.

It can be seen that the structure below the CEO is quite different from that under the director of MGTO. There are four departments: Marketing, International, Destinations, and Business Performance and Planning. TQ also operates a number of international offices.

What is the best organizational structure to guarantee effective governance of a DMO? This may be the hardest question to answer in this entire book. There is also not much research that has been done that critically evaluates the effectiveness of different DMO organizational structures. Most of the materials that exist just describe different types of DMOs and do not attempt a deeper analysis or classification. However, d'Angella et al. (2010) compared the governance models of thirteen local and city tourism destinations in Europe and found four archetypes (models or typical examples).

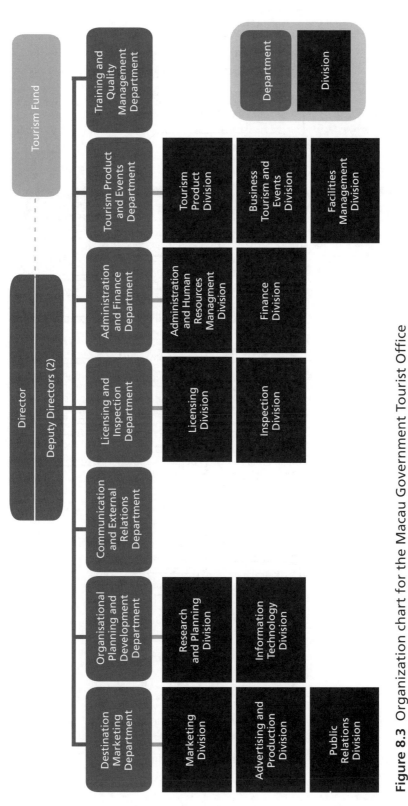

Figure 8.3 Organization chart for the Macau Government Tourist Office
Source: Macau Government Office of Tourism, 2012.

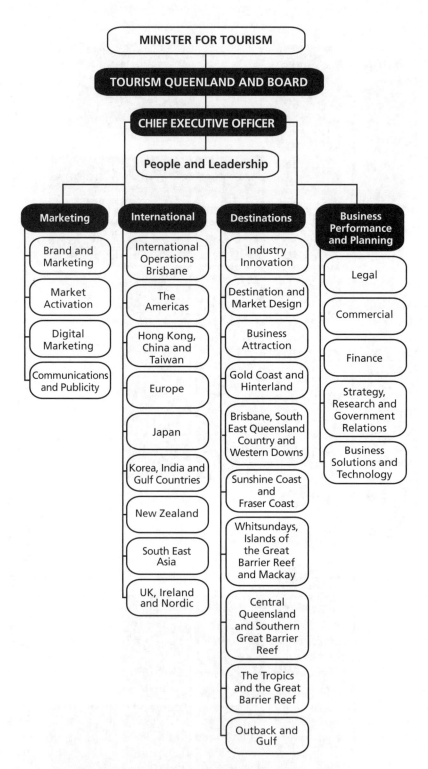

Figure 8.4 Tourism Queensland organization chart 2011

Source: Tourism Queensland, 2011.

The four were called normative/regulatory (concentrated governance functions and strong coordination mechanisms); entrepreneurial (scattered governance functions and strong coordination mechanisms); leading firm (concentrated governance functions and weak coordination mechanisms); and fragmented (scattered governance functions and weak coordination mechanisms).

The research by d'Angella *et al.* (2010) highlighted another aspect of coordination with which DMOs must cope. This is the coordination of multiple government agencies at all levels with some influence on tourism. Additionally, there may also be multiple private-sector associations and non-profit organizations involved, and coordinating them can also be challenging for DMOs.

A good example of coordination among agencies at a city level is Göteborg & Co. in Sweden. It brings together government agencies and the private sector, so it is an example of a public–private partnership (PPP) in destination management. The business concept of Göteborg & Co. is 'to be a leading platform for collaboration on destination development in an international context'. The owners of Göteborg & Co. are the following:

- The City of Gothenburg
- The Gothenburg Region
- West Sweden Chamber of Commerce
- Liseberg
- Got Event
- Stena Line
- Swedish Exhibition and Congress Centre
- The Association of Large Hotels
- The Association of Gothenburg Hotels
- City Association
- Gothenburg Restaurant Association.

As you can see, this ownership structure is a mixture of government agencies at different levels, trade and business associations, and private sector companies. Göteborg & Co. has a 21 person board that represents all of the owners and some other local jurisdictions, tourism attractions and private firms. The CEO of Göteborg & Co. and an employee of Göteborg & Co. are also on the Board. The organization chart for Göteborg & Co. is shown in Figure 8.5. In 2010, Göteborg & Co. had a staff of 116 and an operating income of SEK 216,887,000. It is interesting to note that just 36 per cent of Göteborg & Co.'s operating income came directly from local government in 2010 and that amount from the City was as a 'payment for assignments'.

Göteborg & Co. is a great example of shared governance by the public and private sector, and all of the major 'players' in tourism at the city and region are involved and participate. This sets a great governance model for other DMOs to emulate.

A second model of coordinating the public and private sector in destination is provided by the Catalan Tourist Board (CTB) in Spain. It has a budget of around 25 million euros and a staff of 110 people, and was established in 2007 by the Catalan Parliament. The CTB has two boards:

- The General Council for discussion and consultation with all the sectors represented (private companies, local tourist boards, municipalities, unions, etc.).
- The Management Board for decision taking and control of the agency. The participation in this board is conditioned to make an economic contribution to the agency.

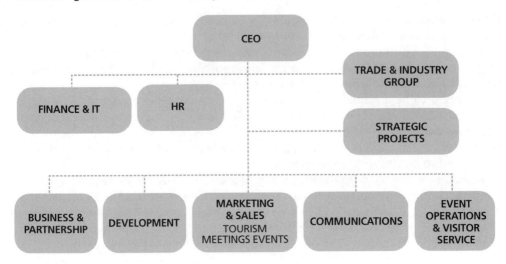

Figure 8.5 Organization chart for Göteborg & Co.
Source: Göteborg & Co., 2011.

The CTB model is one where the tourism stakeholders perform in a consultative and advisory role; and the public sector through the CTB has the control and decision-making responsibilities.

The Göteborg & Co. and Catalan Tourist Board cases are not exactly the same, although both provide for public–private partnerships in destination management. Göteborg & Co. is a blending of the public and private sectors into one management board; the Catalan Tourist Board links but separates the functions of the two groups.

From these examples in Macau, Australia, Sweden and Spain, you can see that there is great diversity in organizational structures. However, the trend towards more public–private partnerships is obvious, especially in the more advanced economies.

Boards of directors

For the DMOs that are not wholly operated by government agencies, the most common structure is for a chief executive officer (CEO) or executive director to be hired and for this DMO leader to work with a board of directors. This is the preferred structure for the growing number of public–private partnerships (PPPs) in destination management. It is typical with this type of structure that the board has to approve all DMO expenditures above a specified level.

Chapter 7 discussed DMO relations with boards of directors and reviewed board composition; board member recruitment, selection, orientation and motivation; board member conduct; board size and members' terms of office; and board performance assessment. There are many other aspects and issues for DMOs in dealing with boards of directors to ensure more effective governance.

Again it needs to be reiterated that many DMOs are non-profit organizations and board members are not compensated for the time they spend at meetings or any other time they dedicate to DMO affairs. Therefore, the motivation and management of DMO board members is difficult and challenging.

How many meetings to schedule for boards of directors seems like a trivial matter, but in fact it is very important to the DMO's governance. If boards meet too infrequently, they may be just 'rubber-stamping' the decisions of the CEO and senior management of the DMO and may not be able to keep up with what is going on within the CVB. Bill Geist in his book, *Destination Leadership for Boards* (2004), believes that when boards meet quarterly (four times per year) this is not frequent enough for them to effectively govern the DMO. He strongly recommends that boards of directors meet monthly, especially when the DMOs are locally based.

Who sets the agenda for board of directors' meetings? This is another seemingly innocuous matter, but again it is an issue that needs to be given great thought. Geist (2004) recommends that the chairman of the board should prepare the agendas for meetings, perhaps with some assistance from the leader of the DMO. However, he suggests that the DMO should not be wholly entrusted with writing the board meeting agendas.

The culture created for boards of directors is another important matter, as well as how board meetings are conducted. The board chair is the key person in the development of the board culture and must ensure that divergent views are encouraged and valued at board meetings.

Motivating board members is a high priority for non-profit organizations and this responsibility falls again to the board chair, who should request the assistance of the DMO executive and other senior management staff. Geist (2004) and others recommend giving 'visibility' to board members in their communities as the main basis for motivation. This means getting favourable publicity and exposure for board members in local media channels and commending them for their contributions to the DMO and the tourism sector in general.

By-laws

Many DMOs are created by acts of legislation and must abide by the conditions specified therein. In addition, most DMOs have by-laws that specify in great detail how the DMO is to be operated and the most important policies and procedures. By-laws are the rules that govern the internal operations of a DMO. They are normally established when the DMO first begins operations and may be changed (amended) by subsequent boards of directors. For example, the Canadian Tourism Commission (CTC) which is a Crown Corporation has by-laws that were set in 2001and amended several times, most recently in 2006. There are three by-laws that govern CTC and these are shown in Figure 8.6.

As you can see from Figure 8.6, the by-laws contain specific instructions and conditions for the management of this DMO including about the composition of the Board of Directors and the sub-committees of the Board. For example, the by-laws specify that there should not be more than twenty-six board members, and seven and nine people should be on the Executive Committee. The by-laws also dictate rules about meetings and reports that must be prepared.

The enforcement of DMO by-laws is therefore important to DMO governance to ensure that the internal rules are strictly followed. The question then becomes who should enforce these by-laws? In the real word, by-laws are often forgotten and neglected by organizations, unless they have particularly meticulous board members or DMO staff. Dealing with by-laws and changing them is often viewed as a 'chore' that not many board members want to deal with. However, by-laws are critical to DMO governance. It is recommended that the board chair takes responsibility for this matter and that the by-laws are reviewed in at least one board meeting per year.

By-Law 1	Management and conduct of the affairs of CTC		By-Law 2	Code of ethics for directors, members of the working committees and employees of CTC
1	Interpretation		1	Code of Ethics
2	General		By-Law 3	Contracting policy for the CTC
3	Board		1	Contracting Policy
4	Committees of the Board			
5	Executive Committee			
6	Governance and Nominating Committee			
7	Audit Committee			
8	Human Resources Committee			
9	Working Committee			
10	Meetings			
11	Corporate Secretary			
12	Officers of the Commission			
13	Banking			
14	Execution of documents			
15	Corporate plan and budgets			
16	Annual Report and Financial Statement			

Figure 8.6 By-laws of the Canadian Tourism Commission
Source: Canadian Tourism Commission, 2012.

Board functions

The by-laws specify the major functions and objectives of boards of directors. Some of the typical functions of boards are to:

- Approve the annual budget of the DMO including expected sources of funding and planned expenditures.
- Assist the DMO with its programmes and activities when necessary.
- Govern the DMO in the manner described in the by-laws.
- Monitor the finances of the DMO.
- Provide overall direction and oversight for DMO operations.
- Monitor and review the annual performance of the DMO.
- Monitor and review the performance of the chief executive officer or executive director.
- Periodically review and amend where necessary the by-laws of the DMO.
- Represent the DMO and the tourism sector within the destination.

Board committees

Most boards of directors have committees to deal with specific matters and these are smaller groups of board members with usually not more than six people. Permanent committees created by by-laws are known as standing committees and these often include an executive committee, finance committee and governance or audit committee. Committees created for a short-term period and not included in the by-laws are most often called *ad hoc* committees.

Board officers

Once again according to by-laws, a number of board officer positions are specified. Most boards have at least four officers including the chair, vice-chair, treasurer and secretary. The by-laws specify how officers are to be selected and the terms of their office.

DMO funding

The funding of DMOs is a topic that always seems to draw much public debate. Funding levels certainly affect the power and influence of DMOs, especially within the tourism sector itself. DMOs with low funding levels struggle to be influential; those with high budgets can 'lead from the front' as they have adequate resources to take fresh initiatives and help other partners. However, the situation is complicated by the fact that DMOs seldom control their own destinies in terms of long-term funding. In reality, their budget levels can vary from year to year based on external factors and the decisions of other actors.

There are many different funding formulas for DMOs and it can also be said that there is great variation in the budget levels of DMOs. How a DMO is funded has a great influence on its governance. There is an old saying that 'he or she that pays the piper calls the tune' and that means that those providing most of the funding tend to play a major role in destination governance.

In many countries, DMO funding comes directly from government. For example, VisitBritain received £26.5 million for 2011/2012 through a grant-in-aid from the Department of Culture, Media and Sport. Tourism Australia received AUD 132.8 million from government, representing 85 per cent of its total revenues for 2011-2012. The Singapore Tourism Board received approximately 90 per cent of its 2010/2011 income of SGD 239.9 million from government funding. The Federal Government in Canada provided support in 2010 for approximately 86.6 per cent of the Canadian Tourism Commission's total expenditures of CAD 124.8 million.

A report prepared by UNWTO and the European Travel Commission was based on a survey of sixty-two national tourism organizations (NTOs) around the world. They found that three-quarters (75 per cent) of the NTOs received more than two-thirds of their income from the central government.

A unique DMO funding formula has been developed in the USA through the introduction of local taxes on rooms. These are called 'bed taxes' or 'hotel occupancy taxes'. These are user-pay taxes, meaning that guests pay the taxes as a percentage on top of their room costs. According to Destination Marketing Association International (DMAI), 86 per cent of the DMOs in the USA that are called convention and visitors bureaus (CVBs), receive funding through hotel occupancy taxes. The average hotel room tax was 7.4 per cent. The other 14 per cent of the CVBs in the USA receive funds either from state or city government allocations. About half of the CVBs have membership programmes and so they receive income through membership dues.

Figure 8.7 shows the sources of funding for the Las Vegas Convention and Visitors Authority (LVCVA), which is the CVB with the largest budget in the USA. For 2012, LVCVA was projecting that 77.5 per cent of its total funding would be through room taxes. The LVCVA operates the Las Vegas Convention Center and the Cashman Center, so it has an additional source of revenues from rentals at these properties. The other revenue sources include $1.95 million of gaming fees from casinos and are based on the numbers of games and slot machines.

There have been mixed fortunes for DMO funding in different places in recent times; some DMO budgets have been slashed while others have been increased. For example, a *USA Today* article in 2011 reported that twenty states had cut their tourism budgets and one state tourism office (Washington) was completely shut down. In Australia, the state tourism offices in South Australia and Tasmania were both expected to have budget cuts in early 2012. Tourism agencies in the UK also experienced budget cuts in 2010 and 2011. Government funding for VisitBritain was reduced in 2011/2012 from 2010/2011 and led to the agency reducing staff numbers. Generally, all of these DMO funding cuts were attributed to overall governmental budgetary problems.

Figure 8.8 highlights one of the major issues with DMO funding when the majority of the funds come directly from government. This shows the budget of the Tourism Office of the Iowa Department of Economic Development in the USA. The issue is that these government-run DMOs have their budgets set annually and the budget levels fluctuate from year to year. In addition, they are usually not able to carry forward surpluses from one year to the next. This is certainly not a situation that is favourable for stable DMO governance.

Some DMOs have been experiencing recent declines in funding due to adverse economic conditions and the resulting impacts on the tourism sector. This has been especially so for those DMOs that depend mainly on room taxes, since their revenues decreased as hotel occupancies declined. For example, the room taxes received by the Las Vegas Convention and Visitors Authority (LVCVA) attained a high of $221 million in 2008 but then dropped in 2009 with a further decline in 2010 to $154 million. Thus LVCVA's major source of funding fell by 32 per cent in 2 years.

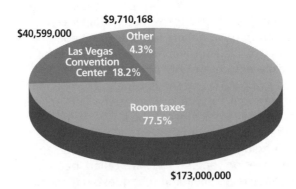

Figure 8.7 Funding sources of Las Vegas Convention and Visitors Authority, 2012
Source: Las Vegas Convention and Visitors Authority, 2012b.

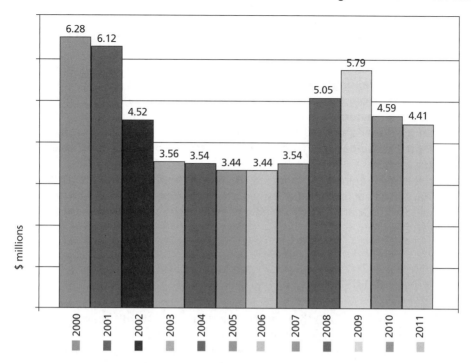

Figure 8.8 Trend in state tourism budget of Iowa, USA, 2000–2011
Source: Travel Federation of Iowa, 2011.

Dr Bill Siegel, Chairman and CEO of Longwoods International, conducted an in-depth study of two successful US cases of destination marketing in the state of Michigan and the city of Philadelphia. The study was published by the US Travel Association under the title of 'The Power of Destination Marketing'. Siegel also reflected on the past closure of the state tourism office in Colorado and the damage that had done to the state's tourism sector. The following is one of Siegel's (2011) conclusions:

'The Power of Destination Marketing'

At a time of budget cutbacks around the country, the issue of tourism funding is more relevant than ever. Over the past decade, the Colorado case has become a cautionary tale for the dangers of cutting back a successful programme. The elimination of tourism promotion in that state caused a severe loss of market share, visitor dollars and tax revenues that took years to recoup.

There was some good news as several DMOs received more funding. The New South Wales government in Australia increased funding for tourism and events to AUD 133 million in 2011/2012. The budgets of the DMOs in Western Australia and Queensland were also higher. Even in the USA where there were many budget cuts, some state tourism programmes experienced budget increases, Wisconsin being one of them with a budget increase from $13.97 to $16.59 million.

Figure 8.9 provides a summary of the major funding mechanisms and sources for DMOs. You should not assume that every DMO receives funds from all the six sources listed in Figure 8.9; rather these are a set of potential funding sources.

There are certain other funding sources in addition to those shown in Figure 8.9 that DMOs are increasingly considering as traditional funding is threatened. These include revenues from the operation of events and festivals, sales of printed and digital collateral materials (e.g. guides, maps, DVDs, etc.), sales of souvenirs and other local goods, and private-sector sponsorships. For example, Göteborg & Co. in Sweden and the Singapore Tourism Board receive part of their revenues from operating events.

Even in the USA where most CVBs rely mainly on room tax revenues, DMOs like Visit Orlando have been successfully diversifying their funding sources. As you will see from the following, Visit Orlando has been able to increase its proportion of 'entrepreneurial funds' to 40 per cent.

Funding of Visit Orlando

We are funded partially through a marketing contract with Orange County, FL that allows us to receive of a portion of the tourist development tax levied on hotel rooms and paid by visitors. In addition, we are one of the most entrepreneurial destination marketing organizations in the United States, supplementing our Orlando marketing efforts from entrepreneurial activities like publishing, membership, destination meeting services, ticket sales and cooperative marketing campaigns. Currently, Visit Orlando's budget is 60 per cent tourist development tax and 40 per cent entrepreneurial funds.

(2012)

Figure 8.9 Potential funding mechanisms and sources for DMOs

Measuring DMO effectiveness

Ensuring the efficiency and effectiveness of operations is another dimension of destination governance. In demonstrating it is accountable, a DMO must prove that it has been efficient and effective in the use of resources. Efficiency usually means doing things at the lowest possible cost, while effectiveness measures the degree of success in attaining goals and objectives. Part of the task in ensuring efficiency is through day-to-day management of the DMO and through the application of an internal control system.

However, measuring effectiveness is about measuring results and you already know that DMO accountability includes projecting results and then measuring results. The projected results should be based upon specific plans that the DMO has prepared, e.g. marketing plan, community relations plan, product development plan, etc. They need to be justified by research that the DMO has conducted or other credible information and assumptions. These must not be 'guesstimates' based upon personal opinions. It is also assumed that the projected results prepared by the DMO and its staff will be reviewed and approved by the governing body, and this most often is a board of directors.

DMOs nowadays express results in key performance indicators (KPIs) within key result areas (KRAs). This topic was discussed earlier in Chapter 3 in the discussion of measuring the effectiveness of destination marketing. Examples were given there for Tourism Queensland (KRAs) and Tourism Malaysia (KRAs and KPIs).

Figure 8.10 displays an overall framework for measuring DMO effectiveness using the six destination management roles as the KRAs.

As you can see in Figure 8.10, KPIs are developed for each destination management role and this is one of the options open to setting KPIs for a DMO. In actual practice, DMOs usually have specific initiatives that have been identified within each destination management role and the KPIs are tied to these initiatives. The initiatives will have been developed within a corporate or business plan, marketing plan, community relations plan, long-term tourism plan or other planning documents.

Visit Wales provides a real-life example of successfully setting and measuring KPIs, although just for the destination marketing and promotion role. Morgan *et al.* (2012) suggested that traditional approaches to evaluating marketing included customer

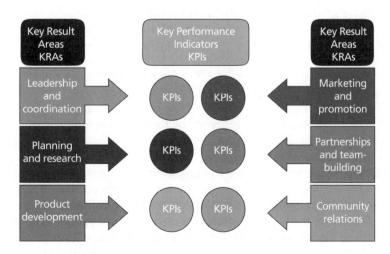

Figure 8.10 KRAs and KPIs for destination management

enquiries (KPI: conversion); financial/response (KPIs: ROI and business value); advertising awareness/impact (KPI: tracking); website usage (KPI: Internet conversion); and brand development (KPI: brand assessment). However, these authors deemed these five approaches that originated around the 1990s as not being appropriate for modern-day destination marketing and promotion. In 2007, Visit Wales established a task force to develop a new set of KPIs to measure its destination marketing effectiveness. The new system of KPIs was introduced by Visit Wales in 2009 and includes seven KPIs that are tied mainly to advertising/promotional campaigns.

The new Visit Wales destination marketing KPIs

- Destination awareness
- Total campaign awareness
- Claimed campaign response/known campaign response
- Emotional proximity (measuring brand engagement)
- Conviction to visit
- Conversion through decision-making process
- Value per respondent.

Here are some more detailed descriptions of these seven Visit Wales KPIs:

- *Destination awareness*: Awareness of Wales as a destination compared to other destinations in the British Isles. This measures the percentage of the people who are aware of Wales as a holiday/short-break destination.
- *Total campaign awareness*: This measures the percentage of people who have been exposed to at least some form of Visit Wales marketing (e.g. direct marketing, advertising, events and conferences, etc.).
- *Claimed campaign response*: The number of people exposed to the campaign who claim they were inspired or persuaded to find out more about Wales as a result of that exposure.
- *Known campaign response*: An estimate of the actual number of people exposed to the campaign that went on to find out more about Wales as a result of the exposure.
- *Emotional proximity*: A measure of how close a person feels towards a particular brand. This closeness is a function of how appealing and how engaging the brand is.
- *Conviction to visit*: The number of people who placed Wales on their 'mental list' of countries they would like to visit in the future.
- *Conversion throughout decision-making process*: The percentage of individuals moving from stage to stage throughout the decision-making process.
- *Value per respondent*: The expected value generated over a given time frame (first visit or 12 months) by people responding to Visit Wales communications who attribute part of their decision to the impact of marketing.

Figure 8.11 shows the measurement of Visit Wales' KPIs for 2009.

The Visit Wales case study is an outstanding example of setting and measuring KPIs; however, these KPIs are only for marketing and promotion and indeed focus mostly on promotion. There is a need to develop a much more comprehensive set of KPIs for DMOs that embraces all of the destination management roles.

1. Destination awareness	• 44 % of UK population rank in top 3
2. Campaign awareness	• 13% spontaneous; 22% prompted
3. Claimed and known response	• 1.8 million; 3% of UK population
4. Emotional proximity	• 15% of UK population rate 9/10
5. Conviction to visit	• 40% visiting vs. 60% non-visiting
6. Marketing effectiveness (conversion)	(not available)
7. Value of marketing	• Appoximately £60 million per year

Figure 8.11 Measurement of KPIs for Visit Wales, 2009
Source: Based on Morgan *et al.*, 2011.

DMOs and their trade associations have recognized the need to demonstrate accountability and to measure their performance. An outstanding example is the work done by Destination Marketing Association International (DMAI) on the *Standard DMO Performance Reporting Handbook* (2011). The following five main areas of performance reporting have been identified by DMAI and for each of the five areas specific activity measures, performance measures and productivity metrics are recommended:

- DMO convention sales performance reporting
- DMO travel trade sales performance reporting
- DMO membership performance reporting
- DMO visitor information centre performance reporting
- DMO return on investment.

DMAI not only believes the *Handbook* it has produced helps DMOs to be accountable, but that it also protects DMOs from audits and reviews that are often conducted by those who do not understand DMO operations.

Value of the *Standard DMO Performance Reporting Handbook*

In addition to internally reviewing their operations, DMOs are often required, due to their unique funding sources, to undergo external performance reviews by various stakeholders within their local communities. At times, these external audits/ reviews may be done by firms lacking DMO knowledge and experience. In the past, the DMO community had no uniform approach to reporting performance to these audiences. As a result, DMOs would sometimes find themselves limited in their ability to systematically and credibly articulate their contribution to the destination. This Handbook will serve as a basis for standards and best practices among DMOs.

DMAI's work on defining DMO standard performance reporting guidelines began in 2004 and continued until 2011, indicating that the association viewed this as a very high priority. DMAI is to be strongly commended on this pioneering initiative to give DMOs the tools to demonstrate their operational results and to show accountability. The *Handbook* undoubtedly has helped many DMOs to be more systematic in setting and measuring results. However, as with the Visit Wales KPIs, the DMAI standards are mostly oriented to assessing the marketing and promotional role. More work is needed in the future to define measurement standards for other destination management roles.

Before leaving this discussion on DMO effectiveness, you should be aware of one controversial issue. Can the DMO claim to be solely responsible for the numbers of visitors who come to the destination? This is hotly debated and truthfully there is no precise evidence to say that a DMO can or cannot make this claim. However, it is most unlikely that a DMO can take 100 per cent of the credit, because there are other influential parties including airlines, hotels and resorts, attractions, travel trade and the media. It is most prudent for a DMO not to over-exaggerate its influence on visitor volumes, and better to acknowledge that the DMO played a major role but with the assistance of others. Additionally, DMOs should do research and information-gathering to identify those visitors who were drawn specifically because of the DMO's marketing and promotional efforts.

Involvement

Figure 8.2 identified involvement as one of the dimensions of governance. The idea of involvement is strongly associated with political governance and the desirability of citizen involvement. However, the concept still has application to corporate governance and to destination management.

It is important that DMOs encourage involvement in their affairs and that they are open to inputs, especially from tourism stakeholders. This topic was discussed extensively in Chapters 6 and 7. Chapter 6 discussed building involvement with the DMO through partnerships and team-building. Chapter 7 reviewed many ways to involve local community residents and tourism sector stakeholders in DMO programmes and activities.

Göteborg & Co. (2012) again provides an outstanding case study in encouraging the involvement of other entities in strategic efforts, as evidenced by its Trade and Industry Group.

Collaboration and involvement at Göteborg & Co.

One excellent example is the company's [Göteborg & Co.'s] Trade and Industry Group. Twenty-five of Gothenburg's largest companies work together in the group to develop Gothenburg as a destination, which also enhances their own competitiveness in the long term. But this partnership also extends to many other areas that are important to the city. Examples include collaboration with the city's restaurant association and hotel associations.

Risk management

Effective destination governance includes giving adequate attention to risk management. As mentioned earlier, DMOs are exposed to different types of risks, some of which are internal to their own operations and others that affect tourism within their destinations. For the latter type of risk to destinations through natural and other disasters, some DMOs have prepared crisis management plans. New Orleans was devastated by Hurricane Katrina in 2005. Its DMO has prepared a Tourism Crisis Management Plan (2011a) in case an event like this happens again.

Tourism Crisis Management Plan, New Orleans CVB

The New Orleans CVB Tourism Crisis Management Plan, along with diligent and thorough preparation with an emphasis on safety, will assist visitors in responding appropriately to emergencies.

The City of New Orleans and State of Louisiana have implemented a unified emergency communications plan to ensure the timely flow of information across the region in emergency situations. A comprehensive and effective city-wide emergency communications plan for the Greater New Orleans tourism industry has been developed for visitors.

(New Orleans Convention and Visitors Bureau, 2011a)

DMOs face risks other than crises and these result directly from and within their operations. These include fraud and misappropriation of funds by the DMO's staff members. They also face risks if part of their funding is used inappropriately for personal rather than business purposes. In addition, there are risks from the major projects and other initiatives of the DMO. The following materials are the risk management rules at Tourism Australia that are the responsibility assigned to the Audit and Finance Committee of its Board.

Risk management at Tourism Australia

- Consider whether management have in place a current a comprehensive risk management framework, and associated procedures for the effective identification and management of the financial and business risks.
- Review the risk management plans of major projects or undertakings to consider whether the plans appropriately identify, assess and address risk and any potential impact on the internal control environment or other Audit and Finance Committee responsibilities.
- Consider the impact of the risk management framework on its insurance arrangements.

Ensuring adequate insurance coverage is one of the ways to manage risk at DMOs, as is DMO management planning ahead and anticipating what risks might be present in their programmes and activities.

Destination leadership

DMOs must assume a leadership role for the tourism sector in their destinations and so must their senior executives. In fact, it is rather a unique situation since the DMO must be leaders of their organizations and among the leaders of the tourism sector for their destinations. This leadership role is accentuated in communities where tourism is not given a high priority and where the benefits of tourism are not well understood.

Leadership roles of DMOs

What initiatives must a DMO take to demonstrate its leadership? The following are eight of the key leadership roles that the DMO must assume within the destination:

Setting the tourism agenda: In Chapter 1, it was suggested that the DMO should set the agenda for tourism and coordinate all tourism stakeholder efforts toward achieving the agenda. Of course, you now know from the previous six chapters that the DMO does not and should not do the agenda-setting on its own. It needs to do this with the active involvement and input from tourism stakeholders within the destination.

Setting the agenda really means defining a long-term vision for tourism and engaging the tourism sector in long-range planning. The visionary role of the DMO is one of the key requirements for its leadership.

Guiding and coordinating tourism sector stakeholders: The DMO needs to guide and coordinate the efforts of tourism sector stakeholders. This is a difficult task given the diversity of stakeholders and their opinions and viewpoints on tourism. The coaching role of the DMO is to bring all of the team together to focus on a shared set of goals and objectives.

Championing tourism: As mentioned in Chapter 1, tourism is generally not well understood and under-appreciated as an economic sector. It is often afforded the role of a second-class citizen when compared to manufacturing, agriculture and even mining. It does not always get the respect it deserves. The championing role of the DMO is to continuously communicate and confirm the positive contributions to their destinations.

Educating about tourism: By conducting research and keeping up to date about tourism, the DMO is a source of data, information and facts for tourism sector stakeholders and community residents. DMO management and staff should continuously participate in training and professional development, since tourism is a dynamic and fast-changing economic sector. The scholar/teacher role of the DMO makes everybody in the destination better understand tourism and the trends in the sector and its markets.

Leading tourism marketing: The DMO is the body entrusted with marketing the destination as a whole. It needs to set the directions for tourism sector stakeholders to follow and provide partnering opportunities to achieve marketing goals and objectives. The DMO should develop the destination positioning and branding approaches that provide a promotional platform for all involved in tourism. The promoter role of DMOs increases awareness and brings in more visitors to the destination.

Serving visitors: The DMO serves visitors in many different ways, especially in providing information about tourism in the destination. It must assist in taking steps to assure the safety and security of visitors, and their ease of movement within the destination. The visitor servant role of the DMO enhances the satisfaction of people who come to the destination on business or for leisure.

Maintaining tourism quality standards: The DMO must participate in the setting and monitoring of tourism quality standards. It must ensure that quality standards match with the positioning and branding of the destination. The quality controller role of the DMO enhances the experiences of visitors in the destination and makes them want to return.

Stewarding resources: The DMO must advocate a sustainable approach to tourism development. The DMO must also be a careful steward of the funds and other resources with which it is provided. The steward role of the DMO means that resources are used prudently and that natural and cultural resources are preserved for future destinations.

Figure 8.12 provides a summary of these eight major leadership roles of DMOs. All of these roles are important and it is very difficult to say which leadership roles should be given the highest priority. Certainly being visionary is one of the key roles in leadership of all types and this would apply to DMOs as well. Of course, being accountable requires that the DMO be a good steward of resources, so this is also a high priority leadership role. Leading tourism marketing is essential, as is setting the tourism agenda.

Figure 8.12 Major leadership roles of DMOs

Tourism Queensland (TQ) has developed a very clever Leadership Charter with six elements:

Tourism Queensland Leadership Charter

At Tourism Queensland, leadership is encouraged at every level of our organisation. The leadership charter is an expression of leadership qualities that are valued and encouraged at Tourism Queensland. It provides an ethos to describe the work values that we support and encourage.

- Lead by example
- Embrace change
- Be Approachable
- Inspire a shared direction
- Empower others to act
- Respect the values and beliefs of other

Destination leadership styles

There have been so many books and articles written about leadership styles that it is difficult to know where to start this discussion. However, Hankinson (2007) in his article about destination branding listed strong, visionary leadership as one of the guiding principles. So leading the tourism sector toward a shared vision is one of the requirements of the DMO leadership role. Chapters 2 and 3 both emphasized the need to develop long-term visions for the destination and the DMO. Of course, there is more to visionary leaders than just having a vision, and this has been highlighted by many previous authors including Westley and Mintzberg (1989). They viewed visionary leadership as a psychological gift that only certain people have.

There are many different leadership styles, and one of those that can fit with some DMO situations is servant leadership, which was introduced as a concept by Greenleaf (1977). Servant leaders focus on others rather than on themselves and they are not motivated by self-interest. The primary objective is to serve and meet the needs of others. Servant leaders help other people develop, provide vision and gain the trust and credibility of others (Stone, 2003). Figure 8.13 shows the twenty attributes of servant leadership based on a literature review by Russell and Stone (2002). The nine functional attributes are the ones most often found in the literature on service leadership. The accompanying attributes complement the functional attributes and are prerequisites to effective service leadership.

Some of the attributes in Figure 8.13 may not be as instantly recognizable as others, so here are some explanations. Modelling means leading by example and by behaviour. Pioneering means taking the initiative and showing the way for others to follow. Stewardship is managing the properties or business affairs of other persons.

Functional attributes	Accompanying attributes
❑ Vision	❑ Communication
❑ Honesty	❑ Credibility
❑ Integrity	❑ Competence
❑ Trust	❑ Stewardship
❑ Service	❑ Visibility
❑ Modelling	❑ Influence
❑ Pioneering	❑ Persuasion
❑ Appreciation of others	❑ Listening
❑ Empowerment	❑ Encouragement
	❑ Teaching
	❑ Delegation

Figure 8.13 Attributes of servant leadership

Summary

Destination governance is a concept that is receiving increasing attention. This is how a DMO is administered and who does the administering. Governance involves the policies, systems and processes to ensure that all stakeholders are involved and that the DMO is accountable for its results and resource usage and has a high level of transparency.

Two of the key dimensions of destination governance are accountability and transparency. Accountability is the obligation of a DMO to justify and account for its programmes and activities; and to accept responsibility for results. The DMO must disclose these results in a transparent manner and take responsibility for the use of all resources with which it has been entrusted. Transparency means openness in operations and communications. The tourism stakeholders in the destination should be able to see what the DMO is doing and understand its decision-making.

There are many different types of organizational structures for DMOs. However, public–private partnerships (PPPs) with independent boards of directors are becoming more of the norm. The operation of boards of directors affects governance and board chairs have a key role to play in ensuring that boards function effectively. By-laws set out the rules for boards of directors and they must be checked periodically to guarantee compliance.

The funding of DMOs in many places in the world has been under threat due to government budget deficits and downturns in tourism business levels. Several DMOs are looking for new ways to earn revenues in the face of significant cost-cutting.

The effectiveness of DMO operations needs to be measured, and this is done mainly through defining key result areas (KRAs) and setting key performance indicators (KPIs). KPIs need to be set for all of the destination management roles and not just for marketing and promotion.

Risk management is another dimension of effective destination governance. The DMO in particular must ensure that it is fully protected from all potential risks, and some that may even threaten its future existence.

DMOs need to be leaders of the tourism sector in their destinations. The major leadership roles of DMOs are to be visionaries, coaches, champions, scholars/teachers, promoters, visitor servants, quality controllers and stewards. DMOs and their leaders may adopt different leadership styles. Servant leadership is one style that seems very well suited for destination management.

The specific steps to be taken for a DMO to accomplish its destination governance role are to:

- Take all the steps necessary to demonstrate the accountability of the DMO.
- Ensure that the operations and decision-making of the DMO have transparency.
- If applicable, ensure that the board conducts its functions effectively and follows the rules specified in the DMO's by-laws.
- Be a good steward of the funds and other resources with which the DMO is entrusted.
- Have an internal control system and other policies and procedures to ensure the efficiency of DMO operations.
- Measure the effectiveness of the DMO's programmes and activities by estimating results and then calculating the degree of attainment of these results.
- Identify key results areas (KRAs) and key performance indicators (KPIs).
- Encourage the involvement of all tourism stakeholders in the DMO's programmes and activities.
- Implement a risk management programme.
- Perform the major leadership roles that are expected of DMOs.

Review questions

1 How would you define destination governance?
2 What are the main dimensions of destination governance?
3 What is accountability and which actions does a DMO need to take to prove it is being accountable?
4 How can a DMO demonstrate transparency and what is the relationship between transparency and accountability?
5 How do DMO organizational structures affect destination governance?
6 In the operations of boards of directors, who should take the responsibility for setting board culture, scheduling meetings and preparing meeting agendas? How should these tasks be approached?
7 What are by-laws and how do these relate to destination governance?
8 What are the different funding mechanisms and sources that are used for DMOs?
9 What have been some of the recent trends in the funding of DMOs?
10 What steps should a DMO take to measure its effectiveness?
11 Why is it important for a DMO to plan for risk management and what are some of the risks that might be encountered?
12 What are the major leadership roles that DMOs should assume within their destinations?

References

Baggio, R., Scott, N., and Cooper, C. 2010. Improving tourism destination governance: A complexity science approach. *Tourism Review*, 65(4), 51–60.

Beaumont, N., and Dredge, D. 2010. Local tourism governance: A comparison of three network approaches. *Journal of Sustainable Tourism*, 18(1), 7–28.

Beritelli, P., Bieger, T., and Laesser, C. 2007. Destination governance: Using corporate governance theories as a foundation for effective destination management. *Journal of Travel Research*, 46(1), 96–107.

Canadian Tourism Commission. 2012. By-Laws for CTC Crown Corporation.

Carver, J. 2006. Boards That Make a Difference. A New Design for Leadership in Nonprofit and Public Organizations, 3rd edn. San Francisco: Jossey-Bass.

Catalan Tourist Board. 2012. http://www.act.cat

Cooper, C., Scott, N., and Baggio, R. 2009. Network position and perceptions of destination stakeholder importance. *Anatolia*, 20(1), 33–45.

d'Angella, F., De Carlo, M., and Sainaghi, R. 2010. Archetypes of destination governance: A comparison of international destinations. *Tourism Review*, 65(4), 61–73.

Del Rosso, L. 2011. Tourism offices under scrutiny as states cope with budget cuts. *Travel Weekly*, 23 May. http://www.travelweekly.com/Travel-News/Government/Tourism-offices-under-scrutiny-as-states-cope-with-budget-cuts/

Destination Marketing Association International. 2011. Standard DMO Performance Reporting Handbook. Washington, DC: DMAI

Ford, R.C., and Peeper, W.C. 2008. Managing Destination Marketing Organizations. Orlando, FL: ForPer Publications.

Ford, R.C., Gresock, A.R., and Peeper, W.C. 2011. Board composition and CVB effectiveness: Engaging stakeholders that can matter. *Tourism Review*, 66(4), 4–17.

Gartrell, R.B. 1988. Destination Marketing for Convention and Visitor Bureaus. Dubuque, IA: Kendall Hunt Publishing.

Geist, B. 2004. Destination Leadership for Boards. Miami Shores, FL: Neverland Publishing.

Göteborg & Co. 2011. Göteborg & Co. Annual Report 2010.

——2012. About Göteborg & Co. http://corporate.goteborg.com/about/we-create-opportunities/?lang=en

Greenleaf, R.K. 1977. Servant Leadership: A Journey into the Nature of Legitimate Power and Greatness. Mahwah, NJ: Paulist Press.

Hall, C.M. 2011. A typology of governance and its implications for tourism policy analysis. *Journal of Sustainable Tourism*, 19(4/5), 437–457.

Hankinson, G. 2007. The management of destination brands: Five guiding principles based on the recent developments in corporate branding theory. *Brand Management*, 14(3), 240–254.

Hong Kong Tourism Board. 2012. Annual Report 2010/2011: Corporate Governance.

Hotel Association of Canada. 2011. Why Tourism Budgets should be Increased.

Las Vegas Convention and Visitors Authority. 2012a. About LVCVA. http://www.lvcva.com/about/index.jsp

——2012b. Las Vegas Convention and Visitor Authority, Annual Budget – Fiscal Year 2011/2012, vi.

Laws, E., Richins, H., Agrusa, J., and Scott, N. 2011. Tourist Destination Governance: Practice, Theory and Issues. Wallingford: CABI Publishing.

Macau Government Tourist Office. 2012. Press Conference of the Macau Government Tourist Office, 10 January.

Morgan, N., Hastings, E., and Pritchard, A. 2012. Developing a new DMO marketing evaluation framework: The case of Wales. *Journal of Vacation Marketing*, 18(1), 73–89.

Moscardo, G. 2011. Exploring social representations of tourism planning: Issues for governance. *Journal of Sustainable Tourism*, 19(4/5), 423–436.

Munro, J., Ryan, J., and Hall, T. 2011. Managing Reputation in a Multi-channel World. Presentation at ENTER, Innsbruck, Austria.

New Orleans Convention and Visitors Bureau. 2011a. Emergency Planning: New Orleans Tourism Crisis Management Plan. http://www.neworleanscvb.com/meeting-planners/plan-your-meeting/emergency-planning/

——2011b. Frequently Asked Questions for Visitors to New Orleans. http://www.neworleanscvb.com/visit/faq/

Nordin, S., and Svensson, B. 2007. Innovative destination governance: The Swedish ski resort of Åre. *Entrepreneurship and Innovation*, 8(1), 53–66.

Palmer, A. 1998. Evaluating the governance style of marketing groups. *Annals of Tourism Research*, 25(1), 185–201.

Partners Andrews Aldridge. 2008. Visit Wales Marketing Evaluation: Project Summary Document, March.

Perdue, R.R., and Pitegoff, B.E. 1990. Methods of accountability research for destination marketing. *Journal of Travel Research*, 28(4), 45–49.

Ruhanen, L., Scott, N., and Tkaczynski, A. 2010. Governance: A review and synthesis of the literature. *Tourism Review*, 65(4), 4–16.

Russell, R.F., and Stone, A.G. 2002. A review of servant leadership attributes: Developing a practical model. *Leadership and Organization Development Journal*, 23(3), 145–157.

Sainaghi, R. 2006. From contents to processes: Versus a dynamic destination management model (DDMM). *Tourism Management*, 27, 1053–1063.

Siegel, B. 2011. The Power of Destination Marketing. US Travel Association.

Singapore Tourism Board. 2011. Singapore Tourism Board Annual Report 2010/2011.

Stone, A.G. 2003. Transformational versus Servant Leadership: A Difference in Leader Focus. School of Leadership Studies, Regent University.

Torrent, P. 2010. The Catalan Tourist Board. 5th meeting of the UNWTO Destination Council, Berlin.

Tourism Australia. 2011. Tourism Australia Annual Report 2010–2011.

Tourism New Zealand. 2011. Why Have a Tourism Marketing Board? http://www.tourismnewzealand.com/about-us/why-have-a-tourism-marketing-board/

——2012. CE Expenses. http://www.tourismnewzealand.com/about-us/corporate-responsibility/ce-expenses/

Tourism Queensland 2011. Tourism Queensland Annual Report 2010/2011.

Travel Federation of Iowa. 2011. 2011 Tourism Fast Facts Booklet.

UNESCAP. 2012. What Is Good Governance? Bangkok, Thailand: UNESCAP. www.unescap.org/padd/prs/ProjectActivities/Ongoing/gg/governance.asp.

UNWTO. 2007. A Practical Guide to Tourism Destination Management. Madrid: UNWTO.

——2010. Survey on Destination Governance. Evaluation Report. Madrid: UNWTO.

UNWTO and European Travel Commission. 2010. Budgets of National Tourism Organizations 2008–2009. Madrid: UNWTO.

Visit Orlando. 2012. How We Are Funded. http://corporate.visitorlando.com/who-we-are/how-we-are-funded/

VisitBritain. 2012. Transparency. http://www.visitbritain.org/aboutus/transparency/index.aspx

Westley, F., and Mintzberg, H. 1989. Visionary leadership and strategic management. *Strategic Management Journal*, 10(S1), 17–32.

Yardley, W. 2011. A tourism office falls victim to hard times. *New York Times*, 11 July. http://www.nytimes.com/2011/07/12/us/12tourism.html

Yuksel, F., Bramwell, B., and Yuksel, A. 2005. Centralized and decentralized tourism governance in Turkey. *Annals of Tourism Research*, 32(4), 859–886.

Zhang, H. 2011. Studies on tourism destination governance from the perspective of institutional economics: Retrospect and prospect. *3rd International Conference on Information and Financial Engineering IPEDR*, vol. 12.

PART II

Destination communications and promotions

Chapter 9

Destination branding

Learning objectives

1 Explain the positioning–image–branding approach and define these three interconnected concepts.

2 Discuss the relationships among destination positioning, image and branding.

3 Identify and describe the importance and benefits of destination branding.

4 Elaborate upon the major challenges in implementing destination branding.

5 Review the characteristics of a good destination brand.

6 Explain the classic concepts of branding.

7 Outline and describe the steps to be followed in destination branding.

8 Describe the brand promise concept.

Introduction

You already heard about destination branding as part of the discussion of destination marketing planning in Chapter 3. Although it was briefly introduced earlier in this book, it is such an important marketing topic that you need to have a more in-depth explanation and exposure to how it is actually practised in destination management.

Destination branding has been one of the hottest topics among destination marketers and tourism academic scholars since the late 1990s. In 1998, the Travel and Tourism Research Association (TTRA) held its annual conference under the theme of 'Branding the Travel Market' and J.R. Brent Ritchie and Robin Ritchie were also advocating a more rigorous and well-planned approach to the branding of tourism destinations. Thanks to pioneering work by Morgan *et al.* and their 2002 book on the topic, the concept of destination branding finally attained a high professional status in tourism and became better understood and appreciated.

Of course, there was a sort of branding for destinations that existed before these pioneers made their contributions, but this was mainly within the world of advertising agencies and thus its main focus was on slogans, logos and commercials. Not much thought was given to destination image research or to a consensus-based approach involving tourism stakeholders to building destination brands. Moreover, the destination brand was something that existed only in advertising; it was not a concept that was to be experienced in the destination.

Destination branding is surely not an exact science yet, but it has progressed in its understanding and applications by leaps and bounds over the past 15–20 years. The destination branding topic now is often considered within the concepts of 'place branding' and even 'country branding' and these broader perspectives are helping to further deepen the understanding of destination branding.

There are many tourism destination brands in the world; some are outstanding and some are not so good. This chapter explains a systematic, step-by-step process to develop a long-term destination brand. You will see that this is not a 'how to' description of the ways to develop logos and slogans; but rather it is a research-based and stakeholder-involved process.

Positioning–image–branding (PIB) approach

In Chapter 3 when discussing marketing strategy, the positioning–image–branding (PIB) approach was introduced. You learned that the concepts of destination positioning, image and branding were closely intertwined, as shown in Figure 9.1. DMO marketing strategies must specify who the destination's target markets are and how destinations are to be positioned (what images are to be created) in the minds of potential visitors within these target markets. DMOs also need to consider how to make destinations unique within their competitive sets. Additionally, DMOs must determine the existing destination images that people have within their markets using the research techniques discussed in Chapter 4. Then, DMOs must decide how to brand destinations given their selected positioning approaches and the types of images that support this positioning.

As illustrated in Figure 9.1, there are two-way feedback links between each pairing of these concepts. Destination positioning impacts destination branding, but it also is intended to affect destination image. Tourists' actual destination images should

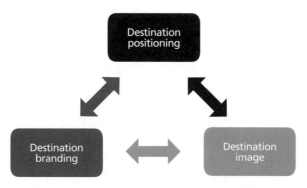

Figure 9.1 The interactions of destination positioning, image and branding

influence both destination positioning and destination branding. Destination branding is a marketing strategy approach intended to have a positive effect on destination image; its results will also impact on future destination positioning decisions. It is best to view the relationship among these three concepts as a cycle rather than a step-by-step, linear process. You should also realize that this is not a static model, but rather it is dynamic and evolving over time. It is also worth knowing that destination image is the hardest of the three concepts to change quickly; tourists' images of places may take several years to modify.

To ensure that you have a complete understanding of these three interconnected concepts, here are their definitions as placed within the contexts of tourism destinations and destination marketing:

Positioning, image and branding

Destination positioning

The steps taken by a DMO, in collaboration with its stakeholders, to identify and communicate a unique destination image to people within its target markets. Therefore, positioning is how the destination decides to make itself unique among competing destinations from the tourist's perspective.

Destination image

The mental 'pictures' people have in their minds of specific tourism destinations. These images are formed from multiple sources of information. Destination images are difficult to change in the short term.

Destination branding

The steps taken by a DMO, in collaboration with its stakeholders, to develop and communicate an identity and personality for its destination, which are different from those of all competing destinations. Some experts also refer to a place's destination brand as its 'competitive identity' (Anholt, 2009).

As you may not know immediately what 'personality' means in the destination branding definition, the case study of the Destination Australia brand is supplied in Figure 9.2 and explained further below:

Tourism Australia's destination brand personality

Our brand personality is a distinct part of our brand. It describes the human characteristics that we associate with our brand. These characteristics are emotionally driven and they relate to how we represent our brand to our target audience.

High spirited, down to earth, irreverent, welcoming.

(2012)

You can see from these three definitions that two of the concepts, positioning and branding, are in the control of the DMO. Destination images are under the control of the tourists and are how they perceive destinations. There are two types of images in these definitions; the images or perceptions that tourists have in their minds about destinations, and the desired images that DMOs want them to have.

DMOs must decide on the desired destination images (positioning) and the identity and personality (branding) for their destinations. This sounds quite simple and straightforward, but as you will soon see, these are difficult tasks for a DMO and its stakeholders to accomplish and much more complex than branding consumer goods. Developing a destination brand can be time-consuming and expensive, so it is vital to fully understand why it is important to design a destination brand. Additionally, the potential benefits to the destination and its marketing, and to tourists, need to be recognized.

Figure 9.2 Australia's destination brand personality is high-spirited
Source: Shutterstock, Inc. (Pawel Papis).

Importance and benefits of destination branding

Why is branding so important in destination marketing and what are its specific benefits to destinations and tourists? Blain *et al.* (2005) identified three reasons for the importance of destination branding:

Enhances destination image

Branding clarifies and improves the image of the destination among potential travellers. This was as suggested in Figure 9.1. For example, the classic case of '100% Pure New Zealand' enhanced the image of New Zealand as a natural, clean and environmentally-sensitive destination. The 'Incredible India' branding fundamentally changed and improved the image of India as a tourism destination.

Reinforces unique image or personality

Branding can reinforce what potential travellers already perceive about the destination in terms of a unique image or personality. For example, Las Vegas has a reputation of being a sort of adult vacation playground; so the branding around the theme of 'What happens in Vegas, stays in Vegas®' reinforces this image.

Assists DMOs in measuring achievements

DMOs with destination brands find it easier to measure results through research. They have a definite concept that can be reviewed and discussed with consumers, and can track changes in perceptions and attitudes over time.

Some other aspects of the importance of destination branding are as follows:

Articulates ambition, raises expectations and makes a quality promise

According to Sean Young (2006) of Locum Consulting in the UK, a successful destination brand articulates ambition, raises expectations and makes a promise of quality. Kotler and Gartner (2002) also agree that brands offer consumers a promise of value. Articulating ambition means putting in words and images what the destination wants to be; the desired identity and personality of the destination are made more concrete and less vague. Raising expectations is two-sided; the DMO and tourism stakeholders raise their sights on what will be achieved through destination branding; tourists increase their expectations of the experiences and quality that they will receive within the destination.

Differentiates destination among competitors

An effective brand makes the destination stand out among its competitors and this is definitely one of the most important purposes of destination branding. As mentioned above in the definition of destination branding, some of the leading experts in place branding refer to this process as creating a 'competitive identity'.

The specific benefits of destination branding for tourists have been identified by Clarke (2000) and others, and include the following:

- *Lowering risks in decision-making*: Destination brands give consumers more confidence in their choices of holidays and destinations. This lowers their perceived risks as they have a clearer idea of what to expect.
- *Reducing impact of intangibility*: As you will learn quite soon, tourism is an experience good and is intangible at the time when a trip purchase decision is being made. Destination branding provides clues and cues to potential tourists that help to reduce the impact of intangibility.
- *Conveying greater consistency*: If the destination branding is widely applied in the destination, this creates greater consistency in brand implementation across multiple tourism sector stakeholder outlets and continuously over several years.

For DMOs and destinations, the benefits of destination branding are (Clarke, 2000; Baker, 2010):

- *Facilitating precise market segmentation*: Branding forces destinations and DMOs to think very clearly about their audiences and to take aim at specific segments of the market.
- *Integrating stakeholder efforts*: A destination brand provides a platform and a focus for tourism sector stakeholders to work together toward a mutually-beneficial outcome.
- *Generating increased respect, recognition, loyalty and renown*: A place can gain more respect, recognition and renown from having an outstanding destination brand. For example, the 'Malaysia Truly Asia' branding (Figure 9.3) has definitely helped Malaysia earn greater respect and recognition as a tourism destination. Here is how Tourism Malaysia explains the 'Truly Asia' concept:

What makes Malaysia 'Truly Asia'

There is only one place where all the colours, flavours, sounds and sights of Asia come together – Malaysia. No other country has Asia's three major races, Malay, Chinese, Indian, plus various other ethnic groups in large numbers. Nowhere is there such exciting diversity of cultures, festivals, traditions and customs, offering myriad experiences. No other county is 'Truly Asia' as Malaysia.

'Malaysia, Truly Asia' captures and defines the essence of the country's unique diversity. It sums up the distinctiveness and allure of Malaysia that make it an exceptional tourist destination.

(Tourism Malaysia, 2008)

- *Correcting inaccurate perceptions*: Sometimes people within the destination itself have outdated and inaccurate perceptions of their own place. Negative attitudes often exist internally and the process of destination branding should counter this pessimism with fresh new ideas and accurate market and competitive information.

Figure 9.3 'Malaysia Truly Asia' is a well recognized destination brand
Source: Shutterstock, Inc.

- *Increasing tourism's economic benefits*: Effective destination branding should, with continued implementation over several years, improve stakeholders' incomes and profits, and increase tax revenues for government.
- *Enhancing community pride and advocacy*: Good brands make local people feel a greater sense of pride in the places where they live. This also helps to increase community support and advocacy for tourism.
- *Expanding the primary market for all to share*: Expanding the size of the 'pie' (or primary market) for stakeholders to get a larger share, rather than having to rely on lowering prices to get a share of a smaller 'pie'.

The Montana Office of Tourism (2011) describes the benefits of the state's tourism destination brand as follows:

What is the Montana brand?

- The essential attributes that distinguish Montana from its competitors.
- The direct or indirect experience guests have with our state.
- The public perception of those who visit or live in Montana.
- A strategic roadmap for advertising, marketing and promotion.
- Something that does not change from year to year.

Branding is critical and strategic to the marketing of tourism destinations and it has many potential benefits. Now that the importance of destination branding has received much higher recognition in the past 15–20 years, highly professional procedures and practices are now available to DMOs. However, destination branding faces a set of daunting challenges that need to be confronted and overcome. These challenges are now discussed.

Challenges of destination branding

Destination branding is very challenging in practical terms and branding is difficult to accomplish and maintain over long time periods. Yet the world's best destination brands have been around for decades. The following are some of the added complexities of branding tourism destinations:

Destinations are a mix of different products and services

Unlike physical products that have finite and known characteristics, tourism destinations are complex and variable. They are not single products but rather an amalgam of products and services under different ownerships. You learned about the destination mix concept in Chapters 1 and 5, and it has several dimensions including attractions and events, facilities, transportation, infrastructure and hospitality resources. All of these quite different elements need to be integrated under one brand.

DMOs do not have total control over the destination mix that is being branded

DMOs do not own or manage the products and services that are covered under the destination branding. In reality, other companies and organizations are responsible for 'delivering' the destination brand. A diverse range of tourism sector and other stakeholders are involved; their quality standards may vary quite widely. This is a very different situation than that experienced by a company, since a company has total control over product quality and brand delivery. It is much more challenging for a DMO that has to rely on the quality and experiences delivered by multiple tourism sector stakeholders. Moreover, the DMO usually has no direct power or control over stakeholders, but can only act in an advisory capacity.

Needs a team effort

A DMO should not do destination branding on its own; in fact, it requires a team effort. The team should include tourism sector stakeholders and others in the community who can make useful contributions. Past and potential tourists should also be recruited for the team, and provide their valuable inputs. Figure 9.4 shows that four major groups of people are involved in developing and using the destination brand: tourism sector stakeholders, community residents, the DMO and tourists.

Of course, there will be others on the destination branding team. These will include a tourism destination branding consulting company and a creative design company. These professionals will work along with the DMO's marketing department, especially for the development of the brand strategy and brand identity design.

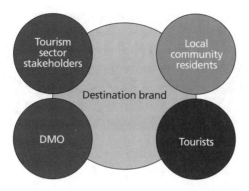

Figure 9.4 Team effort and players for destination branding

Requires a long-term commitment

The *Slovenia Times* (2010) likened destination branding to a relay race, in which the baton is passed from person to person until the finish line is reached. What a great metaphor that is, since destination branding needs a long-term commitment and may not produce immediate results. Also the players may change at the DMO and within the destination, but destination branding must continue on its course. The challenges are to be patient and to ensure that the continuity of destination branding is maintained. The 'Virginia is for Lovers®' destination branding is an outstanding example of a state DMO making a long-term commitment to a destination branding approach (Figure 9.5).

'The power of love: Virginia is for Lovers, 42 years and still strong'

In addition to the state's superior tourism product and accessibility, Virginia is for Lovers® is one of the most highly recognized tourism slogans in the world. The year 2009 marked the 40th anniversary of the popular state tourism slogan and logo. In June of 2009, Forbes.com named Virginia is for Lovers® one of the top ten tourism marketing campaigns of all time. Forbes had this to say about Virginia is for Lovers®: 'Forty years later, the Virginia is for Lovers® state tourism campaign is still going strong – and still ranked as one of the top travel campaigns in history. Who after all is against love?' says travel journalist and Forbes judge Rudy Maxa. Virginia is for Lovers®, launched in 1969, and is a brand that has endured and is supported by superior product and vacation experience. Today, Virginia is for Lovers® represents love, pure and simple, and tells visitors that love is at the heart of every Virginia vacation.

(Virginia Tourism Corporation, 2011)

Figure 9.5 An outstanding brand from Virginia
Source: Virginia Tourism Corporation, 2012.

Tourism is an experience good

Tourism is not bought and consumed like physical products; tourism and destinations are experience goods. The quality of destinations cannot truly be observed and assessed in advance; destinations must be experienced to determine their real quality. So tourism destinations cannot be 'tried on' or 'tried out' before booking them to see if they 'fit' the tourist's needs and wants. This level of uncertainty about the destination experience makes branding more challenging.

You will see the word 'experience' used repeatedly throughout this chapter and in many of the destination branding examples. This is not accidental but rather it mirrors the need to promise and deliver the experiences that tourists most desire in destinations.

Lack of sufficient funding to support destination branding efforts

The biggest DMOs around the world can afford to do destination branding as their marketing budgets are large enough. However many small and medium-sized DMOs find it difficult to come up with the funds to hire branding consultant specialists and to pay for the approaches and materials that the consultants recommend.

What does destination branding usually cost? This is an extremely difficult question to answer as the costs vary widely from destination to destination. You will see some figures quoted in the examples in this chapter, and they vary from $100,000 to over one million US dollars. Of course, the costs vary according to what is actually included in the estimates. The minimum cost would be for the fees and expenses of hiring an expert consulting organization in destination branding and presumably this would not be much less than $100,000 and could also be significantly higher than this.

Political influences may be felt

Destinations are places and places have governments with political leaders. Politicians are very sensitive about the images of the places within their jurisdiction. If a powerful politician does not personally like a suggested destination branding approach, it might not get the approval of government.

For example, a new 'Always Natural' destination branding was developed for the Maldives at a cost reported to be around $100,000. However, with the political crisis and change of government there, the political leaders have opted to have another new destination brand.

In fact, this is one of the real threats to the longevity of a destination brand. When political parties and leaders change, as they do frequently, there is a tendency to want to 'sweep clean' all that was done by previous administrations. Weak destination brands that do not have the complete support of stakeholders are in grave danger of being scrapped and replaced. Outstanding brands that are deeply embedded in consumers' minds and wholeheartedly embraced by stakeholders have a much better chance of surviving a political house-cleaning.

Brands and destination advertising are subject to public discussion and criticism

'Everybody is a tourism expert.' Because almost everybody travels and becomes a tourist themselves, they all have opinions about how to put across the images of the places where they live. Reporters and editors in the media also like to talk and write about local tourism branding and advertising approaches. Therefore, destination brands often become the topic of widespread debate in the local media. This can be a difficult process for a DMO to manage, since some opinions may be misinformed, but still influential.

Pure New Zealand under attack

New Zealand should be prepared for international criticism for its plan to open conservation land to mining, a tourism expert says.

Tourism Research Institute director Simon Milne said the plan was likely to be picked up on by international media, and tourist businesses should be prepared for the fallout.

(Gibson, 2010)

With the introduction of worldwide communications through social media networks, there is now much more public scrutiny and discussion of destination brands. For example, when the Philippine Department of Tourism launched its new brand with the slogan, 'It's more fun in the Philippines', many observers in cyberspace noted this was the same slogan as was used in Switzerland decades before. The previous campaign, *'Pilipinas Kay Ganda'*, was short-lived and drew huge criticism from netizens. One of the criticisms came within one week after its launch when bloggers noticed the logo was strikingly similar to the logo for Poland's tourism.

The Tourism Australia advertising campaign, 'So where the bloody hell are you?' was withdrawn amid widespread criticism online and offline. Non-English speakers could not understand what was meant by the phrase, and some countries banned the advertisements deeming them to be too risqué.

These are just a few examples of what can happen after a tourism destination brand 'goes public' in today's instant communication society. As you will see later in this chapter, it is much better to take more time and reveal preliminary ideas for the brand identity to tourism sector stakeholders and test them with consumers.

Before starting to discuss how to do destination branding, it is good for you to first know about what makes an effective destination brand. It is important to have some basic criteria for what constitutes a good destination brand before starting the process of developing a new brand. This provides 'benchmarks' against which the destination brand can be compared to ensure that it meets certain standards.

Characteristics of a good destination brand

Based upon their successful experiences around the world in the past 40–50 years, effective destination brands have certain shared characteristics:

- *Attractive*: While a destination brand is not only visual, it is important that its visual elements are attractive and appealing to people in the target markets. For example, the destination brand logo for Spain's tourism is beautiful in its design and colour scheme, and was created by a famous Spanish painter.
- *Communicates destination quality and experiences*: As an experience good, an effective destination brand puts across the types of experiences that tourists will have, as well as promising a certain level of quality. The 'Canada: Keep Exploring' destination branding approach by the Canadian Tourism Commission (CTC) is excellent at communicating the experiences that tourists will have in this vast country. Here is how CTC (2012) justifies this approach:

Canada is for explorers

In 2004, we set out to change this outdated idea of Canada. Going back to this country's roots, we put our stake in the ground. We aren't a specialty destination for sun-worshippers who want to lie on the beach for a week. We're a country built by – and for – explorers. We attract travellers who want the freedom to express themselves through travel. If Canada is an adventure story, our hero is the curious traveller who thrives on surprising, unexpected and out-of-the-ordinary experiences.

- *Consistent with positioning*: The destination brand must convey the desired image that has been selected. For example, an eco-oriented tourism destination like Costa Rica is well-advised to use a good deal of green in its communications supporting the destination branding.
- *Expresses the destination's personality*: The tone projected by the destination brand fits well with the character of the place. For example, the Newfoundland and Labrador, Canada tourism personality is 'the natural and spontaneous expression of who we are' and is as follows:
  - Natural and uncomplicated.
  - Warm and friendly.
  - Genuine and authentic.
  - Quietly and proudly independent.
  - Spontaneous, rather than practised or self-conscious.
  - Witty and funny, with a natural spontaneity.
  - Creative – not only in art and culture, but in our natural ingenuity and inventiveness.
  - Comfortable in our own skin.
- *Is supported by marketing activities*: A good destination brand is the foundation for and supported by effective integrated marketing communications (IMC) campaigns. You will learn all about how this is done in the next chapter.

- *Memorable:* A good destination brand is not easily forgotten. For example, how many of us can forget, 'I Love New York'? Many people think this is the brand of New York City, but it was actually introduced by the state DMO on Valentine's Day 1977. This memorable brand has been a huge benefit to tourism in the state of New York and New York City (Figure 9.6).
- *Simple*: It is better that a destination brand be not too complex as consumers may not be able to interpret what is meant by the brand. Many of the truly successful destination brands of the past decades, including 'I Love New York' and '100% Pure New Zealand', are the essence of simplicity. In contrast, the failed brands include many that were too hard to interpret and understand.
- *Market-tested*: A good destination brand has been market-tested in a preliminary form with a representative group of people in the intended target markets. It also has been given the 'stamp of approval' by tourism sector stakeholders.
- *Transportable to the Web as a domain name*: You have already heard about integrated marketing communications (IMC) in Chapter 3 and it is a real bonus if the destination branding can yield some text or an expression that can be transported to the Web as a domain name. For example, Travel Alberta created a new consumer website, http://www.remembertobreathe.com that reflects its new destination branding programme of the same name.
- *Unique*: Being different is one of the keys to the success of destination branding and this means standing out among competitors. The Tourism Ireland destination brand is very unique and not just in the shamrock-shaped logo. The uniqueness of the Tourism Ireland branding is how it blends together four factors: physical experience of holidaymaking in Ireland, the personality for communications, the experiences and the benefits that holidaymakers receive. These are based upon the people, culture and place that is Ireland (Figure 9.7).

Figure 9.6 New York and New York City both benefit from 'I Love New York'
Source: Shutterstock Inc., (ARENA Creative).

Figure 9.7 The beauty and history of Ireland are a strong part of its brand
Source: Shutterstock, Inc. (Patryk Kosmider).

- *Well-accepted by all stakeholders*: The destination brand must have acceptance of the stakeholders within the destination, and especially the tourism sector stakeholders. If stakeholders oppose the destination brand or are not particularly impressed by it, it has a low probability of succeeding.

Classic concepts in branding

Branding is one of those topics in management and marketing that is a real 'alphabet soup' of terminology; there are so many concepts thrown about that it confuses even the experts. So that you will not be confused, a few of the classic concepts in branding are defined below:

- *Brand equity*: Aaker (1991) defined brand equity as having five elements: brand loyalty, brand awareness, perceived quality, brand associations and other proprietary brand assets. Brand equity is the total accumulated value or worth of a brand.
- *Brand essence*: The main or core characteristics or values that are the main platform for the brand's competitive identity.
- *Brand identity*: This has two meanings according to branding experts. First, it is the perception of a brand in the tourism marketplace that is based on its positioning and brand personality. The second is the visual design of the brand, which normally includes a logo and some words and symbols.
- *Brand positioning*: The image of the brand in the minds of customers and potential customers.
- *Brand personality*: The outward characteristics of the brand sometimes associated with human traits.
- *Brand promise*: The expectations that customers have of the brand based upon what they have seen in marketing communications.

Steps in destination branding

In Chapter 3, you learned about the destination marketing planning system and destination branding falls within the second step that addresses the question of 'Where would we like to be?' As Figure 9.8 illustrates, the first part of the process of destination branding is the situation analysis, consisting of destination analysis (or destination audit), competitive analysis, market analysis, destination image analysis (or marketing position analysis), resident analysis and analysis of past marketing programmes. The destination image analysis determines the existing perceptions of the destination among past and potential tourists.

Before starting the description of the brand development process, you might be curious about how long it takes to develop a destination brand. Unfortunately there are no 'industry averages' for this, so a few case examples are cited. Travel Alberta's ('Remember to Breathe') destination branding for the province was 18 months in development. The new destination brand for the nearby state of Montana took almost a year to develop. Tourism Queensland stated that it spent AUD 4.16 million over 2 years to develop its new state brand, 'Queensland, Where Australia Shines'. Seattle's 'Metronatural™' destination brand was in development for 1 year. These four examples show that destination brand development can be time-consuming and can take more than a year from the basic research to the brand launch. Having said this, there are no doubt some cases where destination brands have been designed in less than a year; but as you will see now, it is hard to believe that all the following steps can be accomplished that quickly.

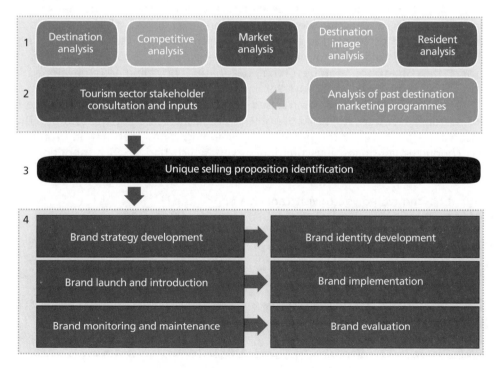

Figure 9.8 Steps involved in destination branding

1 Situation analysis

Chapter 3 explained how a situation analysis is done as a step in developing a marketing plan. The different parts (destination, competitive, market, destination image, resident and past marketing programmes) of the situation analysis also provide rich and necessary information for destination branding. There is no doubt that these analyses can be very time-consuming but they should not be skipped over in developing a destination brand. Just doing one or two quick focus groups with a few handfuls of people is not sufficient, although it happens quite often in brand-building.

Potential tourists are the main audience for a new destination brand. Therefore, the development of the destination branding should be based on a thorough understanding of these people and what they want to experience within the destination. The brand must be built to resonate with customers and not just to reflect what is available in the destination. This means that research needs to be conducted on the current images of the destination among people within the target markets.

A good case study here is the market research that preceded the development of the 'Shaoxing: Vintage China' destination branding in Zhejiang Province, China. Belle Tourism International (BTI) Consulting conducted extensive research with consumers in China and abroad to provide the support for brand development. Consumer surveys were conducted in Japan, South Korea, Macau and Taiwan, as well as in several cities in China (Shanghai, Beijing, Guangzhou, Hangzhou, Nanjing, Suzhou, Wuxi and Wenzhou). A travel agency survey was completed in Hong Kong. Respondents were asked about their awareness of the existing major attractions in Shaoxing. The two items in which there were the highest levels of awareness were Shaoxing yellow rice wine and Lu Xun, a famous Chinese contemporary writer who lived in Shaoxing and wrote about life in the city. Respondents were also asked which activities and experiences they most wanted to engage in when travelling to China and Shaoxing.

Meetings were held with tourism sector stakeholders in Shaoxing; and after this analysis, the 'Shaoxing: Vintage China' destination branding was developed for international tourist markets (Figure 9.9).

A second example of a research-based approach to destination branding comes from Tanzania in eastern Africa. At the time of preparing this book, the country's DMO (Tanzania Tourism) was in the process of developing a new destination brand. The DMO conducted an image investigation survey, which had 2,548 respondents. The questions included in this survey were:

- What has motivated you to visit Tanzania on this trip?
- What image did you have of Tanzania prior to your first visit?

Figure 9.9 Visual expressions of 'Vintage Shaoxing' destination branding
Source: Belle Tourism International Consulting, 2008.

- What image do you have of Tanzania now?
- What is the strength of Tanzania's destination image?
- What brand (name, slogan, etc.) could best promote Tanzania as a tourist destination?

2 Tourism sector stakeholder consultations and inputs

Input should be gathered from tourism sector stakeholders on their suggestions about the image and positioning of the destination. In particular, stakeholders should be asked to express what they see as being the most unique features of the destination. Stakeholders' opinions cannot and should not be taken as substitute for those of tourists; however, there is no point in having a destination branding that they do not support. Additionally, it is essential that tourism sector stakeholders adopt the destination brand and use it in their own marketing and promotional programmes.

As an example here, the Montana Office of Tourism in the USA conducted eight meetings across the state and received input from more than 350 stakeholders. The input from stakeholders was placed against the results of consumer focus groups in developing the most relevant and believable attributes of the Montana brand.

3 Unique selling proposition identification

The destination's unique selling propositions (USPs) are one of the most critical inputs to destination branding, as these articulate what is truly different in the place when compared to competitors. For example, in the Shaoxing example discussed above, six USPs were identified; (1) Shaoxing yellow rice wine; (2) ancient canal city; (3) celebrities; (4) nature; (5) artistic impression; and (6) beauty and love. The visual expressions of five of these USPs are illustrated in Figure 9.9. The Shaoxing yellow rice wine is shown in the containers in each of the four images.

Tourism Queensland in Australia (2010) identified the Queensland lifestyle, islands and beaches, natural encounters and adventure as the state's four attributes that represented its USPs. However, in coming up with its new destination brand with the slogan of 'Queensland, Where Australia Shines', it wanted to reflect more on the tourism experiences that people could have in Queensland and their emotional responses to these experiences:

Queensland's USPs from a tourist perspective

- The thought and line are born out of something Queensland already owns – a beautiful climate and laid back attitude.
- When people are happy, they shine. Their faces radiate the same joy, warmth and love that Queensland does.
- Queensland's unique destinations are all shining examples of what makes Australia great.
- We want people to see Queensland as the one place in the world where they'll get their chance to shine too.

4 Destination brand development

Destination brand development comprises six sequential steps as shown earlier in Figure 9.8. This is much like a 'micro' version of the destination marketing planning process described in Chapter 3.

Branding strategy development

This represents the approaches used to develop the destination brand, and the following questions need to be answered in this step:

- *Why does the destination need a new tourism brand?* A clear rationale or reasoning behind starting the process of developing a new brand must be given.
- *What are the objectives for the destination branding?* A set of specific destination branding objectives must be articulated.
- *What image will the new destination brand communicate?* The way the destination will be positioned in the new brand must be explained.
- *Who are the targets for the destination brand?* The target markets to which the new destination brand will be communicated must be identified and described.
- *How will the new destination brand look?* A basic and general idea of the new destination brand needs to be developed.

The starting point for designing a destination brand is the development of branding objectives; what is it that the destination brand is expected to achieve and by when? The *Handbook on Tourism Destination Branding* prepared by the European Travel Commission and UNWTO suggested a set of destination branding objectives, and these were adapted for this book and are shown below:

Destination branding objectives

- To differentiate the destination from competitors.
- To increase awareness, recognition and memorability of the destination over time among potential visitors.
- To create a positive image of the destination that makes people responsive to the DMO's marketing messages and therefore more likely to visit.
- To give the destination a strong and compelling brand identity.

The next stage in branding strategy development is deciding on the brand positioning. Destination positioning has already been defined in this chapter as the image that the destination wants to create in the minds of people within its target markets. You might say these are the perceptions that it wishes people to have about the destination.

Brand positioning of destination Australia

The people of Australia are friendly, straight talking and open. Their sense of 'mateship' and their 'no worries' attitude make everyone feel welcome and make it easy to enjoy adventures beyond the imagination. Whether it's in Australia's wide open landscapes, pristine oceans or vibrant cities, a holiday in Australia is an opportunity to experience a vast yet accessible adventure playground.

You don't just visit Australia, you live it.

(Tourism Australia, 2012)

The branding strategy must be aligned with the destination's market segmentation strategy and in particular give consideration to the target markets that have been selected. It is likely that the destination brand will have to be adapted and applied differently for dissimilar target markets; although it is most desirable that there is consistency among the different applications.

Based upon the situation analysis results, the inputs from stakeholders, along with the branding objectives and positioning and marketing segmentation strategy, the DMO then prepares a brief or written summary document, that is the foundation for the creative development. This gives a basic and general picture in words about how the new destination brand should feel and look.

For example, Montana identified the following three 'brand pillars' to guide its branding process. The first one was its strongest characteristic, which it called its 'ace card'.

- *More spectacular unspoiled nature than anywhere else in the lower 48* (the ace card; Differentiator)
- *Vibrant and charming small towns that serve as gateways to our natural wonders* (the surprise card; Mitigator)
- *Breathtaking experiences by day and relaxing hospitality at night* (card that ties the hand together; Brand Builder)

Brand identity development

This is the creative stage of destination brand development. Here the brief or summary document is interpreted into a creative strategy that can encompass a new logo, colour scheme and other visual image (VI) guidelines, slogan (or strapline), musical score and other elements.

The wording and the typography are extremely important elements of brand identity. Two of the most highly commended destination brands attest to this point. Launched in 1999, '100% Pure New Zealand' has undoubtedly been the 'world champion' of destination branding for at least 10 years. Set on a black background when it was first introduced (Figure 9.10), this destination branding by Tourism New Zealand set the standard for others to follow.

Figure 9.10 The 'world champion' of destination branding from Tourism New Zealand
Source: Tourism New Zealand, 2009.

Another highly-acclaimed brand is very simple (two words) but conveys so much meaning about tourism in a vast country. 'Incredible India' was launched in 2002 and has been hugely beneficial to tourism in India (Figure 9.11).

Figure 9.11 India is truly an incredible destination with sites like the Taj Mahal
Source: Shutterstock, Inc. (Luciano Mortula).

Although beautiful logos are not destination brands, it really helps if the logo is highly attractive and memorable. A great example here is the logo developed by the famous Catalan painter Joan Miró in 1982 for Tourism Spain (Figure 9.12).

Figure 9.12 A beautiful image accompanies Spain's destination branding
Source: Tourism Spain, 2012.

The colours used with the brand identity can be very crucial. For example, the Netherlands Board of Tourism and Conventions uses orange in the destination logo and accompanying elements. Switzerland Tourism (2012) uses red and the reasons are explained below:

Switzerland's tourism identity

Switzerland Tourism's visuals are defined largely by two main elements: the colour red and the sender. The colour red is an allusion to the colour of the Swiss flag. The Switzerland Tourism sender, meanwhile, consists of the word 'Switzerland', the gold flower signet and claim 'get natural'. The word 'Switzerland' communicates what we stand for. The gilt edelweiss with a Swiss flag in its centre is a combined allusion to the natural beauty of our country and to our high standards of quality and independence. It depicts Switzerland as a jewel. 'Get natural' is our brand promise to our guests.

The brand promise reflects the expectations that tourists have, based upon what is contained in the DMO's marketing communications and how the communications are delivered. Travel Alberta in Canada introduced a new destination brand for the province in late 2011 and the new approach had a very clear and strong brand promise. 'Give them Goosebumps' was the brand promise, meaning that based upon the Travel Alberta marketing campaign, visitors to the province could expect many exciting and unforgettable experiences.

Brand launch and introduction

The brand launch is when a new destination brand is revealed to the public for the first time. Normally this is done with some 'pomp and ceremony' and is a major public relations event in the destination. For example, the 'YourSingapore' destination brand was launched at the Singapore Tourism Board Tourism Industry Conference in March 2010.

The following advice from Arcade Brands (2010) is excellent in designing the brand launch as well as differentiating between a logo and a destination brand:

A logo is not a destination brand

The real danger in including a new logo when you launch your finely crafted and painstakingly developed destination brand is that no one will listen to a single word you say. They'll fixate on the logo. And it won't matter how many hundred 'consultations' and 'workshops' you did, or that you surveyed every man, woman and child in all your key markets and reviewed three hundred years of third party research, all of which was time and money well invested. It won't even matter whether your idea for the destination brand is any good. The scope of your multi-year project will be reduced to headlines that read 'City spends $1 million on logo'. And you'll only have yourself to blame.

As pointed out above by Arcade Brands (2010), it is dangerous to put the main focus on a new logo in launching a destination brand. Again, a destination brand is much more than just a logo; but if the DMO focuses on the logo in the launch, others will also focus on it as well. It seems that many DMOs are not listening to this advice and their launches are mainly for presenting new tourism logos and slogans.

The brand launch above all needs to relay information on the research that was done with consumers and explain how stakeholders' input was collected and integrated. In fact, the whole 'brand story' must be related to the audience. Some DMOs refer to the entire process as a 'destination branding journey' and that indeed is a very good metaphor, since the launch should be more like a starting point rather than an ending to the journey. If the logo and slogan are seen as being the final outcome of the destination branding process, that is definitely not the impression to be communicated in a brand launch. You just need to consider the longevity of the world's most successful destination brands to realize that the lifespan of a good brand will be 10 or more years. So, even if the brand takes 2 years to develop, it will have many more years ahead of it. Thus, the logo and slogans may be modified in the future, but the basic ideas underpinning the destination branding will not.

After the launch, tourism sector stakeholders will be anxious to get going with the new destination brand. The DMO needs to develop a variety of materials for the introduction of the brand and the use of the brand internally and by tourism sector stakeholders. These materials include the following items:

- *Brand manual*: This is a complete guide to the new destination brand and explains how and why it was developed, and how it is to be implemented. This is sometimes called the 'brand story' (Knapp and Sherwin, 2005). You will hear about some outstanding examples soon.
- *Photo library or gallery*: Photographs are tremendously important in tourism communications and they are even more critical in supporting the images of the destination brand.
- *Style manual*: Guidelines on how and how not to use the brand logo; a colour palette; and directions on how to apply the brand.

The brand introduction includes steps taken by the DMO to educate tourism sector stakeholders to the new destination brand. This is not just the launch event but a concerted campaign to make stakeholders aware of the reasons for the brand and how to use it. There are different ways to accomplish this; one is to prepare a brand book or manual providing all the details on the destination brand. *Discovering the Montana Brand* describes the new destination brand for the state in great detail.

Tourism Australia published a *Brand Book* and describes the information contained therein as follows:

Tourism Australia *Brand Book*

The first type (of information) outlines Destination Australia's brand positioning, proposition and personality, as well as our target audience. The second gives you all the specific details you need to form a clear and comprehensive picture of our brand, including tips on how the brand influences how you promote Australia. And, of course, we also show the experiences that make Australia not only unique, but also unforgettable.

(Tourism Australia, 2012)

Travel Alberta also did an excellent job of introducing its new destination branding, which included an online video of the launch event. This was accompanied by a very practical *Brand Experiences Workbook*.

Several DMOs have designed special training programmes including seminars and workshops that present their new destination brands to tourism sector stakeholders. These programmes are supplemented with information and materials on DMOs' websites that explain the branding in greater detail and are always there for reference purposes.

It is also very helpful in introducing and communicating a brand if it can be expressed in a visual representation that captures the main features of the brand. A great case study is the Britain brand that was developed by VisitBritain (2012) (Figure 9.13).

Figure 9.13 An excellent visual representation of the Britain brand
Source: Copyright VisitBritain, 2011.

The Britain brand

The three words at the heart of the essence that define Britain as a tourist destination are Timeless, Dynamic and Genuine. In turn, they describe the Place, the Culture and People of Britain. We use people at the heart of brand and marketing. These three essence words, woven together, give a real sense of the nature of the experience that tourists expect. Rich in history but with stories to tell; a real warmth and informality of spirit combined with a spark and dynamism that gives Britain its unique sense of place.

The place (destination), people and culture are what differentiates Britain from competitors. Britain is a timeless place with castles, museums, countryside, gardens and legends. It has very genuine people and they can be encountered at pubs, markets, B&Bs, villages and festivals. Britain has a dynamic culture that can be experienced in its cities, music, arts, sports and shopping. So in one diagram, VisitBritain neatly but also comprehensively communicates the tourism brand for Britain.

Brand implementation

Instead of saying brand implementation, this could have been titled 'living the brand'. Knapp and Sherwin (2005) call this process 'brand culturalization' or the roadmap for how the destination will deliver the brand promise. Once the destination brand is launched and introduced, it must be embedded within the destination and appear in every communication and interaction with tourists and potential tourists. Embedded in the destination means that the brand must be practised; it is not just a vague concept that just appears on paper or in a video. Remember that the brand is a promise and a promise builds expectations of what will be experienced in the destination. Therefore, every service encounter with tourism staff and local residents, the ways in which tourism sector stakeholders deliver the experiences, and all the marketing that is done by stakeholders, must support and enhance the destination brand. Ensuring the consistency of the message delivered within the destination is critical to effective destination branding.

Brand implementation also involves incorporating a new destination brand in all of the DMO's marketing and promotion programmes and activities. Chapters 10 and 11 discuss how marketing communications are accomplished, so it is unnecessary to go into great detail here about integrated marketing communications using traditional (offline) and information and communication technology (online) channels. It just needs to be said that the destination branding must be reflected in all the DMO's communications, and that it be consistently applied at all times.

A brief example of brand incorporation is provided here and follows on from one of the previous examples. The 'Shaoxing Vintage China' destination brand was implemented in the development of a new English-language website, http://www. vintageshaoxing.com, and thereafter several other language versions were developed (Japanese, Korean, Spanish and German). An event was created for a group of foreign expatriates living in nearby Shanghai and was staged just before the 2,500th anniversary of the city. The event was called the '25 @ 100% Vintage Shaoxing Experiences' and generated much positive publicity for Shaoxing. The participants at the event kept diaries of their experiences and many photos were taken of their trips within Shaoxing. These were later used in the production of an English guidebook, *Experience Vintage Shaoxing* (Figure 9.14). As you can see, these were a well-integrated set of marketing and promotion activities to implement a new destination brand.

Figure 9.14 *Experience Vintage Shaoxing* English guidebook
Source: Belle Tourism International Consulting, 2010.

Brand monitoring and maintenance

It is very important that the performance of the brand be monitored and maintained. Monitoring implies tracking the implementation of destination branding and assessing the progress towards the achievement of objectives. This monitoring can be accomplished using a variety of research techniques including content analysis of travel blogs and consumer destination reviews (qualitative), surveys (visitor profile surveys; post-visit surveys; random surveys of visitors and non-visitors) (quantitative) and focus groups (qualitative). The items to be measured here include awareness and recall of the brand; impact on intentions to visit the destination; and image of the destination.

The DMO acts as the 'brand guardian' making sure that the initial excitement from the launching of the new brand is maintained over the long term, which will be years rather than months. As such, the DMO must monitor how tourism sector stakeholders are applying the brand in their marketing and operations; and make suggestions on how usage can be enhanced. This is one part of the task of brand maintenance.

There are other brand maintenance tasks that occur in the lifetime of good and long-lasting destination brands. Usually these are not major repair jobs but the fine-tuning of aspects of the brand identity to keep up with contemporary design trends and with changes in market priorities and customer expectations. For example, although the tourism brand logo for Spain has remained the same since 1982, the words accompanying it have been changed. Additionally, the highly-successful '100% Pure New Zealand' brand became '100% Pure You' in 2011.

Brand evaluation

The true test of the effectiveness of a destination brand is if it achieves its objectives. Here again, solid research is needed to conclusively determine if the destination branding impacted the target market as intended. Winning awards for excellent destination branding is nice and makes for great publicity; however, awards do not prove that destination brands have achieved their objectives. The types of research that should be completed are similar to those mentioned above for brand monitoring.

There are several universal questions that should be addressed in any destination brand evaluation, and these include the following:

- Did the brand increase the levels of awareness of the destination in target markets?
- Did the brand increase intentions to visit the destination in target markets?
- Did the brand improve the destination's image among people in the target markets?
- Did the brand create a unique competitive identity for the destination?
- Was the brand an instrumental factor in increasing tourist volumes and expenditures in the destination?
- Does the brand have a high level of recall and memorability among people within the target markets?

These are good questions and there are undoubtedly others that can be addressed in brand evaluation. The results of the evaluation are critical and especially if another new destination branding cycle is being contemplated.

Summary

Destination branding has become a hot topic in tourism during the past 15–20 years. This is an element of destination marketing strategy, and its perceived importance has increased as destination competitiveness has intensified worldwide. There is a trio of interrelated concepts that work together in this aspect of destination marketing strategy: destination positioning, destination image and destination branding.

Destination branding is important in several ways but particularly in establishing a place's competitive identity and communicating what makes it unique among all destination choices. Many benefits are created for destinations and tourists through effective destination branding. Above all, effective destination branding makes places stand out among competitors and, as a result, the destinations draw more tourists than they did before the brands were launched.

Branding tourism destinations is very challenging given the diversity of the destination mix and the experience good characteristic of tourism. Destination branding often requires time to be successful, so patience is required as well as continual investment in the brand. The classic success stories in tourism destination branding have withstood the test of time and have been in place for 10 to more than 40 years. These include 'Virginia is for Lovers®', 'I Love New York®', '100% Pure New Zealand' and 'Incredible India'. Many destinations tend to chop and change approaches very often and this is a clue that they are really not following the principles of professional destination branding. Instead, they are on a never-ending search for the perfect slogan and logo.

The past 15–20 years have brought great professionalism and flair into destination branding. However, political interference often gets in the way of excellent destination branding and spoils the continuity of professional branding efforts. Also destination marketers often face a barrage of criticism online; although some of this is deserved, it must be said. The best advice for DMOs is to invest in solid research to prove the value and contributions of their destination brands, and also to continue to keep tourism stakeholders informed and onside.

Brand development starts with a situation analysis that provides the facts, figures and conclusions for the rest of the process. This includes analyses of the destination, competitors, market, destination image, residents and past marketing programmes. Then, there are consultations with tourism sector stakeholders to get their vital inputs into the destination branding process. The third step is to identify the destination's unique selling propositions (USPs) that make it different from competitors.

The actual development of the destination brand takes place in six steps: brand strategy development; brand identity development; brand launch and introduction; brand implementation; brand monitoring and maintenance; and brand evaluation. A brand is not just a logo and a slogan; in fact, it is a promise that the destination makes to potential visitors about the experiences they will have. So delivering on the brand is not just about marketing and promotion, it involves the service quality in the destination and how tourism sector stakeholders deliver experiences. If a brand is not actually 'lived' in the destination, then it is not truly a destination brand.

Here is what a DMO must accomplish to do destination branding effectively:

- Carefully document the reasons for needing a new destination brand, noting why the previous destination brand is to be discontinued.
- Conduct a situation analysis.
- Obtain input from tourism sector stakeholders on the destination brand.
- Identify the destination's unique selling propositions.
- Develop a destination brand strategy including objectives, positioning and target markets.
- Write a brief summary as the basis for the creative development of the brand.
- Work with vendors for brand identity development.
- Launch the new destination brand.
- Introduce the new destination brand to the market and tourism sector stakeholders.
- Implement the brand in marketing communications and within the destination.
- Monitor and maintain the brand.
- Evaluate the brand.

Review questions

1. Destination positioning, image and branding are interconnected concepts. How are these three concepts interrelated and in which ways do they impact each other?
2. Why is destination branding important?
3. What are the benefits that can accrue to destinations and tourists from destination branding?
4. What are the major challenges involved with doing destination branding?
5. What are the characteristics of a good destination brand?

6   What are the steps involved in destination brand development?
7   Which items are included in a destination brand strategy?
8   How would you describe the brand promise?
9   How long should a destination brand last? Please explain your reasoning based on actual practice.

References

Aaker, D. A. 1991. Managing Brand Equity: Capitalizing on the Value of a Brand Name. New York: The Free Press.

Anholt, S. 2009. Why national image matters – an essay by Simon Anholt. In European Travel Commission and UNWTO, Handbook on Tourism Destination Branding. Madrid: ETC/UNWTO.

Arcade Brand Strategies. 2010. A destination Brand is Not a Logo (and Not Just for the Reasons you May Think). http://brandarcade.com/?p=476

Baker, B. 2007. Destination Branding for Small Cities: The Essentials for Successful Place Branding. Oregon: Creative Leap Books.

——2010. Twenty benefits of a city branding strategy. Total Destination Marketing. http://www.destinationbranding.com/articles/Benefits_of_Strong_City_Brand.pdf

Balakrishnan, M.S. 2008. Dubai – a star in the east: A case study in strategic destination branding. *Journal of Place Management and Development*, 1(1), 62–91.

——2009. Strategic branding of destinations: A framework. *European Journal of Marketing*, 43 (5/6), 611–629.

Belle Tourism International Consulting. 2008. International Tourism Marketing Implementation Plan for Shaoxing.

——2010. Experience Vintage Shaoxing. A Guidebook for Travelers. Shanghai, PRC.

——2012. Experience Vintage Shaoxing English Guidebook. Shanghai, PRC.

Bendel, P. 2007. Destination marketing 3.0: A look back – and forward – as 'I Love NY' turns 30. *Travel Marketing Decisions* (Fall), 8–11.

Blain, C., Levy, S.E., and Ritchie, J.R.B. 2005. Destination branding: Insights and practices from destination management organizations. *Journal of Travel Research*, 43(4), 328–338.

Buncle, T. 2010. Destination Brand Architecture: Combined Strength or Constrained Image? http://www.insights.org.uk/articleitem.aspx?title=Destination+Brand+Architecture%3A+Combined+Strength+or+Constrained+Image%3F

Cai, L.A. 2002. Cooperative branding for rural destinations. *Annals of Tourism Research*, 29(3), 720–742.

Cai, L.A., Gartner, W.C., and Munar, A.M. eds. 2009. Tourism Branding; Communities in Action. Bingley: Emerald Group Publishing Limited.

Caldwell, N., and Freire, J.R. 2004. The differences between branding a country, a region and a city: Applying the Brand Box model. *Brand Management*, 12(1), 50–61.

Canadian Tourism Commission. 2012. Canada's Tourism Brand. http://en-corporate.canada.travel/resources-industry/canada%E2%80%99s-tourism-brand

Clarke, J. 2000. Tourism brands: An exploratory study of the brands box model. *Journal of Vacation Marketing*, 6(4), 329–345.

D'Hauteserre, A.-M. 2001. Destination branding in a hostile environment. *Journal of Travel Research*, 39(3), 300–307.

Dinnie, K. 2004. Place branding: Overview of an emerging literature. *Place Branding and Public Diplomacy*, 1(1), 106–110.

——2011. City Branding: Theory and Cases. Basingstoke: Palgrave Macmillan.

Dioko, L.A.N., and Harrill, R. 2011. Affirmation, assimilation, and anarchy: Critical undercurrents in destination branding. *International Journal of Culture, Tourism and Hospitality Research*, 5(3), 215–226.

Elson, S. 2008. 29th Annual TTRA Conference: June 7–10, 1998. Radisson Plaza Fort Worth, Fort Worth, Texas. *Journal of Travel Research*, 36(4), 102–103.

European Travel Commission and UNWTO. 2009. Handbook on Tourism Destination Branding. Madrid: ETC/UNWTO.

Foley, A., and Fahy, J. 2004. Incongruity between expression and experience: The role of imagery in supporting the positioning of a tourism destination brand. *Journal of Brand Management*, 11(3), 209–217.

Galarpe, K. 2010. 'Pilipinas Kay Ganda' Logo Lifted from Poland Logo? http://www.abs-cbnnews.com/lifestyle/11/18/10/pilipinas-kay-ganda-logo-lifted-poland-logo

Gartner, W.C., and Ruzzier, M.K. 2011. Tourism destination brand equity dimensions: Renewal versus repeat market. *Journal of Travel Research*, 50(5), 471–481.

Gibson, E. 2010. Excavation jars with pure image: Expert. *New Zealand Herald*, 24 March.

Govers, R., and Go, F. 2009. Place Branding: Glocal, Virtual and Physical Identities, Constructed, Imagined and Experienced. Basingstoke: Palgrave Macmillan.

Hanna, S., and Rowley, J. 2008. An analysis of terminology use in place branding. *Place Branding and Public Diplomacy*, 4(1), 61–75.

Hassan, S.B., Fayoum, M.S.H., and Al Bohairy, H. 2010. Perception of destination branding measures: A case study of Alexandria destination marketing organizations. *International Journal of Euro-Mediterranean Studies*, 3(2), 269–288.

Henderson, J.C. 2007. Uniquely Singapore? A case study in destination branding. *Journal of Vacation Marketing*, 13(3), 261–274.

Hosany, S., Ekinci, Y., and Uysal, M. 2006. Destination image and destination personality: An application of branding theories to tourism places. *Journal of Business Research*, 59(5), 638–642.

Hudson, S., and Ritchie, J.R.B. 2009. Branding a memorable destination experience. The case of 'Brand Canada'. *International Journal of Tourism Research*, 11(2), 217–228.

Insch, A. 2011. Conceptualization and anatomy of green destination brands. *International Journal of Culture, Tourism and Hospitality Research*, 5(3), 282–290.

Jago, L., Chalip, L., Brown, G., Mules, T., and Ali, S. 2003. Building events into destination branding: Insights from experts. *Event Management*, 8(1), 3–14.

Kant, A. 2009. Branding India: An Incredible Story. Noida, India: Collins Business.

Kaplanidou, K., and Vogt, C. 2003. Destination Branding: Concept and Measurement. Department of Park, Recreation and Tourism Resources, Michigan State University.

Keller, K.L. 1993. Conceptualizing, measuring, and managing customer-based brand equity. *Journal of Marketing*, 57(1), 1–22.

Knapp, D., and Sherwin, G. 2005. Destination BrandScience. Washington, DC: Destination Marketing Association International (IACVB).

Kneesel, E., Baloglu, S., and Millar, M. 2010. Gaming destination images: Implications for branding. *Journal of Travel Research*, 49(1), 68–78.

Konecnik, M., and Go, F. 2008. Tourism destination brand identity: The case of Slovenia. *Brand Management*, 15(3), 177–189.

Kotler, P., and Gartner, D. 2002. Country as a brand, product and beyond: A place marketing and brand management perspective. *The Journal of Brand Management*, 9(4/5), 249–261.

Lee, I., and Arcodia, C. 2011. The role of regional food festivals for destination branding. *International Journal of Tourism Research*, 13(4), 355–367.

Malkin, B. 2010. Australia drops controversial tourism campaign for 'safer' slogan. *The Telegraph*, 31 March.

Marzano, G., and Scott, N. 2009. Power in destination branding. *Annals of Tourism Research*, 36(2), 247–267.

Montana Department of Commerce. 2011. Montana Branding Initiative: Uncovering Montana's Brand. http://travelmontana.mt.gov/branding/

Montana Office of Tourism. 2011a. Discovering the Montana Brand.

——2011b. Using the Montana Brand.

Morgan, N., Pritchard, A., and Pride, R. 2002. Destination Branding: Creating the Unique Destination Proposition. London: Taylor & Francis Group.

——2011. Destination Brands: Managing Place Reputation, 3rd edn. Abingdon: Butterworth-Heinemann Elsevier.

Morgan, N.J., Pritchard, A., and Piggott, R. 2003. Destination branding and the role of stakeholders. *Journal of Vacation Marketing*, 9(3), 285–299.

Munar, A.M. 2011. Tourist-created content: rethinking destination branding. *International Journal of Culture, Tourism and Hospitality Research*, 5(3), 291–305.

Murphy, L., Moscardo, G., and Benckendorff, P. 2007. Using brand personality to differentiate regional tourism destinations. *Journal of Travel Research*, 46(1), 5–14.

Nelson, P. 1970. Information and consumer behavior. *Journal of Political Economy*, 78(2), 311–329.

Netherlands Board of Tourism and Conventions. 2012. New Focus: Holland Marketing from 2012 and Beyond.

Newfoundland and Labrador Department of Tourism, Culture and Recreation. 2011. Newfoundland and Labrador Brand. http://www.tcr.gov.nl.ca/tcr/tourism/tourism_marketing/newfoundland_and_labrador_brand.html

O'Connor, N., Flanagan, S., and Gilbert, D. 2008. The integration of film-induced tourism and destination branding in Yorkshire, UK. *International Journal of Tourism Research*, 10(5), 423–437.

Ooi, C.-S. 2010. Familiarity and uniqueness: Branding Singapore as a revitalized destination. Creative Encounters Working Paper 47, Copenhagen Business School.

Park, S.-Y., and Petrick, J.F. 2005. Destinations' perspectives of branding. *Annals of Tourism Research*, 33(1), 262–265.

Philippine Department of Tourism. 2012. http://itsmorefuninthephilippines.com/

Pike, S. 2005. Tourism destination branding complexity. *Journal of Product and Brand Management*, 14(4), 258–259.

——2009. Destination brand positions of a competitive set of near-home destinations. *Tourism Management*, 30(6), 857–866.

Qu, H., Kim, L.H., and Im, H.H. 2011. A model of destination branding: Integrating the concepts of the branding and destination image. *Tourism Management*, 32(3), 465–476.

Ritchie, J.R.B., and Ritchie, R.J.B. 1998. The Branding of Tourism Destinations: Past Achievements and Future Challenges. Annual Congress of the International Association of Scientific Experts in Tourism, Marrakech, Morocco.

Samath, F., and Hudoyo, F. 2012. Brand Maldives up in the air. *TTG Asia*, 23–29 March.

Saraniemi, S. 2010. Destination brand identity development and value system. *Tourism Review*, 65(2), 52–60.

——2011. From destination image building to identity-based branding. International *Journal of Culture, Tourism and Hospitality Research*, 5(3), 247–254.

Schmitt, B., and Simonson, A. 1997. Marketing Aesthetics: The Strategic Management of Brands, Identity, and Image. New York: The Free Press.

Singapore Tourism Board. 2010. Singapore Tourism Board Forecasts Record Numbers for 2010 and Unveils 'Your Singapore' Destination Brand. http://app.s+b.gov.sg/asp/new/newoza.asp?d+11384

Slovenia Times. 2010. The relay race of destination branding. 5 November.

Switzerland Tourism. 2012. Brand Switzerland's New Communications Presence. http://www.stnet.ch/fr.cfm/st/strategie/offer-Ueber_uns-Strategie-255954.html

Szondi, G. 2007. The role and challenges of country branding in transition countries: The Central and Eastern European experience. *Place Branding and Public Diplomacy*, 3(1), 8–20.

Tanzania Tourism. 2012. New Destination Branding Campaign for Tanzania.

Tasci, A.D.A., and Kozak, M. 2006. Destination brands vs. destination images. Do we know what we mean? *Journal of Vacation Marketing*, 12(4), 299–317.

Tourism Australia. 2012. Our Brand. http://www.tourism.australia.com/en-au/marketing/brand-australia.aspx

Tourism Ireland. 2004. Understanding our Brand. http://www.tourismireland.com/CMSPages/GetFile.aspx?guid=89dd5625-e64e-488e-aad0-e4cbf30eb575

Tourism Malaysia. 2008. History. http://corporate.tourism.gov.my/trade.asp?page=malaysia_truly&subpage=history

Tourism New Zealand. 2009. 10 Years Young. 100% Pure New Zealand. http://10yearsyoung.tourismnewzealand.com/.

Tourism Queensland. 2010. Got questions about our new brand? http://www.tq.com.au/about-tq/tq-brand/got-questions-about-our-new-brand.cfm

Tourism Spain. 2012. http://www.tourspain.es/es-es/Paginas/index.aspx

Travel Alberta. Our Brand Journey. http://industry.travelalberta.com/Marketing%20Toolbox/Our%20Brand%20Journey.aspx

Vardhan, J. 2008. From a Desert to a Dreamland: The Case of Successful Destination Marketing of Dubai and Lessons for India. Indian Institute of Management, Conference on Tourism in India – Challenges Ahead, 17 May, Kozhikode.

Vasudevan, S. 2008. The role of internal stakeholders in destination branding: Observations from Kerala Tourism. *Place Branding and Public Diplomacy*, 4(4), 331–335.

Virginia Tourism Corporation. 2011. Virginia Tourism Corporation Strategic Marketing Plan FY 12.

VisitBritain. 2012. The Britain Brand. http://www.visitbritain.org/aboutus/marketing/brand/index.aspx

Wagner, O., and Peters, M. 2009. Can association methods reveal the effects of internal branding on tourism destination stakeholders? *Journal of Place Management and Development*, 2(1), 52–69.

Young, S. 2006. What Makes a Great Destination? Locum Consulting.

Yu, R. 2010. Cities use destination branding to lure tourists. *USA Today*, 12 February.

Chapter 10

Destination integrated marketing communications

Learning objectives

1 Describe the elements of the basic model of communications.

2 Define integrated marketing communications and explain the benefits that DMOs derive by following this approach.

3 Identify and elaborate upon each of the major components of integrated marketing communications.

4 Explain the importance and roles of advertising in promoting a destination.

5 Describe how personal selling is essential for DMOs in securing business from specific market segments and identify the roles of personal selling in destination marketing.

6 Review why public relations and publicity are required for a DMO to build and maintain relationships with its multiple publics.

7 Identify a DMOs' internal and external publics.

8 Point out the roles played by sales promotion and merchandising for DMOs.

9 Describe the different sales promotion and merchandising techniques.

10 Identify the main digital marketing techniques and venues.

11 Explain the concept of crowdsourcing and the different ways that this concept can be applied in destination integrated marketing communications.

12 Elaborate on the relationship between movies and films and destination marketing and development.

13 Review the concept of theme and event years as a basis for DMO integrated marketing communications.

14 Discuss the steps involved in the planning, implementation and evaluation of an IMC campaign.

Introduction

Marketing and promotion represent one of the roles of destination management. Chapter 3 provided an in-depth description of destination marketing planning and briefly touched upon the promotion sub-role; Chapter 10 elaborates on destination promotion and explains all of its components. Promotion is a traditional activity of DMOs, with most organizations historically putting the greatest emphasis on advertising and sales (personal selling). Public relations and publicity, sales promotion and merchandising are the three other traditional components of the so-called 'promotional mix'.

DMOs are now making heavy use of information and communication technologies (ICTs) in their promotions. Sometimes referred to as digital or interactive marketing, these technologies include websites, e-mail, social network sites, blogging, mobile phones and smartphones, GPS and several others. These are reviewed in detail in Chapter 11.

Although this used to be called the promotional mix or simply advertising or advertising and promotion, it is now known as IMC or integrated marketing communications. This chapter reviews all of the IMC components, their roles and functions, and how their effectiveness is measured. Before discussing IMC, this chapter explains a basic model of communications and highlights the usefulness of IMC in overcoming some of the challenges of communications. A definition of IMC is then provided and the six major IMC components are identified and explained.

The chapter reviews some overall approaches for destination marketing and IMC including using crowdsourcing, films and movies, and theme and event years.

Elements of communications model

Before getting into the detailed discussion on integrated marketing communications for destinations, it is best that you first know about how communications work. Figure 10.1 depicts a basic model of communications comprising of nine different elements. The model is very useful in showing how a DMO can be successful with its communications, as well as highlighting the reasons why sometimes communications do not work.

- *Sender*: The sender of the communication to the intended receiver is the DMO or its vendors (e.g. advertising agency).
- *Encoding*: To make the DMO message in the communication appealing and to get the receiver's attention, the DMO must design an arrangement of words, graphic images, sounds or music. This is called 'encoding' the message.
- *Message*: The message is the basic idea that the DMO wants to communicate to the intended receiver.
- *Medium*: The medium is the specific channel in which the message is placed by the DMO or its vendors. This could be a website, a magazine, a TV programme, etc.
- *Receiver*: The receiver is the intended target of the DMO's communication within a particular audience. This could be pleasure travellers, planners of business events, travel trade professionals or others.

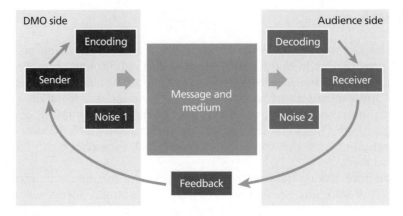

Figure 10.1 Elements of the basic model of communications

- *Decoding*: This is how the receiver interprets the message from the DMO. Each person may take a unique meaning from the message and how it has been encoded by the DMO.
- *Feedback*: This is the response given back by the receiver to the sender. This may be via a phone call, e-mail message, SMS, filling out a web-based form, through the mail, by visiting in person, etc.
- *Noise 1*: There are so many competing messages for the receiver's attention that the receiver may not notice or pay attention to the DMO's message. This can be called 'competitive noise' in the medium. It means that the message may not get through to the intended receiver.
- *Noise 2*: This represents barriers to receiving the communication on the receiver's side due mainly to distractions that cause the person not to see or pay attention to the message.

The basic model of communications highlights the potential challenges that DMOs face in communicating with their intended audiences. Because of the interference of 'noise' on both the sender's and receiver's sides, messages may not get through. Moreover, due to errors in the encoding of messages by the DMO and its vendors or the misinterpretation of the encoded messages by the receivers, the communication may not work as the DMO had planned. Integrated marketing communications (IMC) can assist DMOs in overcoming some of these challenges, by aggregating and making messages in different media consistent with each other.

The next topics for discussion therefore are IMC and its components. This begins with a clear definition of the IMC approach.

Definition of integrated marketing communications

The concept of integrated marketing communications (IMC) was briefly discussed in Chapter 3 and illustrated in Figure 3.22. The basic idea behind IMC is that DMO promotions are types of communications and it is essential that DMOs integrate all types of promotions, making sure that they are consistent.

Definition of integrated marketing communications

Integrated marketing communications or IMC is the coordination and integration of all of a DMO's external communications and promotions to increase their effectiveness and consistency. This is much superior to using each IMC component separately and independently.

Components of integrated marketing communications

Integrated marketing communications (IMC) for DMOs have six major components (Figure 10.2). Definitions of these six components are provided below:

- *Advertising*: The placement of persuasive messages by a DMO in any of the mass media to remind, inform or persuade potential pleasure travellers, business event planners, travel trade companies and others to consider the destination for future travel.
- *Sales*: Sales or personal selling involves communications between DMO sales staff and prospective customers (prospects). These communications can be face-to-face, by telephone or SMS, by e-mail or an instant messaging programme, or through other web-enabled services.
- *Public relations and publicity*: All the programmes and activities that a DMO initiates or participates in with the purpose of maintaining or improving its relationship with other organizations and individuals. Publicity is a PR technique involving non-paid communications of information about the destination of the DMO.
- *Sales promotion*: Approaches used by DMOs to give short-term inducements for people to visit, and special communication methods and techniques not included in other promotional components.
- *Merchandising*: Retail merchandising materials and point-of-purchase advertising done by DMOs in places such as visitor information centres, transportation terminals, attractions and accommodations.
- *Digital marketing*: The use of digital-format information and communication technologies to liaise with various audiences, to provide destination information and to promote the destination.

Benefits of integrated marketing communications

DMOs that follow the IMC approach realize significant benefits and six of the most important of these benefits are as follows:

Greater consistency in communication messages

Greater consistency in DMO communications is the major benefit from using IMC. You will hear about a great example of this in Chapter 11 from Switzerland Tourism. Switzerland uses one colour, red, consistently in its promotions and always features that distinctive cross that is also on its national flag (Figure 10.3).

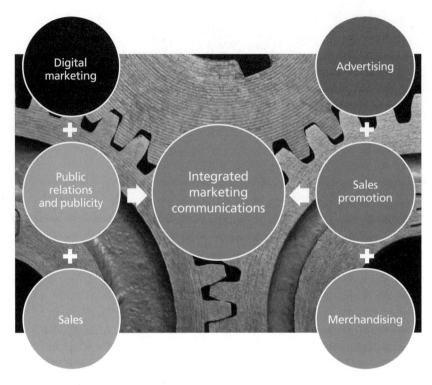

Figure 10.2 Integration of DMO communication components
Source: Switzerland Tourism, 2012.

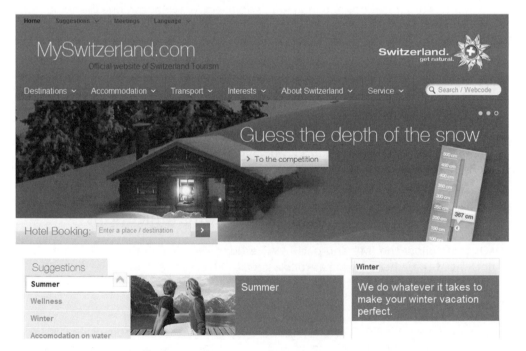

Figure 10.3 Outstanding quality of communications from Switzerland Tourism

Added impact since messages are repeated

The basic model of communications described above demonstrated that one message from a DMO may not get to the intended receiver. However, if the same or a similar message is passed through multiple channels, there is a much greater probability that they will get to the receiver successfully.

More importantly, if the receiver gets the same message from multiple channels, the messages reinforce each other and are more effective collectively. The repetition of the DMO's messages makes it more likely that they will be recalled and remembered by individual receivers.

Reflects different customer buying stages

You will learn in Chapter 12 about consumer buying process stages. One of the most accepted of these buying-stage models has five sequences: need awareness; information search; evaluation of alternatives; purchase; and post-purchase evaluation. Past research has shown that different IMC elements work better at specific buying-process stages; for example, advertising is more influential in the need awareness stage, but a sales promotion can be more powerful at the purchase stage. Since the DMO's audience will have people spread across all the buying-process stages, it is better for the DMO to be simultaneously using all of the IMC components and not just one of them.

More effectively puts across positioning and branding

Using all of the IMC components in a consistent way more convincingly communicates the destination's chosen positioning and branding approach. Each component has individual advantages for expressing images and branding; some are highly visual including advertising and websites, so they are good at visually communicating these concepts. PR and publicity and sales rely more on words and text, so they convey more in-depth explanations about the image and branding of destinations.

Better accommodates different consumer learning styles

Different people have different learning styles. Some people learn best by reading text on printed materials or online. Other people find it easier to absorb facts and knowledge by listening to people speaking. Still others prefer to see visuals to make their learning more effective. The IMC components vary in their use of text, visuals and spoken narratives, and so when used together by the DMO they will accommodate all the different consumer learning styles.

Components complement and support each other

Each IMC component has its unique strengths and weaknesses. For example, advertising is not particularly good at 'closing the sale' and that means getting the customer to actually make the purchase. However, sales and sales promotion tend to be much more effective in convincing people to make the buying decision. So the weakness of one IMC component (advertising) is compensated for by using other IMC components (sales or sales promotions).

A second very good example of integrated communications is from the Philippines Department of Tourism. The initial advertising campaign had the simple slogan of, 'It's more fun in the Philippines'. Two examples of this effective advertising are demonstrated in Figures 10.4 and 10.5 ('Getting upstairs. More fun in the Philippines' and 'Commuting. More fun in the Philippines'). Demonstrating its use of IMC, the Philippines Department of Tourism extended the campaign to social network sites including Facebook and Twitter.

The impact of this IMC has been extended even further and into what is called viral marketing. Viral marketing means the original message is spread even further by other people; in this case by Filipinos and fans of the Philippines who are posting their additions to the campaign on social network sites with an ever-expanding list of what is 'more fun in the Philippines'.

Figure 10.4 A terraced rice field scene was used with the strapline of 'Getting upstairs. More Fun in the Philippines'
Source: Shutterstock, Inc. (Suronin).

Figure 10.5 'Commuting. More fun in the Philippines' was the strapline with a shoreline scene like this one
Source: Shutterstock, Inc. (Maugli).

Advertising

The advertising of destinations has existed for decades and is still a major component of many DMOs promotional campaigns. Destination advertising tends to be quite expensive and for some DMOs it occupies a significant share of the total budget for marketing and promotion. Based upon data from Destination Marketing Association International (DMAI), DMOs spend almost half (43 per cent) of their budgets on sales and marketing efforts, with media advertising the top activity (17 per cent of total expenses). The rest of their costs were for staff (40 per cent) and administrative expenses (17 per cent). These statistics from DMAI are more skewed towards North American convention and visitor bureaus. In Australia, in 2010/2011, the South Australian Tourism Commission spent 15.1 per cent of its total expenses of AUD 68.5 million on consumer advertising (about AUD 10.4 million). However, Tourism Australia in 2011 devoted 41.3 per cent (AUD 59.2 million) of its total expenses of AUD 143.2 million on advertising. In the Las Vegas Convention and Visitors Authority's budget for 2011/2012, 43.7 per cent ($79.7 million) of total expenses of $182.4 million was allocated for advertising. While these figures can in no way be taken as representative of all DMOs in the world, they demonstrate that destination advertising expenditures are significant and may be in the range of 15–45 per cent of total expenses.

Importance of advertising for destinations

How important is advertising to tourism destinations? This is a difficult question to answer as there is some variation in importance according to different destinations. The variation is impacted partly by the Tourism Area Life Cycle (TALC) of which you learned in Chapters 3 and 5. For example, advertising can be instrumental in building destination awareness in the early stages of the TALC; and again be crucial in more mature destinations that are facing intense competition. In the intermediate stages, advertising may not be as important as other IMC components.

Some people have argued that advertising a destination is not that effective in bringing people in and that advertising budgets can be cut and nothing much will happen. However, the case of Colorado in the USA provides outstanding evidence of what transpires when a DMO completely stops its promotions. This case has been carefully documented by Dr Bill Siegel, CEO of Longwoods International of Toronto, Canada (2011). As shown in the following quote, the Government of Colorado made the unprecedented decision to take this drastic action in 1993:

What happened when Colorado stopped destination advertising?

In 1993, Colorado became the only state to eliminate its tourism marketing function, when it cut its $12 million promotion budget to zero. As a result, Colorado's domestic market share plunged 30 per cent within two years, representing a loss of over $1.4 billion in tourism revenue annually. Over time, the revenue loss increased to well over $2 billion yearly. In the important summer resort segment, Colorado dropped from first place among states to seventeenth.

Colorado is a well-established and popular tourism destination and is beautiful and has much to offer tourists. It is not a new destination and is more towards the mature stages of the TALC. Some might say, therefore, that Colorado 'advertises itself' with respect to tourism. Based on this experience, however, this was definitely not the case and a cessation of destination advertising corresponded with a significant decline in tourism.

Roles of advertising

Destination advertising plays three major roles for DMOs:

- *Informing*: This is the very basic value level of destination advertising in making markets aware of destinations and their tourism products. New and emerging destinations tend to suffer from a lack of market awareness, and advertising, especially in the mass media, is one way to get their messages out to thousands or even millions of people.
- *Persuading*: When destinations are mature and are facing close substitutes, they have to be more concerned that advertising is persuasive. Many destinations in Europe and North America find themselves in this situation and the creativity in their advertisements is at a premium.
- *Reminding*: For some audiences, DMOs need to do advertising as a reminder of the destination and typically this means the advertising is towards people who have already visited. It is frequently used in domestic tourism marketing campaigns where the audience is already quite familiar with the destinations.

Advertising tends to be one of the more expensive of the IMC components along with sales where a sales staff must be maintained. Just one quick cost example will prove this point for you. The 2012 national rates for *Travel + Leisure* magazine have a rate base of 950,000; this means that *Travel + Leisure* guarantees that the circulation of the magazine will be 950,000 copies. If a DMO decided to place a four-colour ad just once in *Travel + Leisure*, the 2012 rate was $124,350.

Advertising media alternatives

DMOs are faced with a choice of several advertising media alternatives and must weigh up their costs and relative advantages. These include television, radio, magazines, newspapers, outdoor, transit and online advertising. Advertising of tourism tends to work best in colour rather than black and white, and it is better if the ads are large rather than small. Magazines are, therefore, a favoured place for destination advertising due to their quality and also because they tend to be read in a relaxed way. Outdoor and transit advertising are also very popular because of the large size and potential visual impact, along with their ability to be viewed by commuters and other passing traffic. The two Philippines tourism ads shown in Figures 10.4 and 10.5 demonstrate the effectiveness of these types of advertising placements. The introduction of tablets, especially iPads, has provided an exciting set of new advertising opportunities for traditional magazine publishers. For example, *Travel + Leisure for iPad* only allows only ten advertisers and this helps these advertisers to stand out. Advertising in this way on iPad also has 'hotspot layers' that allow DMOs to embed videos, JPG images and links to their websites.

The other favourite is television advertising which adds so many more dimensions to the 'still' advertisements placed in magazines, outdoor and transit venues. A good example here is VisitScotland's 'Surprise Yourself' advertising campaign on television that was run in 2011 and 2012. The dramatic scenery of Scotland with a great Scottish voice-over and inspiring music show the true strengths of TV advertising and its emotional pull.

Recently, DMOs have been doing much more online advertising to catch the attention of the ever-expanding number of Internet users around the world. There are several different formats for this type of online advertising, including display or banner advertising, and using keywords in search engines and paying on a 'pay-per-click' (PPC) basis. Banner advertisements are ads that are embedded on website pages and they are often animated to draw the user's attention. When the page is opened and the ad appears, this is called an 'impression' which means the ad is potentially viewed. If the user clicks on the ad, that is called a 'click-through'. The other option is to use keywords, for example on major search engines. For example on Google.com, 'AdWords' are keywords chosen by advertisers. When users of the search engine enter one of the advertiser's key words, their 'AdWords' may appear to the right of the search results.

Online advertising can certainly be considered to be a part of digital marketing, which is discussed later in this chapter as well as in Chapter 11. One of the major advantages of online advertising is the measurability of its results, and measuring advertising effectiveness is the next topic for discussion.

Measuring the effectiveness of advertising

Measuring advertising effectiveness has traditionally presented challenges to marketers. In the past, some DMOs have claimed that all of the tourists came to their destination as a result of the DMO's advertising and promotions. This is a dangerous claim for a DMO to make and quite unrealistic as well. The leading professional associations of DMOs, including Destination Marketing Association International (DMAI), strongly warn against such exaggerated claims (2012):

A strong caution from Destination Marketing Association International

The ultimate measure of marketing productivity is the number of individuals whose visit to the destination was clearly and significantly generated by the DMO's marketing efforts.

DMOs are strongly cautioned against using their destination's total number of visitors as it is extremely unlikely that the DMO generated each and every visitor to its destination.

One of the traditional methods for measuring advertising effectiveness was to conduct conversion studies. These studies were used for direct-response advertising campaigns, in which people were asked to telephone a certain number, mail in a request for more information or click on a link online. Samples of people who responded were drawn and the researchers determined what percentages of those who enquired actually went to the destination later. This percentage was called the conversion rate on the advertising. Undoubtedly this is a useful advertising effectiveness research technique and has been widely applied by DMOs, but it has a major flaw. It tends to over-estimate the number of tourists that came as a result of the advertising, since some people have already decided to visit before seeing the advertisements.

Another type of research on advertising is called tracking, and is done by market research companies while the advertising campaign is under way. A good example here is from the advertising tracking research by Longwoods International of the 'Pure Michigan' campaign by the state of Michigan DMO in the USA. For the 2009 'Pure Michigan' campaign, Longwoods found that 65 per cent of respondents in regional markets (specific cities in Illinois, Ohio, Wisconsin, Missouri and Ontario) were aware of this advertising. Additionally, 35 per cent of the respondents in national markets were aware of 'Pure Michigan'. Longwoods also estimated that the 2009 summer campaign generated two million extra trips to Michigan, $588 million in added visitor spending and $41 million more in state taxes. Later in 2010, Longwoods conducted a conversion study on respondents from outside the Great Lakes region; they found that an added 1.5 million trips were generated, with $622 million in added visitor spending, and $43.5 million in incremental state taxes. Since the national 'Pure Michigan' campaign cost $7.8 million to run, the return on investment was over 5:1 (comparing added state tax revenues with the campaign cost).

Sales (personal selling)

Personal selling or sales is very important for certain DMOs, especially those that have a strong focus on attracting business events. This is certainly the case in the USA where most of the DMOs are called convention and visitors bureaus with the 'convention' indicating that business events are their top-most priority. Personal selling by DMOs plays several distinct roles:

- *Promoting to travel trade, associations, corporation and other groups*: Some communications in tourism need a personal touch and require more direct contact with potential clients. This is certainly so for 'industrial buying' where people are making large purchases on behalf of an association, company or other group.
- *Providing detailed and up-to-date information to event planners and travel trade*: It is important to keep business event planners and travel trade companies updated on new developments in the destination. This is the case at travel shows and exhibitions where sales persons dispense much detailed information at their booths.
- *Maintaining a personal relationship with key clients*: Sales is very much about one-to-one relationships between sales persons and their clients and prospects. Making sales calls on clients and keeping in touch with them in other ways maintains these important personal relationships.
- *Identifying decision makers, decision processes and qualified buyers*: Part of the sales activity is called prospecting and that means finding and qualifying organizations and people that can buy.
- *Gathering information on competitors*: Sales team members often gather information on competitive destinations through their communications with clients and prospects.

An example of a DMO sales department is described below for the Reno-Sparks Convention and Visitors Authority in Nevada, USA. You will notice that they have fifteen full-time and forty part-time staff; so there is a significant investment in sales at this DMO. You will also see that this Convention Sales and Services Department targets conventions, exhibits, trade shows, corporate meetings, incentive programmes, association activities and special events.

Convention Sales and Services Department at Reno-Sparks CVA, Nevada, USA

The Reno-Sparks Convention and Visitors Authority's Convention Sales and Services Department is made up of 15 full time employees and over 40 part time registration employees. The role of the Convention Sales department is to prospect and maintain relationships with potential customers to utilize hotels and RSCVA facilities for their conventions and meetings including, but not limited to, conventions, exhibits, trade shows, corporate meetings, incentive programs, association activities and special events. The role of the Convention Services department is to provide event marketing assistance and event management services to all of our incoming convention and meeting clients.

(2012)

Typically DMOs that have sales departments divide up staff according to geographic territories and sometimes also by type of business event. Special training is required for this type of work in DMOs and sales management approaches are applied. For example, the senior sales executive will develop a sales plan for each year with the input of all the sales team. Team members may be assigned sales quotas based on this plan. Given the relatively high costs of maintaining sales teams and support for their sales efforts, the measurement of sales performance is critical for DMOs. The following materials discuss the types of performance reporting approaches that can be used.

Measuring the effectiveness of sales

The results of sales activities are more easily tracked than advertising and can more directly be attributed to the work of DMOs and their sales staff teams. Figure 10.6 shows Destination Marketing Association International's recommendations for measuring the effectiveness of DMO sales efforts, aimed at generating conventions (business events). As you can see, sales performance is primarily measured by leads (prospective conventions for the destination) and bookings (actual conventions held in the destination).

DMAI also recommends travel trade sales performance reporting procedures that include activity measures, performance measures and productivity metrics. In the case of travel trade sales, the performance measures are expressed only in leads and bookings.

Activity measures	Performance measures	Productivity measures
• Number of bids • Trade shows attended/exhibited • Sales missions • Familiarization tours • Number of sales calls • Number of client site inspections • Client events • Sponsorships • Number of accounts with activity	• Leads • Bookings (hotel events/citywide and convention centre events) • Lost opportunities • Cancellations • Number of leads per trade show attended/exhibited • By-year production • Post-event measures (total attendance; room night pick-up) • Tentatives	• Personnel productivity metrics (number of leads per sales manager; number of bookings per sales manager; number of booked rooms per sales manager) • Repeat business ratios • Cost productivity metrics • Lead conversion ratios • Convention booking/room supply ratio • Demand ratios for total room nights sold

Figure 10.6 DMAI activity measures, performance measures and productivity metrics for DMO convention sales

Public relations and publicity

You already know about some aspects of a DMO's public relations efforts from the discussion of community and stakeholder relationships in Chapter 7. It is crucial for DMOs to maintain and enhance these 'at home' connections with local community residents, the tourism sector and other stakeholders.

Roles of public relations and publicity

PR and publicity serve three major roles for a DMO:

- *Maintaining a positive public presence*: The DMO definitely wants to ensure that the destination has a positive image externally, and within the destination as well. This component is called public relations because the DMO has several 'publics' with whom it interacts. Figure 10.7 identifies the internal and external publics with which DMOs must maintain positive relationships.
- *Enhancing effectiveness of other IMC components*: Getting publicity enhances and extends the effects of other IMC components. For example, the 'It's more fun in the Philippines' IMC campaign discussed earlier, has attracted significant media attention and this has augmented the positive impacts of the promotion.
- *Handling negative publicity*: A destination can receive negative publicity for a number of reasons including natural disasters, acts of terrorism, outbreaks of serious illnesses, etc. The DMO must handle these situations tactfully and in the best interests of the destination. The following quote from Bahrain highlights how adverse media reports can cause great damage to the tourism sector in a destination. It also emphasizes the need to 'counter' such negative publicity to give a more balanced picture of the destination.

Bahrain needs to combat negative foreign media reports

A tourism chief has called on Bahrain to step up its public relations war to combat foreign media reports, which he said were killing Bahrain's travel industry.

It follows the temporary suspension of visits by a major cruise ship operator, which cancelled stops in Bahrain on February 8, last Wednesday and this coming Wednesday over security concerns.

Bahrain Chamber of Commerce and Industry (BCCI) tourism committee chairman Nabeel Kanoo said more needed to be done to counter negative reports about Bahrain in the West.

'The hotels and tourism sector have lost more than 40 per cent in revenues over the last year', he said.

(Eturbonews.com, 2012)

The media relations portion of this IMC is particularly important since the media or press are the source of publicity. Here the DMO may attend media tradeshows, organize media missions, conduct media familiarization tours, visit media contacts, prepare press releases, participate in media interviews and handle media enquiries. Most DMOs prepare newsletters and public service announcements (PSAs), and these are considered to be within public relations and publicity.

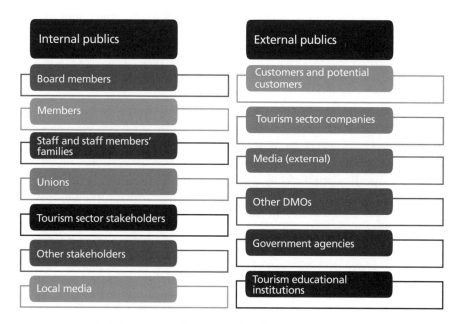

Figure 10.7 DMO's internal and external publics

As Figure 10.7 shows, the internal publics are those within the DMO and the destination. The DMO has staff members and it may also be partly unionized. Many DMOs have boards and some have membership programmes. The stakeholders outside of the DMO include the tourism sector stakeholders, other stakeholders and local media.

The external stakeholders are outside of the destination and two of the most important ones are customers/potential customers and the media (press). Tourism sector companies include airlines, travel trade companies, hotel and resort companies, and others with connections to the destination. Other DMOs, including competitors, government agencies and tourism educational institutions are the remaining external publics.

As was mentioned in Chapter 7, DMOs in the past did not pay as much attention to their internal publics as they devoted to their external publics. This has changed drastically in recent times as DMOs have begun to develop a greater appreciation of the value of having solid support and backing within their destinations.

Measuring the effectiveness of public relations and publicity

Some of the outcomes of public relations are quite difficult to measure; however, there are some traditional ways of measuring the publicity generated by a DMO for its destination. Usually this is accomplished by measuring the 'placements' or 'stories' about the destination that result from the DMO's own public relations efforts or are initiated by the media. News in the form of press releases prepared by DMOs are commonly the major source of publicity coverage. DMOs track publicity by where it occurs (e.g. domestic v. international) and in which media the stories appear (e.g. television, radio, newspaper, magazine, online, etc.).

In addition to counting the number of stories in the media, DMOs will estimate the numbers of impressions (e.g. the circulation of a magazine) and advertising equivalency value of these stories. DMOs may do the tracking of publicity coverage themselves or may outsource this to specialized companies that are typically called 'media clipping services'. Burrelles Luce and Bacon's are two of the most famous of these companies in North America.

Sales promotion and merchandising

Sales promotions and merchandising are often closely connected, so they have been grouped together for this discussion. These techniques are generally used tactically, meaning that they are used in the short term for specific purposes, like attracting more tourists in the off-season.

Types of sales promotion and merchandising

There are many types of sales promotion and merchandising techniques available to destination marketers. These fall into two main categories: (1) special offers, and (2) special communication methods. Figure 10.8 identifies most of the techniques that fall into these two categories:

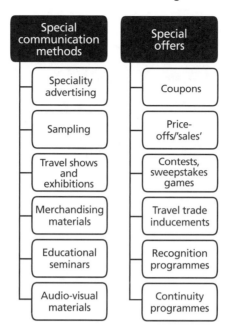

Figure 10.8 Sales promotion and merchandising techniques

The following is a brief description of the techniques within these two categories of sales promotions and merchandising.

Special offers

Some of these sales promotion techniques give tourists a value offer so that they will make a purchase in the short term, including coupons and price-offs or 'sales'.

Contests, sweepstakes and games create excitement and also encourage people to take immediate action. Figure 10.9 provides an example of a sweepstake from VisitBritain to encourage locals to invite their friends and relatives to visit the UK. This promotion was included on Facebook and to enter the sweepstake people had to 'like' this VisitBritain Facebook page.

Travel trade inducements typically involve some type of commission paid to travel agencies or discount offered on services and facilities within the destination. Recognition programmes are promotional approaches that 'recognize' travel trade companies, other organizations or individual tourists for their past contributions or demonstrated interest level in destinations. The Brown County 'Valued Visitor' programme described earlier in Chapter 6 is a good example of a recognition programme designed for individual tourists that have an interest in this destination in southern Indiana, USA. Another example of a type of recognition programme is actually a combination of a special communication method and a special offer. The Aussie Specialist programme offered by Tourism Australia is a very good example. Continuity programmes are sales promotions in which people must continue to make repeated purchases, sometimes over a long period of time. If they do not, their status levels within the programmes will be lower. Frequent-flyer and frequent-guest programmes are continuity recognition programmes. There have not yet been many applications of continuity programmes by DMOs.

Figure 10.9 VisitBritain sweepstake on Facebook
Source: Copyright VisitBritain, 2011.

Special communication methods

This is a sort of catch-all for methods that do not exactly fit into other IMC components and it also includes all the merchandising techniques. As the name suggests these are special ways to communicate with potential tourists, travel trade companies and planners of business events. Actually within this category are several approaches that are commonly used by DMOs including exhibiting at travel shows and exhibitions, arranging familiarization tours and site investigations, designing posters, and arranging educational seminars and workshops.

Speciality advertising involves the preparation of many types of items bearing the name and/or brand mark of the destination. These items are most often given away as gifts and usually in conjunction with sales, sales promotion and public relations programmes and activities. These include t-shirts, cups and other containers, logo-bags, books and diaries, desk ornaments and many other items.

Sampling for DMOs typically means inviting people to visit the destination to see what it has to offer. There are two main sampling formats; familiarization tours and site investigations. Familiarization tours are arranged for travel agents, tour operators, travel writers and media companies. The Arizona Office of Tourism divides the purposes of 'FAMs' into travel industry marketing and media relations. As you will see, AZOT points out that the purposes of FAMs for these two groups are not the same; for the travel trade the purpose is to build product knowledge, but for the media, they are used to generate more publicity for the destination.

Purposes of FAM tours: Arizona Office of Tourism

- *Travel industry marketing*: The purpose of hosting a travel agent or tour operator FAM tour is to either increase product knowledge or the amount of product an agent or operator is selling.
- *Media relations*: The purpose of hosting a media FAM tour is to garner positive editorial publicity about a destination and/or organization. This is different than paid advertising in the sense that the publicity generated through media relations efforts is the editorial opinion of the writer, which is often considered more valuable than paid advertising.

Site investigations are conducted by associations, companies and other organizations that are seriously considering the destination as a place for a future event such as a convention, exhibition, trade show or other type of meeting. These meeting planners are especially interested in viewing the hotels that they may be using and the venues for events, such as convention and exhibition centres. It is common for DMOs to pay for all of the costs of the site investigation team while they are in the destination. For example, Business Events Sydney in Australia says,

> During the bid process, we often invite representatives from the association's international committee to visit Sydney and take a tour of our congress infrastructure, to ensure the city and its venues meet their requirements. All their expenses are covered while they're in Sydney.

(2012)

Many major travel shows and exhibitions are held around the world each year and they attract numerous DMOs to exhibit. Some of the largest of these international events are the following:

- ITB Berlin, Germany
- World Travel Market, London, England
- The Motivation Show, Chicago, USA
- Salon Mondial du Tourisme, Paris, France
- BIT, Milan, Italy
- FITUR, Madrid, Spain
- Arabian Travel Market, Dubai
- MITT, Moscow, Russia
- Rendez-vous Canada
- China International Travel Market, Shanghai/Kunming, China.

Most of these shows and exhibitions are operated by private companies and DMOs pay fees based upon their exhibit space and locations at the events. However, in some cases the shows are actually run by the DMOs themselves and the objective is to showcase the destinations and tourism stakeholders within their jurisdictions. These include Rendez-vous Canada, operated by the Canadian Tourism Commission (Figure 10.10) and the China International Travel Mart run by Sunny Communications on behalf of the China National Tourism Administration.

Figure 10.10 'Rendez-vous Canada' operated by the Canadian Tourism
Commission

Source: Canadian Tourism Commission, 2012b.

DMOs produce many merchandising materials for display and distribution in a variety of places. These materials include printed visitor guides, maps and a variety of brochures, as well as posters. Although DMOs do not necessarily operate shops, they often have visitor information centres and have brochure material distribution points at local hotels, attractions and transportation terminals. DMOs also distribute much literature at travel shows and exhibitions. These materials are often called 'printed collateral' by DMOs.

Educational seminars can be very effective sales promotion tools for DMOs, especially when directed at travel agencies and tour operators in key origins of tourists. Tourism Australia's Aussie Specialist programme was mentioned already and it is a truly excellent example of a long-standing and highly successful educational programme by a DMO.

DMOs produce many audio-visual materials that are used in different ways for communication purposes. These include printed collateral materials, videos/DVDs, photo galleries (Figure 10.11), music CDs, MP3s, podcasts, PowerPoint presentations and others. The audio-visual materials are utilized at travel shows and exhibitions and by sales representatives in making presentations to prospective customers. The materials are also made available to media companies for their use in publicity coverage. Materials are given to business event organizers to help them generate greater attendance and participation. Some of the materials are made available to individual tourists; for example, videos can be viewed on YouTube and photo galleries can be perused on Flickr.

Figure 10.11 Photo galleries are important tools for destinations. The Blue Mosque in Shah Alam, Malaysia
Source: Photo by Alastair M. Morrison.

Roles of sales promotion and merchandising

Sales promotions and merchandising perform several specific roles for DMOs. These roles are not necessarily met by other IMC components. For example, sales promotion really means 'to promote sales' and that usually implies providing a short-term inducement to buy. The following are several specific roles of sales promotions and merchandising:

● *Getting people to come to the destination for the first time*: Inviting people to visit the destination for the very first time may be the goal of a sales promotion campaign. Offering some sort of incentive to the first-time visitor or having an invitation extended by a past visitor are two ways to achieve this.
● *Increasing off-peak demand*: Getting tourists to come at off-peak times is one of the most frequent applications of sales promotions. Often this is done through the use of discounted prices (price-offs) that are incorporated into pages.
● *Increasing demand in periods that coincide with major events, vacations or special occasions*: Another very popular time to introduce sales promotions is in the time periods leading up to major events, holidays and other special occasions. The VisitBritain promotion in Figure 10.9 is an example of this, encouraging people to come to UK during 2012, the year of the London Summer Olympics.
● *Encouraging travel trade intermediaries to make a special effort to sell the destination*: Travel agencies and tour operators are very important sources of business for many destinations. Planners of business events are another highly influential group and especially for city tourism destinations.
● *Helping sales staff get business from prospects*: Some DMOs have sales staff and most of these are positioned to generate new demand from business events or travel trade companies. These sales staff are given a variety of audio-visual materials that help them in making sales such as videos, photo libraries, PowerPoint presentations, guides and brochures, etc.

- *Facilitating travel trade intermediary marketing*: DMOs provide materials to travel agencies, tour operators, business event planners and other travel trade companies that help them with their marketing. These include posters, visitor guides and brochures, videos, etc.

Measuring the effectiveness of sales promotion and merchandising

Measuring the effectiveness of some of the special-offer sales promotions is quite straightforward and involves calculating the percentages of people who received the offers that actually went ahead and purchased or booked the offers. Some of the special communications can also be measured, while others are difficult to measure. For example, leads resulting from exhibiting at travel shows and exhibitions can be tracked; and participants in familiarization tours, site investigations, and at educational seminars and workshops can be counted.

For some of the special communication methods, it is much more difficult to assess the exact impacts of posters, printed collateral, merchandising materials and speciality advertising items that are offered as gifts. These may be noticed and appreciated, but no immediate action is taken or response given after exposure to the materials.

Digital marketing

This chapter section has been labelled as digital marketing, but it could have been called interactive marketing or given some other fancy name. Getting past the naming issue, what is really involved here is the DMO working with all forms of information and communication technologies (ICTs) that use digital formats. Earlier in this chapter, online advertising was discussed; Figure 10.12 shows the other digital marketing techniques and venues.

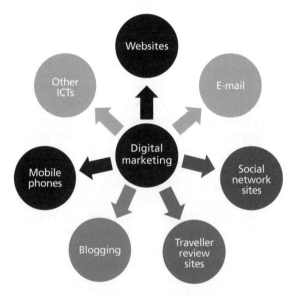

Figure 10.12 Digital marketing techniques and venues

Chapter 11 reviews these techniques and venues in detail and highlights the strategic importance of DMO websites as a platform for connecting with other ICTs (information and communication technologies). Digital marketing has definitely become much more critical for the overall success of destination marketing and promotion. Here is a very brief overview of the items in Figure 10.12:

- *Websites*: Websites are now unquestionably the principal communications platform for most DMOs. Many DMOs have websites in multiple languages as well as sites designed for specific audiences, e.g. visitor sites and corporate sites.
- *E-mail*: E-mail does not get the same attention as websites, but it is essential for online communications and is also a marketing and promotion channel. It is used by salespersons in DMOs and also to respond to people that request information either via e-mail or on the DMO's website. In addition, sometimes DMOs conduct promotional campaigns solely using e-mail.
- *Social network sites*: The most popular of these include Facebook, Twitter, YouTube and Flickr, but there are hundreds of them now. Many DMOs have established their own pages on the major social network sites.
- *Traveller review sites:* These are websites in which travellers provide their comments on hotels, restaurants, attractions, destinations and other travel-related items. The most famous site is TripAdvisor.com.
- *Blogging*: Web logs or simply blogs are a hobby for some and a profession for others. DMOs study these blogs to get feedback about their destinations. Moreover, many DMOs are writing their own blogs and distributing them through their websites and social network sites.
- *Mobile phones*: There are now billions of mobile phones around the world and these are becoming increasingly important for destination marketing and promotion. Several DMOs have developed travel guide applications (apps) for smartphones that can be downloaded free of charge.
- *Other ICTs*: These include GPS (global positioning system), geo-tagging, podcasts, smart cards, virtual visitor guides and brochures, Google maps and Google Earth, e-book readers, wikis and others.
- *Online advertising*: Although not shown in Figure 10.12, online advertising does fit into digital marketing as well. It was discussed earlier in this chapter and involves the use of banner/display advertising and keywords. Placements are made on search engines and social network sites.

There has been a very strong trend toward DMOs placing greater emphasis on digital marketing in recent years and correspondingly making lesser use of some the traditional IMC components. Tourism New Zealand (2012) is an example of this change in emphasis.

Many DMOs now have departments and units that look after their websites, social network site maintenance and communications, and other digital marketing efforts. This is a clear indication of how important these 'new media' have become for DMOs. You might recall from Figure 8.4 , the organization chart for Tourism Queensland, that this DMO has a Digital Marketing unit with its Marketing Department.

Tourism New Zealand making greater use of ICTs

Increasingly Tourism New Zealand's advertising is evolving from print, television, cinema and billboard advertising, to greater use of technology to promote New Zealand as a holiday destination to our target audience wherever they are, and whatever they might be doing, in their daily lives.

This has meant embracing new media such as mobile technology, social media and online advertising. The Internet has become a more influential communication channel, and our advertising has moved to embrace mobile media and social networking tools and to direct consumers to New Zealand's award-winning travel website, www.newzealand.com.

Measuring the effectiveness of digital marketing

Generally, digital marketing is one of the most measurable of the IMC components, since ICTs maintain a 'track record' of interactions. Figure 10.13 identifies some of the performance measures that can be applied to the main digital marketing techniques and venues. For example, log-file analyser programmes can be used to track and analyse all of the traffic to DMOs' websites, providing data on numbers of users, favourite pages, time spent on each page and on the website in total, and many other useful statistics. Additionally, all of the major social network sites maintain their own special sets of statistics so it is easy to measure their traffic.

Crowdsourcing

Before leaving the topic of digital marketing, you should be aware of one newly-minted promotional technique called 'crowdsourcing' that is associated with the use of social network sites. The definition of crowdsourcing is to outsource a task to a group (crowd) of people; in this case, to individuals outside of the DMO. Crowdsourcing has been used by several DMOs in recent years, and Tourism Australia and the Canadian

Websites	E-mail	Social networks	Mobile phones
• User sessions • Unique users • Page views • Average session length • Search engine referrals • Search engine placements • Sign-ups to materials and registrations	• E-mails delivered • Opened e-mails • Clicks and unique clicks • Forwarded e-mails • Unsubscribes • Conversion rates	• Facebook ('likes', page views, unique page views, active users, conversions, etc.) • Twitter (followers, retweets, 'mentions', conversions) • YouTube (channel views, video views, subscibers, etc.)	• Messages delivered • Conversions • Downloads of mobile electronic tourist guides, METGs • Activity levels from METGs

Figure 10.13 Selected performance measures for major digital marketing techniques and venues

Source: Adapted from Destination Marketing Association International, 2011.

Tourism Commission are examples. Under one scenario, basically what happens is the DMO invites local people to upload written materials and photos of their favourite places, experiences and activities in the destination. Tourism Australia used this approach in their campaign, 'There's *nothing* like Australia' (Figure 10.14). Actually the crowd that helped in response to Tourism Australia's request was quite large, at over 64,000 people. Apart from the benefits to IMC campaigns, these initiatives involve local community residents with tourism and the DMO, and that in itself is very positive. Additionally, tourists get truly authentic experiences that have been fully vetted by locals. So this can be called a win–win–win proposition.

Another scenario is to invite a smaller group of selected 'outsiders' to help in building communication campaigns. In Chapter 6 the example was given of the Jordan Tourism Bureau inviting a small group of travel bloggers on a familiarization tour, and they wrote about Jordan on their return home. Belle Tourism International (BTI) Consulting invited 25 foreign expatriates for a weekend in the ancient city of Shaoxing in Zhejiang Province, China. With the sponsorship and assistance of the local DMO, Shaoxing Tourism Commission, the participants were involved in authentic local experiences like being an apprentice Chinese opera singer and cooking a famous local-recipe tofu dish. The expats were asked to keep diaries of their experiences and take photos and videos. BTI collected these and they were later used as part of an English guidebook for Shaoxing.

A final example of crowdsourcing is by the DMO in Philadelphia, USA. Over 101 days, it featured 101 one-minute videos of Philadelphians talking about their favourite places to visit in the city. The programme of videos appeared on Facebook, Twitter, Pinterest, YouTube and a local social network site (uwishunu).

Figure 10.14 'There's *nothing* like Australia' campaign
Source: Tourism Australia, 2012b.

Crowdsourcing from the DMO in Philadelphia, USA

The Greater Philadelphia Tourism Marketing Corporation (GPTMC) has launched a new local-focus digital/social campaign called 'Philly 101' that comprises 101 one-minute videos over the same number of days, each one spotlighting famous, somewhat famous and not-so-famous Philadelphians who talk about what they do every day (in places worth visiting) while offering their own take on something visitors should see or do.

The program, housed on a local-flavor site, uwishunu.com, will also live on social media channels Facebook.com/visitphilly, twitter.com/visitphilly, twitter.com/uwishunu, pinterest.com/visitphilly and youtube.com/visitphilly.

(Greenberg, 2012)

Theme year and event marketing

Several national DMOs have adopted a strategy of consistently having theme years to heighten the interest of tourists in visiting their countries. VisitScotland's Homecoming Scotland 2009 and 2014 are good examples of years with a specific theme. However, this practice is most popular in Asia, with China, Indonesia, Malaysia and Thailand being four of the countries that use this strategy most frequently.

The Tourism Authority of Thailand began its 'Visit Thailand' years in 1987. This first theme year in Thailand had a significant positive impact on inbound international tourism. It also attracted the attention of other destinations in Southeast Asia and they decided to try out a similar strategy.

The impact of 'Visit Thailand Year'

Thanks to a burst of adrenalin that united the industry behind a common cause and grand celebration, Thailand received 3.48 million visitors that year, with the growth rate of 23.6 per cent being the highest since arrivals crossed the one million mark in 1973. The event literally helped double visitor arrivals in the second half of the 1980s, from 2.8 million in 1986 to 5.2 million in 1990.

The massive publicity campaigns and awareness of tourism generated by VTY '87 spawned a whole range of copycat years throughout ASEAN, Asia and the world. It conferred an element of respectability upon travel and tourism as an industry and helped awaken governments worldwide to its potential as a job creator and foreign exchange earner.

(Muqbil, 2007)

Theme years have been a core strategy used by the China National Tourism Administration (CNTA) for many years. For example, China had the following theme years from 2008 to 2012:

- 2008: China Olympic Tourism Year
- 2009: China Ecotourism Year
- 2010: China World Expo Tourism Year
- 2011: China Cultural Tour
- 2012: China Happy and Healthy Tour.

As can be seen from this 5-year list, China used two mega-events as the themes, these being for the 2008 Beijing Summer Olympic Games and the 2010 Shanghai World Expo.

These theme years provide a strong focus and platform for integrated marketing communications. The central concept underpinning the theme can be communicated in a variety of different ways and in various media and at different places. Figures 10.15 and 10.16 show parts of the IMC campaign developed by Sunny Communications for the China National Tourism Administration to support China World Expo Tourism Year 2010.

Figure 10.15 Advertisement for China World Expo Tourism Year
Source: Beijing Sunny Communications and China National Tourism Administration, 2009.

Figure 10.16 Transit advertising and DVD for China World Expo Tourism Year
Source: Beijing Sunny Communications and China National Tourism Administration, 2009.

Movie and film development

Movie- or film-induced tourism has really caught the attention of destination marketers and tourism scholars in the past two decades. This has been because people like to visit the places where famous movies and films were shot. Two of the most discussed case studies here are *Lord of the Rings* for New Zealand and *Braveheart* for Scotland, but there are many more examples. You might wonder what this topic is doing in a chapter about integrated marketing communications and indeed you should know. Some destinations have recognized this phenomenon and used movies and films as part of their promotions. Other destinations have gone even further and put tourism development and marketing together with film development and marketing, knowing the synergies that can occur between the two.

The Virginia Film Office is a unit within the Virginia Tourism Corporation in the USA and it describes the roles of film commissions and their interactions with the tourism sector as follows:

Film Office of the Virginia Tourism Corporation, USA

There are more than 300 officially sanctioned Film Commissions worldwide. Nearly every state and many major cities have one, as well as countries, regions, provinces and towns. Film Commissions are essentially marketing organizations that promote their localities to the film and television industries by publicizing filming locations, crew members and services of their areas. Once a locality has been chosen for filming, staff members assist the production company and function as a liaison between the filmmakers and the community, helping to provide essential services such as parking, police assistance and traffic control.

A film office operates much the same as other marketing organizations, particularly those involved in the tourism industry. Staff members attend trade shows, make marketing calls on prospective clients, conduct familiarization tours and place news stories and advertising in national publications. In fact, since both groups work to promote the remarkable physical and human resources to be found within their jurisdictions, it is not surprising that tourism and film have been found to work so well together. In addition, studies have shown that states with strong film industries usually have strong tourism industries, partially because a successful film can act as a powerful advertisement for the area in which it was shot. In Virginia, the films *Dirty Dancing*, *Gods and Generals*, *Cold Mountain* and *The New World* have been particularly strong tourism generators.

(Virginia Film Office, 2012)

A more recent example of the successful interplay of movies and tourism involves a rather unusual combination: Bollywood in India and Spain. Turespana (Spain Tourism) came up with the basic idea for the hit 2011 Bollywood road-trip movie *Zindagi Na Milegi Dobara*. Turespana provided support and subsidies for the shooting of the film in several locations in Spain but did not directly finance the film production. However, Turespana spent an estimated USD 660,000 on marketing including TV commercials with clips from the film (Munshi, 2012). The film was released in July 2011 and by August 2011 visa applications in India at Spain's embassy and consulates doubled and there was a 65 per cent increase in Indian visitors to Spain in 2011 when compared to 2010.

Planning integrated marketing communications

IMC needs to be carefully planned and there is a definite sequence of events that should be followed. The following is a brief description of the steps for planning a specific IMC campaign:

- *Set IMC campaign objectives*: It is very important to begin by setting clear and measurable objectives for the IMC campaign. These objectives, for example, may be to increase tourist numbers and tourism spending from the intended audience by specific amounts or percentages.
- *Estimate a tentative IMC campaign budget*: The DMO needs to prepare a preliminary budget estimate for the IMC campaign bearing in mind the funds it has available for marketing and promotion.
- *Consider partnership model and potential partners*: The DMO should identify potential partners who share similar objectives and might be interested in participating as a part-sponsor of the IMC campaign. Potential partnership models also need to be identified. Negotiations with these potential partners should take place.
- *Determine mix of IMC components*: The DMO determines which components of IMC will be used in the campaign and how these will be interconnected. The DMO also needs to decide when and how often components will be used and in which sequences, if appropriate.
- *Design and test IMC campaign*: A theme and creative approach is chosen reflecting a specific communication message idea or ideas. Proposed materials should be pre-tested by showing them to members of the intended audience and getting their feedback and suggestions. Materials should be revised accordingly.
- *Prepare final IMC campaign*: The IMC materials for the campaign are finalized based on the pre-test and prepared in a finished format.
- *Develop a final IMC budget*: The tentative budget is reviewed and revised into a final IMC budget based on the finished format materials and their placements.
- *Launch, maintain and monitor IMC campaign*: The IMC campaign is implemented and it is likely that the DMO or its vendors (e.g. advertising, PR or digital marketing consultants) will have to be involved, especially if there is a component for the social network sites that involves interacting with people that respond to the IMC campaign.
- *Measure and evaluate results of IMC campaign*: The results of the IMC campaign are measured and compared to the objectives that were set in the first step.

Summary

The basic model of communications highlights some of the difficulties and challenges for DMOs in getting their messages across to the intended audiences. There are nine elements in the model: sender, encoding, message, medium, receiver, decoding, feedback, noise 1 and noise 2. Using integrated marketing communications (IMC) helps DMOs overcome some of the communications challenges, since messages are repeated in different formats and media channels.

IMC is the coordination and integration of all of a DMO's external communications and promotions to increase their effectiveness and consistency. Advertising, sales, public relations and publicity, sales promotion and merchandising, and digital marketing are the components of IMC. Campaigns involve some combination of the six components, but not all may be employed in a single campaign.

Advertising can be very expensive for DMOs, especially if placed on television or in leading travel magazines. Because of its high costs, destination advertising has attracted criticism in many parts of the world, but media advertising remains an important component of IMC for many DMOs. A case study in Colorado, USA clearly underscored the dangers of closing down a destination's advertising campaigns. Because of its high costs, it is particularly important that destination advertising be tracked and its effectiveness measured.

Advertising plays three major roles for DMOs: informing, persuading and reminding. The traditional media for destination advertising were television, radio, magazines, newspapers, outdoor and transit. In recent times, DMOs have made greater use of online advertising.

Sales or personal selling is of great importance for many DMOs and especially those that place strong emphasis on attracting business events. Among the most important of the sales roles is to appeal to and win group business from associations, corporations and the travel trade.

Public relations and publicity involves developing and maintaining positive relationships with all of the DMO's publics. All DMOs have both internal publics (within the destination) and external publics (outside of the destination). Publicity is sometimes called 'free advertising' but it usually has some costs since the DMO must keep the media informed about key events and stories that are taking place within the destination.

Sales promotion and merchandising are two closely connected IMC components. These are techniques that are used tactically and for short periods of time. There are two categories, special offers and special communication methods. Sampling (familiarization tours and site investigations) and exhibiting at travel shows and exhibitions are two techniques that are especially important for DMOs.

Digital marketing using information and communication technologies (ICTs) is now being given much greater emphasis by DMOs. The most important techniques and venues include websites, e-mail, social network sites, traveller review sites, blogging and mobile phones. Crowdsourcing is a relatively new promotional technique that often involves digital communications, and is where the DMO 'outsources' some of the responsibility for a promotion to a group of people.

Popular films and movies have been instrumental in generating significant tourism increases for the destinations in which they have been shot. In some places, the responsibilities for tourism development and marketing and film development and marketing have been combined into one agency; in other words the DMO and film commission have been integrated together.

An IMC campaign needs to be carefully planned and should follow a distinct sequence. The IMC plan should always start with the setting of objectives and end with the measurement of results.

To meet its destination promotion sub-role, a DMO must take the following initiatives:

- Adopt an integrated marketing communications (IMC) approach for its promotional campaigns.
- Carefully plan IMC campaigns in a step-by-step process.
- Set specific objectives for every IMC campaign.
- Measure the effectiveness of advertising, sales/personal selling, public relations and publicity, sales promotion and merchandising, and digital marketing.
- Consider crowdsourcing as a way to implement IMC campaigns.
- Evaluate the potential of attracting film crews to shoot films and movies within the destination.
- Contemplate the idea of using theme and event years as a marketing strategy and IMC platform.

Review questions

1 Which elements comprise the basic models of communications and what are their roles and functions?
2 What is the definition of integrated marketing communications (IMC) and why is this concept important for DMOs?
3 What are the major components of IMC and how is each of them defined?
4 Which benefits do DMOs gain from following the IMC approach?
5 Why is advertising important for destinations and what are advertising's three main roles for a DMO?
6 What roles do sales or personal selling perform for DMOs?
7 What are the roles played by sales promotion and merchandising?
8 Which techniques comprise special offers and special communication methods?
9 What are the roles of public relations and publicity?
10 Who are a DMO's internal and external publics?
11 What are the major digital marketing techniques and venues?
12 How is the effectiveness of individual IMC components measured?
13 What is crowdsourcing and how can it be applied in IMC by DMOs?
14 Theme and event years have been used by several countries as a tourism marketing strategy. Why are these theme/event years a good platform for IMC?
15 How are tourism and film/movie development inter-related and how can they benefit each other in terms of both marketing and development?
16 What are the steps involved in planning integrated marketing communications?

References

Arizona Office of Tourism. 2007. How to Conduct a Familiarization Tour.

Belle Tourism International Consulting. 2008. International Tourism Marketing Implementation Plan for Shaoxing. Shanghai, PRC.

Bulearca, M., and Bulearca, S. 2011. Romania branding campaign – an IMC perspective. *International Journal of Business, Management and Social Sciences*, 2(3), 35–58.

Business Events Sydney. 2012. How the Bid Process Works. http://www.business eventssydney.com.au/bid-for-an-event/your-bidding-partner/how-conference-bidding-works/

Canadian Tourism Commission. 2012a. Canadians Invite the World! http://en.corporate. canada.travel/content/news_release/35-million-directors-video

——2012b. Rende-vous Canada. http://en-corporate.canada.travel/rendez-vous-canada

China National Tourism Administration. 2011. 2012 China Happiness and Health Tour: Launching Ceremony of China–Russia Tourism Year. http://en.cnta.gov.cn/html/ 2011-11/2011-11-29-14-35-91480.html

Croy, W.G. 2011. Film tourism: sustained economic contributions to destinations. *Worldwide Hospitality and Tourism Themes*, 3(2), 159–164.

Destination Marketing Association International. 2011. Standard DMO Performance Reporting: A Handbook for DMOs. Washington, DC.

——2012. Profile of a Convention and Visitor Bureau. http://www.destinationmarketing. org/resource_center/resource_content_view.asp?Act=VIEW&mResource_ ID=10&mContent_ID=269

Dinnie, K., Melewar, T.C., Seidenfuss, K.-U., and Musa, G. 2010. Nation branding and integrated marketing communications: An ASEAN perspective. *International Marketing Review*, 27(4), 388–403.

Dolnicar, S., and Schoesser, C.M. 2003. Market Research in Austrian NTO and RTOs: Is the Research Homework done Before Spending Marketing Millions? University of Wollongong Research Online.

Eturbonews.com. 2012. Bahrain Needs to Combat Negative Foreign Media Reports. 19 February.

Greenberg, K. 2012. Philadelphia campaign lets Philly talk. *Marketing Daily*, 16 March.

Hartley, B., and Picton, D. 1999. Integrated marketing communications requires a new way of thinking. *Journal of Marketing Communications*, 5(2), 97–106.

Hudson, S. 2011. Working together to leverage film tourism: Collaboration between the film and tourism industries. *Worldwide Hospitality and Tourism Themes*, 3(2), 165–172.

Keller, K.L. 2001. Mastering the marketing communications mix: Micro and macro perspectives on integrated marketing communication programs. *Journal of Marketing Management*, 17(7–8), 819–847.

Kliatchko, J. 2008. Revisiting the IMC construct: A revised definition and four pillars. *International Journal of Advertising*, 27(1), 133–160.

Las Vegas Convention and Visitors Authority. 2011. Annual Budget – Fiscal Year 2011/2012.

Mendiratta, A. 2009. Destination Advertising as a Fuel for Crisis Recovery. CNN Task Group. COMPASS – Insights into Tourism Branding.

Mill, R.C., and Morrison, A.M. 2012. The Tourism System, 7th edn. Dubuque, IA: Kendall Hunt Publishing.

Morrison, A.M. 2009. Hospitality and Travel Marketing, 4th edn. Clifton Hills, NY: Cengage.

Munshi, N. 2012. Spain's starring role in Bollywood movie a boon to tourism. *Advertising Age*, 6 February.

Muqbil, I. 2007. Thai Tourism: 20 Years after 'Visit Thailand Year'. http://www.travel-impact-newswire.com/2007/01/thai-tourism-20-years-after-visit-thailand-year/#axzz1pTJlANLK

Philippines Department of Tourism. 2012. It's More Fun in the Philippines. http://www.itsmorefuninthephilippines.com/

Reno-Sparks Convention and Visitors Authority. 2012. The Reno-Sparks Convention and Visitors Authority's Convention Sales and Services Department. http://www.visitrenotahoe.com/about-us/convention-sales

Siegel, B. 2011. What Happens When You Stop Marketing? The Rise and Fall of Colorado Tourism. Toronto: Longwoods International.

Singapore Tourism Board. 2011. Singapore Tourism Board Annual Report 2010/2011.

South Australian Tourism Commission. 2012. South Australian Tourism Commission Annual Report 2010–11. http://www.tourism.sa-gov.au/assets/documents/About/20SATC/satc-annual-report-2010-2011.pdf

Switzerland Tourism. 2012. http://www.myswitzerland.com

Tourism Australia. 2012a. Welcome to the Aussie Specialist Program. http://www.aussiespecialist.com/

——2012b. There's nothing like Australia. http://www.nothinglikeaustralia.com/index.htm

Tourism Malaysia. 2012. Tourism Malaysia Image Gallery. http://imagegallery.tourism.gov.my/

Tourism New Zealand. 2012. What We Do and How We Do It. Campaign. http://www.tourismnewzealand.com/about-us/what-we-do-and-how-we-do-it/campaign/

US Travel Association and Longwoods International. 2011. The Power of Destination Marketing. Washington, DC.

Virginia Film Office. 2012. http://www.vatc.org/film/index.asp

VisitBritain. 2012. Marketing. http://www.visitbritain.org/marketing/

VisitScotland. 2012. Surprise Yourself! http://surprise.visitscotland.com/

Destination branding and integrated marketing communications

Shaoxing Tourism case study

This case study accompanies the materials for Chapter 9 on destination branding and Chapter 10 on integrated marketing communications. It also provides materials at the beginning on destination marketing strategy and planning that correspond to the materials in Chapter 3 on destination marketing planning.

Introduction

This Shaoxing International Marketing Implementation Plan was completed for the Shaoxing Tourism Commission in Zhejiang Province, China by Belle Tourism International Consulting (BTI). The major goal was to produce an actionable plan for appealing to inbound international tourism markets to Shaoxing. The plan was developed after an assignment called *Tourism Development Plan for Shaoxing*, completed under the Zhejiang Urban Environmental Project for the World Bank. The plan was therefore able to take full advantage of extensive product and market research that was done for the World Bank assignment.

The major steps completed in preparing this plan were as follows:

- Market analysis
- International marketing strategy
- Marketing goals, objectives and initiatives
- International positioning, image and branding approach
- Implementation plan marketing mix
- Marketing implementation plan.

Market analysis

The market analysis was conducted in three parts:

- Analysis of existing inbound tourist markets (review of recent statistics on volumes of tourist arrivals in Shaoxing)

- Analysis of trends in inbound tourist markets (review of recent trends in volumes of tourist arrivals in Shaoxing)
- Analysis of market survey results (awareness of Shaoxing attractions; past rates of visits to Shaoxing; future intentions to travel to Shaoxing).

Market research highlights

The main findings resulting from the market analysis were:

- Awareness levels of Shaoxing attractions vary significantly.
- Some regional attractions are very well-known (e.g. West Lake and Mount Putuo).
- Nature, culture, history, local foods and water villages are the most desired activities.
- Independent travel is a strong market trend.
- Word of mouth and the Internet are the most important sources of travel information.

International marketing strategy

The first step in the international marketing strategy development was to identify the future priority target markets for Shaoxing's tourism. The potential tourism markets for Shaoxing are truly global but resource constraints require that the main focus must be placed on priority markets. It was of the utmost importance in the destination marketing plan for STC that such priorities were established. The establishment of target market priorities was guided by market analysis findings and also the expected return on investment (ROI) from pursuing specific markets.

- *1st priority*: Hong Kong, Macau and Taiwan; and Japan and South Korea.
- *2nd priority*: Southeast and South Asia (Singapore, Malaysia, Thailand, Indonesia, Philippines and India).
- *3rd priority*: North America, Europe and Oceania (USA, Canada, UK, Germany, France, Italy, Spain, Australia and New Zealand).

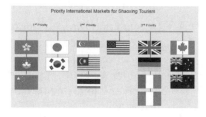

Figure 10A International tourism marketing goals for Shaoxing, 2009–2011

Source: Belle Tourism International Consulting, 2008.

Marketing goals, objectives and initiatives

Twelve sets of international tourism marketing goals were set according to marketing functions:

Table 10A   International tourism marketing goals for Shaoxing, 2009–2011

Marketing functions	Marketing goals: 2009–2011
Positioning, image and branding	• Implement the 'Shaoxing: Vintage China' positioning approach for all inbound markets • Develop the 'Ancient Canal City' image and branding for 2009 and continue to use this approach in 2010 and 2011
Target marketing	• Increase the volume of visitors from priority origin markets
Promotion, Internet marketing and integrated marketing communications	• Communicate consistent images and messages through an Integrated Marketing Communications (IMC) model • Increase awareness of secondary attractions and the number of international visitors to these sites • Integrate the administrative divisions of Shaoxing, Shangyu, Shengzhou, Xinchang and Zhuji into a more unified tourism destination under the 'Shaoxing: Vintage China' umbrella
Partnerships and cooperative marketing	• Develop a stronger local tourism team involving multiple agencies of government and local communities • Design and implement several innovative partnerships and cooperative marketing initiatives with organizations outside of Shaoxing
Programming	• Develop and carry out innovative programming approaches based upon the unique visitor experiences and activities available in Shaoxing • Implement a tourism theme year approach and design and implement related special events and festivals

continued

Table 10A   Continued

Marketing functions	Marketing goals: 2009–2011
Packaging	• Develop an online package sales system • Design selected packages for each priority market • Encourage travel trade intermediaries to add more Shaoxing products
Distribution channels (place)	• Increase awareness of Shaoxing among travel trade intermediaries • Expand the product offerings featuring Shaoxing among travel trade intermediaries
Relationship and database marketing	• Identify priority relationship groups; and design and implement specific programmes for relationship-building with each (e.g. media, local suppliers in Shaoxing, local communities, etc.) • Prepare and continuously maintain a set of relational databases
Product development	• Realize a series of supportive product improvements that enhance international visitor convenience, experiences and trip satisfaction
Human resources and training	• Improve professionalism in destination marketing • Enhance local skills in foreign languages, guiding services for and communications with international visitors, and cultural awareness • Design and implement a series of training programmes in support of the International Marketing Plan
Marketing research	• Design and conduct an annual Visitor Profile Study in Shaoxing • Measure the economic impact of tourism in Shaoxing • Track important domestic and international market trends, and project their implications for future tourism in Shaoxing

continued

Table 10A   Continued

Marketing functions	Marketing goals: 2009–2011
Marketing control and evaluation	• Monitor progress of International Marketing Plan implementation each year • Measure the performance of marketing efforts at the end of each year against these goals and marketing objectives • Measure overall tourism performance in Shaoxing according to specific metrics including: (1) extending average length of stay of visitors; (2) increasing per capita expenditures of visitors; and (3) growing the number of international visitors to Shaoxing each year

Source: Belle Tourism International Consulting, 2008.

Then, detailed, specific initiatives and shorter-term marketing objectives were defined for each of the three groups of priority markets.

International positioning, image and branding approach

Overall positioning concept

The overall concept recommended was to position Shaoxing around the concept of 'Vintage China'. The use of 'China' along with 'vintage' was deliberate and intended to clearly position Shaoxing within China, and also to associate the city with the ancient and historical times in the nation. 'Vintage' is a word with multiple meanings in English and all of these meanings could be applied to Shaoxing and its tourism.

Figure 10B Shaoxing positioning concept: vintage means old and ancient

Source: Belle Tourism International Consulting, 2008.

We can begin with the idea that 'Shaoxing is ancient'. As the first image shows, 'vintage' also means 'ancient' and 'old'. This concept seems to match well with the destination images that are trying to be *induced* by the Shaoxing Tourism Commission. Moreover, it reflects well the *organic images* of Shaoxing that are found on the web and in the printed copies of guidebooks.

Figure 10C Shaoxing positioning concept: vintage means superior, excellent and select

Source: Belle Tourism International Consulting, 2008.

But old or ancient do not fully describe Shaoxing either! Another meaning of 'vintage' is 'superior', 'excellent' or 'select' (second image). By using 'Vintage China' for Shaoxing, this implies that Shaoxing is an outstanding and one-of-a-kind or unique place, and this too seems to be very accurate. Shaoxing is unique in terms of its association with many famous Chinese people, including Lu Xun, Zhou Enlai, Wang Xizhi, Xi Shi, Da Yu and several other noteworthy individuals. Shaoxing is a one-of-a-kind place due to its contributions to various forms of artistic expression, which include novels, calligraphy and Yue opera.

Figure 10D Shaoxing positioning concept: vintage means origin, era and collection

Source: Belle Tourism International Consulting, 2008.

The third set of meanings for 'vintage' is that it represents a 'collection', 'era' or 'origin'. These are, in fact, the connotations of vintage in relation to *wine*. Shaoxing is the origin of the famous yellow rice wine, which of course is generically known as Shaoxing wine. Using the term 'Vintage China', therefore, is a good way to put across the ancient wine culture of Shaoxing. However, another dimension is that it can be used to communicate about different categories of attractions or resources in Shaoxing.

Figure 10E Shaoxing's five unique selling propositions (USPs)
Source: Belle Tourism International Consulting, 2008.

Positioning statement

The following paragraph describes the recommended positioning statement:

> Shaoxing is a famous ancient water city near the Yangtze River in China. With a rich history of 6,000 years, Shaoxing is truly Vintage China, as it has a select collection of cultural, historic, and natural attractions that reflect the very best of what China has to offer to tourists and include:
>
> - *Vintage water city*: Shaoxing is an ancient water city located to the south of the Yangtze River.
> - *Vintage boats*: Shaoxing has a unique gondola-style boat, known as the *wupeng* that has been sailing the city's canals, rivers and lakes for centuries.
> - *Vintage culture and lifestyles*: Shaoxing's ancient culture and lifestyles are still very much alive in its historic blocks and their intricate network of canals. Shaoxing's culture is also ancient, dating back 6,000 years.

- *Vintage personalities*: Shaoxing has been the home and the inspiration to many great people from China, including the greatest modern fiction writer, Lu Xun, and most celebrated calligrapher, Wang Xizhi.
- *Vintage artistic expression*: Shaoxing is an internationally important centre for calligraphy and is the birthplace of Yue Opera that dates back 2,500 years to Shaoxing's time as the capital of the ancient Yue Kingdom.
- *Vintage wine*: Shaoxing is the hometown of the world-famous yellow rice wine that shares the same name as the city.

Figure 10F Shaoxing yellow rice wine
Source: Belle Tourism International Consulting, 2008.

- *Vintage nature*: Shaoxing's nature is abundant and spectacular, sustained by its many water courses, and surrounded by unique hills and mountain ranges.

Implementation plan marketing mix

The implementation plan marketing mix provided a detailed description of the required actions and tasks according to the '8 Ps of Destination Marketing' (Morrison, 2009). The marketing mix elements for the International Marketing Implementation Plan were as follows:

- Programming ('100% Vintage Shaoxing Experiences')
- Packaging
- Pricing
- Promotion (integrated marketing communications, Internet marketing and sales promotions)
- Place (distribution channels)
- Partnerships (cooperative marketing)
- Product (support product development)
- People (human resources development and training).

Recognizing that Shaoxing Tourism's budget for international marketing and promotion was somewhat limited, the greatest emphasis was placed on the most efficient, lower-cost actions and tasks. These included programming, Internet marketing, sales promotions and promotional events.

Figure 10G Yue opera performance
Source: Belle Tourism International Consulting, 2008.

Marketing implementation plan

Programming: '100% Vintage Shaoxing Experiences'

This model comprised pure and authentic experiences that supply tourists with 100 per cent understanding of Shaoxing's culture and 100 per cent enjoyment from their trips around Shaoxing. It was called the '25 @ 100% Vintage Shaoxing Experiences' model. This used the 2,500th anniversary of Shaoxing in 2010 as the starting point for developing new programmes and packages. Certain colours were assigned to represent each of the five themes; for example, blue for Ancient Canal City; green for Nature; pink for Beauty and Love; yellow for Celebrities; and red for Artistic Expression.

The following is the Vintage Shaoxing Experiences Menu:

Figure 10H Vintage Shaoxing Experiences Menu
Source: Belle Tourism International Consulting, 2008.

Packaging and pricing

A new system for packaging was outlined and was based on international visitor experiences rather than on specific sites:

● *Vintage Shaoxing Packages*: The Vintage Shaoxing Packages reflect a 'pay-one-price' pricing strategy that integrates attractions, activities, accommodations, transport and other tourism services. This programme is an application of flexible retail pricing.
● *Tourism Product Pricing System*: The system is a basic pricing model that reflects the factors that must be considered before determining prices. The system should serve as a guideline for all tourism industry sectors.
● *Value-Added Vintage Shaoxing*: These value-added programmes will give visitors more favourable experiences in Shaoxing and help Shaoxing impress its visitors. These value-added programmes are all free for visitors.
● *Vintage Shaoxing Coupons*: This programme creates different coupons for attractions and services, and distributes the coupons to visitors through local channels and guidebooks.

Promotion

Integrated marketing communications

It was essential that all of the promotions and communications for the International Marketing Implementation Plan followed the integrated marketing communications (IMC) concept. Thus, Internet marketing; advertising; sales promotion, merchandising and events; public relations and publicity must be consistent and mutually-supportive. The 'Shaoxing Vintage China' positioning approach was to be reflected in all the future communications with international markets.

Figure 10I Integrated marketing communications (IMC) concept for Shaoxing
Source: Belle Tourism International Consulting, 2008.

As shown in the diagram above, 'Online Vintage Shaoxing Experiences' were included in the IMC model for Shaoxing. This was to ensure that these experiences were given a high priority in Shaoxing Tourism websites and also within social media sites and discussion groups.

Internet marketing

The Internet is one of the most important information sources used by international visitors to China. In 2008, Shaoxing Tourism began the development of English, Japanese and Korean official tourism website versions. This step represents a great improvement in Shaoxing's tourism marketing and positioning efforts. However, to implement all elements of the International Marketing Implementation Plan, it was recommended that Shaoxing Tourism also develop German and Spanish versions of the official tourism website. This would further expand the reach to other major long-haul target markets.

German is one of most-used languages among major tourist-generating European countries in Western Europe. Germany, Austria and Switzerland are large tourist origin countries for China and Shaoxing. Spanish is among the top three spoken languages in the world, along with Chinese and English. A Spanish version will be particularly useful in appealing to the North American market, especially to the USA where the Latino population is expanding rapidly, and to the Spanish and Latin American countries of South and Central America. Therefore, it would be advisable to have German and Spanish as the next two European language versions.

Sales promotions

A wide variety of individual sales promotions were recommended for implementation, consisting of:

- Speciality advertising
- Prizes
- Printed collateral materials
- Displays.

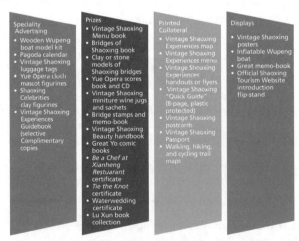

Figure 10J Recommended sales promotion for Shaoxing
Source: Belle Tourism International Consulting, 2008.

Several of these promotional items were integrated with the '100% Vintage Shaoxing Experiences'. Others were stand-alone promotions that emphasized the 'Shaoxing Vintage China' positioning approach in a creative and interesting way for international tourists.

Prototypes of several of the promotional items were developed and are shown in the photograph that follows:

Figure 10K Prototypes of promotional items for Shaoxing
Source: Belle Tourism International Consulting, 2008.

Prototypes of Shaoxing tourism promotional items

- Wooden *wupeng* boat model
- Pagoda calendar
- Vintage Shaoxing luggage tags
- Shaoxing celebrities rice figurines
- Vintage Shaoxing menu book
- Vintage Shaoxing Experiences bookmarks
- Vintage Shaoxing Experiences handout
- Vintage Shaoxing Quick-Guide
- Vintage Shaoxing passport
- Shaoxing Experiences postcards.

Place: distribution channels

A focus on international travel trade intermediaries will prove to be an efficient and lower-cost approach to reaching Shaoxing's priority markets. The main challenge is to properly identify the most effective channels and companies. The range of possible online and offline travel channels in Asia, Europe, North America and Oceania is enormous. These distribution channels can be divided into: (1) online (websites and social media); (2) offline (traditional travel trade and travel media). Three priority groups and twenty specific origin markets were pinpointed for Shaoxing Tourism to focus upon.

The market research results showed that Shaoxing did not have high awareness among China's international visitors or with international travel agencies. To increase international awareness, more promotion and advertising to travel distribution channels is necessary. During the implementation of the plan, a focus on travel trade intermediaries will prove to be an efficient and lower-cost approach to reaching priority markets.

Market travel trade intermediary profiles

Figure 10L Samples of market travel intermediary profiles
Source: Belle Tourism International Consulting, 2008.

To assist Shaoxing Tourism in the selection of the most appropriate channels, a *Market Travel Trade Intermediary Profile* was provided for each of the priority markets. The operations of each company and their ability to target the twenty priority markets were analysed and further categorized into three sub-categories of companies that reach: large/small group; fully independent traveller (FIT); and special-interest traveller (SIT) markets. This categorization was based on survey results and current market trends.

Partnerships (cooperative marketing)

Eight innovative partnership concepts were detailed in the International Marketing Implementation Plan, as shown below:

Figure 10M Partnership concepts for Shaoxing
Source: Belle Tourism International Consulting, 2008.

Two of the most creative of these partnership proposals are described below:

Ancient Town DMO Alliance

In China, there are many famous ancient towns, some of which are listed on the UNESCO World Heritage List, such as Lijiang in Yunnan. These ancient towns serve as important tourism attractions for local DMOs and share similar objectives for attracting tourists and conserving cultural and heritage resources. To enhance cooperation among these, it is recommended that the 'Ancient Town DMO Alliance' be created. Shaoxing and STC will initiate the process in forming this alliance and invite other ancient town DMOs to join. This alliance is not intended to spark greater competition among ancient towns, and so Lijiang and Pingyao should be first priority members. These towns have high market awareness and popularity but are farther from Shaoxing.

Similar alliances have had great success, and the Ancient Town DMO Alliance will increase the international market awareness of China's ancient towns, while making them more recognizable under a single and global image.

Chinese Calligraphy Alliance

Lan Pavilion is unquestionably the Mecca of Chinese Calligraphy, a precious resource of Shaoxing with great potential that has yet to be fully explored. The Lan Pavilion International Calligraphy Festival has been successfully held for 24 years.

Based on the unparalleled reputation of Lan Pavilion in Chinese calligraphy, it is suggested that Shaoxing initiate the 'Chinese Calligraphy Alliance', comprised of both domestic and international calligraphy associations and organizations. Shaoxing has already established solid relationships with domestic calligraphy associations and organizations. The next step is to enhance these by holding other related activities that will motivate international calligraphy associations and organizations to join, not only independent enthusiasts. In order to attract foreign visitors to Shaoxing, the inclusion of international groups in the Chinese Calligraphy Alliance is essential. Shaoxing will organize several new activities in Lan Pavilion, for example, a Chinese calligraphy contest each month for participating countries, that will culminate in a yearly world championship competition.

Product (support product development)

Supportive Product Development

Ancient Canal City Gates
The project implements the conceptual idea of *City Gates* for Shaoxing to the east, north, south, and west. These will actually serve as visitor information centers (VICs).

3D-IINS
A functional prototype for a 3D (three-dimensional) tourism information, interpretation, and navigation system for Shaoxing tourism was created.

Western Tourist Radio
TOURIST RADIO
FM
Discover WA our way

Vintage Shaoxing Passport©

ITS
Intelligent Transportation System is the tourism transportation structure designed to make tourists feel safer, more efficient, more reliable and interesting.

Vintage Shaoxing Passport
This special card encourages people to visit more tourist attractions.

Figure 10N Supportive product development for Shaoxing
Source: Belle Tourism International Consulting, 2008.

People (human resources development and training)

Human resources (people) were judged to be essential for the implementation of this International Marketing Implementation Plan. The human resources development and training recommendations covered branch office establishment, tourism research enhancements, recruitment, training and certification.

Seven specific programmes and initiatives were recommended within the plan:

- Recruitment and training of guides and guide families programme
- Shaoxing Tourism Development and Research Centre
- Shaoxing Tourism branch office in Shanghai
- International Marketing Implementation Plan training
- Tourism destination marketing skills training
- Communication and language skills training
- Vintage Shaoxing international guide certification.

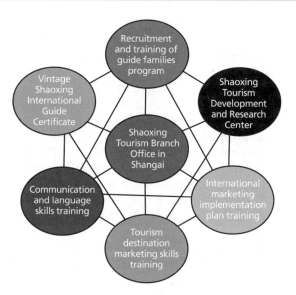

Figure 10O Human Resources developing and training
programmes and initiatives
Source: Belle Tourism International Consulting, 2008.

Figure 10P Ancient canal section in Shaoxing
Source: Belle Tourism International Consulting, 2008.

Case summary

The International Marketing Implementation Plan was a crucial step in
transforming Shaoxing from primarily a place for domestic travel into an

international tourism destination. Shaoxing Tourism demonstrated great wisdom and vision in commissioning the preparation of such a plan.

Starting from a strong foundation of product and market research, this case study had several strengths that have resulted in successful implementation. In particular, the 'Shaoxing Vintage China' positioning, image and branding approach has been widely accepted and used in marketing Shaoxing internationally. The approach has been applied in websites, printed promotional materials, programming and in various consumer and travel trade promotional events and exhibitions.

The plan's recommendations related to Internet marketing have been followed very closely. Shaoxing Tourism now has five foreign-language versions of its official tourism website (English, Korean, Japanese, German and Spanish). The design and contents of these websites have received widespread praise.

Shaoxing Tourism has used the 'Shaoxing Vintage China' theme in several presentations abroad to travel agencies and others in Europe, Southeast Asia, Japan and Korea.

The '100% Vintage Shaoxing Experiences' programming concept has also been adopted and used in Shaoxing Tourism's international marketing. A later case study explains the '25 @ 100% Vintage Shaoxing Experiences Event' that was held with great success in Shaoxing.

Figure 10Q Vintage Shaoxing Experiences map
Source: Belle Tourism International Consulting, 2008.

Destination branding and integrated marketing communications case study questions and exercise

1 The positioning and branding for Shaoxing was based on comprehensive market research and a thorough competitive analysis. Why is it so important to have in-depth analysis of potential markets and competitors when developing the positioning–image–branding approaches for a tourism destination?
2 For a small city like Shaoxing and other small cities around the world that have limited budgets for marketing and promotion, what are the IMC techniques that are likely to be the most affordable as well as effective? Please ensure that you fully justify your answers.
3 Using your local area as the destination of focus, how would you develop positioning–image–branding approaches and an IMC campaign for the area? Who would be involved in these development processes and how would you ensure that the processes would produce effective outcomes?

Chapter 11

Destination information and communication technologies

Learning objectives

1 Define information and communication technologies and give a brief history of their development.

2 Explain the importance of Internet marketing to DMOs.

3 Identify and discuss the major roles of DMO websites.

4 Describe the marketing functions of DMO websites.

5 Name and discuss the functions that websites play for tourists.

6 Review the steps that should be followed in evaluating the effectiveness of websites.

7 Detail the characteristics of effective websites.

8 Review the social media and the ways these channels are used by DMOs and tourists.

9 Discuss the significance of traveller review sites for tourism businesses and destinations.

10 Identify and explain the uses and advantages of blogs for destinations and DMOs.

11 Review the impacts of mobile phones and smartphones on tourism.

12 Elaborate on the concept of augmented reality and how it can be used in tourism.

Introduction

Information and communication technologies (ICTs) have had a major impact on the tourism sector during the past 25 years. The impacts began in the early 1990s and seem to be accelerating more quickly now. The destination marketing and promotion role of destination management was the first to feel the effects of ICT innovations, but the impacts have now spread to all the other destination management roles.

The introduction of the Internet especially had a huge impact on destination management and on tourists. It has affected how tourists search for information about destinations and plan trips. The Internet has had a great impact on how people book travel and has spawned a new breed of intermediaries, online travel agencies. For DMOs, the Internet has become the major information dissemination and marketing tool.

The social media or social network sites have opened up a new world of dialogue among people, including conversations about destinations. DMOs have joined these conversations by building their own sites and pages. The main advantage of social networks for destinations is the stimulation of online word-of-mouth recommendations.

Blogging has become very popular among consumers. Blogs can serve multiple purposes and have distinct advantages for DMOs. This chapter explains how DMOs can take advantage of blogging.

Mobile phones and smartphones have become numerous around the world and their use has had a significant effect on tourism and destinations. In particular, the number of travel and tourism applications ('apps') for smartphones has grown rapidly and now there are several thousand. The development of mobile electronic travel guides (METGs) is advancing rapidly and offers benefits both for destinations and tourists.

Definition of information and communication technologies (ICTs)

Information and communication technologies provide access to information through communication technologies. These technologies include the Internet, social networks, wireless networks, mobile phones, global positioning system and many others. Providing access alone does not do justice to the many roles and functions that ICTs play. ICTs allow people to interact with the information, with other users, and with the sponsors. The following is a more complete definition of ICTs.

Definition of ICTs

Information and communications technologies (ICTs) is an umbrella name that covers communication devices or applications (radio, television, cameras, mobile phones, computer and network hardware and software, satellite systems, etc.), as well as their associated services and applications, including video conferencing, distance education, cloud computing, Wi-Fi, augmented reality, etc.

Brief recent history of ICTs

One of the first major ICT waves came around 1993 with the development of HTML and the World Wide Web. DMOs started developing websites around 1994–1995. The second wave was the introduction of e-commerce into tourism very soon after destinations started using the Internet. The third wave, mobile commerce (m-commerce) came right on the heels of e-commerce around 1997. The fourth wave was the so-called Web 2.0 or the use of social media online, with the first social network site being launched in 1997. However, the most popular social media sites started around 2003–2004. The fifth wave came with the introduction of smartphones, the earliest versions appearing in 2002. The Apple iPhone was introduced in 2007. Mobile broadband Internet access began around 2007.

Figure 11.1 includes data from the International Telecommunication Union (ITU) on the use of the main types of ICT across the world. These data show the number of subscriptions per 100 inhabitants and it can be seen that mobile-cellular telephone subscriptions have the highest penetration rate, followed by the Internet. ITU estimated that there were 5.9 billion mobile-cellular subscriptions in 2011 and a global penetration rate of 86 per cent. ITU found the penetration rate of the Internet was 32.5 per cent in 2011, and that 45 per cent of Internet users were under 25 years old.

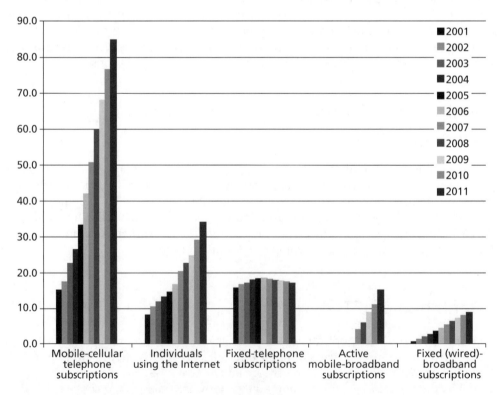

Figure 11.1 Growth in the adoption of ICTs

Source: International Telecommunication Union, 2012.

Importance of Internet marketing

Internet marketing has rapidly become the most important form of marketing and the major information communications tool for DMOs around the world. For travellers, the Internet is also now the most important information source and trip planning tool. The Internet is more than a source of information, a partner for travellers and a tool for the travel trade; it has become an entertaining venue to gain knowledge and get hands-on experiences. One of the best ways to effectively use the Internet is through the creation of interactive and informative websites.

Websites must offer online users a wide array of information while seeming to be personalized for just one visitor. The information provided must span from what the destination is, why it should be visited and what should be visited, to all other components of the experience.

DMOs count on the Internet for its ability to communicate with existing and potential customers whether they are nearby or on the other side of the world. Geographic boundaries do not exist online and when the Internet is well used, it is a highly individualized and targeted medium. The ideal destination website increases awareness and curiosity; therefore, it attracts more visitors.

Internet usage

There were almost 2.3 billion Internet users in the world at the end of 2011 (Figure 11.2); and that was more than 6.3 times the Internet population at the end of 2000. Europe has emerged as the second largest Internet market, having overtaken North

World regions	Internet users*	Percentage of Internet users	Penetration of national markets
Asia	1,016,799,076	44.8%	26%
Europe	500,723,686	22.1%	61.3%
North America	273,067,546	12.0%	78.6%
Latin America and Caribbean	235,819,740	10.4%	39.5%
Africa	139,875,242	6.2%	13.5%
Middle East	77,020,995	3.4%	35.6%
Oceania/Australia	23,927,457	1.1%	67.5%
Total	2,267,233,742	100.0%	37.7%

Figure 11.2 World Internet population 2011
Note: * At 31 December 2011.
Source: Miniwatts Marketing Group, 2012.

America several years ago. The highest market penetration rates of the Internet are in North America, Oceania/Australia and Europe. Asia is the leading region, with 45 per cent of all the world's Internet users. There are over one billion Internet users in Asia. However, the market penetration of Internet users is only 26.2 per cent in Asia. So, there is great potential in the future for growing the Internet user market in Asia, perhaps by two to three times the present level.

China is the leading Internet user market in the world with 477 million Internet users, followed by the USA, India, Japan and Germany (Figure 11.3).

Roles of websites for DMOs

Destination websites have existed since around 1994–1995 and they have now become much more than information channels. Today, websites play multiple roles for DMOs worldwide. In fact, there are at least nine roles for DMO websites (Figure 11.4).

The destination information source role of DMO websites is still a critical function as tourists use them for trip planning and selecting destinations. For example, research done by Belle Tourism International Consulting (BTI) in China indicated that websites and the Internet were the top source of information for international visitors when planning their trips to China. Attractive, informative and engaging websites in multiple languages are a 'must have' for DMOs that are pursuing international tourists.

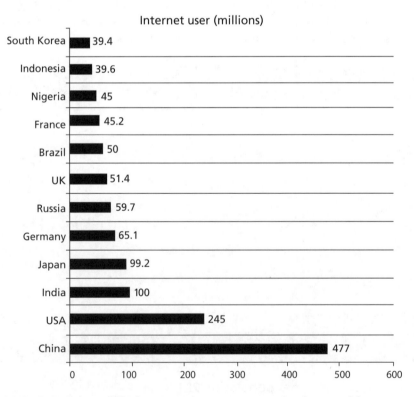

Figure 11.3 Countries with the most Internet users in the world
Source: Miniwatts Marketing Group, 2012.

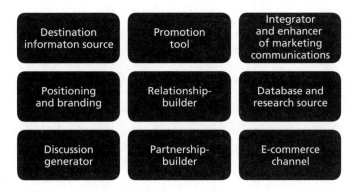

Figure 11.4 Nine main roles of DMO websites

DMO websites have become increasingly important as marketing tools and in engaging in communications with travellers. A majority of the nine roles relate to some aspect of destination marketing. One way of thinking about the multiple roles of a DMO website is to regard it as the hub of communications with potential tourists and other audiences. The website is a place where everyone can go for information and advice on the destination. It is also where the DMO talks one-to-one with individual potential visitors and others. The following is a more detailed description of the nine roles of DMO websites:

- *Provide information on the destination*: When DMOs first started introducing websites, these were like electronic brochures (e-brochures) packed with information about the destinations. They were not very interactive and did not include many features. Nowadays the information is provided in a much more attractive way with considerable scope for interactivity.
- *Promote destination product and services*: Websites are the global shop window for promoting destinations. With great photography, colours, sound and inter-activity, websites allow for a highly convincing and appealing presentation of destinations.
- *Support and enhance traditional promotions*: Websites provide support to the traditional promotional mix elements including public relations and publicity, advertising, personal selling, sales promotions and merchandising. These all now work together as integrated marketing communications built upon an online platform. For example, websites have become the major venue for posting the news releases of DMOs, as well as the place to first introduce major new promotional campaigns.
- *Communicate destination positioning and branding*: Websites reflect the image that the DMO wants to create for the destination and support the chosen approach to branding the place. The outstanding visual qualities and interactivity of websites make for convincing image presentations.
- *Build relationships with tourists and travel trade*: People can sign-up on websites to receive more detailed information, as well as providing more details on their travel interests. Databases of individuals (B2C) and travel trade (B2B) can be built through sign-ups at websites, and then used to maintain ongoing contacts.
- *Engage travellers in discussions via the social media*: The social media channels provide a platform for DMOs to place information content and to engage in conversations and discussions with potential tourists.

Destination communications and promotions

- *Generate visitor databases and research*: Websites can be used to conduct online surveys and to build databases of people who register. This can be a very low-cost alternative to gathering research data when compared to traditional offline methods.
- *Encourage destination partnerships*: Websites are a great tool for partnerships with tourism sector stakeholders and other organizations with which the DMO has established collaboration.
- *Allow bookings and reservations (e-commerce)*: Several DMO websites allow bookings and reservations to be made at hotels, attractions and at other stakeholder locations.

DMO websites are an essential part of marketing strategy and marketing plan implementation. Indeed some experts say websites are now the most important part of destination marketing. There are at least ten different marketing applications of DMO websites (Figure 11.5).

- *Target marketing*: For marketing strategy, official destination websites play a role in target marketing, positioning and destination branding. Often there are different parts of DMO websites for individual target markets, or separate websites are designed for individual markets.
- *Positioning*: A DMO website can be used to visually demonstrate the image that the destination has decided to communicate. For example, using predominantly green colours can give an image of an eco- or nature-based destination.
- *Destination branding*: The destination branding approach selected by the DMO can be reflected in its websites. Depicting images and colours that reflect the branding reinforces brand adoption and equity.

Figure 11.5 Marketing functions of DMO websites

- *Globalization*: Websites allow DMOs and destinations to reach out globally and build awareness around the world. To do this, DMO websites have to be in multiple languages as well as reflective of the cultural differences among countries.
- *Market research*: Websites are great not only for providing information to customers, but also for gathering information from customers. Market research data are collected through online surveys and feedback forms.
- *Relationship marketing*: Information that customers enter about themselves is built into databases, and used to create closer relationships with them. In other words, websites support DMOs' customer relationship management (CRM) efforts.
- *Social media*: Social media environments are places where customers discuss aspects of the destination and thereby provide valuable intelligence for the DMO. This application is discussed in greater detail later in this chapter.
- *Marketing programmes and activities*: Websites are venues for implementing all types of marketing activities and programmes (using the 8 Ps discussed earlier in Chapter 3). Websites are also a key element in integrated marketing communications (IMC).
- *Partnerships*: The online environment is a great place for building partnerships. In Chapter 6, several examples were provided of online partnerships and e-collaborators, including Alps Europe, the BestCities Global Alliance, and the cooperative website of the Korea Tourism Organization and the China National Tourist Office.

Functions of websites for tourists

Websites have also become much more than an information source for tourists. Tourists visit destination websites for multiple reasons and purposes. Websites, therefore, are not purely being used as a source of information. TEAM Tourism Consulting of the UK identified twelve different reasons and purposes for using DMO websites (Figure 11.6).

- *Dreaming, enthusing and informing*: Before booking their trips, websites are used for dreaming, enthusing and informing people about potential destinations.
- *Planning, selecting and booking*: When people make the decision to travel, websites are then used in trip planning and in selecting destinations. People may also use websites for booking their trips.
- *Travelling, visiting and enjoying*: People may refer to the websites when travelling within the destination and for visiting and enjoying places of interest.
- *Repeating, recommending and recollecting*: People may want to go back to the destination, so they revisit websites. They may recommend the websites and destinations to relatives and friends. In addition, they may return to the websites just to remember the details of their trips.

When planning the design of websites, DMOs need to be sure to provide for all of these potential customer reasons and purposes. Content alone is not enough to meet all of these diverse needs and requirements.

Therefore, there are supply requirements (DMO and tourism sector stakeholders) and demand (tourists) requirements to DMO websites and both must be blended together for the most effective Internet presence. It is not surprising that some DMOs have multiple websites that are segmented by audience, and supplement their websites

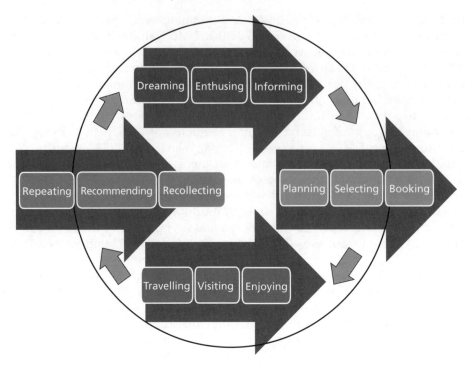

Figure 11.6 Consumer reasons and purposes for using DMO websites
Source: UNWTO and European Travel Commission, 2008.

with pages on popular social media channels that allow different types of interactions with tourists.

Website evaluation

The constant evaluation of destination websites is essential. DMO WebEVAL® is a system developed and owned by Belle Tourism International (BTI) Consulting (Figure 11.7). This system is a comprehensive tool used to measure the effectiveness and quality of DMO websites. In addition, it also provides useful guidelines for developing websites and testing their performance. The system is designed to detect weaknesses that can be improved upon and strengths that can be accentuated. WebEVAL uses four perspectives for DMO website evaluation:

- *Technical perspective*: Is the website free from technical problems and does it have good link popularity?
- *Customer perspective*: How user-friendly and attractive is the website for travellers?
- *Marketing effectiveness perspective*: How effective is the website in marketing, positioning and branding the destination?
- *Destination information perspective*: Does the website provide the complete range of information that travellers, travel trade, media and others expect from a DMO?

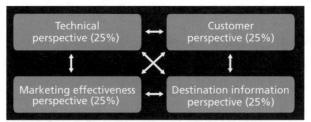

Based on a modified Balanced Scorecard (BSC) approach

Figure 11.7 The DMO WebEVAL® system
Source: Belle Tourism International Consulting, 2012.

Here are some of the specific criteria within each of these four perspectives:

● *Technical*: Download time, browser compatibility, spelling and use of HTML.
● *Customer*: Site accessibility, site navigation, visual attractiveness, ease of contact and currency of information.
● *Marketing effectiveness*: Globalization, market segmentation and targeting, positioning and branding, tangibilizing products, marketing research, relationship and database marketing, partnerships and value-adding.
● *Destination information*: Destination mix information, general travel information and information for meeting planners, media/press and travel trade.

Characteristics of effective DMO websites

The 'I AM OUTSTANDING' model

What are the characteristics of the world's best DMO websites? To demonstrate these characteristics, the 'I AM OUTSTANDING' model is introduced and explained in detail (Figure 11.8). There are 14 important characteristics of excellent international DMO websites and taken one-by-one they spell out 'I AM OUTSTANDING'. They reflect

Figure 11.8 The 'I AM OUTSTANDING' model of effective websites

377

website features that are not only important to customers, but also are critical to effective DMO marketing communications. There are undoubtedly other features of great DMO websites, but these fourteen are considered to be among the most important for a successful Internet presence.

I = International: The website of VisitDenmark (http://www.visitdenmark.com) has 22 different language and country versions. Most of the major countries of Europe are covered but Chinese and Japanese versions are also available. The VisitBritain site (http://www.visitbritain.com) is available in 23 different languages, as well as several versions of English. The foreign languages include two versions of Chinese, Japanese, Korean, Thai, Arabic and many European tongues. The Tourism Australia site (http://www.australia.com) has 34 different country and language versions, including several different English language versions.

A = Address: The great DMO websites treat website users as individuals and allow personalization of the website experience. YourSingapore.com by the Singapore Tourism Board (http://www.yoursingapore.com) is a great example of addressing travellers as individuals. People planning to visit the country can assemble their own Singapore travel guides on the website. They can also access guides that other visitors have previously designed.

Tourism New Zealand's website (http://www.NewZealand.com/) is highly personalized. In the 'Travel Planner', visitors can create a day-by-day itinerary for themselves on a map that can be saved. They can collect contents about scenic highlights, activities and other points of interest in New Zealand.

The Hong Kong Tourism Board's website (http://www.discoverhongkong.com) is full of interest and interactivity. One of the personalized functions is the 'Discover Hong Kong Itinerary Planner' in which visitors enter the length of trip and day parts of arrival and departure. They can then select from an array of possible morning, afternoon and evening activities to fill out their personalized Hong Kong itinerary.

M = Monitored: Excellent international DMO websites are always being constantly checked, evaluated and updated by their owners; evaluation is constant. The Tourism Wyoming site (http://www.wyomingtourism.org) includes a 'Site survey' questionnaire. This is a new website, so the questionnaire asks visitors what they liked or disliked about the site. It also asks if people encountered any navigation problems, and which functions and features they used to browse and navigate the site. A rating scale question is asked about five aspects of the site. The questionnaire is short (just eight questions) and easy to complete.

Tourism Winnipeg's website (http://www.tourismwinnipeg.com) has a pop-up survey that gathers demographic information and intentions to visit the city in the future. It also asks about favourite things to do in Winnipeg.

The Ministry of Tourism of India has a feedback form with its official website (http://www.incredibleindia.org). This form allows site visitors to provide feedback on the site and also about their trips to India.

O = Outstanding: Great DMO websites often win awards or some other recognition. Some of the website award and recognition programmes are the Webby Awards; the PATA Gold Awards; *Travel + Leisure*'s Best Travel Websites and Apps; World

Travel Awards; and WebAward.com. There are also ratings by newspapers including *The Times*, the *Telegraph* and the *Independent* in the UK; and by tourism consultants.

The German National Tourist Board website (http://www.germany.travel) was one of the PATA Gold Award winners in 2012. It is the essence of simplicity on the front page; but is easy to navigate and has all the information that visitors want.

The Tourism Montréal website (http://www.tourisme-montreal.org) gets high ratings from several tourism consultants. This site is praised for its prominent placement of the destination video (*Montréal in Two Minutes*), plus its great use of social media channels.

The EnjoyEngland website (http://www.enjoyengland.com) won the World's Leading Travel Destination Website 2011 award.

U = Updated or Up-to-Date: The excellent international DMO websites are updated frequently and therefore are current. They include timely information and never appear out-of-date. The destination website for New York City (http://www.nycgo.com) illustrates a good case study of introducing timeliness. NYC is famous for its Broadway and off-Broadway shows, and other live performance events. The site is frequently updated to include information on the current shows and events, so it always has a fresh contents look and feel.

The website of Cumbria and the Lake District of England (http://www.golakes.co.uk/) demonstrates one good way to make a website look updated by showing photos that represent the current season of the year.

The Las Vegas Convention and Visitor Authority's website (http://www.visitlasvegas.com) appears very up-to-date as it includes the weather forecast for the upcoming week and a hotel booking function that has the current dates.

T = Targeted: The great international websites segment information according to major target markets. The Paris website (http://convention.parisinfo.com/en/) is aimed at the business events markets and has its own unique website domain name. It describes all the meeting venues in the great French city. An online RFP (request for proposals) is included.

The Jamaica Tourist Board has devoted part of its website (http://www.visitjamaica.com) to the wedding and honeymoon market. The DMO has also appointed a 'Wedding Concierge' to help couples who are planning to be married in Jamaica.

The Tourism Australia site is considered by many to be one of the world's very best DMO websites. The web page (http://www.australia.com/campaigns/season_06/en/index_iv.html) was developed for young travellers going to Australia. It provides information for younger travellers who want to travel and work, spend a gap year, or just simply travel to Australia.

S = Social media: All of the excellent international websites are heavily involved in social media marketing. The most successful DMOs are making frequent use of popular social media channels. Tourism Malaysia created a special page on Facebook (http://www.Facebook.com/FriendofMalaysia) in March 2010, and by March 2012 approximately 37,500 people had indicated they 'liked' the page. It includes the wall, info, photos, notes (where Tourism Malaysia newsletters are posted), discussions and a calendar of events.

Visit Wales has had a special page (http://www.youtube.com/VisitWales) on YouTube since 2007. It is well-designed to complement the DMO's website. In March 2012, there had been over 113,241 video views on this YouTube page.

Tourism Queensland has an official Twitter profile page (http://twitter.com/#!/queensland). There were almost 20,540 followers and over 2,681 tweets on the page in March 2012. This is a great medium for passing along short and timely messages to people interested in Queensland tourism, as well as stimulating user discussions about the state's tourism industry.

T = Telephone-ready: There has been huge growth in the use of smartphones and there will soon be more smartphones than PCs in the world. Several of the outstanding DMOs have developed mobile phone versions of their website materials or special downloadable phone applications. The Netherlands Board of Tourism and Conventions provides the *Amsterdam Mobile Guide* that can be downloaded from its website (http://us.Holland.com). The guide has information on over 200 places to visit in the city.

The *Cityguide Gothenburg* can be downloaded as an iPhone application from Göteborg & Co.'s website (http://www.goteborg.com/en/). Visitors can use the phone application to plan their trips to Gothenburg in Sweden and create lists of favourite places within the city.

Sixteen DMOs in France's Côte Basque joined in a partnership to create a mobile phone website (www.macotebasque.com). This mobile site provides much useful travel information for people visiting the region.

A = Attractive: Bold photography and colours, and eye-catching headlines make these sites stand out. Attractive websites are not cluttered with too much different information, especially on their front pages. The state of Alaska is a destination full of magnificent natural scenery and wildlife. Six different and large photographs of these beautiful scenes are offered on Travel Alaska's website front page (http://www.travelalaska.com) and they have great eye-appeal. A set of five smaller photos demonstrate the reasons or motivations for visiting Alaska.

Namibia, located in southwest Africa, is a fantastic natural destination with great diversity of landforms and animal species. The DMO's website front page is very neatly designed with great colour compatibility (http://www.namibiatourism.com.na). Again, a set of large and bold photographs quickly draw the viewer's attention and interest.

The Czech Republic's tourism website (http://www.czechtourism.com) quickly catches the eye with great background photography and movement in each photo image. This is an outstanding example of how to immediately get the attention of a website visitor through interactivity combined with attractive visual imagery.

N = Networked: Great DMOs often partner with others in Internet marketing. Berlin, Cape Town, Copenhagen, Dubai, Edinburgh, Houston, Melbourne, San Juan, Singapore and Vancouver have joined forces to create a website (http://www.bestcities.net) to gain a larger share of international business events markets. This is a great example of cooperation among top-class cities that have decided it is better to work together than always being competitors. The network has also introduced a set of 'Best City Certified Quality Service' standards.

The four provinces of Atlantic Canada (New Brunswick, Newfoundland and Labrador, Nova Scotia, and Prince Edward Island) along with the Canadian Tourism Commission have partnered together for marketing in the USA and internationally. This is an outstanding example of regional tourism marketing (http://atlanticcanadaholiday.ca/english/index.php).

The 11 states in the southeast of the USA have had a long-standing cooperation in tourism promotion that has been extended into Internet marketing. The website offers downloadable visitor guides, an interactive regional map, video and special travel offers via e-mail (http://www.travelsouthUSA.com).

D = Dynamic: The outstanding international DMO websites have compelling interactive features. The DMO of Austria provides a fantastic interactive map on its website. It outlines Austria's nine tourist regions; identifies the 'Best of Austria'; and provides photos and live webcam images. The map also shows details on activities and experiences; accommodation; eating and drinking; and other useful information (http://www.austria.info/us/interactive-map-austria).

The DMO in Peru offers a 360-degree virtual photo tour of some of its most popular attractions, including Machu Picchu and eight other tourism areas. The nine virtual tours incorporate a video with an audio commentary. They also provide a detailed map of each area (http://tours.peru.info/index_ing.html).

The Kentucky Department of Travel's website features an interactive Official Visitor's Guide (http://www.kentuckytourism.com/). Site visitors can flip through the pages just like they would do with a real book or magazine. The publication can also be printed out (http://guides.weaver-group.com/kyg/12/index.html).

I = Integrated: The best websites of international DMOs are part of carefully crafted and multi-element integrated marketing communication (IMC) programmes. Switzerland Tourism is the DMO for this European country and it provides a good example of an IMC programme delivered on the Internet. As can be seen, the three examples here are all linked together for greater communications consistency.

The website has bold red colours and eye-catching photographs. The very distinctive logo line, 'Switzerland. Get natural', is prominently shown (http://www.myswitzerland.com).

Switzerland Tourism has developed its own page on Facebook and a similar photographic image to the website is included (http://www.facebook.com/MySwitzerland). This site had 158,000 'likes' in March 2012. Switzerland Tourism also has sites on Twitter, YouTube and Flickr, again all reflecting the same theme.

Switzerland Tourism has an online shop where visitors can download various travel brochures. The design of all of the brochures is similar to that found on the website (https://www.myswitzerlandshop.com/).

N = Niche markets: The outstanding international websites often pick out good potential niche or special-interest markets and appeal directly to them.

Tourism Niagara in Canada promotes its 'Wine Country' to wine lovers on its website (http://www.tourismniagara.com). With 70 wineries in the Niagara region, there is much to be explored by these special-interest travellers. The site also provides a hyperlink to all the wine regions of Ontario (http://www.winecountryontario.ca/).

Belgium is famous for chocolate and so the Belgian Tourist Office includes a section for chocolate lovers in its website section on gastronomy. There is a special part about 'The Chocolate Makers' in Brussels and Wallonia, including the famous Godiva brand (http://www.belgique-tourisme.net).

Medugorje is located in Bosnia-Herzegovina and is a sacred site for pilgrimages by Catholics. It is said that in 1981 six teenagers saw a vision of the Virgin Mary on a hillside in Medugorje and that she talked with them. The vision reappeared several times thereafter. The site in Herzegovina has now been visited by about 15 million people (http://www.bhtourism.ba).

G = Great contents: This is a hallmark of excellent DMO websites. But giving very obvious and convenient ways of accessing these great contents is also very important. The colourful map of the Bahamas makes it easy to get information on each island. By clicking on the interactive map which forms from The Islands of the Bahamas logo, the site visitor is taken to the contents and a special video on fourteen different islands or groups of islands (http://www.bahamas.com).

The Canadian Tourism Commission's website for the US market provides fast access to specific travel experiences. A specific activity or event is described for each province and territory. This is a great way to organize contents according to the experiences that visitors can have in Canada (http://us.canada.travel/things-to-do/all).

The Argentinean DMO website provides excellent contents in a well-organized manner for the 5,000-kilometre Road 40 that runs from the north to the south of this South American country. This website section also incorporates an interactive map of sites along Road 40 (http://www.turismo.gov.ar/eng/menu.htm).

Summary of effective website characteristics

It can be fairly said that these effective international websites resemble the most glossy, modern magazines. They are sophisticated and eye-catching, and creative as well. They are often the essence of simplicity, while being deep in content and highly potent as marketing tools. The 'I AM OUTSTANDING' model identifies 14 important characteristics and features of excellent DMO websites. The following summary explains and connects these aspects of effective DMO websites:

- *Recognized for excellence*: The world's most effective DMO websites often win awards or gain some other type of recognition for excellence.
- *Address travellers as individuals and are dynamic*: The effective international DMO websites treat website users as individuals and allow for personalization. Dynamic, interactive features are included to provide each user with an individualized experience.

- *Global, attractive and contain great contents*: The effective DMO websites have multiple foreign language versions and make other adjustments to fit the cultures of different originating regions. With bold photography and colours, and eye-catching headlines, they stand out and attract users. They have great and in-depth contents with very obvious and convenient ways of accessing the detailed information.
- *Targeted and appeal to niche or special-interest markets*: Effective DMO websites are target marketing tools and provide contents for different segments of the market. Many of them address markets with specialized travel interests and give these customers the unique information that they are seeking online.
- *Up-to-date and are monitored*: The excellent international DMO websites are updated frequently and are very current. They are constantly being watched, evaluated and improved.
- *Have smartphone applications available*: There will soon be more smartphones in the world than personal computers. The great DMO websites have noticed this trend and have developed mobile phone applications that can be downloaded from their websites.
- *Use social media channels and generate user content*: The most successful DMOs have been making extensive use of popular social media channels for several years. They encourage users to provide their own contents in words, photos or videos; and then use some of these materials in DMO promotions and share it with other potential visitors.
- *Are part of integrated marketing communications (IMC)*: The best websites of international DMOs are part of carefully crafted and multi-element IMC programmes. Each online and offline component fits together well and they all reinforce each other.
- *Networked with partners and partner sites*: Great DMOs recognize the value of cooperation and often partner with others in Internet marketing. Sometimes they work together with other nearby DMOs to form regional websites that create greater online exposure for all partners.

There was a time when websites were stand-alone marketing and communication tools but that has changed greatly over the past 10 years or so. DMO websites now provide a platform for connecting with other ICTs and applications, and for informing and communicating with DMOs' audiences. For example, some DMO websites incorporate 'virtual communities' where interested people discuss various aspects and features of destinations and recollect their trips for others to read and enjoy. Many people write blogs within these communities. Additionally, most DMO websites have the 'widgets' linking site visitors to the most popular social network sites such as Facebook, Twitter and YouTube. Increasingly, websites are including download information for DMO apps for smartphones. People can sign-up for RSS (really simple syndication) feeds from DMO websites to automatically get updated information from the destination. DMO websites now provide many types of downloads that offer a variety of communication tools for potential tourists.

So, in other words, a website is no longer just a website for a DMO, but rather an online location to interconnect with different audiences using an integrated set of ICTs. One of these ICTs is the social networks, which is the next topic for discussion in this chapter.

Social networks and destination management

Since around 2003–2004, social network services and sites have had a major influence on destinations and DMOs. Now most DMOs are active in the social media and are using them for information dissemination, communications and marketing purposes. However, the use of this branch of ICTs is in a relatively early stage and research about its effectiveness is still not mature.

Use of social media channels

A scan of the websites of many leading DMOs around the world shows you that many of them have established sites on Facebook, Twitter and YouTube. Figure 11.9 illustrates the channels used by ten of the top country destinations in the world and it can be seen that all are using these three popular social media channels. Flickr is also quite popular, as is linking to TripAdvisor.com. RSS feeds are also a very common feature.

Among these Facebook sites, the Spanish is one of the most popular with over 745,000 likes in March 2012. However, the Tourism Australia Facebook site may be the most popular among DMOs in the world with 2.4 million likes in March 2012 and a Facebook 'fanbase' of over one million people. The following is some basic information on the most popular of these social network sites:

Country	Facebook	Twitter	YouTube	Other	RSS
Spain	☑	☑	☑	Formspring	☑
Italy	☑	☑	☑	Foursquare Google+ JoinItaly	☑
UK	☑	☑	☑	Flickr Google+	☑
Germany	☑	☑	☑		☑
Malaysia	☑	☑	☑	TripAdvisor	☑
Mexico	☑	☑	☑	Flickr TripAdvisor	☑
Hong Kong	☑	☑	☑	Flickr	☑
Austria	☑	☑	☑	TripAdvisor	☑
Canada	☑	☑	☑	Flickr	☑
Australia	☑	☑	☑	Flickr Google+	☑

Figure 11.9 Use of popular social media channels by leading destinations

- *Facebook*: Started in 2004 and by the end of 2011 had 845 million monthly active users. Facebook estimates that 80 per cent of its users are outside of the USA and Canada. The company said that 425 million monthly active users used Facebook mobile products in December 2011.
- *Twitter*: Launched in 2006, Twitter is the one of the world's most popular micro-blogging platforms. There are now micro-blogging sites (called 'weibo') in China that have more users than Twitter.
- *YouTube*: YouTube was launched in 2005 and the company estimated in early 2012 that 800 million unique users visit every month. Approximately 70 per cent of YouTube's traffic is from outside of the USA.
- *Flickr:* Flickr is an online photo management and sharing application that was launched in 2004.

DMO activities on social networks

Social networks provide a great array of online venues for DMOs to distribute information and communicate with others. There are many activities in which DMOs can engage on the social networks, but some of the most important of these are identified below:

- *Building and maintaining communities of interest*: Social networks tend to build communities that share similar interests. For DMOs, the goal is to build communities that have an interest in their specific destinations.
- *Collecting user-generated content*: This is a very important function of social media sites for DMOs as people post their blogs, comments, videos and photographs of trips to destinations.
- *Displaying photography and videos*: Some of the social media channels are designed specifically for displaying visual materials, e.g. YouTube (for videos) and Flickr (for photographs).
- *Distributing topical news stories*: The social networks are a great place for DMOs to 'push out' news stories about their destinations. This is done through websites, but can be more effective when distributing to communities of people that have indicated an interest in the destination.
- *Emphasizing current events and campaigns*: The social networks are very timely and people are constantly checking them. Placing upcoming events and new promotional programmes here gives a freshness to the information.
- *Encouraging word-of-mouth recommendations*: This is another of the most important functions of social networks for DMOs. The positive recommendations of past visitors may influence others to go to the destinations.
- *Getting feedback*: The DMO can request feedback in several ways from people using social networks. Some DMOs conduct polls and place research surveys on social networks.

The use of social networks is increasing in importance among DMOs but it can be said that DMOs are still trying to find out how to use these channels most effectively. One of the related applications within social networks is the concept of traveller review sites, and this concept is the next to be discussed.

Traveller review sites

Traveller review sites are websites that include assessments by people that have visited destinations, hotels, attractions, restaurants or used other travel services and facilities. TripAdvisor.com is the most used among these websites. The main appeal of these websites is the perceived 'objectivity' of the reviews, for people who are considering going to the destination or using a particular tourism operation.

TripAdvisor.com has over 50 million unique visitors every month and has around sixty million reviews and opinions by travellers. VirtualTourist is another popular traveller review site and has an estimated 1.2 million members worldwide.

Other traveller reviews are found in a variety of different sites including the sites of traditional travel guidebook publishing companies. For example, Lonely Planet has the Thorn Tree travel forum which is an online discussion group for travellers. This forum is in several parts including the 'departure lounge' (discussions by geographic regions) and the 'lobby' (discussions by specific interests and topics). Frommer's operates a community on its website and this is broken down into different regions of the world. Rough Guides also operates a travel community, but on its Facebook site. Fodor's has a number of forums on its website called 'Fodor's Travel Talk Forums' and these are mainly organized by geographic region. Travel guidebooks are trusted for their objectivity and lack of commercial ties to destinations and tourism businesses; and this extends to their online forums and discussion groups.

Recent surveys of traveller review sites indicate that a majority of consumers find the reviews to be credible and useful. Using these sites also appears to be growing in popularity. However, you should be aware that there has been some criticism of these sites in recent times. The main lesson here for DMOs is that there must be a willingness to accept both positive and negative reviews by past tourists.

Some of the reviews that are included on these sites are very brief comments, while others are more extensive and can be classified as blogs. The next section of this chapter on ICT covers the broader topic of blogging and how blogging affects and is used by DMOs.

Blogging

The so-called 'blogosphere' of web logs written about tourism destinations and travel in general is another aspect of ICTs that has had a significant impact on destination marketing and management. Blogs appear in many different places on the Internet and have a variety of different types of authors. For example, in Chapter 6 you learned about the Jordan Tourism Board inviting some prominent travel bloggers to come to Jordan on a familiarization tour. This group of professional or semi-professional 'new age' travel writers represents just one type of blogger; many ordinary tourists write blogs about the places they have visited. Some DMOs put together blogs, and in certain ways these replace some of the traditional types of press or news releases.

Blogs have not received as much recent attention as social network sites, but blogging is continuously attracting more writers and readers of these online materials. According to NielsenWire (2012), there were 181 million blogs in the world at the end of 2011 and that was 36 million more than 5 years before in 2006. Schmallegger and Carson (2008) analysed how DMOs and tourism businesses were using blogs and found there were five main applications:

Contents of travel blogs (Vrana and Zafiropoulos, 2010)

Travel blogs can include comments, suggestions, advice, directions, maps, photos and videos, links to related web sites and to external information, links to other travellers, RSS, trackbacks, comments, taglines, archives, permanent links and blogrolls.

(Blogrolls are lists of website links that the blogger finds to be interesting)

- *Communication*: B2C (business-to-consumer) or corporate blogs are being increasingly used by DMOs. B2B (business-to-business) blogs are also prepared by DMOs to communicate with tourism sector stakeholders, travel trade companies, meeting and event planners, and other businesses.
- *Promotion*: DMOs often consider blogging to be a less expensive form of promotional communication than traditional advertising. However, blogs need to provide added value to potential tourists and cannot be 'too commercial'. Some DMOs have turned to sponsored bloggers (like the Jordan Tourism Bureau case) to meet this challenge.
- *Product distribution*: This means using blogs to create online bookings, but this suffers from the same challenges as promotions in blogs. It can make the DMO blogs look more commercial and less objective.
- *Management*: Blogs can be very useful in customer relationship management (CRM) and in monitoring the image and reputation of the destination.
- *Research*: Most of the blogging activity around the world is C2C (consumer to consumer). This massive store of text and graphics is considered a highly valuable source of research information by tourism academic scholars and tourism practitioners, including DMOs.

Schmallegger and Carson (2008) also identified four major advantages of blogs over other types of content including in comparison with website content: (1) relatively easy to update; (2) flexible in structure; (3) encouraging interaction between authors and readers; and (4) allowing people who would not otherwise have the opportunity to exchange information.

User-generated content (UGC)

One of the core concepts about blogging is the generation of user-generated content (UGC) on destinations and how DMOs can use UGC in a variety of different ways. For example, UGC can provide significant positive word-of-mouth (WoM) for a destination, as well as being a valuable repository of research information and feedback. Exploratory research by Mack *et al.* (2008) suggested that UGC was not as much believed as traditional WoM, but was more credible than commercial sources of information.

Consumers are already making significant use of UGC in gathering travel information and making trip decisions. A survey conducted in the USA in early 2012 found that 46.9 per cent of respondents reviewed UGC when planning their leisure travel trips;

and overall, 55.9 per cent used UGC or social media. This compared to 31.1 per cent using print or online DMO resources.

DMO blogging

Some DMOs write their own blogs and share this through their websites or social networks. VisitBlackpool in England is a good example here with its blog, http://blog.visitblackpool.com/ Another case study is the Scottsdale Convention and Visitors Bureau in the USA with its blog, http://blog.scottsdalecvb.com/. A third example is Tourisme Montréal's blog, The Montréal Buzz, at http://www.tourisme-montreal.org/Blog/.

The usual format for DMO blogs is to have staff members and other local experts prepare the written materials. Actually this is not really a completely new activity for DMOs but the online venue is a new place for distributing stories about the destination. The following is an example of a state-level DMO blog from Illinois in the USA.

Enjoy Illinois blog

Welcome! Enjoy Illinois is the official blog of the Illinois Office of Tourism.

On behalf of everyone at IOT, we want to thank you for stopping by. It's truly an honor to share insight about our great state with the rest of the world. We have some excellent contributors from around the state here and we're always looking for more.

If you're an Illinois travel enthusiast, want to share a travel experience, or have any questions at all about travel in Illinois let us know.

(Illinois Office of Tourism, 2012)

Travel and tourism blog sites

There are now hundreds of specialized travel and tourism blog sites on the Internet to which people contribute blogs on their travel experiences. Some of the most popular of these include Blog.Realtravel.com, Travelblog.org, TravelPod.com, IgoUgo.com and Travellerspoint.com. TravelPod.com was one of the earliest of these sites, introduced in 1997. It has around 64,000 new travel blogs per week mainly about members' experiences on their travel trips. There is now a TravelPod app that can be downloaded and members can write blogs on their mobile phones as they are travelling.

Micro-blogging has followed after blogging as more people are using their mobile phones and smartphones to communicate shorter pieces of information to other groups of people. These devices are the next ICT topic in this chapter.

Mobile phones and smartphones

They are called different names in different places, including cell phones, hand phones, mobile phones or mobiles, but there is little doubt about the huge impact these devices have had on society worldwide. These cellular phones and networks got started around 1978–1979 in the USA and Japan. Digital mobile phones were introduced in the early 1990s.

SMS

Tourism destinations have been using SMS (short messaging services) for some time now. One of the applications of SMS is to allow mobile phone users to request destination information. For example, the DMO in Goa, India introduced an SMS service where tourists call a number and then using special codes get information on specific attractions. A second example is a service offered by the DMO for the Canary Islands of Spain. Called a 'tourism guide to the Canary Islands on your mobile phone', tourists call a nine-digit number, select the language they prefer, dial the number on the sign identifying the location, and then receive a message about the location they are visiting.

Mobile electronic tourist guides (METGs)

Traditional paper-based guidebooks are a popular source of destination information for tourists. Guidebook series such as *Lonely Planet* and the *Rough Guides* are excellent sources of detailed information about destinations, and are often taken on trips by people. Now several destinations have introduced mobile electronic tourist guides (METGs) as apps for smartphones, including iPhones, Android and Blackberry. Guidebook publishers are also now providing apps of selected guidebooks.

Peres *et al.* (2011) say that METGs are still an emerging technology but they have promising potential due to several advantages for tourists and DMOs:

- Tourists are more able to better utilize their time in the destination by not having to physically go to get information (e.g. at VICs).
- Tourists can access information anywhere and at any time.
- Time-saving may mean that tourists spend more in the destination.
- DMOs can provide more information and a greater variety of information.
- Tourist loyalty to the destination may be increased.
- DMOs can monitor tourists' experiences.
- DMOs can more directly influence the information available to tourists.

Several DMOs have developed these apps for smartphones and many others plan to do so. Among the earliest adopters of this technology were the Hong Kong Tourism Board, Singapore Tourism Board, Tourism Australia and Instituto de Turismo de España (Spain Tourism). These are very handy tools to have on a mobile phone when travelling within these destinations, but also before going and when planning trips.

i Tour Seoul is a great example of an METG. It can be downloaded to iPhones, iPads and Android phones. On the main page of this Seoul app, there are twelve icons leading to local travel information (About Seoul; Seoul's Best; Attractions; Events; Dining; Shopping; Hotels; Transit; General Information; Tours and Itineraries; Medical Tourism; and Gangnam Tourism). Gangnam is one of Seoul's districts. In addition to these great contents, *i Tour Seoul* has a number of special features. By connecting to phones' Global Positioning System (GPS) software, the app shows users what attractions and other points of interest are near them (by popularity and by distance). The app has an augmented reality feature, a concept that is discussed below. It contains many maps and users can find their current locations on these maps. *i Tour Seoul* shows information on attractions by specific areas of the city and has a search function. Users can also store 'favourites' on this app. Overall the Seoul METG is a very powerful and outstanding example of the usefulness of these ICTs to tourists.

'Smart tourism' is the term now being used for examples like that in Seoul where ICTs are being used in assisting tourists in way-finding and improving their overall experiences and enjoyment in destinations. Seoul is not the only place to have introduced these 'smart' functions for mobile phones. The Singapore Tourism Board's *Your Singapore Guide* allows users to find out what is in close proximity by using GPS and a 'What's Near You' feature. The Discover HK app from the Hong Kong Tourism Board has an AR Mode (augmented reality) that is similar to the one for Seoul.

Augmented reality tourism

Augmented reality is an ICT application involving the use of smartphones. It is done by users pointing phone cameras at specific attractions, points of interest and other locations, and then computer software overlays images, icons or information on the images in their camera screens. The regional tourism DMO in Tuscany, Italy was one of the very first to introduce an AR-enhanced app in 2010 called *Tuscany+*. It allows users to point their smartphones at any scene in Tuscany and balloons pop up with information in four categories: sightseeing, accommodation, dining and entertainment.

As the following quote from Apollo Matrix (2009) indicates, there are many potential applications of augmented reality (AR) for tourism destinations and individual attractions:

Description of augmented reality tourism

With augmented reality tourism, travel guides come to life in real-time. Augmented reality content stored on a central server is available to the person who takes a photo of the historical site. Visitors can visualize in 3D historical places, beautiful landscapes or anything they desire to see in real-time locations. Augmented reality on mobile smartphones can also enhance any tourist's experience. Imagine walking through a museum and having the ability to access additional information or images associated with a priceless, historical work of art simply by viewing it through your smartphone. Augmented reality can further enrich any tourist's experience by enhancing his or her view of the world today with supplementary information and superimposed images of times past. Augmented reality tourism gives us the ability to view historic people, places and objects outside the boundaries of linear time.

As highlighted in this quote, AR can be used to enhance the interpretation at sightseeing spots or at specific attractions such as museums and art galleries. For example, in the camera screens of smartphones the original structure of buildings can be superimposed upon the ruins at which tourists are pointing. This use of ICTs can be very helpful in fulfilling at least some of the roles of interpretation that are discussed in Chapter 5.

Tablet devices

Tablet computers or simply tablets have a flat touch-screen and are highly portable and convenient. While the Apple iPad, considered to be a post-PC tablet, may be the best known of these, there are many other brands and models on the market as well. Because of their portability they have become very popular with travellers and so this has put pressure on DMOs to communicate with and provide applications for these devices.

With larger screens than smartphones, tablets are better for viewing documents and photos. Therefore, some DMOs have produced tablet-ready visitor guides and these are very appealing when viewed. For example, many of the major city DMOs in the USA and Canada now have iPad apps that are for downloading their visitor guides, including Anaheim, Austin, Los Angeles, Philadelphia, Vancouver and others.

Many of the METGs discussed above also have tablet versions and especially for iPads. However using these on tablets is not quite as convenient as using them on smartphones when a person is on foot and travelling within the destination.

Usage of mobile phones when travelling

Although there is not yet any comprehensive worldwide data on the use of mobile phones and smartphones for accessing travel information when travelling, this is undoubtedly on a steep upward trend. A survey conducted in the USA in January 2012 found that 89.2 per cent or respondents used their mobile devices to get travel information during their trips. Some 63.3 per cent used their mobile devices to get travel information before leaving on their trips. The most used functions on mobile devices were finding restaurant information, checking weather, looking at maps and using a GPS-related app for directions.

Mobile phones and smartphones will undoubtedly assume even greater importance for destinations and DMOs in the future, since they will outnumber personal computers. With this scenario, the emphasis in DMO communications and marketing will have to switch more towards mobile phones and smartphones. This trend is already evident with the proliferation of METGs and the development of apps for popular travel guides including *Lonely Planet* and the *Rough Guides* and for traveller review sites including TripAdvisor.com.

Other ICTs

There are many other ICTs available that are being applied in tourism destinations or have the potential to be used. Indeed, there are almost too many to write about, and the focus of this chapter has been on the main ICTs and their usage by DMOs and tourists. There are ICTs that are being applied within specific types of tourism businesses, such as in hotels and restaurants, but it was decided not to review these in detail in this book. However, there are a few additional ICTs that need to be discussed briefly, so you have a more complete picture of their usage within destinations in general.

Global positioning system (GPS)

GPS has multiple applications in tourism destinations. A standard feature in most cars for getting directions to places, GPS is also now a function available on smartphones.

As you read earlier, GPS technology on phones is being used by DMOs including those in Seoul and Singapore in their METG apps for way-finding and for letting users know what is in close proximity to their current locations. There are many other more generic mapping apps that allow people to find their ways around in destinations using mobile phones, as this also can be done with purpose-designed, hand-held GPS devices. A recent study in Sydney, Australia found that just 20 per cent of visitors were using a GPS or smartphone app for way-finding in the city, but this proportion should grow quite rapidly in the future as more people adopt these technologies rather than using paper-based maps and guidebooks.

One very interesting application of GPS for way-finding in tourism is in geocaching, a game that has been created using ICTs (Figure 11.10). Here is a description of geocaching from Groundspeak, Inc. (2012), the originators of the concept:

Geocaching

A real-world outdoor treasure hunting game. Players try to locate hidden containers, called geocaches, using GPS-enabled devices and then share their experiences online.

Tourism Radio® is another application that combines GPS with radio. This technology was developed in South Africa and it delivers audio travel guides to either cars or smartphones. At the time of writing, Tourism Radio® offered 150 free audio travel guides that could either be downloaded as apps to smartphones or listened to in cars using a Tourism Radio® GPS device.

Figure 11.10 Finding a geocache with a GPS device
Source: Shutterstock, Inc. (Tyler Olson).

Geo-tagging

Geo-tagging uses GPS technology to add specific geographic location data to a photo, video, blog or other type of digital file. This is entirely feasible now with smartphones that have built-in cameras and GPS functions. Geo-tagged photos are popular in photo-sharing websites like Flickr and Panoramio since they allow users to see exactly where photos were taken. Geo-tagging is not yet widely used by DMOs but it has considerable potential in interactive mapping and the placement of geo-coded photos on these maps.

Geo-tagging is also popular on some micro-blogging sites as it allows people to know where their friends are located. There has been some backlash against this type of service by some notable people, who do not want others to know where they are or where they have been.

Podcasts

Podcasts are short digital audio or video files that are made available on websites and that are downloaded through RSS feeds. Some DMOs are using podcasts to deliver timely short videos that are coordinated with upcoming events or festivals. One of the potential advantages of podcasting is that it can be done at a relatively low cost and within a short time period.

Smart cards

Smart cards have been available for several years for travel on public transportation systems in major cities around the world. However, their use is expanding to other parts of tourism including paying admission fees at attractions, restaurants and shopping. The traditional smart cards have embedded integrated circuits that are recognized by special reader devices hooked up to computers.

Now these smart cards can be downloaded into smartphones and the phone is used for scanning rather than a card. This technology is being used in a number of urban public transportation systems.

Smartphone boarding passes are another similar application where airline passengers have their phone screens scanned. This is a paperless boarding card system that is facilitated by barcode readers. It was started in 2009 by a number of European airlines.

Virtual visitor guides and brochures

Sometimes called interactive guides, these are online visitor guides that have the appearance of a real visitor guide, and people flip over the pages as they would with a real guide. Of course, these save paper and the photo quality is very good and sharp when viewed online. They also do not have to be delivered to the door of potential tourists or have to be printed out from PDF files. Users can quickly navigate to the guide sections in which they are most interested without having to flip many pages. Another advantage is that these are searchable and can contain embedded videos. Links to the DMO's website are hyperlinked into these guides as well.

As the title suggests, shorter visitor brochures can also be published online in this format. These brochures have the same advantages as virtual guides, but an added benefit is that they can be updated more frequently without wasting an existing stock of printed brochures.

It is very unlikely that these 'virtual' guides and brochures will ever completely replace their printed counterparts; however, in an increasingly environmentally-concerned and technology-savvy world, these types of digital publications will continue to make inroads into the shares held by printed publications.

Google Maps and Google Earth

There are a number of mapping tools available on the Internet that can be useful for DMOs, and two of the prime ones are Google Maps and Google Earth. The National Geographic Society based in the USA also has some great online maps, as well as an app for viewing maps on smartphones.

Several DMOs are using prominent mapping sources like these to provide directions to tourists. They are also trying to embed more sites within their destinations on the maps, and some of these with geo-coded photos.

E-book readers

E-book readers have become more popular among consumers preferring to download books rather than purchase print copies. The idea of the digital book is catching on faster than many expected. The introduction of the Kindle e-book reader by Amazon in 2007 started this trend. Kindle is now available as an app for smartphones, allowing people to read their favourite books on their phones. There are many other e-book readers now on the market apart from Kindle.

The screens on e-book readers are smaller than most tablets, but they are increasingly adding more functions than tablets have. Moreover, these e-book readers are much less expensive than the most popular tablets.

It is not yet clear how DMOs will use e-book readers in the future, but it appears that they may accommodate similar applications as do tablets. They may become another digital venue for longer documents such as guidebooks and visitor guides.

Wikis

Wikis are websites on which the contents are contributed by online communities of people. Theoretically, any user can add, modify or delete content on the wiki; but that basic concept has been modified by some wikis to give more control over the content. Wikipedia is probably the best known wiki. There are several wikis that exist for tourism, travel and hospitality, but DMOs do not seem to make much use of this ICT application at the present time.

Summary

For the past 25 years information and communication technologies (ICTs) have had a major impact on tourism in general. They have revolutionized how DMOs share destination information and communicate with people. It is very likely that they will be even more important for destination management in the future.

The major impacts have come through websites, social network sites and mobile telephony. The Internet has become the most important venue for destination marketing, as well as being the consumer's first-choice place to search for information on destinations. Websites perform a number of specific roles for DMOs and especially for destination marketing and promotions. They have become the main platform for DMO communications interconnecting through other ICTs to all potential audiences.

Websites perform important functions for tourists as well. The reasons and purposes for using DMO websites can be divided into four stages: dreaming/enthusing/informing; planning/selecting/booking; travelling/visiting/enjoying; and repeating/recommending/recollecting.

Effective DMO websites have a number of specific characteristics and the 'I AM OUTSTANDING' model expresses fourteen of these (international; address website users as individuals; monitored or constantly evaluated and improved; outstanding/award-winning; up-to-date; targeted; social media; telephone versions; attractive; networked; dynamic; integrated; niche markets; and great contents).

Most DMOs are now heavily engaged in using social network sites and especially the most popular ones including Facebook, Twitter, YouTube and Flickr. The major activities of DMOs in using social network sites include building and maintaining communities of interest; collecting user-generated content; displaying photography and videos; distributing topical news stories; emphasizing current events and campaigns; encouraging word-of-mouth recommendations; and getting feedback.

Blogging has become tremendously popular among consumers and travel is one of the most discussed themes for people to write about online. Most of the activity is consumer to consumer (C2C) communications about travel trip experiences. DMOs and tourism businesses are using blogs for five different purposes: communication, promotion, product distribution, management and research.

Mobile phones and smartphones are now being used extensively in travel and tourism with multiple applications. Mobile electronic tourist guides (METGs) are one of the major applications being used by DMOs where they distribute these guides to tourists as apps for smartphones. Augmented reality (AR) is enhancing the experiences of phone users within destinations.

There are many other ICTs being applied in various parts of the tourism sector. GPS, smart cards and podcasts are three ICT applications that are being used quite frequently now within destinations and by DMOs. Geo-tagging, e-book readers and wikis are three other ICTs that have good future potential for DMOs.

To take the fullest advantage of information and communication technologies (ICTs), DMOs need to do the following:

- Design and maintain effective websites including continual evaluation of these websites.
- Make effective use of e-mail for communications with potential tourists, stakeholders and others.
- Establish and maintain pages on the most popular social network sites.
- Develop applications for the most popular smartphones and tablet devices.
- Continuously track comments about the destination and tourism stakeholder operations on traveller review sites. Provide feedback and comments when required.
- Continuously track travel blog sites. Provide feedback and comments when required.
- Use blogging to provide ongoing information and stories on the destination.
- Review the feasibility of introducing smart cards within the destination.

- Consider making use of ICTs such as virtual guidebooks and brochures, e-book readers and podcasts.
- Keep updated on the introduction of new ICTs in tourism and related fields.

Review questions

1 Why are information communication technologies so important in today's tourism business?
2 What are the major roles of DMO websites?
3 What are the main marketing functions of DMO websites?
4 How should DMO website effectiveness be evaluated?
5 What are the characteristics of effective DMO websites?
6 Social network sites offer great opportunities for DMOs. What are some of the most important activities in which DMOs can engage on social network sites?
7 What is user-generated content (UGC) and how can these materials be used by DMOs and by tourists?
8 How can DMOs take advantage of blogging?
9 How do traveller review sites like TripAdvisor.com influence the travel decisions of people?
10 What are mobile electronic tourist guides (METGs) and how can these be used by travellers before, during and after their trips?
11 Digital publishing is becoming much more prevalent and popular around the world. What are some of the applications of digital publishing in tourism?
12 What have been some of the applications of the global positioning system (GPS) in tourism?

References

Apollo Matrix. 2009. Augmented Reality Tourism, the Apps and Potential. http://apollomatrix.com/content/augmented-reality-tourism-apps-and-potential

Belle Tourism International Consulting. 2010. Shanghai International Visitor Survey.

——2012. WebEVAL DMO® System. http://belletourism.com

Boyd, D.M., and Ellison, N.B. 2007. Social network sites: Definition, history, and scholarship. *Journal of Computer-Mediated Communication*, 13(1). http://jcmc.indiana.edu/vol13/issue1/boyd.ellison.html

Buhalis, D., and O'Connor, P. 2005. Information communication technology revolutionizing tourism. *Tourism Recreation Research*, 30(3), 7–16.

Carson, D. 2008. The 'blogosphere' as a market research tool for tourism destinations: A case study of Australia's Northern Territory. *Journal of Vacation Marketing*, 14(2), 111–119.

Carter, R. 2010. The evolving impact of ICT on destination management and marketing. ITSA 2010 Conference, Shah Alam, Malaysia.

Davidson, R. 2011. Web 2.0 as a marketing tool for conference centres. *International Journal of Event and Festival Management*, 2(2), 117–138.

Destination Analysts, Inc. 2012. The State of the American Traveler.

Di Pietro, L., Di Virgilio, F., and Pantano, E. 2012. Social network for the choice of destination: Attitude and behavioral intention. *Journal of Hospitality and Tourism Technology*, 3(1), 60–76.

Feng, R., Morrison, A.M., and Ismail, J.A. 2003. East versus West: A comparison of online destination marketing in China and the USA. *Journal of Vacation Marketing*, 10(1), 43–56.

Fritz, F., Susperregui, A., and Linaza, M.T. 2005. Enhancing Cultural Tourism Experiences with Augmented Reality Technologies. The 6th International Symposium on Virtual Reality, Archaeology and Cultural Heritage, San Sebastian, Spain.

Furutani, T. 2005. A study on tourist navigation with the use of application service provider of location positioning system: A case in Kamakura. *Proceedings of the Eastern Asia Society for Transportation Studies*, vol. 5, 1233–1248.

Gretzel, U., Yoo, K.H., and Purifoy, M. 2007. Online Travel Review Study: Role and Impact of Online Travel Reviews. Texas A&M University.

Groundspeak, Inc. 2012. Geocaching. http://www.geocaching.com/

Guarente, M. 2010. The Importance of Social Media. http://www.insights.org.uk/ articleitem.aspx?title=The+Importance+of+Social+Media

Han, J., and Mills, J.E. 2006. Zero acquaintance benchmarking at travel destination websites: What is the first impression that national tourism organizations try to make? *International Journal of Tourism Research*, 8(6), 405–430.

Illinois Office of Tourism. 2012. Enjoy Illinois Blog. http://www.enjoyillinoisblog.com/

International Telecommunication Union. 2012. The World in 2011: ITU Facts and Figures.

Jordan, B. 2011. Seoul's Smart Tourism: How Technology Can Improve the Visitor Experience. Corbin Ball Associates. http://www.corbinball.com/articles_technology/ index.cfm?fuseaction=cor_av&artID=8591

Kasavana, M.L., Nusair, K., and Teodosic, K. 2010. Online social networking: Redefining the human web. *Journal of Hospitality and Tourism Technology*, 1(1), 68–82.

Katsoni, V. 2011. The role of ICTs in regional tourist development. *Regional Science Inquiry Journal*, 3(2), 95–111.

Kim, H., and Fesenmaier, D.R. 2008. Persuasive design of destination web sites: An analysis of first impression. *Journal of Travel Research*, 47(3), 3–13.

Lee, B.C., and Wicks, B. 2010. Tourism technology training for destination marketing organisations (DMOs): Need-based content development. *Journal of Hospitality, Leisure, Sport and Tourism Education*, 9(1), 39–52.

Mack, R.W., Blose, J.E., and Pan, B. 2008. Believe it or not: Credibility of blogs in tourism. *Journal of Vacation Marketing*, 14(2), 133–144.

Mendes-Filho, L., and Tan, F.B. 2009. User-generated Content Consumer Empowerment in the Travel Industry: A Uses and Gratifications Dual-process Conceptualization. Pacific Asia Conference on Information Systems (PACIS).

Miniwatts Marketing Group. 2012. Internet World Stats. http://www.internetworldstats. com/stats.htm

Nielsen Media. 2011. The Social Media Report: State of the Media: Q3 2011.

NielsenWire. 2012. Buzz in the Blogosphere: Millions More Bloggers and Blog Readers.

Osti, L. 2009. Creating UGC areas of official destination websites: Is there a recipe for success? An insight through netnographic research. Munich Personal RePEc Archive.

Park, Y.A., and Gretzel, U. 2007. Success factors for destination marketing web sites. *Journal of Travel Research*, 46(1), 46–63.

Peres, R., Correia, A., and Moital, M. 2011. The indicators of intention to adopt mobile electronic tourist guides. *Journal of Hospitality and Tourism Technology*, 2(2), 120–138.

Promotur Turismo de Canarias. 2012. Tourism Guide to the Canary Islands on your Mobile Phone. http://www.turismodecanarias.com/canary-islands-spain/web/tourist-guide-mobile-phone-ciceron/index.html

Proxima Mobile. 2010. Tourisme et mobile sur la côte basque: macotebasque.com. http://www.proximamobile.fr/article/tourisme-et-mobile-sur-la-cote-basque-macotebasquecom

Rothschild, P.C. 2011. Social media use in sports and entertainment venues. *International Journal of Event and Festival Management*, 2(2), 139–150.

Schmallegger, D., and Carson, D. 2008. Blogs in tourism: Changing approaches to information exchange. *Journal of Vacation Marketing*, 14(2), 99–110.

Sigala, M. 2009. Web 2.0, social marketing strategies and distribution channels for city destinations: Enhancing the participatory role of travelers and exploiting their collective intelligence. In Gasco-Hernandez, M., and Torres-Coronas, T. (eds), Information Communication Technologies and City Marketing: Digital Opportunities for Cities around the World. Hershey, PA: Idea Group Publishing, 220–244.

Singapore Tourism Board. 2012. http://www.yoursingapore.com/content/traveller/en/experience.html

Tourism Australia. 2012. Australia's Fanbase on Facebook Exceeds One Million Milestone. http://www.tourism.australia.com/en-au/news/media-releases_6112.aspx

Tourism Radio. Intelligent travel guides that speak to you! http://www.hummba.com

Travel + Leisure. 2011. Best Travel Websites and Apps. http://www.travelandleisure.com/articles/best-travel-websites-and-apps

Travelution. 2010. Travel Review Sites Overwhelmingly Trusted, Survey Finds. Travel Weekly Group Ltd.

Tyntec. 2011. White Paper. SMS and the Travel and Tourism Industry.

United Nations Conference on Trade and Development. 2002. ICT and Tourism: A Natural Partnership. http://www.unctad.org/templates/Page.asp?intItemID=3609&lang=1

University of Technology Sydney. 2011. Visitor Wayfinding in Sydney.

UNWTO. 2007. A Practical Guide to Tourism Destination Management. Madrid: UNWTO.

UNWTO and European Travel Commission. 2008. Handbook on E-Marketing for Tourism Destinations. Madrid, Spain.

USAID. 2006. Information Communication Technologies and Tourism. Washington, DC: USAID.

Visit Tuscany. 2010. Tuscany+: The First Augmented Reality Tourism Application. http://www.turismo.intoscana.it/allthingstuscany/aroundtuscany/tuscany-the-first-augmented-reality-tourism-application/

VisitBlackpool. 2012. VisitBlackpool Blog. http://blog.visitblackpool.com/

Vrana, V., and Zafiropoulos, K. 2010. Locating central travelers' groups in travel blogs' social networks. *Journal of Enterprise Information Management*, 23(5), 595–609.

Webby Awards. 2012. http://www.webbyawards.com/

Wenger, A. 2008. Analysis of travel bloggers' characteristics and their communication about Austria as a tourism destination. *Journal of Vacation Marketing*, 14(2), 169–176.

Wyman, O. 2009. Ontario Way-finding Research Study. Queen's Printer of Ontario.

PART III

Destination markets

Consumer behaviour, segmentation and market trends

Learning objectives

1   Describe people's motivations in going to tourism destinations for pleasure or leisure trips.

2   Identify and explain the factors that affect tourists' selection of destinations.

3   Explain the process by which destination images are formed and how destination images impact upon destination selection.

4   Review the process of travel purchase behaviour and pinpoint the different stages that tourists tend to go through.

5   Elaborate on market segmentation in tourism and the main ways of classifying tourists into distinct groups.

6   Review the recent market trends in tourism.

Introduction

Chapter 12 begins this book's review of tourist behaviours and market segments. This chapter gives you an overview of how people tend to make decisions about tourism destinations, including their motives, selection criteria, perceptions of destinations and purchasing stages. It is really fascinating to know how complex these processes can be.

This chapter begins by briefly reviewing motivational theories that have been proposed for tourism, leisure and recreation. Although there is no consensus among competing theories, there seems to be some agreement that there are two sides to motivation in pleasure/leisure travel: 'push' (internal to tourists) and 'pull' (destination product and marketing) factors.

There are a variety of factors that influence people when selecting tourism destinations for their trips. These are discussed and a model of destination selection is presented and reviewed. The formulation of people's destination images is also discussed and another model is described of image formation.

Market segmentation is discussed and seven criteria for dividing up markets are explained. Trip purpose and geography have traditionally been used by DMOs to segment markets; but more sophisticated approaches are now being applied in destinations such as Canada and Australia.

The chapter ends by reviewing some of the predominant market trends that are impacting tourism destinations. These trends result from changes in demographics, countries of origin, trip purposes, trip planning and travel arrangements, psychographics and lifestyles, special interests and uses of technology. The implications of these trends for destinations and DMOs are identified.

Motivations for travel

Before starting this discussion, you should know that the focus of this chapter is on what is usually called pleasure or leisure travel, and not on business travel. The motivations for pleasure/leisure and business travel are quite different. Business travel is motivated by organizational needs and priorities, while pleasure/leisure travel is based on personal needs and wants. There is less freedom and flexibility in selecting the destinations for business travel than for pleasure/leisure travel. The motivations for business travel are reviewed later in Chapter 15.

Academic scholars have put forward several different theories and approaches to explain why people decide to travel for vacations and holidays. John Crompton, Graham Dann, Seppo Iso-Ahola and Philip Pearce are four of the most famous of these scholars but there are several others who have attempted to explain tourist motivations. Some scholars have adapted general models of human motivation to tourism including the theories advanced by Abraham Maslow, Frederick Herzberg and others. There is no consensus among scholars on what motivates pleasure and leisure travel, so what follows is a review of the approaches that appear to be the most accepted.

Mill and Morrison (2012) suggest that an analysis of the travel literature indicates that travel motivations can fit into Maslow's *Hierarchy of Needs* model that consists of:

- *Survival*: Hunger, thirst, rest, activity.
- *Safety*: Security, freedom from fear and anxiety.
- *Belonging and love*: Affection, giving and receiving love.

- *Esteem*: Self-esteem and esteem from others.
- *Self-actualization*: Personal self-fulfilment.

These are arranged in a hierarchy and lower-level needs (survival, safety) require more immediate attention and satisfaction before people turn to the satisfaction of higher-level needs. While the application of Maslow's theory to tourist motivations has gained acceptance, some scholars have judged it to be inadequate in dealing with the special situation of tourism destinations.

Dann's (1977) 'push–pull' theory has been one of the most accepted among the more specific explanations of tourist motivation. The 'push' factors are within individuals themselves as people act to take care of certain internal drives such as the need for escape (Figure 12.1). The 'pull' factors are the products and marketing by destinations that attract people to visit. DMOs and tourism sector stakeholders have the most control over the 'pull' factors, although they cannot totally orchestrate how people form images of their destinations, as you learned in Chapter 9.

What comes first, 'push' or 'pull'? Generally, it has been accepted that the 'push' factors start the process of motivating a person to travel and the 'pull' factors are the ones that make them select a specific tourism destination or business within the destination. Klenosky (2002) said that the 'push' factors are related to tourists' needs and wants and include the need for escape, rest and relaxation, adventure, prestige, health and fitness, and social interaction. Lee *et al.* (2002) suggested that push factors determine whether to go, while pull factors determine where to go (Figure 12.2). The diagram shows that vacation destination choices are impacted by internal motivational driving forces ('push') and destination attributes ('pull'). The two-way arrow between the 'push' and 'pull' factors suggests that there is an interaction between the two factors as people are making their travel decisions. This model also implies that the 'push' and 'pull' factors vary according to the origins of tourists; and this may be due to economic, socio-cultural and geographic (e.g. climate) differences.

Figure 12.1 Escaping is one of the strongest 'push' factors
Source: Shutterstock, Inc.

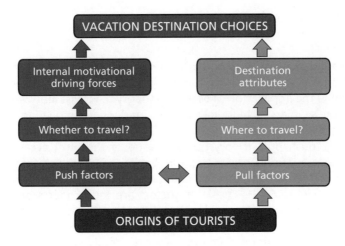

Figure 12.2 'Push' and 'pull' tourist motivation factors
Source: Adapted from Lee *et al.*, 2002.

Another model with seemingly good acceptance is that of Iso-Ahola, who proposed a social psychological model of tourism motivation (1980; 1982; 1983; 1989). He suggested there were two main motives in leisure (including tourism) and these were 'seeking intrinsic rewards' and 'escaping the everyday environment'. These motives can exist simultaneously, and both have personal (psychological) and interpersonal (social) elements (Snepenger *et al.*, 2006). Iso-Ahola proposed four dimensions: (1) personal seeking, (2) personal escape, (3) interpersonal seeking and (4) interpersonal escape.

Crompton (1979), based upon unstructured in-depth interviews with respondents in Texas and Massachusetts, found two categories of motives for travel: socio-psychological and cultural. The seven socio-psychological motives were as follows:

● *Escape from a perceived mundane environment*: Getting away from the place of residence and from home and job environments.
● *Exploration and evaluation of self*: Having the opportunity to re-evaluate and discover more about oneself, or acting out one's self-images.
● *Relaxation*: Taking more time to enjoy activities of interest within the tourism destination.
● *Prestige*: Increasing one's social status through travelling to certain tourism destinations or businesses.
● *Regression*: Doing things that are inconceivable in a person's usual lifestyle.
● *Enhancement of kinship relationships*: Enhancing and enriching family relationships through travelling to and experiencing tourism destinations together.
● *Facilitation of social interaction*: Meeting new people in different locations.

There were two cultural motives: novelty and education. According to Dann's model, the socio-psychological motives could be classified as 'push' factors and the 'pull factors' were the cultural motives.

Another tourist motivation theory is the 'travel career' approach proposed by Philip Pearce. This approach proposes that the motivation to travel changes with the amount of travel experience that individual tourists have accumulated. Pearce and Lee (2005) found that experiencing different cultures and being close to nature were more important motivating factors for experienced travellers. Less-experienced travellers placed a higher priority on stimulation, personal development, relationship (security), self-actualization, nostalgia, romance and recognition. These scholars also found that there was a core set of four motivation factors for all tourists; escape, relaxation, relationship enhancement and self-development.

Beard and Ragheb (1983) developed the *Leisure Motivation Scale* containing four types of motives that were derived from Maslow's Hierarchy of Needs theory. These were as follows:

- *Intellectual*: Engaging in mental activities while travelling including learning, exploring, discovering, thinking and imagining.
- *Social*: Seeking friendship and social esteem from others through travelling.
- *Complete mastery*: Showing mastery, usually of physical activities, by meeting certain challenges or competition.
- *Stimulus avoidance*: Escaping and getting away from over-stimulating life situations.

Other academic scholars have produced typologies of tourist motivations by placing the motives from various research studies and theories into categories. Swarbrooke and Horner (1999) suggested there were six categories of motivators in tourism:

- *Cultural*: Sightseeing; experiencing new cultures.
- *Physical*: Relaxation; sun; exercise and health; sex.
- *Emotional*: Nostalgia; romance; adventure; escapism; fantasy; spiritual fulfilment.
- *Tourist*: Status; exclusivity; fashionability; obtaining a good deal; ostentatious spending opportunities.
- *Personal development*: Increased knowledge; learning a new skill.
- *Personal*: Visiting friends and relatives; making new friends; need to satisfy others; search for economy if on limited income.

Mill and Morrison (2012) developed a set of motives and referenced actions/desires from the tourism research literature, and placed these within Maslow's Hierarchy of Needs dimensions. These are shown in Figure 12.3.

This is not a book solely dedicated to consumer behaviour in tourism; however, this discussion of tourist motivations should have given you a taste of the complexity of this topic. Moreover, you should realize that there are many reasons why people travel on vacations or holidays to tourism destinations. DMOs need to conduct research to determine the motives for pleasure/leisure travel to their specific destinations. Above all, those who are doing destination marketing and promotion must realize that people's motivations vary greatly, even if they are from the same geographic origins or having similar socio-demographic characteristics.

Tourism destination selection

People are faced with a wide array of potential destinations for their travel trips. They can travel locally, regionally, nationally (domestically) and internationally. How do they select their destinations? Once again, the process of destination choice or selection has been a popular topic among tourism academic researchers. They have offered an

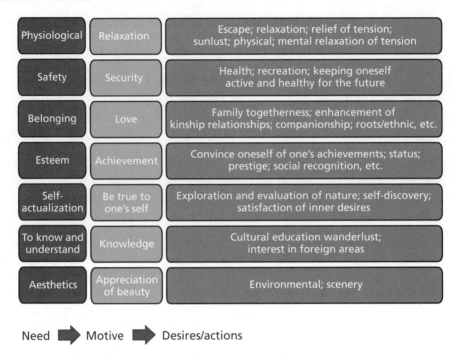

Physiological	Relaxation	Escape; relaxation; relief of tension; sunlust; physical; mental relaxation of tension
Safety	Security	Health; recreation; keeping oneself active and healthy for the future
Belonging	Love	Family togetherness; enhancement of kinship relationships; companionship; roots/ethnic, etc.
Esteem	Achievement	Convince oneself of one's achievements; status; prestige; social recognition, etc.
Self-actualization	Be true to one's self	Exploration and evaluation of nature; self-discovery; satisfaction of inner desires
To know and understand	Knowledge	Cultural education wanderlust; interest in foreign areas
Aesthetics	Appreciation of beauty	Environmental; scenery

Need ➡ Motive ➡ Desires/actions

Figure 12.3 Tourist needs, motives and desires/actions
Source: Adapted from Mill and Morrison, 2012.

assortment of choice models that have proven useful in understanding why people pick certain destinations.

From these models, the factors that have been found to affect destination selection include the following:

- *Socio-psychological (personal)*: According to Um and Crompton (1990), these internal inputs include the personal characteristics, motives, values and attitudes of the tourist. As you saw earlier, these characteristics are linked closely with people's motives for pleasure/leisure travel.
- *Situational factors*: The constraints that individuals or families have in terms of available time and financial resources to travel.
- *Interpersonal (social)*: The influence of family members, other relatives, friends, business associates, opinion leaders and others.
- *Awareness levels*: Tourists have to be aware of destinations in order to consider them for pleasure/leisure travel trips. People have 'awareness sets' and 'evoked sets' of destinations (Um and Crompton, 1990). The 'awareness' set includes all the places that a person has thought or dreamed about going (Figure 12.4). The 'evoked set' is a smaller group of destinations from the 'awareness set' that are feasible for a specific trip based on situational and other factors.
- *Destination images*: These are the perceptions that people have of specific destinations. These images are discussed in more detail in the next section of this chapter.
- *Destination products*: The destination mixes offered by alternative destinations may be influential and especially the specific attractions, events, experiences and activities that they offer tourists.

Figure 12.4 Venice is in many people's 'awareness sets' as a destination they want to visit
Source: Shutterstock, Inc.

- *Marketing and promotional communications*: The messages and images transmitted by DMOs and tourism sector stakeholders through a variety of channels.
- *Information search*: The process of searching for information on 'evoked set' destinations and the information gathered may influence decisions. For example, people may develop more favourable or less favourable perceptions of destinations in reading travel blogs and traveller review sites.
- *Past experience in visiting*: The past history of visits to particular destinations. It is generally accepted that previous visitors to a destination have a higher probability of visiting than those who have not yet visited.
- *Geographic origins and cultures*: Tourist statistics clearly indicate that travel destinations vary by geographic origin and also by people's cultural backgrounds.

Some of these factors are external to the people making the destination selection, including the interpersonal factors, destination products, and marketing and promotional communications. The others are internal factors including the particular circumstances of people, their socio-psychological characteristics and past travel behaviours, and cognitive processes (e.g. awareness levels and destination images).

Moscardo *et al.* (1996) proposed a model integrating the theories relating to these internal and external factors. This *Activities Model of Destination Choice* recognized the contributions of four fields of tourism research (Gilbert and Cooper, 1991):

- Tourist motivation theories and research
- Destination image research
- Destination choice model research
- Market segmentation research.

The Activities Model of Destination Choice suggested tourists' desired activities, experiences and benefits linked motivation with destination choice; this is shown in Figure 12.5. The five components of the model (A to E) are briefly described below:

- *A. Marketing and external factors*: All of the information about destinations' activities and experiences from marketing and interpersonal sources.
- *B. Tourist socio-psychological factors*: Motives, socio-demographic characteristics and situational factors of tourists.
- *C. Images of destinations*: Tourists' perceptions of the activities and experiences as destination attributes of specific places.
- *D. Destination choice*: The choice of destination based on the best match between tourists' preferred activities/experiences and the perceived activities/experiences at specific places.
- *E. Destinations*: The activities and experiences offered by destinations. This is the destination product, as defined earlier in Chapter 5.

The influence of destination images

The topic of people's images of destinations has been introduced already in Chapters 3, 4 and 9, and destination image has been a favourite research subject for tourism academic scholars since at least the early 1970s. It is difficult indeed to summarize all of the research that has been done on this topic. Pike (2002) reviewed 142 papers that

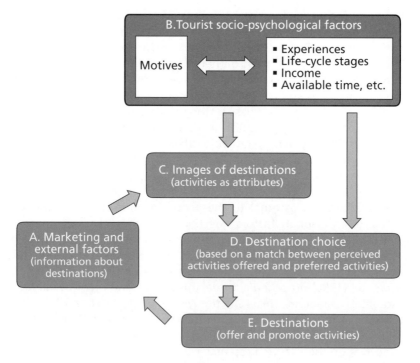

Figure 12.5 Activities model of destination choice
Source: Adapted from Moscardo *et al.*, 1996.

had been published on destination image from 1973 to 2002; and there have been many others that have appeared in the 10-plus years since then.

Chapters 4 reviewed the use of research to measure and assess destination images. You learned there about attributes and holistic images as defined by Echtner and Ritchie (1993). Chapter 4 also showed that destination images are formed in different ways and influenced by a variety of sources of information on places, including previous visits. Eight destination image formation agents suggested by Gartner (1993) were discussed and shown in Figure 4.7. These were divided into three groups of information; organic, induced and autonomous.

Beerli and Martin (2004) tested a proposed model of the formation of destination images and this is shown in Figure 12.6. Most of the terms in this model have already been introduced in this chapter, but 'affective' and 'cognitive' images require more explanation. 'Affective' images are people's feelings about destinations; as such they are subjective. 'Cognitive' images are based on people's knowledge of a destination and an evaluation of the destination's attributes. Figure 4.7 provided the definitions of induced organic and autonomous images.

The model in Figure 12.6 suggests that perceived destination images are formed through the combined effects of information sources and personal factors. The information sources are organized according to Gartner's (1993) classification and divided into primary (previous visits to the destination) and secondary. The personal factors include motivations (as discussed earlier), vacation experience (as per Pearce's 'travel career' concept) and socio-demographic characteristics of tourists. The 'overall' image of a destination is formed from two components: the 'cognitive' and 'affective' images.

Several previous tourism research studies have shown that destination images directly influence the choice of tourism destinations. For example, Chen and Tsai (2007) conducted a visitor survey in southern Taiwan and found that destination image directly impacted the selection of the destination. In addition, they concluded that destination image affected the 'after-decision-making' behaviours of tourists.

This discussion once again highlights how influential destination images are in the selection of tourism destinations. Therefore, as suggested in Chapter 4, it is very important that DMOs conduct research to determine the existing tourist images of

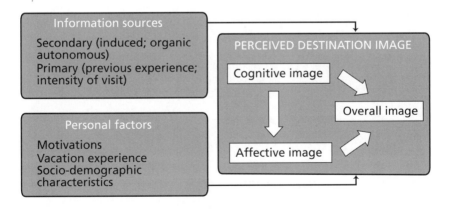

Figure 12.6 Model of the formation of destination images
Source: Adapted from Beerli and Martin, 2004.

their destinations. In addition, although it may require a long-term commitment of resources, DMOs must position the images of their destinations in an optimum way, through both marketing communications and attention to service quality and other aspects of the destination product.

Travel purchase behaviour process

People go through several different stages in planning travel to the destination, experiencing the destination and after returning home from the destination. You may remember the twelve stages of the customer cycle in Chapter 11, and that is just one of the many models suggested for travel purchasing behaviour. A more 'classic' model is shown in Figure 12.7 and consists of seven sequential stages (Morrison, 2010).

A quick note on the model is that the seventh step is traditionally named as 'divestment' but that label was judged inappropriate for tourism destination experiences. The title of 'remembering and sharing' was substituted.

Need recognition

The travel purchasing process begins when people become aware of needs that they feel going on holiday or vacation will satisfy. Usually this awareness is triggered by one or more of a variety of stimuli from three main sources (personal, interpersonal and commercial). The needs are recognized when the stimulus is strong enough.

Commercial: DMOs and their marketing and promotional communications represent the commercial sources; these DMO messages are intended to make potential tourists recognize their needs to travel. It is better for these communications, therefore, to focus on customer needs and desires rather than being purely about the features of destinations.

Interpersonal: For many years, it has been recognized that word-of-mouth is more powerful in influencing tourists than commercial information. It has been verified in study after study that interpersonal information and recommendations are heavily relied upon in tourism, because of their objectivity and credibility. Interpersonal sources include family members and friends, business associates and opinion leaders.

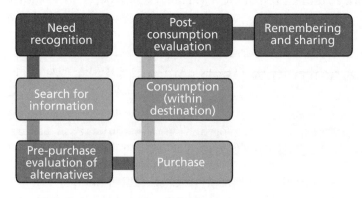

Figure 12.7 Model of travel purchase behaviour process

Chapter 11 mentioned a new 'breed' of interpersonal sources within social network sites, and this might be called 'online word-of-mouth'. This may not be as powerful and believable information and advice as real word-of-mouth, but it seems to be significantly more credible than commercial information.

Personal: Personal (internal) drives to deal with need deficiencies are the third source that can trigger need recognition. You have heard these described as the 'push' factors earlier in this chapter.

People may recognize need deficiencies because of the combined impact of several sources and stimuli. In fact, it may require a combination of two or three of these factors to get people started on their search for information.

Search for information

The second stage in the travel purchase process is an active search for information. Once people become aware of needs, they tend to begin looking for information on tourism destinations, products and services that they feel will satisfy those needs. When people recognize needs, these become wants; if wants exist, people usually start an information search. There are three main sources of information available to people:

- *Destination-dominated information*: These information sources are the marketing and promotions by DMOs and other tourism sector stakeholders. Websites and social network services are now the major sources for finding information about tourism destinations, but there are also the other elements of DMO integrated marketing communications campaigns (advertising, sales, public relations and publicity, and sales promotion and merchandising) described in Chapter 10.
- *Interpersonal and third-party information*: The interpersonal sources include family, friends, business associates and opinion leaders; they are the word-of-mouth sources. Independent, third-party and objective assessments can be gathered from travel guidebooks such as *Lonely Planet*, the *Rough Guides*, *Frommer's*, *Fodor's* and others. Government and independent rating systems like the famous Michelin scheme also are available for helping with decision-making. The traveller review sites like TripAdvisor.com and the travel blogs of other people are also included in this category of information.
- *Internal sources*: This is the information about places stored in people's own memories. It includes past travel experiences in going to places and their memories of destination promotions. Importantly, these also encompass people's perceptions or images of specific destinations.

As mentioned earlier, Um and Crompton (1990) suggested that all people have an 'awareness set' of places that they would like to visit. People may also become aware of other desirable destinations during information searches. Not all the available destinations will be considered. Lack of awareness, perception of places not being affordable, previous bad experiences and negative word-of-mouth information will eliminate some destinations. The final list is the 'evoked set'; the alternative destinations selected for further consideration.

Pre-purchase evaluation of alternatives

The next stage is assessing the short-listed 'evoked set' destinations using objective and subjective criteria developed by the potential traveller. Some people are very careful and organized in their trip planning and write things down on paper or in their computers; others just do the work in their heads. Objective criteria include air fares, destination products, activities and experiences, hotel and other prices, destination locations, etc. Subjective criteria are intangible items such as people's perceived images of destinations.

Purchase

People have now determined which destination best meets their criteria. They develop a definite intention to book their trips to the destination, but the decision-making process may still be incomplete. Whether or not they buy can still be influenced by other factors. They may want to talk over their choices with family members, friends and other interpersonal sources. Social network sites may be checked to confirm selections. Information or opinions might be found that leads to questioning the destination choice. This may cause a postponement of the purchase or a complete re-evaluation of the decision. Additionally, situational factors may change, including employment and financial circumstances, leading to a delay in the purchase decision.

Perceived risk is another factor that may delay purchases or cause them to be postponed. Pleasure/leisure travel to tourism destinations represents the purchase of an 'experience good'. Destinations are booked 'sight unseen' if the person has not visited them before. These decisions, therefore, involve an above-average level of risks. The risks are financial (will my money be well spent at the destination?), psychological (will going to the destination improve my self-image?) or social (will my friends and family think more of me after I have been to the destination?). If the risks are considered too great or the rewards perceived to be too low, people do something to correct the situation. They may postpone purchases, search for more information or choose a better-known or more familiar destination. Risk can also be reduced by continually returning to the same destinations. DMOs must design their communications campaigns and information services to reduce these perceived risks.

You should also realize that picking a destination is not the only decision that needs to be made. In fact, there are numerous other sub-decisions that have to be taken before the final purchase is made. These include when to travel, how to pay, how and where to make bookings, how long to stay, how much to spend, how to get there, what routes to take and what to do at the destination. If the decision-maker is not a solo traveller, these decisions can be complicated and involve several different people (e.g. in a family, the parents and children).

Cognitive dissonance is a psychological state that some people feel after making a booking. They may be unsettled or unsure as to whether they have made the best decision. The intensity of dissonance increases with the importance and value of the purchase. For example, dissonance may be higher for a long-haul trip than travel to a more familiar domestic destination. Here, it is the job of the tourism sector stakeholders and the DMO to do all that they can to reassure people that they have made good decisions.

Consumption

This stage is the experiences that people have within the destination. For the DMO, the priority is to ensure that the destination meets or exceeds tourists' expectations and that they leave very satisfied. This is difficult for the DMO to accomplish since they do not control the products and services consumed by tourists; these are delivered primarily by tourism sector stakeholders. As suggested in Chapter 5, the DMO should have a quality assurance programme in place to provide a better guarantee of satisfaction for tourists.

As suggested in the model proposed by Moscardo *et al.* (1996) (Figure 12.5), tourists expect that the activities, experiences and benefits they will receive in the destinations of their choice will match their preferences. If this expectation is not realized there will be dissatisfaction with the destination. Therefore, the DMO must pay particular attention to this issue and ensure that the activities, experiences and benefits are actually available and are delivered at a level that meets or exceeds tourists' expectations.

Post-consumption evaluation

When tourists are on their way back from the destination or have returned home, they will evaluate their destination experiences against their expectations. Expectations are based on the information they received from destination-dominated sources (DMO and tourism sector stakeholder advertising and promotions) and interpersonal and third-party sources (family, friends, business associates, opinion leaders, travel blogs, traveller review sites, etc.). If tourists' expectations are met or exceeded, they are most likely to be satisfied with the destination. If not, they are more than likely to be dissatisfied. The golden rule for the DMO and its stakeholders is never to promise more than can be delivered.

With the arrival of social network sites, it has become much more convenient for people to write about their good and bad experiences with travelling. DMOs need to be very vigilant in tracking such commentaries online and responding when they deem it to be appropriate.

Figure 12.8 People like to share their travel experiences online
Source: Shutterstock, Inc.

When tourists are satisfied with destinations, the dividends are significant. Satisfied tourists are more likely to be repeat visitors. They have experienced the destinations and know that their expectations were met and the experiences were delivered as anticipated. By telling friends, relatives and associates about positive destination experiences they will influence others to visit through word-of-mouth recommendations.

However, dissatisfied tourists are less likely to be repeat visitors and they will tell others, thereby discouraging other people from visiting the destination. Information from interpersonal sources carries more weight for people than destination-dominated sources. Therefore, DMOs must be especially concerned about having dissatisfied tourists.

Remembering and sharing

Based just upon the huge number of travel blogs and vacation/holiday photographs posted on social media networks, it is clear that many people like to remember and share their travel and destination experiences (Figure 12.8). DMOs and tourism sector stakeholders should do all they can to encourage this tendency to reminisce and tell others about travel experiences. Providing online communities on their websites and spaces on social network sites for comments are two ways to accomplish this.

People derive great enjoyment from this last stage of the travel purchase behaviour process, but last in this case is definitely not the least important. For DMOs, these are a great source of credible testimonials that can be shown to people considering travelling to their destinations.

Tourism market segmentation

Chapter 3 introduced the market segmentation concept as part of marketing strategy and as the foundation for selecting the approaches to destination positioning and branding. Most DMOs carefully select their priority target markets in order to make more effective use of their resources and to generate the best return on investment (ROI).

As mentioned in Chapter 3, the most widely accepted practice in destination marketing is to begin by dividing markets by geographic origin and by trip purpose.

Trip purpose

The four main trip-purpose divisions are pleasure/leisure travel; visiting friends and relatives (VFR); business travel; and other personal travel (Figure 12.9). It is reasonable to assume that the motives for these trips are different. Earlier in this chapter, you learned about the many potential motives for pleasure/leisure travel.

Research has shown that VFR travel is actually more diverse than might initially be thought. People with this trip purpose share some of the same motives as pleasure/leisure travellers, but interpersonal motives are stronger. A study of Australian domestic VFR travellers found six different VFR markets, based on holiday activity participation (Morrison et al., 1995). The VFR travel market is discussed in more detail in Chapters 13 (domestic travel) and 14 (international travel).

Business travel is often the largest market for certain destinations and especially for major cities. This segment is very diverse and includes normal business travel as well as travel related to business events. Hankinson (2005) defined the latter as travel associated with attendance at meetings, conferences, exhibitions and incentives events.

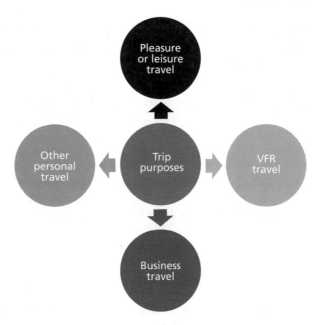

Figure 12.9 Trip purpose segments of tourism markets

Other personal travel can be a very significant market for destinations. People travel for a variety of other purposes beyond pleasure/leisure, VFR and business. These are mostly for personal reasons including medical, educational, job search and legal advice travel.

Geography

Geographic markets are defined by place of residence or source of origin, and this is one of the most common ways to define the markets for tourism destinations. Often the following terminology is used to classify geographic markets into their broadest categories:

- *Domestic travel*: Travel by the residents of a country within their own country.
- *Inbound travel*: Travel into a country by the residents of foreign nations.
- *Outbound travel*: Travel by the residents of a country to places outside of their own country.

Most DMOs very clearly specify their main geographic markets and Tourism Ireland provides a good example of this (Tourism Ireland Marketing Plan 2012):

Tourism Ireland's geographic target markets

- Great Britain (England, Wales and Scotland)
- North America (USA and Canada)
- Mainland Europe (France, Germany, etc.)
- Australia and New Zealand
- Emerging markets (Middle East, China, Thailand, etc.)

The three main components of geographic markets are discussed in detail in Chapters 13 and 14.

Socio-demographics

Socio-demographics are characteristics such as age, education, occupation, income and household composition. Traditionally, these tourist characteristics were much used by DMOs in their market segmentation analyses, and they are still used to profile tourists. The age-cohort classification that you will hear about later in this chapter (Baby Boomers–Generation X–Generation Y) is a good example. If you read through travel trade journals and newspapers, you will also undoubtedly come across the term 'luxury travel' and this usually involves wealthy people and those with very high incomes.

Household composition segmentation is also very popular and much discussed in travel trade publications and among DMOs as well. Within these groups, the family travel market is the most popular target. The family market is an especially important factor in domestic tourism as discussed in Chapter 13.

Several past tourism research studies have shown that the combination of age, income level and education has a strong influence on travel behaviours and spending. However, in recent times several DMOs have moved away from using socio-demographic characteristics for identifying and describing their target markets. The Canadian Tourism Commission (CTC) is one of the DMOs that has moved to a more sophisticated market segmentation approach, based more on personality than socio-demographic characteristics:

EQ, The Explorer Quotient™ from the Canadian Tourism Commission

EQ is one of the most innovative market segmentation tools to come from the science of psychographics – an evolution of the traditional field of demographics. Instead of defining people based on age, income, gender, family status or education level – all of which is valuable information – psychographics looks deeper at people's personal beliefs, social values and view of the world. It's a major leap forward, because these factors are what drive real people to seek out certain types of experiences.

Psychographics

Market researcher Stanley Plog popularized the concept of using psychographics to divide up tourist markets. He called these 'personality profiles', which involves dividing up people by their psychological orientations, lifestyles or AIOs (activities–interests–opinions). The example quoted above from the Canadian Tourism Commission is a good case study in applying psychographic segmentation to tourist markets. The CTC system has identified nine groups of travellers:

- Authentic experiencer
- Cultural explorer

- Cultural history buff
- Personal history explorer
- Free spirit
- Gentle explorer
- No hassle traveller
- Rejuvenator
- Virtual traveller.

Another example of a more personality-based approach to defining target markets is that used by Tourism Australia (TA). TA has defined the main target market for international inbound travel as the 'experience seekers' and a description of this segment is provided below:

Tourism Australia: who are experience seekers?

Who are they? These people:

- Are experienced international travellers.
- Seek out and enjoy authentic personal experiences they can talk about.
- Involve themselves in holiday activities, are sociable and enjoy engaging with the locals.
- Are active in their pursuits and come away having learnt something.
- Are somewhat adventurous and enjoy a variety of experiences on any single trip.
- Place high importance on value and hence critically balance benefits with costs.
- Place high value on contrasting experiences (i.e. different from their day-to-day lives).

What do we know about them? These people typically:

- Come from households that have higher than average household income.
- Are tertiary educated.
- Are open-minded and have an interest in world affairs.
- Are selective about their media consumption.
- Are opinion leaders within their peer and social groups.
- Are not characterised by nationality, preferred holiday style/mode or age.

How large is the segment? This segment constitutes around 30 to 50 per cent of all potential long haul outbound travellers from key source markets.

Behaviour

This approach involves dividing tourists into groups based upon their past purchasing and travel behaviours or future travel purchase intentions. One of the most important behavioural distinctions for tourism destinations is repeat visitors versus those visiting for the first time. Several tourism academic scholars have examined the differences between these two groups. For example, Rittichainuwat *et al.* (2008) compared first-time and repeat visitors to Thailand and found that there were significant differences in the travel motivations of the two groups. First-time visitors to Thailand were most interested in 'seeing people from different cultures'. Repeat visitors to the country were more motivated by 'Thai food' and the 'short distance'.

Related to the repeat visitation concept are the theories of variety-seeking and novelty-seeking. These theories are somewhat similar and suggest that people behave in such a way to get the right balance between familiarity and variety/novelty. Some tourists prefer a high level of familiarity so they may return to the same destination several times. Others are more likely to 'switch' their destinations as they desire more variety and novelty for their tourism experiences.

Product-related

Destinations may have certain products that will focus DMOs' attention on specific segments with the highest interest levels in using these products. The inventory of such products is very long, so only an indicative list is provided below:

- Alpine/downhill ski slopes (skiers and snowboarders)
- Casinos (people who like to gamble)
- Equestrian facilities (horse owners/riders)
- Golf courses (golfers)
- Reefs and shipwrecks (scuba divers and snorkellers)
- Religious structures, sites and legends (believers)
- Health, wellness and spa facilities (medical tourists/spa-goers)
- Marinas for yachts and other pleasure crafts (yacht/boat owners)
- Mountains and peaks (climbers and hill-walkers)
- Wine areas and wineries (wine enthusiasts).

The increasing popularity of pursuing special interests and hobbies when travelling has made product-related segmentation a more viable alternative for certain DMOs.

Channel of distribution (business-to-business or B2B)

This type of segmentation is used in business travel and in marketing to travel trade intermediaries. Business travel market segmentation is discussed in Chapter 15. For travel trade intermediaries, tour operators can be classified geographically or by speciality or destinations served. Travel agencies may also be targeted by geographic origin markets for the destination. Another common approach is to focus on tour operators and travel agencies that have already sent tourists to destinations. Specialized agencies, such as cruise-only agencies and those with a focus on special interests, may be identified and targeted by DMOs.

Market trends

Tourist markets are dynamic and undergoing constant change. Their motivations and desires for specific destination experiences vary over time. Therefore, you should know about the major market trends and this part of the chapter identifies and describes these trends.

Statistics on tourist arrivals are not enough when a DMO is engaged in highly competitive marketplaces. DMOs must dig deeper to develop a more detailed understanding of markets. DMOs need to delve deeper 'behind the statistics' to know how and why tourists are changing. Winning marketing strategies frequently are a result of using good market research results in an appropriate and creative way. It is especially important for DMOs to know the latest trends in markets according to the following seven factors:

- Demographics
- Countries of origin
- Trip purposes
- Trip planning and travel arrangements
- Psychographics and lifestyles
- Special interests
- Technology uses.

Unfortunately, some DMOs are not engaging in this level of market analysis. Perhaps this is because DMOs do not feel the need to invest in market research on markets that still represent a small proportion of total tourism demand. This may be especially so for the 'emerging' markets in international tourism. However, as international tourist arrivals continue to grow, these research data will become more valuable, since competition among destinations will intensify further.

Demographics

All eyes in tourism are currently fixed on three generational cohorts (people born between certain defined years); the *Baby Boomers*, *Generation X* and *Generation Y*. These three age-group cohorts span about 55 years from 1946 to 2000, and they represent the bulk of the decision-making tourism consumers in the world.

Aging but engaging, Baby Boomers: The populations in most Western and some Asian-Pacific countries like Australia, Japan, New Zealand and South Korea are aging. The largest group of older consumers is known as the Baby Boomers and these people were born between 1946 and 1964. According to Hudson (2010), the European 55-plus market will increase by 60 per cent in the next 15 years; and in the USA there will be 76 million Baby Boomers in 2020 and 115 million over 50. Worldwide, Japan has the highest proportion of its population over the age of 65, at 20 per cent.

Older age groups are more willing to travel than previous generations and are interested in active and adventurous travel experiences. ElderTreks ('Small Group Exotic Adventures for Travelers 50 Plus') is a good example of a tourism company that has done a great job in attracting the adventurous Baby Boomers. The company, based in Canada near Toronto, was established in 1987 and offers active holiday tours in over 100 country destinations around the world.

An extra-special market, GenX: Generation X (GenXers) are people in the age group that followed the Baby Boomers. They were born from 1965 to around 1979 and are also sometimes called the Baby Busters. GenXers are known to be very independent thinkers and more adventurous and tougher to please than the Baby Boomers when travelling. GenXers make extensive use of websites and social network services to find travel information and make bookings. They especially like using social network sites including Facebook, Twitter and various blog sites and discussion forums. Being in the age range from 30 to 45, GenXers often have children and travel as families.

A good example of marketing to Generation X is provided in the 'LOVE campaign' being used by the Virginia Tourism Corporation (VTC) in the USA. VTC has very successfully used the slogan of 'Virginia is for Lovers' since 1970; aiming mainly at the Baby Boomers. The 'LOVE campaign' is focused on GenXers, as VTC has found from its research that they are more adventurous and spend more money in Virginia than the Baby Boomers. The DMO's market research showed that those travelling with children in Virginia spent 50 per cent more than those visiting without children.

Y travel? Generating travel from the Internet generation: Generation Y are those people born from around 1980 to 2000; they are also sometimes called the Echo Boomers, the Net Generation or the Millennials. This generation really likes international travel. For example, a survey by STA Travel in Australia found that 70 per cent of Generation Y Australians had already spent significant time overseas and 65 per cent intended to travel outside of Australia in the future.

Generation Y are especially well known for their high propensity to take 'gap years'. This means that they take a year off for travelling and most often this involves international travel. Gap years are usually taken after graduating from university and before commencing full-time employment. They are also taken during work careers; for example, when transitioning between jobs or employers.

This is an important market for many DMOs, because these younger people travel extensively within destinations as their trip lengths tend to be longer than those of Baby Boomers and GenXers. The Queensland Tourism Industry Council (QTIC) in Australia has recognized the importance of this generational cohort and set up a comprehensive project to emphasize the importance of this market segment:

Queensland Tourism Industry Council's QTIC-Y project

QTIC-Y is a project founded by the Queensland Tourism Industry Council. It is a Generation Y tourism network linking tourism students, employees, entrepreneurs and stakeholders. The network will encompass all sectors of the tourism industry, including tour operators, accommodation, travel, events and more. QTIC-Y will endeavour to strive for positive changes in the industry while working on issues affecting or of importance to Generation Y.

> The network has three main objectives:
>
> - Raising awareness of and articulation of Generation Y priorities to wider industry, government and media
> - Networking within the Y community and the wider industry for job referrals, peer mentoring and training
> - Offering training, information sessions and business development support for members.

Countries of origin

DMOs interested in attracting international tourists are constantly tracking the trends in the major countries of opportunity. According to UNWTO, in 2010 the five countries with the greatest expenditures on international tourism were Germany, the USA, China, the UK and France (UNWTO, 2012). However, other countries, including Brazil and Malaysia, are moving up the world rankings very rapidly, so DMOs should not overlook the 'emerging markets'. The BRICs are a good example here:

Building with BRICs: taking advantage of the travel boom: The acronym of BRIC refers to Brazil, Russia, India and China. They are the world's four fastest-growing country economies. Goldman Sachs, the investment company, claims to have originated the BRIC concept in 2001.

The four BRIC countries are expected to have above-average growth in outbound tourism in the next 10–20 years, so they require special attention from DMOs that decide to target them. According to Goldman Sachs, outbound travel from the BRICs will grow at twice the average rate, and the market expansion will be especially high for China and India. The company attributes this expected growth to huge increases in the middle classes in the BRIC countries.

Trip purposes

While trip purposes have tended to be enduring over many decades, external forces and especially tough economic conditions and shifting lifestyles have been reshaping them. The combinations of multiple trip purposes in one trip have been a noticeable trend.

Multi-purpose tourism: blended travel on the rise: Most destination marketers neatly divide the tourist market into pleasure/leisure, VFR, business travel/business events and personal travel segments. However, this apportionment of the market is not totally accurate and the distinctions between the four segments are becoming blurred. Increasingly, people are pursuing multiple trip purposes and are especially combining business and pleasure/leisure on trips. Time poverty is a factor influencing this trend.

Some have started to refer to these trips with multiple purposes as 'blended travel'. A survey conducted by Meredith Corporation in the USA in 2010 found that 77 per cent of business travellers took a family member or significant other along with them on their last business trip. Some 47 per cent did this most of the time (Mohn, 2010).

Two articles from the USA and New Zealand discuss this trend of adding vacations and family travel to business trips. 'Add a vacation to a business trip' was a special advertising section in *Business Week* magazine in 2007. 'Add family to the trip' indicated that many workers in New Zealand are reluctant to take long breaks from work, so combining business with pleasure was a good alternative for them (South, 2007):

Add family to the trip (New Zealand Herald)

While business trips traditionally mean solo jaunts of all work and little play, there's a growing trend towards taking the family along – and it can make good financial sense. If one adult fare and the accommodation is sorted, it can be relatively inexpensive to add the family to the trip. If you're a frequent flyer, air points trim the cost even further.

Research has shown that long-haul destinations experience higher levels of multi-purpose travel trips. This is particularly important for destinations considering inbound business tourism from Europe, North America, Australia, New Zealand and other long-haul origin countries. For the highly desirable travel destinations in people's 'awareness sets', those taking business trips may seriously consider bringing family members or friends along with them.

'Breakationing' due to time poverty: short breaks gain in popularity: With the pressures of modern society and work, many people have the money to travel but they do not have enough free time to take the long vacations that previous generations did (time poverty). These people can be called 'cash-rich, but time-poor'. The recently difficult economic times in many developed countries have accentuated this phenomenon, which has resulted in more frequent and shorter-duration trips being taken by these busy people.

The types of trips made by these travellers are called 'short breaks' or 'breakations' (mixture of breaks and vacations). For example, Visit Wales' website provides a good example of short-break and weekend trip marketing in the UK, including many 'Short Break Itineraries' that can be searched online. 'Breakations with Virgin Blue' is a case from the airline industry in Australia and the Pacific.

This is not a particularly positive trend for long-haul destinations, but benefits destinations and countries within a specific country or region. Therefore, it is good news for domestic travel and for international markets that are close to countries of origin.

Trip planning and arrangements

Hu and Morrison (2002) used the terms 'tripography' and 'tripographics' to describe the characteristics of the travel trips to destinations that people arrange. There have been some definite trends in both trip planning and the resulting 'tripographics' in recent years. One of these trends has been the increased popularity of independent travel:

Going it alone: the increasing popularity of independent travel: During the past 20 years there has been a significant increase in the popularity of independent travel. Sometimes this is referred to as 'free independent travel' or FIT for short. Actually, there are two somewhat different meanings to the term independent travel. The first is where a person travels alone without any companions; the second is where the person travels with others but is not part of an organized group tour with a fixed itinerary.

Let's start with the first definition of independent travel, i.e. people travelling alone without travel companions. Solo independent travellers tend to be younger and some are what are commonly referred to as 'backpackers' (Figure 12.10). These may be 'gap year' travellers from Generation Y, as was discussed earlier. However, older singles may also be travelling alone and can even be from among the Baby Boomers.

It is important to know that independent travellers do not use tour companies, and they may also not work with traditional travel agencies. Instead, they rely heavily on information from websites and social network sites, and independent travel guidebooks such as *Lonely Planet*, the *Rough Guides*, *Frommer's*, etc. To communicate with independent travellers, the key information channels that must be used are the Internet and guidebooks; independent travellers will not be as effectively reached through the travel trade.

Psychographics and lifestyles

People have been changing the ways they live and this has definitely spilled over to tourism destinations. These changes have, for example, spurred the increased popularity of spas and health/wellness tourism and environmentally-sensitive travel and tourism.

Figure 12.10 Surfers are one of the segments of independent travellers
Source: Shutterstock, Inc.

Getting and staying healthier: eating well and getting fitter when travelling: Consumers are increasingly concerned about health and wellness and this affects both their everyday lives and also how they travel. While travelling, some want to maintain their fitness levels or just stay active; and to ensure they keep with their dietary regimens. Others desire to use travel to improve their well-being or lifestyle habits.

This trend has had numerous impacts on tourism and destinations, including the increasing popularity of spas, medical and fitness resorts; more active vacation and holiday products including soft- and hard-adventure; health-oriented menus including vegetarian meal options; and greater preference levels for 'green' travel destinations such as New Zealand, Costa Rica and Australia.

Decompressing in style: the spectacular growth of hotel and day spas: The stress in consumers' daily lives is creating a need for pampering and spas are a way to escape pressures and get re-energized. Moreover, people of all genders are seeking different ways of looking and feeling younger.

Spas have been popular at least since the Roman times, but today's spas have much greater variety and sophistication. The International Spa Association (IPSA) estimates that the number of spas in the USA has grown by almost five times, from 4,140 in 1999 to 19,900 in 2010.

Today's spas can be divided into two main groups; beauty, healthcare and retreat spas; and natural hot springs spas. There is also a distinction between 'day spas' (people do not stay overnight at the property) and resort/hotel spas (people stay overnight).

Blumenthal (2008) supplies the following top ten reasons for going to a spa, but there are undoubtedly others:

- Stress management and relaxation
- Detoxification
- Increased self-esteem and confidence
- Improved circulation and blood pressure
- Anti-aging and healthy skin
- Psychological benefits
- Pain management
- Improved sleep patterns
- Improved breathing
- Improved flexibility, range of motion and athletic performance.

Greening with meaning: the green traveller market is getting larger: Consumers are showing increasing concern for the environment and this is extending into the travel trips that they take. As a result, the demand for nature-based and ecotourism destinations and packages is growing.

People who place a special emphasis on eco-friendly destinations and practices are sometimes called 'green travellers'. The *Green Traveler Study 2010–2011* conducted by CMI Green Community Marketing, Inc. (2011) in the USA, found that green travellers have the following characteristics:

- Forty per cent look for a third party certification that a destination is 'environmentally friendly' (e.g. Green Globe).
- Peer influence has the greatest impact on travel by eco-conscious consumers, not advertising.
- They feel that Costa Rica is truly a destination with a green identity.

Destinations such as Costa Rica, Belize, Australia and New Zealand, to name just a few, have had outstanding success with ecotourism and other types of nature-based tourism.

Getting gayer in travel: the importance of GLBT tourists: The gay, lesbian, bisexual and transgender (GLBT) market is now a mainstream segment of tourism. Many major tourist destinations consider GLBTs to be an important market with great potential. For example, according to Roy Morgan Research of Sydney, Australia, 'the gay and lesbian market is recognized throughout the tourism industry as an important niche segment, representing differences in holiday behavior, attitudes and yield opportunities when compared with the Australian population average'.

Some destinations are very popular with GLBT tourists and it is not surprising that they also do a great job of marketing to this market segment. They include San Francisco, New York and Montreal in North America; Amsterdam in Europe; and Sydney in Australia. The San Francisco GLBT website page has the welcoming heading of 'The gate is always open for you' (referencing the famous Golden Gate); while Amsterdam has a 'Gay and lesbian stay and play' page.

Special interests

Another predominant trend has been 'niche marketing' or appealing to tourists that have special interests when they travel:

Finding their niche: the expansion of special-interest travel (SIT) markets: Special-interest (SIT) or niche travel has been one of the hottest trends in tourism in recent times. The main reason behind this trend has been that consumers' interests today have become much more diverse than before. Some of the SIT segments that have emerged include the following:

- Adventure travel
- Cruise travel
- Casino gaming
- Culinary/gastronomic tourism
- Cultural tourism
- Dark tourism
- Ecotourism and nature-based tourism
- Health/wellness tourism
- Heritage/historic tourism
- Industrial tourism
- Religious tourism
- Voluntourism
- Wine tourism.

There are many other SIT activities and segments and two excellent sources of information on these are SpecialtyTravel.com and InfoHub.com. SpecialtyTravel.com (*Specialty Travel Index*) has information on more than 300 travel interests/activities worldwide. The *InfoHub Specialty Travel Guide* claims to be the largest Internet portal on speciality travel with more than 20,000 speciality trips in 150 countries included.

Technology uses

Chapter 11 provided an in-depth discussion of information communication technologies (ICTs) and how DMOs are using these channels and tools. People are increasingly making use of various technologies in selecting and booking destinations, as well as during and after their visits to destinations.

Looking and booking: the Internet has become the most important venue: There were 2.27 billion Internet users in the world in December 2011 (Miniwatts Marketing Group). Asia is the biggest regional market with 1.02 billion users. However, Internet penetration is highest in North America, Oceania/Australia and Europe.

Information sources of international visitors to China

Based upon surveys conducted by Belle Tourism International Consulting (BTI) with international visitors to China, websites and the Internet are the most important information source for planning trips to China:

- Websites and the Internet: #1 rank
- Guidebooks: #2 rank
- Friends and relatives: #3 rank
- Travel agencies: #4 rank
- Tour operators: #5 rank
- Blogs of other people: #6 rank
- Magazine articles: #7 rank
- Newspaper articles: #8 rank
- Marketing materials from tourism bureau: #9 rank
- Advertising by tourism organizations: #10 rank.

Therefore, in terms of reaching and communicating with potential tourists, the Internet is now the most important channel for DMOs to use. Internet marketing is part of the application of ICTs and has several elements that include websites, e-mail and social network sites.

Because tourists are increasingly using the Internet and smartphones to get travel and tourism information and to make bookings, every DMO needs to develop an integrated ICT strategy. For DMOs, this means having effective websites in multiple languages; initiating multi-lingual e-mail marketing communication programmes; making extensive use of social network sites, blogging and discussion groups; providing applications (apps) and other information services through smartphones; and implementing other ICT elements.

Meet you online: social networking is connecting the world: There is no doubt that social network sites on the Internet have drawn in millions of people around the world. This has had a huge impact on the volume and types of information available about tourism destinations. Additionally, it has significantly affected how DMOs are marketing to domestic and international tourists.

Through blogs and micro-blogs, consumers themselves have become travel writers and critics. For many people, blogging is not only a way to communicate with others; but it has also become a pastime or hobby. For DMOs, blogs are a good source of information about tourists' satisfaction and experiences in their destinations.

Social media or social network site marketing is now a vital part of destination marketing and almost all international DMOs are heavily engaged in this information and promotion channel.

Many more pages could have been written about consumer behaviour, segmentation and market trends. In fact, entire books have been written on each of these topics. However, space was limited in this book and the intention was to give you a broad overview on the topics. Many other theories and models could have been introduced and discussed; but the preferred route was to give you a straightforward and practical introduction to tourism consumer behaviour and not to lose you in the intricacies of complex models. A major message that it is hoped you took onboard is that all tourism consumers are different. To treat people as if they are all alike is unlikely to be a winning strategy for a destination!

Summary

Why do people travel to tourism destinations for pleasure or leisure reasons? This has been a topic of academic debate for many decades and several competing theories have been proffered. Among these, Dann's 'push–pull' theory appears to have gained the greatest acceptance. The 'push' factors are internal drives that vary from person to person; the 'pull' factors are destinations' products and marketing communications.

There is a set of factors that influence tourists' choice of destinations. These include socio-psychological (personal), situational factors, interpersonal (social), awareness levels, destination images, destination products, marketing and promotional communications, information search, past visitation, and geographic origins and cultures.

One of the powerful factors affecting the selection of destinations is the images that people have of the places. This has been the focus of many research studies over 40-plus years and many image measurement models have been suggested by academic models. People form images of destinations based upon multiple sources of information. They are also influenced by personal factors.

People tend to go through several distinct stages in planning travel, experiencing the destination and after returning home. One travel purchase behaviour process model has tourists passing through seven sequential steps: need recognition, search for information, pre-purchase evaluation of alternatives, purchase, consumption (within destination), post-consumption evaluation, and remembering and sharing. For DMOs, it is worth emphasizing that their job does not finish after the purchase or booking has been made. They also need to play an active role in the last three of the seven steps.

Tourism market segmentation is important for destinations in more sharply focusing their attention on specific groups of travellers. Today, there is really no concept of a 'mass market' and indeed tourism has become more of a 'one-to-one' phenomenon. There are seven main variables that can be used to segment tourism markets; trip purpose, geography, socio-demographics, psychographics, behaviour, product-related and channel of distribution. These can be applied separately or in combinations.

DMOs need to constantly stay on top of market trends as customers and their behaviours are changing more quickly than before. It is especially important to keep a focus on market trends caused by changes in demographics, countries of origin, trip purposes, trip planning and travel arrangements, psychographics and lifestyles, special-interests, and technology uses.

With respect to consumer behaviour, segmentation and trends, it is recommended that DMOs take the following actions:

- Use research to better understand the reasons why tourists visit their destinations (note: it is often hard to find out people's underlying motives).
- Find out which sources of information tourists used in planning trips to the destination.
- Conduct destination image research among past visitors and non-visitors.
- Develop marketing/product strategies for consumers according to all stages in the tourism purchase process.
- Analyse the online reviews and comments about their destinations; respond to reviews/comments when appropriate.
- Develop special marketing and incentive programmes for past visitors in order to encourage repeat visits.
- Segment markets scientifically based upon data that has been generated from visitor profile studies and other studies.
- Constantly track market trends and consider ways to capitalize on these trends in the future.
- Regularly share recent market trends and segmentation approaches with tourism sector stakeholders.

Review questions

1 How does the 'push' and 'pull' theory originally developed by Graham Dann explain why people travel?
2 What are the main factors that influence tourists in selecting destinations? In your opinion, which of these factors are the most important and why?
3 How do people's images or perceptions of tourism destinations affect their decisions on where to travel?
4 What are the stages that people tend to go through when purchasing, consuming and recalling trips to tourism destinations?
5 How can tourist markets be divided into groups that share common characteristics? What are the segmentation criteria that can be applied and which of these do you consider to be the best for a DMO to use and why?
6 How have recent market trends affected tourism? Which of these market trends do you believe will have the greatest impact on tourism in the future and what are your reasons?

References

Baloglu, S., and McCleary, K.W. 1999. A model of destination image formation. *Annals of Tourism Research*, 26(4), 868–897.

Beard, J.G., and Ragheb, M.G. 1983. Measuring leisure motivation. *Journal of Leisure Research*, 15(3), 219–228.

Beerli, A., and Martin, J.D. 2004. Factors influencing destination image. *Annals of Tourism Research*, 31(3), 657–681.

Belle Tourism International Consulting. 2010. Shanghai International Visitor Survey.

Benckendorff, P., Moscardo, G., and Pendergast, D. (eds). 2010. Tourism and Generation Y. Wallingford: CABI.

Bieger, T., and Laesser, C. 2004. Information sources for travel decisions: Toward a source process model. *Journal of Travel Research*, 42(4), 357–371.

Bigné, J.E., Sánchez, I., and Andreu, L. 2009. The role of variety seeking in short and long run revisit intentions in holiday destinations. *International Journal of Culture, Tourism and Hospitality Research*, 3(2), 103–115.

Blumenthal, B. 2008. Top 10 Reasons to Go to the Spa. http://shine.yahoo.com/healthy-living/top-10-reasons-to-go-to-the-spa-245803.html

Bronner, F., and de Hoog, R. 2011. A new perspective on tourist information search: discussion in couples as the context. *International Journal of Culture, Tourism and Hospitality Research*, 5(2), 128–143.

Business Week. 2007. Add a vacation to a business trip. http://www.businessweek.com/adsections/2007/pdf/09172007_Destinations.pdf

Canadian Tourism Commission. 2009. Discover your Best Customer and Speak to Them Like Never Before.

——2012. Traveller Types. http://caen.canada.travel/traveller-types

Cha, S., McCleary, K.W., and Uysal, M. 1995. Travel motivations of Japanese overseas travelers: A factor-cluster segmentation approach. *Journal of Travel Research*, 34(2), 33–39.

Chen, C.-F., and Tsai, D.C. 2007. How do destination image and evaluative factors affect behavioral intentions? *Tourism Management*, 28(4), 1115–1122.

Cohen, E. 1974. Who is a tourist? A conceptual clarification. *The Sociological Review*, 22(4), 527–555.

Community Marketing, Inc. 2011. Green Traveler Study 2010–11. http://www.cmigreen.com/

Crompton, J.L. 1979. Motivations for pleasure vacation. *Annals of Tourism Research*, 6(4), 408–424.

——1992. Structure of vacation destination choice sets. *Annals of Tourism Research*, 19(3), 420–434.

Crompton, J.L., and Ankomah, P.K. 1993. Choice set propositions in destination decisions. *Annals of Tourism Research*, 20(3), 461–476.

Dann, G. 1977. Anomie, ego-enhancement and tourism. *Annals of Tourism Research*, 4(4), 184–194.

——1981. Tourist motivation: An appraisal. *Annals of Tourism Research*, 8(2), 187–219.

Dann, G.M.S. 1996. Tourists' images of a destination: An alternative analysis. *Journal of Travel and Tourism Marketing*, 5(1/2), 41–55.

Dunne, G., Flanagan, S., and Buckley, J. 2011. Towards a decision making model for city break travel. *International Journal of Culture, Tourism and Hospitality Research*, 5(2), 158–172.

Echtner, C.M., and Ritchie, J.R.B. 1993. The measurement of destination image: An empirical assessment. *Journal of Travel Research*, 31(Spring), 3–13.

ElderTreks. 2012. Small Group Exotic Adventures for Travelers 50 Plus. http://www.eldertreks.com/

Gartner, W.C. 1993. Image formation process. In Uysal, M., and Fesenmaier, D. (eds). Communication and Channel Systems in Tourism Marketing. New York: Haworth Press, 191–215.

Gilbert, D.C., and Cooper, C.P. 1991. An examination of the consumer behaviour process related to tourism. *Progress in Tourism, Recreation and Hospitality Management*, 3, 78–106.

Goldman Sachs. 2010. Is this the BRICs' Decade? What's Next for the World's Key Emerging Markets? http://www.goldmansachs.com/our-thinking/brics/brics-decade.html

Hankinson, G. 2005. Destination brand images: a business tourism perspective. *Journal of Services Marketing*, 19(1), 24–32.

Herzberg, F. 1964. The motivation-hygiene concept and problems of manpower. *Personnel Administration*, 27(1), 3–7.

Hu, B., and Morrison, A.M. 2002. Tripography: Can destination use patterns enhance understanding of the VFR market? *Journal of Vacation Marketing*, 8(3), 201–220.

Hudson, S. 2010. Wooing zoomers: Marketing to the mature traveler. *Marketing Intelligence and Planning*, 28(4), 444–461.

I amsterdam. 2009. Gay and Lesbian Stay and Play. http://www.iamsterdam.com/en/visiting/spotlight/gay-lesbian-stayandplay

InfoHub, Inc. 2012. Info Hub. http://www.infohub.com/

International Spa Association. 2012. Industry Stats. http://www.experienceispa.com/media/facts-stats

Iso-Ahola, S.E. 1980. The Social Psychology of Leisure and Recreation. Dubuque, IA: Brown.

——1982. Toward a social psychological theory of tourism motivation: A rejoinder. *Annals of Tourism Research*, 9(2), 256–262.

——1983. Towards a social psychology of recreational travel. *Leisure Studies*, 2(1), 45–56.

——1989. Motivation for leisure. In Jackson, E.L., and Burton, T.L. (eds). Understanding Leisure and Recreation: Mapping the Past, Charting the Future. State College, Pennsylvania: Venture Publishing Inc.

Jang, S. and Feng, R. 2007. Temporal destination revisit intention: The effects of novelty seeking and satisfaction. *Tourism Management*, 28(2), 580–590.

Klenosky, D. 2002. The 'pull' of tourism destinations: A means-end investigation. *Journal of Travel Research*, 40(4), 385–395.

Krippendorf, J. 1986. The new tourist: Turning point for leisure and travel. *Tourism Management*, 7(2), 131–135.

Lee, G., O'Leary, J.T., Lee, S.H., and Morrison, A.M. 2002. Comparison and contrast of push and pull motivational effects on trip behavior: An application of a multinomial logistic regression model. *Tourism Analysis*, 7(2), 89–104.

MacCannell, D. 1976. The Tourist: A New Theory of the Leisure Class. Berkeley: University of California Press.

Mannell, R., and Iso-Ahola, S.E. 1987. Psychological nature of leisure and tourism experience. *Annals of Tourism Research*, 14(3), 314–331.

March, R., and Woodside, A.G. 2005. Tourism Behaviour: Travellers' Decisions and Actions. Wallingford: CABI.

Maslow, A.H. 1943. A theory of human motivation. *Psychological Review*, 50(4), 370–396.

Mayo, E.J., and Jarvis, L.P. 1981. The Psychology of Leisure Travel. Boston: CBI Publishing Company, Inc.

Mill, R.C., and Morrison, A.M. 2012. The Tourism System, 7th edn. Dubuque, IA: Kendall Hunt Publishing.

Miniwatts Marketing Group. 2012. Internet World Stats. http://internetworldstats.com/stats.htm

Mohn, T. 2010. Business Travelers Bringing Families on the Road. MSNBC.com. http://www.msnbc.msn.com/id/39101711/ns/travel-business_travel/t/business-travelers-bringing-families-road/

Morrison, A.M. 2010. Hospitality and Travel Marketing. Clifton Park, NY: Cengage Delmar.

Morrison, A.M., Hsieh, S., and O'Leary, J.T. 1995. Segmenting the visiting friends and relatives market by holiday activity participation. Journal of Tourism Studies, 6(1), 48–63.

Moscardo, G.M., Morrison, A.M., Pearce, P.L., Lang, C., and O'Leary, J.T. 1996. Understanding vacation destination choice through travel motivation and activities. Journal of Vacation Marketing, 2(2), 109–122.

Pearce, P.L. 1982. The Social Psychology of Tourist Behaviour. Oxford: Pergamon Press.

——2005. Tourist Behaviour: Themes and Conceptual Schemes. Clevedon: Channel View Publications.

Pearce, P.L., and Lee, U.-I. 2005. Developing the travel career approach to tourist motivation. Journal of Travel Research, 43(3), 226–237.

Pike, S.D. 2002. Destination image analysis: A review of 142 papers from 1973–2000. Tourism Management, 23(5), 541–549.

Pine, B.J., and Gilmore, J.H. 1999. The Experience Economy: Work is Theatre and Every Business is a Stage. Cambridge, MA: Harvard Business Press.

Plog, S.C. 2002. The power of psychographics and the concept of venturesomeness. Journal of Travel Research, 40(3), 244–251.

Prayag, G., and Ryan, C. 2011. The relationship between the 'push' and 'pull' factors of a tourist destination: the role of nationality: An analytical qualitative research approach. Current Issues in Tourism, 14(2), 121–143.

Queensland Tourism Industry Council. 2012. http://www.qtic.com.au/project-service/qtic-y-mentoring-program

Records, L. 2010. San Francisco Travel's New Gay Travel Website Reminds Visitors 'The Gate is Always Open'. http://www.sanfrancisco.travel/media/media-resources/San-Francisco-Travels-New-Gay-Travel-Website-Reminds-Visitors-The-Gate-is-Always-Open.html

Rittichainuwat, B.N., Qu, H., and Mongkhonvanit, C. 2008. Understanding the motivation of travelers on repeat visits to Thailand. Journal of Vacation Marketing, 14(1), 5–21.

Ross, G.F. 1994. The Psychology of Tourism. Wallingford: CABI.

Roy Morgan Research. 2009. Market Insight – Gay and Lesbian Leisure Travellers.

Ryan, C. 2002. The Tourist Experience. Andover: Cengage Learning EMEA.

Seddighi, H.R., and Theocharous, A.L. 2002. A model of tourism destination choice: A theoretical and empirical analysis. Tourism Management, 23(5), 475–487.

Snepenger, D., King, J., Marshall, E., and Uysal, M. 2006. Modeling Iso-Ahola's motivation theory in the tourism context. Journal of Travel Research, 45(2), 140–149.

South, G. 2007. Add family to the trip. New Zealand Herald, 15 October.

Specialty Travel Index. 2012. Adventure and Specialty Travel. http://www.specialtytravel.com/

STA Travel. 2007. Gap Year Survey: Gen Y Aussies Travel as Far as the Resume Reaches. http://www.statravel.com.au/gay_year_survey.htm

Stepchenkova, S., and Morrison, A.M. 2006. The destination image of Russia: From the online induced perspective. *Tourism Management*, 27(5), 943–956.

——2008. Russia's destination image among American pleasure travelers: Revisiting Echtner and Ritchie. *Tourism Management*, 29(3), 548–560.

Swarbrooke, J., and Horner, S. 1999. Consumer Behavior in Tourism. Oxford: Butterworth Heinemann.

Tapachai, N., and Waryszak, R. 2000. An examination of the role of beneficial image in tourist destination selection. *Journal of Travel Research*, 39(1), 37–44.

Teichemann, K. 2011. Expertise, experience and self-confidence in consumers' travel information search. *International Journal of Culture, Tourism and Hospitality Research*, 5(2), 184–194.

Tian-Cole, S., and Crompton, J. 2003. A conceptualization of the relationships between service quality and visitor satisfaction, and their links to destination selection. *Leisure Studies*, 22(1), 65–80.

Tourism Australia. 2006. A Uniquely Australian Invitation: The Experience Seekers.

——2012. Our Target Market. The Experience Seeker. http://www.tourism.australia.com/en-au/marketing/experience-seekers.aspx

Tourism Ireland. 2011. Competing to Win. Tourism Ireland Marketing Plan 2012.

Um, S., and Crompton, J.L. 1990. Attitude determinants in destination choice. *Annals of Tourism Research*, 17(3), 432–448.

UNWTO. 2012. UNWTO World Tourism Barometer. Madrid: UNWTO.

Virgin Australia Airlines. 2012. Breakations. http://www.virginaustralia.com/us/en/specials-offers/holiday-specials/breakations/

Virginia Tourism Corporation. 2010. Virginia Tourism Corporation Marketing Plan FY11.

Visit Wales. 2012. Short Break Itineraries. http://www.visitwales.co.uk/things-to-do-in-wales/tour-operators/short-break-itineraries/

Woodside, A.G., and Lysonski, S. 1989. A general model of traveler destination choice. *Journal of Travel Research*, 27(4), 8–14.

Woodside, A.G., and Sherrell, D. 1977. Traveler evoked set, inept set, and inert sets of vacation destinations. *Journal of Travel Research*, 16(1), 14–18.

You, X., O'Leary, J., Morrison, A.M., and Hong, G.-S. 2000. A cross-cultural comparison of travel push and pull factors: United Kingdom vs. Japan. *International Journal of Hospitality and Tourism Administration*, 1(2), 1–26.

Chapter 13

Domestic pleasure and leisure travel markets

Learning objectives

1 Explain the benefits of domestic tourism.

2 Discuss the size and importance of domestic tourism in selected countries and compare the domestic and international tourism contributions.

3 Elaborate upon the recent trends and future prospects for domestic tourism.

4 Review the major challenges in the marketing and development of domestic tourism.

5 Describe the major segments of domestic tourism.

6 Discuss a systematic, step-by-step approach to the marketing of domestic tourism.

7 Identify and describe a select number of domestic tourism marketing and promotion campaigns.

8 Examine the visiting friends and relatives (VFR) market and explain its importance for domestic tourism.

9 Pinpoint the reasons why the positive impacts of the VFR market are sometimes underestimated.

Introduction

Domestic travel in several countries is what sustains the tourism sector and not international tourism. You might think of it as the 'staple food' or 'bread-and-butter' market for many DMOs and tourism sector stakeholders. While domestic tourism may not hold the same glamour for some destinations as international tourism, it is hugely important to many parts of the world. Moreover, many local people say they want to 'discover their own countries first' before venturing abroad.

The current status of domestic tourism varies across the world. In the developed countries of Europe, North America and the Asia-Pacific, domestic tourism is very mature with decades of development, marketing and promotion. With large middle classes and reasonably high household incomes, most people can afford to travel within their own countries for pleasure and leisure. Domestic tourism in most of the developed countries is growing rather slowly and, in a few cases, is declining. Competition from outbound tourism destinations is just one of the reasons.

The situation is not the same in the poorer, developing countries and indeed domestic tourism is a fairly new concept to these nations. Several of these countries are experiencing high rates of economic growth and personal disposable incomes, so domestic tourism is starting to boom. China and India are two good examples of places where domestic tourism is on a sharp upward trend.

There are many benefits of developing domestic tourism within a destination, and this chapter starts with that particular topic.

VFR travel is closely linked with pleasure and leisure travel and it is significant in both domestic and international tourism. Despite its size and importance, the value of VFR travel is often underestimated and undervalued. There are no reasons for any DMO to ignore this important market.

Benefits of domestic tourism

Many countries in the world, particularly the developing nations, have had a strong orientation towards generating foreign currencies through international tourism development and promotion. Domestic tourism for these countries has had a much lower priority. This has not necessarily been the case in developed economies where domestic tourism has had a 'mainstay' status and is well recognized and appreciated. Mendiratta (2011) suggested that many destinations have relegated domestic tourism to a secondary status in tourism marketing and development.

However, domestic tourism offers significant economic, social and cultural benefits for tourism in a country. Some of the benefits that have been attributed to domestic tourism are the following (Heath, 2011; Mendiratta, 2011; Sri Lanka Tourism Development Authority, 2011):

- *Enhancement of national pride*: Creating more pride and ambassadorship for one's own country through enhanced understanding, experience and appreciation of all that it offers. Local residents may become better 'tourism ambassadors' for their countries if they have travelled and experienced the country more extensively.

Domestic tourism on the B-list for many destinations

Sadly, the A-list profile and appeal of the International inbound segment of the tourism sector has meant that domestic tourism has, for many destinations, been relegated to the B-list. Promotion of the tourism sector to people of the destination itself has, for many nations, become an additional extra within the overall destination growth strategy. Secondary attention is applied, along with secondary budget.

(Mendiratta, 2011)

- *Greater appreciation of environmental conservation and local culture*: Better educating local people so they develop a deeper awareness of the natural and cultural resources of their countries. They attach a higher value to these resources after experiencing them first-hand.
- *Greater geographic spread of tourism*: Dispersing travellers across, and deeper into the destination, stretching tourism activity and attractions beyond the main cities. People leave heavily populated urban areas and visit the countryside, rural and resort locations.
- *Hard currency retention*: Retaining the hard currency that would otherwise leave the country in the form of outbound travel expenditures in foreign destinations.
- *Increased employment*: Generating more jobs for local people in the tourism sector (both direct and indirect) as a result of greater and ongoing tourism activity.
- *Leisure-time experiences*: Enabling domestic residents who have growing disposable incomes to participate in productive and satisfying experiences during their leisure time.
- *Lower carbon footprint*: Travelling domestically may have a lower carbon footprint than travelling to other parts of the world.
- *Reduction of seasonality*: Creating year-round tourism activity and lessening the valleys in seasonality curves, enabling tourism operators to operate longer.
- *Social and cultural benefits*: Giving social and cultural benefits to domestic residents who might not otherwise be able to experience the cultural and natural richness of their own nations.
- *Wealth redistribution*: Redistributing wealth within a country's boundaries. For example, people from the cities go to rural and poorer areas of a country and spend money in these more economically depressed regions.

The significance of domestic tourism is well demonstrated in the case of Ireland, as explained by the Irish Tourist Industry Confederation (2009):

The importance of domestic tourism to Ireland

The domestic tourism market is now the source of:

- 38 per cent share of holiday bednights in the country
- Almost two out of every three hotel bednights (for all purposes of travel)

- An increasing share of tourism revenue to most regions
- Almost one third of spend by tourists in Ireland (all expenditure by domestic travel vs. overseas expenditure in Ireland).

An even more pronounced indicator of the importance of domestic tourism is for Brazil. For 2011, the World Travel and Tourism Council (2012) estimated that 94.9 per cent of travel and tourism's contribution to the Brazilian GDP was from domestic expenditures; only 5.1 per cent was from foreign visitor spending in Brazil (Table 13.1). Japan was another country with a very high economic contribution of domestic tourism, at 95.4 per cent.

Table 13.1 Population and GDP characteristics of world's most populated countries

Pop. rank	Country	Population (2012)	GDP per capita (2011)	Real GDP growth rate (2011)	Domestic tourism GDP % contribution
1	China	1,343,239,923	8,400	9.2%	88.1%
2	India	1,205,073,612	3,700	7.8%	82.2%
3	United States	313,847,465	48,100	1.5%	81.3%
4	Indonesia	248,216,193	4,700	6.4%	79.1%
5	Brazil	205,716,890	11,600	2.7%	94.9%
6	Pakistan	190,291,129	2,800	2.4%	89.7%
7	Nigeria	170,123,740	2,600	6.9%	88.3%
8	Bangladesh	161,083,804	1,700	6.3%	97.8%
9	Russia	138,082,178	16,700	4.3%	77.3%
10	Japan	127,368,088	34,300	− 0.5%	95.4%
11	Mexico	114,975,406	15,100	3.8%	87.7%
12	Philippines	103,775,002	4,100	3.7%	59.1%

Sources: Central Intelligence Agency, 2012; World Travel and Tourism Council, 2012.

Size and importance of domestic tourism

In the world's most populated countries, the potential domestic travel markets are vast in size. For example, China's domestic travel market is huge and involves hundreds of millions of people moving about the country. According to Liu (2011), there were 2.1 billion domestic tourists in China in 2010. There are massive movements of people at the time of major national holidays and especially at Chinese New Year. The growth of domestic tourism continued in 2012 according to statistics released by the China National Tourism Administration (CNTA):

Domestic tourism expands further in China in 2012

Domestic tourists made 875 million trips from January to March, up 15.1 percent year-on-year, Shao Qiwei, head of the National Tourism Administration (NTA), said in a statement posted on the NTA's website.

The tourism industry has been playing an increasingly important role in stimulating domestic demand and generating jobs. Rising domestic living standards and the country's unremitting efforts to open wider to the outside world will provide fresh opportunities for the development of the tourism sector, Shao said in the statement.

The Market Research Division of the Ministry of Tourism in India (2011) found there were 740 million domestic tourist visits to the states and union territories of India in 2010. This was an increase of 10.7 per cent in 2010 over 2009. The top ten states in terms of number of domestic tourist visits (in millions) during 2010 were Andhra Pradesh (155.8), Uttar Pradesh (144.8), Tamil Nadu (111.6), Maharashtra (48.5), Karnataka (38.2), Madhya Pradesh (38.1), Uttarakhand (30.2), Rajasthan (25.5), West Bengal (21.1) and Gujarat (18.9).

The US Travel Association (2011) estimated that US residents took 1.5 billion person-trips for leisure purposes in 2010. The top activities of US residents on these trips were: (1) visiting relatives, (2) shopping, (3) visiting friends, (4) rural sightseeing and (5) beaches.

For Europe as a whole, domestic tourism represented 77 per cent of the all the holiday trips taken by Europeans in 2010 according to Eurostat (2011), and that agency highlighted a common misperception about holiday-taking:

'Home' destinations are the most popular among Europeans

Tourism is generally considered to be an international phenomenon. People travel to other countries to discover new cultures or enjoy unseen nature or heritage, or simply to enjoy a mild climate for a week or so. However, statistics show that the destination of most trips made by Europeans is within their own country.

For Canada, Statistics Canada (2011) estimated that Canadians made 229.1 million person-trips within Canada in 2010. About 66 per cent of these trips were to destinations in Ontario and Quebec. There were 119.4 million domestic trips taken in the UK in 2010 and about 66 per cent were for holiday purposes (The UK Tourist 2010). Australians made 69.8 million overnight trips and 156.4 million day trips within Australia in 2011 (Tourism Research Australia, 2012).

While many of these numbers are not directly comparable due to differences in definitions of trips and visits, they clearly underline the magnitude of domestic tourism in the selected countries. Table 13.2 further confirms the size and importance of domestic tourism and in an interesting way: it lists the top ten destinations in the world in terms of international tourist arrivals, according to UNWTO. However, the percentages in Table 13.2 are from the World Travel and Tourism Council and are estimates of the contributions of domestic tourism to the total travel and tourism GDPs of the top destinations. You can see that the domestic tourism contribution percentages vary from a high of 88.1 per cent for China to a low of 42 per cent for Malaysia. If the ten percentages are averaged, the result is approximately 64 per cent. These are many numbers to think about, but what is the main take-away point? The answer is that, even for most of the top international tourism destinations in the world, domestic tourism is larger and more important economically than international inbound tourism. This is particularly true for the top three destinations, France, the USA and China.

While the main point may already be made about the critical importance of domestic tourism in several top destinations, there is a follow-on point that also requires some emphasis and you need to know about it. You will learn in Chapter 14 about the susceptibility of international tourism to crises, and this has been demonstrated with 9/11 (2001), SARS (2003) and the worldwide economic problems in 2008–2009. When crises such as these are encountered, inbound international tourism is particularly affected and can drop precipitously. So what are the potential solutions for destinations that rely very heavily on tourism? The answer has been to focus marketing and promotion 'closer to home' and especially on domestic tourists. In some ways, domestic tourism provides an 'insurance policy' for times when international tourism experiences a downturn and, therefore, domestic tourism should never be neglected or given an inferior status in national tourism.

As a final postscript on this discussion, there are some destinations in the world where international tourism is massively important to their economies and where domestic tourism is minimal. Macau SAR is one of these destinations, where the very small resident population contributes just 1.8 per cent of total travel and tourism GDP (World Travel and Tourism Council, 2012). Two other well-known destinations where the domestic contributions are very low are the Maldives (4.7 per cent) and the Bahamas (18 per cent).

Table 13.2 Domestic tourism contributions to world's top international tourism destinations

International tourism rank (UNWTO)	Country	Domestic tourism contribution to travel and tourism GDP (WT&TC)
1	France	71.4%
2	USA	81.3%
3	China	88.1%
4	Spain	55.8%
5	Italy	67.5%
6	UK	67.8%
7	Turkey	53.1%
8	Germany	62.0%
9	Malaysia	42.0%
10	Austria	49.0%

Sources: UNWTO; World Travel and Tourism Council, 2012.

Domestic tourism is the primary and sometimes exclusive focus of many DMOs around the world. These DMOs pay very little attention to international tourism marketing and promotion, leaving this task to higher-level DMOs within their countries. This is true of many of the convention and visitors' bureaus (CVBs) operating in the USA and of many regional tourism associations around the world.

Trends and future prospects for domestic tourism

What are the principal trends that have been impacting upon domestic tourism and what are the future prospects for this very important branch of the tourism sector?

Trends and influences on domestic tourism

Chapter 12 highlighted seven categories of overall trends that have been occurring in tourism worldwide and six of these have definitely affected domestic tourism in recent times:

- *Demographics*: Baby Boomers; Generation X; Generation Y.
- *Trip purposes*: Multi-purposing trips; short-break vacations/holidays.
- *Trip planning and travel arrangements*: More independent travel.
- *Psychographics and lifestyles*: Health and wellness; spa usage; green travel; GLBT market.
- *Special interests*: Adventure; cruises; casino gaming; culinary; cultural; dark tourism; nature-based and ecotourism; health and wellness; heritage/historic; industrial; religious; voluntourism; wine.
- *Technology uses*: Searching and booking travel online; use of social network sites.

Added to this mixture of influential factors has to be the recessionary or poorer economic conditions in many developed countries, with the main effects being experienced in 2008 and 2009. Another factor has been the relative pricing levels within domestic versus outbound tourism destinations. In some cases, domestic prices have risen to much higher levels than available in the outbound destinations. Additionally, the development of low-cost carrier (LCC) airlines on international routes has encouraged more outbound tourism, and this has particularly been the case in Europe and the Asia-Pacific region.

Without wanting to be too repetitive here, some of these trends will be briefly mentioned again in the context of their impacts on domestic tourism:

- *Demographics*: The changing demographic structures in society are affecting domestic tourism. Later in this chapter, you will hear about multi-generation domestic travel, one of the outcomes of demographic changes.
- *Multi-purposing travel trips*: This trend has clearly helped domestic tourism destinations in many countries and Chapter 12 mentioned that this situation is occurring in New Zealand and the USA. In the tougher economic times and because of time-poverty, people have been increasingly combining business and leisure trip purposes.
- *Psychographics and lifestyles*: Domestic tourism is experiencing the impacts of changes in psychographics and lifestyles. One of the trends noted here is the growth

in 'green travellers', i.e. these are people who are particularly concerned about environmental protection and conservation.

- *Short-break holidays (breakations)*: The trend toward taking shorter holidays favours places close to the residences of tourists and is not beneficial for long-haul destinations.
- *Special-interest travel*: The trend toward more special-interest travel applies both to domestic and international tourism. This topic is discussed later in this chapter as well as in Chapter 14.
- *Technology uses*: The effects of ICTs on tourism are universal and are pervasively impacting upon domestic tourism. For example, domestic travellers are now relying most heavily on websites and social network sites to gather information on destinations.
- *Trip planning and travel arrangements*: Trips are being planned on shorter time frames than before and last-minute travel arrangements are gaining in popularity in domestic and international tourism.

Although there has been strong recent growth in domestic travel in several countries (including China and India), other countries have noted a softness in demand and even declines in domestic tourism (including Australia, New Zealand and the UK). This negative trend in domestic tourism is attributed mainly to the global economic problems in 2008 and 2009, and the impact that had on local residents of the nations that were most adversely affected by the recessionary conditions.

The UK Tourist: Statistics 2010, based on the results from the United Kingdom Tourism Survey for the UK's statutory tourist boards, noted a decline in domestic tourist volumes between 2009 and 2010:

A fall in the number of UK holidays

Pure holiday (pleasure/leisure, which exclude VFR on holiday) trips also reported a decrease (4.1 million) between 2009 (60.7 million) and 2010 (56.6 million) in the UK. There was a noticeable increase in trips in June but this was more than offset by a fall in demand for trips during April and May and July through to December. In fact, just three months (February, March and June) recorded increases on 2009. Analysing the situation more closely, it was holiday trips of 4+ nights in length that contributed most to the decrease with 4–7 night holidays falling by 7 per cent and longer 8+ night holidays by 13 per cent. Shorter breaks (1–3 nights) also decreased compared to 2009 by 6 per cent.

Future prospects

It appears that the prospects for the further expansion of domestic tourism in many countries are very bright indeed. Table 13.2 shows the twelve countries in the world with populations of over 100 million people. In all of these countries, the potential for future expansion of domestic tourism is significant, although some will be hampered by low per capita incomes and other unique local constraints and conditions. Countries with high growth rates in real GDP are particularly primed for domestic tourism growth, including China, India, Nigeria and Indonesia. Other countries such as the USA and Japan are slowly emerging from very poor economic conditions, and domestic tourism is expected to grow only modestly.

Despite the favourable conditions in many countries for domestic tourism in the future, there are issues and challenges that will undoubtedly be encountered and these are now reviewed.

Issues and challenges

Domestic tourism faces some overall issues as well as some specific challenges in development, marketing and promotion.

Whose responsibility is domestic tourism?

Generally, there is an acceptance that the official national DMO should do the destination marketing and promotion for its country abroad. The consensus is not as strong on who should market and promote domestic tourism. The Tourism Industry Association New Zealand (2005) conducted an analysis of domestic tourism and identified the following issue about promoting New Zealand to New Zealanders:

Why not promote New Zealand to New Zealanders?

The issues identified in this document also raises the question: is New Zealand 'out of step' by not actively promoting the concept of domestic tourism within New Zealand: and, should New Zealand be actively promoting New Zealand to New Zealanders as a way of encouraging New Zealanders to see their own country and spending their hard earned discretionary incomes here rather than overseas?

This issue is further complicated by the fact that in many countries, local residents travel mainly within their own states, provinces or territories. For example, the Government of Canada (2011) noted that nine out of ten domestic trips by Canadians were taken within their own provinces. While not quite as high, 75 per cent of the domestic visits within California were made by Californians.

The question then becomes, why not have the states, provinces or territories, and cities market and promote domestic tourism, since they are the major beneficiaries? It's a good question since every state, province and territory has an official DMO as well as many city/county-level DMOs and sometimes also RTOs or RTAs. In fact, these sub-national DMOs are generally very active in domestic tourism marketing and promotion. However, there is still a need for an NTO to promote the concept of domestic tourism as a whole within a country.

Competition between domestic and international tourism and tourists

In several ways, domestic and international tourism are competing with each other. At one level, they are competing for increasingly scarce government tourism resources to support the tourism sector. At another level, domestic and international tourism are competing for business from the residents of a given country. The relative price levels and convenience of travel are key factors in who wins this competition.

There are varying tendencies among the citizens of different countries to take holidays at home (domestic) and travel outbound (international); and this is well demonstrated for Europe. For example, 53 per cent of the trips by residents (15 years and older) of the Netherlands were taken outside of their country in 2010; but for France, the comparable figure was 11 per cent. For the UK, 61 per cent of the trips were domestic; 39 per cent outbound. The average for the EU-27 (excluding Malta) was 77 per cent domestic and 23 per cent outbound (Eurostat, 2011).

Another aspect of competition comprises situations when domestic and international tourists are mixed together at tourism attractions and facilities within a specific country. In the vast majority of cases, this blending of the two markets is good for tourism and presents no visitor management problems. However, there are a few situations where the differing behaviours and expectations can cause some tension between the two groups. For example, some international visitors to famous sites in China are disturbed and put off by the large numbers of domestic tourist groups who do not tend to follow the same manners and rules of etiquette to which they are accustomed in their home countries.

Impacts of currency rate fluctuations

Changes in currency exchange rates can have a significant influence on tourist volumes, including those for domestic tourism. For example, when a country's currency is stronger, the buying power of its citizens when travelling abroad increases. Australia provides a good recent example of this currency rate exchange issue. Tourism Research Australia (2011) conducted a special study and concluded that domestic tourism was losing market share to outbound tourism by Australians due to the high value of the Australian dollar, rising incomes and increased airline capacity to places outside the country:

Australian domestic tourism being challenged by outbound tourism

Domestic tourism contributes significantly to the economic value of the industry and the Australian economy. Worth around $25 billion in gross domestic product (GDP), this accounts for almost three quarters of tourism GDP (with $21 billion generated by households and $4 billion by business/government). However, the price of the Australian (domestic) tourism product has been steadily increasing relative to the outbound tourism product over the last decade, due to a stronger Australian dollar. Rising incomes and increased air capacity have provided improved access to a range of destinations, and the appeal of outbound tourism for Australians is strong.

These types of challenges are impossible for the tourism sector to deal with on its own and reflect the susceptibility of tourism to forces and crises outside of its own realm.

Is a day-tripper a tourist?

Often a significant portion of domestic travel involves day-trips where there are no overnight stays in the destinations. UNWTO says there are 'tourists' and 'excursionists' and excursionists are temporary visitors who stay less than 24 hours in a destination. This is a particularly important point in counting international tourist arrivals at very busy cross-border points between two countries. Counting excursionists as international tourist arrivals is discouraged by UNWTO for the sake of uniformity of counting around the world.

However, in a domestic tourism situation is it really as necessary to make this distinction between overnight tourists and day-trippers? This is not just an important point for market researchers, but it has implications for product development, marketing and the management of visitor attractions. In some cases, there seems to be a type of resentment against day visitors perceiving them as low-spenders when compared to 'real' tourists. The following quote from Robinson (2009) about the size of the day visitor market shows that their economic impact must not be underestimated.

Fifty per cent of tourism revenues in UK from day visitors

Over 50 per cent of tourism revenue in the UK comes from day visitors. But the focus of much tourism effort, policy and investment is on longer-term visitors – from mini-breaks to holidays. In the current economic climate the day visitor market is particularly valuable and could benefit from greater understanding and specific product development.

Some destinations have decided that day-trippers or day visitors are important and need attention from the DMO as well. For example, the US Travel Association defines a person-trip as a trip by one person 'away from home overnight in paid accommodations or on a day or overnight trip to places 50 miles or more (one-way) away from home'. This type of definition for domestic tourism based on the distance travelled is a much fairer and reasonable way to consider the day visitor market.

Unfortunately it is difficult to compare day visitors across different countries, because the definitions vary. For example, Tourism Research Australia defines day visitors as

> those who travel for a round trip distance of at least 50 kilometres, are away from home for at least four hours and who do not spend a night away from home as part of their travel. Same day travel as part of overnight travel is excluded, as is routine travel such as commuting between work/school and home.

You can see this is different from the definition by the US Travel Association.

Slower development of tourism for domestic markets

In some countries, domestic tourism has been neglected in favour of product development and marketing towards international tourists. This has been a practical decision based on the desire to earn more in foreign currencies and to take advantage of the higher spending power of foreign tourists. Facilities developed for international tourists may be priced at levels that are too high for residents and this may lead to some resentment among local residents, as well as excluding them from buying.

Market segments

There are different ways in which domestic travel market segments can be described. They are usually divided by geographic origin and then into pleasure/leisure or holiday travel, VFR, business travel and other.

As you know from Chapter 12, there are at least seven different ways to form segments of tourist markets (trip purpose; geography; socio-demographics; psychographics; behaviour; product-related; and channel of distribution). All of these segmentation approaches can be applied to domestic tourists. In this chapter, part of the focus is on trip purpose segments; pleasure/leisure/holiday travel and VFR; and business travel is discussed in Chapter 15.

Because we are dealing with nearly 200 different countries in the world, it is very difficult to deal with geographic origin segmentation; as a result that topic is not discussed here. So, the focus is now placed on socio-economic, psychographic/lifestyle and product related segmentation, beginning with the family travel market.

Family travel market

Families travelling with children represent a significant proportion of most domestic tourism markets. For example, a number of studies on leisure travel markets in North America indicate that the family travel market represents about 30–40 per cent of total demand (Saltzman, 2010).

The United Kingdom Tourism Survey (UKTS) divides UK adults into four categories: (1) pre-nesters (under 35 years and no children); (2) families (all ages and with children); (3) older independents (35–54 years and no children); and (4) empty nesters (55 years and above and no children). For 2010, the families category accounted for the largest proportion of 'pure holidays' taken in the UK, at 35.9 per cent. Empty nesters were next at 30.5 per cent; older independents were 18.7 per cent; and pre-nesters were 14.9 per cent. There was some variation among the countries of the UK; for example, empty nesters outnumbered families for holidays in Scotland (31 per cent vs 30 per cent), while families had an above-average share (42 per cent) for Wales.

Families have several decision-makers (parents and children) and there are several vacation/holiday sub-decisions, as was mentioned in Chapter 12. From the research that has been completed on family vacation decision-making, it appears quite clear that the female head of household (mother) plays the key role. The Virginia Tourism Corporation (VTC) in the USA decided to mainly focus on the family travel market in 2012. Based upon VTC's research, the key planner and booker within the family is the female head of household and DMOs need to pay attention to this finding (VTC 2011):

Role of the female head of household

While the primary information-gatherer and trip-booker is the female head of household, she takes into consideration the input from all in the family-travel party and discusses the options and ideas with her partner. She is the one making the vacation destination short list and presenting the options to the group. Once the travel party arrives at a decision, she makes the majority of the travel plans including researching all trip options. The female head of household therefore remains the primary person with whom the marketing needs to connect emotionally. She has to connect while in the planning stage of the vacation and she must see a connection that the Virginia travel experience will appeal to the vacation desires of all in the family/travel party.

Sometimes tourism marketers focus on the children in families to attract them to their destinations. For example, the DMO in New York City, NYC & Company, teamed up with the Muppets to encourage families to visit NYC in 2012:

Muppets will encourage families to travel to New York City in 2012 by highlighting family-friendly destinations and attractions

In 2011, New York City welcomed fifteen million family visitors, contributing approximately $14 billion to New York City's economy. New York City Mayor Michael R. Bloomberg and NYC & Company, New York City's tourism and marketing organization, announced that the Muppets will return to New York City in 2012 as the official NYC Family Ambassadors. As part of the year-long collaboration, the Muppets will encourage family travel to the City by highlighting the best ways for families to experience and enjoy the many dining and shopping venues, cultural institutions, parks and attractions across the five boroughs.

The Family Ambassador program began in 2009. Since then, family visitation to New York City has increased by 14.4 percent.

(NYC & Company, 2012)

Helsinki in Finland is another destination with a family travel marketing campaign. The campaign has created a special character called 'Helppi'. A family travel brochure was produced in cooperation with the travel trade (Figure 13.1).

Multi-generational travel market

Some experts regard this as one of the hottest growth markets in pleasure and leisure travel, and particularly for domestic tourism. Multi-generational travel is defined as a trip party that includes three or more generations, e.g. grandparents, parents and children.

Figure 13.1 Vacation experiences for children brochure

Source: Helsinki City Tourist and Convention Bureau, Finland, 2012.

One of the reasons for the growth in multi-generational travel is that families are increasingly being dispersed and living far apart. Another reason is that the Baby Boomers are fit and more active and want to spend more time with their grandchildren. A study prepared by Preferred Hotels (2011) found that 40 per cent of all active leisure travellers in the US had taken a multi-generational trip in the previous 12 months. Preferred Hotels offer the following four main reasons for the growth in multi-generational travel:

Reasons for growth of multi-generational travel

- Families are living geographically farther from each other than at any time in history.
- A multi-generational trip is often the only option for today's modern and mobile family to gather in one place.
- The hyper-fast pace of life in the twenty-first century means evenings and weekends are no longer untouchable family time, creating a greater need for the escape that only travel can provide.
- Baby boomers are trading in their briefcases for a roller bag. Boomers now have the time, health and disposable income to make travel with their families a top priority.

Luxury travel market

Luxury travel is partly socio-demographic and partly lifestyle in nature. The luxury travel market is a segment of domestic and international tourism markets that seeks exclusivity and social distinction, and this has a price dimension (International Luxury Travel Market/Horwath HTL, 2011):

The price dimension of luxury

Luxury refers to extremes in terms of price:

- High price points help maintain exclusivity for affluent customers.
- While luxury travellers will pay a premium price for top quality, value is a key consideration.
- Social distinction remains important in the luxury sector.

There are many articles written about luxury travellers, but precious few statistics have ever been published on their numbers and characteristics. It is easier to identify the tourism products they prefer, like first-class air travel and the top five-star hotels and resorts like Aman, Shangri-la and Banyan Tree (Figure 13.2).

Special-interest travel markets

Special-interest travel markets are usually drawn to destinations by particular types of tourism products; for example, golfers go to destinations that have courses they want

Figure 13.2 The luxurious Banyan Tree Resort in Lijiang, Yunnan Province, China
Source: Banyan Tree Hotels & Resorts, 2012.

to play; scuba-divers go to ocean areas where they can see reefs or shipwrecks; and those who want to gamble seek out casino destinations. Therefore, special-interest travel is closely aligned with product-related segmentation. However, there is also a human side to special-interest travel as it reflects the psychographics and lifestyles of particular people.

Domestic tourism has experienced an increase in special-interest travel (SIT) markets. In Chapter 14, fifteen market segments with growth potential are identified and briefly described. These are identified in Figure 13.3. All fifteen segments are significant and growing as part of the domestic tourism in many countries.

Since the fifteen SIT segments are described in Chapter 14, they are not elaborated upon in this chapter. Obviously a list of fifteen items does not cover every possible special-interest travel activity that can take place in a country.

Agritourism market

Another special-interest category not included is agritourism, also sometimes called agrotourism. 'Agritourism is the crossroads of tourism and agriculture: when the public visits working farms, ranches or wineries to buy products, enjoy entertainment, participate in activities, shop in a country store, eat a meal or make overnight stays' (Figart and Nelson, 2005). Traditionally associated with Europe, agritourism has spread throughout the world to the Americas, Australia and New Zealand and is even very popular in China through the *nong jia le* (happy farm family homes) concept.

Agritourism has been especially popular in domestic tourism as it allows urban dwellers to experience a simpler lifestyle at a reasonable cost. Veeck et al. (2006) carried out a research study on agritourism operations in Michigan, USA and placed these operations into ten categories (animal products; berries; Christmas; fall harvest; farm market; farm experience; honey/maple syrup; nurseries; orchards; vineyards). Veeck et al. found agritourism to be a 'win–win' proposition for the farmers and tourists and identified the following specific benefits:

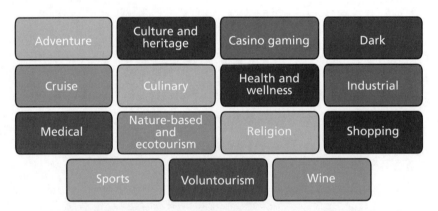

Figure 13.3 Market segments with growth potential: domestic and international tourism

Benefits of agritourism in Michigan

Michigan agritourism offers many benefits to the rural areas where these farms are located and should be supported. Beyond wages and taxes, these farm activities help many families stay on the farm, and provide a new draw of customers to area businesses. Further, keeping farm families on the farm slows urban sprawl, while maintaining an important aspect of state history and heritage. Finally, and perhaps more important than all the money is that fact that these businesses give all of us wonderful opportunities to 'go back to the farm'.

Agritourism is particularly important in sustaining the livelihoods of farm families and 'keeping them on the land'. A great example of a successful agritourism attraction is Amish Acres in Indiana, USA. This is located in Elkhart County, which is home to the third largest population of Amish people in the USA (Figure 13.4).

Golf travel market

Some experts consider golf to be a sub-set of sports tourism (Kim and Ritchie, 2012). However, golf tourism is a popular mode of travel in both domestic and international tourism and requires separate attention. Kim *et al.* (2008) define golf tourism as 'travel for more than one night to destinations where golf is played as a major tourism activity (active golf holiday) to meet travel motivations'.

The golf market is large in several developed countries (Figure 13.5). For example, the National Golf Foundation (NGF) estimated that there were 26.1 million golfers in the USA in 2010. NGF also estimated that 11.4 million golfers in 2007 travelled and played golf while on holiday or business trips. Kim and Ritchie (2012) reported that 635,000 Koreans played golf overseas in 2006 and spent USD 1.183 billion on their golf holidays in the Philippines, China, Thailand and other parts of Asia. Canadian travellers made more than one million trips involving golf, spending an estimated C\$1.9 billion annually on golf-related travel within Canada (Strategic Networks Group, 2009).

Figure 13.4 Amish Acres: a highly successful agritourism attraction in Indiana
Source: Shutterstock, Inc. (Tammy Venable).

Kim and Ritchie (2012) completed a study on the motivations of Korean golfers for golf tourism. Using Dann's 'push and pull' theory of tourist motivation, they found five 'push' factors (business opportunity; benefits; learning and challenging; escape/relax; social interaction/kinship factors). The 'pull' factors of destinations were: natural environment; golfing-related availability and accessibility; golf resort/course facilities and services; tourism attractions; tourism facilities and services; nightlife and entertainment; price and ease of access.

A great example of a domestic golf tourism destination, that is also a great partnership example, is the Robert Trent Jones Golf Trail in Alabama, USA. It joins together 11 different sites with 468 holes of golf. The first course was completed in 1992, with all the courses being designed by the world's most famous golf course designer, Robert Trent Jones. About 550,000 rounds of golf are played on the trail each year, and it has become an attraction for international golfers as well.

Theme park travel market

The segment of the domestic tourism market visiting theme parks is substantial in many countries. According to the *2010 Theme Index* from AECOM, the top 25 theme parks in the world had a combined annual attendance of 189.1 million in 2010. The top 20 theme parks in North America had combined attendances of 123.6 million; the top twenty in Asia had 83.3 million; and the top 20 in Europe had 56.3 million. So the audiences for theme parks are huge and a large proportion of the attendances result from domestic tourism.

Other market segmentation approaches

As you will see later in this chapter, there are other ways to segment domestic markets. Two further examples are provided from Queensland, Australia and South Africa. The Tourism Queensland segmentation approach is a psychographic one; while the South African segmentation is a combination of life-cycle stage and income levels.

Figure 13.5 The home of golf, St Andrews, Scotland
Source: Shutterstock, Inc. (Adam Edwards).

Domestic pleasure/leisure travel marketing procedures

Almost every DMO needs to prepare a marketing strategy and plan for domestic tourism and its component market segments. Typically, these strategies and plans are focused on specific geographic regions and cities within the home country. It is recommended that the *Destination Marketing System* model (Morrison, 2010) be followed for the marketing and promotion of domestic tourism.

Where are we now?

A situation analysis should be completed each year that identifies the destination's strengths, weaknesses and marketing opportunities for domestic tourism. Conducting a situation analysis was discussed in detail in Chapter 3, so there is no need to repeat that discussion here. However, it is important to emphasize that the DMO should conduct a thorough market analysis of domestic tourism as a foundation for developing a marketing strategy and plan for domestic pleasure and leisure tourists. This task is easier in countries that have regular national surveys of domestic travellers, and is much more difficult in places where no such data are available.

Two good case studies here are for New Zealand and the UK. The Domestic Travel Survey (DTS) uses a stratified random sampling of 15,000 people aged 15 years or older in New Zealand. People are interviewed at their households via telephone. The five purposes of the DTS are to:

- Measure the amount of expenditure of domestic visitors.
- Determine the activities domestic visitors participate in, the transport and accommodation types used and places visited.
- Provide data for determining tourism expenditure in the tourism satellite account.
- Provide demographic information about domestic visitors and their reasons for travelling.
- Provide data about residents who haven't travelled in New Zealand recently and their reasons for not travelling.

The DTS does an outstanding job of determining the specific activity participation of New Zealanders when travelling domestically, as well as pinpointing the attractions they visit. More than sixty individual activities (ranging from abseiling to walking in a city) are included in the survey questionnaire.

The United Kingdom Tourism Survey (UKTS) has been referred to several times in this chapter. For 2010, 100,000 face-to-face interviews were conducted in the UK. A description of the UKTS methodology (VisitEngland, 2011) is provided below:

Description of UKTS methodology

The UKTS survey is conducted continuously throughout the year, using face-to-face Computer Assisted Personal Interviews or CAPI interviewing, as part of TNS's in-home omnibus surveys. Weekly omnibus surveys are conducted with a representative sample of 2,000 adults aged sixteen and over within the UK. Respondents are asked whether they have taken trips in the UK in the previous four calendar weeks that involved at least one night away from home.

For 2011, Northern Ireland dropped out of UKTS, and the survey will become the GBTS.

Survey data like these in New Zealand and the UK provide a solid foundation for domestic tourism marketing and promotion. Without such data, DMOs are left to guess about domestic markets based on anecdotal evidence that may or may not be accurate. Countries such as Australia, Canada, New Zealand, the UK and the USA are setting a great example for other nations with their continuing surveys of domestic travellers. There are still some countries that do not have such data available on a regular basis for DMO marketers, and China and Russia are two of these.

The major outcomes of the domestic tourism situation analysis should be an articulation of the destination's strengths and weaknesses and unique selling propositions (USPs) vis-à-vis domestic tourism.

Where would we like to be?

The second step in domestic marketing and promotion is to select target markets and then develop a positioning–image–branding approach for domestic tourism markets. As you know from Chapter 3, this is part of the development of the marketing strategy.

Tourism Queensland (TQ) has done an excellent job of picking out the state's domestic tourism markets. TQ conducted a research study about Australia's ideal holiday needs and wants, and this resulted in six segments that were named as the: (1) active explorers (11 per cent); (2) stylish travellers (5 per cent); (3) self-discovers (12 per cent); (4) unwinders (15 per cent); (5) connectors (32 per cent); and (6) social fun-seekers (25 per cent).

A second good example of developing a unique market segmentation approach and strategy is from South Africa. The Department of Environmental Affairs and Tourism prepared a 'Domestic Tourism Growth Strategy, 2004 to 2007'. In this strategy, seven different consumer segments of South Africans were defined: (a) young and up-coming; (b) independent young couples and families; (c) striving families; (d) well-off homely couples; (e) home based low income families; (f) basic needs older families; and (g) 'golden active' couples.

The Domestic Tourism Market Growth Strategy for South Africa had six objectives:

- Match products to consumer segments.
- Extract greater levels of value from established and emerging holiday travellers through promoting: (1) more short breaks; (2) staying longer; and (3) providing more to do.
- Convert emerging and untapped segments into holiday travellers by providing: (1) group travel options; (2) travel vouchers; and (3) affordable breaks.
- Promote year round travel by encouraging more trips outside of school holidays through: (1) quiet season specials; and (2) winter experiences.
- Encourage greater levels of inter-provincial travel through: (1) touring options; (2) publicizing hidden secrets; and (3) providing new experiences.
- Utilize events to reduce seasonality and provide a full package option with events.

Marketing goals and objectives for domestic tourism need to be specified by the DMO as the platform for building the domestic tourism marketing plan.

How do we get there?

The third step is to develop a marketing plan that meets the objectives for the domestic marketing by using the 8 Ps (as described in Chapter 3). Sometimes the 8 Ps are covered in an integrated marketing communications campaign like 'Holidays at Home are GREAT' in the UK (VisitEngland, 2012).

'Holidays at Home are GREAT' (in the UK)

With backing from the Government, VisitEngland and the host nation tourist boards of Scotland, Wales, Northern Ireland and London, on the biggest ever domestic marketing campaign to date, the campaign called Holidays at Home are GREAT is designed to encourage Brits to take more domestic short breaks and holidays in this momentous year.

The campaign will kick off with a TV advertising campaign fronted by four of our best-loved actors Stephen Fry, Julie Walters, Rupert Grint and Michelle Dockery. The ad features the themes of coast, countryside and city, with a call to action to visit a specially designed website portal for the campaign. The website will feature special deals from our industry partners including 20.12 per cent off and other great offers and will link directly through to individual businesses' websites for further information and to book directly with the provider.

The aim of the campaign is to showcase the wide range of experiences to be had in this country and the exceptional value they present in this special year. It will feature the opportunities presented throughout the nation under the London 2012 Festival programme, the Torch Relay and the Queen's Diamond Jubilee.

A second domestic tourism marketing campaign at a national level that also had a good level of creativity was Tourism Australia's 'No Leave No Life'. This campaign was based on the knowledge that Australian's were stockpiling their holiday leave entitlements.

The 'No Leave No Life' campaign not only targeted employees, but also their companies. The message was simple, if you do not take holidays it is not good for you, and also not good for your employers either. Australians had stockpiled a staggering total of 129 million days of leave entitlement (unused holiday time). A special website was created for the campaign and it included a number of 'employer tools'. In these materials, five programme benefits were identified:

- It helps reduce your financial liability.
- It helps you attract and take care of employees.
- It increases productivity.
- It provides a framework for discussion.
- It encourages executives to lead by example.

Useful programme materials were also provided for use by employers, including information sheets about 'No Leave No Life', CEO letter/e-mail templates, holiday planning checklist, wallpaper and screensaver downloads, etc. As you can see, this was a truly creative and well thought-out domestic tourism marketing campaign.

How do we make sure we get there?

Domestic tourism marketing and promotion programmes need to be carefully monitored during their implementation to ensure that they are on track to achieving objectives. Periodic checks should be made at least every quarter to see if the preliminary results are satisfactory or if changes need to be made in the implementation of programmes and activities.

How do we know if we got there?

The DMO must demonstrate its accountability by evaluating the results and outcomes from its domestic tourism marketing and promotion. A good example here is from the Kansas City Convention and Visitors Association (KCCVA) in Missouri, USA. KCCVA has defined its four audiences as: (1) meeting and convention planners; (2) leisure travellers; (3) local community; and (4) KCCVA Organization. In its annual report, KCCVA specifically and comprehensively details the results and outcomes of the previous year's marketing and promotions for the four audiences.

KCCVA implemented a domestic leisure travel advertising campaign in 2011 and it generated 242,000 additional hotel room nights:

KCCVA generated 242,000 incremental hotel room nights

[KCCVA] executed a $1.1 million destination advertising campaign that generated 242,000 incremental hotel room nights and $94.6 million in incremental economic impact. The campaign realized a record-setting $88 return on investment for every KCCVA media dollar spent – a 42-percent hike from 2010.

(KCCVA, 2012)

Visiting friends and relatives (VFR) market

The VFR market in many countries represents a significant proportion of domestic tourism. As you will see in Chapter 14, VFRs are also important in international tourism. Evidence from around the world indicates that VFR represents from 30 per cent to 50 per cent of domestic tourist travel. For example, the UK Tourism Survey (UKTS) found that 35.8 per cent of all trips in the UK in 2010 involved visiting friends and relatives. For 2011, the National Visitor Survey estimated that 34 per cent of all overnight domestic trips by Australians had a VFR purpose. For Ireland in 2009, 32.5 per cent of the domestic trips by residents were for VFR.

Although this book classifies VFR and pleasure/leisure travel to be two different trip-purpose segments, there is some overlap between the two concepts. This is demonstrated in the treatment of these two markets in the United Kingdom Tourism Survey (UKTS). The UKTS divides the VFR market into two parts: (1) VFR-Holiday; and (2) pure VFR. The latter category of VFR is defined by UKTS as 'visiting friends and relatives' or 'VFR' is the term used for trips where the main reason for taking the trip is initially described as 'visiting friends and relatives', and which on subsequent probing is described as being mainly for some other reason rather than a holiday.

Since VFR is such a significant element of domestic and international tourism, it will be described in more detail in this chapter of the book. A special issue of the *Journal of Tourism Studies* in 1995 was a watershed event for research on the VFR market. Guest editors Joseph T. O'Leary and Alastair M. Morrison bemoaned the lack of respect that was given to VFRs by the tourism sector.

Moscardo *et al.* (2000) used an empirical research study to prove that the VFR market was not one large homogeneous market, but it was in fact composed of multiple sub-segments. These researchers pointed out that there was a difference between VFR as a trip purpose and VFR as an activity. Five factors were defined that differentiated VFRs: (1) type (VFR as a primary motivation or trip purpose vs. VFR as an activity); (2) scope (domestic vs. international); (3) range (short-haul vs long-haul); (4) accommodation used (accommodated with friends/relatives vs not accommodated with friends/relatives; and (5) focus of visit (visit friends vs visit relatives vs visit friends and visit relatives) (Figure 13.6).

The importance of the VFR is quite often underestimated for a variety of reasons. Elisa Backer of the University of Ballarat in Australia says this is mainly because VFRs have not been as deeply researched as other types of tourists:

VFR is well-known, but not known well

In comparison to its size, there has been little research into VFR travellers, their motivations, behaviours and characteristics, and the factors that influence their choices. This has led to their lack of recognition as a market segment and an assumption that they contribute little to local economies and tourism industries. While VFR travel is one of the largest and most significant forms of travel, 'VFR travel remains well-known but not known well.'

(Backer, 2009, p. 2)

The first reason is that there is an assumption that VFRs only stay at the homes of friends and relatives, and do not use hotels or other commercial accommodation. However, research has proven that this assumption is inaccurate as some VFRs do use commercial accommodation. Based on research conducted on the Sunshine Coast of Australia, Backer (2010) found that 26 per cent of VFRs stayed in commercial accommodation and she classified them as CVFRs. Braunlich and Nadkarni (1995) also reached a similar conclusion based upon research in the US. They found that over one-fifth of the VFR travellers in the East North Central Census region were hotel users.

The second reason is that the expenditures by VFRs and their hosts in a destinations' tourism sector are often assumed to be modest. However, several research studies have proven that this too is inaccurate. Some of the research suggests that VFRs outspend other domestic tourists in certain categories of expenditures (but not for lodging).

Another apparent reason why VFRs tend to be neglected is that some DMOs feel they cannot influence these people to travel to their destinations. The assumption is made that VFRs are most influenced by word of mouth and by invitations from their

Type	Scope	Range	Accommodation	Focus
		Short-haul	AFR	VF, VR, VFVR
		Long-haul	NAFR	VF, VR, VFVR
VFR as a major motive or trip type	Domestic	Short-haul	AFR	VF, VR, VFVR
		Long-haul	NAFR	VF, VR, VFVR
VFR as one activity on a trip	International	Short-haul	AFR	VF, VR, VFVR
		Long-haul	NAFR	VF, VR, VFVR
		Short-haul	AFR	VF, VR, VFVR
		Long-haul	NAFR	VF, VR, VFVR

Figure 13.6 Typology of visiting friends and relatives (VFR) market

Note: VFR = visiting friends and relatives; AFR = accommodated solely with friends and/ or relatives; NAFR = accommodated at least one night in commercial accommodation; VF = visit friends; VR = visit relatives; VFVR = visit both friends and relatives.

Source: Adapted from Moscardo et al., 2000.

friends and relatives. In fact, this is an erroneous assumption as many VFRs plan trips exactly the same way as do other tourists. Additionally, DMOs can promote the idea of VFR travel to local community residents.

There are several DMOs that have realized the value of the VFR market and they have implemented special marketing and promotion programmes aimed specifically at VFRs. Destination Melbourne in Australia is one of these and it introduced the 'Discover Your Own Backyard' VFR marketing campaign in 2011.

'Discover Your Own Backyard' VFR marketing campaign, Melbourne, Australia

Visiting friends and relatives (VFR) continues to be the largest driving factor for people visiting Melbourne. It is worth $2.8 billion to Melbourne's economy. Visitors spend on average $255 per night in Melbourne and are most likely to stay with a friend or relative during their stay. This represents a massive opportunity for communities throughout Melbourne.

In 2011, Destination Melbourne commenced the roll-out of Discover Your Own Backyard, a VFR marketing campaign aimed at increasing local residents' awareness of tourism related products and experiences in their region. The aim is to build community pride in residents and encourage dispersal and yield. Discover Your Own Backyard was built on the understanding that the host (the resident) has the greatest influence over visitor behaviour. If we can educate the host, we create a social and economic dividend for communities and support the visitor experience for people visiting their friends and relatives.

Destination Melbourne has developed an outstanding toolkit that explains to local communities and partners how they can implement the 'Discover Your Own Backyard' campaign.

Destination Melbourne conducted research on the VFR market in Melbourne and VFRs' economic impacts on the city. They found that about one-third of all the visitors to Melbourne were VFRs and that overnight VFR travellers spent an average of AUD 570 per trip in 2009.

Summary

Domestic tourism is a 'mainstay' of the tourism sectors in many parts of the world, particularly in the developed nations. It is less important in the developing world, but domestic tourism is rapidly expanding in some of these countries and notably in China and India. Unfortunately domestic tourism is often given a second-class status compared to international tourism.

The benefits of domestic tourism are significant albeit somewhat less well recognized than the advantages of international tourism. It is more dispersed within a country than international tourism, and also tends to be less seasonal. Local residents have the opportunity to have a first-hand experience of the natural and cultural resources of their own countries. Domestic tourism enhances national pride and has social and cultural benefits. Local residents also become more effective ambassadors for their tourism sectors.

There are several significant issues and challenges in the development and marketing of domestic tourism. The first issue is to whom the responsibility for domestic tourism should be assigned. Another issue is the competition between domestic tourism and international tourism and this has several levels; for example, competition for increasingly scarce government funding; domestic vs. outbound destination competition for local resident travel; and behavioral conflicts between local and international tourists.

Another issue with domestic tourism – and it also is present in international tourism – is whether day visitors (day-trippers) should be included. There are parts of the tourism sector that believe only overnight visitors should be classified as tourists. However, day visitors have a major positive economic impact on several destinations and many destinations include them within domestic tourism.

The future growth potential for domestic tourism varies by country, but overall the prospects are positive, and particularly in the countries with the highest populations. Factors such as growing housing incomes and increases in car ownership will spur domestic tourism in developing countries. The growth rates of domestic tourism will be more muted in developed countries due to unfavourable economic conditions and competition from sometimes cheaper outbound tourism destinations.

The trends and influences on domestic tourism have included changes in demographics, trip purposes, trip planning and travel arrangements, psychographics and lifestyles, special-interests, technology uses, recessionary or poorer economic conditions in many developed countries, relative pricing levels within domestic versus outbound tourism destinations and the development of low-cost carrier (LCC) airlines.

There are several market segments in domestic tourism that are significant and enjoying growth. These include the family travel, multi-generational travel, luxury travel, special-interest travel, agritourism, golf tourism and travel to theme parks.

The destination marketing system should be followed in developing and implementing a marketing strategy and plan for domestic tourism. As a top priority, the DMO must have in-depth research data on the characteristics of domestic tourists and use these data in forming its approach to market segmentation. The DMO needs to select domestic tourism target markets and a positioning–image–branding approach to communicate with and attract these tourists. Several DMOs design and implement integrated marketing communications (IMC) campaigns for their domestic markets.

The VFR market is significant in domestic tourism but it is often underestimated and has not been as deeply researched as other market segments. DMOs often do not engage in VFR marketing and promotion because of erroneous assumptions about VFRs. These mistaken assumptions are that VFRs never use commercial accommodations; that VFRs do not spend as much money as other tourists; and that DMOs cannot influence VFRs to travel to their destinations.

To accomplish its domestic tourism marketing and promotion role, a DMO must complete the following tasks:

- Analyse the trends in domestic tourism volumes and within specific market segments of domestic tourism.
- Conduct research on the characteristics of domestic tourism markets.
- Complete a market segmentation analysis and then select domestic tourism target markets.
- Prepare a positioning–image–branding approach for domestic tourism.
- Develop and implement an integrated marketing communications campaign for domestic tourism, integrating the 8 Ps of marketing (product, price, place, promotion, packaging, programming, partnership and people).
- Continuously monitor the implementation of domestic tourism marketing and promotion.
- Demonstrate accountability by evaluating the results and outcomes from domestic tourism marketing and promotional programmes.
- Conduct research on the size and impacts of VFR travel in the destination.
- Engage in marketing and promotions aimed at encouraging more VFR travel to the destination.

Review questions

1 What are the major benefits of developing and promoting domestic tourism?
2 How large is the domestic tourism market? Answer this question by considering the domestic tourism market in selected countries.
3 How important is domestic tourism vis-à-vis international tourism?
4 What have been the recent trends in domestic tourism?
5 What are the future prospects for domestic tourism?
6 What are the overall issues and challenges with domestic tourism?
7 Who should be responsible for domestic tourism marketing and promotion within a country and what are the reasons behind your opinion?

8 Should day travellers (day-trippers) be included in domestic tourism? Why or why not?

9 Why is it difficult to effectively market and promote domestic tourism, without in-depth research data on domestic travellers and their segmentation?

10 What have been some of the outstanding domestic tourism marketing and promotion campaigns in recent times?

11 How important is the visiting friends and relatives market in domestic tourism?

12 What are some of the reasons for underestimating the contributions of VFRs to the tourism sector?

References

AECOM. 2011. 2010 Theme Index. The Global Attractions Attendance Report.

Agarwal, S. 2002. Restructuring seaside tourism: The resort lifecycle. *Annals of Tourism Research*, 29(1), 25–55.

Agnew, M.D., and Palutikof, J.P. 2006. Impacts of short-term climate variability in the UK on demand for domestic and international tourism. *Climate Research*, 31, 109–120.

Athanasopoulos, G., and Hyndman, R.J. 2006. Modelling and Forecasting Australian Domestic Tourism. Department of Econometrics and Business Statistics, Monash University.

Backer, E. 2007. VFR travel: An examination of the expenditures of VFR travellers and their hosts. *Current Issues in Tourism*, 10(4), 366–377.

——2009. The VFR Trilogy. Refereed paper. In Carlsen, J., Hughes, M., Holmes, K., and Jones, R. (eds). See Change: Proceedings of the CAUTHE Conference, 10–13 Feb, 2009, Fremantle, WA, Australia. CD-ROM, Curtin University, WA, Australia.

——2010. Opportunities for commercial accommodation in VFR travel. *International Journal of Tourism Research*, 12(4), 334–354.

——2012. VFR travel: It *is* underestimated. *Tourism Management*, 33(1), 74–79.

Banyan Tree Hotels & Resorts. 2012. http://www.banyantree.com/image_gallery

Beditz, J.F., and Kass, J.R. 2010. Golf Participation in America, 2010–2020. Jupiter, FL: National Golf Foundation.

Bigné, J.E., Andreu, L., and Gnoth, J. 2005. The theme park experience: An analysis of pleasure, arousal and satisfaction. *Tourism Management*, 26(6), 833–844.

Braunlich, C.G., and Nadkarni, N. 1995. The importance of the VFR market to the hotel industry. *Journal of Tourism Studies*, 6(1), 38–47.

Canadian Tourism Commission. 2008. US Travel Market Behavioural Study. Summary Report.

Central Intelligence Agency. 2012. The World Factbook. https://www.cia.gov/library/publications/the-world-factbook/geos/ch.html

China Daily USA. 2012. China's Q1 tourism revenues rise 23 per cent. 14 April.

China National Tourism Administration. 2012. News. http://en.cnta.gov.cn

Destination Melbourne. 2011. Visiting Friends & Relatives. http://www.destinationmelbourne.com.au/industry/research/visiting-friends-relatives/

Eijgelaar, E., Peeters, P., and Piket, P. 2008. Domestic and International Tourism in a Globalized World. International Conference, 'Ever the twain shall meet – relating international and domestic tourism', of Research Committee RC50 International Tourism, International Sociological Association Jaipur, Rajasthan, India.

Eurostat. 2011. Domestic Tourism Europeans Spend 77 Per Cent of their Holiday Trips in their Own Country.

Fáilte Ireland. 2010. Domestic Tourism 2009.

Fair Oaks Farms. 2010. Fair Oaks Farms. http://www.fofarms.com/en/home#Scene_1

Figart, F., and Nelson, L. 2005. The growing market for special-interest tours. *The Courier*, May.

Government of Canada. 2011. Tourism Sector – Key Facts 2010.

Heath, E. 2011. International Best Practices in Stimulating Domestic Tourism. University of Pretoria.

Helsinki City Tourist and Convention Bureau. 2012. Strategy for Domestic Marketing. http://www.visithelsinki.fi/en/professional/get-know-helsinki/strategy/strategy-domestic-marketing

International Luxury Travel Market/Horwath HTL. 2011. The Future of Luxury Travel.

Irish Tourist Industry Confederation. 2009. Review and Outlook for Ireland's Domestic Travel Market.

Jolly, D.A., and Reynolds, K.A. 2005. Consumer Demand for Agricultural and On-Farm Nature Tourism. UC Small Farm Center Research Brief.

Kansas City Convention and Visitors Association. 2012. 2011 Annual Report. Kansas City Convention and Visitors Association.

Kim, J.H., and Ritchie, B.W. 2012. Motivation-based typology: An empirical study of golf tourists. *Journal of Hospitality and Tourism Research*, 36(2), 251–280.

Kim, S., Kim, J.H., and Ritchie, B.W. 2008. Segmenting overseas golf tourists by the concept of specialization. *Journal of Travel and Tourism Marketing*, 25(2), 199–217.

Liu, D. 2011. Analyses and prospects of China's domestic tourism 2010–2011. In Zhang, G., Song, R., and Liu, D. (eds). Green Book of China's Tourism 2011: China's Tourism Development Analysis and Forecast. China Outbound Tourism Research Institute.

Mendiratta, A. 2011. Domestic Tourism: Home-Grown Growth. CNN's TASK Group.

Ministry of Economic Development, New Zealand. 2012. About the DTS. http://www.med.govt.nz/sectors-industries/tourism/tourism-research-data/domestic-tourism/domestic-travel-survey-information

Ministry of Tourism, Government of India. 2011. Domestic Tourism Registers an Impressive Growth During 2010. http://tourism.gov.in/TourismDivision/AboutDivision.aspx?Name=MarketResearchandStatistics

Mishell, D. 2011. California Tourism Outlook 2011–2012.

Morrison, A.M. 2010. Hospitality and Travel Marketing. Clifton Park, NY: Cengage Delmar.

Moscardo, G., Pearce, P., Morrison, A.M., Green, D., and O'Leary, J.T. 2000. Developing a typology for understanding visiting friends and relatives markets. *Journal of Travel Research*, 38(3), 251–259.

National Golf Foundation. 2010. Golf Industry Overview – 2010. http://www.ngf.org/pages/golf-industry-overview

Northern Ireland Tourist Board, VisitEngland, VisitScotland, Visit Wales. 2011. The UK Tourist: Statistics 2010.

NYC & Company, Inc. 2012. Mayor Bloomberg and NYC & Company Announce the Muppets as New York City's Official Family Ambassadors. http://www.nycand

company.org/communications/mayor-bloomberg-and-nyc-company-announce-the-muppets-as-new-york-citys-official-family-ambassadors

Pangaea Network. 2012. Luxury Market Trends. 2nd edn. Milan: Pangaea Network.

Pearce, D.G., and Schott, C. 2011. Domestic vs. outbound booking and channel choice behavior: Evidence from New Zealand. *International Journal of Culture, Tourism and Hospitality Research*, 5(2), 112–127.

Petrick, J.F., and Backman, S.J. 2002. An examination of the determinants of golf travelers' satisfaction. *Journal of Travel Research*, 40(3), 252–258.

Preferred Hotel Group. 2011. Multi-Generational Travel. The Next Powerful Growth Opportunity in the Travel Industry.

Prideaux, B. 2000. The resort development spectrum – a new approach to modeling resort development. *Tourism Management*, 21(3), 225–240.

Robert Trent Jones Golf Trail. 2012. The Robert Trent Jones Golf Trail. http://www.rtjgolf.com/

Robinson, P. 2009. Valuing the Day Visitor. http://www.insights.org.uk/articleitem.aspx?title=ValuingtheDayVisitor

Saltzman, D. 2010. Tapping into lucrative family travel markets. http://www.travelmarketreport.com/leisure?articleID=3149&LP=1

South African Tourism. 2004. Domestic Tourism Growth Strategy 2004–2007.

Southall, C. 2010. Family Tourism. http://www.insights.org.uk/articleitem.aspx?title=Family+Tourism

Sri Lanka Tourism Development Authority. 2011. Guidelines for Local Domestic Tourism. http://www.sltda.gov.lk/domestic_tourism

Statistics Canada. 2011. Travel Survey of Residents of Canada (TSRC). http://www23.statcan.gc.ca:81/imdb/p2SV.pl?Function=getSurvey&SDDS=3810&lang=en&db=imdb&adm=8&dis=2

Strategic Networks Group. 2009. Economic Impact Study of Golf for Canada.

Tourism Australia. 2009. No Leave No Life. Rewarding Hard-Working Aussies with a Holiday. http://www.noleavenolife.com/

Tourism Industry Association of New Zealand. 2005. Domestic tourism promotion: A discussion paper.

Tourism Queensland. 2011. Understanding Our Consumers. TQ's Domestic Market Segmentation. http://www.tq.com.au/marketing/understanding-our-consumer-tq-domestic-market-segmentation/understanding-our-consumers-tq-domestic-market-segmentation_home.cfm

Tourism Research Australia. 2011. What is driving Australians' travel choices?

——2012. Travel by Australians. December 2011 Quarterly Results of the National Visitor Survey.

US Travel Association. 2011. US Travel Answer Sheet. Facts about a Leading American Industry That's More Than Just Fun.

Veeck, G., Che, D., and Veeck, A. 2006. America's changing farmscape: A study of agricultural tourism in Michigan. *The Professional Geographer*, 58(3), 235–248.

Virginia Tourism Corporation. 2011. Virginia Tourism Corporation Strategic Marketing Plan FY12.

VisitEngland. 2011. Methods and Performance Report. http://www.visitengland.org/Images/UKTS%202010%20-%20Methods%20Performance%20Report_tcm30-29926.pdf

——2012. Holidays at Home are GREAT. http://www.visitengland.org/marketing/HAHAG/index.aspx

World Travel and Tourism Council. 2012. Travel and Tourism Economic Impact 2012 Brazil.

Wu, B., Zhu, H., and Xu, X. 2000. Trends in China's domestic tourism development at the turn of the century. *International Journal of Contemporary Hospitality Management*, 12(5), 296–299.

Young, R. 2010. Not Quite so Much Domestic Bliss. http://luxurysociety.com/articles/2010/05/not-quite-so-much-domestic-bliss

Chapter 14

International pleasure and leisure travel markets

Learning objectives

1 Indicate the size of the worldwide international tourist market and the distribution of tourist arrivals by region and for the leading destinations.

2 Elaborate on the trends and future prospects for international tourist arrivals.

3 Discuss the major challenges involved with inbound international tourism to a destination.

4 Identify and profile the emerging geographic origin markets.

5 Review selected market segments that have demonstrated recent growth potential.

6 Explain a general procedure for marketing and promotion towards international pleasure and leisure travel markets.

Introduction

Destinations are normally very keen to attract international visitors, both for economic and political prestige reasons. Domestic travel is often seen as not being as 'glamorous' as inbound tourism and politicians tend to talk more about the numbers of international tourists to their countries and the economic benefits they generate. The rationale for this is rather simple; international tourists inject 'new money' into a country's economy; domestic tourists just 'recycle' money within the country's economy. This argument tends to be quite unfair to domestic tourism, as it has major beneficial impacts on various regions within countries. However, from a macro perspective, there is truth to this argument (see VisitBritain quote below).

International tourism has been on a long-term growth trend, although there have been some short-term downturns due to economic and other crises. Regionally, the Asia-Pacific has been gaining market share and Europe's proportion of total worldwide tourist arrivals has been declining. This trend is forecast to continue until 2030.

Marketing and promoting to international pleasure and leisure markets has a unique set of challenges. The 'openness' of the tourism sector to the influences of external factors is great and tourism is particularly vulnerable to economic and political dislocations, natural disasters, and health and security crises.

For international tourism, every DMO needs a market strategy: this is a clear and well-justified set of country origin markets upon which the DMO will focus its marketing and promotions. A general marketing approach for international markets using the *Destination Marketing System* is explained in this chapter.

'Inbound tourism = export earnings for Britain'

Inbound tourism can be thought of as export earnings for Britain, and during 2011 these exports amounted to £17.76 billon for the British economy: that is more than the total construction costs of the new Crossrail scheme that will ease congestion and bring 1.5 million more people within 45 minutes commuting distance of London's key business districts, as well as making it far easier for visitors to get around the capital and to reach transport hubs that will link them with other parts of Britain such as the Midlands and West of England.

(VisitBritain, 2012a)

Size of the international tourist market

The most comprehensive worldwide statistics of tourist numbers are maintained by the UN World Tourism Organization (UNWTO). This chapter begins by reviewing recent statistics from UNWTO, starting with the total arrivals by region and then for the top destinations. You should realize when viewing these statistics that they include other trip purposes in addition to pleasure/leisure travel. In other words, the figures do not separate out pleasure/leisure travel from business, VFR and other personal travel.

There are no universal averages for worldwide travel by trip purpose according to the definition used in this book, but a few indicative figures are provided in Table 14.1. Based on these seven countries' statistics, pleasure and leisure travel represents the major market share of inbound travel, followed generally by VFR and then business. For these countries, pleasure/leisure travel represents from approximately 38–83 per cent. Spain has the highest proportion (82.6 per cent) suggesting it is primarily a vacation/holiday destination for international tourists.

VFR as an inbound travel market is significant for six of these seven countries; and for these six, it is in the range of 25–35 per cent of all international tourist arrivals. Inbound international business travel is also significant, but only for five of these seven countries. For these five countries, business travel represents from approximately 13–22 per cent of all international tourist arrivals.

The UNWTO does provide a breakdown by trip purpose, but it does not exactly match this book's definition. For 2010, UNWTO estimates that 'leisure, recreation and holidays' were 54.5 per cent of all international tourist arrivals; 'business and professional' travel represented 16 per cent. The remaining 29.5 per cent was for 'VFR, health, religion, other'.

Total arrivals by region

The UNWTO World Tourism Barometer estimated there were 980 million international tourist arrivals worldwide in 2011 (UNWTO, 2012). This was the highest level for one year in the history of the world.

Europe received the highest proportion of these arrivals, at 51.2 per cent (Figure 14.1). Asia and the Pacific had the second largest share, at 22.1 per cent; and the Americas had 15.9 per cent. The Middle East and Africa each had just over 5 per cent of the total arrivals. The split between arrivals in advanced economies (53.3 per cent) and emerging economies (46.7 per cent) was quite even.

Total arrivals by destination country

According to the UNWTO's 2010 figures, France was the top destination in the world, followed by the USA and China (Figure 14.2). Spain and Italy were in the fourth and fifth places. As you will learn in the discussions on trends and emerging markets, China has been steadily climbing the world ranks in recent years and may soon overtake the USA to earn the second spot after France. Turkey and Malaysia are two other countries that have been gaining ground in terms of total arrivals.

Table 14.1 Trip purpose distributions for selected countries (2009–2010)

Trip purpose	Australia	Canada	Ireland	New Zealand	Spain	UK	USA
Holiday	44.0%	50.3%	44.7%	38.2%	82.6%	38.0%	53.5%
VFR	25.0%	26.6%	34.9%	32.6%	5.5%	29.0%	20.2%
Business	17.0%	15.2%	13.3%	5.6%	8.3%	22.0%	21.9%
Other	14.0%	7.9%	7.1%	23.6%	3.6%	11.0%	4.4%
Total	100.0%	100.0%	100.0%	100.0%	100.0%	100.0%	100.0%

Source: UNWTO, 2012.

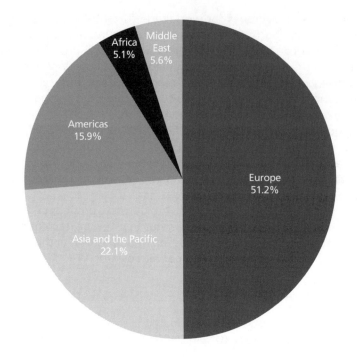

Figure 14.1 International tourist arrivals by region, 2011
Source: UNWTO, 2012.

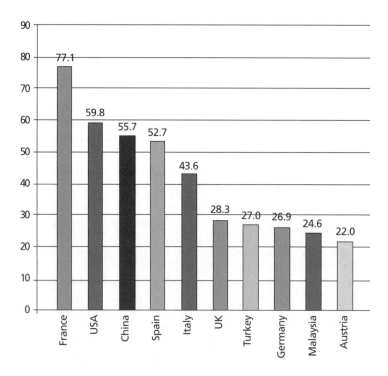

Figure 14.2 Top ten country destinations by total arrivals, 2010
Source: UNWTO, 2012.

When considering the international tourist figures for individual countries, there is variation in origin markets. Eleven examples are shown below of the top ten origins for individual countries (in either 2010 or 2011).

- *Australia*: 1. New Zealand; 2. UK; 3. China; 4. USA; 5. Japan; 6. Singapore; 7. Malaysia; 8. South Korea; 9. Hong Kong; 10. Germany
- *Canada*: 1. USA; 2. UK; 3. France; 4. Germany; 5. Australia; 6. China; 7. Japan; 8. South Korea; 9. India; 10. Mexico
- *China*: 1. Korea; 2. Japan; 3. Russia; 4. USA; 5. Malaysia; 6. Singapore; 7. Philippines; 8. Mongolia; 9. Canada; 10. Australia
- *Germany*: 1. Netherlands; 2. USA; 3. Switzerland; 4. UK; 5. Italy; 6. Austria; 7. France; 8. Belgium; 9. Denmark; 10. Spain
- *Italy*: 1. Germany; 2. USA; 3. France; 4. UK; 5. Austria; 6. Spain; 7. Netherlands; 8. Switzerland; 9. Japan; 10. Russia
- *Malaysia*: 1. Singapore; 2. Indonesia; 3. Thailand; 4. China; 5. Brunei; 6. India; 7. Australia; 8. UK; 9. Japan; 10. Philippines
- *New Zealand*: 1. Australia; 2. UK; 3. USA; 4. China; 5. Japan; 6. Germany; 7. South Korea; 8. Canada; 9. Singapore; 10. Taiwan
- *Spain*: 1. UK; 2. Germany; 3. France; 4. Italy; 5. Netherlands; 6. Portugal; 7. Belgium; 8. Ireland; 9. Switzerland; 10. USA
- *Turkey*: 1. Germany; 2. Bulgaria; 3. Iran; 4. Georgia; 5. Syria; 6. Greece; 7. Russia; 8. Azerbaijan; 9. France; 10. UK
- *UK*: 1. France; 2. Germany; 3. USA; 4. Irish Republic; 5. Spain; 6. Netherlands; 7. Italy; 8. Belgium; 9. Poland; 10. Australia
- *USA*: 1. Canada; 2. Mexico; 3. UK; 4. Japan; 5. Germany; 6. France; 7. Brazil; 8. South Korea; 9. Australia; 10. Italy.

While this is only a small selection of countries, there are some noticeable similarities in sources. The UK, Germany and the USA appear in almost all the top ten lists. In most cases, nearby and adjacent countries represent the main sources of international tourists.

International tourism expenditures by country

Which countries' residents spend the most on international tourism? Table 14.2 provides the answer. Germany was at the top of the table with $78.1 billion in 2010, followed by the USA and China. The UK and France were in fourth and fifth positions respectively.

In addition to the total spending by the residents of a particular country, DMOs must also consider factors related to the 'yield' of the market. Yield can be expressed in different ways, but typically it means the trip per capita expenditures or daily average expenditures in the destination. For example, the UK's top two markets in terms of total inbound visits are France and Germany; however, the USA is the top-yielding market with trip per capita spending of £2,133 compared to £1,142 for France and £1,193 for Germany. This means a US visitor is almost twice as valuable to the British economy as a visitor from France or Germany.

The seasonality or distribution of expenditures over the 12 months of the year is another important issue when assessing the yield from different country markets. For example, if the spending from a specific country market tends to be concentrated in a

Table 14.2 International tourism expenditures, 2010

Country	International tourism expenditures, 2010 (USD billions)
1. Germany	78.1
2. USA	75.5
3. China	54.9
4. UK	50.0
5. France	38.5
6. Canada	29.6
7. Japan	27.9
8. Italy	27.1
9. Russia	26.5
10. Australia	22.2

Source: UNWTO, 2012.

destination's off-peak season, the DMO may decide that the yield from that market is more valuable and attractive.

The 'import content' required to serve particular country markets must also be taken into account. For example, serving certain countries may require the importation of foodstuffs from their countries, resulting in a 'leakage' from the local economy. They may also stay in hotels and resorts owned by companies and travel with branches of travel trade companies from their home countries. So economic leakages from the local destination's economy should be considered when yield levels are being estimated.

Trends and future prospects for international tourism

The long-term trend has been for international tourism to be increasing (Figure 14.3). In fact, worldwide tourism arrivals have grown from 528 million in 1995 to 980 million in 2011. As you can see from the trend lines in Figure 14.3, there were just three years from 1995 to 2011 where international tourism arrivals declined: 2000, 2003 and 2009.

The impact of 9/11

The impact of terrorism on tourism was brought to the fore after the September 11 bombing of the World Trade Center and the Pentagon. The events of September 2001 sent shock waves through the travel and tourism industry. The industry lost 10 percent or more of its business worldwide, with some countries experiencing losses of up to 30 percent.

(Crawford, 2012)

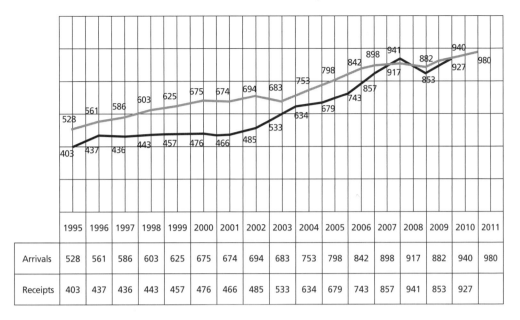

	1995	1996	1997	1998	1999	2000	2001	2002	2003	2004	2005	2006	2007	2008	2009	2010	2011
Arrivals	528	561	586	603	625	675	674	694	683	753	798	842	898	917	882	940	980
Receipts	403	437	436	443	457	476	466	485	533	634	679	743	857	941	853	927	

Figure 14.3 Trends in world tourist arrivals and receipts, 1995–2011
Source: UNWTO, 2011c; UNWTO, 2012.

The future prospects for international tourism are bright, but growth will be at a slower pace than before. In October 2011, UNWTO released its new long-term forecast for international tourism, *Tourism Towards 2030*. UNWTO predicted that international tourist arrivals would grow at an average annual rate of 3.3 per cent and reach 1.8 billion by 2030:

Tourism towards 2030 (UNWTO)

International tourism will continue to grow in the period 2010–2030, but at a more moderate pace than the past decades, with the number of international tourist arrivals worldwide increasing by an average 3.3 per cent a year. As a result, an average 43 million additional international tourists will join the tourism marketplace every year.

At the projected pace of growth, arrivals will pass the 1 billion mark by 2012, up from 940 million in 2010. By 2030, arrivals are expected to reach 1.8 billion, meaning that in two decades' time, five million people will be crossing international borders for leisure, business or other purposes such as visiting friends and family every day.

All the world's regions will experience growth in international tourist arrivals to 2030. However, according to this UNWTO forecast, Europe and the Americas will continue to lose market share to the Asia and Pacific region. Europe's share will fall from 51.2 per cent in 2011 to 41 per cent in 2030; the Americas' share will drop to 14 per cent from 15.9 per cent. The Asia and Pacific region's share will grow from 22.1 per cent in 2011 to 30 per cent in 2030 (Table 14.3).

Table 14.3 Distributions of international tourist arrivals, 1980–2030

Regions	1980 shares (%)	2010 (arrivals in millions)	2020 (arrivals in millions)	2030 (arrivals in millions)	2030 shares (%)
Europe	64%	475.3	620.0	744.0	41%
Asia and the Pacific	8%	204.0	355.0	535.0	30%
Americas	22%	149.7	198.0	248.0	14%
Middle East	3%	60.9	101.0	149.0	8%
Africa	3%	50.3	85.0	134.0	7%
World	100%	940.2	1,359.0	1,810.0	100%

Source: UNWTO, 2011a.

Challenges

Marketing and promoting to international pleasure and leisure travel markets presents a unique set of challenges, most of which are not found with domestic tourism. The scale and complexity of international markets is perhaps the most serious challenge.

Where to focus marketing and promotion?

The world is so big with so many countries that the major challenge for DMOs is where to market and promote their destinations. They obviously cannot afford to be marketing in every country of the world, so choices have to be made about where to focus effort to produce the best return on investment (ROI). One of the most obvious solutions to this challenge is to focus on the markets that are presently generating the most tourists and this type of strategy is the most popular, especially for those DMOs with limited resources. The Canadian Tourism Commission (CTC) operates in its top ten inbound markets plus Brazil:

'Where we market Canada'

The Canadian Tourism Commission operates in eleven countries* around the world. Our global marketing and sales teams provide expert knowledge and support to the local travel trade, conduct media relations and promotional activities, launch consumer advertising and promotional campaigns, and maintain a strong presence at consumer and trade shows. We are a vital resource for the Canadian tourism industry in international markets.

(2012)

(* Australia, Brazil, China, France, Germany, India, Japan, Mexico, South Korea, UK, USA)

VisitBritain has decided to focus on twenty-one priority markets that offer the best immediate return and best future prospects for Britain.

Another type of strategy is to assume that the productivity and benefits of markets will change in the future and to try to forecast the markets' future potential. This is the market strategy being followed by Tourism Australia (TA), which has divided its target markets by country into three categories. TA has identified nineteen countries/regions for its major focus until 2020 (Figure 14.4). As you can see, the top-priority markets (Category 1) are China, UK, USA, Australia, New Zealand, Japan and South Korea.

Some academic scholars have suggested other ways to select international target markets. For example, Soo Cheong Jang and his co-researchers have recommended a portfolio approach in which the risks and rewards from each market are calculated and balanced. The unique contribution of these works in the assessment of market 'risks' in addition to 'rewards' and in suggesting that DMOs need to balance the risk and rewards to derive the optimum scenarios for country market selections.

Balance of payments deficits

There are several countries that have balance of payments deficits for tourism. This means that their own residents spend more for tourism in other countries than international tourists spend in their countries. Among the top ten destinations, three countries have deficits: Germany, the UK and China (Figure 14.5). The other seven destinations have positive balances, with Spain and the USA having the largest surpluses. For those with balance of payments deficits, this means that their tourism 'exports' are less than their tourism 'imports'. This is not a good long-term situation for a country's tourism sector.

What can a country do that has a deficit in its balance of payments in tourism? There are three main strategy options: (1) attract more international visitors; (2) convince residents to holiday or vacation at home rather than going abroad; and (3) change the proportions of international tourist country sources. The third strategy

Category 1

- **Potential to be worth over AU$5 billion by 2020**
  - China, UK, USA, Australia
- **Potential to be worth over AU$3 billion by 2020**
  - New Zealand, Japan, South Korea

Category 2

- **Potential to be worth over AU$1.5 to $3 billion by 2020**
  - Singapore, Gulf countries, Malaysia, Germany, Indonesia, Hong Kong, India, Canada, France

Category 3

- **Fast emerging**
  - Brazil, Vietnam
- **High piority**
  - Italy

Figure 14.4 Market strategy of Tourism Australia
Source: Tourism Australia, 2012.

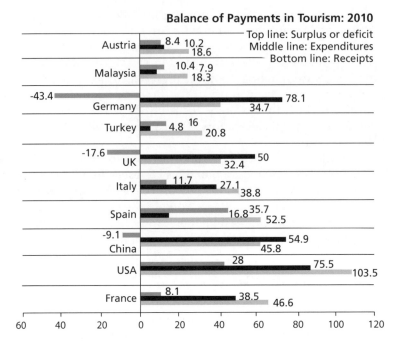

Figure 14.5 Tourism balance of payments situation for world's top country tourism destinations in 2010
Source: UNWTO data, 2012.

may not be as obvious to you, so a little further explanation is given. Often, destinations have positive tourism balances with certain countries, but run deficits with other countries. For example, Canadians spend more in tourism in the USA than US residents spend in Canada. Thus, the USA has a positive balance in tourism vis-à-vis Canada. In fact, the USA has positive tourism balances with seven of its top ten inbound markets; and runs relatively small deficits with Mexico, Italy and South Korea. By more intensive marketing to its seven 'positive' contributors (Canada, UK, Japan, Germany, France, Brazil and Australia), the USA might further improve its tourism balance of payments.

One example of a country that has had a 'deficit' turned into a 'surplus' in tourism is, in fact, the USA. The so-called 'travel gap' was a huge economic issue for decades in the USA. It became so bad that one of their presidents asked people to not travel as much abroad.

Marketing and promotion challenges

Gretzel *et al.* (2006) identified six major marketing and promotion challenges that DMOs are facing. These apply to both international and domestic marketing; however, they become even more acute when marketing abroad.

- *Adapting to technological change*: It is fair to say that many DMOs are still adapting to the changes that information communication technologies (ICTs) have brought to destination management and marketing. There is still a need to invest more in ICTs in many destinations and to train staff to use ICTs more effectively. Additionally, websites and related tools need to be improved to meet tourists' unique needs and expectations. As you can imagine, the challenge of ICTs is greater and is more complex when a DMO is communicating in several international markets.

- *Managing expectations*: DMOs serve a variety of different publics, internally in their communities and externally outside of their destinations. DMOs must play a leadership role and this is particularly true for international marketing and promotion. They must constantly monitor changes in consumer behaviour in a variety of origin countries, and this alone is very difficult to accomplish.
- *From destination marketing to destination management*: This was an issue that was addressed in Chapter 1 and you learned there that there has been a transition from destination marketing to the broader concept of destination management. DMOs need to get more involved in planning and development projects, and must make sure that the needs of international guests are considered in destination planning and development.
- *Confronting new levels of competition*: Competition in tourism is now global and becoming increasingly intense. DMOs must also deal with internal competition from other economic sectors apart from tourism, in environments where funding support from government is becoming more limited. It is noteworthy here that there have been significant budget cuts for several major national DMOs, including the Canadian Tourism Commission and VisitBritain.
- *Recognizing creative partnering as the new way of life*: Chapter 6 was devoted to partnership and team-building and highlighted the growing importance of this role for DMOs. Partnering in international marketing takes on even greater importance as the challenges are greater, and joining up with others can help to enhance effectiveness and reduce risks. There may be a lack of incentives for partnering but the positive outcomes of successful partnerships can be substantial. You may remember the partnership of the Scandinavian country DMOs in operating a joint office in the USA, and this is a great case study in how to partner for mutual benefit.
- *Finding new measures of success*: The importance of showing accountability for effective governance was stressed in Chapter 8. Performance measurement is especially important in international marketing and promotion, since there are alternatives available for the investment of resources, e.g. different countries can be targeted. More sophisticated models may be required in future to demonstrate the viability and the outcomes from international market and marketing strategies.

In order to market effectively at an international level, a DMO needs the authority to do so and must have adequate financial and human resources to carry out the mandate. The USA represents an interesting case study here, since up until 2012 it did not have such a body with the official mandate and budget to market and promote towards international tourists. After much lobbying by the tourism sector and demonstrating that the US share of world tourism dropped from 2000 to 2010, the Federal Government passed the Travel Promotion Act of 2010. A new body was created, Brand USA, and was hoping to raise $150 million for promoting the country abroad by means of tourism private sector contributions plus a $14 fee per person from the thirty-six countries in the visa waiver programme.

'Brand USA to sell America abroad'

The law created a nonprofit travel promotion corporation, now known as Brand USA, which is being financed with both public and private money, to run the marketing campaign. The first three targets are Britain, Canada and Japan, said James Evans, chief executive of Brand USA. Later, the promotion may move on to Germany, France, Japan, Brazil, China and India.

(Edleson, 2012)

Another major marketing challenge is in adapting approaches and campaigns for different languages and cultures. For example, DMO websites must be translated into several languages and great care must also be taken in adapting to the varied cultural nuances among countries. Many countries have their own social network sites and adjustments must also be made for these.

Susceptibility to crises

The trend lines for worldwide international tourism shown earlier in Figure 14.3 clearly prove that tourism is quite susceptible to major crises that can cause declines in tourist movements and expenditures, albeit short-term in duration. For example, this can be seen in the visitor arrivals for five different countries in 2011 that suffered from such crises:

- *Egypt*: Arrivals declined by 32 per cent in 2011 compared to 2010.
- *Japan*: Arrivals declined by 28 per cent in 2011 compared to 2010 (due to natural disaster).
- *Lebanon*: Arrivals declined by 24 per cent in 2011 compared to 2010.
- *Syria*: Arrivals declined by 41 per cent in 2011 compared to 2010.
- *Tunisia*: Arrivals declined by 31 per cent in 2011 compared to 2010.

Tourism is an 'open system' economic sector and therefore it can be rapidly and extensively affected by developments and incidents in external environments. For example, the tropical island paradise of Jamaica is under threat from its well-publicized and above-average rates of crime and violence:

Trouble in Paradise? Jamaica deals with crime and violence

Reports of Jamaica's corruption, crime and violence are frequently published in the local and international media. It is widely believed that these well-publicized incidents have serious negative implications for Jamaica's international image and reputation, and by extension, the tourism industry.

(Hall, 2012)

Although not necessarily a crisis, fluctuations in currency exchange rates can have a major impact on inbound tourism. If a destination's currency rate increases versus inbound origin countries' currencies, this may have a negative impact on arrivals; if the rate falls, a positive impact may be experienced.

Uneven distribution of tourists

It is common for international tourists to flock to the most popular destinations within countries, while other regions in the countries receive very few of them. A good example here is the distribution of international visitors to the UK. As you can see from Figure 14.6, there were 14.7 million visits to London, but there were only 2.4 million visits to Scotland, 0.9 million to Wales and 0.4 million to Northern Ireland.

In geographically larger countries than the UK, including Australia, Canada, China and Russia, this phenomenon is even more pronounced since tourists cannot possibly visit all the destinations within these nations in a short space of time. For Australia in 2011, 51 per cent of international tourists visited New South Wales; 35 per cent went to Queensland; and 32 per cent went to Victoria. However, the percentages were much lower for other parts of Australia; 13.6 per cent for Western Australia; 6.5 per cent for South Australia; 5.3 per cent for Northern Territory; 3.2 per cent for Australian Capital Territory; and 2.8 per cent for Tasmania.

This is a difficult challenge to deal with as it tends to be market-driven and thus hard to change. A DMO that represents an entire country cannot show favouritism to a region that attracts a below-average share of international tourists. However, the national DMO can encourage local DMOs to become more aggressive in marketing international tourism and try to convince travel agencies and tour operators to provide more products for international markets.

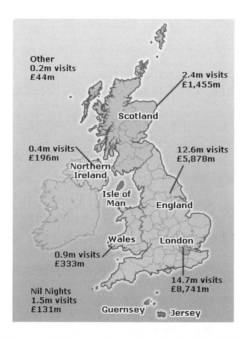

Figure 14.6 Distributions of international visits to the UK
Source: Copyright VisitBritain, 2012b.

Emerging geographic origin markets

The term 'emerging markets' is used by many DMOs around the world and usually these markets are defined by geography. When designated in this way, 'emerging' means that these geographic origin markets are growing at above-average rates when compared to the world as a whole. The four BRIC (Brazil–Russia–India–China) countries were already discussed in Chapter 12 and they are commonly pinpointed as being among the most promising emerging markets.

Brazil

With a population estimated at 205.7 million in 2012, Brazil is the fifth most populated nation in the world. Brazil's GDP in 2011 was around $2.28 trillion and $11,600 per capita (Central Intelligence Agency, 2012).

According to UNWTO estimates, the Brazilian outbound market was in 18th place in terms of international tourism expenditures in 2010 ($16.4 billion) (UNWTO, 2012). The favourite destination for Brazilians is the USA. The 'Market Snapshot' prepared by VisitBritain in the 'Brazil Market and Trade Profile' (January 2012), estimated there were 6.2 million outbound trips from Brazil in 2010.

Russia

Russia is the ninth most populated country in the world with 138.1 million people. The GDP of Russia in 2011 was $2.38 trillion and $16,700 per capita (Central Intelligence Agency, 2012). The Russian outbound market ranked ninth in the world in international tourism expenditures in 2010 ($26.5 billion) (UNWTO, 2012). VisitBritain (2012) reported that there were 24.3 million outbound trips from Russia in 2010.

India

India is the second most populous nation in the world with 1.21 billion people. Its GDP was estimated at $4.46 trillion in 2011 but only $3,700 per capita (Central Intelligence Agency, 2012).

UNWTO (2012) had the Indian outbound market in 23rd place in 2010 ($10.6 billion). There were 9.9 million outbound trips from India in 2010 according to VisitBritain (2012).

China

The People's Republic of China is the world's most populated country with 1.34 billion people. China's GDP was $11.29 trillion in 2011 and $8,400 per capita. It has one of the three largest economies in the world.

The Chinese outbound market ranked third in 2010 in terms of international tourism expenditures ($54.9 billion) (UNWTO, 2012). The outbound market from Mainland China has been growing rapidly. From 2005 to 2010, the volume grew from 31 to 57.4 million. The Chinese Tourism Academy (CTA) predicts further growth in 2011 up to 65 million. By 2020, it is expected that the outbound tourism volume will climb to approximately 100 million.

It is important to look further behind the overall volume statistics on Chinese outbound tourism and especially to analyse the destinations for these trips. Included in these statistics is the travel by Mainlanders to both Hong Kong and Macau, which are the two most popular destinations for Chinese outbound travellers. In fact, in 2010 approximately 67 per cent of all the outbound tourism from Mainland China was to Hong Kong and Macau. About 76 per cent of all the trips were to Hong Kong, Macau, Taiwan, Japan and South Korea. For other countries, the largest recipients were Vietnam (1,210,000); the USA (1,080,000); Thailand (1,010,000); Singapore (830,000); and Russia (710,000).

There is also a destination-specific way of defining 'emerging' markets, and you should be aware of that as well. For example, a single destination may have a unique situation where certain origin markets have above-average growth, but overall growth in that market is not as high. For example, the Canadian Tourism Commission classifies Japan as an emerging market, but most other countries view Japan as a mature market. Tourism Australia identifies Vietnam as one of its emerging markets.

Market segments with growth potential

In addition to looking at markets by geographic origin and trip purpose, the markets can also be analysed in greater detail by interests, activities and desired experiences. Within each country origin and trip purpose market, there is still much variety in tourism motivations and what people do on their trips.

There are international market segments that have been demonstrating growth potential in recent years, and these include several of the special-interest (SIT) markets that were identified in Chapter 12. In briefly reviewing 15 of these market segments, it needs to be said that they are found in both domestic and international pleasure and leisure travel, but here they are being discussed in the context of international tourism. There are very few accurate estimates on the size of these markets on a worldwide basis, so the discussion that follows is mainly descriptive. The following descriptions are just 'snapshots' of these market segments and much more could be said about each of them.

Adventure tourism

Adventure tourism is defined as 'any domestic or international trip that includes at least two of the following three aspects: physical activity, interaction with nature and cultural learning or exchange' (Adventure Travel Trade Association, 2010). Generally, adventure tourism is divided into 'hard' and 'soft' adventure based upon the physical demands and potential risks involved (Figure 14.7).

Destinations with rich and spectacular natural resources tend to be the most popular destinations for adventure tourism. According to the 2010 Adventure Tourism Development Index (ATDI), the top ten adventure tourism destinations in developed countries were Switzerland, Iceland, New Zealand, Canada, Germany, Sweden, Ireland, Norway, Finland and Austria. The top ten for developing countries were Israel, Slovak Republic, Chile, Estonia, Czech Republic, Bulgaria, Slovenia, Jordan, Romania and Latvia. Among these twenty destinations, New Zealand stands out as a place that has done an outstanding job of building and marketing adventure tourism:

New Zealand: a popular adventure tourism destination

New Zealand's landscape and temperate climate lends itself to outdoor activity. New Zealand is renowned for its range of adventure activities, including bungy jumping, jetboat riding, rafting and skiing.

But adventure means different things to different people, and the best aspect of the New Zealand adventure scene is that it provides activities rated from 'soft' to 'extreme' - from hiking and waterskiing, to mountain climbing and caving.

New Zealand's adventure tourism industry makes the most of a landscape surrounded by sea, criss-crossed by rivers and lakes, covered in native bush and with a central spine of spectacular snow-capped mountains. There's something for everyone who enjoys the outdoor lifestyle and the special sense of freedom the relatively sparsely populated land provides.

(New Zealand Ministry of Economic Development, 2012)

Figure 14.7 identifies adventure tourism activities and categorizes them into the 'hard' and 'soft' categories. As you can see, most of the activities are classified under 'soft' adventure tourism.

Cruise tourism

Cruising has enjoyed significant growth in past decades and is an important source of demand for destinations in the Caribbean, Mediterranean and other maritime and riverfront destinations. Cruise tourism has been fast gaining in popularity and its volume has been steadily increasing. However, the capsizing of the *Costa Concordia* off of Italy and resulting passenger deaths, as well as some well-publicized onboard food poisoning incidents, has led to some public concern about this mode of international pleasure and leisure travel.

The major destination for cruise tourism in the world is the Caribbean and the markets for Caribbean cruise tourism are primarily from North America. The Cruise Lines International Association (CLIA) estimated the worldwide average annual growth rate of cruise passengers at 7.2 per cent between 1990 and 2009. The 2009 worldwide cruise market was 13.4 million, with 76 per cent of the demand from North America. Approximately 92.5 per cent of the North American passengers are from the USA. The Florida–Caribbean Cruise Association predicted that there would be sixteen million cruise passengers worldwide in 2011.

The average length of a cruise is around 7 days and passengers are very satisfied after experiencing this type of tourism. The cruise line associations believe market penetration is still relatively low and that significant growth will continue into the future in cruise tourism. For example, CLIA estimates that only 20 per cent of the US population has been on a cruise.

While the Caribbean and the Mediterranean are the two main hubs of cruise tourism, other regions are experiencing growth and investing more in this market segment. One of these growth regions is in the Asia-Pacific.

Adventure tourism activities	Hard	Soft
Archeological expeditions		☑
Backpacking		☑
Birdwatching		☑
Camping		☑
Canoeing		☑
Caving	☑	☑
Climbing	☑	☑
Cycling		☑
Ecotourism		☑
Educational programmes		☑
Environmentally sustainable activities		☑
Fishing/fly-fishing		☑
Hiking		☑
Horseback riding		☑
Hunting		☑
Kayaking/sea/whitewater		☑
Orienteering		☑
Rafting		☑
Research expeditions		☑
Safaris		☑
Sailing		☑
Scuba diving		☑
Snorkelling		☑
Skiing/snowboarding		☑
Surfing		☑
Trekking	☑	☑
Voluntourism (volunteer tourism)		☑

Figure 14.7 Adventure tourism activities: hard and soft

Source: Adventure Travel Trade Association, 2010.

Asia-Pacific region is a cruise tourism growth market

As Asia Pacific gains space in the global cruise category, the region will see increased investment in port infrastructure, a critical factor to guarantee the delivery of exceptional service and compete against well-established cruising markets like North America and the Caribbean.

Early in 2010, China inaugurated a new terminal in Tianjin, and in 2012 it will debut a second facility in Shanghai, boosting its capacity to handle eight cruise ships per day. Hong Kong and Singapore are also developing new port terminal facilities capable of handling ships as large as the Oasis class from Royal Caribbean.

(CLIA, 2010)

Casino gaming

Casino gaming is booming around the globe and being introduced in places where this activity was previously illegal. While destinations such as Monte Carlo have always been associated with casinos, other destinations have drawn more attention recently. These include Las Vegas and Atlantic City in the USA, Macau SAR in China, Singapore, the Philippines and several others. There are also plans to expand the casino capacity around Incheon International Airport in South Korea, mainly to cater to the Mainland China market.

The international 'star' of casino development in the past 10–12 years has been Macau. Las Vegas-based Sands opened a new $4 billion dollar casino resort in the Cotai area of Macau in April 2012:

'Macau's gaming market is growing at a healthy pace'

Sands is opening the Cotai Central property at a time when the Macau gaming market is growing at a reduced, but still very healthy, pace. The growth rate slowed to 27 per cent in the first quarter (of 2012), down from 42 per cent in 2011 and 58 per cent in 2010, but we do not expect a precipitous decline in visitation or gaming spending trends this year.

We have not adjusted our original full year 2012 gaming revenue growth forecast of 20 per cent, which reflects our broader view that economic growth in China will slow to 8 per cent this year.

(Reuters, quoting Fitch Ratings, 11 April 2012)

Singapore, as part of its so-called 'integrated resort' developments on Sentosa Island, introduced two casinos during 2010. According to recent reports, there will be further expansion of integrated resorts including casinos in Spain and Vietnam (Thomas, 2012).

Casino gaming has expanded rapidly in the USA, although most of the gaming revenues are being earned from US residents rather than international tourists. According to the American Gaming Association, consumer spending on casino gaming in 2010 was $34.6 billion, with twenty-one states that allow casinos.

It is also worth mentioning the overlap between cruise tourism and casino gaming. Cruise ships and riverboats have become popular casino venues, particularly in places where gambling is not allowed on land. This trend has been evident in both the USA and Hong Kong.

Culinary tourism

This form of tourism is either called culinary or gastronomic tourism, or even food tourism. The Ontario Ministry of Tourism and Culture (2011) defined culinary tourism as including 'any tourism experience in which one learns about, appreciates and/or consumes food and drink that reflects the local, regional, or national cuisine, heritage, culture, tradition or culinary techniques'.

Several DMOs have developed culinary tourism strategies for their destinations and this is a great idea where there is a rich food and wine tradition. Ontario has been one of the leaders in developing this market segment and has prepared a 'Four-Year Culinary Tourism Strategy and Action Plan 2011–2015'. This Action Plan cites the following trends in food and beverage consumption as being responsible for the growing interest in culinary tourism:

- Growing consumer interest in farm/producer branded products with a story
- The marketing of new cuts of meat (e.g. flat iron pork)
- Growing interest in heritage vegetables, fruits and breads
- Growing demand for healthy herbs, spices and fruits such as blueberries, rhubarb, shallots and pumpkin seed
- Innovative, non-alcoholic beverages particularly those incorporating local ingredients or flavours
- A growing recognition of the value of partnerships and strategic alliances in tourism for both marketing as well as product innovation
- Increasing use of social media by consumers to access information about culinary tourism, as well as web-coupons and location-based social media (tied to visitors in specific regions)
- Wider use of technology including kiosk ordering for restaurant meals and i-Pad wine lists and apps.

While every tourist has to eat while visiting a destination, culinary tourism transforms the food and local wines, and their preparation, into an attraction and sometimes also an event. The Canadian Tourism Commission (2003) identified the following culinary activities as comprising this type of tourism:

- Festivals (food and wine)
- Agricultural tours
- Themed agricultural tours (e.g. wine routes)
- U-pick agricultural tours
- Culinary packages offered by tour operators
- Agricultural tours featuring grower–restaurant partnerships

- Associations of restaurants featuring regional cuisine
- Events promoting regional products
- Agricultural fairs.

'L'Assiette de Pays' in France is a great example of cooperation among restaurants to feature regionally distinctive cuisine. This programme was established in 1995 and is now operating in Aquitaine, Brittany, Languedoc-Roussillon and Normandy. Another example that has been developed into a culinary tourism route is 'La Route des Saveurs de Charlevoix' in Quebec, Canada.

Cultural and heritage tourism

Many definitions of cultural tourism have been proposed, and it tends to be associated with heritage and historic tourism. Lord Cultural Resources, a Canadian company, defines cultural tourism as, 'travel from outside the host community motivated wholly or in part by interest in the historical, artistic, scientific or lifestyle/heritage offerings of a community, group or institution' (Lord, 2011). The National Trust for Historic Preservation in the USA defines cultural heritage tourism as 'traveling to experience the places and activities that authentically represent the stories and people of the past and present. It includes historic, cultural and natural resources.' Another definition from Pennsylvania says that heritage tourism 'is a leisure trip with the primary purpose of visiting historic, cultural, natural, recreational and scenic attractions to learn more about the past in an enjoyable way.' So this is a mixture of history and traditional and modern-day culture.

Obviously cultural and heritage tourism is of great importance to many destinations around the world. For example, the UNESCO World Heritage List in 2012 included 936 'properties' spread throughout 153 countries of the world that are the globe's most significant cultural and natural treasures. Some 725 of these 'properties' were classified as cultural, 183 as natural and 28 as mixed (cultural and natural). For example, the Tower of London (UK), Route of Santiago de Compostela (Spain) and the Great Wall (China) are cultural 'properties'; the Great Barrier Reef (Australia) and the Canadian Rocky Mountain Parks are natural 'properties'. These 900-plus 'properties' are representatives of 'tangible' heritage, but there is also 'intangible' heritage. UNESCO also maintains a list of intangible cultural heritage and this includes 'traditions or living expressions inherited from our ancestors and passed on to our descendants, such as oral traditions, performing arts, social practices, rituals, festive events, knowledge and practices concerning nature and the universe or the knowledge and skills to produce traditional crafts' (UNESCO, 2012). For example, Chinese acupuncture and calligraphy are on the intangible culture list, as is Spain's flamenco dancing.

There are many significant cultural and heritage/historical tourism sites and resources that are not transcribed on the World Heritage List, but they are still visited and enjoyed by international tourists.

Several scholars and experts have tried to classify cultural and heritage tourists into groups. Often these classifications have been based on the involvement of people with the places they are visiting or the cultural performances they are experiencing. Poria *et al.* (2003) suggested that only 'tourists motivated by the heritage attributes of the site, and consider the site as part of their own heritage' are truly core heritage tourists. Lord (2011) classifies tourists into three groups, those motivated wholly, partially or incidentally by culture. The basic idea here is that there are 'serious' cultural and heritage/historical tourists who are motivated by the inherent characteristics of sites; and at the other end of the spectrum there are people who 'accidentally' visit but are not truly interested in the sites' inherent cultural and heritage assets.

Dark tourism

Some people seem to have a fascination with travelling to places that are associated with disasters, human suffering, wars and battles, famous murders and assassinations, and other death-related sites. According to Stone and Sharpley (2008), these types of attractions have drawn tourists for a long time:

Dark tourism sites have attracted tourists for many years

Travel to and experience of places associated with death is not a new phenomenon. People have long been drawn, purposefully or otherwise, towards sites, attractions or events linked in one way or another with death, suffering, violence or disaster.

A few examples here might bring this concept into clearer focus for you. Some of the most famous dark tourism sites include Ground Zero (New York City), Auschwitz Concentration Camp (Poland) and the Pont de l'Alma Road Tunnel in Paris. Stone (ibid.) divides dark tourism destinations and products into the following seven categories:

- Dark fun factories (e.g. Schloss Dracula at Erlebnispark Strasswalchen near Salzburg, Austria; and the London Dungeon)
- Dark exhibitions (e.g. Tuol Sleng Genocide Museum in Phnom Penh, Cambodia)
- Dark dungeons (e.g. Port Arthur in Tasmania, Australia)
- Dark resting places (e.g. various cemeteries including the World War I and World War II cemeteries in Europe)
- Dark shrines (e.g. the Hiroshima Peace Site in Japan; and Nanjing Massacre Memorial Hall in Jiangsu, China)
- Dark conflict sites (e.g. Normandy landings and battlefields)
- Dark camps of genocide (e.g. Auschwitz in Poland).

There has been a vigorous debate among scholars about what constitutes dark tourism, but not much research has been done on the characteristics and behaviours of the tourists that consume it. Additionally, not much work has been done on how to market dark tourism.

Health and wellness tourism

There has been a great spurt in interest in health and wellness tourism as people are becoming more concerned about their fitness and overall health. There are many traditional spas around the world that have relied on the healing qualities of their natural spring waters. Places like Bath in England, Baden-Baden in Germany and Carlsbad (Karlovy Vary) in the Czech Republic are among the most famous for these sorts of experiences.

According to Smith and Puczkó (2009), there are many different definitions of health and wellness tourism and they tend to vary by country and region of the world. These authors define five types of health tourism:

- Holistic (wellness)
- Leisure and recreation (wellness)
- Medical wellness
- Medical (therapeutic)
- Medical (surgery).

Medical tourism is discussed below under a separate category. Smith and Puczkó define holistic wellness as incorporating spiritual, yoga and meditation, and new age experiences. Wellness leisure and recreation includes beauty treatments, pampering, and sports and fitness. So, the great upward trends in the use of spas at numerous types of location (day spas, airports, hotels and resorts, cruise ships, etc.) is included in this market segment.

Industrial tourism

Industrial tourism is where people visit the sites or buildings of existing or former industries. These include tours of factories, mines, farms and orchards, docklands and other current or heritage industries.

Factory infatuation in Japan?

In Kawasaki, Japan, tourists are flocking to a new kind of attraction: a power plant. It is a monument of sorts, but not one made from marble or granite. Rather than celebrating history or culture, it memorializes how our societies run. And its tall smokestacks, shooting up clouds like industrial geysers, inspire awe in the minds of *kojo moe* tourists. *Kojo moe*, meaning 'factory infatuation', is a growing subculture of people who travel around Japan to see oil refineries, steel manufacturing plants, chemical factories and other such fortresses of industry. They find grandeur and beauty in what many see as unsightly sources of pollution.

(Sood, 2011)

A very good and successful industrial tourism attraction is the Dole Plantation in Hawaii, USA. The focus at the Dole Plantation is on the production of pineapples, and one of the key attractions is the world's largest and longest pineapple garden maze. The Guinness Storehouse® in Dublin, Ireland is a second great industrial tourism case study.

Medical tourism

Medical tourism is where people leave their own countries for medical treatment or surgery in other countries. This has been a popular trend as the medical costs are lower, but the standards of medical care are still high. Some of the top medical tourism destinations in the world include Hungary, India, Malaysia, Singapore, South Korea and Thailand (Figure 14.8) and Ukraine.

The medical treatments sought in different places vary. For example, some destinations are famous for cosmetic surgery, while others are known for dentistry, including some Eastern European countries.

Nature-based tourism and ecotourism

The International Ecotourism Society (TIES) defines ecotourism as 'responsible travel to natural areas that conserves the environment and improves the well-being of local people'. TIES also suggests that ecotourism involves conservation, communities (participation) and interpretation, and that ecotourism must follow six principles:

- Minimize impact.
- Build environmental and cultural awareness and respect.
- Provide positive experiences for both visitors and hosts.
- Provide direct financial benefits for conservation.
- Provide financial benefits and empowerment for local people.
- Raise sensitivity to host countries' political, environmental and social climate.

According to SNV (2009), the motivations of nature-based tourists are usually as follows:

- Want to see wildlife in natural settings. Gratified, feel in touch with nature.
- Are sensitive to the environment and want to do no harm.

Figure 14.8 Thailand actively markets medical tourism
Source: Shutterstock, Inc.

- Exploration. Go to remote locations. Want to see more of the world, interested in landscape, flora and fauna. Want to see things before they are gone.
- Looking to be up close and personal with animals and nature.
- Get away from city life. Likes to be out in nature and does not mind moderate physical activity.

Strong demand for nature-based tourism

Nature-based tourism (including ecotourism) accounts for 20 per cent – 40 per cent of international tourists. Demand is expected to remain strong as more urban dwellers seek authentic and natural experiences and want to see exotic destinations and endangered species. Due to the influence of ecotourism within this segment, consumer interest is strong for tourism companies to adhere to responsible practices.

(SNV, 2009)

Religious tourism

Travelling with a religious pilgrimage purpose is a significant part of the inbound international tourism for several countries, including Saudi Arabia, Italy, Portugal, Spain, Croatia, India, Sri Lanka and several others. Additionally, many other international tourists visit religious sites and buildings. Religious tourism is hard to define, according to a special study conducted by UNWTO on Asia and the Pacific:

Difficulties in defining religious tourism

Statistics on religious tourism of Asia and the Pacific are limited or vague. This is partly due to the close link between religion and culture in Asia where it is difficult to separate the motivation of travel except in the specific case of pilgrimages and religious festivals.

Practically all Asian archaeological monuments have some connotation to religion and form the backbone of tourist circuits. Therefore, it is difficult to differentiate between the cultural and the religious tourist.

(UNWTO, 2011)

Rinschede (1992) divided religious tourism into two parts: short-term and long-term religious tourism. Short-term religious tourism is mainly local and regional travel to pilgrimage sites or to participate in a religious celebration, religious conference or church meeting. Long-term religious tourism involves national or international travel for several days or weeks. These include major religious pilgrimage sites like Mecca (Saudi Arabia), the Vatican City in Rome, Benares (India), Jerusalem (Israel), Lourdes (France), Fátima (Portugal), Guadalupe (Mexico) and Santiago de Compostela (Spain).

Shopping tourism

Shopping is an activity in which most international pleasure and leisure tourists engage and greatly enjoy. However, there is a difference between shopping as one of several activities engaged in when travelling and shopping as the principal purpose and reason for a trip. When people travel to places like the Mall of America (Bloomington, Minnesota), West Edmonton Mall (Edmonton, Alberta, Canada) and the Dubai Mall, or to duty-free shopping zones, their main desired travel experience might be the shopping.

Several places around the world have been aggressively promoting themselves as shopping destinations for international tourists, including Malaysia:

'Malaysia has become a premier shopping destination'

Malaysia is a premier shopping destination in Southeast Asia. Malaysians love shopping, which explains the vast number of luxury malls, stores and street-side stalls in the capital, Kuala Lumpur. If you are a shopaholic, the best time of the year to visit is during the Malaysia Mega Sale Carnival, around August September when the entire country offers great discounts. Please check our listings to find out when the next Mega Sale Carnival is on.

The exemption of duty on a range of items has resulted in more competitive pricing and makes shopping in Malaysia an even more attractive option. Malaysian duty-free zones are the islands of Labuan and Langkawi. There are also some duty-free shops in Kuala Lumpur and Penang, international airports and city centres. Duty-free items like cameras, watches, pens, cosmetics, perfumes, mobile phones, computers, cigarettes and liquor are among the cheapest in the world.

(Tourism Malaysia, 2012)

Shopping tourism can be classified as 'leisure shopping' and there are three distinctive environments for leisure shopping: ambient shopping (typical shopping at a mall); magnet leisure in a new-generation shopping mall (such as the Mall of America; and heritage-destination leisure (shopping in historic areas) (Timothy, 2005).

Sports tourism

Tourism associated with both professional and amateur sports is a market that is receiving increasing attention from DMOs. Ireland is one of the countries that has put an emphasis on the development of sports tourism:

Sports tourism sponsorship programme (Fáilte Ireland)

The Sports Tourism Initiative is designed to attract major sporting events with tourism potential to Ireland. The strategy is to concentrate on those events that have the ability to showcase Ireland's natural landscape through

> the international media. Such events include: outdoor events, which take place against a backdrop of stunning scenery; or those events with capacity to attract large numbers of overseas visitors, which bring great economic benefit to the area in which the event is taking place. The main focus of the initiative is the promotion of Ireland as a 'natural sports arena'. Sports like sailing, cycling, car rallying, golf and equestrian feature prominently.
>
> (Fáilte Ireland, 2012)

Weed and Bull (2004) defined sports tourism as, 'a social, economic and cultural phenomenon arising from the unique interaction of activity, people and place'. Therefore, sports tourism is a very broad concept that offers a wide spectrum of opportunities for destinations. These opportunities range from mega sporting events like the Olympics and the World Cup to amateur sports tournaments, and everything in between.

Voluntourism

This is a form of tourism in which people volunteer their time when they are travelling. People who engage in voluntourism are on holiday but they also want to help local destinations through volunteer elements within their trips. They feel good by giving something back to local communities and believe they get a more authentic cultural exchange.

Holmes *et al.* (2010) define tourism volunteering broadly as encompassing

> individuals volunteering in their own community (i.e. host volunteering) and tourists volunteering at a destination (i.e. volunteer tourism). Volunteers in tourism on the whole are engaged in the process of assisting the leisure experiences of others while simultaneously undertaking a recreational activity either in their home community or in a destination further afield.

Actually this definition is rather narrow; many voluntourism trips are not for 'assisting with leisure experiences' but involve teaching/education, medical and dental care, help with construction projects, etc. Sometimes these are referred to as 'missions' rather than tours.

Wine tourism

Wine tourism has become very popular in many parts of the world, including North and South America, Europe, South Africa and Australia and New Zealand. Hall *et al.* (2000) define wine tourism as visits 'to vineyards, wineries, wine festivals and wine shows for which grape wine tasting and/or experiencing the attributes of a grape wine region are the prime motivating factors for visitors'. Getz and Brown (2006) add that there are three perspectives on wine tourism; the wine producers, DMOs and consumers. The Winemakers' Federation of Australia (a producer group) has prepared 'A Strategic Framework for the Future of Wine and Food Tourism to 2020'. In this strategy, the WFA (2011) emphasizes the importance of all destination attributes and not just the wine:

More to wine tourism than wine

The wine sector traditionally has regarded tourism as a channel to connect with consumers, build relationships and increase sales. It would benefit more significantly if it were to collaborate in activities that can be packaged and bundled to add value that augments the Australian tourism experience.

The opportunity for wine tourism destinations is to leverage the wine experience and connect it with the other narratives around food, landscape and culture to create compelling reasons for visitation.

In Chapter 6, you learned about the wine tourism product clubs and the 'Wine Routes' of Spain from the perspective of creating destination partnerships.

International pleasure/leisure travel marketing procedures

The *Destination Marketing System* model (Morrison, 2010) was described in Chapter 3. It is recommended that this model should be followed when marketing to international pleasure and leisure travel markets. The five questions in the model should be applied to each origin country that is being targeted.

Where are we now?

What is the existing situation in the market that is being considered? The DMO needs to analyse the recent past history of visits from this market as part of a market analysis. Several DMOs do this very professionally and share their summary results with tourism sector stakeholders as part of a series of 'market profiles'. These DMOs include the Office of Travel and Tourism Industries (USA), Tourism Australia, Tourism Ireland, Tourism New Zealand, VisitBritain and others.

The market analyses by origin country should include the following contents (Table 14.4):

It can be very helpful here if the DMO has conducted a survey of previous visitors from the country of origin, as this provides more in-depth information on what people do and what they most like and dislike about the destination. Having more detailed information like this better informs the subsequent marketing strategy and plan for that country of origin. For example, the Shanghai International Visitor Survey was conducted for the Shanghai Municipal Tourism Administration (SMTA) in late 2009 and early 2010. The goals of the project were to profile the characteristics of international visitors; determine visitor opinions of Shanghai as a tourism destination; and suggest the most appropriate marketing strategies for the top ten international leisure markets and for international business/MICE markets. The top ten origin countries were: Australia, France, Germany, Japan, Malaysia, Russia, Singapore, South Korea, the UK and the USA (Hong Kong, Macau and Taiwan were excluded). Individual marketing recommendations were prepared for each of the top ten origin countries and also for the other countries as a group. These were called the 'Top 10 for 2010' and overall 110 separate recommendations were provided.

Table 14.4 Contents of market analysis by origin country

General information	Tourism information
• Current and projected population	• Total outbound departures
• GDP and GDP per capita	• Total outbound expenditures
• Economic trends and prospects	• Top 10 favourite destinations
• Major cities and their populations	• Recent inbound arrival statistics from origin country to the destination
• Public holidays and annual leave	• Destination's market share
• Cultural and other past associations between origin country/destination	• Air services and other transport connections
• Country expatriates and expatriate companies in the destination	• Major travel fairs and exhibitions held in origin country
• Major media companies/channels	• Major travel trade companies
• Major social network sites	• Major consumer/travel trade publications

Some countries conduct regular international visitor surveys, usually on an annual basis, and their results provide a good foundation for future marketing. Australia, for example, has the International Visitor Survey, which has an impressive number of respondents:

40,000 international visitors surveyed each year by Australia

Since 1 January 2005, interviews have been conducted with 40,000 international visitors on an annual basis. The sample was increased in order to enhance the estimates for smaller states, territories and regions. Increasing the sample size of the IVS by 100 per cent has improved the reliability of survey estimates.

(Tourism Research Australia, 2012)

The Australian IVS contains over ninety-six questions, with particular sections including:

● Usual place of residence
● Repeat visitation
● Group tours
● Travel party
● Sources for obtaining information about Australia
● Purpose of visit and places visited
● Transportation and accommodation
● Activities
● Expenditure
● Demographics.

The Office of Travel and Tourism Industries in the USA conducts the Survey of International Air Travelers that provides data on thirty-five individual characteristics of international tourists. New Zealand has an International Visitor Survey (IVS), which is a sample survey of approximately 5,200 international visitors to New Zealand aged 15 years or older per year. In the UK, the Office for National Statistics conducts the International Passenger Survey (IPS).

Of course, surveys such as this tend to be somewhat expensive and not all DMOs can afford to do them, especially on a regular basis. Most often then DMOs have to rely on secondary data sources. For example, some DMOS use the FutureBrand Country Brand Index (CBI) for information on other country's' perceptions.

Where would we like to be?

To complete this step, DMOs must develop a marketing strategy that they will apply to each market and set goals for each market. A great example of this is the Canadian Tourism Commission's 'Global Marketing and Sales Plan 2011'. As mentioned earlier, CTC has chosen Brazil, China, India, Japan, Mexico, South Korea, Australia, France, Germany, the UK and the USA as its eleven focus markets. CTC considers Brazil, China, India, Japan and Mexico to be its 'emerging' markets and the other five to be its 'mature and traditional markets'. CTC uses the 'Market Portfolio Analysis' (MPA) rating system and the 'Market Investment Model' (MIM) to validate its selection of markets and to suggest the allocation of its marketing budget to the selected country markets. For 2011, the MIM suggested the following budget allocations by country:

- UK: 16.2 per cent
- South Korea: 10.8 per cent
- China: 10.4 per cent
- Australia: 9.6 per cent
- Germany: 9.6 per cent
- France: 9.1 per cent
- Japan: 9.1 per cent
- India: 9.0 per cent
- Mexico: 8.4 per cent
- Brazil: 7.7 per cent.

In addition to target country selection, the international marketing strategy must also encompass a destination PIB (positioning–image–branding) approach. Here there are different options available; using a 'global approach' that does not significantly vary by country, or an 'individualized approach' where the PIB approach is customized for each market or each region.

How do we get there?

A mini marketing plan should be designed for each international market to guide the implementation of marketing and promotion programmes and activities. These plans should be based on specific objectives for each market and should detail how the 8 Ps will be applied (product, price, place, promotion, packaging, programming, partnership and people).

Product: It is important to have information on the activities and experiences most desired by the tourists from each origin country. This chapter has discussed several tourism product categories that appear to have increasing appeal for international tourists. Earlier in this chapter, you heard about fifteen market segments with growth potential for domestic and international tourism; these segments are based on different aspects of the tourism product.

Certain slight adjustments to normally-delivered products may be required to meet the requirements of international tourists. Food and dietary restrictions is an obvious example here and DMOs should educate tourism sector stakeholders about the product modifications needed for specific origin markets and according to religious and traditional requirements.

Price: Price levels and value for money are undoubtedly very important decision attributes for international tourists. However, DMOs seldom are directly involved in setting prices for tourism products within their destinations.

Place: As mentioned in Chapter 3, place in tourism means the distribution channels that DMOs use. These include online distribution comprising websites, social network sites, online travel agencies, mobile phones, etc.; and traditional distribution channels through travel trade companies such as travel agencies and tour operators.

Using the available distribution channels is exceptionally important for marketing to international pleasure and leisure tourists. This is because traditional consumer promotions such as advertising can be very expensive when conducted in foreign countries, particularly if the return on investment is considered.

Promotion: Different types of sales promotions are most often used in marketing to international pleasure and leisure tourists. For example, having booths at travel shows and exhibitions in origin countries is a very common approach as it is a very efficient way to meet with the travel trades and consumers. 'Road shows' or promotional seminars/workshops are another favoured promotional approach. Typically these events are for travel trade companies and representatives of the media.

Familiarization tours or 'fams' are another very popular approach in the marketing for international pleasure and leisure tourists. They give influential people a first-hand view and experience with the destination that they can pass along to potential tourists.
    Travel agent training and certification programmes are a great way to develop an influential group of travel professionals to help to sell destinations. The *Aussie Specialist* programme operated by Tourism Australia has already been mentioned as an outstanding example of such training.

Packaging: A significant proportion of inbound tourists buy packaged vacations/holidays and others are on pre-arranged itineraries. These are usually designed and operated by travel trade companies, hotels and resorts, airlines and other tourism sector stakeholders, and are not a DMO responsibility. However, the DMO should act in an advisory role in encouraging other players to develop the most appropriate packages and tours for inbound international tourists.

Sometimes DMOs have to play a regulation and control role with inbound tours and packages in order to protect international guests and ensure their satisfaction. For example, there have been several instances with the Chinese inbound market where unscrupulous tour operators and their guides have been forcing their customers to shop in particular stores and insisting that they spend large amounts of money.

Programming: Many of the 15 market segments discussed in this chapter require elements of programming to provide interpretation, activities and participatory experiences for international tourists. For example, adventure tourism requires experienced guides and instructors; sports tourism may require that tournaments are organized; and voluntourism needs special programme development.

Additionally, destinations may create events and festivals mainly for international markets. For example, the Malaysia Mega Sale Carnival 2012 is from mid-June to early September and is designed to attract shoppers from around the world to hunt for bargains.

Partnership: Partnering is an essential for marketing internationally as a DMO is unlikely to be successful on its own. The partners may include airlines flying between the origin country and the destination, other DMOs, and major hotels and attractions in the destination.

People: Human resources are another extremely important consideration when catering to international pleasure and leisure tourists. For example, it may be essential to have staff members that are completely fluent in the language of the origin country, as well as being very familiar with the country's culture and traditions.

The training of guides may be essential to ensure that inbound tourists have an enjoyable and hassle-free stay in the destination, and also extract the maximum value from the sites they see and the shopping in which they engage.

How do we make sure we get there?

The marketing and promotions for each international market must be carefully monitored to ensure that they remain on track. In Chapter 3, you learned about the concepts of destination marketing control and evaluation. For each international market, DMOs will have specific activities and programmes identified in their respective mini marketing plans. The completion of these activities and programmes is one type of control measure, e.g. if the DMO arranges a 'fam' or attends a travel exhibition or fair.

As well as having activity tracking, DMOs must also have productivity and performance measures. The productivity measures show the efficiency and effectiveness of the DMO in using resources, e.g. how many people came on 'fams' to the destination or attended the DMO's promotional seminars. The performance measures are the actual outcomes or results from implementing the activities and programmes for each international market.

How do we know if we got there?

A careful assessment of marketing and promotional performance must be completed for each international market. Here it is essential that DMOs define key result areas (KRAs) and key performance indicators (KPIs) for each market.

Many national DMOs have offices abroad in their major focus countries, and these become a very important element of DMO operations. There are several different models for establishing these offices and the first one is to operate the offices with full-time staff of the DMO. The second model is not to have any full-time staff, but to work with a vendor or contractor known as a 'representative' or 'general sales agent' (GSA). The third model is for a DMO to have a combination of self-operated and representative offices. A fourth model is just to have a consular or embassy unit or attaché with the responsibility of tourism as well as other commercial and trade activities.

Summary

International tourism has been on a long-term growth trend and is predicted to continue this upward pattern until 2030. International tourism arrivals are forecast to grow from 980 million in 2011 to 1.8 billion in 2030. Despite the growth, tourism remains highly susceptible to negative impacts from various types of crises, as has been well demonstrated in the period from 2000 to 2009.

There are several unique challenges for international tourism and in marketing to international leisure and pleasure travel markets. From the broader perspective, balance of payments in tourism deficits are an issue for several countries, and the uneven distribution of international tourists within a host country destination is a second concern. From a marketing viewpoint, the major challenge is in selecting which origin countries to target. Many DMOs consider the yields of various origin countries in determining their market strategies.

Outbound markets including Brazil, Russia, India and China (the BRICs) are expanding at an above-average pace and are attracting the attention of more DMOs. These four nations are among the top ten most populated countries and are experiencing significant economic growth that is stimulating outbound travel.

Not all international tourists are alike and in fact they may be looking for different types of experiences within the destination. Certain specific market segments have demonstrated strong growth and are expected to continue to have good future potential for destinations. A growing proportion of international tourists are visiting destinations to pursue special interests and specific forms of tourism (adventure, casino gaming, cruise, culinary, cultural/heritage/historic, dark, ecotourism and nature-based, health and wellness, industrial, medical, religion, shopping, sports, volunteering and wine tourism).

It is recommended that DMOs follow the destination marketing system when marketing and promoting internationally. The operation of DMO offices in other countries is an important part of the international tourism marketing role.

For the most effective marketing to international pleasure and leisure travel markets, DMOs need to do the following:

- Become familiar with and continuously track the trends and future prospects for international tourism.
- Prepare individual market analyses or 'profiles'.
- Conduct periodic surveys of international tourists to their destinations.
- Develop a market strategy that is based on an understanding of the market yields and market growth forecasts.

- Define the destination's emerging markets and identify market characteristics.
- Examine the destination's potential for various growth market segments.
- Prepare a marketing strategy and mini marketing plan for each country market.
- Follow a systematic approach to marketing and promoting to international tourists, including careful performance measurement.

Review questions

1 What have been the trends in international tourism arrivals in recent years according to UNWTO?
2 What are the future prospects for international tourism for the next 10–15 years?
3 What are the major challenges facing DMOs in the international marketing for pleasure and leisure travel?
4 Which geographic origin markets are considered to be 'emerging' and why have they earned this designation?
5 Which market segments have shown substantial growth potential in recent years and are expected to continue to increase in the future?
6 What are the procedures that DMOs need to follow in marketing to international pleasure and leisure tourists?

References

Adventure Travel Trade Association. 2010. Adventure Tourism Market Report.

Adventure Travel Trade Association/The George Washington University/Vital Wave Consulting. 2011. ATDI Adventure Tourism Development Index 2010 Report.

American Gaming Association. 2011. 2011 AGA Survey of Casino Entertainment.

Belle Tourism International Consulting. 2007. A Strategic Marketing Plan for Tourism in Jiangsu Province. Europe and North America: 2008–2012. Shanghai, PRC.

——2010. Shanghai International Visitor Survey.

Brown, S., and Lehto, X. 2005. Travelling with a purpose: Understanding the motives and benefits of volunteer vacationers. *Current Issues in Tourism*, 8(6), 479–496.

Bruwer, J. 2003. South African wine routes: Some perspectives on the wine tourism industry's structural dimensions and wine tourism product. *Tourism Management*, 24(4), 423–435.

Burmon, A. 2010. Dark tourism. Cambodia tries to turn its bloody history into a sightseeing boom. *The Atlantic*, November.

Canadian Tourism Commission. 2003. How-to Guide: Develop a Culinary Tourism Product.

——2010. Global Marketing and Sales Plan 2011.

——2012. Where we Market Canada. http://en-corporate.canada.travel/markets/where-we-market-canada

Central Intelligence Agency. 2012. The World Factbook. https://www.cia.gov/library/publications/the-world-factbook/geos/ch.html

Chen, M.-H., Jang, S.C., and Peng, Y.-J. 2011. Discovering optimal tourist market mixes. *Journal of Travel Research*, 50(6), 602–614.

China National Tourist Office. 2011. China Tourism Statistics. http://www.cnto.org/chinastats_2010ArrivalsByAgeSex.asp

China Tourism Academy. 2010. Annual Report of China Outbound Tourism Development 2009/2010.

Cohen, M. 2012. Upstart Singapore outstrips Las Vegas. *Asia Times Online*, 5 January.

Corti, I.N., Marola, P.N., and Castro, M.B. 2010. Social inclusion and local development through European voluntourism: A case study of the project realized in a neighborhood of Morocco. *American Journal of Economics and Business Administration*, 2(3), 221–231.

Crawford, D. 2012. Recovering from terror: The Egyptian and Balinese experiences. *Worldwide Hospitality and Tourism Themes*, 4(1), 91–97.

Cruise Lines International Association. 2010. The Overview. 2010 CLIA Cruise Market Overview.

Dole Plantation. 2012. Welcome to Dole Plantation. http://dole-plantation.com/

du Rand, G.E., and Heath, E. 2006. Towards a framework for food tourism as an element of destination marketing. *Current Issues in Tourism*, 9(3), 206–234.

Edleson, H. 2012. Selling America abroad. *New York Times*, 2 April.

Ehrbeck, T., Guevara, C., and Mango, P.D. 2008. Mapping the marketing for medical travel. *The McKinsey Quarterly*, May.

ENIT Italia. 2012. Studies and Research. http://www.enit.it/en/studies-and-research.html

Erlebnispark Strasswalchen. 2012. http://www.erlebnispark.at/

Fáilte Ireland. 2010. Overseas Visitors and Holidaymakers to Ireland 1999–2009.

——2012. Sports Tourism. http://www.failteireland.ie/sportstourism

Fédération Régionale des Pays d'Accueil Touristiques. 2012. Presentation. http://www.bienvenueaupays.fr/

Florida–Caribbean Cruise Association. 2011. Cruise Industry Overview – 2011.

FutureBrand. 2011. FutureBrand Country Brand Index 2011–12.

German National Tourist Board. 2011. Sales and Marketing for Destination Germany.

Getz, D., and Brown, G. 2006. Critical success factors for wine tourism regions: A demand analysis. *Tourism Management*, 27(1), 146–158.

Gray, H.P. 1967. The balance-of-payments cost of foreign travel expenditures. *Southern Economic Journal*, 34(1), 17–26.

Gretzel, U., Fesenmaier, D.F., Formica, S., and O'Leary, J.T. 2006. Searching for the future: Challenges faced by destination marketing organizations. *Journal of Travel Research*, 45(2), 116–126.

Guinness Storehouse. 2012. http://www.guinness-storehouse.com/en/Index.aspx

Hall, A. 2012. The response of the tourism industry in Jamaica to crime and the threat of terrorism. *Worldwide Hospitality and Tourism Themes*, 4(1), 59–72.

Hall, C.M., Sharples, L., Cambourne, B., and Macionis, N. (eds). 2000. Wine Tourism around the World. Oxford: Butterworth-Heinemann.

Holmes, K., Smith, K.A., Lockstone-Binney, L., and Baum, T. 2010. Developing the dimensions of tourism volunteering. *Leisure Sciences*, 32(3), 255–269.

Horng, J.-S., and Tsai, C.-T. 2012. Exploring marketing strategies for culinary tourism in Hong Kong and Singapore, *Asia Pacific Journal of Tourism Research*, 3, 1–24.

Instituto de Estudios Turísticos. 2011. Movimientos Turísticos en Fronteras (Frontur); Encuesta de Gasto Turístico (Egatur).

IPK International. 2012. Global Travel Trends 2011/12.

Jang, S., Morrison, A.M., and O'Leary, J.T. (2004a). A procedure for target market selection in tourism. *Journal of Travel and Tourism Marketing*, 16(1), 17–31.

——(2004b). The tourism efficient frontier: An approach to selecting the most efficient travel segments. *Journal of Travel and Tourism Marketing*, 16(4), 33–46.

La Route des Saveurs de Charlevoix. 2007. http://www.routedesaveurs.com/

London Dungeon. 2012. http://www.the-dungeons.co.uk/london/en/index.htm

Lord, B. 2011. Cultural Tourism, Cultural Change and Museum Planning in India. http://www.lord.ca/Media/Barry-New-Delhi-April2011.pdf

McKercher, B., and du Cros, H. 2003. Testing a cultural tourism typology. *International Journal of Tourism Research*, 5(1), 45–58.

Ministry of Economic Development, New Zealand. 2012. IVS Methodology. http://www.med.govt.nz/sectors-industries/tourism/tourism-research-data/international-visitor-survey/about-the-international-visitor-survey/methodology

Morrison, A.M. 2010. Hospitality and Travel Marketing, 4th edn. Clifton Hills, NY: Delmar Cengage.

Nanjing Massacre Memorial Hall. 2005. http://www.nj1937.org/english/default.asp

National Trust for Historic Preservation. 2012. Heritage Tourism. http://www.preservationnation.org/information-center/economics-of-revitalization/heritage-tourism/

Nides, T. 2012. Delivering Jobs with International Tourism. US Department of State. http://www.state.gov/s/dmr/remarks/2012/183849.htm.

New Zealand Ministry of Economic Development. 2012. International Visitor Survey. http://www.med.govt.nz/sectors-industries/tourism/tourism-research-data/international-visitor-survey

Nolan, M.L., and Nolan, S. 1992. Religious sites as tourism attractions in Europe. *Annals of Tourism Research*, 19(1), 68–78.

Ontario Ministry of Tourism and Culture. 2011. Ontario's Four-Year Culinary Tourism Strategy and Action Plan 2011–2015.

Ontario Tourism Marketing Partnership Corporation. 2010. Ontario's Emerging Markets: China, India, Brazil.

Partners in Tourism: Culture and Commerce. 2011. Cultural Heritage Tourism. http://www.culturalheritagetourism.org/howtogetstarted.htm

Pennsylvania Department of Conservation and Natural Resources. 2001. Moving Heritage Tourism Forward in Pennsylvania.

Pole Touristique du Bessin. 2012. http://www.bessin-normandie.com/

Poria, Y., Butler, R., and Airey, D. 2003. The core of heritage tourism. *Annals of Tourism Research*, 30(1), 238–254.

Republic of Turkey Ministry of Culture and Tourism. 2012. Number of Arriving–Departing Foreigners and Citizens. http://www.kultur.gov.tr/EN/belge/2-27503/number-of-arriving-departing-foreigners-and-citizens.html

Rinschede, G. 1992. Forms of religious tourism. *Annals of Tourism Research*, 19(1), 51–67.

Robinson, P. 2008. The role of shopping in tourism destinations. *Tourism Insights*. http://www.insights.org.uk/articleitem.aspx?title=TheRoleofShoppinginTourismDestinations

Simone-Charteris, M.T., and Boyd, S. 2010. Developing dark and political tourism in Northern Ireland: An industry perspective. In Contemporary Issues in Irish and Global Tourism and Hospitality, Dublin: Dublin Institute of Technology.

Smith, M., and Kelly, C. 2006. Wellness tourism. *Tourism Recreation Research*, 31(1), 1–4.

Smith, M., and Puczkó, L. 2009. Health and Wellness Tourism. Kidlington: Butterworth-Heinemann/Elsevier.

SNV Netherlands Development Organisation. 2009. The Market for Responsible Tourism Products.

Sood, S. 2011. The complicated allure of industrial tourism. *BBC Travel*, 10 October.

Statistics Canada. 2012. Service Bulletin: International Travel: Advance Information, December 2011.

Stone, P., and Sharpley, R. 2008. Consuming dark tourism: A thanatological perspective. *Annals of Tourism Research*, 35(2), 574–595.

Strange, C., and Kempa, M. 2003. Shades of dark tourism: Alcatraz and Robben Island. *Annals of Tourism Research*, 30(2), 386–405.

The International Ecotourism Society (TIES). 2012. What is Ecotourism? http://www.ecotourism.org/what-is-ecotourism

Thomas, N. 2012. Casino billionaire Sheldon Adelson plans 'mini Las Vegas' in Spain. *The Telegraph*, 11 April.

Timothy, D.J. 2005. Shopping Tourism, Retailing and Leisure: Aspects of Tourism. Bristol: Channel View Publications.

Tourism Australia. 2011. Exchange rates: Challenges and opportunities for Australian tourism.

——2012. Market Strategy. http://www.tourism.australia.com/en-au/markets/market-strategy.aspx

Tourism Authority of Thailand. 2012. Thailand Medical Tourism Portal. http://www.thailandmedtourism.com/Home/28

Tourism Ireland. 2012. Our Markets. http://www.tourismireland.com/Home/Our-Markets.aspx

Tourism Malaysia. 2012a. Activities and Sports: Shopping. http://www.tourism.gov.my/activities/?xtvt_id=6

——2012b. Tourist Arrivals to Malaysia for January–December 2011.

Tourism Research Australia. 2012. International Visitors in Australia: December 2011.

Tourismreview.com. 2010. Mega Ships: Asia Pacific Ready to Go Cruising. http://www.tourism-review.com/travel-tourism-magazine-cruising-industry-in-asia-going-up-article1431

UNESCO. 2012. World Heritage List. http://whc.unesco.org/en/list

UNWTO. 2011a. International Tourists to Hit 1.8 Billion by 2030. http://media.unwto.org/en/press-release/2011-10-11/international-tourists-hit-18-billion-2030

——2011b. Religious Tourism in Asia and the Pacific. Madrid: UNWTO.

——2011c. UNWTO World Tourism Highlights. 2011 Edition. Madrid: UNWTO.

——2012. UNWTO World Tourism Barometer. Volume 10. March. Madrid: UNWTO.

US Department of Commerce, International Trade Administration, Office of Travel and Tourism Industries. 2011a. Top 10 International Markets: 2010.

——2011b. United States Travel and Tourism Exports, Imports, and the Balance of Trade: 2009.

VisitBritain. 2012a. Foresight, March 2012: Britain's International Tourism Balance of Payments.

——2012b. Inbound Tourism Facts. http://www.visitbritain.org/insightsandstatistics/inboundtourismfacts/index.aspx

——2012c. Brazil Market and Trade Profile.

——2012d. India Market and Trade Profile.

——2012e. Russia Market and Trade Profile.

Weed, M. 2006. Sports tourism research 2000–2004: A systematic review of knowledge and a meta-evaluation of methods. *Journal of Sport and Tourism*, 11(1), 5–30.

——2009. Progress in sports tourism research? A meta-review and exploration of futures. *Tourism Management*, 30(5), 615–628.

Weed, M.E., and Bull, C.J. 2004. Sports Tourism: Participants, Policy and Providers. Oxford: Elsevier.

Winemakers' Federation of Australia. 2011. A Strategic Framework for the Future of Wine and Food Tourism to 2020.

Wood, R.E. 2000. Caribbean cruise tourism: Globalization at sea. *Annals of Tourism Research*, 27(2), 345–370.

World Travel and Tourism Council. 2012. Travel and Tourism Forecast to Pass 100m Jobs and $2 trillion GDP in 2012.

Xu, J. 2011. Tourism Trends and Emerging Markets. 5th UNWTO-PATA Forum on Tourism Trends and Outlook, Guilin, China.

International pleasure and leisure travel markets

Jiangsu Province case study

This case study accompanies the materials included in Chapter 14 on international pleasure and leisure travel markets. In particular, it shows how a provincial DMO in China developed a plan to attract international visitors from Europe and North America.

Introduction

The Strategic Marketing Plan for Tourism in Jiangsu Province was conducted for the Jiangsu Provincial Tourism Bureau (JPTB). It was one of the first-ever comprehensive destination marketing plans completed for a province in China. It was prepared during a 1-year period in 2006 and 2007. Two official documents were produced in both Chinese and English: the *Marketing Plan* and a *Technical Report*.

The specific steps completed were as follows:

- Attraction and resource assessment
- Past visitor market analysis
- Analysis of past marketing strategies and programmes
- Analysis of potential markets and marketing opportunities
- Identification of marketing goals and strategies
- Development of marketing objectives and action plans
- Development of organization and management plan
- Measurement of strategic marketing plan performance.

Unique selling propositions (USPs)

The first step was to assess the existing tourism attractions and resources in Jiangsu Province, with particular attention to those within the thirteen major cities. Site visits to the thirteen cities were made in order to identify major product themes and unique selling propositions (USPs).

The USPs were categorized into two distinct groups: culture-heritage resources; and natural resources.

Culture-heritage resources

- Bridges of Jiangsu
- Chinese classical gardens
- Chinese medicine, tea, health and longevity
- City walls
- Cuisine and food
- Famous people or icons
- Grand Canal
- Great folk stories of China
- Han Dynasty culture
- Handicrafts and unique shopping products
- Historic streets
- Ming Dynasty culture
- Museums
- Performing arts and music
- Religious buildings and sites
- Revolutionary and red tourism
- Silk manufacturing and silk products
- Water towns.

Natural resources

- Birds and animals
- Golf
- Hot springs
- Lakes and lake resorts
- Mountains and hills
- Natural wetlands
- Sea coast and seaside resorts
- Yangtze River.

Figure 14A Wall window at Suzhou classical Chinese garden
Source: Shutterstock, Inc. (Robert Paul Van Beets).

Figure 14B Buddhist pagoda at Changzhou
Source: Shutterstock, Inc. (Shao Weiwei).

Figure 14C Terracotta warriors and horses from the Han Dynasty in Xuzhou
Source: Shutterstock, Inc. (Craig Hanson).

Market research

To give the most solid and market-oriented foundation for the marketing plan, extensive research was conducted in North America and Europe.

- US consumer survey (sample = 1,245)
- North American international visitor survey (sample = 529)

- North American tour wholesaler survey (sample = 17)
- North American tour wholesaler programme analysis (sample = 30 companies with 256 programmes in China)
- European international visitor survey (sample = 851)
- European tour operator survey (sample = 20)
- European tour operator programme analysis (sample = 29 companies with 284 programmes in China).

Primary data were collected by BTI from North American and European travellers and travel trade intermediaries that more clearly focused the marketing strategy for Jiangsu tourism. For example, this research provided information on awareness levels of Jiangsu's major destinations and attractions, and previous trip history to China and Jiangsu. In addition, the data gave an indication of the types of destination activities in which travellers and trade channels were most interested in pursuing while in China. For example, a list of 31 specific places, sites and attractions in Jiangsu was included in the US consumer survey questionnaire and the respondents were asked to indicate their awareness of each of these on a 'yes' or 'no' basis. With the exception of the Yangtze River, of which 61.8 per cent were aware, the majority of the respondents were not aware of the individual places, sites and attractions in Jiangsu.

The rankings of these places, sites and attractions deserved further comment because of their relevance to the future marketing of Jiangsu. First, it was clear that there was no single 'hallmark' attraction in Jiangsu in the minds of these respondents in the US, such as the Great Wall for Beijing and the Terracotta Warriors for Xi'an. Instead, there were seven attractions that were moderately well-known among US consumers including the Yangtze River, the Grand Canal, the Confucius Temple area in Nanjing, Suzhou silk embroidery, the Classical Chinese gardens of Suzhou, the Presidential Palace in Nanjing and Nanjing itself.

Country profiles

Twenty-five country profiles were completed on the major nations within North America and Europe. The profiles included extensive secondary research on each market and information was collected from multiple sources around the world over a period of 8 months.

DMO case studies

Case studies were completed on ten top international DMOs. Information was gathered on how these DMOs were marketing in North America and

Europe. The DMOs were from Australia, Brazil, Canada, Hong Kong, Ireland, New Zealand, Singapore, South Africa, the UK and the USA. Each of the case studies detailed the current marketing activities of these DMOs in the following countries:

- France
- Germany
- Italy
- UK
- Canada
- USA.

Marketing goals

Based upon the USPs, research results, country profiles and case studies, a set of thirteen marketing goals for Jiangsu Province Tourism were identified in the following twelve categories of marketing initiatives:

Positioning

- To consistently implement the new positioning, 'Taste Jiangsu: To taste Jiangsu is to know China', over a period of 3–4 years.

Target markets

- To continually increase the volume of visitors to Jiangsu from the USA, UK, Germany, France, Canada and Italy each year from 2008 to 2012.
- To design and implement a strategy for attracting selected special-interest travel (SIT) markets to Jiangsu.

Marketing planning

- To develop a systematic template and annual programmatic procedure for developing marketing strategies and plans for major market sources.

Marketing research

- To design and conduct a marketing research programme plan on an annual basis from 2008 to 2012 inclusive.

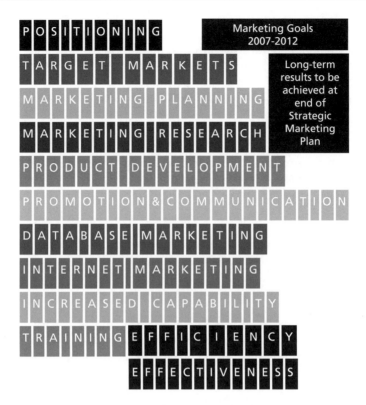

Figure 14D International marketing goals 2007–2012 for Jiangsu Province

Source: Belle Tourism International Consulting, 2007.

Product development

● To develop a series of product development, packaging, programming and partnership initiatives that correspond with the unique selling propositions (USPs).

Promotional communications

● To develop and implement an annual promotion and communications plan for each major geographic market in Europe and North America.

Database marketing

● To prepare systematic and relational databases covering the local tourism industry; foreign travel trade; past and potential visitors; media representatives; and an image library.

Internet marketing

- To implement an aggressive Internet marketing strategy and plan that addresses the individual traveller market, travel trade, MICE markets, media and press and other JPTB publics.

Increased capability

- To expand the Marketing and Promotion Division of JPTB in accordance with the new roles and specific demands of the Strategic Marketing Plan for Europe and North America.

Training

- To implement a systematic, annual training programme of marketing planning and implementation.

Efficiency

- To develop a set of measures to quantify the efficiency of JPTB's marketing, promotion and communications programs, e.g. measuring the number of unique visitors to the English-language version of the JPTB website.

Effectiveness

- To measure the effectiveness and impacts and return on investment of major marketing and promotional programmes.

Target markets

Six high-priority country markets were identified in the USA, Canada, UK, Germany, France and Italy. It was recommended that a special emphasis should be placed on attracting independent travellers from North America and Europe. This was because the market research had shown that a majority of the international visitors surveyed in China were independent travellers.

However, the group tour market to China from Europe to North America is significant, and it therefore was also recommended for priority attention. Special-interest travel (SIT) markets have been growing rapidly around the world. Given the characteristics of Jiangsu Tourism's USPs, it was recommended that attention be paid to SIT markets in North America and Europe.

Figure 14E High-priority international country markets for Jiangsu Province

Source: Belle Tourism International Consulting, 2007.

Positioning approach

'Taste Jiangsu: to taste Jiangsu is to know China'

The recommended positioning statement for Jiangsu tourism was designed as an *active* invitation to Europeans and North Americans to visit the province. Furthermore, it encouraged Europeans and North Americans to sample (*taste*) Jiangsu and in so doing to better understand China itself. However, this was just one of four dimensions to this positioning approach and statement, as can be seen in the description and diagram that follow.

- First, it sent a strong and enticing message that is an invitation for Europeans and North Americans to explore Jiangsu Province (*consumer invitation*).
- Second, it aptly characterized the tourism products and attractions of Jiangsu as being *tasteful* and *refined*, as well as being rich, valuable and in-depth (*product characterization*).
- Third, it provided an opportunity to personalize communications to visitors with such phrases as 'It's your taste' (*consumer personalization*).
- Fourth, it offered a platform to feature all of the city destinations in the province's tourism positioning, using such phrases as 'A garden classic. Taste Jiangsu in Suzhou' and 'A presidential resting place. Taste Jiangsu in Nanjing' (*city destination associations*).

Taste
Consumer invitations
Sample
Explore
Discover
Experience
Try
Jiangsu
Product characterizations
Refined taste
Rich culture and history
Sophisticated taste
Unique taste or flavour
Huaiyang cuisine
TASTE
JIANGSU
Consumer Personalizations
It's your taste
Your taste of China
Become a China expert
Taste Jiangsu
Know
City destination associations
Taste Jiangsu in Suzhou
Taste Jiangsu in Nanjing
Others
China

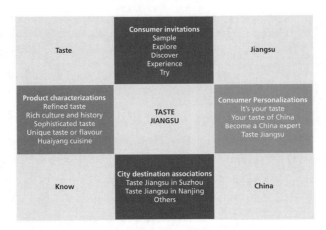

Figure 14F Four dimensions of international tourism positioning approach for Jiangsu Province
Source: Belle Tourism International Consulting, 2007.

The positioning approach had great flexibility of expression, as shown in the following chart. For example, as a consumer invitation, it could simply be expressed as 'Taste Jiangsu' or be used in its fullest form of 'To taste Jiangsu is to know China.'

Consumer invitations
Consumer personalization
Product characterizations
City destination associations
To taste Jiangsu is to know China
Your taste of China. In Jiangsu
The home of sweet & sour. Taste Jiangsu
A garden classic. Taste Jiangsu in Suzhou
Taste Jiangsu
It's your taste. Jiangsu, China
The genuine fried rice. Taste Jiangsu
It's your cup of tea Taste Jiangsu in Yixing
Jiangsu. Taste our Culture
Your China discovery. Taste Jiangsu
The birthplace of Huaiyang. Taste Jiangsu
The home of fried rice. Taste Jiangsu in Yangzhou
Acquire a taste for China ... in Jiangsu
Your complete menu of China
Savour our flavours. Taste Jiangsu
Sweet & sour. Taste Jiangsu in Zhenjiang
Get sweet on China. Taste Jiangsu
Your China sampler. Made in Jiangsu
Jiangsu. A refined taste
See the China Sea. Taste Jiangsu in LYG
Take a taste test of China ... In Jiangsu
Jiangsu. Your taste test of China
A tasteful place. Jiangsu, China
A presidential resting place. Taste Jiangsu in Nanjing

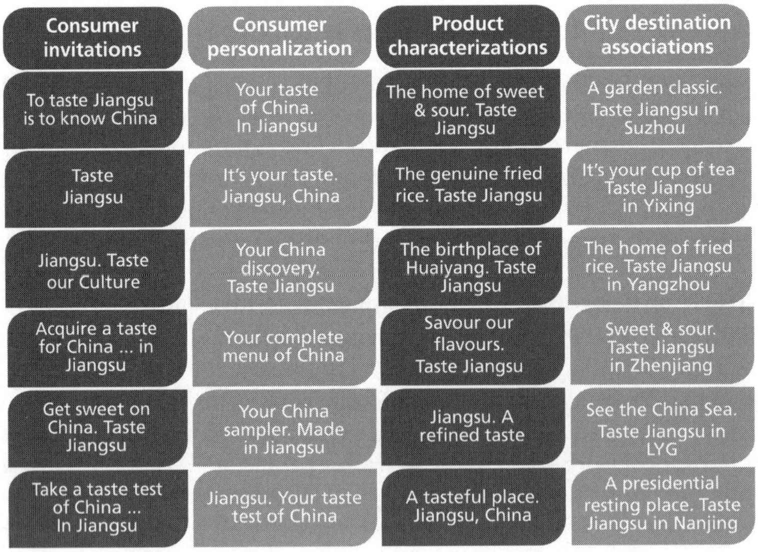

Figure 14G Expressions of international tourism positioning for Jiangsu Province
Source: Belle Tourism International Consulting, 2007.

Following the completion of this marketing plan, an English website was developed for Jiangsu tourism with the domain name of TasteJiangsu. com. So the selected positioning approach was now very well reflected in Jiangsu Tourism's Internet marketing.

The recommended target markets along with the positioning approach represented the marketing strategy for Jiangsu Province tourism for North America and Europe.

Marketing plan

The marketing plan included the following components:

- Marketing plan rationale; marketing strategies; and marketing goals
- Annual marketing objectives and action plans for Europe and North America
- Specific marketing ideas and approaches
- Measurement of strategic marketing plan performance, including the control and evaluation blueprint (efficiency and effectiveness measures)
- Market and marketing research programme
- Marketing organization and management plan
- Follow-up system and tracking timetable
- Training programmes.

Marketing objectives

Marketing objectives were developed for each year from 2008 to 2012 inclusive based upon the marketing goals.

Marketing action plans

Then annual marketing action plans were designed to achieve each year's objectives. Action tasks were specified for the achievement of each objective in each year.

Specific marketing ideas and approaches

Many specific ideas and approaches were put forward during the preparation of the marketing plan for the international tourism promotion of each of the cities. Some of the ideas were recommendations on how to position the individual cities in the North American and European markets. Four examples are provided below:

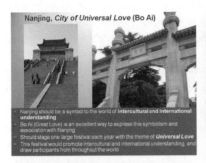

Figure 14H International positioning of individual cities in Jiangsu Province

Source: Belle Tourism International Consulting, 2007.

International event presentations

Another practical outcome of the marketing plan was the design of a professional PowerPoint presentation for English-language audiences around the world. These slides were creatively designed to incorporate the 'Taste Jiangsu' positioning approach.

Figure 14I Taste Jiangsu international presentation for Jiangsu Province

Source: Belle Tourism International Consulting, 2007.

The presentation featured tourism in each of Jiangsu's thirteen major cities. The text emphasized the USPs of each city:

Figure 14J Postcard format for Taste Jiangsu event presentation
Source: Belle Tourism International Consulting, 2007.

Measurement of strategic marketing plan performance

The step identified ways to track and measure the results of the marketing objectives and action plans within the Strategic Marketing Plan for Europe and North America. These consisted of: (1) marketing efficiency measures; and (2) marketing effectiveness measures. These represented the performance measurement of JPTB with respect to these plans.

Marketing efficiency measures monitor progress on activities as each marketing objectives and action plan is being implemented (or formative evaluation). Generally, they track the volume of responses by potential visitors or travel trade intermediaries to specific promotional activities or campaigns.

Marketing effectiveness measures are collected at the completion of each marketing objectives and action plan and assess to what extent the plan's objectives were achieved (or summative evaluation). Marketing efficiency measures are associated with activity or activities; marketing effectiveness measures are indicators of satisfaction of marketing objectives for:

- Control and evaluation blueprint
- Public relations and communications
- Sales and sales promotion
- Internet and database marketing
- Market and marketing research.

Control and evaluation blueprint

The control and evaluation blueprint specified the marketing efficiency and effectiveness measures and questions for each of the annual marketing objectives and action plans.

Marketing efficiency measures

PUBLIC RELATIONS AND COMMUNICATIONS MEASURES

- General and travel media and press contacts
- Travel writer contacts
- Media and press relations
- Familiarization trips
- Printed promotional materials distribution.

SALES AND SALES PROMOTION MEASURES

- Tour operator, wholesaler and travel agency contacts
- MICE planner contacts
- MICE planner site inspections
- Travel fairs and exhibitions
- Sales missions
- Sales calls
- Special-interest travel markets
- Packages
- Festivals and events
- Partnerships and cooperative marketing.

INTERNET AND DATABASE MARKETING MEASURES

- Website traffic
- Digital materials distribution.

Marketing effectiveness measures

- Measure 1: To count the number of new general and travel media and press contacts when they are successfully entered into the computer database.
- Measure 2: To count the number of new travel writer contacts when they are successfully entered into the computer database.
- Measure 3: To measure the responses of the media and press to promotional activities and also count public presentations by JPTB officials and staff.
- Measure 4: To measure participation levels and financial investment in familiarization trips.
- Measure 5: To count the number of printed promotional material items requested and distributed to potential visitors and others.
- Measure 6: To count the number of new tour operator, wholesaler and travel agency contacts when they are successfully entered into the computer database.
- Measure 7: To count the number of new meeting planner contacts when they are successfully entered into the computer database.
- Measure 8: To count the number of site inspections by MICE planners in Jiangsu for which JPTB provides assistance.
- Measure 9: To measure the levels of activity associated with attendance and participation in travel fairs and exhibitions.
- Measure 10: To measure the volume of activity involved with sales missions.
- Measure 11: To measure sales call activity levels.
- Measure 12: To measure the activities involved with investigating the potential of individual special-interest travel markets and developing strategies for appealing to them.
- Measure 13: To track the number of packages partly or wholly designed and created by staff in the JPTB.
- Measure 14: To count the number of new festivals and events partly or wholly designed and created by staff in the JPTB.
- Measure 15: To measure the number of partnerships and the levels of participation in these partnerships.
- Measure 16: To track and measure the traffic to JPTB's English and Spanish websites.
- Measure 17: To count the number of digital promotional material items requested and distributed to potential visitors and others.
- Measure 18: To track the number and value of projects and studies commissioned that are awarded to external vendors.
- Measure 19: To count the number of speeches and presentations for which statistics or data were provided to JPTB officials and staff, and others.
- Measure 20: To track the number of releases of the research digest or compendium of statistics.

Market and marketing research programme

The sixth project goal was to develop a set of objectives and action plans for each of the 5 years from 2008 to 2012. As part of the work required for meeting this goal, a market and marketing research programme plan was highly recommended.

The seventh project step was an elaboration of the marketing objectives and action plans with respect to market and marketing research projects. The outcome was the development of an outline for an ongoing programme of market and marketing research related to the European and North American markets.

The detailed components of the market and marketing research programme were as follows:

- Within-Jiangsu visitor market research
- Current long-haul market research
- Emerging markets and trends research
- Special-interest travel (SIT) market research
- MICE market research
- Travel trade intermediary research
- Internet marketing tracking and research
- Media and public relations (PR) research
- Pre- and post-testing of promotions
- Control and evaluation research.

Marketing organization and management plan

- Recommended structure of Marketing and Promotion Division
- Staffing requirements
- Training requirements
- New partnership structures.

Follow-up system and tracking timetable

Follow-up system

The control and evaluation blueprint provided a comprehensive set of measures to keep track of marketing efficiency and performance, as well as to judge if annual marketing objectives were attained or not. However, the blueprint did not guarantee that all of the items will be measured as proposed; nor did it account for unforeseen circumstances that might require some adjustments in the plans. Therefore, it was necessary to recommend a follow-up system with an appropriate timetable to conduct more formal and comprehensive reviews of the plans from 2008 onwards. This system incorporated the following three main elements:

- Semi-annual report
- Annual review meeting
- Recommendations for following year.

Timetable

A timetable was recommended for implementing this follow-up system.

Training programmes

The step proposed a series of training programmes in support of the marketing plan implementation. It recognized that the new marketing emphasis on Europe and North America would be new and challenging for JPTB and for others in the Jiangsu tourism industry. Interest was very high everywhere in Jiangsu in further penetrating these markets, but there was not much prior experience in doing so. Thus, training would be a key factor in better preparing JPTB staff and others in the industry for the new marketing initiatives in North America and Europe. The nine priority topics for the series of training programmes were:

- Destination marketing planning processes and steps
- Communications with Europeans and North Americans
- The travel trade distribution system and outbound travel markets in individual European and North American countries
- Designing effective websites and measuring website effectiveness
- Internet and database marketing
- Promotional communications techniques for North America and Europe
- Destination positioning and branding strategies
- Product development, packaging and programming for Europe and North America
- Service standard expectations of North Americans and Europeans.

Case summary

This is an excellent case study for showing how the professional principles of destination marketing have been applied to the international marketing of a province in China. The Destination Marketing Planning

Process (DMPP) as described earlier in this book was closely followed in the preparation of the Strategic Marketing Plan for Tourism in Jiangsu Province.

The Destination Marketing System (DMS) and the PRICE model were also used as guiding frameworks for this marketing plan and the annual action plans specified tasks according to the 8 Ps of destination marketing.

Another outstanding feature of the preparation of this plan in Jiangsu was the detailed assessment of the tourism attractions and resources in the main destinations throughout the province. This was greatly facilitated by the excellent cooperation among all of the marketing officers at the provincial and city government levels.

A significant amount of market research was completed as a foundation for this destination marketing plan; and this could be considered as another major strength of this case study.

International pleasure and leisure travel markets case study questions and exercise

1 The Jiangsu marketing strategy and plan had a focus on Europe and North America, which are both long-haul markets for the province. How would the approaches used need to be adapted for continents and countries where English is not predominantly used and the underlying cultures are quite different?
2 Should a province, state or region market the whole country first and then secondly market itself? What is your reasoning for your answer? Please provide some real examples to explain your arguments.
3 Taking your own province, state or region as the destination of focus, how would you develop a marketing strategy and plan to attract international pleasure and leisure travellers? What would be included in the strategy and plan, and on which countries would you concentrate and why?

Chapter 15

Business travel and business event markets

Learning objectives

1 Define the major segments of business travel and business events.

2 Discuss the size and importance of business travel and business events in selected countries.

3 Explain the benefits of business travel and business events.

4 Review the major challenges in the marketing and development of business travel and business events.

5 Elaborate upon the recent trends for business travel and business events.

6 Explain the roles played by professional congress/conference organizers and independent meeting or event planners.

7 Detail the roles of incentive travel planning companies and explain the trend of convergence of meetings and incentive travel trips.

8 Describe the role of RFPs (requests for proposals) in the business event markets.

9 Discuss a systematic, step-by-step approach to the marketing of business events.

10 Identify and describe a select number of excellent business event marketing and promotion campaigns.

Introduction

The business travel and business event markets are the 'backbone' of the client base for many city destinations around the world. For some DMOs, they are the main focus of activity and pleasure and leisure travellers are of secondary concern. For example, this is true for hundreds of convention and visitors bureaus in North America, as well as for many other larger city DMOs in other parts of the world.

While DMOs cannot directly influence what is considered to be 'regular' business travel, they play a major role in attracting business events to their destinations. As you will understand, regular business travel motivations are quite different from the motivations of pleasure and leisure travellers that were discussed in Chapter 12. Unlike regular business travel where the choice of destination is fixed, business event organizers have a choice of potential destinations and tourism products play a role in their site selection decision-making.

Business travel and business events represent a significant proportion of domestic and international tourism in many destinations around the world. The global economic crisis in 2008 and 2009 had a major adverse impact on these markets, but this chapter will show that they have been recovering.

DMOs are very professional in their marketing approaches to business events, and this is required because of the high level of competition and bidding situations. This chapter introduces some outstanding examples of marketing and promotional approaches for business events markets.

Definition of market segments

One of the toughest challenges in this chapter is how to define the market segments of business travel and business events. Why is this so? The answer is because people use terminology interchangeably and definitions tend to vary from region to region and even by country. For example, there was a period where the term 'MICE' was used quite widely and particularly in Asia. However, there has now been a movement in the tourism sector not to use this term anymore.

Before providing the definitions, you should know that an alternative collective term for all of them is 'business tourism'. In this book, the preferred terminology is 'business travel and business events' since this is more descriptive of the two major components of this form of tourism.

Regular business travel

The types of business-related travel tend to fall into the following seven categories (US Travel Association/Oxford Economics, 2009):

- Customer visits
- Sales and marketing
- Internal meetings
- Employee training
- Conferences and conventions
- Trade shows and exhibitions
- Incentive and reward.

For the purposes of this book, the first four categories are included in regular business travel and the last three are within business events.

Business events

There is a huge variety of definitions of business events and it is really confusing to try to make sense out of all of these. In the following materials, this book will attempt to remove the confusion for you. The following is a set of definitions for the most commonly held business events:

- *Business events*: The US Travel Association says that business events include, 'meetings, conventions, conferences, trade shows, exhibitions and incentive travel. They last at least 4 hours, include a minimum of ten participants and take place at a contracted venue'. This definition is useful since it specifies a minimum duration and a minimum number of participants (4 hours; ten participants). The other useful part of this definition is that it specifies that events must be held at 'contracted venues' and this means that the events are held at places where there is a contract between the organizers and the facility owners (e.g. convention centre, hotel or resort, cruise ship, etc.).
- *Citywide*: A citywide is an 'event that requires the use of a convention centre or event complex and multiple hotels in the host city' (APEX Industry Glossary) (APEX = Accepted Practices Exchange).
- *Conference*: ICCA defines a conference as a 'participatory meeting designed for discussion, fact-finding, problem solving and consultation. As compared with a congress, a conference is normally smaller in scale and more select in character – features which tend to facilitate the exchange of information. The term "conference" carries no special connotation as to frequency. Though not inherently limited in time, conferences are usually of limited duration with specific objectives.'
- *Congresses*: ICCA defines congresses as the 'regular coming together on a representational basis of several hundred, or even thousands, of individuals belonging to a single professional, cultural, religious or other group. A congress is often convened to discuss a particular subject. Contributions to the presentation and discussion of the subject matter come only from members of the organising body. The frequency is usually established in advance and can be either multi-annual or annual. Most international or world congresses are of the former type; while national congresses are more frequently held annually. A congress will often last several days and has several simultaneous sessions.' ICCA took this definition from the International Association of Professional Congress Organisers (IAPCO).
- *Conventions*: The APEX Glossary defines a convention as a 'gathering of delegates, representatives, and members of a membership or industry organization convened for a common purpose. Common features include educational sessions, committee meetings, social functions, and meetings to conduct the governance business of the organization. Conventions are typically recurring events with specific, established timing.' Typically, the organizations involved are associations. Unlike with meetings, there may be an exhibit component at conventions, but they are a secondary part of the event.
- *Exhibitions*: Exhibitions are 'events at which products, services or promotional materials are displayed to attendees visiting exhibits on the show floor' (APEX Glossary 2011). These events focus primarily on business-to-business (B2B) relationships, but consumers are also allowed to attend on certain days (Figure 15.1).

Figure 15.1 BIT in Milan, Italy is a travel exhibition
Source: Shutterstock, Inc. (Adriano Castelli).

- *Incentive travel*: SITE International Foundation (2010) defines incentive travel as 'a global management tool that uses an exceptional travel experience to motivate and/or recognize participants for increased levels of performance in support of organizational goals'. You should note that these are commonly called 'incentives'.
- *Meetings*: The APEX Industry Glossary 2011 specifies that at a meeting the 'primary activity of the participants is to attend educational sessions, participate in discussions, social functions, or attend other organized events'. Meetings do not have an exhibit component according to the APEX definition.
- *Trade shows*: These are B2B (business-to-business) events. They are exhibitions of products and/or services held for members of common or related industries (Convention Industry Council, 2012). Trade shows are not open to the general public.

You may be a little confused since there seems to be some overlap among some of these definitions; so some further explanation is in order. The main issue is because of differences in terminology between North America and Europe. The term 'convention' is more of a North American term and encompasses the ideas of 'congresses' and 'conferences'. The term 'congress' is more of a European term and you might think of it as being synonymous with 'convention' although the two are not exactly the same.

The terms 'exhibition' and 'trade show' are quite similar, but the difference in meaning is that trade shows are exclusively B2B. Exhibitions have a consumer component as well.

There are terms that are used for meetings including forums, seminars, symposiums and workshops. For the sake of keeping things simple, this book will not define these additional terms. However, there are some further definitions about the participants of business events that you need to know about:

ICCA also tracks the number of international association meetings by city and for 2010, the top ten cities were: (1) Vienna, (2) Barcelona, (3) Paris, (4) Berlin, (5) Singapore, (6) Madrid, (7) Istanbul, (8) Lisbon, (9) Amsterdam and (10) Sydney.

Vienna, Austria: ICCA's top-ranking city destination for international association meetings does a wonderful job of reporting on its business event activity each year. In the *Vienna Meetings Industry Report 2011*, the Vienna Convention Bureau, a branch within the Vienna Tourist Board, indicated that a total of 3,151 association congresses and corporate events were held in the city during 2011. These meetings had a total of 475,298 participants spending 1,412,133 bednights in Vienna (about three nights on average). Business events contributed 12.4 per cent of all the bednights in Vienna in 2011. The number of business events in 2011 in Vienna was up 7 per cent over 2010, and bednights increased by 6 per cent.

Barcelona, Spain: For 2010, there were 2,138 business events in Barcelona (310 congresses; 226 seminars and symposiums; and 1,602 conventions and incentives). These events had a total of 616,833 participants. The average attendances at these events were: 976 for congresses; 169 for conventions and incentives; and 191 for seminars and symposiums.

Singapore: Some 27 per cent of the 9.7 million visitor arrivals to Singapore in 2009 had business/MICE as the purpose of visit.

Benefits of business travel and business event markets

This is an interesting topic because of the differences between regular business travel and business events. The benefits of business events are typically expressed in economic terms and particularly in total expenditures and expenditures per capita. However, the advantages of regular business travel trips that are not associated with a business event, are most often expressed through the benefits that accrue to the companies, rather than the destinations.

Benefits of business travel

For example, an interesting study was conducted by Oxford Economics on behalf of the US Travel Association (USTA) and published in 2009. It was called *The Return on Investment of US Business Travel*, and was a unique perspective on business travel and its benefits. The study pinpointed four benefits of business travel: (1) keeping customers, (2) converting prospects, (3) building relational networks and (4) investing in people.

Business travel benefits companies and individuals

Business travel is an essential business function which produces a broad range of benefits to both companies and individuals. This rather obvious claim is supported by 82% of executives whom believe travel is important for business results.

(US Travel Association/Oxford Economics, 2009)

One of the key findings of this study was that for every dollar invested in business travel, companies earned $12.50 in additional revenues. The study was conducted during the economic recession of 2009 in the USA and companies were already cutting back on business travel in order to reduce their costs. However, the research study concluded that cutting back on business travel could reduce a company's profits for several years. On average, a company would give up 17 per cent of its profits in the first year of eliminating business travel and then it would take more than 3 years for profits to recover.

There are also costs to regular business travel that need to be controlled by companies in the same way as other costs. These are often called 'T&E' or travel and entertainment expenses. T&E costs are difficult to control since many different individuals incur travel expenses and companies must rely on their honesty and integrity in reporting T&E expenses accurately. It is strongly recommended that every company should develop, implement and enforce a T&E policy for all of their travellers. American Express (2007) says that organizations only have four points at which they can control T&E expenditures:

'When companies can control T&E costs by American Express'

Organizations have only four chances to exercise control over any given T&E expenditure. The first opportunity, which occurs before the expense has been incurred, involves the development of a T&E policy. This is simply a matter of exercising control by letting travellers know the ground rules. The second control opportunity is the point at which prices are determined. This can occur at the time reservations are made (airline tickets, hotel rooms, car rentals) or at the point of sale (restaurants). The third control opportunity involves the usage of comprehensive and efficient payment methods that verify actual costs and collect vendor data. The fourth and last chance an organization has to control and reduce travel expenses is at the time expense reports are audited and processed for payment.

Benefits of business events

The benefits of business events tend to be quoted in terms of delegate expenditures. The strongest argument is often that business event participants spend more than other tourists on a per capita daily basis. This point is well demonstrated for the inbound market from the USA to Canada in 2010. The average per night spending for a meeting, convention and incentive traveller was C$ 248 compared with C$ 117 for a leisure traveller from the USA (Canadian Tourism Commission, 2011). Although these business event tourists represented 14.8 per cent of all the US resident trips to Canada, they accounted for 22.7 per cent of the total spending. A second example of this above-average spending is from Vienna, Austria. According to the Vienna Convention Bureau, business event participants spent 475 euros per bednight compared to an average of 260 euros for all visitors to the city (Vienna Convention Bureau, 2012).

Additionally, business events are one the highest yielding market segments in Australia. In 2010, total business events delegate visitor expenditures were AUD 8.5 billion and by 2020, they have the potential to contribute up to AUD 16 billion annually.

The US Travel Association (USTA) (2012) divides the benefits of meetings into three categories: (1) impacts on the national economy, (2) impacts on local communities and (3) impacts on businesses:

Impacts of business events on the USA

- Impacts on national economy (2009)
  - Contributed $458 billion to the nation's GDP.
  - Directly employed 1.7 million Americans and supports 4.6 million indirect jobs.
  - Generated $64 billion in tax revenue for the federal government.
- Impacts on local communities
  - The value of meetings extends far beyond the convention centres and local tourist destinations.
  - Meeting participants spent $145 billion at local businesses including hotels, restaurants, shops and meeting vendors.
  - State and local governments earned $46 billion in tax revenue from meetings-related travel.
- Impacts on businesses and job creation
  - In-person meetings provide bottom line value for thousands of US businesses and are vital to driving job creation.
  - Approximately 35 per cent of all business travel is meeting-related.
  - Meetings provide the greatest financial return of any form of business marketing; every dollar invested in business travel generates a $10–15 dollar return.

The USTA definition of benefits tend to be more economic and short-term in measurement; however, business events have impacts that may spread over several years. For example, the Association of Australian Convention Bureaux (AACB) (2007) provides another perspective of the benefits of business events as they emphasize the longer-term advantages to communities:

Business events: long term legacies for Australian society

The legacy of business events can be felt long after these high-yield visitors have departed:

- Exposure to, and promotion of, world's best practice
- Networking and enhancing business-to-business relationships

- Education
- Trade opportunities from exhibitions and commercial sponsorships
- Exposing original research to the marketplace
- Leveraging existing exports such as mining, medicine and technology
- Fundraising opportunities
- Enhancing international prestige
- Business migration inflow
- Showcasing host-nation infrastructure.

Therefore, business events have both short-term economic benefits and long-term community benefits. Their strongest economic benefit is the above-average daily spending rates of participants.

However, business travel and business events are not without challenges and there are important issues as well. This chapter now reviews the most significant of these challenges and issues for destination marketing and development.

Challenges

Business travel and business events have just passed through a very challenging time period; due to the adverse global economic conditions in 2008 and 2009 and their after-effects. Companies have been cutting back on their business travel costs and less people have been attending business events. The US Travel Association (USTA) has called this difficult phase the 'perfect storm' as destinations were also being challenged by technology that was providing an alternative to face-to-face meetings.

Competitive intensity

The competition for many major business events is global and very intense nowadays. Most events are bidding situations where competing destinations must vie against each other to try to find the edge that will allow them to win. Prices are always a major factor in site selection decisions and some destinations can offer larger price 'incentives' than others to secure events. Some call this 'buying the business' but, in fact, financial support from host destinations to event organizers has become more common.

Cost control and policy compliance

Particularly for regular business travel, the control of travel expenses and having employees comply with corporate travel policies is a major challenge. Cost control is also a major issue for meeting planners. This may not at first glance seem to be of direct concern to DMOs, but they should do what they can to assist the organizations involved to control their costs.

Incorporating use of social network sites

Chapters 10 and 12 highlighted the explosion in consumer use of social network sites, and these so-called Web 2.0 tools are presenting a host of new challenges as well as opportunities for business travel and business events. Is the use of social media sites a help or hindrance to business travel and business events? Does using SNSs distract business people from doing their real work? These are good questions indeed, but the majority of opinion is that the use of SNSs is a positive development for corporations and non-profit organizations.

Some academic tourism scholars have suggested that many meetings are not adapting to these new technologies but are still following antiquated models (Fenich *et al.*, 2011; Lee, 2011). Lee's study concluded that meeting professionals believed that Twitter and Facebook were valuable tools in transforming meetings into interactive sessions. Moreover, the SNSs are now critical to successful marketing and communications of business events.

There appear to be generational differences of opinions on this issue, with older people favouring traditional styles of business communications, and younger people preferring to make the use of SNSs and other Internet functions.

Negative economic conditions

Government agencies and private companies have recently been cutting back on business-related travel due to the negative economic conditions that have adversely affected many of the major developed countries. This has particularly been true in Europe and North America in the period 2008–2010, with some recovery being experienced in 2011 and 2012. Many government agencies are operating with reduced budgets; and the private sector has been cost-cutting to maintain profitability of operations.

Unfortunately when unfavourable economic conditions are encountered, travel is one of the first candidates considered for cost-cutting. This is unfortunate for destinations, but as yet the value of business-related travel is still considered inferior to other cost centres.

'Perk' perceptions of business travel and business events

Fear of adverse public relations in difficult economic times is another issue that governments and companies have had to contemplate. The US Travel Association argues that 'business travel has been inaccurately portrayed as an unnecessary perk rather than a critical component of job creation and innovation'. In the USA, this issue was not helped by a 'scandal' that the Federal Government's General Services Administration (GSA) held a training conference in Las Vegas and spent $822,000 on the event, and $440,000 on an employee awards programme. *Federal Times* (2012) expects that the US government will cut back on its travel, based on the negative publicity this scandal created and the increased scrutiny it caused:

Expected fallout from GSA conference scandal

Many federal employees interviewed by Federal Times — most on the condition they remain anonymous — said they expect lawmakers to cut deeply into federal travel, conference and training budgets in the aftermath of the scandal. And they expect that getting approvals for legitimate business trips will almost certainly get harder and more time-consuming.

Reliance on other tourism sector stakeholders' performance

DMOs do not control and operate the facilities that are used by the business travel and business event markets; they have to rely on the performance of tourism sector stakeholders. DMOs market and promote the hotels/resorts and convention/exhibition centres within their destinations, but it is the performance levels of these facilities that ultimately determine customer satisfaction. This is challenging for DMOs since they make the promises but it is up to others to deliver on these promises. Therefore, it is very important that DMOs conduct post-event audits of participant and event planner satisfaction levels.

Technology as a substitute for travel

Information and communication technologies (ICTs) were discussed in Chapter 11 and they are definitely having a very positive impact on destination management and marketing, by providing DMOs with many new tools and channels. But is it possible that ICTs could be both 'friend' and 'foe' for travel to tourism destinations? The answer would have to be a definite 'yes'.

Video conferencing and teleconferencing have been touted for many years as a low-cost and more convenient alternative to traditional business events. However, DMOs and their associations have strongly argued that nothing can replace the value and benefits of real, face-to-face meetings, as evidenced in the following statement by the US Travel Association:

'Technology cannot replicate the unique value of meetings'

The meetings industry is a critical driver of economic growth for communities and businesses across the country. Meetings are core to our national fabric as a means to educate, collaborate, and innovate. From walking trade show floors to sharing ideas in a group setting, to launching new ventures, the unique value of meetings cannot be replicated by conference calls or emails.

(US Travel Association, 2012)

However, ICTs are getting much better and will improve further in future. Two-way video and audio is now available in many more ICTs including PCs, mobile phones, tablet devices, as well as the dedicated video conferencing software and hardware applications. Webinars are very popular due to their convenience and the comfort of 'attending' in a person's own office or even at home. It is noteworthy that several tourism sector associations and businesses are themselves making extensive use of webinars including the Pacific Asia Travel Association (PATA).

While older generations tend to favour face-to-face meetings over technology-assisted 'get-togethers', this may not be so strong a sentiment in the future when Generation Y and subsequent groups move into the decision-making positions. These tech-savvy, Internet generation business travellers will probably make greater use of ICTs for all types of business communications. After all, this is not just an issue of whether to travel or not, but these ICTs can greatly improve business communications at a global level while also boosting productivity and profitability.

All of these challenges and issues are putting greater pressure on those who coordinate business travel and those who plan business events to become more professional and accountable.

Trends for business travel and business event markets

There is no doubt that business travel and business events are undergoing some fundamental changes at the present time and the future will see even more change occurring. Just as tourism in general, business travel and business events are not immune from the economic, political, social and cultural, technological and natural environments surrounding them.

Green meetings

There is increasing concern around the world about the potential adverse effects on the environment that can be caused by business events. Green meetings is a movement designed to have environmental considerations in mind when planning and implementing business events. The United Nations Environmental Programme (UNEP) has published the *Green Meeting Guide 2009* that provides guidelines for organizers and hosts. The *Guide* suggests the following environmental targets for meetings:

- Reduce energy use, and the resulting greenhouse gas emissions, e.g. choose convenient locations where participant transportation is minimized.
- Reduce materials consumption and waste generation, e.g. avoid use of disposable items.
- Reduce water use, e.g. minimize the distribution of bottled water to participants.
- Reduce indirect environmental impacts to air, water and soil, e.g. use organic foods.

A Green Meetings Industry Council (GMIC) has been established with its office in Oregon, USA. GMIC says it

> seeks to inspire, educate and support leaders of all levels and disciplines who will manifest the transformation of the global meetings industry towards

sustainability. We champion the implementation of sustainability practices and provide advocacy, education, resources, industry research and recognition of industry leadership.

Several DMOs from North America, Europe and Asia have joined GMIC and are listed in the *GMIC Green Supplier Directory*.

Some individual DMOs have developed their own green meetings initiatives, and one of the outstanding cases has been Travel Portland in Oregon, USA. This DMO has a dedicated website for green meetings and has prepared a 'Green Meetings Toolkit' for meeting planners. The Toolkit includes a book with the title of *Saving Green by Going Green* that provides meeting planners with a guide to saving money while holding sustainable events.

Vienna, Austria is another place that is serious about green meetings. The Vienna Convention Bureau announced in early 2012 that it would certify 'green meetings' according to the requirements and conditions of the 'Austrian Green Meetings EcoLogo'.

'Hybrid' meetings

Carlson Wagonlit Travel (2011) suggests that there will be a trend towards more hybrid meetings. These are meetings that combine traditional meetings with ICTs; some attendees meet in the traditional way, but others are 'connected' by ICTs to the event.

Multi-purposing trips

As mentioned in Chapter 12, people are increasingly combining business travel with other trips purposes and particularly with pleasure and leisure travel. This is mainly as a result of 'time poverty' but also a way for people to get more value out of their travel trips.

Figure 15.2 Portland is a major proponent of green meetings
Source: Shutterstock, Inc. (Josemaria Toscano).

Shorter stays

A number of different sources of research on business travel and business events indicate that lengths of stay in destinations are being reduced. For example, the Vienna Convention Bureau (2012) found that meeting delegates were staying for appreciably shorter time periods and travelling less with companions. VCB said, therefore, that the only way to increase delegate bednights was to attract more events.

Strategic meetings management programmes (SMMPs)

According to Corbin Ball Associates (2009), a strategic meetings management programme (SMMP) is 'the strategic management of enterprise-wide meeting related processes, spend, volumes, standards and suppliers to achieve quantitative cost-savings, risk mitigation and superior service. SMMP can help your company reduce meeting costs, reduce contractual risks and improve service.'

An SMMP is an integrated and comprehensive approach to meeting planning across an organization (e.g. company or association) supported by a complete set of policies. The components covered in an SMMP are the registration of meeting or event; approvals; sourcing and procurement; planning and execution; payment and expense reconciliation; and data analysis and reporting. Various application technologies support the execution of all of these components.

Sperstad and Cecil (2011) have published an article in the *Journal of Convention and Event Tourism* using the title of the 'Changing paradigm of meeting management'. Their major message is that meeting management has changed 'from an industry to a profession'. In particular, these two authors mention the creation of international competency standards for meeting and business event management. Known as the 'Meeting and Business Event Competency Standards', these were developed by the Canadian Tourism Human Resource Council. These standards cover twelve skill areas:

- Strategic planning
- Project management
- Risk management
- Financial management
- Administration
- Human resources
- Stakeholder management
- Event design
- Site management
- Marketing
- Professionalism
- Communication.

Use of technology

Undoubtedly as has already been said in the chapter, the use of technology is a major trend that is affecting business travel and business events. The Canadian Tourism Commission (2011a) has made the following assessment of technological applications for business events:

Canadian Tourism Commission says more digital event strategies are ahead

There is a growing trend toward incorporating a virtual component to meetings and conventions worldwide. Whether through live webcasting, twitter feeds, delegate tracking and polling tools, smart phone meeting apps, social media or online rebroadcasting – the MC&IT market is embracing these new technologies. Contrary however to initial theories, online technology has not reduced delegate participation in meetings. It has actually opened a new market of virtual delegates catering to students and third world participants, giving organizations greater exposure and notoriety. According to meeting professionals surveyed by the Center for Exhibition Industry Research and George P. Johnson Experience Marketing, 72 per cent expect to have a digital event strategy in place by the end of 2010, 44 per cent intend to build internal digital marketing capabilities in the future, 78 per cent say digital marketing increases exhibition marketing effectiveness and 40 per cent indicate that up to 10 per cent of their exhibition budget is spent on digital offerings.

Professional congress or conference organizers (PCOs)

Companies and associations that are holding business events have to make one very fundamental decision: do we plan and implement the event all by ourselves or should we outsource the tasks to professional event planners? You can call this a sort of 'make or buy' decision. If you ever get involved with an event in the future, you will soon realize how complex and complicated they are to plan and operate. This is not something to take on without much previous experience.

Therefore, before delving into DMO business event marketing and promotions, you need to know a little about PCOs and their roles. PCOs are either called Professional Congress Organizers or Professional Conference Organizers. In Continental Europe 'congress' is preferred, while in the UK 'conference' will more likely be used. Actually, the term PCO is not much used in the USA and people performing similar functions tend to be called independent meeting planners. In Canada, they are called event planners.

According to Visit London (2010), Professional Conference Organisers (PCOs) are 'companies that specialize in conference organisation and administration. They have a vast experience and knowledge in planning meetings and are vital for the management of budgets and the securing of sponsorship opportunities.' The types of services offered by PCOs include those listed in Table 15.4.

Basically then PCOs are expert professionals at planning, organizing and implementing business events. Although not called PCOs, the functions of independent meeting or event planners in North America are much the same. For example, the Professional Convention Management Association (PCMA) provides the following description of independent meeting planners:

Independent meeting planners by PCMA

Independent meeting planners are one of the fastest growing segments in the meetings industry today. As independent contractors, they act as a third party, managing the details of finding venues and negotiation of contracts for the corporations and associations they represent. To do so successfully requires independent meeting planners to be knowledgeable in a wide range of areas including site selection, contracts, negotiating, legal issues, hotels, transportation, logistics, tourism and a variety of other planning components.

Table 15.4 Types of services offered by PCOs

- Assistance with congress bids
- Venue research and feasibility
- Advice and consultancy services
- Help in defining objectives
- Guidance on tax issues
- Project planning
- Draft income and expenditure budget preparation
- Financial consultancy
- Book-keeping
- Control of bank accounts
- Negotiation with suppliers and venues
- Meetings with organising committees
- Risk assessments
- Liaison with production companies
- Conference registration
- Delegate management
- Scientific programme development
- Abstract handling

- Exhibition and sales management
- Web design and management
- Speaker liaison and support
- Marketing and public relations
- Venue management
- Staffing on site
- Social event management

- Liaison with airlines and convention bureaus
- Transportation management
- Event evaluations
- Closure of accounts
- Design and print services
- Insurance advice
- Simultaneous interpretation
- Translation of congress documentation
- Accommodation management
- Tour programmes
- Study tours

Source: Visit London, 2010.

Incentive travel planners

Incentive travel planners are companies that specialize in designing and operating incentives and they primarily serve corporate clients. Maritz Travel and Carlson Marketing in the USA are two of the largest incentive travel planning firms in the world. The main trade association for incentive travel planning companies is the Society of Incentive Travel Executives (SITE), which has chapters around the world.

Destination markets

The trips arranged by incentive travel planning companies are given to employees or dealers of their clients as a reward for outstanding sales or work performance. Companies pay for the incentive travel planner's services through a mark-up on the incentive trip costs or pay an agreed-upon fixed fee.

Maritz Travel identifies five aspects of the incentive planning services and these provide a good outline for the roles played by incentive travel planning companies:

- *Design*: Incentive travel planners design customized travel trips for the winners from their client companies. They suggest the destinations for trips as well as the activities and events programme.
- *Communications*: Incentive travel planners prepare and implement programmes to promote the incentive trips to the pool of potential winners within the client company.
- *Operations*: Incentive travel planners operate their trips and this may be done with or without of destination management companies (DMCs) within specific destinations.
- *Measurement*: Incentive travel planners do surveys of trip winners' satisfaction and about the elements of the trip they liked most. They also estimate the benefits of the incentive trip to the company.
- *Technology*: Incentive travel planners use many types of technological applications to operate trip programmes and for communicating with potential participants and winners. These include online registration systems, smartphone app design and using social network sites for communication and discussions.

Maritz Travel below describes how it makes its incentive trips always fresh and exciting:

'You won't find "Wow Factor" on a map, but our clients always end up there'

How do you top your incentive travel programs year after year? It's difficult to keep up with the latest trends, newest experiences and current hot spots. With our patented research approach you can unlock the power of your travel program by connecting with your participants in new and unique ways. You'll have a better understanding of the needs and aspirations of your audience and identify which elements and activities are most meaningful to them. Even better, you'll deliver the kind of travel program your attendees expect and the business results stakeholders demand. With Maritz, the wow just keeps coming.

Incentive travel is truly a mixture of business and pleasure travel, and the incentive winners want to go to popular tourism destinations. Popular destinations for pleasure travel such as Canada, Dubai, Hawaii, Hong Kong and Queensland, Australia are very active in marketing toward incentive travel planners. For example, Tourism Queensland has developed a dedicated website for incentives (http://www.queenslandincentives.com/).

Before leaving the topic of incentive travel, one more predominant trend needs to be mentioned. This is usually referred to as the 'convergence' of meetings and incentives, in other words a combination of business meetings and incentive travel. Business meetings are being scheduled during incentive trips more frequently as companies try to eke out the greatest value and ROI from their investments in travel. A special joint research study has been completed by the SITE Foundation and the MPI Foundation, and its results confirmed this strong trend towards convergence.

Requests for proposals (RFPs)

RFPs are used very frequently in the planning and organizing of business events and you should definitely know about them. Basically, RFPs are forms that meeting planners complete to request proposals for their events from DMOs or hotels. DMOs now have these posted on their websites to make it easier for meeting planners to complete them than the traditional hard-copy versions. Completed RFPs represent 'leads' that DMOs can pass along to hotels and meeting venues that satisfy the meeting planner's needs and requirements.

Most RFPs ask for the following categories of information about planned events:

- Meeting planner contact details
- Title or name of the event
- Proposed dates of event
- Number of attendees
- Meeting room requirements
- Hotel room requirements
- Site inspection required or not required.

You can see that RFPs are very useful tools for all parties involved with business events. For DMOs they provide a 'sure-fire' way of demonstrating their value to tourism sector stakeholders by passing along these leads; for meeting planners, they represent a convenient way of expressing event requirements; and for hotel, resorts and meeting venues they provide the basic information for developing proposals and sales approaches.

Business event marketing procedures

Generally DMOs do not specifically target individual regular business travellers, assuming that this type of travel cannot be influenced. Tourism sector stakeholders and particularly local hotels aggressively sell to locally-based companies, government agencies and non-profits to accommodate their so-called 'transient' guests.

However, this does not mean that DMOs should completely ignore the companies and government agencies located within their destinations. 'Soft sell' approaches should be used, including supplying companies with brochures and other information on the local destination, that can be given out to their visitors and prospective employees.

Additionally, local organizations may be very helpful in assisting the DMO in attracting business events to the destinations. For example, there may be local chapters of state/provincial, national or international associations in the destination. Additionally, there may be local people who are holding executive positions on associations or other non-profit groups. Striking up partnerships with local chapters and with the officers of non-profits is a worthwhile effort for DMOs to initiate.

For business events, DMOs must develop a dedicated set of approaches to destination marketing and promotion. In contrast to the pleasure and leisure markets, potential business event customers and primary competitors are easier to identify. Many DMOs have developed highly professional approaches to business event marketing and promotion. This is partly due to the relative ease of market and competitor identification, but mainly because there is intense competition for business events and DMOs have in-depth experience in business event sales and servicing.

Before getting started on this topic, you need to know a little more about the different types of organizations that get involved in business event marketing and promotion, because it is not just DMOs.

Some countries have established business event divisions or convention bureaus at the national level. For example, Business Events Australia is one of these cases, as is the Singapore Exhibition and Convention Bureau™. Most city DMOs also are actively marketing towards business event organizers.

Another important player is convention and exhibition centre facilities. Sometimes these are under the direct jurisdiction of city DMOs, but more often they are independent entities with their own marketing programmes. Many local governments themselves operate convention/exhibition centres, but in other situations they are contracted out to private companies that specialize in managing these types of venues. For example, SMG is a company based in Pennsylvania, USA that operates around 60 convention centres in the USA, Canada, Jamaica and Puerto Rico. SMG is aggressively marketing the centres that they are operating, as are other facility-operating companies.

Companies that specialize in organizing large events are another important player in business event marketing. Reed Exhibitions is a good example and in 2011, six million participants attended their events. With its headquarters in Surrey, England, Reed has a portfolio of 500 events in 39 countries, including 'trade and consumer exhibitions, conferences and meetings, ranging across forty-four industry sectors; from aerospace and aviation to beauty and cosmetics to sports and recreation'. (2011)

There are also numerous trade associations serving different aspects of business events and they are too many to mention here. Arcodia and Reid (2005) have provided a very good analysis of event management associations and the types of services they provide. There are associations for meeting planners, professional congress organizers (PCOs), destination management companies (DMCs), trade shows, conference centres and several other categories. All these associations are advocating on behalf of business events and marketing the business event concept to multiple audiences.

The individual organizers of business events are also very much involved in promoting their events to potential participants and to the media. This marketing is, of course, beneficial to the event destinations.

Now you know that there are many different parties involved in business event marketing and promotion. However, the materials that follow focus solely on DMOs and their marketing and promotions for business event markets.

Where are we now?

The completion of a situation analysis based upon facilities, clients, and competitors is the starting point for the DMO's business event marketing efforts. As shown in Figure

3.12, the business event situation analysis must cover five topics: (1) destination, (2) competitors, (3) business event visitors, (4) marketing position and (5) residents. The results of these five areas of analysis should be an identification of the destination's strengths and weaknesses and USPs related to business event markets.

An excellent model is provided in the Canadian Tourism Commission's 'International Meetings, Conventions and Incentive Travel Strategic Plan 2011–2016'. This planning document includes a situation analysis, SWOT analysis, market analysis for five countries (USA, UK, France, Germany and Belgium), and the plan.

The site selection criteria used by meeting and event planners are the key to assessing the strengths and weaknesses of a destination for business events. Academic scholars have conducted many research studies on site selection criteria, and other experts have also offered their opinions on this topic. Crouch and Louviere (2004) identified the following eight categories of convention site selection factors and this represents a very good summary:

- *Accessibility*: Cost, time, frequency, convenience, barriers.
- *Local support*: Local chapter, support from DMO/convention centre, subsidies.
- *Extra-conference opportunities*: Entertainment, shopping, sightseeing, recreation, professional opportunities.
- *Accommodation facilities*: Capacity, cost, service, security, availability.
- *Meeting facilities*: Capacity, layout, cost, ambience, service, security, availability.
- *Information*: Past experience, reputation, marketing.
- *Site environment*: Climate, setting, infrastructure, hospitality.
- *Other criteria*: Risks, profitability, association promotion, novelty.

Crouch and Louviere (2004) conducted a survey of meeting planners in Australia and they found that the most influential factors in convention site selection were (in order): (1) cost of (meeting) venue; (2) food quality; (3) plenary room (a large room where all the participants meet); (4) on-site/off-site accommodation (on-site much preferred); (5) participant proximity (to meeting venue); (6) exhibition space; (7) break-out rooms; (8) accommodation rates; (9) physical setting; and (10) entertainment opportunities. This study showed that the meeting venue characteristics were particularly important in site selection.

Pinpointing and assessing the relative strengths of competitive business event destinations is crucial in this type of marketing and promotion. For example, the Louisville Convention and Visitors Bureau (LCVB) in Kentucky, USA identified its 'competitive and comparable' cities as Charlotte (North Carolina), Cincinnati (Ohio), Columbus (Ohio), Indianapolis (Indiana), Kansas City (Missouri), Memphis (Tennessee), Milwaukee (Wisconsin), Minneapolis (Minnesota), Nashville (Tennessee), Pittsburgh (Pennsylvania) and St Louis (Missouri). LCVB has clearly identified one of its most important USPs for business events and it is shown in Figure 15.3. This USP is the availability of 2,300 hotel rooms connected with each other and the Kentucky International Convention Center by skywalks. Based on Crouch and Louviere's (2004) study, Louisville's USP fits well with many of the most important convention site selection criteria.

It is important that destinations gather detailed statistics on their business events and the characteristics of these events. This is not only important for guiding marketing decisions, but also for demonstrating the DMO's performance accountability. One outstanding example of reporting statistics about its business events activity is from the Amsterdam Tourism and Convention Board (ATCB) in the Netherlands. ATCB

LOUISVILLE WILL HAVE YOU WALKING ON AIR.

Marriott
Louisville
Downtown

Fourth Street
Live!

Hyatt Regency Louisville

Kentucky International
Convention Center

Galt House
Hotel & Suites

Galt House East
Hotel & Suites

KFC Yum Center!

The skywalks connect 2,300 downtown hotel rooms to
convention space and entertainment in downtown

Figure 15.3 Louisville's business event 'Convenience' USP
Source: Louisville Convention and Visitors Bureau, 2012a.

produces a highly informative and beautifully designed report each year under the title of *Amsterdam as a Conference Destination: Key Figures*. Included in the 2011 report were figures for both 2009 and 2010 on: (1) number of conferences by duration (2-3 days; 4-5 days; more than 5 days); (2) number of participant days according to the size of meeting (40–999 participants; 1,000 to 4,999 participants; over 5,000 participants); and (3) percentage of overnight stays from meetings). The report also showed the percentages of corporate meetings and non-corporate events using five- and four-star hotels, and the month-by-month distribution of meetings.

Because of the scale and potential impact of business events on local communities, it is advisable for DMOs to periodically survey local residents about their perceptions of these events. In practice, this is seldom done, but that does not mean that such an analysis should not be conducted.

Where would we like to be?

Next, the DMO needs to develop a business events marketing strategy, comprising the target markets and the positioning–image–branding approach. For business events, the typical approach is to divide up potential targets by organizational type (association vs corporate), geography (international, national, regional, state/province/territory) and type of event (e.g. convention/conference/congress/meeting vs trade show/exhibition vs incentive travel). One example of target market identification is for Tourism Toronto (Toronto Convention and Visitors Association) in Canada. Its 2011 Business Plan and Annual Budget had the following budget allocations for meetings, conventions and incentive travel sales:

- US associations (28.4 per cent)
- US corporate (8.3 per cent)
- Canadian associations (3.3 per cent)
- Canadian corporate (2.5 per cent)
- International congress sales (9.3 per cent)
- Regional sector sales (11.2 per cent)
- Client services (10.7 per cent)
- Convention development fund (19.7 per cent)
- Promotional incentive fund (3.3 per cent)
- Targeted meeting incentive fund (3.3 per cent).

The DMO should give consideration to developing a unique positioning–image–branding (PIB) approach for business events, but this should be linked in some way to the approach used for pleasure and leisure travel markets. A good case study here is from the US Virgin Islands in the Caribbean, which is a popular meeting and incentive destination. The PIB approach for USVI is the 'unscripted Caribbean experience' as explained in the following:

The US Virgin Islands: an 'unscripted Caribbean experience'

Following a series of focus groups and months of rigorous market research by Atlanta-based advertising agency, J. Walter Thompson, the colorful image of a traditional stilt dancer, known as a Mocko Jumbie, was selected by the Department of Tourism as the icon that best represents the elements of the US Virgin Island experience. Originating in West Africa and believed to be a guardian of the people, the Mocko Jumbie is a popular character at cultural events, parades and other festivities in the US Virgin Islands.

The logo is the first step in a larger brand repositioning for the Territory that is designed to highlight the 'unscripted Caribbean experience' offered in the US Virgin Islands, in response to market research that indicates travelers are seeking more than a 'cookie-cutter' Caribbean vacation.

The branding transition will culminate in January 2009, when all of the new branding elements will be used together for the first time with the launch of a new Web site for the Department of Tourism.

(United States Virgin Islands Department of Tourism, 2011)

USVI prepares a meetings and incentives guide and within the guide there is a background image similar to that in Figure 15.4. On that image there is a tie-in with the overall PIB approach with the use of the phrases, 'Unscripted discoveries' and 'You unscripted'.

One earlier example from Travel Portland is a good case study of positioning a city as a business events destination. As you will remember, Travel Portland is communicating that the city is a great place for green meetings; so the positioning is based on the sustainable use of resources at business events.

The DMO must also develop a specific set of marketing objectives for business-related markets. These should be expressed according to key result areas (KRAs) and as KPIs (key performance indicators). These KRAs and KPIs can be built upon the Standard DMO Performance Reporting system from Destination Marketing Association International (DMAI), which is discussed in more detail later in this chapter.

A good example of setting measurable objectives for business events is from San Antonio in Texas. The Convention Sales Division of the San Antonio Convention and Visitors Bureau set the following specific booking objectives for 2010:

- Achieve 830,000 definite group room nights.
- Generate 1,700 group sales leads.
- Book 690 group meetings.
- Additionally, the Sales Leadership Team will be measured on the following:
  - Increase in convention centre revenues;
  - Hotel Occupancy Tax collection;
  - Customer satisfaction surveys; and
  - Progress against all future years booking pace, as measured by the TAP Report.

Figure 15.4 Charlotte Amalie in St Thomas, US Virgin Islands
Source: Shutterstock, Inc. (Steve Heap).

How do we get there?

DMOs need to develop specific marketing plans directed towards business travellers and particularly for business events. Personal selling or sales is the most important promotional element in pursuing business events and, as such, larger DMOs maintain substantial sales forces. These sales efforts need to be placed within a carefully-orchestrated business event integrated marketing communications campaign.

Again, the Louisville Convention and Visitors Bureau (LCVB) (2012) provides a highly creative example of how to launch an effective IMC campaign for business events.

Convention campaign: seven secrets

In today's marketplace, most CVBs and DMOs sell their destinations to meeting planners using their skyline without being able to really drive home a specific attribute that makes their city stand out above the rest. So rather than blend in with what other destinations are doing, we decided to focus our advertising elements, not on the skyline, but on the unique selling points of Louisville as a meetings destination.

We defined the top seven unique selling points of Louisville that our salespeople use in pitches to meeting planners. We repackaged those selling points into a fully integrated campaign, called, The 7 Secrets of Highly Effective Meeting Planners.

As you can see, LCVB's approach was very business-like in defining the seven most important USPs of its meeting products, but then putting them a very creative but also client-oriented communications format. The seven secrets were:

- Secret 1: *Be in the middle of it all*: A state-of-the-art, 22,708 seat, 700,000 square foot waterfront arena connected to all kinds of hotels and meeting spaces.
- Secret 2: *Size matters*: More than 1.3 million square feet of downtown exhibition space.
- Secret 3: *Hotel choice can make or break a visit*: 3,800 downtown hotel rooms; with 2,300 rooms linked to convention rooms by pedestrian skywalks.
- Secret 4: *Don't spend more. Spend better*: Get more. Spend less.
- Secret 5: *Wow them with the culinary experience*: Louisville has been named one of Bon Appetit's top food cities.
- Secret 6: *Make it easy to get to, and easy to get around*: Louisville is less than a day's drive from half the US population, and the airport's just 10 minutes from downtown.
- Secret 7: *The entertainment should be entertaining*: Louisville has a diverse and authentic nightlife and an entertainment district.

If you check these seven secrets against the most important convention site selection criteria in the Crouch and Louviere (2004) research study, you will see that LCVB is doing an outstanding job in addressing the meeting planner's major priorities and concerns.

How do we make sure we get there?

Control and evaluation procedures are essential tools for DMOs in demonstrating accountability. As mentioned in Chapters 3 and 8, Destination Marketing Association International (DMAI) has developed a standard performance reporting system for DMOs, and this system is particularly detailed for business event marketing performance reporting. Included in the system are three components: (1) activity measures, (2) performance measures and (3) productivity metrics.

For convention sales (business event sales), DMAI created the following very important definitions:

- *Lead*: The forwarding by the DMO of a request for a minimum of ten sleeping rooms per night (peak rooms) over a specific set or range of dates. The request is related to an event being organized by a corporation, association, organization or independent meeting planner. The DMO sales staff sends the lead only to those local hotels that satisfy the event planner's event criteria. A lead is not just a DMO passing business cards along to local hotels.
- *Bid*: A proposal submitted by the DMO (with or without a local hotel) to an event planner that includes defined dates and room blocks. DMAI emphasizes that a bid is an activity and not a performance measure.
- *Tentative*: A bid that has been submitted to an event planner and the DMO is awaiting the decision. This is not a performance measure.
- *Booking*: a. Hotel event: A future event where a written contract has been signed between the hotel and the event organizer. b. Citywide/convention centre event: (1) confirmed booking: a future event confirmed in writing; and (2) contracted booking: a future event where a written contract has been signed between the event organizer and the event facility.
- *Lost opportunity*: A potential event that has been classified as a 'lead' or a 'tentative' but the destination subsequently loses the event. The reasons for losing the business may include: dates not available at hotels; hotel room rates too high; lack of hotel interest; dates not available at the convention centre; convention centre costs too high; no hotel adjacent to convention centre; safety concerns; meeting cancelled or postponed; union or labour costs; transportation or access issues; national or international incidents; and Board preference or internal politics.
- *Cancelled business*: An event that was booked (contracted or confirmed) that subsequently does not take place because of cancellation by the event organizer.

Table 15.5 shows the nine convention sales activities identified by DMAI and their 23 individual measurements.

Activities are the tasks that the DMO decides to complete for its business event marketing and sales, but they do not reflect the performance of the DMO is so doing. Therefore, DMAI has suggested a set of seven performance items and twenty-one performance measures that are listed in Table 15.6.

Table 15.5 Convention sales activities and measures from DMAI

	Convention sales activities	Convention sales activity measures
1	Number of bids	
2	Trade shows attended/exhibited	Number of trade shows Number of co-op partners attending Co-op monies generated
3	Sales missions (with sector partners)	Number of sales missions Number of co-op partners participating Co-op monies generated
4	Familiarization tours	Number of familiarization tours Number of participants (event organizers only) Number of accounts Number of co-op partners participating Co-op monies generated
5	Number of sales calls	
6	Number of client site inspections	
7	Client events	Number of client events Number of participants (event organizers only) Number of accounts Number of co-op partners participating Co-op monies generated
8	Sponsorships	Number of client events Trade show elements/sessions Monies spent Number of people at sponsored events ('customer-exposed impressions')
9	Number of accounts with activity	

Source: Destination Marketing Association International, 2011.

Finally, DMAI suggests that a set of six productivity metrics be measured in relation to business event marketing and sales. These metrics are shown in Figure 15.5 and include:

- *Personnel productivity metrics*: These measure the productivity of the DMO's business event sales staff.
- *Repeat business ratios*: The DMO does these calculations to measure repeat business, which is an indication of meeting planner satisfaction.
- *Cost productivity metrics*: These ratios measure the DMO's costs based upon leads, bookings and booked room nights.
- *Lead conversion ratios*: These ratios calculate the percentage of leads that are converted into bookings and also the lost opportunity percentage.
- *Convention booking/room supply ratio*: This is a key ratio vis-à-vis the hotels within the destination. The ratio measures the DMO's contribution to total hotel room nights by year.
- *Demand ratios for total room nights sold*: Another key ratio, this measures by year the DMO's contribution to all business event booked room nights.

Table 15.6 Convention sales performance items and measures from DMAI

Convention sales performance items	Convention sales performance measures
1 Leads	Number of leads Lead room nights (estimated)
2 Bookings	Hotel events (number of bookings; booked room nights, estimated; booked attendance, estimated; booked attendee spending, estimated)
	Citywide/convention centre events (number of confirmed bookings; booked room nights, estimated; booked attendance, estimated; booked attendee spending, estimated) and (number of contracted bookings; booked room nights, estimated; booked attendance, estimated; booked attendee spending, estimated)
3 Lost opportunities	a. Number of lost opportunities; b. Reason for lost opportunity; c. Lost room nights, estimated; d. Lost attendance, estimated; e. Lost attendance spending, estimate
4 Cancellations	a. Number of lost cancellations; b. Reason for cancellation; c. Cancelled room nights, estimated; d. Cancelled attendance, estimated; e. Cancelled attendance spending, estimate
5 Number of leads per trade show attended/ exhibited by DMO sales staff	
6 By-year production	Estimates for each year ahead of: a. Number of bookings; b. Number of booked room nights, estimated; c. Number of booked attendees, estimated; d. Booked attendee spending, estimate
7 Post-event measures	a. Room night pick-up; b. Total attendance

Source: Destination Marketing Association International, 2011.

How do we know if we got there?

The fifth step in applying the destination marketing system to business events marketing and promotion is to evaluate the success or performance in implementing the marketing strategy and plan. In Chapter 3, you saw some excellent reporting of performance results from Meet Minneapolis in the USA (Figures 3.34 and 3.35). You have also seen a detailed description in this chapter of how DMAI recommends that DMOs report their performance for business events marketing. The main yardstick to be applied here is to answer the question, 'Did we achieve our marketing objectives?' Also as you already know, this involves the results for the KPIs that the DMO has set for business event marketing.

1. Personnel productivity metrics:	2. Repeat business ratios:	3. Cost productivity metrics:
a. Number of leads per sales manager b. Number of bookings per sales manager c. Number of booked room nights per sales manager	a. Number of repeat business bookings/total number of bookings b. Room nights from repeat business bookings/total booked room nights	a. Convention sales function direct and indirect operating costs/number of leads b. Convention sales function direct and indirect operating costs/number of bookings c. Convention sales function direct and indirect operating costs/number of bookedroom nights
4. Lead conversion ratios:	5. Convention booking/room supply ratio:	6. Demand ratios for total room nights sold:
a. Booking ratio: number of bookings/number of bookings + number of lost opportunities b. Lost opportunity ratio: number of lost opportunities/number of bookings + number of lost opportunities	a. Booked room nights (by-year production)/total (available) convention hotel room nights	a. Booked room nights (by-year production)/total meeting-convention room nights sold b. Booked room nights (by-year production)/total room nights sold (destination-level)

Figure 15.5 Productivity metrics for convention sales from DMAI
Source: Destination Marketing Association International, 2011.

Taking an example again from the Louisville Convention and Visitors Bureau, here is how that DMO succinctly summarized their performance:

'Louisville: unconventionally smart about conventions'

In 2010/2011, the Louisville Convention and Visitors Bureau's convention development department exceeded its sales goals in every category. Sales leads to potential new clients were up 3 per cent and room nights were up 3 per cent as well. On average, every convention delegate spends $965 while in Louisville.

Because of the unique, and state-of-the-art, characteristics of the Kentucky Exposition Center (KEC), ten significantly large conventions have been retained. Each of these conventions average nearly 4,000 hotel rooms on its peak attendance night. The Bureau's goal is to add at least one new citywide annual show at the Expo Center each year while retaining our existing client base.

Summary

The business travel and business event markets are the 'backbone' of tourism for many cities around the world. In recent years, they have been adversely affected by the poor global economic conditions, but are recovering.

Business events are of different types and these include conferences, congresses, conventions, exhibitions, incentives, meetings and trade shows. Unfortunately there are no universally accepted definitions of these terms and different usages can cause confusion.

Business travel and business events are significant in size and have a major beneficial economic impact on many countries and individual communities. The higher-than-average yield of these markets makes them very appealing to destinations.

The major challenges and issues facing business travel and business events are competitive intensity; cost control and policy compliance; incorporating use of social network sites; negative economic conditions; 'perk' perceptions of business travel and business events; reliance on other tourism sector stakeholders' performance; and technology as a substitute for travel.

Some of the major trends that are being felt in business travel and business events include green meetings, 'hybrid' meetings, multi-purposing trips, shorter stays, strategic meetings management programmes (SMMPs) and more use of digital technology applications. All of the challenges, issues and trends impacting on business travel and business events are forcing planners and managers to become more professional, comprehensive and integrated in their planning and implementation efforts.

There has been a definite movement towards greater professionalism in business travel and meeting management. New standards are being developed, including professional skill competencies and these will undoubtedly benefit DMOs and destinations in the future. DMOs should not be 'silent partners' in this process but should do all that they can to assist their client partners to achieve their goals.

Professional congress or conference organizers are specialists in planning, organizing and implementing meetings and other events. These are highly qualified and experienced meeting professionals that can take care of all aspects of an event on behalf of companies and non-profits.

Incentive travel planning companies are specialists in arranging motivation-oriented trips for companies. Their services typically include programme design, communications, operations and measurement, and they apply various technologies in so doing. Because of the tighter economic conditions and the desire for companies to get a greater return on investment from incentive travel, there has been a movement towards converging business meetings and incentive travel.

RFPs (requests for proposals) are forms that meeting planners complete and submit to DMOs or hotels and meeting venues. Now most DMOs provide online versions of RFPs. Completed RFPs summarize the meeting planner's requirements for an upcoming event. RFPs are beneficial to all the parties involved including the meeting planners, DMOs, and hotels, resorts and meeting venues.

The DMO's marketing and promotions for business events are usually the most scrutinized areas of its operations. Therefore, it is vitally important that the DMO's performance reporting be thorough and cover all the relevant activity measures and productivity metrics. It is particularly important that a DMO demonstrates its contributions to the hotels and resorts within the destination, so it must measure room nights generated through its business event marketing and promotions.

For the most effective marketing to business travel and business event markets, DMOs need to do the following:

- Become familiar with and continuously track the trends and future prospects for business travel and business events.
- Encourage technology application adoption and use by tourism sector stakeholders to ensure they meet the needs and requirements of business travellers and meeting planners and their delegates.
- Prepare individual market analyses of the various segments of the business event market.
- Continuously work to develop good and supportive relationships with meeting planners, professional congress/conference organizers, incentive travel planners and corporate travel managers.
- Operate a professional and efficient system of requests for proposals (RFPs) and lead sharing.
- Assist meeting planners and local hotels/resorts/meeting venues to ensure that events are 'delivered' according to expectations.
- Conduct periodic surveys of business event planners and participants to determine satisfaction levels with events help within the destination. Provide feedback on survey results to local hotels, resorts and meeting venues.
- Prepare a specific marketing strategy and marketing plan for business events.
- Follow a systematic, step-by-step approach to marketing and promoting to business event planners.
- Carefully document performance in business event marketing and promotions.

Review questions

1 How would you define regular business travel and can it be influenced by DMOs? Why or why not?
2 What are the different business event markets and how is each of them defined?
3 What are the benefits of regular business travel?
4 What are the benefits of business events?
5 Business travel and business events are facing which major challenges and issues at the moment?
6 Which trends are impacting upon business travel and business events?
7 What is a PCO and what services do these specialists provide?
8 What are the roles played by incentive travel planning companies and what is the meaning of 'convergence'?
9 What are the roles played by incentive travel planners and who are their clients?
10 Why are RFPs convenient for meeting planners and at the same time a good marketing tool for DMOs, hotels and meeting venues?
11 Why is it important for a DMO to gather research data on the business events held within its jurisdiction and what types of statistics should be collected?
12 How should a DMO demonstrate its accountability with respect to its marketing and promotions aimed at business events?

References

American Express Company. 2007. Building a Best-in-Class T&E Policy.

Amsterdam Tourism and Convention Board. 2011. Amsterdam as a Conference Destination. Key Figures 2011.

Arcodia, C., and Reid, S. 2005. Event management associations and the provision of services. *Journal of Convention and Event Tourism*, 6(4), 5–25.

Association of Australian Convention Bureaux. 2007. Business Events: Long Term Legacies for Australian Society.

Barcelona Convention Bureau. 2012. Barcelona Convention Bureau. About Us. http://professional.barcelonaturisme.com/Professionals/bcb/bcb-que-fem/About-us/_Ukvru92jxZCAP7IRa9C4GqE_LnCqWZWMx57q3-3CnvQ

M. Booth and Associates. n.d. US Virgin Islands Unveils New Logo: Additional Rebranding Initiatives to Launch in 2009.

Business Events Australia. 2011a. 2020 Tourism Industry Potential ... The Business Events Sector.

——2011b. Business Events Arrivals December 2011.

Canadian Tourism Commission. 2011a. International Meetings, Conventions and Incentive Travel Strategic Plan 2011–2016.

——2011b. Travel Characteristics Q4 2010.

Canadian Tourism Human Resource Council. 2010. Emerit International Competency Standards. Event Management – International. Version 1.0.

Carlson Marketing. 2012. Incentives. http://www.carlsonmarketing.com/services/incentives/

Carlson Wagonlit Travel. 2011. Business Travel Market Trends in 2012. The Business Travel Landscape at a Glance.

Center for Exhibition Industry Research. http://www.ceir.org/

Chen, S.C. 2011. Residents' perceptions of the impact of major annual tourism events in Macao: Cluster analysis. *Journal of Convention and Event Tourism*, 12(2), 106–128.

Convention Industry Council. 2011. The Economic Significance of Meetings to the US Economy.

——2012. APEX Industry Glossary – 2011 Edition. http://www.conventionindustry.org/StandardsPractices/APEX/glossary.aspx/

Corbin Ball Associates. 2009. Strategic Meetings Management Program (SMMP) Implementation and Idea Guide.

Crouch, G.I., and Louviere, J.J. 2004. The determinants of convention site selection: A logistic choice model from experimental data. *Journal of Travel Research*, 43(2), 118–130.

Destination Marketing Association International. 2011. Standard DMO Performance Reporting. Washington, DC: DMAI.

Douloff, D. 2011. 2011 Market Report. MeetingsCanada.com.

EIBTM. 2011. EIBTM 2011 Industry Trends and Market Share Report.

Eventia. 2010. UK Events Market Trends Survey 2010.

Fáilte Ireland. 2010. Domestic Tourism 2009.

Federal Times. 2012. GSA Scandal. Heavy Fallout Expected. http://www.federaltimes.com/article/20120416/DEPARTMENTS07/204160301/

Fenich, G.G., Scott-Halsell, S., and Hashimoto, K. 2011. An investigation of technological uses by different generations as it relates to meetings and events: A pilot study. *Journal of Convention and Event Tourism*, 12(1), 53–63.

Green Meetings Industry Council. http://www.gmicglobal.org/

HVS International. 2007. Revitalising the Convention and Exhibition Industry in Sydney.

IMEX Research. 2010. New Survey Shows Resilience Remains Defining Feature of Association Meetings Market. Regent Exhibitions Ltd.

International Association of Professional Congress Organisers. 2012. Welcome to IAPCO's Website. http://www.iapco.org/

International Congress and Convention Association. 2011. Statistics Report 2000–2010.

Lee, S. 2011. To tweet or not to tweet: An exploratory study of meeting professionals' attitudes toward applying social media for meeting sessions. *Journal of Convention and Event Tourism*, 12(4), 271–289.

Louisville Convention and Visitors Bureau. 2011. 2011–2012 Destination Marketing Plan. http://www.lcvb.info/bureau-reports/conventions-and-meetings

——2012a. Conventions and Meetings.

——2012b. The 7 Secrets of Highly Effective Meeting Planners. http://www.gotolouisville.com/forms/Default/seven_secrets.aspx

Maritz Travel. 2012. Incentive Travel. http://www.maritztravel.com/Incentive-Travel/Design.aspx

Meeting Professionals International. 2005. Defining a Strategic Meetings Management Program: How Meetings Drive Business in Partnership-Focused Companies.

National Business Travel Association. 2008. Building a Strategic Meetings Management Program.

Northern Ireland Tourist Board, VisitEngland, VisitScotland, Visit Wales. 2011. The UK Tourist: Statistics 2010.

Professional Convention Management Association. 2011. The 20th Annual Meetings Market Survey. PCMA Convene, March.

——n.d. Independent Planners. http://www.pcma.org/Resources/Meeting-Management-Resources/Independent-Planners.htm

Reed Exhibitions. 2011. About Us. http://www.reedexpo.com/about-us/

The Right Solution Limited. 2012. British Meetings and Events Industry Survey 2011. http://www.rightsolution.co.uk/projects/the-british-meetings-and-events-industry-survey-2011/

San Antonio Convention and Visitors Bureau. 2009. Convention Sales.

Singapore Exhibition and Convention Bureau. 2012. Singapore Exhibition and Convention Bureau™. http://www.yoursingapore.com/content/mice/en/why-singapore/singapore-exhibition-convention-bureau.html

Singapore Tourism Board. 2010. Annual Report on Tourism Statistics 2009.

SITE. 2012. SITE Index. The Annual Analysis and Forecast for the Motivational Events Industry.

SITE International Foundation. 2010. 2010 Study of the German Incentive and Motivational Travel Market.

SITE International Foundation/MPI Foundation. 2011. The Convergence of Incentive Travel and Meeting Planning Activities.

SMG. 2012. Convention Centers. http://www.smgworld.com/convention_centers.aspx tmf GmbH. 2010. Results MICE Market Monitor 2010 – IMEX Presentation.

Sperstad, J., and Cecil, A.K. 2011. Changing paradigm of meeting management: What does this mean for academia? *Journal of Convention and Event Tourism*, 12(4), 313–324.

Toronto Convention and Visitors Association. 2010. Tourism Toronto Business Plan and Annual Budget 2011.

Tourism Queensland. 2011. Queensland Incentives. http://www.queenslandincentives.com/

Tourism Research Australia. 2012. Travel by Australians. December 2011 Quarterly Results of the National Visitor Survey.

Travel Portland. Meet Portland. Meet Green. 2012. http://greenmeetings.travelportland.com/

Union of International Associations. 2011. International Meeting Statistics for the Year 2010.

United Nations Environment Programme. 2009. Green Meeting Guide 2009. http://www.unglobalcompact.org/docs/issues_doc/Environment/Green_Meeting_Guide_WEB.pdf

US Travel Association/Oxford Economics. 2009. The Return on Investment of US Business Travel.

——2011. US Travel Answer Sheet.

——2012. Keep America Meeting. Securing the Future of Meetings Industry.

United States Virgin Islands Department of Tourism. 2011. Business Meets Tranquility. A Meetings and Incentives Guide to the US Virgin Islands.

Vienna Convention Bureau. 2012a. Vienna Convention Bureau to Certify Green Meetings. http://www.vienna.convention.at/Home/News/Vienna-Convention-Bureau-zertifiziert-ab-sofort-Gr.aspx

——2012b. Vienna Convention Bureau Reports Record Turnover.

——2012c. Vienna Meetings Industry Report 2011.

Visit London. 2010. Professional Conference Organisers.

World Travel and Tourism Council. 2012. Country Reports.

Xiang, Z., and Formica, S. 2007. Mapping environmental change in tourism: A study of the incentive travel industry. *Tourism Management*, 28(5), 1193–1202.

PART IV

The future of destination management and marketing

Chapter 16

The future of destination management and marketing

Learning objectives

1 To identify and explain the current and future issues affecting destination management and marketing.

2 To pinpoint expected future trends and potential challenges for destinations and DMOs.

3 To suggest some of the characteristics of future DMOs.

Introduction

What does the future hold for destination management and destination marketing? Will DMOs survive all the issues and challenges with which they are now faced? This chapter addresses these questions by reviewing the major issues, challenges and trends that are impacting upon destinations and DMOs now and that are expected to have an effect in the future.

DMOs have been around for more than 100 years but they have never before felt the impact of the winds of change as they are experiencing now. In this chapter, seven authoritative sources are reviewed that identify the key issues and trends currently affecting destination management, marketing and DMOs. As you will see, these sources are unanimous in their opinion that DMOs need to significantly adapt their ways of operating in the future.

Destination marketing and management is an emerging professional field in tourism. It will have to become even more professional in the future and this book has tried to suggest what needs to be done to achieve this outcome. A summary of the main issues and trends noted in the first fifteen chapters is, therefore, also provided.

This chapter also previews the expected future trends and potential challenges for destinations and DMOs and provides some ideas on the future characteristics of DMOs.

Current and future issues in destination management and marketing

Earlier chapters have identified various issues and challenges that destinations and DMOs are currently encountering. These included funding sources and levels, competition, changes in technology, economic and other crises, and several others. In the materials that follow, you will learn about the issues that have been identified by one DMO professional association and a number of company and individual experts in destination management and marketing.

The *DMAI Futures Study*

In 2007–2008, Destination Marketing Association International (DMAI) and Karl Albrecht International conducted a landmark study that was called the *DMAI Futures Study 2008* with the sub-title of *The Future of Destination Marketing*. While this research is most relevant for DMOs based in the USA, it does have broader implications for DMOs in other countries.

Three high-level strategic themes emerged from this study related to DMOs: (1) relevance, (2) value proposition and (3) visibility.

● *Relevance*: DMOs operate in a space between tourism sector stakeholders and potential visitors. That space is becoming increasingly crowded with other players and this is eroding the traditional and unique position that DMOs once held. According to DMAI and Karl Albrecht International and the DMO executives they interviewed, this is challenging the relevance of DMOs:

The challenges to relevancy

The increasing disintermediation of the visitor services marketplace, the rise of new business entities contending for the attention of visitors and meeting organizers, the wealth of free information made available online, and increasing local competition for funds formerly earmarked for destination marketing all conspire to erode or marginalize the traditional role of the DMO as the 'marketing department' of a particular locality.

(2008)

- *Value proposition*: What is the unique contribution of DMOs? Or stated another way, what is their core value proposition? According to the *DMAI Futures Study*, new players have been 'nibbling away' at the traditional value package offered to local tourism sector stakeholders and their communities in general.
- *Visibility*: DMO executives interviewed for the *DMAI Futures Study* were extremely concerned about their organizations' visibility and consumer recognition. This concern was especially about visibility on the Internet where competing sources of destination information were judged to be doing a superior job to many DMOs:

Consumers know little about DMOs

DMAI's branding research indicates that consumers typically know very little about CVBs and have little inclination to seek them out. Valid measures are difficult to find as of the publication of this report, but it appears that many DMOs rely on statistical good fortune in search engine listings, as an adjunct to whatever population of 'loyal' visitors they may have who go directly to their websites for information.

Relatively few DMO websites demonstrate the level of sophistication, user-friendly design and interactiveness needed to compete with other sources. City-operated websites, sites operated by city-specific magazines, and sites of individual local attractions all compete with the DMO site for visitor attention. Some DMOs, particularly small ones, have merely moved their print brochures online, so to speak.

(2008)

The *DMAI Futures Study* identified the following eight 'super-trends' that were impacting destination marketing:

- *Customer*: Called 'Proliferating preferences' this trend was about pleasure/leisure and business travellers constantly seeking new products and experiences at tourism destinations.

- *Competitor*: Termed 'the battle for attention' this trend concerned the increasing competitive intensity in travel and tourism and the movement towards online travel purchases.
- *Economic*: 'Dodging asteroids' was about DMOs becoming increasingly vulnerable to economic downturns and other types of global crises (terrorism, political unrest, pandemics, rising energy prices, etc.).
- *Technological*: This trend stressed the increasing importance of information and communication technologies (ICTs) and particularly the Internet. It was named 'smart and friendly websites'.
- *Social*: 'The electronic society' was the trend towards much greater use of social network sites and the creation of user-generated content about tourism destinations.
- *Political*: This trend was about the funding of DMOs from local government agencies. Billed as the 'Quest for relevance', this trend concerned the greater difficulties that DMOs were having convincing stakeholders of their value. There was also a growing trend for governments to use more of room tax collections for non-tourism purposes.
- *Legal*: Under the title of 'Mixed signals from government' this trend concerned how tourism organizations were constantly being affected by changes in government policies, legislation and regulations.
- *Geophysical*: 'Going green' was the eighth super-trend and related to the increasing emphasis on sustainable tourism development and green practices.

The *DMAI Futures Study* identified twenty DMO-related trends based upon rankings from DMO executives (Table 16.1).

Some of these twenty trends are definitely relevant mostly to DMOs operating in the USA, particularly 1, 5 and 14. However, the other seventeen trends are thought to apply to DMOs in most other countries as well. Eight of the trends involve customers, while another five of the trends relate to the Internet. Two of the trends were about DMO funding sources.

Based upon the eight 'super trends' and the twenty DMO-specific trends, DMAI and Karl Albrecht International recommended a new 'strategic map' for destination marketing, which is shown in Figure 16.1. The key part of this new strategic map was the four key roles for DMOs:

- *Informing, educating and advising the visitor*: The key contribution here is serving as the 'official face and voice' of the tourism sector within a destination.
- *Advising and supporting marketers*: The DMO should perform the role of a 'matchmaker', bringing those together who buy and sell the destination's services and products.
- *Advocating the total visitor experience*: The DMO needs to convince tourism sector stakeholders to focus on all aspects of the total visitor experience within the destination.
- *Supporting and developing the destination strategy*: The DMO needs to take a strategic perspective on destination development and insist on the master planning of tourism.

Overall, the *DMAI Futures Study* was a realistic portrayal of the current issues affecting DMOs, albeit with a strong US orientation. This research study emphasized the changes among customers, as well as in information and communication technologies and

Table 16.1 DMO-specific trends identified by executives of DMOs

Rank and trend	Score
1. Hotel occupancy tax is increasingly vulnerable to alternative politically based projects. (This trend is typically relevant to US-based DMOs more than those in other countries. Some destinations impose additional taxes, generally referred to as visitor taxes.)	4.60
2. Website design and implementation will be increasingly critical to the success of DMOs, particularly in the leisure travel segment.	4.58
3. The massive shift of 'content' to the Internet continues at an accelerating pace.	4.50
4. Consumers are becoming increasingly comfortable with ordering products online.	4.46
5. The perceived barriers to entering the US (e.g. visa requirements, security) are inhibiting foreign travel.	4.42
6. The era of cheap oil is over; prices of petroleum-based products will increasingly dominate economic development, energy allocation and international politics.	4.36
7. Travel customers are becoming increasingly more segmented in their interests.	4.36
8. People increasingly expect businesses and organizations to 'know it's me' and deliver an individualized value package.	4.36
9. Nearly all teenaged children of middle- and upper-class families have cell phones and Internet access, or soon will.	4.36
10. There is ever more information clutter, more 'noise'.	4.33
11. Web-based distribution of information predisposes people to want results immediately.	4.33
12. Baby boomers have more disposable income to allocate to travel and other forms of leisure.	4.21
13. Funding sources are increasingly questioning/evaluating DMO's financial contribution.	4.21
14. The need to repair the US image abroad will increase the political value of attracting inbound tourism.	4.20
15. The Internet, as a perceived 'system', is steadily becoming smarter as content migrates to the Web, search capability improves and cyber-communities proliferate.	4.17
16. Short-stay trips and mini-vacations are becoming increasingly popular.	4.14
17. Travel customers are becoming increasingly more fickle, self-reliant and predatory.	4.14
18. Travel customers increasingly seek greater value for their money.	4.14
19. DMOs are losing the advantage of uniqueness as many other entities provide free information and assistance to visitors and meeting organizers.	4.14
20. Global warming is becoming more 'real' in the public perception.	4.08

Source: Destination Marketing Association International, 2008.

funding sources. However, perhaps more importantly it carried a serious warning for DMOs: increase relevancy, value and visibility or slowly be replaced by a variety of other entities performing similar roles.

Actually, the recommendations of the *DMAI Futures Study* very much reflect an expansion of the role from just destination marketing to the broader perspective of destination management. Throughout this book, this transformation of roles has been strongly advocated and you have learned about all aspects of destination management, and not just destination marketing.

15 Cs framework

Fyall and Leask (2006) suggested a 15 Cs framework for describing the strategic challenges in destination marketing. These two authors examined the application of the 15 Cs in terms of the DMOs in London and Edinburgh in the UK.

These 15 Cs are shown in Figure 16.2 and briefly explained below in the words of this book's author:

Complexity: The tourism product is very complex and, therefore, extremely difficult to manage. DMOs have to build positive relationships with multiple stakeholders within their destinations and form collaborative relationships outside. Moreover, DMOs must perform multiple roles, at a time while they are adapting to new technologies and shrinking government funding.

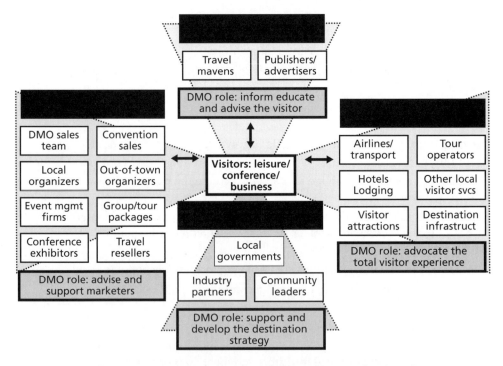

Figure 16.1 The new strategic map for destination marketing from DMAI and Karl Albrecht International (modified by author)

Source: Destination Marketing Association International, 2008.

Control: DMOs do not have direct control over the tourism product within their destinations, and this has been mentioned several times already in this book. Additionally, there is a danger that tourism sector stakeholders might launch their own communication programmes that do not support the overall destination branding approach.

Change: The winds of change are buffeting DMOs from many different directions. You have heard that many DMOs have moved away from being purely government-run to being public–private partnerships (PPPs). In addition, DMOs have been transforming from being only promotional agencies and are becoming destination management organizations with greater responsibilities for product development, tourism planning, community involvement and participation.

Crisis: Many destinations have had to deal with major crises that have caused great trauma in their tourism sectors. These crises have been caused by economic difficulties, natural disasters, civil disturbances, acts of terrorism, onsets of diseases, etc. They have undermined tourists' confidence in travelling to certain destinations. Nowadays DMOs must be proactive and have crisis management plans. Moreover, they need to avoid having 'too many eggs in one basket' market-wise; they need to expand their portfolios of target markets and collaborations. DMOs, as emphasized in Chapter 13, should never neglect their nearby and domestic markets, as these can become critical business sources amidst a period of crisis.

Complacency: 'Nothing lasts forever' is a phrase that DMOs need to remember, so they do not become complacent in today's dynamic external environments. DMO complacency can set in when the organization has enjoyed long-running success, where the destinations' market demand sources have been steady for many years, and when the funding sources have been stable for a long time. DMOs must guard against becoming complacent in this era of global competition, and one of the best ways to do this is with 'zero-based' planning, which means that no programmes or markets are sacred and each is constantly being re-evaluated.

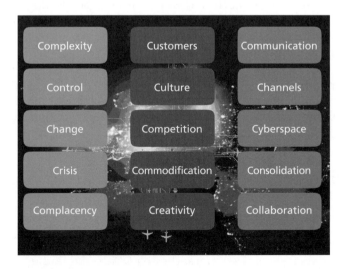

Figure 16.2 The 15 Cs framework
Source: Adapted from Fyall and Leask, 2006.

Customers: Customers are constantly changing and for DMOs it is worthwhile remembering that 'no two customers are exactly alike'. People even from the same markets go to destinations with differing motives and expectations. Although market segmentation analysis is essential in destination marketing, it is still an approximation of reality, and even within distinct market segments there is considerable diversity.

Culture: Many destinations rely on their unique cultural and heritage resources to attract tourists. These resources tend to be a destination's key point of differentiation. Many of these buildings and sites are owned and operated by government agencies and, therefore, are reliant on government support. They are often among the most popular tourism attractions in a destination and so the issue becomes, who should pay for their upkeep? Should governments pay and use local residents' tax contributions in so doing, or should the predominant users (tourists) be required to pay through admission fees? This is becoming a delicate issue, particularly in Europe, when governments want to operate such buildings and sites on a free-admission basis, to provide greater educational and cultural experiences for local people.

Competition: Most DMOs are facing new competitors as global travel opens up further. Fyall and Leask (2006) suggest that the expansion of low-cost airline carriers (LCCs) has opened up many new destinations for Europeans; and the same can be said about the Asia-Pacific region where LCCs have started many new routes, plus offering better deals for passengers on well-established routes.

Commodification: Globalization has blurred the differences among places and even between destinations that are geographically far apart. For example, almost everywhere you travel you can find McDonald's, Starbucks and KFC; and downtowns, shopping centres and airports look increasingly alike. Commodification is the process of taking a resource that is truly unique and turning it into a commodity that can be consumed by many people. In the transformation, the true meaning of the resource is lost. In tourism, the commercialization of resources means they often lose their intrinsic authenticity and uniqueness. Several tourism scholars have conducted research on this particular issue. For example, Halewood and Hannam (2001) found evidence of commodification with the Viking culture around different destinations in Europe; Cloke and Perkins (2002) noted a similar trend with the commodification of adventure in New Zealand.

Although commodification makes tourism resources such as culture and heritage more 'consumable' for some people, it is not a favourable trend for destinations in terms of their uniqueness and sustainability. DMOs must constantly try to find and communicate what is truly unique about their destinations, and not what makes them like their competitors.

Creativity: DMOs must be creative in their destination marketing and management approaches in the face of intensifying competition. Having a highly creative approach to positioning–image–branding (PIB) is certainly part of this requirement, but it is not enough. This creativity also has to be present in the experiences and products that tourists can have within destinations. Earlier in this book, you have learned about several creative approaches by DMOs and you may remember the Signature Experiences Collection® example from the Canadian Tourism Commission (CTC). Based upon thorough market research, the CTC has responded with uniquely Canadian experiences that are desired by people within its targeted markets.

Communication: DMOs must be outstanding at communications, both within their destinations and externally. DMOs need to listen to their various publics and then respond with the initiatives, services and programmes that these publics need and expect. You have heard about many clever DMO communication campaigns in this book, and one of these was from the Louisville Convention and Visitors Bureau in Kentucky, USA, described in Chapter 15. The '7 Secrets of Highly Effective Meeting Planners' campaign is a brilliant example of effective communications for business event markets. Why brilliant? The communication campaign matches the resources within Louisville to the priority requirements of business event planners.

Channels: DMOs need to adopt a multi-channel approach to communications, and in most cases this includes both traditional media and travel trade channels and the newer ICT channels, particularly DMO websites, social network sites and mobile phones.

Cyberspace: DMOs need to become more active and sophisticated in their use of ICTs. Online travel agencies (OTAs) and travel review websites are increasingly offering more detailed information, features and services related to tourism destinations.

'Consumers becoming incredibly powerful'

Consumers are becoming incredibly powerful and are increasingly able to determine elements of their tourism products. They are also much more sophisticated and experienced and therefore are much more difficult to please. Innovative tourism enterprises will have the ability to divert resources and expertise to servicing consumers and provide higher value added transactions.

(Buhalis and Law, 2008)

Consolidation: Consolidation is a trend in many sub-sectors of tourism including, for example, among airlines, hotels and resorts, and travel agencies and tour companies. Interestingly this is also happening, perhaps more quietly, in the management of convention centres, arenas and sports stadiums, and other public performance venues. This is putting more marketing power and political 'clout' in fewer hands. This is not a trend that DMOs should ignore or view as outside of their domain.

Collaboration: According to Fyall and Leask (2006), greater collaboration by DMOs is a necessity and not a luxury.

Fyall and Leask (2006) did an outstanding job of pinpointing a large number of issues and challenges for DMOs, and in this case the examples were drawn mainly from the UK rather than the USA. In many ways, the issues defined by these two authors were mirrored in the *DMAI Futures Study*, although Fyall and Leask identified issues that were not in the US study, such as crisis, complacency, culture and consolidation.

The PhoCusWright destination marketing study

The US online travel market research company, PhoCusWright, Inc., published a research study, *Destination Marketing: Understanding the Role and Impact of Destination Marketers*, in 2009 (Schetzina, 2009). This study had three main research objectives: (1) analyse consumer trends; (2) profile destination marketers and identify best practices; and (3) identify the opportunities to serve and/or partner with destination marketing organizations. The research included a web-based consumer survey about using DMOs and their websites; a web-based survey of destination marketers; phone interviews with fifty destination marketers and partners/suppliers; analysis of traffic to DMO websites; and an analysis of fifteen specific websites.

The key findings of this study was that DMO websites were most important to consumers and were the most preferred way for potential tourists to interact with DMOs. They visited DMO websites at different times, including both before and after making their bookings. Some 57 per cent of the users said the DMO websites influenced their activity selections at destinations. Deals, packages and promotions posted on websites were of particular interest to tourists.

The study also concluded that DMOs were highly engaged online and have gradually been increasing their online marketing spending. However, the DMOs reported spending just 37 per cent of their marketing budgets online. It was also found that DMOs had been slow to integrate interactive features on their websites.

usdm.net is an interactive agency and media company which was one of the sponsors of the PhoCusWright research study on destination marketing. In 2010, usdm.net produced the *Leadership Report: Are You a Revolutionary DMO*? that summarized and commented upon the results of both the *DMAI Futures Study* and the PhoCusWright research study. The company made a number of very important conclusions and recommendations:

- Travellers view DMOs primarily as sources of information.
- DMOs can greatly enhance their visibility and relevancy by investing more in online content and interactivity.
- DMOs should promote events, specials and packages on their websites and across social network sites and to mobile phones.
- DMOs should particularly focus on activity development and marketing, since consumers look for these contents on DMO websites.
- It would be preferable to allow consumers to book online at DMO websites.
- DMOs are wasting their marketing budgets on newspaper, magazine, radio and outdoor advertising; they should divert more of their budgets online, including to search engines.
- The Internet offers immediate and detailed tracking of consumer and meeting planner responses. This enhanced measurability quantifies and validates the DMO's value proposition and relevance.

Overall, the PhoCusWright research study and the follow-up recommendations by usdm.net emphasized that DMOs should be making much greater use of ICTs and especially the Internet. They suggested, however, that DMOs were not moving rapidly enough in that direction and so other parties were entering that space. The implication here is that DMOs have been reluctant to give up their years-old practices, especially in using traditional media advertising.

DestiCorp conceptual development paper

Anna Pollock of DestiCorp in the UK is a well-known expert on destination marketing and management. In 2010, her company released a 'conceptual discussion paper' under the title of 'Speculation on the Future of Destination Marketing Organizations (DMOs)'. This paper indicated that there were seven main drivers of change that were affecting destination marketing:

Information technology enables global connectivity and digital platforms that mirror reality: ICTs and particularly the Internet have completely removed the barrier of distance and offer consumers instant and continuous information about destinations. However, although the digitization of content has been pervasive for more than a decade, DestiCorp felt that DMOs have changed relatively little and only some DMO websites are interactive. This needs to change in the future as DMOs become 'orchestrators of DMO experiences' rather than 'promoters of tourism products':

The DMO as an orchestrator

If a destination is to convince visitors it can offer a unique set of distinctive experiences that reflect a specific place, the DMO will need to think of itself as less of a marketer in the promotion sense and more of an orchestrator. Creation of an agile, flexible, electronic platform that enables collaboration, distribution, cross selling, intelligence gathering and exchange to occur will be essential.

(DestiCorp, 2010)

Marketing is being turned upside-down, from push to pull; from promotion to attraction: DMOs have traditionally been promoters of the tourism products within their destinations. This worked when the supply of information was more limited, but it is not that way anymore. Now consumers are in the driver's seat and they want to be involved in designing their own tourism experience products. DestiCorp argued that DMOs need to put less emphasis on promotion now, and need to give a much greater priority to creating and staging the types of experiences that tourists want within destinations.

Emergence of the creative/experience economy: Tourists are buying experiences at their destinations and not products. DestiCorp suggests, therefore, that DMOs need 'to recognize their role is more of a stage manager and conductor than promoter'.

Changing economic realities: globalization vs localization: There are two trends that are going in different directions at the same time. The world has become more globalized in the past 20–25 years. There is a greater need for places to stand out in this global environment and not only for tourism but in attracting more inward investment, talented workforces and students. However, as mentioned in Chapter 13, economic downturns and rising energy costs are forcing more people not to travel so far and to discover more things locally.

Biophysical realities: DMOs need to pay more attention to environmental considerations and play their part in the low-carbon economy. This is due to global warming, as well as the steadily increasing world demand for energy, food and water.

Fiscal realities: There are increasing pressures on governments to deal with huge national debt situations, plus funding major infrastructure improvements and greater demand for social and health services for aging populations. In these testing circumstances for governments, it is very likely that the funds available for destination marketing will dwindle and DMOs will be required to look elsewhere for support.

Changing models and mindsets: Today's society and business requires a network model and mindset, where there is collaboration and transparency among DMOs, partners, suppliers and customers. This is a change from the traditional 'command and control' model and mindset that many DMOs have become accustomed to over many past decades.

Based upon these seven drivers of change, DestiCorp recommended that DMOs respond and adapt in the following eight ways:

DMOs need to change their perceptions and mindsets: The main point here is that DMOs were formed many decades ago and have maintained a fairly similar model since then. This model views destinations as 'value chains' with linear relationships. However, this model does not fit with today's realities and DMOs need to view destinations as a 'network of self-organizing agents' that need to collaborate and offer tourists some level of consistency.

DMOs should do less and enable more: DMOs need to focus on developing an enabling digital infrastructure. DestiCorp calls this a 'destination web' that is an electronically connected community of autonomous interdependent users in the destination.

DMOs should promote less and attract more: The DMO needs to engage all parts of the host community, including tourists, in 'conversations' about the destination.

DMOs need to align and integrate with other organizations: In most communities, economic development and other agencies charged with attracting inward investment usually have much greater resources than DMOs. Rather than fearing the competition from these agencies, DMOs need to find new ways to align and integrate their efforts with these bodies.

DMOs should engage suppliers and visitors during and after experiences: DMOs should enlist the help of suppliers and tourists in assisting with destination marketing. DestiCorp recommended that DMOs put more emphasis on becoming 'platform builders' for others and less emphasis on being purely one-dimensional promoters. For example, Chapter 10 highlighted some outstanding examples of 'crowdsourcing' within the context of digital marketing. This is an example of recruiting the help of local residents and/or visitors in engaging in conversations about destinations and posting content on the Internet.

DMOs should nurture the intelligence of destinations: DMOs need to find new and quicker ways for gathering research on what is happening within their destinations. In particular, this 'intelligence' needs to be real-time and it can be gathered by using smartphones and social network sites.

'Faking the truth no longer possible'

Through these modern communication enabling facilities, customers are empowered to discuss their travel experiences and to share their opinions about destinations with the rest of the world. In this dynamic environment, destinations' product offerings are analyzed and the best offerings become prevalent. Therefore, destinations can no longer hide their weaknesses from their customers and cannot promote their products and services faking the truth. The truth is the most prevalent characteristic of customer generated communications and it will be widespread regardless of the effort the destination may try to put in to stop it.

(Machlouzarides, 2010)

DMOs should rationalize to a higher degree: There tends to be some overlapping and redundancy among the various levels of DMOs in given countries, from the national to the community level. DMOs need to collaborate and make use of new technologies to rationalize their efforts to a higher degree.

The M in DMO should become management: This has been a predominant and recurring theme throughout this book. DMOs must be engaged in many more activities than just purely promotion and sales. For example, the biophysical realities mentioned earlier require DMOs to get more involved with sustainable tourism development. They must also be more involved in quality assurance and visitor management programmes.

'The future of destination marketing' (Anna Pollock)

Figure 16.3 shows a diagram based on a presentation by Anna Pollock from DestiCorp that was delivered in Norway in 2009. The main idea within the diagram is that DMOs must move more from 'pushing' (or promoting) their destinations to potential tourists, towards 'pulling' (or attracting) people to destinations. The '5 Ps' have to change into the '5 Cs':

- *Customer*: DMOs need to focus more on the experiences that customers want rather than on the features of their products. Customers have the greatest power now in the digital content era.
- *Connections*: DMOs must find the most appropriate ways of connecting with customers, and not worry so much about positioning their products.
- *Conversations*: Markets have become conversations and DMOs must engage others to have good conversations about their destinations.
- *Content*: Traditional types of promotion need to give way to the creation of digital content.
- *Community*: DMOs need to build online communities and then engage others (residents, suppliers, tourists, etc.) to have conversations about their destinations.

These ideas from DestiCorp and Anna Pollock, about how destination marketing needs to adapt, are very thought-provoking and again strongly advocate a move towards greater integration and use of ICTs by DMOs. But the ideas are not just about using technologies, they are as much about adapting new DMO business models which involve much higher levels of collaboration and networking. Overall, the implication is that the old model for DMOs is unlikely to be successful in the future.

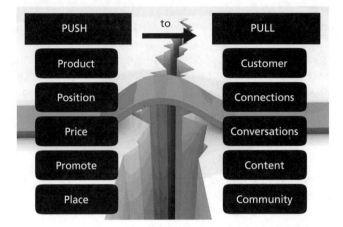

Figure 16.3 From 5 Ps to 5 Cs
Source: Adapted from diagram in Pollock, 2009.

As a postscript to this sub-section, you should realize that many DMOs are already in the process of transforming from the 'old' to the 'new' model of destination marketing and management. Additionally, although many of the foregoing comments and ideas have been about pleasure and leisure travel, the same applies to business travel and business events. As an example of these two points, in *CVB Smackdown*, Loomis and Gloudeman (2011) quote Tom Norwalk, CEO of the Seattle Convention and Visitors Bureau in Washington, USA, as saying the following:

Seattle CVB using the power of social media with meeting planners

SCVB's Twitter and Facebook channels are increasingly followed by meeting attendees. Our convention services team promotes the Seattle Maven, our lead tweeter, who offers the latest Seattle travel tips and deals, news of events, dining, cultural performances and much more. Anecdotally, we hear from planners who say they appreciate the service. Many include our Twitter and Facebook links in their convention promotions, on their websites, in blog posts and in other communications with their membership.

Implications of global trends for destination management

Dwyer *et al.* (2009) published an article in *Tourism Management*, 'Destination and enterprise management for a tourism future', that, among other things, outlined the implications of five global trends for destination management. The research team conducted tourism sector workshops in Brisbane, Melbourne and Sydney, Australia, as well as reviewing all of the published forecasts on tourism until 2020. Six drivers of change in tourism were identified as: (1) economic, (2) political, (3) environmental, (4) technological, (5) demographic and (6) social.

The five global trends and a brief statement of their implications are provided below:

- *Sustainable tourism development*: DMOs should focus on the 'yield per capita' rather than on just growth in visitor numbers. They should adopt sustainability principles as a foundation for tourism development. Community residents should be more involved in determining the directions for future tourism development.
- *Climate change*: DMOs should encourage tourism sector stakeholders to minimize their impacts on climate change.
- *Target marketing*: Destination product development and marketing in the future will be increasingly targeted and theme-based. Emotional benefits of tourism products should be emphasized more than their functional benefits. Once again, this group of authors emphasized the use of technologies in achieving this new emphasis in destination marketing:

Technology assisting move from functions to emotions

While conceding that many new Internet technologies empower the consumer, greatly enhancing their power in the marketplace, workshop participants argued that tourism operators must inevitably shift from the promotion of the functional benefits of their products and services to the emotional benefits such as reverie/escape, status enhancement, stress-alleviation, and reward and social-skill confirmation. There was strong support for the view that the use of electronic technology will enable firms to more readily and accurately identify market segments and niches and to communicate with them more effectively.

(2009)

- *Risk management*: DMOs along with their stakeholders must introduce risk management strategies that make sure that tourists feel safe and secure in their destinations.
- *Education for tourism management*: The tourism sector needs to increase its knowledge and skill base to improve its innovative capabilities.

The contributions from Dwyer *et al.* (2009) are very valuable and offer some additional issues and challenges that deserve careful consideration by DMOs. For example, the concept of tourist safety and security, and with it the destination's risk management strategy, is extremely important in an era of frequent crises. These authors also raised the topics of sustainable development and education to a higher level than the previous works.

Managing Destination Marketing Organizations (Ford and Peeper)

Robert C. Ford is a professor at the University of Central Florida; while William C. Peeper is a former president of the Orlando/Orange County Convention and Visitors Bureau and worked at that Bureau for more than 25 years. They wrote a book, *Managing Destination Marketing Organizations*, which was published in 2008. This book focused mainly on the tasks, roles and responsibilities of CVB executives. They conducted twenty-four in-depth interviews with the CEOs of large, medium and small DMOs, and most of these were based in the USA.

In the final chapter, Ford and Peeper identified five future challenges for CVB executives:

Funding and governance: The CEOs that were interviewed highlighted the continuing difficulties in securing funding for their DMOs. In the USA, this was because other community agencies were vying for shares of the hotel room tax. As shown by the following quote from the book, this meant that the DMOs had to do a more effective job of proving their economic contributions to their communities:

'Value of DMOs not yet fully understood'

The CVB leaders interviewed recognized that the increased competition for funding required them to more aggressively and effectively market their value to their own communities and local stakeholders. They felt a strong need to do a better job of telling their communities about their contributions to its economic health. But most of the interviewed believed that their stakeholders did not understand either what they did or the value of their work to the community.

These two authors also pointed out that local hotels exerted the greatest power in DMO governance, but they tended to have a 'heads in beds' and short-term outlook on DMO objectives and performance.

Job responsibilities: DMO executives' job responsibilities are rapidly expanding and this is to be expected in the shift from destination marketing to destination management. Ford and Peeper pointed out that in addition to marketing and promotion, DMO CEOs have similar responsibilities to those that run companies, including financial management and human resources management. They are also playing a much greater role in the brand management of their destinations than before. However, they tend to be evaluated solely on the results from their sales and marketing responsibilities.

Technological change: DMOs are experiencing competition from online providers of destination information and they need to adapt to these changes. These two authors not only viewed technology as a great opportunity for DMOs, but also as a huge threat, as explained below.

Online travel agencies offer stiff competition

Commercial travel information websites such as Expedia.com and Travelocity. com already compete with one of the CVB's traditional roles, the distributor of destination information. While CVBs have websites, which in many larger cities receive millions of visits, they cannot go head-to-head against the business model of the commercial sites, especially on a non-profit CVB's limited budget.

The availability of lower hotel room rates on these and other OTA sites meant that business event participants were booking their rooms there and not within the block of rooms that the hotels and meeting planners had contracted for. This was causing a serious problem for the hotels, meeting planners and DMOs.

Information: Providing destination information in a variety of different ways has been a traditional DMO role. In addition, in North America, DMAI and its forerunner, International Association of Convention and Visitor Bureaus (IACVB), has maintained a databank of information about meeting resources and venues for many years; now called empowerMINT. However, other online providers have come along in recent years and now offer comparable and sometimes more complete information for meeting planners. Other online providers such as Google Maps and MapQuest also offer great map and direction information that was traditionally given out by DMOs. So the traditional information role of DMOs is rapidly being undermined by for-profit online companies.

Competition: Ford and Peeper (2008) argued that many cities have greatly expanded their convention centre and hotel capacities, and this was placing greater pressure on DMOs to bring in even more business events. They pointed out that in the USA there was more supply of meeting space than there was demand, and this was leading to a high level of discounting on meeting space and even giving convention centre space away for free as an incentive.

The increased competition from a variety of different online information providers has already been mentioned. These two authors, also through their CEO interviews, found two further sources of new competition. The first source was an internal one and was from city-owned convention/exhibition centres. These venues in many cases were desperately seeking any business to cover their operating costs, and the deals they were making were undermining the DMO's efforts to attract high-yielding business events for hotels that meet the room tax goals of their communities. The second source of competition was from mega-meeting-planning services companies including Experient, ConferenceDirect, HelmsBriscoe and others. These companies now provided many of the similar services for business events that were traditionally performed by DMOs. However, they have a much different funding model than DMOs, getting their revenues via commissions from business event suppliers such as hotels. So they are able to offer these planning and meeting logistics services to meeting planners free of charge.

The Ford and Peeper book paints a highly challenging future picture for DMOs, particularly in the USA. The issues they raise are in many ways quite similar to those that you have heard about earlier in this chapter. However, they draw particular attention to the problems and challenges that US CVBs have related to the system of hotel room taxes. These two authors predicted the following future directions for DMOs:

- *Financing*: DMOs, and especially the North American style CVBs, will have to aggressively compete for commission incomes, and reduce their reliance on hotel room tax revenues.
- *Spokesperson*: DMOs need to assume the role of not only marketing their communities; they must become more involved in managing their destination's resources. They must ensure that the promises made in marketing are actually delivered to tourists. DMOs must also act as the 'spokespersons' for tourism in their communities.

- *Cooperation*: DMOs need to form new partnerships and collaborative models, sometimes with other DMOs that previously were deemed to be competitors. The BestCities Global Alliance that was discussed in Chapter 6 is a great example of what needs to be done.
- *Business models*: Ford and Peeper (2008) predicted a very different future for CVBs. They recommended consideration of six alternative business models for the future: (1) outsource model, (2) RFP model, (3) national-consolidation model – privatization version, (4) national-consolidation model – cooperative version, (5) franchise model and (6) status quo.

The foregoing materials have comprehensively reviewed the current and expected near future issues in destination management and marketing. To recap, the following seven sources of information were discussed:

- *DMAI Futures Study*, 2008
- 15 Cs framework (Fyall and Leask), 2006
- The PhoCusWright destination marketing study (Schetzina), 2009
- DestiCorp conceptual discussion paper, 2010
- 'The Future of Destination Marketing' (Pollock), 2009
- 'Destination and Enterprise Management for a Tourism Future' (Dwyer *et al.*) , 2009
- *Managing Destination Marketing Organizations* (Ford and Peeper), 2008.

These sources have provided a wide variety of perspectives on the operation of DMOs and from different geographic regions and types of professionals. There were many similarities in the opinions expressed in the seven sources, although each of them offered certain unique views on important issues.

Summary of issues and trends from Chapters 1–15

Before discussing the future trends and potential challenges, it is also worth reviewing the issues and trends that have been cited in this book. Some of these reinforce the sentiments from the seven sources, while others were not covered in these sources:

- *Destination management and marketing*: The success of a DMO is at least in part measured by how well it communicates and interacts with its stakeholders (Chapter 1).
- The field of destination management is receiving greater recognition and becoming more professional (Chapter 1).
- *Destination planning*: Tourism planning for destinations is still maturing and there remain many destinations around the world that are without long-term tourism plans. It is difficult to contemplate professional destination management without long-term planning (Chapter 2).
- *Destination marketing planning*: Many DMOs are not yet following a long-term and systematic, step-by-step approach to destination marketing and promotion (Chapter 3).
- *Destination management research*: There is not enough investment in various forms of consumer and product research by DMOs (Chapter 4).
- *Destination product development*: DMOs are generally becoming more involved in destination product development as the competition for tourists intensifies. There is also greater recognition that destination marketing and product development

are closely intertwined, and that those involved in destination marketing should have an interest and involvement in product development (Chapter 5).

- Destination quality is important for destinations and all of the dimensions of quality (hardware, software and environment) need to be managed. Significant benefits accrue to those destinations that make a concerted effort to manage quality (Chapter 5).
- All destinations are facing serious challenges with respect to human resource availability and quality (Chapter 5).
- *Destination partnership and team-building*: Although the potential benefits from destination partnerships are substantial, there are many barriers and challenges to setting up such cooperation and collaborations. Lack of adequate financial resources, communication problems, uneven benefit distribution and unwillingness to cooperate are just a few of the roadblocks to destination partnerships (Chapter 6).
- *Destination community and stakeholder relations*: Community relations are becoming a more important role of destination management, as DMOs increasingly recognize that they must have the support of local community residents and tourism sector stakeholders. This is putting much more pressure on DMOs not only to perform at a high level in external markets, but also to be outstanding at building and maintaining relationships at home (Chapter 7).
- *Destination governance and leadership*: Destination governance is a concept that is receiving increasing attention. This is how a DMO is administered and who does the administering. Governance involves the policies, systems and processes to ensure that all stakeholders are involved and that the DMO is accountable for its results and resource usage and has a high level of transparency (Chapter 8).
- The funding of DMOs in many places in the world has been under threat due to government budget deficits and downturns in tourism business levels. Several DMOs are looking for new ways to earn revenues in the face of significant cost-cutting (Chapter 8).
- *Destination branding*: Branding tourism destinations is very challenging given the diversity of the destination mix and the experience good characteristic of tourism. Destination branding often requires time to be successful, so patience is required as well as continual investment in the brand (Chapter 9).
- *Destination integrated marketing communications and promotion*: Digital marketing using information and communication technologies (ICTs) is now being given much greater emphasis by DMOs (Chapter 10).
- *Destination information and communication technologies*: For the past 25 years information and communication technologies (ICTs) have had a major impact on tourism in general. They have revolutionized how DMOs share destination information and communicate with people. It is very likely that they will be even more important for destination management in the future (Chapter 11).
- *Consumer behaviour, market segmentation and trends*: DMOs need to constantly stay on top of market trends, as customers and their behaviours are changing more quickly than before (Chapter 12).
- *Domestic pleasure and leisure travel markets*: Domestic tourism is a 'mainstay' of the tourism sectors in many parts of the world, particularly in the developed nations. Unfortunately domestic tourism often is given second-class status compared to international tourism (Chapter 13).
- *International pleasure and leisure travel markets*: Despite the growth, international tourism remains highly susceptible to negative impacts from various types of crises, as has been well demonstrated in the period from 2000 to 2009 (Chapter 14).

- *Business travel and business event markets*: The major challenges and issues facing business travel and business events are competitive intensity, cost control and policy compliance, incorporating use of social network sites, negative economic conditions, 'perk' perceptions of business travel and business events, reliance on other tourism sector stakeholders' performance and technology as a substitute for travel (Chapter 15).

As well as providing a good summary of some of the main points of this book, these bulleted points bring out some additional issues regarding DMOs and destination management. For example, this book emphasizes that the professionalization of destination management is under way, but this still requires greater recognition and attention. Programmes such as DMAI's Certified Destination Management Executive have done much to focus attention on this issue, as also have DMAI's Standard DMO Performance Reporting System and its Destination Marketing Accreditation Program. These truly have been visionary initiatives to improve the professionalism in destination marketing and management.

The seven sources described earlier appeared to make the assumption that DMOs were doing a good job of destination marketing and promotion, but needed to focus more attention elsewhere. However, if we take more of a global focus, this is not entirely accurate as the destination marketing, promotion and research practices in many countries still require great improvement.

Another issue that was not heavily touched upon by the seven sources is how DMOs need to allocate priorities among different markets (domestic vs international; pleasure/leisure vs VFR vs business travel/business events, etc). Too many experts are very quick to say that DMOs must get more engaged online, but exactly where is still a practical question that they leave unanswered.

One must also wonder if the issues being experienced by DMOs and destination management are, in fact, a symptom of a lack of understanding and respect for tourism in general in many nations of the world. The late American comedian, Rodney Dangerfield, always used the line, 'I don't get no respect.' In many ways, tourism is a 'don't get no respect' economic sector that is not given the priority that it deserves. So, in the bigger picture, the issues that face destination management are also issues faced by tourism in general.

Expected future trends and potential challenges for destinations and DMOs

It is difficult to predict exactly what will happen with DMOs in the next 10–20 years, but in all probability many of the current issues and trends will continue into the foreseeable future. However, the following eight future trends and potential challenges are anticipated:

- *Consolidation of place marketing and branding entities*: There has been a strong movement towards place marketing and branding in recent times, and this has been extended to all economic sectors of nations, states/provinces/territories and cities. Places are becoming increasingly aggressive in trying to attract inward investment, human talent, university and other students, major events, etc. DMOs have shown other sectors how to be successful at place branding, but ironically the greater visibility gained from these efforts may make them targets for consolidation into more comprehensive and integrated economic development agencies. In the continuing fragile economic times ahead and tight public sector funding, this consolidation or rationalization of place marketing and branding entities seems inevitable.

- *Digitalization of content continues*: Everyone expects that DMOs will continue to digitalize content and that the primary way to communicate with all audiences will be through ICTs. DMOs have made great strides in this respect since around 1995 but other for-profit entities have innovated more rapidly. DMOs need to quickly catch up with these other entities or else they will eventually be overlooked online by consumers and meeting planners.

- *Funding sources remain troublesome*: The funding of DMOs will continue to be a very troubling issue in many countries and it is very likely that many DMOs will have to 'make do' with lower budgets than they have been accustomed to. Retail travel agencies have been able to survive by changing their revenue source models; so too must DMOs in the future.

- *Greater investment in technology-enabled marketing*: As suggested by several of the seven sources described earlier in this chapter, DMOs need to make a much heavier investment in technology-enabled marketing, probably by diverting funds away from the expensive traditional media that they have been using for decades.

- *More collaboration among DMOs and associations*: Greater collaboration and more partnerships among DMOs and other entities seem to be highly likely and also definitely needed. DMOs will increasingly be sharing resources to achieve common goals and desired outcomes. Also, and as suggested by Ford and Peeper (2008), associations that are active in destination marketing will need to work more collaboratively in the future to support the efforts of DMO practitioners.

- *New DMO business models appear*: As Ford and Peeper (2008) have predicted, many DMOs will have to make radical changes in their business models in the future. The USA, for a long time the 'sleeping giant of world tourism' finally awoke in May 2012 due to a new business model and launched its first-ever global tourism marketing campaign. Associated Press (Bomkamp, 2012) provided the following commentary:

'"Come and Find Your Land of Dreams" campaign to encourage US tourism launches'

How do you sell Times Square and the Grand Canyon? The Carolinas and California?

Residents of Japan, Canada and the United Kingdom are getting a taste Tuesday of the United States' first-ever marketing campaign aimed at boosting tourism. The print, web and video ads released Tuesday were created by Brand USA, a partnership of government agencies and private companies. The consortium was developed to act like the tourism ministries of countries such as Ireland, Italy or Israel.

It's the first time that the US has marketed itself as a tourist destination to people living in other countries.

- *Professionalization of destination management gains pace*: Undoubtedly these past 15–20 years have witnessed increasing professionalism in destination marketing and management. Destination marketing and management associations have been pioneering this movement to better prepare DMO professionals for the future. In the future, it is anticipated that academic institutions will join in this effort by offering degree programmes in destination marketing and management.
- *Sustainable tourism development gets a higher priority*: In some parts of the world, such as Australia and New Zealand, DMOs are placing a high priority on environmental concerns as well as the social-cultural impacts of tourism. However, many DMOs have still to fully engage in this movement and seem to be giving it 'lip service' rather than allocating resources to it. This will change in the future and DMOs will generally give sustainable tourism development a much higher priority.

The DMO of the future

What will the future DMOs look like? One could say that the 'writing is already on the wall' for DMOs to see how they must change to be more responsive to consumer and external environmental trends. Many DMOs need to change from being mainly 'sales' organizations to becoming well-rounded and officially-endorsed destination management organizations. The following seven future DMO characteristics are likely:

- *Professional destination managers*: The DMO of the future is operated by professional destination managers who have attended universities and obtained degrees in this field. The universities have worked closely with destination marketing and management associations in creating curricula and sit on the advisory boards for these programmes.
- *Tourism network hubs*: The DMO of the future is a hub of many networked organizations. Local sector stakeholders go to DMOs for market and industry intelligence and research. DMOs coach local tourism sector stakeholders on how to make their products and services have greater appeal in the marketplace.
- *Collaboration experts*: DMOs are experts in collaborations, partnerships and team-building. DMO staff members are tasked with reaching out to other organizations and are rewarded for establishing effective collaborative models. Collaborative models are established at all geographic levels from international to local; across markets and tourism sub-sectors; and according to major issues (e.g. the environment; professional education and training; crisis/risk management; quality assurance, etc.).
- *Digital content masters and facilitators*: DMOs are also masters at managing digital content. They encourage local residents, tourism sector stakeholders and tourists to develop content and to engage in discussions and conversations about the destination. They teach tourism sector stakeholders how to put content online.
- *Experience brokers*: DMOs arrange experiences for tourists within their destinations. They find out what experiences consumers want and work with tourism sector stakeholders to design these experiences. They stay in touch with tourists to ensure that their experiences go well and meet their expectations. DMOs encourage tourists to write and develop digital content about their experiences. DMOs provide feedback to tourism sector stakeholders and coach them to make necessary improvements in the experiences they offer.

- *Environmental and cultural champions*: DMOs are at the forefront in promoting low-carbon tourism and other initiatives designed to protect the environment. They champion all efforts in their communities to conserve and protect heritage resources, and insist on the authentic portrayal of local culture.
- *Official consumer and tourism advocates*: 'Official' is the word that separates DMOs from all other players in destination marketing. DMOs have been ratified by local government policies to serve the best interests of tourists and of the local tourism sector. Consumers deeply trust DMOs since they are truthful, honest and ethical in all that they do.

Many experts predicted that the days of 'bricks-and-mortar' travel agencies were over when airlines, particularly in North America, removed the commissions to which they had become accustomed. However, although fewer in numbers than in their heyday, traditional travel agencies are still around. DMOs likewise are very likely to survive because they can play an essential role in tourism.

Summary

Destination management is an emerging field in tourism and it is not yet well understood by political decision-makers and the general public. At the same time, DMOs are struggling for recognition while doing much more in proving their worth to their communities. Additionally, DMOs are experiencing new and intensifying competition from across the globe to within their own destinations. In particular, their traditional exclusive space as information providers for tourists and meeting planners has been invaded by many new online, for-profit providers.

This chapter has comprehensively reviewed seven authoritative sources providing expert commentary and ideas on the future of destination management and marketing, and DMOs. Although drawn from different parts of the world, there is a strong consensus among these sources that DMOs need to change fundamentally if they are to survive.

Many issues are affecting destination management and DMOs at the current time. These include the availability of funding for operations, increasing importance of ICTs, emergence of new competitors, global environmental problems, continual economic and other crises, growing concerns for personal safety and security, expanding market fragmentation, changing consumer expectations, requirements for more community resident involvement, and tightening controls on DMO operations and accountability. The broad scope of these issues and dealing with all of their implications means that DMOs cannot just be 'sales offices' or 'community megaphones' for their tourism sectors; they must become 'strategic champions' for their destinations, involved in all aspects of planning, research, development and marketing.

The DMO of the future will probably look quite different from the one of today. It is envisaged that future DMOs will be: professional destination managers; tourism network hubs; collaboration masters; digital content masters and facilitators; experience brokers; environmental and cultural champions; and official consumer and tourism advocates. DMO executives and managers will have to have a much broader skill set in the future in order to deal with all the issues and challenges that they will undoubtedly face. It is incumbent on industry associations, DMO practitioners and academic institutions to work together to prepare future professionals for these challenges.

Review questions

1 Relevance, value proposition and visibility were the three high-level strategic themes identified in the *DMAI Futures Study* (2008). What are the implications of these themes for DMOs?

2 What are the 'super trends' identified in the *DMAI Futures Study* and in which ways are these impacting upon destination marketing?

3 Which four key roles for DMOs are suggested in the new 'strategic map' developed by DMAI and Karl Albrecht International?

4 What is the 15 Cs framework for describing the challenges facing destination marketing as suggested by Fyall and Leask (2006)?

5 The PhoCusWright destination marketing study (2009) found that DMOs' Internet marketing efforts were lacking in certain respects. What were the weaknesses that this study found in DMOs' Internet marketing?

6 DestiCorp of the UK (2010) in its paper, 'Speculation on the Future of Destination Marketing Organizations', suggested that DMOs need to change their models and mindsets. In what ways should DMOs change in the future according to this source?

7 Anna Pollock of DestiCorp says that DMOs need to become 'orchestrators' and 'stage managers' rather than today's destination promoters. What does this mean in terms of how DMOs should work with local tourism sector stakeholders and in how they communicate with potential tourists?

8 What are the five global trends identified by Dwyer *et al.* (2009) and what are their future implications for DMOs?

9 Ford and Peeper (2008) described five future challenges for DMOs. What were these challenges and how will they affect DMOs? How will DMOs need to change in order to adapt to these challenges?

10 Which future trends and potential challenges will destinations and DMOs be facing?

11 What are the likely characteristics of the DMO of the future?

References

Bomkamp, S. 2012. Campaign to encourage US tourism launches. *Associated Press*. May.

Buhalis, D. 2000. Marketing the competitive destination of the future. *Tourism Management*, 21(1), 97–116.

Buhalis, D., and Law, R. 2008. Progress in information technology and tourism management: 20 years on and 10 years after the Internet: The state of eTourism research. *Tourism Management*, 29(4), 609–623.

Canadian Tourism Commission. 2012. Signature Experiences Collection®. http://en-corporate.canada.travel/resources-industry/signature_experiences_collection

Cloke, P., and Perkins, H.C. 2002. Commodification and adventure in New Zealand tourism. *Current Issues in Tourism*, 5(6), 521–549.

ConferenceDirect. 2012. ConferenceDirect®. http://www.conferencedirect.com/

DestiCorp. 2010. Speculation on the future of destination marketing organizations (DMOs): A conceptual discussion paper. DestiCorp UK .

Destination Marketing Association International. 2008. DMAI Futures Study 2008: The Future of Destination Marketing.

Destination and Travel Foundation. 2009. Destination Excellence. Investing in the Future of Destination Marketing. Campaign Case for Support.

DiscoverAmerica.com. 2012. Brand USA Campaign Creative Assets. http://www.multivu.com/mnr/55891-usa-international-travel-campaign-discover-this-land-like-never-before

Dwyer, L., Edwards, D., Mistilis, N., Roman, C., and Scott, N. 2009. Destination and enterprise management for a tourism future. *Tourism Management*, 30(1), 63–74.

empowerMINT. 2012. empowerMINT: Planners. Destinations. Experts. Destination Marketing Association International. http://www.destinationmarketing.org/page.asp?pid=353

Experient Inc. 2012. Experient. A Maritz Travel Company. http://www.experient-inc.com/

Ford, R.C., and Peeper, W.C. 2008. Managing Destination Marketing Organizations. Orlando, FL: ForPer Publications.

Fyall, A., and Leask, A. 2006. Destination marketing: Future issues, strategic challenges. *Tourism and Hospitality Research*, 7(1), 50–63.

Gretzel, U., Fesenmaier, D.F., Formica, S., and O'Leary, J.T. 2006. Searching for the future: Challenges faced by destination marketing organizations. *Journal of Travel Research*, 45(2), 116–126.

Halewood, C., and Hannam, K. 2001. Viking heritage tourism: Authenticity and commodification. *Annals of Tourism Research*, 28(3), 565–580.

HelmsBriscoe. 2012. HelmsBriscoe. http://www.helmsbriscoe.com/

King, J. 2002. Destination marketing organisations: Connecting the experience rather than promoting the place. *Journal of Vacation Marketing*, 8(2), 105–108.

Loomis, C., and Gloudeman, N. 2011. CVB Smackdown. http://www.smartmeetings.com/event-planning-magazine/2011/09/cvb-smackdown

Machlouzarides, H. 2010. The future of destination marketing: The case of Cyprus. *Journal of Hospitality and Tourism Technology*, 1(1), 83–95.

Pollock, A. 2009. The Future of Destination Marketing: Why All Marketing is Social Marketing. Presentation to BIT Reiseliv, Oslo, Norway.

Schetzina, C. 2009. Destination Marketing: Understanding the Role and Impact of Destination Marketers. PhoCusWright Inc.

usdm.net. 2010. Leadership Report. Are You a Revolutionary DMO?

Index